TEXAS

the Lone Star State

3RD EDITION

Rupert Norval Richardson
Senior Professor of History, Hardin-Simmons University

Ernest Wallace
Horn Professor of History, Texas Tech University

Adrian N. Anderson
Assistant Professor of History,
Lamar State College of Technology

Prentice-Hall, Inc., Englewood Cliffs, New Jersey

© 1970 by Prentice-Hall, Inc., Englewood Cliffs, New Jersey

13–912436–5

Library of Congress Catalog Card Number 70–92380

Current Printing (last digit)
10   9   8   7   6   5   4   3

PRINTED IN THE UNITED STATES OF AMERICA

Prentice-Hall International, Inc., London
Prentice-Hall of Australia, Pty. Ltd., Sydney
Prentice-Hall of Canada, Ltd., Toronto
Prentice-Hall of India Private Limited, New Delhi
Prentice-Hall of Japan, Inc., Tokyo

PREFACE

The History of Texas is replete with adventure and heroic action. The reader meets with self-denying priests and mail-fisted conquerors of Spain, with filibusters and *empresarios* from beyond the Mississippi, with frontiersmen from Tennessee and planters from Alabama. The Anglo-Americans vied with the Mexicans for supremacy until 1848 and took the country from the Indians by 1875. Thereafter came the struggle for law and order, the lusty cattle industry, the surge of land-hungry farmers seeking virgin soil, the rapid approach of railroads, and the discovery of oil fields. In recent times the challenge of space travel and the explosive growth of urban Texas have continued the tradition of adventure and progress.

Since the last edition of *Texas the Lone Star State* appeared eleven years ago, much history has been made and much has been written. Certain groups in Texas have continued to create tension by protests and demonstrations; contests between political factions and political parties have enlivened the story of public affairs. Campuses have been expanded and new colleges and universities built to meet swelling enrollments. Education, care of the unfortunate, and new state agencies have made new taxes mandatory. Meanwhile, the rank and file of Texans have known prosperity greater than ever before, and one Texan has become President of the United States.

For this new edition the authors have not only brought the text up to date but have also revised the chapters on the past. The greater part of the book has been rewritten, and in several places the organization has been changed to present certain subjects more fully and clearly. We have added a number of new maps, charts, and photographs, and incorporated recently published books and articles in the bibliographies.

In trying to provide a complete survey of the history and current state of Texas we sought to give a fair amount of space to certain less interesting but important affairs, without neglecting the more colorful and romantic. The general reader or the college student can easily follow chronologically the main course of public affairs, breaking the sequence from time to time for a closer look at important movements and life and society in general. Those who prefer to follow the topical units will find the Table of Contents and the Index adequate.

We are deeply grateful to the teachers, students, and general readers whose criticism and constructive suggestions have helped greatly in the work of revision.

R.N.R.

E.W.

A.N.A.

CONTENTS

MAPS

TEXAS

1

THE COUNTRY AND
ITS NATIVE PEOPLES

The name Texas comes from *Tejas*, meaning "friends" or "allies," a word applied by Spanish explorers and missionaries to an Indian confederacy, the Hasinai, that they found in this country. The early Spaniards thought of Texas as just the land of the Hasinai (Texas) Indians, that is, the territory between the Trinity and the Red rivers, including part of present-day Louisiana. Early in the eighteenth century, however, the borders of Texas were extended westward to include Spanish settlements which had been planted on the San Antonio River and Matagorda Bay. A definite boundary on the west was first fixed in 1746, when it was declared that the Medina River should separate Texas from the province of Nuevo Santander. Later the boundaries were extended far to the west and north, while a part of the territory on the east was sliced off. A large part of the border of the state consists of natural boundaries: the Rio Grande on the west and south from the thirty-second parallel to the Gulf of Mexico; the Gulf shore line; the Sabine River to the thirty-second parallel; and the Red River for about 300 miles on the north. The remainder of the boundary consists of straight lines established by surveyors at one time or another in conformity with various treaties and agreements.

With its 267,339 square miles of territory, extending from the High Plains of the Panhandle to the Gulf of Mexico, Texas is, except for Alaska, by far the largest state in the Union. One can travel 800 miles

THE NATURAL REGIONS OF TEXAS

Texas contains a number of regions determined by geological makeup and the resultant physiographic forms. Grasses, timber, soils, and other natural resources have affected its history greatly. (Adapted from Stanley A. Arbingast, Lorrin G. Kennamer, and Michael E. Bonnie, Atlas of Texas, Bureau of Business Research, The University of Texas at Austin, 1967.)

in a straight line within its borders; Texarkana, on the Arkansas border, is closer to Chicago than it is to El Paso, on the Rio Grande.

THE COUNTRY

A glance at a relief map of the United States reveals that Texas is not physiographically uniform but that it is made up of parts of at least three great physical divisions, namely the Atlantic-Gulf coastal plain, the Great Plains of central North America, and the Rocky Mountain system. The fact that these great physiographic provinces join within the state means that there is variety and contrast in topography, climate, and resources.

The state is divided into a number of natural regions, determined mainly by soil and climate. The Gulf Coast Plain, which extends from the shore a little south of Corpus Christi to the Sabine River and inland from about a hundred miles to about two hundred miles. Near the coast the land is low and marshy; inland it is well drained and there is much heavy soil with a great variety of vegetation. Its better clay and loam soils were once savannas affording excellent grazing, but they are now farmed.

East Texas is a country of forests and farm lands. Its pine lands are the western edge of the great Southern pine forest that extends eastward to the Atlantic Ocean. Lumber is exported. West of the pine lands is an extensive area of sandy soils and post oak, extending far into Central Texas. The region produces pork, beef, poultry, and dairy products.

The Central Texas Prairies extend from the Colorado River in the vicinity of Austin northward to the Red River; the same type of terrain continues on into Oklahoma. The prairie is broken by the Eastern Cross Timbers, a thin wedge of trees extending northward from the vicinity of Waco through the Dallas country to the Red River valley. East of this narrow belt of timber is the Blackland Prairie, and to the west lies the Grand Prairie. Rich, black soils predominate, now largely cultivated except where too thin, producing grain and cotton and supporting live-stock. Dallas, Forth Worth, and ten or so lesser cities lie within this region, and Austin and San Antonio share its trade and draw on its resources.

The Cross Timbers, lying between Fort Worth and Abilene and extending from the vicinity of the Colorado River to the Red River and beyond, is a farming and stock raising country, producing peanuts, vegetables, dairy products, and poultry. Its soils range from belts of loose, blowing sand to black clays.

The Rolling Plains, or North Texas Plains belt, includes the Abilene, Vernon, and Wichita Falls country. It is separated from the High Plains to the west by the Caprock, a prominent limestone escarpment. Some of the Rolling Plains terrain is highly eroded; other areas consist of spacious prairies. Cotton and maize cultivation is interspersed with cattle raising.

The greater part of the High Plains is arable, and this region, once a sea of grass, is one of the foremost farming sections in the world. Cotton, maize, and several other crops are grown in stupendous quantities, made possible by irrigation from wells. Within the area have grown up the cities of Amarillo, Lubbock, Plainview, and a score of thriving towns.

The Edwards Plateau is a broken tableland, an extension of the Great Plains. In most places its soil is too shallow for farming. It is widely known as a livestock region, and San Angelo, on its periphery, is a leading wool and mohair market. The South Texas Plain consists of highly eroded localities interspersed with prairies. Light loam soils are prevalent and brush has impinged on much of the grasslands. There is considerable farming and livestock raising. The Winter Garden region south of San Antonio, the lower Rio Grande Valley, and a few other localities produce vegetables and citrus fruits in quantity.

In pictographs like these at Paint Rock, prehistoric Indians recorded the significant events of their lives. (Texas Highway Department)

Except for a few relatively small irrigation centers, the vast Basin and Mountain region, lying mainly west of the Pecos, is a livestock country. On the best soils and under favorable conditions good grass will grow; but yucca, catclaw, and creosote bush dominate much of its surface. With the splendor of its scenery, however, nature compensates for the harsh features of this land. Here are Guadalupe Peak, the highest mountain east of the Rockies, and the wild Chisos of the Big Bend. Under azure skies bald peaks of stone shimmer like giant jewels; silhouettes of massive crags take a thousand fanciful shapes; and myriad-colored canyon walls create an ever-changing vista.

PREHISTORIC PEOPLE

Texas lies between the three areas in which native civilization reached its highest development in North America: the Mayan in Mexico and Central America; the Pueblo of the upper Rio Grande; and the Mound

Builder of the Mississippi Valley. Although Texas was a meeting place of these three cultures, it appears that none was ever extensively established within its boundaries, and archaeologists differ as to what influence each culture had upon it. However that may be, the archaeology of Texas is as diversified as are its natural resources. The ways of life of its early inhabitants differed even more widely from region to region than do those of modern people.

Discoveries during the last third of a century indicate that man has been in America much longer than had previously been believed, and some of the very earliest relics discovered in the New World have been found in Texas. Among the explored sites that indicate the presence of these Paleo-Americans are those near Abilene, Midland, and Plainview, Texas, and Clovis and Folsom, New Mexico—all in the plains country, principally the High Plains, the Llano Estacado. In this region, which E. H. Sellards has named the Llano Complex, the Paleo-Americans hunted and at least occasionally killed in numbers a species of elephant now long extinct. Their spear and dart points, known as the Clovis fluted point, were widely distributed. By measuring the remaining radioactivity of organic materials taken from sites where spearheads and fossils of elephants indicate kills, it has been estimated that the Llano people lived some 12,000 or more years ago.

Somewhat later than the Llano Culture was the Folsom Culture, named after a town in northeastern New Mexico. Here highly-finished projectile points were found, characterized by longitudinal flutes or channels in the blade faces. The meat supply of these people was, in part at least, a huge bison, also long extinct. Folsom fluted points have been found imbedded in the vertebrae of these beasts, and the radiocarbon tests of charred bones taken from an excavation near Lubbock indicate an age of some 10,000 years. Within the city limits of Plainview shallow excavations have revealed more than two dozen flint tools and skeletons of perhaps a hundred bison, which radiocarbon tests indicate have been there for about 9,000 years.

In the Trinity River gravel beds near Malakoff and Trinidad, three stone images were found that may be 30,000 or more years old, but the evidence is too slender to warrant certainty.

About 5000 B.C. either the Paleo-American culture gave way to another culture, or the way of life of these people changed. Perhaps the ending of the ice age and the disappearance of the elephant, the great bison, and other animals that they had hunted were factors in the change. Also, other peoples may have migrated to America during the centuries following 5000 B.C. These changes brought in the Archaic peoples. They were hunters and gatherers of nature's products, as their predecessors had been, but instead of a few well-made stone implements they had a great variety of stone points and tools. For instance, 27 types of dart points have been found in the Edwards Plateau. They also made

Large mammals, like this elephant, and dinosaurs were once plentiful in Texas. (Texas Highway Department)

use of polished stones. Pestles and mortars indicate that they relied more on seeds for food than did their predecessors.

In time the Archaic peoples domesticated the dog, they began to locate in more favored localities, they grew maize (which probably was brought in from the south after about 2500 B.C.) and other foods. The making of pottery and the building of more substantial places of abode followed.

THE INDIANS

The history of any American commonwealth may well begin with its native peoples. It was the hope of finding Indians who could be exploited that brought the first Spanish expeditions into Texas; the desire for trade with the natives was a great factor in bringing other adventurers into the country; and the yearning of zealous priests to win the natives to the Christian religion constituted a powerful motive for extending the influence of the Europeans. The Indian was the best teacher the white frontiersman had. From the Indian he learned of crops and crude but effective means of tillage; of foods and their preparation and preservation; of wild game and its habits and the methods of taking it.

Indeed, the Indians more than the white men determined the nature of frontier institutions. If the Indians were friendly, the white people explored and settled the country rapidly; if they were docile, it was easy to exploit them or, at least, to ignore their rights. If the red men were organized in weak and fragmentary tribes, the white men easily drove them away; but if they were powerful and warlike, they retarded the advance of the intruders for decades, and even for centuries. Furthermore, the Indians determined largely the type of warfare that was carried on. The Caddo of the timber, the Comanche of the plain, and the Apache of the mountain had different tactics, and the Euro-Americans had to meet them in a fashion suited to the conditions that prevailed.

It is true that both the Spaniards, who approached from the west and south, and the Anglo-Americans, who came from the east, had already developed pioneering institutions before they reached Texas; but these institutions proved unsatisfactory in certain important respects. For instance, we shall see that the Spanish mission system, which had been designed for compact pueblos or for docile Indians brought together in colonies, failed among the spirited Caddos of eastern Texas, who lived in scattered hamlets and refused to move to the missions. Likewise, the Anglo-Americans, who had learned to meet Indians who fought on foot, had to develop new tactics for coping with mounted savages of the plains, who struck and retreated with the swiftness of a pilfering coyote.

The first Europeans found many Indian tribes in Texas and a great variety of native cultures—the Caddoan peoples of eastern Texas; the savage Karankawas along the Gulf Coast; the Wichita and Tonkawa groups of tribes in Central Texas; the Coahuiltecans consisting of a number of small tribes who lived south of San Antonio; and the fierce Apaches, who lived in the western part of the state but were forced during the eighteenth century to share their country with the Comanches, no less fierce and even more warlike.

Most of the Indians of East Texas belonged to the great Caddoan family and were included in two confederacies: the Caddo, located in Arkansas, Louisiana, and the part of Texas near present-day Texarkana; and the Hasinai, on the upper Angelina and Neches rivers. In Texas history the Hasinai confederacy is the more important of the two. It was in this confederacy that the Spaniards first established missions in the interior of Texas. Probably a dozen tribes belonged to the confederacy, the more important being the Nabedache, the Nacogdoche, the Hainai, the Nasoni, and the Neche. In about 1690, when the first Spanish missionaries came, these tribes together probably numbered from 3,000 to 5,000 persons. It seems that each tribe had its own chiefs and tribal government but owed a measure of allegiance to the *caddi*, that is, the chief of the Hainai tribe and head chief of the confederacy. More powerful than the grand *caddi*, however, was the *chenesi*, or the head priest, who kept the fire temple. The fire in it was never extinguished and from it the fires of all the confederacy were lighted.

These Indians lived in domelike houses, reinforced with stakes, thatched with twigs, daubed with mud, and covered with grass. According to the descriptions left by early French and Spanish chroniclers, the furnishings suggest beauty as well as solid comfort. In the houses were many-colored rugs, woven of reeds; beds, made of reeds resting on a framework of poles and covered with buffalo hides; reed baskets, filled with beans, acorns, and nuts; jars, filled with corn and covered over with ashes to keep out the weevils; and corn, shucked and hung where exposure to smoke would drive away the weevils. We are told that each year these Indians kept enough seed for two years, lest one crop should be a total failure. Of course, a great part of their food was secured by hunting. Deer and bear were abundant, and hunting parties frequently visited the buffalo range, which was not more than a hundred miles to the west. The Hasinai did not live in large, compact villages similar to the pueblos in Mexico and along the Rio Grande, but rather in hamlets of from seven to fifteen houses divided by woodlands and farms. The diseases and vices of the Europeans took a heavy toll from among the Hasinai tribes during the late eighteenth century. Then, when the Anglo-Americans came, in the nineteenth century, they drove the Indians from their homes into Central Texas and finally into the Indian Territory. Most of the tribes lost their identity and were referred to by the common appellation "Caddo." Associated with the Caddo in southeast Texas lived the Atakapans, consisting of several small tribes, among them the Orcoquisacs and the Bidais. They were hunters, gatherers, and fishermen.

The Karankawa Indians, a small tribe, lived near Matagorda Bay. They were a tall, well-formed people; but their savage customs, including even cannibalism, made them hated by the white men. They anointed their bodies with shark and fish oil, a practice that repelled mosquitoes but gave them a disgusting odor. A few were eventually Christianized, or, at least, lived at the Spanish mission Espíritu Santo, but the large majority were exterminated by wars with the Anglo-Americans during the first half of the nineteenth century.

In south central Texas lived the Tonkawa, a powerful tribe or association of tribes that farmed on a small scale and subsisted mainly on deer and buffalo. They were alternately at peace and at war with the Spaniards during the eighteenth century; and their relations with the Hasinais on the east, the Wichitas and Comanches on the north, and the Apaches on the west were unstable. In the nineteenth century, by the time the Anglo-American colonists arrived, the Tonkawa had been reduced by war and disease to a few hundred souls, tolerated but generally not trusted by the white frontiersmen. During the last Indian wars in Texas they served well as scouts for the military.

From the Arkansas River in Kansas, southward to the vicinity of the present Waco, lived the Wichita tribes. Of these tribes, the Wichita proper (probably identifiable with the Taovayas, or Tawehash of the Spanish era) lived along the Red River, and during the nineteenth century became the most adept horse thieves along the entire border. The Tawakoni and Waco tribes lived in north central Texas and belonged to Texas until they were expelled in 1859. In some respects they lived much like their Caddoan kinsmen to the east; in other respects they were like the Indians of the plains. They farmed to a limited extent and from time to time made hunting trips into the plains. They were proud and warlike and preferred death to imprisonment.

When the Spaniards first came to Texas all of the western part of the state from the Panhandle to the Rio Grande seems to have been dominated by the Apache Indians. Probably the Querechos, whom Coronado met on the plains in 1541, were Apaches. They moved with the buffalos and from the herds supplied all their wants. When they struck camp they packed their belongings on the backs of dogs. The Apaches began to harass San Antonio immediately after that outpost was established in 1718, and their maraudings continued until late in the nineteenth century.

The most troublesome Apache tribes in Texas were the Lipan, the Natagés, and the Mescalero. Many military expeditions were sent against them, and if we are to believe the reports of the white men, large numbers of Indians were slain; but always enough were left to return and renew the depredations. Missionary efforts among them during the eighteenth century were as unsuccessful as were later efforts to exterminate them by aligning against them the friendly tribes of the north. The history of the Jicarilla and other Apache tribes that frequented the northwestern part of Texas at an early date is mainly linked with that of New Merico.

Either an Apache tribe or a tribe associated with the Apaches was the Jumano, found by the Spaniards in the seventeenth century from the vicinity of present-day Presidio eastward to the mouth of the Concho. When the Spaniards first knew them they were enemies of the Apaches and received the white men kindly. Later, however, they became allies of the Apaches and enemies of the Spaniards. The Taovayas (Tawehash) along the Red River also came to be called by the name Jumano, but it may well be doubted that they had any connection with the Jumanos of West Texas.

During later historic times the Great Plains of Texas and a part of the adjacent territory were occupied by the Comanche Indians. They came from the north in the early eighteenth century and drove a wedge between the Apache country on the west and the Caddoan country on the east that extended to the vicinity of Austin and San Antonio. There were several Comanche tribes, or Comanche bands with the status of independent tribes. Of these tribes or bands the better known were: the

A great part of Texas was once Comanche country. Pictured here are Quanah Parker, one of the last Comanche war chiefs and the son of Chief Nocona and Cynthia Ann Parker, a captive white woman; and a Comanche camp in 1872. (Bureau of American Ethnology)

Penatekas, or Honey-eaters, on the south; the Kotsotekas, or Buffalo-eaters, and Nokonies, along the Red and Canadian rivers; the Yamparikas, or Root-eaters, along the Arkansas; and the wild Kwahadis of the High Plains. The Penatekas lived in Texas and the other Comanche divisions either lived in it or visited it from time to time. The Kiowas, loyal allies of the Comanches, occasionally came along with these northern bands.

The Comanches were a nomadic people who never planted crops of any kind. Although each tribe or band regarded a given region as its home and always returned to it after its wanderings, the Comanches never remained for long in any one place. They would break camp on the slightest excuse or on no excuse at all. If a prominent person died, or if an epidemic caused several deaths at a certain camp, the site would be abandoned at once and the Indians would never return there—a practice which, in spite of its obvious inconveniences, no doubt checked the ravages of diseases. More advanced people fumigate after an epidemic; the Comanches moved. Superb horsemen and fierce warriors, the Comanches harried the settlements of Texas and other north-Mexican provinces during the Spanish and Mexican regimes and made life unsafe on the Anglo-American frontier until 1875.

Selected Bibliography

The foremost bibliographies pertaining to Texas are Thomas W. Streeter, *Bibliography of Texas*, 1795–1845 (2 vols., Cambridge, Mass., 1956); E. W. Winkler, *Check List of Texas Imprints*, 1846–1876 (Austin, 1949); E. W. Winkler and Llerena Friend, *Check List of Texas Imprints, 1861–1876* (Austin, 1963); Seymour V. Connor, "A Preliminary Guide to the Archives of Texas," *Southwestern Historical Quarterly*, LX, 255–334; Chester V. Kielman, *The University of Texas Archives* (Austin, 1967).

It is well to be acquainted with *Resources of Texas Libraries* by Edward G. Holley and Donald D. Hendrick (Austin, 1968). The most comprehensive work on the history of Texas is the *Handbook of Texas*, edited by Walter Prescott Webb and H. Bailey Carroll (2 vols., Austin, 1952). A supplementary volume will appear in 1969. The *Texas Almanac*, published biennially by the *Dallas News*, is a dependable reference work on Texas.

The greatest collection of writings on Texas history is the *Quarterly of the Texas State Historical Association* (I–XV, Austin, Texas) from 1897 to 1912, and its successor, the *Southwestern Historical Quarterly*, beginning with July 1912. Much Texas material may be found also in the *Mississippi Valley Historical Review* (and its successor, the *Journal of American History*), since 1914; the *Journal of Southern History*, since 1934; the *Southwestern Social Science Quarterly*, since 1920; the *American West*, since 1963; and *Texana*, a quarterly journal of Texas history published since 1962 at Waco. Some regional publications contain a great deal of Texas history: the *East Texas Historical Journal,* since 1963; *Texas Gulf Coast Historical Publications,* since 1957; the *Panhandle-Plains Historical Review,* since 1927; and the *West Texas Historical Association Year Book,* since 1925.

A convenient and useful collection of source materials on the history of Texas is *Documents of Texas History,* edited by Ernest Wallace with the assistance of David M. Vigness (Austin, 1963). On natural resources, useful are Elmer H. Johnson, *The Natural Regions of Texas* (University of Texas *Bulletin,* No. 3113; Austin, 1931); Frederick W. Simonds, *The Geography of Texas* (Boston, 1914); W. T. Carter, *The Soils of Texas* (College Station, 1931); W. A. Silveus, *Texas Grasses* (San Antonio, 1933); Roy Bedicheck, *Adventures with a Texas Naturalist* (New York, 1947); and W. T. Chambers, *The Geography of Texas* (Austin, 1952).

A basic source on Texas archeology is Dee Ann Suhm and Alex D. Krieger, *An Introductory Handbook of Texas Archeology,* Texas Archeological Society *Bulletin,* Vol. 25 (Austin, 1954). Useful also is E. H. Sellards, *Early Man in America: A Study in Pre-History* (Austin, 1952). An authoritative book on archeology and Indians, containing a comprehensive bibliography is *The Indians of Texas* by W. W. Newcomb, Jr. (Austin, 1961). Rich in source material is Dorman H. Winfrey and James M. Day (eds.), *The Indian Papers of Texas and the Southwest, 1825–1916* (5 vols., Austin, 1966.) Some histories of Indian tribes are: Mildred P. Mayhall, *The Kiowas* (Norman, 1962); Rupert N. Richardson, *The Comanche Barrier to South Plains Settlement* (Glendale, 1933); and Ernest Wallace and E. A. Hoebel, *The Comanches, Lords of the South Plains* (Norman, 1952).

2

EXPLORATION AND OCCUPATION OF TEXAS, 1519–1763

EXPLORATION

Texas came within the orbit of Spain's interests early in the sixteenth century. Commissioned by the governor of Jamaica to explore the lands beyond those claimed by Ponce de León and to search for a strait that linked the Atlantic and Pacific Oceans, Alonso Alvarez de Piñeda in 1519 mapped the coast of the Gulf of Mexico from Florida to Vera Cruz. Piñeda spent forty days at the mouth of the Rio Grande, his "River of Palms," and recommended that a settlement be planted there. This goal was not attained, however, until more than two centuries later.

The first Spaniards to enter the interior of Texas were Alvar Núñez Cabeza de Vaca and three companions, survivors of the ill-fated Pánfilo de Nárvaez expedition, which had landed on the coast of Florida in 1528. Having despaired of finding rumored riches, the 242 stranded survivors in overcrowded, crude boats had tried to reach Pánuco by sailing westward along the coast. The party was shipwrecked in November on the coast of Texas, and only a few men escaped from the sea. After nearly six years of servitude to the Indians, four of the group by persistence and ingenuity managed to escape into the interior. Thence, after wandering many hundreds of miles, probably by the sites of San Antonio and Presidio, they arrived on May 18, 1536, at the northern outpost of Culiacán, near the Gulf of California.

The tales of adventure brought to Mexico by Cabeza de Vaca created great excitement and brought about the expedition of Francisco Vásquez de Coronado, governor of Nueva Galicia on the northwestern frontier, who left Compostela in February 1540, to penetrate the mysterious north country. Under his command marched three hundred horsemen, seventy footmen, and more than a thousand Indians.

Instead of the splendid Seven Cities of Cíbola, which the conqueror had hoped to find, he reached, near the present Arizona-New Mexico line, shabby pueblos inhabited by hostile Indians. Neither did he find anything precious at Tiguex on the Rio Grande near Albuquerque, where he spent the winter of 1540–1541. When spring came, he set out in search of Quivira, a gilded land which an Indian slave told him lay somewhere to the east. He spent many days wandering over the treeless and level plains of Texas and probably crossed Palo Duro Canyon. After 77 days of marching across a land where he had seen "nothing but cows and the sky," he found Quivira—several Wichita Indian villages of squalid grass houses in central Kansas. The chief wore a copper plate about his neck, but there was no gold. Thoroughly discouraged, Coronado returned by way of Tiguex to Mexico, and reported to King Charles I that he did not consider the country he had explored of sufficient value to warrant its being occupied by Spaniards. He had found no precious metals, and the natives were either nomads, who lived in skin lodges, or semi-sedentary barbarians, who lived miserably in little villages. His report destroyed for many years to come the interest of Spaniards in the great northern interior.

While Coronado was searching the southwestern United States for fabulous cities that did not exist, another Spaniard, Hernando de Soto, with about 600 men was exploring the region north of the Gulf of Mexico for wealth with no better success. After De Soto's death, at the Mississippi River in May 1542, the expedition under the command of Luis de Moscoso de Alvarado set out by land for Mexico. After passing through the piney woods of the Tejas in eastern Texas, it marched for many days through a very poor and thinly populated country, probably as far west as the Brazos River in the western Cross Timbers. Unable to get in touch with Coronado, of whom they had heard from the Indians, and beset by a lack of food and inhospitable natives, Moscoso and his followers returned to the Mississippi. Here they built seven crude boats, and on July 3 began floating downstream. Eleven weeks later the 311 survivors, after having been forced ashore near present-day Beaumont, reached the Spanish town of Pánuco. Like Coronado, the men of the De Soto force found nothing in the interior that made them wish to return. For half a century thereafter the Spaniards gave little thought to the region now known as New Mexico and Texas.

During the seventeenth century the history of Texas was closely linked with that of New Mexico. By 1563 the frontier of New Spain had been extended to Santa Bárbara, on the headwaters of the Conchos, a stream that flows northward into the Rio Grande. Zealous Franciscans laboring in that vicinity heard of Indians living in the upper valley of the Rio Grande who were comparatively advanced and lived like those in Mexico. They visited the country, military expeditions followed, and in 1598 Juan de Oñate established Spanish settlements in the upper valley of the Rio Grande. Later, in 1609 Santa Fé had its beginning. This northward advance was followed by the establishment of several missions along the Rio Grande border of southwestern Texas. A mission was founded in 1659 on the site of modern Juarez at El Paso del Norte. After the Indian revolt in New Mexico in 1680, the retreating Spaniards and friendly Indians established the mission pueblo of Corpus Christi de la Isleta a few miles east of El Paso where the village of Ysleta now is. This was the first permanent European settlement within the present boundaries of Texas.

From El Paso, the Spaniards attempted to expand their missionary activities eastward. In 1683 they established a group of missions and pueblos near the junction of the Rio Grande and the Conchos River in the vicinity of present-day Presidio. Also that year, emissaries of the Jumano Indians, a friendly tribe living along the Concho River, came to El Paso asking for missionaries. In response to their request, the governor of New Mexico sent Father Nicolás López and a military escort commanded by Don Juan Domíngues de Mendoza. Near the junction of the Concho and Colorado rivers, where they arrived in February 1684, Mendoza and López built a combination chapel and fort. During their six-weeks sojourn here the soldiers gathered an abundant number of buffalo hides and Father López baptized a bountiful harvest of red souls. The two leaders liked the country and the Indians, and afterwards Mendoza made a trip to Mexico to ask for authorization to plant a mission in the Jumano country. The petition was never granted, for at about that time reports began to reach New Spain that the French had established a settlement on the Gulf Coast, a flagrant intrusion on Spanish claims. These aliens must be found and expelled, and toward that end the best efforts of New Spain were directed.

FRENCH INTRUSION: LA SALLE

The Frenchman whose settlement in Texas provoked Spain's ire was Robert Cavelier, sieur de La Salle, a trader from Canada. In 1682 La Salle had descended the Mississippi to its mouth and claimed for his king all the country that it drained, even "to the mouth of the River of Palms" (Rio Grande). Returning to France, La Salle obtained from Louis XIV a commission to found a colony at the mouth of the Mississippi. On August 1, 1684, he set sail with a company of about three hundred persons in four ships to carry out the plan. Missing the mouth of the Mississippi, La Salle landed at Matagorda Bay on the Texas coast in February 1685. He erected a crude stockade, Fort St. Louis, on Garcitas Creek in the general vicinity of present-day Vanderbilt, and set out to explore the country. After a six-months' journey to the south and west, he returned (with only eight of the 30 men who had started) to find that he was stranded. Not one of his four ships was left. The *St. François* had been lost to Spanish corsairs, the *Amiable* had grounded on the shoals of Matagorda Bay, the *Belle* had wrecked on Palacios Bay, and the *Joli* had sailed back to France. Furthermore, the first crop had failed, the supplies were gone, the Karankawa Indians were making life unsafe, and of the 180 people left behind when the *Joli* sailed for France only 45 were still alive. La Salle thus determined to find the Mississippi and go to Canada for help. On his third expedition (his second toward the east) he was assassinated on March 20, 1687, by one of his men, probably in present-day Cherokee County. Six of the survivors, led by Henri Joutel, La Salle's faithful lieutenant, and guided by a Tejas Indian, finally made their way to Canada and thence to France, but they were unable to persuade Louis XIV to send aid to the ill-fated colony in Texas.

Meanwhile, Fort St. Louis had been destroyed and most of its inhabitants slain. Through French pirates, whom they happened to capture, the Spaniards learned of La Salle's establishment some six months after it was founded. Several expeditions by both land and sea, however, failed to discover the intruders. At last, on his fourth expedition into Texas, Governor Alonso de León of Coahuila, marching from the vicinity of Monclova, reached the ruins of Fort St. Louis on April 22, 1689. Afterwards, De León found two of La Salle's men living among the Indians and learned the sad history of the colony.

THE FIRST MISSIONS IN EAST TEXAS

Although fate had removed the French menace from the Gulf Coast, thoughtful and patriotic Spaniards realized that Spain's claim to the region would always be disputed until she took possession of it. On his return to Mexico De León sent to the viceroy a glowing report regarding the country of the Tejas. The land was fertile; the climate salubrious; and the people were more highly civilized than most primitive groups. Spain should occupy the country at once. Father Damian Massanet, who had accompanied De León and had visited with the chief of the Tejas, was even more eager for the Spaniards to move into the region. He had promised the Tejas chief that he would return. Thus the priest and the soldier made a joint petition asking the viceroy, the Count of Galve, to authorize and support a missionary expedition to the Tejas.

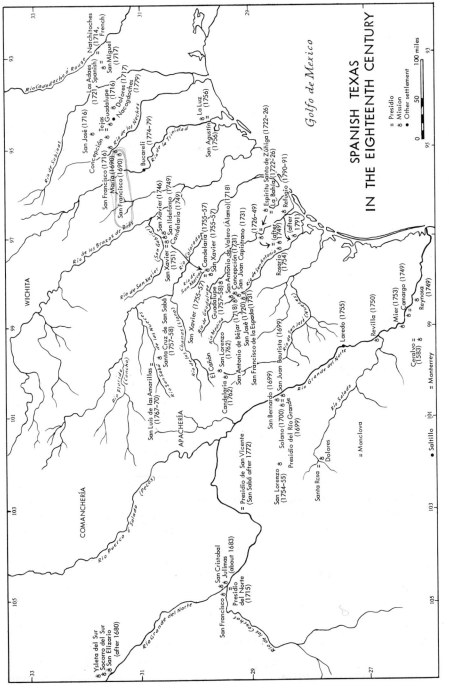

From Robert S. Weddle, The San Saba Mission, Spanish Pivot in Texas (Austin, 1964), p. 4. (By permission of the author and publisher, the University of Texas Press.)

Map labels (top to bottom, as oriented):

COMANCHERÍA

WICHITA

Natchitoches (1714, French)
Los Adaes (1721, Spanish) = San Miguel (1717)
Guadalupe (1716)
Dolores (1717)
San José (1716)
Concepción (1716) Tejas
San Francisco (1690) Nacogdoches (1779)
María (1690)
San Francisco (1690)
Bucareli (1774–79)
Río Cadodacho o Rouge
Río de Sabinas
Río de los Neches
Río de la Trinidad

San Agustín = (1756)
La Luz = (1756)

Golfo de Mexico

SPANISH TEXAS
IN THE EIGHTEENTH CENTURY

= Presidio
ö Mission
• Other settlement

0   50   100 miles

San Gabriel = San Xavier (1746)
San Xavier = San Ildefonso (1749)
San Xavier (1751) Candelaria (1749)
Candelaria (1755–57)
San Xavier (1755–57)
Río de San Xavier
Río Colorado
San Antonio de Valero (Alamo) (1718)
Guadalupe (1757–58) ö Concepción (1731)
San José (1720) ö San Juan Capistrano (1731)
San Francisco de la Espada (1731)
San Antonio de Béjar (1718)
Río de San Antonio = (after 1749)
Rosario ö (1754)
Espíritu Santo de Zúñiga (1722–26)
La Bahía (1722–26)
Refugio (1790–91) (after 1791)

San Luís de las Amarillas (1767–70)
Santa Cruz de San Sabá (1757–58)
Río San Sabá
Río de las Nueces
Río Chanas (Llano)
El Cañón ö San Lorenzo (1762)
Candelaria ö (1762)
San Lorenzo (1754–55)
Presidio de San Vicente (San Sabá after 1772)
Río Florida (Conchos)

APACHERÍA

Río Puerco o Salado
Río Salado (Pecos)

San José
San Bernardo (1699)
San Juan Bautista (1699)
Solano = (1700) ö
Presidio del Río Grande (1699)
Laredo (1755)
Revilla (1750)
Mier (1753)
Camargo (1749)
Reynosa (1749)
Río Medina
Río Guadalupe
Río San José (Cibolo)

Cerralvo (1583)
= Monterrey
Río Grande del Norte
Río Salado

Santa Rosa = ö Dolores
= Monclova
= Saltillo

Ysleta del Sur
ö Socorro del Sur
ö San Elizario (after 1680)
San Cristóbal
ö Julimes (about 1683)
San Francisco ö
= Presidio del Norte (1715)
Río Grande del Norte
Río de los (...chos)

Their petition having been officially approved, Father Massanet, accompanied by three other priests, and De León, with a military escort of more than a hundred soldiers, set out from Monclova in late March of 1690 for Texas. Massanet's friend, the Tejas chief, with a welcoming party of fourteen Indians, met them at the Trinity, and on May 22, 1690, they arrived at the principal village of the Nabedache, a division of the Tejas. Fields of corn, beans, and melons gave the Spaniards confidence in the value of the country, and the chief demonstrated Indian hospitality by serving his guests tamales and mush. Twelve days later the Spaniards celebrated mass and sang *Te Deum Laudamus* in the first mission in the land of the Tejas—San Francisco de los Tejas, located a few miles west of the Neches River, near the present-day village of Weches in Houston County. On the next day De León and Father Massanet began their homeward trek, leaving behind three priests and three soldiers to man this remote post in the land of the Tejas against further French intrusion.

In 1691 Domingo Terán de los Rios, who had been commissioned governor of the province of the Tejas and Coahuila with orders to explore and establish additional missions in Texas, led a second expedition, including nine priests, to the Tejas, where diligent priests had already founded a second mission. Affairs at the missions were going badly, however. An epidemic had taken many of the Indians and a priest had died; drought had destroyed the crops; and the natives had grown first indifferent, then insolent, and finally hostile. Early in 1692 Terán departed, leaving behind only the stouthearted Massanet, two companions, and a guard of nine soldiers. In June 1693, a relief expedition from Monclova brought them food and equipment, but their cause seemed hopeless. Now even Father Massanet agreed that it would take the strong arm of the military to sustain the missions. On October 25, 1693, even before word had been received authorizing the abandonment of the place, the Spaniards set fire to their mission and stole away.

The efforts of De León, Terán, and Massanet had not been altogether in vain. They had acquainted the Spaniards with the geography and the Indians of Texas, and their failure proved that missions in that country could not succeed unless sustained by presidios and settlements.

OCCUPATION OF EAST TEXAS

Although the administration of New Spain had abandoned the Tejas country, the priests and the captains of the frontier did not forget the land of sturdy oaks and stately pines. One of the priests, Father Francisco Hidalgo, spent most of his time on the frontier of Coahuila, hoping anxiously for an opportunity to return to Texas. The dedicated missionary had to wait many years.

For a decade after the failure of La Salle's enterprise France did not press her claim to the lower Mississippi Valley. Costly wars absorbed the energy of Louis XIV. When the Peace of Ryswick gave him a breathing spell and word came that the English were threatening to take the Gulf country, the Grand Monarch moved with energy. His expedition under Pierre Le Moyne, sieur d'Iberville, sailed from France to occupy Pensacola Bay. But the Spaniards, aroused by reports of renewed French activity, had just beaten him to that location. The French expedition then sailed away to establish a post at Biloxi in April 1699. Three years later the French founded a post at Mobile.

In 1712 the crown granted the colony of Louisiana to Antoine Crozat as a commercial monopoly, and La Mothe Cadillac became its first proprietary governor. Meanwhile, Philip of Anjou, grandson of Louis XIV, had ascended the throne of Spain, and the Spanish government had given its tacit consent to French occupancy of the Gulf region. Thenceforth Spanish relations with the French were cordial, but the Spaniards were loath to engage in international trade. This trade Crozat sought, and in 1713 he was planning to send an overland expedition to New Spain when a strange communication reached him. He received a letter from a former Spanish missionary to the Tejas, Fray Francisco Hidalgo, suggesting that the French might be interested in helping to establish a mission for the Tejas. Accordingly, Cadillac made an arrangement with Louis de St. Denis, a Canadian who had been active in Louisiana since 1699, to go to the country of the Tejas, find Father Hidalgo, if possible, and inaugurate a trading program with the Spaniards. St. Denis proceeded leisurely, building a storehouse in October 1713, at a village of the Natchitoches on the Red River, trading with various Indians, inquiring among the Tejas about Father Hidalgo, and arriving finally with a small party at San Juan Bautista on the Rio Grande on July 18, 1714.

St. Denis' coming excited and alarmed the Spaniards. There were positive orders against the introduction of foreign goods or the admission of foreigners into New Spain for any reason whatsoever. Both St. Denis and Father Hidalgo were called to Mexico City for explanations. They fared well, nevertheless; the Frenchman managed to win the hand of the granddaughter of Captain Diego Ramón, the commander of the presidio at San Juan Bautista, and in addition was given a contract to serve as guide to the party of soldiers and missionaries which the government of New Spain determined to send to Texas, and the priest was granted permission to return to the Tejas.

Once again the encroachment of the French had spurred the Spaniards into action. They had learned that missions among the Tejas must be sustained by forts and civil settlements. Hence, in the party of about 70 persons that arrived in the land of the Tejas under the command of Captain Domingo Ramón in June 1716, there were 25 soldiers and several families in addition to a dozen missionaries. The mission work was to be divided among the two noted Franciscan missionary colleges or seminaries which were located at Zacatecas and Querétaro. Fray Antonio Margil de Jesús represented the Zacatecans and Fray Felix Isidro de Espinosa was in charge of the Querétarans.

Like that accorded to De León and Massanet more than a quarter of a century before, the reception by the Indians was most cordial. The first mission, founded on July 3, 1716, and called Nuestro Padre San Francisco de los Tejas, was located just east of the Neches River and a few miles north of the site of the mission which had been founded in 1690. It was fitting that Father Hidalgo should be placed in charge of this mission. During the next few days three other missions were established in the same general vicinity: La Purísima Concepción, eight or nine leagues northeast of San Francisco, near present-day Linwood Crossing; Guadalupe, at present Nacogdoches; and San José, in northwestern Nacogdoches County, two and a half miles north of the village of Cushing.

To offset French influence the Spaniards founded San Miguel among the Adaes Indians, at the site of Robeline, Louisiana, about fifteen miles west of the French post of Natchitoches. Still later, in the autumn of 1716, Ramón and Father Margil planted Mission Dolores among the Ais Indians, near the modern San Augustine and about halfway between the Tejas group and Los Adaes. Thus, by the close of 1716, the Spaniards had established six missions, five of them extending in a line from the Neches to Los Adaes, within a few miles of the Red River. The troops were quartered at Presidio Dolores which Ramón built on the Neches River at the western end of the line of missions.

As a result of a request for supplies and reinforcements for East Texas and a petition from Father Antonio de Buenaventura Olivares, who had accompanied Ramón in 1716, Spanish officials assigned Martín de Alarcón, the governor of Coahuila and Texas, the task of establishing a supporting mission post in Texas. It was at present-day San Antonio that Alarcón left his monument. In May 1718, he founded there *Villa de Bexar* and Mission San Antonio de Valero, later known as the Alamo, which was entrusted to Father Olivares. The *villa* was destined to become the most important Spanish settlement in Texas and was the capital during the last half-century of Spain's control. The founding of the mission was the beginning of the most successful missionary enterprise in Texas. The Alamo later became the shrine of Texas freedom.

The missionary activities of the Spaniards in East Texas were soon interrupted by a war between Spain and France. By order of Governor Celeron de Bienville of Louisiana, M. Blondel, commander of the post at Natchitoches, in June 1719, moved against Mission San Miguel de los Adaes with seven men. The French took the mission and its two occupants, a soldier and a lay brother, and all the mission property. In a moment of confusion, however, the lay brother escaped and made his way hurriedly to Mission Dolores, where he reported that the French were moving with a superior force against the Spanish outposts. The invasion did not materialize, but in the panic that the report created the Spaniards retired to San Antonio.

Convinced that vigorous action was needed, the viceroy appointed the Marqués de San Miguel de Aguayo, a wealthy citizen of Coahuila, governor and captain general of the province of the Tejas and Coahuila and ordered him to recruit a force sufficient to drive the French from Texas and reestablish the Spaniards there. Setting out with 500 men, 5,000 horses and mules, and large herds of cattle and sheep, Aguayo marched into Texas, arriving at the Trinity River on July 9, 1721. The Indians, as ever, were friendly and welcomed the Spaniards with evident delight.

St. Denis, now commander at Natchitoches, on July 31 met Aguayo and informed him that peace had been made by the powers. Aguayo reestablished all the abandoned Spanish missions and turned them over to the churchmen with impressive ceremonies. Then, in spite of St. Denis' protests, he established at Los Adaes, in the autumn of 1721, the presidio of Nuestra Señora del Pilár and left in charge a garrison of a hundred men, equipped with six brass fieldpieces and plenty of powder and shot. This place, with its garrison, mission, and small civil settlement, became the capital of Texas. Here at Los Adaes and the neighboring French post of Natchitoches, the prongs of empire touched. The Spanish advance toward the northeast was ended, as was the French penetration westward from the Mississippi. In the spring of 1722 Aguayo went to La Bahía del Espíritu Santo (Lavaca Bay), and directed the construction of a presidio and a mission near the site of La Salle's old fort. When he returned to Coahuila, Aguayo left behind him 269 soldiers, quartered in presidios at San Antonio, on the Angelina, at Los Adaes, and at La Bahía. Each of the four presidios marked a mission center and altogether they guarded ten missions.

But the complete and adequate establishment left by Aguayo was not permitted to remain undisturbed for long. King Philip V directed the viceroy of New Spain, the Marqués de Casa Fuerte, to make reforms in the interest of economy. Pedro Rivera was sent to make a complete inspection of the frontier posts and to recommend reforms, keeping in mind always the necessity for economizing. Rivera reached Texas in 1727, and as a result of his recommendations the number of soldiers at Los Adaes was cut from 100 to 60 men and the presidio on the Angelina was abolished. The abandonment of the presidio forced the removal of three of the missions in its vicinity to the Colorado in 1730, and to San Antonio the following year. As Spanish influence declined, French influence increased. To Rivera's recommendations also must be charged many of the losses and sufferings endured by the people of San Antonio from raids by the Apaches. At the very time the beleaguered community needed more soldiers to protect its expanding settlements the military force was reduced.

Franco-Spanish relations on the border of Texas, from Rivera's visit to the cession of Louisiana to Spain in 1762, generally speaking, were quiet and peaceful. Representatives of both nations generally accepted in practice the Arroyo Hondo, a small stream running between Los Adaes and Natchitoches, as the dividing line between the two empires. In the contest for the Indian trade the French were more successful. By means of the Nassonite post, established by Bénard de la Harpe in 1719 on the Red River a few miles northwest of the present-day Texarkana, the French controlled the Cadodacho and associated tribes in that vicinity. Likewise they appropriated the trade of the Wichita and the Tawakoni in northern Texas and of the Tonkawa farther south. In about 1750 the Taovayas located their villages at the site of Spanish Fort, far up the Red River in present-day Montague County, and this place became a center of French influence. As early as 1730 French traders from Louisiana passed the Sabine River and traded among the Orcoquizac on the Texas coast. Spurred by this threat, the Spaniards in 1756 established the presidio of San Agustín de Ahumada and a mission, Nuestra Señora de la Luz del Orcoquisac, near the mouth of the Trinity in the general vicinity of modern Anahuac and maintained them for about fifteen years. The place was commonly referred to as El Orcoquisac.

EFFORTS AT EXPANSION

The Spanish occupation of the Gulf region along the lower Trinity River in 1756 was, in a way, only one part of a general program of expansion in practically all of northern New Spain. These efforts at expansion were prompted by a combination of forces both external and internal. Spain's northern outposts were threatened all along her frontiers. The French from Canada and Louisiana were edging into Texas and across the Great Plains toward Santa Fé; the English had founded Georgia and were threatening Spanish supremacy in Florida; a number of Indian tribes were menacing the settlements on the frontier; and reports of the discovery of precious metals in the Apache country north of San Antonio made the occupation of that region seem imperative. In Texas, the expansion movement got under way about 1745 and continued, with various interruptions, until the cession of Louisiana to Spain by France in 1762. One of its more important phases, the Spanish activity along the lower Trinity, has been related briefly. Three other topics, the founding of Nuevo Santander, the San Xavier missions and presidio, and the San Sabá establishment call for more consideration.

In the northward advance of New Spain into Nuevo León, Coahuila, Chihuahua, New Mexico, and Texas, the Spaniards had left uncon-

Mission and (restored) Presido La Bahia, Goliad. Before he withdrew from the Presido in one of the bloodiest battles in Texas history, James Fannin buried the ancient hand-poured cannon shown (below) *to prevent its being taken by the Mexicans. On the prairie a few miles away, Fannin's force of some four hundred troops was captured and later shot by Mexican firing squads.* (Texas Highway Department)

quered a vast coastal area from Tampico to the San Antonio River, called Nuevo Santander, extending inland in certain places as far as 300 miles. Spanish officials feared that the English might attempt to plant a settlement in this vast unguarded region. Furthermore, it was a place of refuge for various remnants of tribes and Indian renegades. The task of subduing them and colonizing the region was assigned in 1746 to José de Escandón, a veteran Indian fighter, who had established Spanish authority in the Sierra Gorda, the mountainous part of the region.

After two years of making preparations and exploring the country, he gathered at Querétaro more than 3,000 soldiers and settlers, and as he advanced northward others joined him. At various sites he left colonists and garrisons under whose protection the priests founded missions. Beginning with the villas of Camargo and Reynosa in 1749, he had founded 23 settlements by 1755, representing the homes of more than 6,000 colonists. Among the most important of these settlements were Dolores and Laredo north of the Rio Grande. Meanwhile, the Franciscan missionaries of the College of Zacatecas had founded 15 missions. Later, Spanish ranchmen appropriated a considerable part of the territory lying between the lower Rio Grande and the Nueces River.

Modern Goliad also had its beginning with Escandón. In 1726 Mission La Bahía del Espíritu Santo de Zuñiga and Prisidio Nuestra Señora de Loreto, which had been founded by Aguayo, were moved to the Guadalupe River in the vicinity of present-day Victoria. Because of the unhealthy climate and the inability to irrigate the surrounding lands, Escandón had the mission and presidio moved in 1749 to the San Antonio River at the present site of Goliad. Although many miles in the interior, the new establishment continued to be known simply as La Bahía. In 1754, as a result of rivalry between Zacatecan and Querétaran missionaries, Mission Nuestra Señora del Rosario was founded about three miles to the southwest for the Karankawas. Around these establishments grew up one of the three principal settlements in Spanish Texas, La Bahía or Goliad.

Along the San Gabriel River, 150 miles northeast of San Antonio in present-day Milam County, there lived during the first half of the eighteenth century various Indian tribes and remnants of tribes commonly referred to as *Ranchería Grande*. Apparently the Tonkawas and certain associates made up a considerable part of this Indian conglomeration.

Father Mariano de los Dolores, a missionary located at San Antonio, began work in this mission field as early as 1746. Three missions and a presidio, all commonly referred to as San Xavier, were established between 1748 and 1751 on the San Xavier (San Gabriel) River, near the present-day town of Rockdale; but their history is a story of continuous turmoil and strife. Unfaithful Indians, smallpox, measles, hostile Apaches, and drought harassed the place. The commander, Captain Felipe Rábago y Terán, quarreled with a priest, Father Ganzabal; and when the churchman was slain, Rábago was charged with murder but was never convicted. One mission was broken up in the confusion, and the two remaining were removed to the San Marcos River in the summer of 1755, and thence, after a year, to the Guadalupe.

The mission enterprise on the San Xavier was followed by the most ambitious and the most ill-fated mission extension program undertaken by the Spaniards in Texas, the San Sabá post for the Apaches.

Apache hostility toward the Spaniards dates back to early *entradas* into the upper Colorado River country. Following the founding of San Antonio in 1718, their marauding expeditions came to be regular occurrences. To these raids the Spaniards frequently replied with retaliatory thrusts, which never brought them more than temporary relief. The missionaries, among them the veteran Francisco Hidalgo and Father Santa Ana, urged that the Spaniards try the gospel where the sword had failed. By 1745 the Apaches, hard pressed by the fierce Comanches to the north, were at San Antonio asking for missions. Four years later the Spaniards negotiated a peace treaty with them, and the priests urged that a mission be established at once. After the Apaches had destroyed in 1755 a mission built for them in Coahuila, the viceroy, pursuant to the recommendation of a general *junta*, by decree of May 18, 1756, ordered that missions be established in the Apache country of Texas. Don Pedro Romero de Terreros, a rich mine-owner philanthropist, agreed to support for three years as many missions for the Apaches as were deemed necessary. The royal government was to bear all the military expense and the missions were to be turned over to the government at the end of the three-year period.

In the spring of 1757 Colonel Diego Ortiz Parrilla, in command of about 400 persons (including 100 soldiers, and 237 women and children) and Father Alonso de Terreros (cousin of the philanthropist, in charge of the religious) founded Mission San Sabá de la Santa Cruz, Presidio San Luis de las Amarillas, and a settlement on the San Sabá River near the present-day town of Menard. The Apaches came in swarms that summer but never found it convenient to stay and become Christians. The alliance of the Spaniards with the Apaches had antagonized the fierce Comanches, who with their allies, the Wichitas, from north Texas attacked the mission and fort in March 1758, killing ten persons, among them Father Terreros. In an attack again a year later, they killed 19 persons. To avenge these deaths—and this insult to the flag of Spain—Parrilla led a mixed force of about 600 militiamen, presidial troops, mission Indians, and Apache warriors against the enemy Indians, who were entrenched at the villages of the Taovayas (present-day Spanish Fort) on the Red River. Parrilla was beaten in October 1759, and driven by the Indians hurriedly back to San Sabá. Spanish arms had suffered the most humiliating defeat at the hands of Indians in the entire history of Texas.

The mission on the San Sabá was never rebuilt. Missionary activities on behalf of the Apaches were transferred to the upper Nueces River, near the present-day Barksdale, where two missions, San Lorenzo de la Santa Cruz and Nuestra Señora de la Candelaria del Cañon, were established in 1762. For a while these missions prospered, but they were never given any support by the government and were abandoned seven years later. The presidio at San Sabá was strengthened and maintained until 1769.

Thus, Spain's efforts at expansion in Texas, except at Goliad and Laredo on the Rio Grande, were failures. El Orcoquisac, placed at the mouth of the Trinity River to expel French intruders, may have been of some value, but it never developed into a civil settlement or even a mission center of any consequence. The mission efforts on the San Xavier and the San Sabá ended in calamity, proving that Spain's chief pioneering institutions, the mission and the presidio, could not be made effective north of San Antonio.

Selected Bibliography

A satisfactory bibliography on Spanish Texas for the material available at the time it was published is Henry R. Wagner, *The Spanish Southwest, 1542–1794; An Annotated Bibliography* (Berkeley, 1924). The history of Texas in its relation to that of the rest of New Spain is dealt with in H. E. Bolton and Thomas M. Marshall, *The Colonization of North America, 1492–1783* (New York, 1921); H. E. Bolton, *The Spanish Borderlands* (New Haven, 1921); Edward G. Bourne, *Spain in America* (New York, 1904). Of the older histories of Texas the most satisfactory for the Spanish period are H. H. Bancroft, *History of the North Mexican States and Texas* (2 vols., San Francisco, 1884 and 1889); and Henderson Yoakum, *History of Texas* (2 vols., New York, 1855). A comprehensive history of early Texas is C. E. Castañeda's *Our Catholic Heritage in Texas 1519–1936* (7 vols., Austin, 1936–1958). Some recently published shorter accounts of the history of Spain in Texas are Odie B. Faulk, *A Successful Failure* (Austin, 1965); O. B. Faulk, *The Last Years of Spanish Texas* (The Hague, 1964); Hodding Carter, *Doomed Road of Empire: The Spanish Trail of Conquest* (New York, 1963).

A voluminous amount of Spanish source material is available. The best source of primary material is the Bexar Archives, located at the University of Texas. The best collection of translated sources is Charles W. Hackett (ed. and trans.), *Pichardo's Treatise on the Limits of Louisiana and Texas* (4 vols., Austin, 1931–1947). Other useful sources include Juan Agustín Morfi, *History of Texas, 1673–1679* (2 vols.,

Albuquerque, 1935); E. Wallace and D. M. Vigness (eds.), *Documents of Texas History; Documentos para la Historia Eclesiástica y Civil de la Provincia de Texas o Nueves Philipinas, 1720–1779* (Madrid, 1961).

There is an abundance of material on early explorers. General accounts are H. E. Bolton (ed.), *Spanish Exploration in the Southwest, 1542–1706* (New York, 1925 and 1959); F. W. Hodge and T. H. Lewis (eds.), *The Spanish Explorers in the Southern United States, 1528–1543* (New York, 1907 and 1959). See also Harbert Davenport and Joseph K. Wells, "The First Europeans in Texas, 1528–1536" (Cabeza de Vaca), *Southwestern Historical Quarterly,* XXII, 111–142, 205–259; Morris Bishop, *The Odyssey of Cabeza de Vaca* (New York, 1933); G. P. Winship, "The Coronado Expedition, 1540–1542," *Fourteenth Annual Report of the Bureau of American Ethnology, 1892–1893,* I, 329–637 (Washington, 1896); C. W. Hackett (ed.), *Historical Documents Relating to New Mexico, Nueva Vizcaya, and Approaches Thereto to 1773* (2 vols., Washington, D. C., 1923–1926); George P. Hammond, *Coronado's Seven Cities* (Albuquerque, 1940); G. P. Hammond and Agapito Rey (eds.), *Narratives of the Coronado Expedition, 1540–1542,* II (Albuquerque, 1940); H. E. Bolton, *Coronado, Knight of Pueblos and Plains* (New York, 1949); David Donoghue, "The Route of the Coronado Expedition in Texas," *The Southwestern Historical Quarterly,* XXXII, 181–192; W. C. Holden, "Coronado's Route across the Staked Plains," *West Texas Historical Association Year Book,* XX, 3–20; Francis Parkman, *LaSalle and the Discovery of the Great West* (Boston, 1893); Rex W. Strickland, "Moscoso's Journey through Texas," J. W. Williams, "Moscoso's Trail in Texas," and Albert Woldert, "The Expedition of Luis de Moscoso in Texas," *Southwestern Historical Quarterly,* XLVI, 109–166.

The best available material on the history of early missions and presidios is C. E. Castañeda, *Our Catholic Heritage in Texas;* Robert C. Clark, *The Beginnings of Texas, 1684–1718* (University of Texas *Bulletin,* No. 98, Humanistic Series, No. 6; Austin, 1907); H. E. Bolton, "The Location of LaSalle's Colony on the Gulf of Mexico," *Southwestern Historical Quarterly,* XXVII, 171–189; George L. Crocket, *Two Centuries in East Texas* (Dallas, 1932); Walter F. McCaleb, *Spanish Missions of Texas* (San Antonio, 1954); E. W. Cole, "LaSalle in Texas," *Southwestern Historical Quarterly,* XLIX, 473–500; Robert S. Weddle, *San Juan Bautista: Gateway to Spanish Texas* (Austin, 1968); R. S. Weddle, *The San Sabá Mission: Spanish Pivot in Texas* (Austin, 1964) Lesley Byrd Simpson (ed.), *The Sabá Papers: A Documentary Account of the Founding and Destruction of San Sabá Mission* (Paul D. Nathan, trans.; San Francisco, 1959); James Day, Joe B. Frantz, Ben H. Procter, Joseph W. Schmitz, Lon Tinkle, and Dorman H. Winfrey, *Six Missions of Texas* (Waco, 1965); Kathryn Stoner O'Connor, *The Presidio La Bahía del Espíritu Santo de Zuniga, 1721–1846* (Austin, 1966), F. C. Chabot, *San Antonio and Its Beginnings, 1691–1731* (San Antonio, 1931).

On border relations and efforts at expansion two scholarly studies by H. E. Bolton are *Texas in the Middle Eighteenth Century* (Berkeley, 1915) and *Athanase de Mézières and the Louisiana–Texas Frontier, 1768–1780* (2 vols., Cleveland, 1914). Useful also are C. W. Hackett, "Policy of the Spanish Crown Regarding French Encroachments from Louisiana, 1721–1762," in *New Spain and the Anglo-American West* (Los Angeles, 1932); William E. Dunn, "Missionary Activities among the Eastern Apaches . . . ," *Quarterly of the Texas State Historical Association*, XV, 186–200; I. J. Cox, "The Louisiana-Texas Frontier," *ibid.*, X, 1–75; XVII, 1–42, 140–187; W. E. Dunn, "The Apache Mission on the San Saba River . . . ," *ibid.*, XVII, 379–414; Ralph A. Smith (ed. and trans.), "Account of the Journey of Bénard de la Harpe: Discovery Made by Him of Several Nations Situated in the West," *ibid.*, LXII, 75–86, 246–259, 371–385, 525–541.

3

SPANISH TEXAS, 1763–1821

Late in the Seven Years' War Spain entered the conflict on the side of France. She lost Florida, but at the Peace of Paris in 1763 she was permitted to keep western Louisiana, which France had secretly ceded to her.

READJUSTMENTS FOLLOWING THE ACQUISITION OF LOUISIANA

Louisiana had cost France "eight hundred thousand *livres* a year, without yielding a *sou* in return," and it was to prove no less a burden to Spain. It was a vast domain which the declining Spanish Empire did not have the resources to defend and develop. On the northeast border the aggressive English rather than the tolerant French were now Spain's neighbors. Twenty years later the Republic of the United States had its beginning, and its frontier people were even more restless than they had been as British subjects. Furthermore, on the Pacific slope both the English and the Russians were threatening to appropriate a part of the Spanish Empire. Internal troubles in New Spain (Mexico) were even more threatening than the dangers from without. In Texas and other northern provinces hordes of savage Indians were becoming more and more destructive.

Drastic reforms and energetic measures were necessary to meet such problems. Fortunately for Spain, the king at this time was Charles III, one of the ablest men of the Bourbon line. Of the various officials whom he sent to America to carry out his reforms José de Gálvez, *visitador general*, was chief; and of those associated directly with Texas the most important was the Marqués de Rubí, inspector of the northern frontier. Accompanied by Nicolás de la Fora, his engineer, Rubí set out in 1766 to explore the frontier from the Gulf of California to Louisiana. Entering Texas during the summer of 1767, he visited El Cañon, on the upper Nueces River; San Sabá; San Antonio; Nacogdoches; Los Ais; Los Adaes; San Agustín de Ahumada (Orcoquisac), on the lower Trinity River; and La Bahía, on the lower San Antonio River. At the end of his journey, in Mexico City, Rubí had traveled about 7,000 miles in less than three years. The inspector discovered what Spanish frontier officers had long been trying to impress on their superiors, that the far-flung posts could not be maintained with the resources available. His very comprehensive and informative reports brought forth on September 10, 1772, a royal order, "Regulation for the Presidios," which followed substantially his recommendations.

In short, as it applied to Texas, the new Regulation called for: (1) the abandonment of all missions and presidios except San Antonio and La Bahía, (2) the strengthening of San Antonio de Bexar by moving to it settlers from Los Ais and Los Adaes, and (3) the inauguration of a new Indian program calling for friendly relations with the northern tribes and a war of extermination against the Apaches. Thus Spain had determined not only to give up all attempts to occupy the country north of San Antonio but also to abandon the settlements in East Texas and the presidio and mission on the Trinity, no longer needed to prevent intrusions from the east.

It did not take a royal order to bring about the abandonment of San Sabá and El Cañon; the Comanches forced that in 1769. Two years later the presidio at Orcoquisac was abandoned, and shortly thereafter the missionaries left their post in that vicinity. These readjustments took place before the new Regulation went into effect.

The abandonment of the East Texas settlements, however, was a different matter; these settlers were removed not because of the problem of maintaining them but because they were no longer needed there as a barrier against French aggression and could be used to strengthen San Antonio. Baron Ripperdá, governor of Texas, supervised the cruel removal, a task not to his liking. In the summer of 1773 more than 500 persons were torn away from their homes and forced to leave behind ripening grain and even livestock. The missions at Los Adaes, Los Ais, and Nacogdoches were abandoned, and the missionaries went along with the people.

Dissatisfied at San Antonio, the East Texans petitioned to return to

Los Ais, where their leader Gil Ibarvo, had a ranch. Ripperdá endorsed their petition, but the viceroy would only assent that they locate at least one hundred leagues from Natchitoches. At Paso Tomás, later known as Robbins' Ferry, on the Trinity River in present Madison County, the refugees in August 1774, laid out the Pueblo of Bucareli, which three years later was the home of 347 persons. Plagued by floods and raids by Comanche Indians, they again moved in 1779, this time without permission, to Nacogdoches. The authorities reluctantly gave their approval, and eventually a number of people scattered to their former homes.

Another part of the new Regulation called for the pacification of the northern tribes and a war of "reduction or destruction" against the Apaches. After Louisiana was taken over from the French in 1769, the Spaniards were wise enough to adopt in part the French system and to employ Frenchmen to deal with the Indians. The plan adopted, be it said, was substantially what Rubí had recommended. The guiding genius in this arrangement was Athanase de Mézières, who was appointed lieutenant governor of the Natchitoches district in 1769. De Mézières, a man of unusual influence and ability, was a son-in-law of St. Denis, a brother-in-law of the Duke of Orleans, and had been seasoned by thirty years of service in Louisiana as a soldier, planter, and Indian trader. By 1771 he had made peace with the Taovayas and Wichitas. Then, in the summer of 1772, he visited the Tawakoni villages (near the present Waco), proceeded up the Brazos about 100 miles, visited the Wichitas, got in touch with the Taovayas, and turned about and proceeded 300 miles over an unknown trail to San Antonio. One Comanche division, the Naytane, signed a treaty with J. Gaignard, a trader from Natchitoches, at Taovayas villages in 1774; the other Comanche tribes continued to harass San Antonio. For several years De Mézières and Ripperdá worked on plans to unite the northern tribes in a joint campaign with the Spaniards against the Apaches. In 1779 De Mézières was appointed governor of Texas in order to control the Indian situation better, but before he took office death ended the career of the great French frontiersman.

De Mézières' task of pacifying the northern tribes was never completed. Nor was a united campaign against the Apaches ever made, although parties from different tribes occasionally joined the Spaniards on campaigns against the hated mountain Indians. The military strength of the province was rarely sufficient to cope with the many hostile Indians. With fewer than 200 troops to divide between three or four presidios or outposts, to furnish escorts for traveling parties, and to supply guards for the various missions, there were never enough soldiers to go around. The peace with the Apaches in 1749 brought only a respite; the treaty with a northern Comanche tribe in 1774 was of little benefit to San Antonio; and the treaty with the southern Comanches in 1785 was a mere temporizing measure.

Baron de Ripperdá, who came to San Antonio as governor in 1770, sent to his superiors dramatic accounts of the plight of that place and urgent pleas for more troops. Additional troops were sent, but Ripperdá never felt secure. Domingo Cabello, Ripperdá's successor, wrote to Teodoro de Croix, the viceroy in 1780: "There is not an instant by day or night when reports do not arrive from all these ranches of barbarities and disorder falling on us. Totally unprotected as we are, they will result in the absolute destruction and loss of this province." In 1792 Governor Manuel Muñoz complained that peace agreements and presents did not stop Comanche raids and that Apache depredations were chronic. The Indians accepted the gifts but did not stop their marauding expeditions.

A desire to strengthen their influence over the Comanche and Wichita Indians so that they might serve as a barrier against Anglo-American intrusion, and the imperative military need to connect the three widely separated pivotal points (San Antonio, Santa Fé, and Natchitoches) on the northern frontier with direct routes prompted the Spaniards to make in the 1780's some notable explorations in Texas. In Pedro Vial, a Frenchman who had traded with the Indians of the Red River, Governor Cabello had a man well equipped to find the most direct the route from San Antonio to Santa Fé. With a small party, Vial set out on October 4, 1786. Vial went northward to a few miles east of present-day Brownwood, then eastward to the Tawakoni village near Waco; thence northwest and north to the Taovayas villages on the Red River in the vicinity of Spanish Fort, and from there by way of the Red and Canadian rivers to Santa Fé, where he arrived in May 1787.

Not satisfied with Vial's report, Governor Fernando de la Concha of New Mexico in July dispatched Corporal José Mares to find a more direct route linking the two outposts. Accompanied by Christóbal de los Santos, who had come to Santa Fé with Vial, Mares went eastward and southeastward by way of Tule Creek and the site of Quanah to the Taovayas villages and thence southward by present-day Jacksboro to San Antonio, where he arrived in October 1787. He had reached San Antonio by traveling about 980 miles, 210 less than Vial but considerably farther than necessary. Guided by friendly Comanches, he started on his return trip in January 1788, determined to go as directly as possible. Traveling northward and slightly westward, he went by or near the sites of Coleman and Abilene, Double Mountain near Aspermont and the Salt Fork of the Brazos, to the lower Tule Creek, and thence proceeded to Santa Fé by his outgoing route. The distance by this route was 845 miles; had Mares continued up the Brazos by the site of Lubbock, he would have traveled one hundred miles less and almost as direct as the shortest modern highway.

The most ambitious journey of all was made by Pedro Vial in 1788–1789. Setting out from Santa Fé on June 24, 1788, he pursued a comparatively direct route by the site of Tucumcari and along the Prairie Dog Fork (main) of Red River to the Taovayas villages; thence he went through the vicinity of Gainesville and Greenville to Natchitoches. He left Natchitoches with its 3,000 inhabitants and proceeded to San Antonio, passing by the site of San Augustine and visiting the settlement of Nacogdoches, which at that time had about 250 inhabitants. He estimated that San Antonio then had about 700 inhabitants. In 1789 the tireless explorer returned to Santa Fé by a route that veered eastward from the trail that Mares had followed the year before.

The route from Santa Fé to Natchitoches may have resulted in a slight increase in travel between those two far-flung outposts; the route from San Antonio to Santa Fé was never used, however, because the inhospitable plains and the Comanches made it impracticable. In 1808 Don Francisco Amangual with the aid of Comanche guides was able to go from San Antonio to Santa Fé with 200 troops. The expedition, a demonstration in answer to the expedition made by the United States Army under Zebulon Pike into Spanish territory two years before, was made to impress both the Americans and the Comanche Indians with Spanish strength and mobility. Amangual went considerably to the west of the routes of Vial and Mares. Going first to the old San Sabá post, he then marched by the site of San Angelo and west of Double Mountain, along the eastern side of the Caprock to the Quitaque, across the High Plains by way of present Amarillo to the Canadian River, and then westward to Santa Fé. He returned by a still more westerly route which followed the Pecos for some distance.

READJUSTMENTS FOLLOWING THE RETROCESSION OF LOUISIANA

In 1800 Napoleon inaugurated a grand scheme for reestablishing the French Empire in America, and wheedled the king of Spain into transferring Louisiana again to France. Then in 1803, realizing that it would be difficult to hold the province in the event of a war with Great Britain, he broke his pledge to Spain not to alienate it and sold it to the United States. Now Texas was once again on the border of New Spain, and an indefinite boundary separated it from the land-hungry Americans. To meet the new situation Spain adopted a threefold imperial policy: first, to hold the territory with its ancient boundaries unimpaired; second, to increase its garrisons and colonize the territory with loyal Spanish subjects; and third, to keep out Anglo-American intruders. Although these three phases are closely related, it seems expedient to develop each of them separately.

A controversy over the western boundary of Louisiana was inevitable. President Thomas Jefferson believed that the territory extended to the Rio Grande, while the Spaniards, with more justification, contended that it did not extend west of Los Adaes. The Spaniards placed additional troops in Texas, including detachments at the old post El Orcoquisac at the mouth of the Trinity and at points east of the Sabine, and thwarted efforts of the United States to explore the disputed territory. The Thomas Freeman expedition, sent up the Red River in 1806, was stopped at a point near the western boundary of the present State of Arkansas, and Zebulon Pike, who succeeded in reaching the upper stretches of the Rio Grande, was captured by a Spanish force.

The United States, on the other hand, sent troops into Louisiana, drove the Spanish troops from Los Adaes, and made preparations for war. Fortunately, a clash of arms was avoided. In November 1806, General James Wilkinson, in command of the United States forces, made with General Simón Herrera, in command of Spanish troops on the border, what is known as the Neutral Ground Agreement, providing that the Spaniards should remain west of the Sabine River and the Americans east of the Arroyo Hondo until their respective governments had reached an agreement. Strained relations between the two countries were aggravated by the report that Aaron Burr, formerly vice-president of the United States, was planning to lead a filibuster expedition into Texas or some other Spanish province. Burr's force disintegrated, however, before it reached New Orleans. When Wilkinson, who is believed to have been both in league with Burr and in the secret pay of Spain, realized that the Burr expedition was doomed to failure, he readily entered into the Neutral Ground Agreement and hurried to New Orleans, where he made much ado while preparing the place for defense against attack from Burr's force.

The diplomatic controversy concerning the western boundary of the Louisiana purchase was long and involved and was linked with the claims of the United States to West Florida. Because of the confusion incident to the Napoleonic wars in Europe, negotiations were discontinued in 1807 and were not resumed until ten years later. At last the Adams-De Onís, or Florida Purchase, Treaty was signed in 1819 and became effective by exchange of ratification two years later. By that agreement the United States acquired Florida from Spain and gave up any shadowy claim she might have had to Texas. Also, the Louisiana-Texas boundary was fixed as follows: the west bank of the Sabine from its mouth to the 32nd parallel, thence north to the Red River, along the south bank of that stream to the 100th meridian, thence north to the Arkansas River, along the south or west bank of that stream to its source, and thence northward to the 42nd parallel. The eastern boundary of Texas as determined by the agreement remains unchanged to this day.

Notwithstanding all her efforts to people Texas, Spain had only the settlements of San Antonio de Bexar, La Bahía (Goliad), and the pueblo of Nacogdoches at the time the United States acquired Louisiana. Faced with the threat of Anglo-American aggression she renewed her efforts to populate the province. In 1805 she established the *villa* of

Salcedo on the Trinity River, opposite the ruins of Bucareli, the *villa* of San Marcos, eight miles above the site of present-day Gonzales, but in 1809 there were only 16 persons living at Salcedo and 82 at San Marcos. The entire population of Texas at that time was estimated at only 4,155 persons, more than 1000 of whom were soldiers. There were still very few foreigners in the province. The efforts of officials to introduce foreigners were offset in great measure by the opposition of Nemesio Salcedo, commandant general of the Interior Provinces, who looked with suspicion on all immigrants from Louisiana, and stoutly forbade commercial relations with that country.

In September 1820, after the Spanish liberals had forced Ferdinand VII to accept the Constitution of 1812, the *Cortes* issued a decree opening all Spanish dominions to any foreigners who would respect the constitution and laws of the monarchy. But the evening of Spain's empire in America was spent, and it was given to the independent Mexican nation to put into effect such a policy.

THE FILIBUSTERS

During the early nineteneth century the Spanish authorities were repeatedly harassed by the fear of Anglo-American intruders with political designs. Traders from Louisiana appropriated much of the Indian trade and offered a market for horses which the Indians stole from the Spanish outposts. Some of these traders defied the authority of Spain. The best known of them is Philip Nolan, whose career is partly shrouded in mystery. Nolan was a protégé of General James Wilkinson (commander of the United States forces in Louisiana), whose capacity for doubledealing has never been surpassed in all American history.

Nolan came to Texas as a trader as early as 1791, and with permission of the Spanish officials took horses out of the country. On one trip he drove out 1,300; on another he rounded up about 2,000. The Spaniards lost confidence in him, however, and when he returned in the autumn of 1800 with a party of 17 armed followers, a superior force of soldiers was sent to arrest him. In the fight that ensued in March 1801, near present-day Waco, Nolan was killed; his followers were imprisoned and later cast dice to see who should die to satisfy the decree of the Spanish monarch. Some evidence indicates that Nolan was planning a more ambitious expedition against Texas.

The severe reception accorded Nolan did not frighten away other American adventurers. The second Anglo-American filibuster movement into Texas originated from a combination of revolutionary developments within New Spain. At the town of Dolores on September 16, 1810, the priest Miguel Hidalgo, representing the underprivileged classes, raised the standard of revolt against the Spanish government. With a few soldiers and a straggling horde of Indians, the priest captured and sacked Guanajuato, where he set up a government, then captured Guadalajara, and soon added Nuevo Santander and Coahuila to the revolutionists' territory.

The people of Texas at first declared their loyalty to the king, but soon became indifferent and critical. Then, on January 22, 1811, Juan Bautista de las Casas instigated at Bexar a revolt against the Spanish authorities, seized Simón Herrera, commander of the troops, and Governor Manuel María de Salcedo, and had himself elected governor *ad interim*. The season of his power was short; the deposed authorities were reinstated in July and soon afterwards Las Casas was executed. The patriots' cause in Texas was seriously weakened by the charge of the royalists that they were tools of Napoleon who, now that he was master of Spain, believed that a revolution in America would further his designs to obtain control of the Spanish colonies.

Although Hidalgo was captured and put to death, the revolution went on under other leaders. Bernardo Gutiérrez de Lara, a wealthy citizen of the city of Revilla (now Guerrero) went to the United States in 1811 as the envoy of the revolutionists. Although he was not recognized by the United States government, he was well received by some cabinet members and various other persons. The Texas republicans got interested in his plan to organize a filibustering force on the border of the United States, and agents from Bexar and Nacogdoches assured him that Texas would revolt on the approach of his invading army. The nucleus of this army was a number of men recruited by Lieutenant Augustus W. Magee, an adroit young officer who had made a good record on the Louisiana-Texas frontier. Dissatisfied at not being promoted in the United States Army, Magee resigned his commission in January 1812 to accept command of the "Republican Army of the North." Gutiérrez was the commander-in-chief, but Magee was in immediate command and the real military authority.

With a conglomerate array of Anglo-Americans, Frenchmen, Mexican revolutionists, and Indian allies, Magee arrived at Nacogdoches in August 1812. The Gutiérrez propaganda pamphlets, letters, and broadsides had made the way smooth. The Spanish soldiers deserted or fled, and the people drove away their officers and went out in a procession to greet the liberators. Gutiérrez followed the army to Nacogdoches and renewed his attack by propaganda. The army followed up his barrage of messages and proclamations and took La Bahía in November; but Magee became ill, and the offensive stalled. Magee died and was succeeded by Samuel Kemper. Then the advance was renewed, and the invaders defeated a Spanish army of 1,200 men and took Bexar on April 1, 1813. Five days later Gutiérrez issued a "Declaration of Independence of the State of Texas," a worthy document written according to the best traditions of American liberalism. The Spaniards, however, now in control at Bexar, could not grasp the ideals of republican liberalism, and the constitution written by Gutiérrez and his henchmen a few days later was, according to Anglo-American standards, a burlesque on free government. It set up a governor and a *junta* with dictatorial powers in no way responsible to the people. Also, by declaring that the "State of Texas" formed "a part of the Mexican Republic, to which it remains inviolably joined," the instrument destroyed the hopes of the Americans that Texas would become a dependency of the United States.

Disgusted with the course of events, including the execution of Governor Salcedo, Simón Herrera and twelve other Spanish officers, many of the Americans returned to the United States. Torn by dissension in their ranks, the heterogeneous collection of 1,400 Americans, Mexicans, and Indians at San Antonio was no match for the 1,830 troops which Joaquín de Arredondo, commandant general of the Eastern Interior Provinces, brought against them. On the Medina River, west of San Antonio, on August 18, 1813, the liberals were put to rout, and most of the Americans were slain. Thus the Mexican State of Texas came to an end after a troubled career of four months.

Arredondo followed up his victory with a purge calculated to rid Texas of all Anglo-Americans and liberal Mexicans. Rebels were shot, their property confiscated, and their wives and daughters imprisoned and forced to labor for the loyalist army. So thoroughly did he do his work that the province was virtually depopulated save for the settlement at Bexar. Indeed, he was unable to put into effect the new liberal Constitution of 1812 because there were not enough suitable persons to fill the offices! No serious effort was again made to populate Texas until 1820, and meanwhile the officials forbade with vehemence any trade with Louisiana.

But the rich lands of Texas constituted an invitation that offset the harshest decrees of the Spanish government. In 1818 the military had to drive away a band of exiled Napoleonic sympathizers who had settled on the lower Trinity River under a Frenchman named Lallemand. The next year a more serious threat to Spanish sovereignty appeared under the leadership of James Long, a merchant of Natchez, who had married a niece of General Wilkinson. The signing of the treaty of 1819, granting the Floridas to the United States in consideration of the acknowledgment of Spain's claim to Texas, angered certain Anglo-Americans who referred to it as the "surrender of Texas." At a meeting in Natchez plans were formulated for driving out the few royalist troops in Texas, organizing a liberal government, and attracting immigrants by the offer of generous land grants. Under Long's leadership, the party set out for Nacogdoches and gained recruits as it advanced until it had 300 fighting men, among them Bernardo Gutiérrez. Shortly after their arrival at Nacogdoches in

June 1819, the invaders established a civil government, adopted a declaration of independence, and invited immigrants to share the blessings of liberty with them.

In order to hold various outposts, Long divided his forces into details and left to visit Jean Lafitte on Galveston Island where he hoped to secure aid. For several years Galveston Island had served as headquarters for various adventurers or buccaneers, including Colonel Henry Perry, a survivor of the Gutiérrez-Magee expedition, and Luis Aury who held a naval commission from the Mexican revolutionists, and Lafitte. Lafitte's tenure dated from April 1817, when he set up his "republic" on the island and made it the headquarters for his privateering activities. While Long was absent, a Spanish force under Colonel Ignacio Pérez captured a part of his men and put the others to flight. Long made his way to New Orleans and with another group of adventurers returned to Texas in 1820. In October Long marched with fifty men into La Bahía where he was warmly received as a revolutionary. Mexico, however, had already won her independence, and a few days later Long and his men were captured and sent to Mexico City. While there on parole, Long was mysteriously shot.

It has already been observed that the abortive rebellion instigated by the priest Hidalgo in 1810 was soon suppressed. The underlying cause of its failure was that the higher classes of the Mexican people did not support it; neither the clergy nor the merchant class joined it. Yet the death of Hidalgo did not bring an end to the insurrection. The flames of rebellion were beaten out, but the smoldering embers of discontent remained. Dissatisfaction with the government in Spain was general, now that Napoleon had made Ferdinand VII a prisoner and had placed Joseph Bonaparte on the Spanish throne. Even the Mexican clergy, staunch supporters of the monarchy, were alienated because they knew that Napoleon was disposed to take many liberties with the church.

Under such leaders as José María Morelos and Vicente Guerrero, the revolution was carried on. After the close of the wars in Europe, however, it seemed that the royal government would suppress the rebels entirely. In 1819 Viceroy Juan Ruíz Apodaca reported to the king that no additional troops were necessary. At this time, however, the character of the revolution completely changed. Because of an insurrection in Spain, Ferdinand was forced to restore the liberal Constitution of 1812. This move antagonized the privileged classes in Mexico, especially the clergy, who resented certain anticlerical policies of the *Cortes*. Old Spain had become too liberal for New Spain. The upper classes in Mexico threw their support behind Agustín de Iturbide. With a command of 2,500 troops he marched against Guerrero, the liberal leader, not to fight but to negotiate. The two leaders soon came to an agreement known as the Plan of Iguala, proclaimed on February 24, 1821. The plan declared that New Spain was an independent, moderate, constitutional monarchy, guaranteed the Catholic religion, and proclaimed racial equality. In August, Juan O'Donojú, the last viceroy, recognized the independence of Mexico, and on September 27 Iturbide entered Mexico City. Thus, through a strange combination of liberals and conservatives the independence of Mexico was attained with little bloodshed.

THE MISSION SYSTEM

Our survey of the history of Spanish Texas has made many references to the missions and the mission system. It would not do justice to the superb work of the priests to leave the subject without some special notice. The missionary projects such as those of San Xavier and San Sabá, which must be given most space in the secular history of the province, are not fairly representative of the work of the churchmen.

The Spanish mission system as it was introduced in Texas was developed in Mexico, where the Europeans found the Indians living in relatively compact and permanent pueblos. The purpose of the mission was threefold: first, to Christianize the Indian; second, to teach him the habits and customs of civilized life and make him a creditable and self-sustaining subject of the king; and third, to extend the influence and authority of Spain and to hold the territory in its vicinity against all intruders. It belonged both to the church and the state. Indeed, the missionaries were employees of the king. Although they were selected by the evangelical colleges, their stipend, generally 450 pesos a year, was paid out of the royal treasury, and their appointment had to be approved by the viceroy. The stipend was not used as a salary for the missionaries but by the college to maintain the mission. New missions could not be established without viceregal assent, and the undertaking was a function of both church and state. The government bore the initial expense of founding a mission, and the evangelical colleges maintained it. A mission was generally maintained for about ten years, after which time it was secularized; that is, its lands and property were distributed among the neophytes and its church taken over by the secular clergy. The time limit was not enforced, however, and in Texas the most successful missions continued in operation for many decades.

The missionaries who served in Texas belonged to the Franciscan order; and nearly all of them were sent either by the College (or seminary) of Santa Cruz de Querétaro, established at Querétaro in 1683, or by the College of Nuestra Señora de Guadalupe de Zacatecas, founded at Zacatecas in 1707.

The chief mission centers in Texas were, first, the East Texas group, extending from the upper Neches River, eastward to Los Adaes, at present-day Robeline, Louisiana; second, the La Bahía group, along the lower San Antonio and Guadalupe rivers; and third, the establishments at

San Antonio. The East Texas group was composed of six missions, founded by Domingo Ramón in 1716 and reestablished by Aguayo in 1721. Three belonged to the College of Querétaro and three to the College of Zacatecas. The three Querétaran missions were moved, first to the Colorado and in 1731 to San Antonio. The three Zacatecan missions, Guadalupe, on the site of the city of Nacogdoches, Dolores (Ais), near present San Augustine, and San Miguel, at Los Adaes, were maintained until the abandonment of East Texas in 1773.

In 1722 Aguayo established and delivered to Father Patrón, representing the College of Zacatecas, the Mission La Bahía Espíritu Santo de Zuñiga, generally known simply as La Bahía mission. At the same time he established nearby, north of Lavaca Bay, and in the vicinity of La Salle's old Fort St. Louis, the presidio of Loreto, also commonly called La Bahía. In 1726 the entire establishment was moved about 25 miles northwestward to the Guadalupe River; and in 1749, as a part of the readjustment made in connection with Escandón's settlement of Nuevo Santander, it was again moved, this time to Santa Dorotea, the site of present-day Goliad. Mission Espíritu Santo and Mission Rosario, established nearby in 1754, met with a measure of success.

In this general vicinity the last mission established in Texas was founded in 1793 at the junction of the Guadalupe and San Antonio rivers and called Nuestra Señora del Refugio. Two years later it was moved to a better site in the general vicinity of the town of Refugio. It seems that its faithful padres were no more successful than their predecessors had been in converting and civilizing the savage Karankawas and neighboring tribes.

The center of Spanish mission efforts in Texas was San Antonio. Here mission activity attained its highest success. San Antonio de Valero, established by Alarcón and Father Olivares in 1718, was a Querétaran mission and was followed two years later by San José y San Miguel de Aguayo, founded for the Zacatecan brotherhood. Added to these were the three East Texas missions, moved to San Antonio in 1731 and commonly called Concepción, San Juan de Capistrano (formerly San José de los Nazonis), and Espada (the old San Francisco de los Neches).

A typical day for a mission Indian was about as follows: religious service at dawn followed by thirty minutes or an hour of instruction in the catechism; breakfast; then work in the fields or the shops, or more frequently for the women, work on the looms, at the pottery wheel, or in the kitchen; and school for the children. All work and instruction was under the direction and personal supervision of the priests, or of the soldiers assigned to the mission for such purposes. In the evening all gathered in front of the church for another hour of instruction and the rosary. Life was hard indeed for the religious when the governor or the presidial officials were hostile toward them, a condition that prevailed occasionally. The most serious quarrel of this kind was with Governor

Mission San José y San Miguel de Aguayo, founded in 1720 for the Zacatecan brotherhood in San Antonio, was the center of Spanish mission efforts in Texas. The Rose Window shown right is renowned as a masterpiece of art. (Texas Highway Department)

Franquis de Lugo (1736–1737), who seems to have used every device within his power to annoy the missionaries and discredit them with the Indians and the populace at San Antonio. The priests appealed to the viceroy; Franquis de Lugo was reprimanded and later removed; but before they were rid of his presence many of the Indians had fled and the whole mission field was demoralized.

Yet the missions enjoyed comparative prosperity, and reports made from time to time indicate that they did effective work. An inspector of the four Querétaran missions at San Antonio in 1745 reported 2,441 baptisms since 1718. At the time of the report 885 Indians, most of whom had been baptized, were living in the missions. They had more than 5,000 head of cattle, about half that many sheep, and large herds of goats and horses. The mission produced annually about 8,000 bushels of corn and quantities of beans, melons, watermelons, sweet potatoes, and cotton.

In 1768 Father Gaspar José de Solís, inspector of the Zacatecan missions, described San José thus: "It is so pretty and well arranged both in a material and in a spiritual way that I have no voice, words, or figures with which to describe its beauty."

The establishment consisted of a perfect square, 220 varas (or about 204 yards) on the side, enclosed by a stone wall with towers in two corners opposite each other. Quarters for the Indians were built against the wall, each supplied with a little kitchen and loopholes on the outside for defense. There was an arch granary of stone, a workshop where very good cotton and woolen cloth was woven, a carpenter shop, an iron shop, a tailor shop, a furnace for burning lime, and an irrigation ditch so large that it "seemed like a small river." There were fields fenced in for more than a league where in season were grown corn, brown beans, lentils, melons, watermelons, peaches (some a pound in weight, more or less), sweet potatoes, Irish potatoes, and sugar cane. So abundant were the crops that the mission supplied in part the presidios at San Antonio, La Bahía, San Sabá, El Orcoquisac, and Los Adaes. The Indians were described as energetic, skilled, and versatile laborers who worked even without supervision. They maintained their own guard and patrol for the defense of the establishment and had their own government with much the same officers and courts as a Spanish pueblo. More than 350 Indians lived at the mission, most of whom spoke Spanish.

Soon after Father De Solís made his inspection, the missions began a decline that continued until the close of the Spanish era. In 1773 the Querétarans, burdened with demands from other fields, turned over their four missions at San Antonio to the Zacatecans. There were only nine missionaries officially active in 1785. Mission Valero (present Alamo), which had only 42 persons in 1777, all fully civilized, was secularized in 1793. Concepción, San Juan, and Espada were given up by the missionaries a few years later. Some mission work was carried on at San Antonio until 1823, and Mission Refugio continued to exist until 1830.

CIVIL AND MILITARY ADMINISTRATION

The first civil settlement in Texas was established at San Antonio by Alarcón in 1718. It consisted of ten families under the protection of a military guard and was called Villa de Bexar. In 1731 55 persons, most of them from the Canary Islands, were moved to San Antonio and located at public expense. The place was now called San Fernando de Bexar. The settlement grew slowly and not until about 1750 did it secure an adequate church. Then it was given a church by royal aid. The population in 1770 was about 800, but this number may not include persons living on ranches in that general vicinity. There were no schools of consequence before the nineteenth century. With the coming of Baron Ripperdá as governor in 1770, San Antonio became the de facto capital, and after the abandonment of Los Adaes three years later, it was officially the seat of government in the province.

The only other civil settlements in Spanish Texas worthy of notice were Goliad, Nacogdoches, and Adaes. After their removal to the site of Goliad in 1749, there grew up about the Mission La Bahía del Espíritu Santo and the presidio of Loreto a settlement and important ranching interests. The population of the community in 1782 was 512. Likewise, Nacogdoches experienced considerable growth after Gil Ibarbo and his exiled Adaesians settled there in 1779. Ibarbo, the lieutenant governor, assigned lands to the people. A commissary for Indian trade was established, and there was considerable illicit trade with Louisiana. A census in 1790 showed a population of 480. Los Adaes, the capital of Texas from 1722 to 1773, was always a small struggling settlement.

The political system of Texas was similar to that of other provinces in New Spain. It was subject directly to the viceroy, who in turn referred important matters to the fiscal of the Royal Audiencia and to the *auditor de guerra*. In important cases, before a final decision was made, a *junta*, or general council, composed of various dignitaries might be called together. All important decisions of the viceroy were subject to royal approval, and, except in emergencies, policies of great consequence were not adopted until the king passed on them. In 1776 the Interior (northern) Provinces of New Spain were organized under a commandant general who was responsible to the king and practically independent of the viceroy.

Except for the *villa* of San Fernando de Bexar, which had self-government in some measure, the government of Texas was almost wholly military. At the head of the administration was a governor appointed by the crown. He commanded the army and the militia of the province, and had the authority to grant land titles, issue licenses, hear appeals from the alcalde court, supervise fiscal matters, and administer and execute laws and decrees. The terms of the governors varied in length, but the average term was about four years. Inspectors from time to time checked on the governors, and at the end of their term a *residencia* or investigation of their administration was made.

Evidently the presidios were frequently badly managed. The common soldiers received about 450 pesos a year out of which they had to purchase their equipment and maintain themselves and their families. They spent a great deal of time working on the private estates of the officers. The captain of a presidio served as the merchant of the post, sometimes charging the soldiers exorbitant prices for their supplies in spite of regulations intended to prevent that abuse. Probably the case of Governor Martos y Navarrete (1759–1767), who was charged with making $80,000 in profits on goods sold to soldiers at Los Adaes, is too extreme to be typical, but it suggests the weaknesses in the system. No doubt this graft lowered the efficiency of commands greatly. In 1737 Governor Franquis de Lugo reprimanded Captain Gabriel Costales at La Bahía for failure to pay and to supply his men adequately, alleging that certain soldiers came to San Antonio from La Bahía practically naked, their arms out of order, and their horses so poor that they were a disgrace.

FAILURE AND LEGACY

The causes of the comparative failure of Spain in Texas were partly within and partly beyond her control. Her exclusive commercial policy, which prohibited trade even between the different parts of her dominions, was certainly a retarding factor. Strict and tyrannical methods of government, strangely mixed with laxity and the tolerance of graft, were also causes of the failure. Certain unfavorable conditions, chief of which was the hostility of nomadic Indian tribes, were beyond her control. Yet Spain might have changed her pioneering institutions, the *villa*, the presidio, and the mission, to meet better the conditions peculiar to the northern frontier.

In general it may be said that Spain suffered most because of a lack of realism in her policies and the stubborn adherence to tradition in administration. For instance, she held doggedly to the notion that the pueblo type of mission was suited to Texas, although it soon proved of little value except along the Rio Grande and in the vicinity of San Antonio. She adhered rigidly to the high ideal that Indians should not have firearms, and thereby compelled them to trade with her rivals. She never gave up the theory that, since Texas was an extension of New Spain, the province should trade with New Spain only; thus she impoverished her settlements and compelled men of enterprise to violate the law. Notwithstanding abundant evidence that conditions were otherwise, she clung to the fiction that poorly paid captains of isolated posts would be scrupulously honest, would sell supplies to their soldiers at fair prices, would keep the men employed in the public service, and would not use them for their own gain. The fact that occasional rigid inspections were made and that sometimes the guilty were punished did not insure honesty.

Spain's achievement in Texas must not be despised, however. She held it against all contenders until her empire in America collapsed, and left upon it an imprint that will endure throughout the ages. Many streams and towns bear Spanish names. In almost every section there are land titles that go back to Spanish grants. The law shows Spanish influence, particularly that pertaining to the property rights of women. Fortunately a few specimens of Spanish architecture still remain. At San Antonio some of the chapels of the old missions have withstood almost two centuries of assault by the elements and the occasional ravages of unfriendly hands. Their stateliness and gentle beauty command a reverent interest. They are worthy monuments to the idealism of the Spaniard and fitting symbols of immortality in a transitory world.

Selected Bibliography

The general accounts mentioned in the preceding bibliography also apply to this chapter. The best sources on the readjustment following the acquisition of Louisiana by Spain are H. E. Bolton, *Texas in the Middle Eighteenth Century*; H. E. Bolton, *Athanase de Mézières*; C. E. Castañeda, *Our Catholic Heritage in Texas, 1519–1936*, Vol. IV; O. B. Faulk, *A Successful Failure*; Noel M. Loomis and A. P. Nasater, *Pedro Vial and the Roads to Santa Fé* (Norman, 1967). See also E. Wallace and D. M. Vigness (eds.), *Documents of Texas History*; H. E. Bolton, "The Spanish Abandonment and Reoccupation of East Texas, 1773–1779," *Quarterly of the Texas State Historical Association*, IX, 67–137; A. B. Thomas (ed. and trans.), *Teodoro de Croix and the Northern Frontier of New Spain, 1776–1783* (Norman, 1941); Elizabeth Ann Harper, "The Taovayas Indians in Frontier Trade and Diplomacy, 1769–1779," *Southwestern Historical Quarterly*, LVII, 181–201.

For a description of various missions see C. E. Castañeda, *Our Catholic Heritage*, Vol. IV; H.E. Bolton, *Texas in the Middle Eighteenth Century*; F. C. Chabot, *San Antonio and Its Beginnings, 1691–1731*; Margaret K. Kress (trans.; introduction by M. A. Hatcher), "Diary of a Visit of Inspection of the Texas Missions Made by Fray Gaspar José de Solís in the Year 1767–'68," *Southwestern Historical Quarterly*, XXXV, 28–76; W. E. Dunn, "The Founding of Nuestra Senora del Refugio, the Last Spanish Mission in Texas," *ibid.*, XXV, 174–184; William H. Oberste, *History of Refugio Mission* (Refugio, 1942); K. S. O'Connor, *The Presidio La Bahia del Espiritu Santo de Zuniga, 1721–1846*; Billie Persons, "Secular Life in the San Antonio Missions," *Southwestern His-*

torical Quarterly, LXII, 45–62; E. Wallace and D. M. Vigness (eds.), *Documents of Texas History;* Mattie Austin Hatcher (trans.), "A Description of Mission Life," in E. C. Barker (ed.), *Readings in Texas History* (Dallas, 1929).

On Spanish civil and military administration the best source is H. E. Bolton, *Texas in the Middle Eighteenth Century.* See also M. A. Hatcher, "The Municipal Government of San Fernando de Bexar, 1730–1800," *Quarterly of the Texas State Historical Association,* VIII, 277–352; I. J. Cox, "Educational Efforts in San Fernando de Bexar," *ibid.,* VI, 27–63; F. C. Chabot, *San Antonio and Its Beginnings;* Sidney B. Brinckerhoff and O. B. Faulk, *Lancers for the King: A Study of the Frontier Military System of Northern New Spain, with a Translation of the Royal Regulations of 1772* (Phoenix, Ariz., 1965); B. E. Bobb, *The Viceregency of Antonio María Bucareli in New Spain, 1771–1779* (Austin, 1962); Nettie Lee Benson, "Texas Failure to Send a Deputy to the Spanish Cortes, 1810–1812," *Southwestern Historical Quarterly,* LXIV, 14–35; Virginia Taylor (ed. and trans.), *Letters of Antonio Martínez, Last Governor of Texas, 1817–1822* (Austin, 1957).

For the last years of Spain in Texas, the best scholarly studies are M. A. Hatcher, *The Opening of Texas to Foreign Settlement, 1801–1821* (University of Texas *Bulletin,* No. 2714; Austin, 1927); O. B. Faulk, *The Last Years of Spanish Texas;* D. M. Vigness, *The Revolutionary Decades* (Austin, 1965); N. L. Benson (ed. and trans.), "A Governor's Report on Texas in 1809," *Southwestern Historical Quarterly,* LXXI, 603–615; L. Friend, "Old Spanish Fort," *West Texas Historical Association Year Book,* XVI, 3–27; Kathryn Garrett, "Dr. John Sibley and the Louisiana-Texas Frontier, 1803–1814," *Southwestern Historical Quarterly,* XLVIII, XLIX; Harris G. Warren, *The Sword Was Their Passport* (Baton Rouge, 1943). Texas-Louisiana relations of that period are dealt with in Thomas M. Marshall, *A History of the Western Boundary of the Louisiana Purchase, 1819–1841* (Berkeley, 1914).

On the filibusters, see the general references previously cited and also: K. Garrett, *Green Flag over Texas* (New York, 1939); D. M. Vigness, *The Revolutionary Decades;* H. S. Thrall, *Pictorial History of Texas* (St. Louis, 1879); M. A. Hatcher, "Joaquin de Arredondo's Report of the Battle of the Medina...," *Quarterly of the Texas State Historical Association,* XI, 220–236; K. Garrett, "The First Constitution of Texas, April 17, 1813," *Southwestern Historical Quarterly,* XL, 290–308; Lois Garver, "Benjamin Rush Milam," *ibid.,* XXXVIII, 79–121; Henry P. Walker (ed.), "William McLane's Narrative of the Magee-Gutiérrez Expedition of 1812–1813," *ibid.,* LXVI, 234–251, 457–479; 569–588; E. Wallace and D. M. Vigness (eds.), *Documents of Texas History.*

4

ANGLO-AMERICAN COLONIZATION, 1820–1835

On the eve of the independence of Mexico a movement was launched which was destined to people Texas with Anglo-Americans and to open the way for the extension of the United States to the Pacific. The history of this movement is largely the story of two men, Moses Austin and his son, Stephen Fuller Austin.

Of all the men who figured in American history [wrote Professor George P. Garrison], there are no other two who have attracted so little attention from their contemporaries and have yet done things of such vast and manifest importance, as Moses Austin and his son Stephen. Their great work consisted in the making of Anglo-American Texas, an enterprise planned and begun by the one and carried into execution by the other.

THE AUSTINS MAKE THE WAY

It was on December 23, 1820, that the elder Austin, Connecticut born and seasoned by many years of business experience in Virginia and Missouri, appeared before Governor Antonio de Martínez in San Antonio and asked his permission to establish in Texas a colony of three hundred families. Austin had moved to Missouri in 1798, when it was a part of the Spanish province of Louisiana, and he came as a former Spanish subject who wished now to renew his allegiance to the king. Thanks to the aid of his old friend, the Baron de Bastrop, whom he happened to meet in San Antonio, his application was received and finally endorsed by Governor Martínez. Then, on January 17, 1821, the petition was approved at Monterrey by a board of superior officers, known as the provincial deputation.

Moses Austin died soon after his return to Missouri and it was left to the son to complete the task begun by the father. Although only 27 years old, Stephen F. Austin was already a man of rich experience. He was well educated; he had served five years in the legislature of the Missouri Territory and had been appointed district judge in the territory of Arkansas; and he had engaged in a variety of business undertakings in Missouri, Arkansas, and Louisiana. More important still, he was, as Professor Eugene C. Barker, his biographer, states, "patient; methodical; energetic; and fair-spoken; and acquainted from childhood with the characteristic social types that mingled on the southwestern border."

With a small party Austin went to San Antonio in the summer of 1821. There Governor Martínez received him cordially, recognized him as the heir to his father's commission, and authorized him to explore the country and to make other arrangements for his colony. News about the project had already traveled far; and on his return to Natchitoches, Louisiana, he found nearly a hundred letters from persons who were interested. With the aid of his partner, Joseph H. Hawkins, he purchased the schooner *Lively* and sent it to Texas with a cargo of 18 or 20 settlers and essential supplies. Austin returned to Texas by way of Nacogdoches where in December he met a group of waiting colonists. Following the San Antonio Road to the Brazos, he found a few colonists already selecting choice lands along the Brazos and Colorado rivers. He suffered a heavy loss and was greatly disturbed when the *Lively* failed to meet him. Later he learned that it had landed at the mouth of the Brazos rather than at the mouth of the Colorado as had been planned, and that most of the immigrants on board had become discouraged and returned to Louisiana.

The first settler to enter the colony, Andrew Robinson, crossed the Brazos River at the La Bahía Road crossing in November 1821. The ferry he operated marked the settlement of Washington-on-the-Brazos. Two or three days later the three Kuykendall brothers and their families joined the Robinsons; others came, among them Josiah H. Bell, whom Austin had known in Missouri; and soon there were settlements in that community and also westward near the site of Independence. At Christmastime Robert and Joseph Kuykendall and Daniel Gilliland followed the La Bahía Road to the Colorado and settled near present Columbus. On January 1, 1822, Thomas Boatright settled on a little stream he called New Year's Creek. Jared E. Groce, planter, lumberman, and capitalist of Alabama, arrived with his 50 wagons and 90 slaves early

Moses Austin. When in 1820 hard times came to Potosi, Missouri, which Austin had founded in 1798, he went to Texas and obtained the governor's permission to settle 300 families there. (E. C. Barker History Center, University of Texas)

in 1822, and settled near the site of Hempstead. Many others came before spring, most of them by land, but some by sea.

After being delayed for some time in the colony, Austin was again in San Antonio in March 1822. There Governor Martínez was obliged to tell him that the officials at Monterrey had refused to recognize his authority to introduce settlers under his father's grant; that the new government of the Mexican nation had under consideration a colonization policy for Texas and the Californias; in short, that he had better go to Mexico and look after his interests. Without delay Austin turned the affairs of the colony over to Josiah Bell and set out for Mexico City.

At the capital he viewed a complex and confusing political scene, but in spite of the many difficulties, he patiently and methodically set to work to secure the approval of the contract. A quarrel between the "Liberator," Agustín de Iturbide, and the liberal Constituent Congress was approaching a crisis when Austin reached the city on April 29, 1822. A few days later a popular revolution, which Iturbide prompted, made the liberator emperor. On August 1, Iturbide forced the Congress to adjourn and replaced it with a handpicked *junta* of 45 members. Austin, who by this time had mastered the rudiments of the Spanish language and some cardinal principles of Mexican politics, talked with each member of the *junta* individually, and secured the passage of a general colonization law on January 3, 1823, through which he could secure relief.

Iturbide's power had begun to wane, however, and Austin dared not leave the capital lest a new government undo all that had been accomplished. At last Iturbide was forced to abdicate; the Congress, now restored, readily ratified Austin's application under the terms of the Imperial Colonization Law, and the new executive department approved it on April 14, 1823. Congress at the same time suspended the Imperial Colonization Law, leaving Austin's the only concession granted under its terms.

It was not until early August 1823 that the proprietor, accompanied by Baron de Bastrop, the commissioner empowered to grant land titles, arrived in the colony. Conditions were critical. The drought of 1822, the hostile Karankawas, and Austin's long absence had caused a number of people to return to the United States. The morale of the colony improved considerably, however, when Baron de Bastrop was sent by the governor at the end of 1822 to supervise the election of alcaldes and militia officers; and when Austin returned with the assurance that his contract had been validated and that land titles soon would be issued, the crisis passed.

The seat of government was established on the Brazos River at the Atascosito crossing, and christened by Governor Luciano García, San Felipe de Austin. By the close of the summer of 1824 when he was called away, Bastrop had issued 272 titles.[1] The "Old Three Hundred," as these settlers came to be known, selected the rich plantation lands along the Brazos, Colorado, and Bernard rivers, from the vicinity of present Navasota, Brenham, and La Grange to the coast. By the terms of the imperial law each family was to receive one *labor* (177 acres) if engaged in farming, and a *sitio* (a square league or about 4,428 acres) for stock raising. Of course, most of the colonists preferred to be classed as stock raisers, and only about 20 titles called for less than a *sitio*. Special grants were made to a few men as compensation for substantial improvements such as mills; and Jared E. Groce, the owner of many slaves, received ten *sitios*. Austin, as *empresario*, received about 22 *sitios*. The law required that land should be occupied and improved within two years after the receipt of the deed, that colonists must profess the Catholic religion, that for six years they would be exempt from the payment of tithes and duties on imports, and that children of slaves born in the empire would be free at the age of fourteen.

A COLONIZATION PROGRAM

It must be repeated that the Imperial Colonization Law did not provide a colonization program for the nation, but was merely a special arrange-

---

[1]The remainder, issued in 1827 and 1828, brought the total number of families introduced, including the "families" of single men who formed partnerships to meet the requirements of the law, to 297. Single men were entitled to 1,476 acres (one-third of a square league). Only seven of the 297 titles actually issued were forfeited.

ment for the relief of Austin. The subject of colonization continued before the Congress and on August 18, 1824, that body issued a general law on the subject. By this act the national government turned over to the states the administration of the public lands and authorized them to prescribe regulations for settlement with only a few reservations. The most important of these were (1) that all state laws had to conform to the constitution then being framed; (2) that except by special approval of the federal executive, foreigners were not to settle within ten leagues of the coast or 20 leagues of the international boundary; (3) that no person should hold more than 11 *sitios*; (4) that no alien should receive a land grant; and (5) that "until after the year 1840, the general congress shall not prohibit the entrance of any foreigner, as a colonist, unless imperious circumstances should require it, with respect to individuals of a particular nation."

By a federal act of May 7, 1824, the two old Spanish provinces of Coahuila and Texas were united as one state until the population of Texas should become large enough for the maintenance of a separate government. The state constituent body was installed at Saltillo on August 15, 1824, and on March 24, of the following year, it passed a colonization law. The law invited Catholic immigrants, requiring that they give satisfactory evidence as to their Christian beliefs, morality, and good habits. They might receive titles as individual families or through an *empresario*. The liberal land policy of the imperial law was continued in a provision allowing families to receive, after payment of a fee of $30, a *sitio* of land for $62.50 ($87.50 for irrigated land), payable in three annual installments, the first being due at the end of the fourth year. They were required to cultivate or occupy the land within six years. For his services an *empresario* should receive five *sitios* of grazing land and five *labors* of farming land for each 100 families up to 800. *Empresario* contracts were to run six years and to be absolutely void if at least one hundred families had not been settled before the expiration of that time. Native-born Mexicans might purchase for small fees as much as eleven *sitios*. There should be no essential changes in the law for a period of six years. Colonists were exempted from general taxation for ten years. This plan was in keeping with the decree of the national congress in 1823, exempting the colonists from customs duties for a period of seven years.

EARLY EMPRESARIO CONTRACTS
AND COLONIZATION

Even before the passage of the state immigration law Austin had determined to ask permission to enlarge his colony. Permits granted him under the colonization law of 1825 amounted to 900 families, and in

CHIEF
COLONIZATION
GRANTS

Miles

0   85

Austin's contract called for 300 families under the Imperial colonization law of April 14, 1823. Three contracts under the state law, 1825, 1827, 1828, called for 900 additional families in the area of his first colony; and, with Sam M. Williams, he had a contract to settle 800 families north and west of his first colony. He located over 1500 families.

On April 15, 1825, Green DeWitt got a contract for 400 families to be located on the Guadalupe, San Marcos, and Lavaca rivers. He issued 166 titles. The Nashville Company, known by the name of its agent, Sterling C. Robertson, as Robertson's colony, secured a contract for 800 families in 1825. After the revolution it was allowed premium lands for 379 families.

David G. Burnet, Lorenzo de Zavala, and Joseph Vehlein secured colonization rights in 1826 for territory on the eastern border of Texas between the twenty-ninth and thirty-third parallels. These rights were transferred to the Galveston Bay & Texas Land Company, which issued between September, 1834, and December, 1835, titles to over 916 leagues.

On March 9, 1826, Arthur G. Wavell, an Englishman, secured a contract for 500 families to be located in northeast Texas. His associate, Benjamin R. Milam, located a number of families, but the United States contended that they were settled east of the boundary set by the treaty of 1819, with Spain, and the contractors never secured premium lands. Power and Hewetson granted almost 200 titles, McMullen and McGloin, 84. The Mexican empresario, De León, settled between 100 and 200 families.

1831 Austin and his partner, Samuel M. Williams, were authorized to settle 800 Mexican and European families. Before the end of 1833, 1,055 land titles had been issued under Austin's various grants. Tabulations made after his death indicate that the great *empresario* authorized, all told, 1,540 grants to colonists. Census returns best reveal the growth of his colony or colonies; the total population was 2,021 in March 1828; 4,248 in June 1830; and 5,665 a year later.

The boundaries of Austin's colony were not defined until 1824, when they were described as extending from the Lavaca River to Chocolate Bayou, and from the seashore to the San Antonio Road. They were enlarged in November of that year to take in a settlement along the west bank of the San Jacinto. The "Little Colony," authorized in 1827, was located on the east side of the Colorado River above the old colony. Bastrop, the colony headquarters, was established in 1832. By a special concession of the President of the Republic, Austin was permitted to locate colonists in the ten-league reserve strip along the coast, where in fact some of the "Old Three Hundred" had already settled. Finally, Austin and Williams were granted colonization rights to a large area north and northwest of Austin's colony. This contract included the territory of the Nashville or Robertson colony, and involved Austin and Williams in a long and bitter controversy over proprietary rights there.

Next to Austin the most important proprietor was Green DeWitt, another Missourian, whose colony lay southwest of Austin's along the Lavaca and Guadalupe rivers. Gonzales, DeWitt's colony town, was located in 1825, but an attack by Indians in July of the following year caused the people to retire to another settlement on the lower Lavaca. Here their troubles did not end, for the neighboring *empresario*, Martín de León, was irascible and even bellicose.

De León's contract, which specified no exact boundaries, was unique among the colonies in that it was authorized by the provincial delegation of San Fernando de Bexar in 1824, before the passage of the national and state colonization laws. Furthermore, the settlers in the colony were predominantly Mexican. In October 1824, De León with a few settlers established himself at Guadalupe Victoria on the Guadalupe River. This location was within the territory later assigned to DeWitt. Disputes over land and other subjects soon developed, and DeWitt's settlers withdrew to Gonzales and vicinity. By 1831 DeWitt's colony had more than one hundred families, the number required before titles to land could be issued. José Antonio Navarro served as commissioner and the colonists were soon given their deeds. At the expiration of DeWitt's contract, April 15, 1831, 166 titles had been issued in his colony, but the greater part of the land within his grant was still vacant.

Haden Edwards, another *empresario* of the early group, secured a contract for a colony in eastern Texas, but a quarrel with the Mexican officials ended his efforts before much had been accomplished. The unfortunate Fredonian Rebellion with which he was associated will receive consideration later.

In addition to the concessions to Austin, DeWitt, and De León, the State of Coahuila and Texas made about 22 other contracts with *empresarios* under the law of March 24, 1825, calling in all for about 8,000 families. The great majority of these *empresarios* located no families or only a negligible number. Others were more successful, but their colonists, almost without exception, came during the second period of colonization, 1834–1836; this period will be given some notice later.

One other colonization movement, the earliest of all, calls for attention. Before Moses Austin had visited San Antonio, his fellow countrymen were making their way into extreme northeast Texas. These men had no connection with *empresarios*. "They came," says R. W. Strickland, historian of the movement, "from Kentucky and Tennessee by the way of Missouri and Arkansas. Their fathers had followed Boone and Harrod over the Wilderness Road to Harrodsburg and Bryant's Station or pioneered with Sevier along the waters of the Holston or French Broad."

In June 1815, George and Alex Wetmore set up a trading house at Pecan Point on the Red River in present Red River County. Settlers joined them and soon there were communities at Pecan Point and at Jonesborough, about thirty miles up the river. Horse thieves, trafficking in animals taken in Missouri and sold in Nacogdoches, laid out Trammel's Trace, a spur of which linked these settlements with the outside world. At first they were under the jurisdiction of Missouri; then in 1820 they became a part of Miller County, Arkansas; and, strange to say, Miller County, Arkansas, as reshaped in 1828 lay wholly within what later proved to be Texas. When Austin's colony was opened to settlers, a number of these people (among them Daniel Gilliland, Martin Varner, Andrew Robinson, and Jesse Burnam) left the Red River settlements and joined the new colony. Other settlers, however, soon took the places they had vacated. As early as 1821 there were about eighty families in the Northeast Texas settlements; and in 1825 the population increased rapidly through the influx of settlers from north of the river, who were driven from their homes to make way for the Choctaws.

In about 1820 word came of the Florida Purchase Treaty, which fixed the northeast boundary of Texas at a line running from the intersection of the Sabine River and the 32nd parallel north latitude to the Red River, but not until the revolution were these settlers united politically with the rest of Texas.

THE DECREE OF APRIL 6, 1830

The very success of the colonization movement all but destroyed it. The stream of immigration from the United States that had been flowing into

Texas in ever-increasing volume since 1823 was stopped without notice by an act of the federal government on April 6, 1830. The decree was the direct outgrowth of the reports of General Manuel Mier y Terán, soldier, scholar, and statesman, who spent much time in Texas in 1828 as the representative of the general government. Terán reported that with their homes, their schools, their energy and enterprise, the "North Americans" were taking the country. Mexico must act "now" or Texas "is lost forever." He proposed that the Mexican government should (1) colonize Mexicans in Texas; (2) colonize Swiss and Germans; (3) encourage coastal trade between Texas and the rest of the Republic; and (4) place more troops in Texas, among them convict soldiers who would become permanent settlers after their terms had expired. Mexicans in high places had become alarmed at the Anglo-American threat to Mexican solidarity. General José María Tornel feared them and used his influence to persuade President Vicente Guerrero to exercise the dictatorial powers that Congress had given him and abolish slavery. On September 15, 1829, he secured Guerrero's signature to a decree that would have put an end to slavery in the entire nation; but because of her protestations, Texas was excluded from its operation.

When Tornel's idea of scaring away Americans by striking at slavery was not carried out, the Mexican government used a more direct approach. Lúcas Alamán, Minister of Foreign Relations, urged Congress to adopt Terán's proposals with certain modifications which he suggested. The decree, signed April 6, 1830, contained in addition the drastic Article 11, a part of which reads: "Citizens of foreign countries lying adjacent to the Mexican territory are prohibited from settling as colonists in the states or territories of the Republic adjoining such countries," meaning that no more Anglo-Americans could settle in Texas. The article, furthermore, declared suspended "all contracts not already completed and not in harmony with this law."

To the Mexican government, the law was a mandatory act to meet an emergency; to the colonists, however, the law seemed nothing less than a calamity. Austin succeeded in fending the blow slightly, in so far as his colony and that of DeWitt were concerned, by an ingenious interpretation that permitted them to complete their quota of families without respect to the law. Thus, the population of Austin's settlements increased from 4,248 in June 1830 to 5,665 a year later. DeWitt's contract and one of Austin's soon expired by limitation, however; Austin's other contracts were soon filled; and in November of 1831 Austin had to admit that immigration of North Americans was totally prohibited. He and his secretary, Samuel M. Williams, then secured a grant to settle European and Mexican families, but in this they did not succeed.

As the unfilled *empresario* contracts made under the state law of 1825 expired, the forfeited lands they had encompassed again became available for new grants. Furthermore, the Law of April 6, 1830, sought to encourage European and Mexican families to settle in Texas. In 1832 the legislature of Coahuila-Texas passed an act promoting the same plan. Under its terms two or three contracts were made, but the results were negligible.

Meanwhile, considerable pressure was exerted for the repeal of the act. The colonists in their convention in April 1833, made repeal of the act their major aim; and Austin, who carried the petition to Mexico City, managed to secure its repeal, effective May 1, 1834.

THE RENEWAL OF COLONIZATION

The renewal of the liberal colonization policy in 1834 made it possible for the state government to renew several of the contracts that had been voided in 1830 and to make new colonization contracts. Now that the legal barrier was removed, the stream of immigrants reached unprecedented proportions. One observer reported that during January and February of 1835, about 2,000 persons landed at the mouth of the Brazos alone. The best known of the later colonization projects is that of the Galveston Bay and Texas Land Company, which in October 1830 had acquired claims in eastern Texas under contracts granted originally to David G. Burnet, Joseph Vehlein, and Lorenzo de Zavala. Although the company did not own any land and did not have the right to sell an acre, it advertised in a fashion similar to that used by the western railroads fifty years later; it sublet huge grants to subordinate contractors; and it sold scrip aggregating nearly 7,500,000 acres at from one to ten cents an acre to prospective settlers or to eager speculators, many of whom evidently believed that they were buying land. Although hesitant because of its irregularities, the authorities finally recognized the company and extended the three contracts it held. Thereafter came a stream of immigrants, and by the close of 1835 the land commissioner had issued approximately one thousand titles.

Another colonizing concern, the Nashville Company, obtained through Robert Leftwich a contract for colonizing lands north and northwest of Austin's colony. This company also sold scrip and otherwise prejudiced people against Texas. Since the company agent, Sterling C. Robertson, apparently had done little to make settlements before the passage of the Law of April 6, 1830, the governor declared the contract forfeited and the territory included awarded to Austin and Williams. The colony was restored to the Nashville Company in April 1834, but Austin and Williams regained the colony in May of the following year. After the revolution a jury, which seems to have been in a very generous mood, allowed Robertson premium lands for 379 families.

Two colonies in the southern part of Texas, contracted in 1828 for 200 families each, are entitled to special consideration, because the efforts of their proprietors were the most successful that were put forth to bring people from across the Atlantic. One was the colony of James Power, a native of Ireland, and James Hewetson, a resident of Monclova. By special approval of the federal government the colony lay within the ten league coastal reserve between the Lavaca and the Nueces rivers. The other was that of John McMullen and James McGloin, natives of Ireland but residents of Matamoros, which lay in the interior, in back of the Power and Hewetson grant.

Beset by trouble and misfortune, Power and Hewetson failed to fulfill their contract but finally did manage to settle their colony. Like DeWitt, they were involved in controversies with the quarrelsome De León. Their central town, Refugio, was established on the site of the old mission by that name, which brought them close to the *ayuntamiento* of Goliad and led to complications in that quarter. In 1834 two shiploads of their 350 Irish immigrants were attacked by cholera. They were forced to leave 70 persons at New Orleans. Numbers of others had been buried at sea. Then on the coast of Texas the immigrants found it necessary to abandon the vessels and thereby lost all their farm implements and other equipment. Nevertheless, almost 200 titles were granted, many of which were, no doubt, to North Americans. The colony of McMullen and McGloin, its headquarters at San Patricio or Hibernia, was known as the Irish colony. Its proprietors were even less successful than their Irish neighbors, since only 84 grants of land were issued to their colonists.

Still another attempt to establish a colony of Europeans ended in complete failure. Dr. John Charles Beales and Dr. James Grant in 1832 contracted to introduce 800 families into the region between the Nueces River and the Rio Grande. Late in 1834 Beales with 59 immigrants established the village of Dolores; but because of a crop failure, Indian hostility, and Santa Anna's invasion of Texas, the settlers fled from the colony.

THE END OF COLONIZATION

The Texas colonization era, which began with the coming of Austin's first settlers late in 1821, ended, so far as legally taking possession of land was concerned, with the decree of the Texas provisional government in November 1835, that closed the land offices. By an act of the Congress of the Republic in June 1837, it was declared that all *empresario* contracts had ceased on the day of the declaration of independence, March 2, 1836. It may be stated in review that the majority of the 25 or more colonization contracts for Texas were without results of any consequence. Preeminent among the *empresarios* stands Austin, who settled almost as many families as all the others combined. After Austin, the most successful during the early period, that is before the passage

Stephen F. Austin, The Father of Texas, earned his title by his outstanding efforts as the greatest colonizer of the state. (University of Texas Library) Also shown, a replica of his home near Sealy. (Texas Highway Department)

of the Law of April 6, 1830, were DeWitt and De León. Of the later group (those who colonized mainly after May 1834), the Galveston Bay and Texas Land Company and the Nashville Company were most successful. In colonizing Europeans, Power and Hewetson made most progress; but their slender accomplishments sustain the statement made by the English historian William Kennedy that "The North Americans are the only people who, in defiance of all obstacles, have struck the roots of civilization deep into the soil of Texas." The colonists were distributed from the Sabine to the Nueces, but an overwhelming majority were located east of the Guadalupe and south of the old road from San Antonio to Nacogdoches. About 3,500 land titles were issued through the different *empresarios* and a few titles were granted without the aid of proprietors. Estimates of population vary. In 1834 the Mexican soldier and statesman, Juan N. Almonte, after a visit to Texas, placed the population at 24,700 including slaves, or at a little more than 20,000 for the Anglo-Americans and their slaves.

Who were these people? Whence had they come and what were the forces that brought them? The evidence available indicates that they were in the main farmers and people of some means, although many had left behind them debts they could not pay. That they were honest and law-abiding is evidenced by the small amount of crime committed in the colonies. The *empresarios* were required to see that lawless characters did not remain. Among the settlers literacy was high for that date. Of more than 266 of Austin's "Old Three Hundred," only four could not write. Data kept by Austin for his colony show that the majority of his people came from Louisiana, Alabama, Arkansas, Tennessee, or Missouri in the order named. A total of 699 registered from the trans-Appalachian states as compared with a total of 107 from the Atlantic Seaboard. Yet, since most adults living west of the mountains at that time had been born in the seaboard states, it is most certain that a majority of the colonists had come originally from east of the mountains. Many of the colonists were people, who, like the Austins, had fared badly in their old environment and were seeking a new country.

The land system of the United States was modified in 1820 in a way that caused men to seek acreage elsewhere; the credit system was abolished and the minimum price was set at $1.25 an acre, cash. By comparison, in Texas the head of a family could obtain 4,428 acres of land for a little more than the cost of 80 acres in the United States.[2] Moreover, in Texas settlers could select land which was as good or even better than any available in the United States.

[2]The cost of land varied slightly under the different laws and in the different colonies. Apparently in Austin's colony under the law of 1825, the fee to the state was $30; the fee to Austin $60, to the land commissioner $15, to S. M. Williams, for clerical work, $10; and for stamped paper, $2; making a total of $117. Generous terms of credit were allowed on a part of the charges. Austin stated with pride that he never turned a man away because he was poor.

COLONIAL INSTITUTIONS

When they crossed the Sabine River, the Anglo-American colonists entered a country where government, religion, customs, and attitudes differed greatly from those they had known before. They ran their own affairs with a minimum of interference from Mexican officials, and they modified Mexican institutions as much as possible to conform to Anglo-American patterns. As Yoakum states: "They brought with them here, as household gods, their own first lessons in politics, morals, religion, and business, and they wished not to unlearn those lessons to learn others."

On October 4, 1824, the Constituent Congress, which had assembled in November 1823, framed and published a constitution much like that of the United States. Perhaps the greatest difference was that the Mexican instrument established the Roman Catholic Church as the official religion. In this congress Erasmo Seguin represented Texas, the farmers of Austin's colony loyally subscribing several hundred bushels of corn to help pay his expenses. The legislature for the State of Coahuila and Texas was organized at Saltillo on August 15, 1824, when Baron de Bastrop represented Texas. Most of its efforts before March 11, 1827, went toward framing a state constitution which was published at that time. The constitution provided for 12 deputies. Of these, Texas was allotted only one, but the number was later increased to three. The deputies, like the members of the national congress, were to be chosen by an indirect electoral process.

In 1825 Texas was made a department within the State of Coahuila and Texas, to be presided over by a political chief who was appointed by and responsible to the governor. This officer, a kind of subgovernor, was to reside at Bexar, watch over public tranquility, inflict punishments, command the local militia, see that the laws were enforced, and make reports to the governor. Later, Texas was divided into three departments, with headquarters and political chiefs at San Antonio, Nacogdoches, and San Felipe.

The most important unit of local government was the municipality, which included one or more towns and adjacent territory. It might cover thousands of square miles. The *ayuntamiento*, or governing body of the municipality, had broad duties that suggest the combined functions of a modern city commission and a county commissioners' court. At its head was an alcalde, the chief executive officer, whose duties were similar to those of sheriff, judge, and mayor of a city. The *regidores*, like members of our own city commissions, had certain legislative powers as well as some administrative responsibilities. The *sindico* may be described inexactly as a municipal city attorney and state's representative. Then there was the *alguacil* or sheriff, appointed by the alcalde, and a secretary appointed by the *ayuntamiento*. Each subdivision of a municipality, known as a district or precinct, had its *comisario*, a sort of subalcalde, generally thought of by Anglo-American colonists as a justice of the peace; and also a *sindico* for the district. Austin's first colonists were given local self-government by the order of Governor José Trespalacios in November 1822, when alcaldes were elected by the settlers on the Colorado River and the Brazos River respectively. New districts were created from time to time, so that when constitutional government was established in 1828, Austin's colony had seven. At that time the municipalities of Texas were Bexar, La Bahía or Goliad, Nacogdoches, and San Felipe (Austin's colony). The municipalities of Brazoria and of Gonzales were created in 1832. Other municipalities were added later, until by the close of 1834 there were 13. Municipal taxes were light and payable largely in kind. The early colonists, it will be recalled, were exempted from state taxes, church tithes, and national customs duties.[3]

Into this pattern of government the *empresario* system was fitted. The duties of the *empresario* were numerous and trying. He had to deal not only with state and national governments that seemed foreign and unsympathetic; but also with the Anglo-American pioneers, a people sturdy, worthy, and well-meaning, yet often prejudiced, stubborn, ignorant, jealous of their freedom, and ever disposed to find fault with those in authority. Austin's burden was much greater than that of his fellow proprietors; for his colony was seven years old before regular constitutional government was established. He was responsible for the selection of his colonists and for seeing to it that they were of good character and properly recommended. Although Bastrop, his land commissioner, actually issued the titles, Austin had to see to the surveying of the land and to conduct all business connected with obtaining and recording titles. He was responsible in general for the government of the colony. Indeed, he was a lawgiver, for he wrote civil and criminal codes for the alcaldes, based on the Mexican laws but adapted to conditions in the colonies. He was commander in chief of the militia and responsible for defense and the maintenance of satisfactory relations with the Indians.

He had to shoulder many informal obligations which in the aggregate were even more burdensome than those required by law. Prospective colonists expected entertainment at his home while they were getting located; frequently he was called on to settle petty disputes; many persons apparently regarded him as a collecting agent; others expected him to make purchases for them, and to advance the money until they should

[3]The Imperial Colonization Law exempted the colonists for six years from tithes, excises, or taxes of any kind whatever. By decree of September 29, 1823, congress exempted from duties for seven years all merchandise from any country. In its colonization law of 1825 the state exempted colonists from taxes for ten years. The Law of April 6, 1830, permitted for two years the importation of provisions, lumber, tools, and so forth, free of duty. In 1832 the exemption on certain articles was extended again for two years.

pay him; and sometimes parents in distant states insisted that he keep an eye on their sons in Texas. Most difficult of all was the burden of serving as intermediary between grumbling colonists on the one hand and a strange government on the other. With the establishment of constitutional government in 1828, the greater part of Austin's formal responsibilities ceased, but he continued to be the counselor of the colonists and their officers.

During its early history, DeWitt's colony was apparently governed similarly to Austin's. In 1826 the *empresario* appointed James Norton alcalde; an irregular act, but the governor approved it. Then, for a period the colony was under the jurisdiction of Bexar, but in response to a petition it was placed, in 1828, under the jurisdiction of San Felipe, where it remained until the municipality of Gonzales was organized in 1832.

The Anglo-Americans, with a love for legislating that equaled the love of the Mexicans for regulating, passed many local laws, but they had little interest in enforcing the laws they made, primarily because the court system was most unsatisfactory. In all important cases the alcalde or *comisario* was required to send a record of the testimony to a higher official at Saltillo and wait for the return of his decision. Even if there were no errors, the sentence had to be approved by the supreme court before the decree could be executed.

Such a system would have been intolerable except for the fact that there was very little crime in the colonies and that most offenders could be dealt with outside of the courts. Austin drove a number of undesirables from his colony; the *ayuntamientos* compelled some to leave; and occasionally the people persuaded certain ill-disposed persons that their health and happiness would be greater beyond the confines of the community.

A special judiciary act passed in 1834 was meant to correct the worst features of the court system by providing for jury trial in both civil and criminal cases and for an appellate circuit court for Texas. Certain features of the act were, however, impracticable, and it never went into effect.

For the first colonists, hostile Indians added to other perils. The savage Karankawas on the coast pillaged and murdered in small bands. In the interior were the Tonkawas, generally nominally at peace with the whites, but sometimes dangerous and always troublesome. And along the Brazos River, above the San Antonio Road, were the Wacos and Tawakonis, spirited and periodically dangerous. In eastern Texas were a few hundred Cherokees and Choctaws who had moved into the country from east of the Mississippi, and also bands of indigenous sedentary Indians.

For defense against the Indians the colonists had to depend mainly on their own strength. The militia in Austin's colony was first organized in the fall of 1822. From time to time new districts were created, until by the close of 1824 six companies had been organized. By 1830 the Indian menace for Austin's colony was a thing of the past, and interest in the militia organizations began to decline. The people of Bexar, Gonzales, and Goliad did not fare so well as those to the east. In 1830 DeWitt wrote the governor that unless troops were sent to his colony, his settlements would be broken up. The settlers managed to hold out, although troops were not sent until the following year, and then only 15. A six-pounder cannon loaned to Gonzales in 1831 for protection against the Indians was destined to be the cause of the first bloodshed in the Texas Revolution.

The status of slavery in colonial Texas is hard to describe. The Imperial Colonization Law (for the benefit of Austin) recognized slavery, but forbade the slave trade and declared that slaves born in the empire should be free at the age of fourteen. The national colonization law of 1824 probably was intended to forbid the bringing in of slaves, but it was not so interpreted. The state constitution of 1827 recognized existing slavery and permitted the introduction of slaves for six months after its publication, but it declared that children born of slaves thereafter should be free. Meanwhile, the Mexican government began to undo with its left hand what it had done with its right: it legalized the domestic slave trade by providing that a slave might "change" his master, "if the new master would indemnify the old"; and a law of 1828 legalized slave importation by recognizing labor "contracts made in foreign countries. . . ." Afterwards, on entering Texas the Negroes were nominally servants under contract, but actually they were still slaves. Mention has been made already of the great excitement provoked in Texas by a decree of President Guerrero, in 1829, abolishing slavery, apparently for the purpose of checking immigration to Texas. Evidently it seemed more expedient to exempt Texas from the proclamation and stop immigration by a law specifically designed for that purpose. The resulting decree of April 6, 1830, recognized existing slavery but prohibited the further introduction of slaves. An act of the legislature in 1832 strengthened the antislavery laws and limited to ten years contracts with slaves and day laborers. Thus, by 1832, the introduction of slaves was positively barred and peonage contracts were limited to ten years.

First and last, many slaves had been brought to Texas; yet, their ratio to that of the whites declined in the later colonial years. In 1825 Austin's colony had 443 slaves and 1,347 whites. In 1834 Almonte estimated the number of slaves in the Department of the Brazos (composed mainly of Austin's colonies) at 1,000, out of a total population of about 10,000. The subject of slavery does not appear extensively in the discussions and protests of the colonists preceding the Revolution, but the uncertain status of the institution frequently caused anxiety and must have frightened away many prospective immigrants.

Judging from letters of inquiry sent to Austin and from other sources, it seems that a few potential colonists stayed away from Texas because of their hostility to Catholicism. By constitution and law, the Roman Catholic Apostolic was the religion of Mexico, to the exclusion of any other. The Catholic faith was supposed to go with Mexican citizenship, and heretics were subject to banishment and other punishment.

Although he always stated these facts plainly to prospective colonists, Austin emphasized them less and less as his colony grew, and other proprietors apparently took much the same attitude. In fact, very few of the colonists were Catholics by faith and not many were even nominally so.

Most of the settlers apparently had little interest in formal religion. One observer, while praising them for the small amount of crime in Texas, added that in respect to the gospel, conditions were "bad—bad! superlatively bad," and another wrote from the Colorado River country in 1831 that there was little regard for the Sabbath which "is generally spent in visiting, driving stock, and breaking mustangs."

The people had more cause to complain of spiritual neglect than of persecution. Repeatedly Austin petitioned the authorities to send a priest to his colony to christen children, legalize marriage contracts, and perform various other services that were expected in a Catholic country, but for ten years he was put off with promises and excuses, the chief reason being, it seems, that there was no provision for paying the priest as long as the colonists were exempted from taxes and tithes. Finally, in 1831, Father Michael Muldoon, an Irish priest, arrived. He was good-natured, loyal, and kind, but apparently he did not always live up to the Anglo-American standards of piety for the ministry. At Nacogdoches, where there had once been a Catholic church and where many Catholics still resided, the established church under Father Antonio Diaz fared better.

In spite of official opposition and the indifference of the colonists, the Protestants made considerable progress in colonial Texas. In 1820, Joseph E. Bays, a Baptist preacher, came from Missouri to Louisiana with Moses Austin, and soon was preaching in Texas. William Stevenson, a Methodist, also was preaching in the colony at an early date and continued to do so despite warnings from Austin and James Gaines, alcalde of the Sabine district. As early as the winter of 1818–1819, Stevenson had preached at Pecan Point.[4] A little later came several missionaries, including Sumner Bacon, Cumberland Presbyterian, who traveled through Austin's and DeWitt's colonies distributing Bibles, and Thomas J. Pilgrim, a Baptist, credited with organizing the first Sunday school in

---

[4] Pecan Point (in present Red River County) was a part of the regular circuit of the Missouri Conference from 1818 to 1825. At different times Thomas Tennant, Green Orr, and Joseph Reed rode that circuit. Freeman Smalley, a Baptist, preached there in 1822.

Texas. There is evidence of a gradual growth of a spirit of tolerance toward dissenters.

After the colonists drove out the Mexican garrisons in 1832, Protestant camp meetings became common. A notable one on Caney Creek in 1835 had five ministers present. Horatio Chriesman, the alcalde, and Dr. James B. Miller, political chief, presumably encouraged the meetings and helped to support the ministers. Also, a few churches were organized during this period. In 1834 a measure of religious tolerance was afforded in a state law which seems to have violated the constitution. It stated that no person should be molested on account of his religious or political opinions, provided he did not disturb the public order.

There was no system of public education in colonial Texas. A public school had been established at San Antonio as early as 1746, and shortly after 1813 the Spaniards had erected a building there to provide for seventy pupils. We hear of books being purchased for a primary school in San Antonio in 1828; but when Colonel Almonte visited Texas in 1834, he lamented the fact that the school once maintained by the *ayuntamiento* of Bexar had been discontinued. He added, however, that there were schools at Nacogdoches, San Augustine, and Johnsburg (Jonesborough, on the Red River).

A small private school in Austin's colony was taught by Isaac M. Pennington as early as 1823, and we hear of other teachers. There was no school in Harrisburg in 1833, but a little later a school with about ten pupils was maintained in a nearby community.

The chief industries in early Texas were farming and trade. Farming will be given consideration in a later chapter. A few trade centers were established at an early date. San Felipe became a thriving town, although as late as 1830 it had only one house that was not built of logs. Brazoria had approximately forty houses and was perhaps the leading shipping point by 1832. Soon, however, it shared some of its trade with the new town of Matagorda, at the mouth of the Colorado. Galveston, with the best harbor on the Texas coast, remained uninhabited during most of the colonial era. The old Spanish town of Nacogdoches, which had only 36 inhabitants when Austin saw it in 1821, grew into a business center with stores well supplied with dry goods, notions, and foodstuffs. San Antonio, or Bexar, as it was more commonly called, was the most populous town throughout the entire period, but it did not grow as rapidly as some of the younger towns.

Two conditions hampered business severely in colonial Texas: the lack of money or banking facilities and the absence of roads or other means of transportation. The account of George B. Erath, the Austrian-American, is typical. Erath traded clothes, which he had brought from Germany, for cattle and hogs; and he traded a horse for corn. He tells of his partner who gave an ox for a sow valued at five dollars, a feather bed for three cows and calves, a gun for a mare, and another gun for a cow, calf, and yearling. The *ayuntamiento* recognized the paucity of money by permitting a person to pay two-thirds of his local taxes[5] in kind, and gave an official stamp to bovine currency by stating that a cow and calf should be valued at ten dollars. Interest rates were exorbitant.

Save for small quantities of salt from the Rio Grande, horses brought into Texas from Mexico, and occasional illicit purchases of tobacco in Mexico, there seems to have been virtually no trade between Texas and Mexico. In 1821, when on his first visit to Texas, Stephen F. Austin found a good trade already established between Natchitoches, Louisiana, and Goliad. Apparently, Natchitoches continued to be a favorite trading post of Texans, and most shipments into the colonies by land originated there. Trade by sea with New Orleans increased throughout the period.

Inadequate ports constituted a great handicap to shipping. Galveston was not convenient to the principal settlements. Even small vessels had to be partly unloaded to cross the bar in order to reach Brazoria and other points on the lower Brazos. Likewise, Matagorda Bay had its perils, and small schooners had difficulty in reaching either the mouth of the Lavaca or the town of Matagorda, at the mouth of the Colorado.

Austin stated in 1829 that the chief possibilities for export from Texas were "cotton, beef, tallow, pork, lard, mules, etc." Almonte, whose data are the best extant but probably little more than a collection of guesses, valued Texas exports for 1833 at $500,000. Of this, cotton made up $353,000; "furs" (probably hides of all kinds), $140,000; and cattle, $25,000. His estimate on cotton certainly is too high, but it may be offset by the miscellaneous items which he ignored, and his failure to credit the Department of the Brazos[6] with the shipment of any cattle. The importation for that year he said amounted to $630,000.

It is well to remember that most families brought with them quantities of goods which are not considered in these estimates. These imports supplied approximately 20,000 colonists with necessities and a few, a very few, luxuries; the exports proved the great potential wealth of the land. Of great political importance, also, is the fact that these imported goods—almost wholly from the United States—kept alive the interest of the Texans in the land of their birth.

Selected Bibliography

Material on Texas colonization is comparatively abundant. Of the older accounts the best is H. Yoakum, *History of Texas*. His text, with some supplementary material, is reproduced in Dudley G. Wooten, *A Compre-*

[5]The tax exemptions granted the colonists did not apply to local taxes.

[6]It will be recalled that at this time Texas was divided into three departments: that of Bexar, with headquarters at San Antonio; the Brazos, with headquarters at San Felipe; and Nacogdoches, with headquarters at the town of that name.

hensive History of Texas (2 vols., Dallas, 1897). Other general accounts are William Kennedy, *Texas* (2d. ed., London, 1841; Fort Worth, 1925); H. H. Bancroft, *History of the North Mexican States and Texas*; John Henry Brown, *A History of Texas, 1685–1892* (2 vols., St. Louis, 1892–1893); Louis J. Wortham, *A History of Texas* (5 vols., Fort Worth, 1924); Clarence R. Wharton, *Texas under Many Flags* (5 vols., Chicago and New York, 1930); and H. S. Thrall, *Pictorial History of Texas.*

A rich mine of source material is *The Austin Papers*, edited by E. C. Barker, and published as *The Annual Report of the American Historical Association*, 1919, II, and 1922, II (Washington, 1924 and 1928), and a supplementary volume (Austin, 1926); E. Wallace and D. M. Vigness (eds.), *Documents of Texas History.*

The most scholarly studies are E. C. Barker, *The Life of Stephen F. Austin* (Nashville and Dallas, 1925); E. C. Barker, *Mexico and Texas, 1821–1835* (Dallas, 1928); and D. M. Vigness, *The Revolutionary Decades.* For the Decree of April 6, 1830, see Ohland Morton, *Terán and Texas* (Austin 1948).

Articles on colony planting are to be found in the *Quarterly of the Texas State Historical Association* (I-XV) and the *Southwestern Historical Quarterly* (XVI-). Among them are: "Journal of Stephen F. Austin on His First Trip to Texas, 1821," VII, 286–307; W. S. Lewis, "Adventures of the *Lively* Immigrants," III, 1–32; L. G. Bugbee, "What Became of the *Lively*?", III, 141–148; L. G. Bugbee, "The Old Three Hundred," I, 108–117; E. C. Barker, "Notes on the Colonization of Texas," XXVII, 108–119; Mary Virginia Henderson, "Minor Empresario Contracts for the Colonization of Texas, 1825–1834," XXXI, 295–324; XXXII, 1–28; Robert W. Amsler, "General Arthur G. Wavell: A Soldier of Fortune in Texas," LXIX, 1–21, 186–209; Andrew Forest Muir, "Humphrey Jackson, Alcalde of San Jacinto," LXVIII, 362–366; Charles A. Bacarisse, "The Union of Coahuila and Texas," LXI, 341–349; Henry W. Barton, "The Anglo-American Colonists under Mexican Militia Laws," LXV, 61–71; Roger N. Conger, "The Tomás de la Vega Eleven-League Grant on the Brazos," LXI, 371–382. R. W. Strickland, "Miller County, Arkansas Territory, the Frontier That Men Forget," *Chronicles of Oklahoma*, XVIII, 12–34, 154–170; XIX, 37–54, gives the only satisfactory account available of the settlement of extreme northeast Texas. Excellent studies of the colonies in southern Texas include W. H. Oberste, *Texas Irish Empresarios and Their Colonies* (Austin, 1953), comprehensive; Leroy P. Graf, "Colonizing Projects in Texas South of the Nueces, 1820–1845," *Southwestern Historical Quarterly*, L, 431–448; Carl Coke Rister, *Comanche Bondage* (Glendale, 1955), about Beale's colony.

On colonial institutions there are in the *Southwestern Historical Quarterly*: E. C. Barker, "The Government of Austin's Colony, 1821–1831," XXI, 223–252; supplemented by the "Minutes of the *Ayuntamiento of San Felipe de Austin,* 1828–1832," XXI, 299–326, 395–423; XXII, 78–95, 180–196, 272–278, 353–359; XXIII, 69–77, 141–151, 214–223, 302–307; XXIV, 81–83, 154–166. Useful also is E. C. Barker, "The Influence of Slavery in the Colonization of Texas," *Southwestern Historical Quarterly,* XXVIII, 1–33. J. H. Kuykendall, a colonist, gathered a series of interesting and valuable reminiscences of colonists; they are printed in the *Quarterly of the Texas State Historical Association* VI, 236–253, 311–330, and VII, 29–64; others, somewhat similar, are found in V, 12–18; XIII, 44–80; XIV, 24–73. Worthy of special mention are *Travel and Adventures in Texas in the 1820's: Being the Reminiscences of Mary Crownover Rabb* (Waco, 1962), and "Reminiscences of Mrs. Dilue Harris," *Quarterly of the Texas State Historical Association,* IV, 85–127, 155–189, 387, written in part from a journal kept by Mrs. Harris' father, Dr. Pleasant W. Rose. Noah Smithwick, *The Evolution of a State* (Austin, 1900), written when the author was ninety years old, is rich in detail and bears evidence of a high degree of accuracy. The best descriptive book of Texas written by a contemporary is Mary Austin Holley, *Texas* (Baltimore, 1833; Lexington, Ky., 1836). Mrs. Holley's text is included in M. A. Hatcher, *Letters of an Early American Traveller: Mary Austin Holley. Her Life and Works,* 1784–1846 (Dallas, 1933). For another biography of this remarkable observer of the Texas scene, see Rebecca Smith Lee, *Mary Austin Holley: A Biography* (Austin, 1962). Religion in early Texas is best discussed in W. S. Red, *The Texas Colonists and Religion, 1821–1836* (Austin, 1924).

Useful is *Texas: A Guide to the Lone Star State* (American Guide Series, compiled by workers of the Writers' Program of the Work Projects Administration in Texas, and sponsored by the Texas State Highway Commission; New York, 1940).

5

THE DEVELOPMENT OF
THE TEXAN REVOLUTION,
1827–1835

"This is the most liberal and munificent Govt. on earth to emigra[n]ts—after being here one year you will oppose a change even to Uncle Sam—." Thus wrote Stephen F. Austin in 1829 to his sister and brother-in-law, urging them to come to Texas. As late as 1832, to his partner and boon companion, Samuel M. Williams, he wrote: "My standing motto—'Fidelity to Mexico'—ought to be in every man's mouth and repeated. . . ." Yet, three years later, Austin, the most loyal of all of Mexico's adopted sons, was leading troops in rebellion against that government. This reversal in sentiment did not take place in one week or even in one year, but was the natural reaction to racial and cultural differences and to a long chain of developments that all together led from fidelity through alienation to rebellion. The development of the Texan Revolution may be considered under six topics, namely: (1) underlying causes, the most important of which were the racial and cultural differences between the Mexicans and the Anglo-American colonists, the Edwards or Fredonian Rebellion, the efforts of the United States to buy Texas, the Emancipation Proclamation of 1829, and the Law of April 6, 1830; (2) the quarrel between Texans and the customs and military officials, climaxed by the insurrection at Anahuac in 1832; (3) the conventions of 1832 and 1833 and developments result-

69

ing from them; (4) Santa Anna's abrogation of the Constitution of 1824 and other acts of tyranny; (5) confusion at the seat of state government from early in 1833 to the spring of 1835; and (6) Santa Anna's effort to enforce his will upon Texas.

UNDERLYING CAUSES

A study of the Texan Revolution reveals striking resemblances to the American Revolution: both can be traced to the disposition of the superior government to assert its authority after the colonists had learned to expect from it laxity and neglect. Customs duties and officious customs collectors play an important part in both stories. The Texans resented Mexican troops quartered among them, just as their forebears hated the British red coats in the days of Samuel Adams. In this connection the grievances of the Texans were even greater than those of the English colonists from whom most of them were descended: first, because the Mexican government even more than the British used the military to enforce civil law; and, second, because the Texans looked upon the Mexicans as an inferior race with whom they had little in common. The Anglo-Americans were aggressive and self-reliant individualists, rebels against centralist authority, and tenacious adherents to the doctrine that their civil liberties could best be preserved by constitutional and local self-government. Furthermore, they were violently averse to the subordination of the civil to the military power and to any connection whatsoever of church and state. They came to Texas with a long heritage of successful experience in self-government.

The Mexicans, in contrast, were sensitive, subtle and indirect in their ways, subservient to authority, and adherents to the Roman Catholic religion. After 300 years of subjugation to Spain, they were not prepared for self-government. Nevertheless, they promulgated a federal republican constitution that provided for a political system which the majority neither well understood nor regarded as sacrosanct. To the Anglo-American colonists, the constitution was not satisfactory: it did not guarantee trial by jury or the right of the accused to bail, it established Roman Catholicism as the official religion, and it did not adequately curb military power. Such contrasts, accentuated by a difference in language, naturally bred mutual suspicion, misunderstanding, and distrust, and consequently the two peoples made poor yokefellows.

Because the Mexicans were preoccupied with political instability at home and the Anglo-American colonists were busy building homes and clearing farms, it was five years after Austin arrived with the first colonists before the first clash between the two cultural groups occurred. In 1825 Haden Edwards secured an *empresario* grant which permitted him to locate colonists in a large area of eastern Texas. Within the boundaries of the grant were the old settlement of Nacogdoches and other communities. When Edwards discovered that certain persons, both Mexicans and Anglo-Americans, were claiming lands under old Spanish grants, he made an arbitrary ruling that required claimants under the old laws to prove title to their lands. This ruling alarmed and antagonized the old settlers, many of whom because of the inconvenience had been careless in perfecting their land titles. Also, through his son-in-law, Chichester Chaplain, Edwards became involved in an election contest and further antagonized the old settlers' party. Austin wrote Edwards, cautioning him against antagonizing the Mexican officials, but his advice went unheeded. Edwards' enemies took their cause to the superior officers, and without notice or hearing the president of the Republic on June 3, 1826, cancelled his contract and ordered that he be expelled from the country. Benjamin Edwards, brother of the proprietor, raised the standard of revolt and in December proclaimed the Republic of Fredonia; but his followers were few and spiritless, and his proposed alliance with the Cherokee Indians did not materialize. Austin loyally sent militiamen to Nacogdoches to aid in the suppression of the rebellion. On the report of the approach of the militia and troops in January 1827, the insurgents fled to the United States. The Fredonian uprising, led by about 15 men, had a greater impact on Mexican sentiment than it deserved. Mexican officials concluded that the Fredonians had intended to add Texas to the United States and became increasingly suspicious of the Anglo-Americans.

The Mexican mind linked inseparably the Fredonian affair with the effort of the United States to acquire, by purchase or otherwise, all or a part of Texas. In 1825, President John Quincy Adams, who had often asserted that the Louisiana Purchase extended to the Rio Grande, through Joel R. Poinsett, minister to Mexico, inaugurated efforts to obtain for the United States a "more suitable" boundary. Poinsett was authorized to offer Mexico one million dollars for the removal of the line to the Rio Grande. President Andrew Jackson raised Adams' offer to five million and continued the effort through Poinsett and Poinsett's successor, Anthony Butler, with no results other than to aggravate the suspicions Mexicans entertained concerning both the United States and the Anglo-American colonists. "The Yankees have failed to take Texas through rebellion," said the Mexicans, "and now they are trying to purchase it. Soon they will renew their efforts to acquire it by violence." The fact that such charges were altogether unfair, both to the United States government and to the Texan colonists, did not lessen their effectiveness in promoting discord.

In turn, a feeling of anxiety and suspicion was aroused among the Anglo-American colonists as a result of President Guerrero's proclamation of emancipation of slavery on September 15, 1829. Upon receipt of the decree, the Mexican political chief at San Antonio petitioned and obtained an exemption for Texas, but the colonists, nevertheless, were left with a feeling that their interests were not safe.

Greater than the emancipation proclamation in promoting ill feeling was the decree of April 6, 1830. It will be recalled that this law prohibited further colonization by people from the United States and provided for the collection of customs duties and for the garrisoning of troops in Texas. Alamán, who drafted the bill, feared that when the Americans became a preponderant majority they would first petition for changes or reforms, then create disturbances, and finally by violence or diplomacy take possession of the province. The law caused exactly what Alamán had hoped to prevent by it; out of it grew the chain of events, listed above, that led from disturbances and petitions to rebellion and independence.

DISTURBANCES OF 1831 AND 1832

In keeping with its program "to maintain the integrity of Mexican territory" as set forth in the Law of April 6, 1830, the federal government sent a customs collector to Texas in May of that year and soon thereafter began to send more troops. The selection of officers for these duties was exceedingly unfortunate. The customs collector for ports east of the Colorado was George Fisher, a Serbian adventurer, once a citizen of the United States, and a Mexican citizen since 1821. He not only took his position too seriously, but had a weakness for interfering in other people's affairs. In command of the important post of Anahuac was John Davis Bradburn, a stubborn, tactless Kentuckian, then in Mexican service.

When Fisher took up regular duties as customs collector in November 1831, he located the customhouse at Anahuac, at the head of Galveston Bay, where troops were stationed under Bradburn. Here he issued a strange decree that required shipmasters who wished to leave Texas from the mouth of the Brazos or certain other ports to secure clearances from him at Anahuac before sailing. Since to do this sometimes required an overland journey of two hundred miles or more, the order provoked much dissatisfaction. When in December 1831 some shippers ignored the order and ran by the guard on the lower Brazos, shots were exchanged and one soldier was seriously wounded.

Fisher's superior officers did not sustain him in this unreasonable ruling, and thereafter a deputy collector was placed at Brazoria on the lower Brazos. Still the colonists protested and in September 1832 the government abandoned the collection of duties. Apparently, there was little or no collection of customs duties in Texas from that date until the spring of 1835.

Ill will over tariffs was closely linked with a more serious contest that arose because of the presence of Mexican troops. Colonel Bradburn at Anahuac soon provoked the bitter resentment of the people. His first serious offense was the arresting, early in 1831, of Francisco Madero, who had come to Texas with authority to grant land titles to settlers living east of the San Jacinto River. Bradburn ordered Madero to desist, on the ground that to issue these titles would violate the decree of April 6, 1830. Madero explained that he had been commissioned by both the state and federal governments, but Bradburn was obdurate and arrested him. Bradburn, furthermore, annulled for a period the *ayuntamiento* of the town of Liberty which Madero had set up by authority of his superiors. To the settlers of East Texas this affair was more than a dispute between two Mexican officers. They felt that Bradburn had tyrannically deprived them of their property and legal rights.

Bradburn's conduct continued to enrage the colonists, and soon some of them, notably William B. Travis and Patrick Jack, began, it seems deliberately, to annoy him with mysterious messages about an armed force that was coming from Louisiana to recover some runaway slaves which Bradburn apparently refused to release. Then the irate Bradburn arrested Travis, Jack, and other citizens, placed them in a jail improvised from an old brick kiln, and refused to deliver them to the civil authorities for trial.

The prolonged imprisonment of Travis and Jack brought the colonists to resistance. William H. Jack, brother of Patrick, having tried unsuccessfully to secure his brother's release, returned to San Felipe and called on his fellow colonists to join him in an attack on Bradburn. In early June men began to gather at Liberty, and soon John Austin (who may have been distantly related to Stephen F. Austin, the colonizer) was on hand with ninety men from Brazoria. By June 10, 1832, 160 angry Texans were before Anahuac. After some parleys, which accomplished nothing, and some skirmishing, the colonists withdrew to await the arrival of cannon from Brazoria. The quarrel at Anahuac ended, however, without the use of artillery.

Colonel José de las Piedras, commander of the garrison of Mexican troops at Nacogdoches, arrived on the scene with a part of his force and with orders to adjust the matter if possible. He entered into an agreement with the colonists to have the prisoners released to the civil authorities for trial, to see to it that owners were indemnified for the property that Bradburn had taken illegally, and to endeavor to have Bradburn removed from command of the post. Bradburn soon resigned; and the garrison thereupon declared for Santa Anna and sailed away to join his army.

The contest at Anahuac had been almost bloodless, but events on the Brazos meanwhile were taking a more serious turn. John Austin had returned to Brazoria, where he secured three cannon (also reinforcements of men) and started by boat down the river for Anahuac;

but Colonel Domingo de Ugartechea, commander of the fort at Velasco, would not permit the schooner to pass, and a bloody engagement was fought, ending with the surrender of the post. By the terms of surrender the garrison was allowed the honors of war, and was to be provided transportation to Matamoros.

Once under way the movement of resistance spread and the colonists determined to drive every Mexican soldier from the settlements. Anahuac and Velasco were emptied of troops by midsummer; Piedras and his command were driven from Nacogdoches; and the post of Tenoxtitlan on the upper Brazos was evacuated. Thus the Anglo-American part of Texas was rid completely of Mexican troops. All this was nothing less than rebellion and war, and save for good luck and the adroit work of Stephen F. Austin and other leaders, it would most surely have brought upon the colonists severe retribution.

Developments in Mexico favored the Texan cause. General Anastacio Bustamante had made himself dictator of Mexico in January 1830. After two years of his tyranny, the troops at Vera Cruz revolted and soon Antonio Lopez de Santa Anna, a president-maker, was at their head. The Texans knew little of Mexican politics, but they knew that Bradburn was serving under Bustamante and that Santa Anna was fighting Bustamante. Therefore, they should be against Bustamante and for Santa Anna, who was posing as a liberal and champion of the constitution. While waiting near Anahuac, the angry colonists on June 13, 1832, had adopted the Turtle Bayou Resolutions in which they professed their "deepest interest and solicitude" in the cause of "the highly talented and distinguished chieftain, Gen. Santa Anna"; and as *freemen* devoted to a correct interpretation and enforcement of the constitution and laws," they pledged their "lives and fortunes" in his support. Likewise, in late July the people of eastern Texas pledged themselves to rally around the standard of Santa Anna as the champion of their freedom, and drove Piedras from the country because he refused to declare for Santa Anna. On August 30, Ramón Músquiz, the political chief at San Antonio, tardily declared for Santa Anna.

A sharp reaction against the war party developed; but the conservatives could not undo what the radicals had done. The insurrection was an accomplished fact. It had been the policy of the Texans to hold themselves aloof from Mexican imbroglios; but forces beyond their control made it imperative that they stand united in defense of what John Austin and his men had done.

In early July at Matamoros, Colonel José Antonio Mexia was in command of the Santanista forces. Nearby was Colonel José Mariano Guerra in command of the Bustamante troops. When Mexia overhauled a mail packet from Brazoria and learned of the disturbances in Texas, he proposed to Guerra that they declare a truce and pool their resources to save Texas for the Mexican confederation. Guerra agreed, and soon

Mexia with about 400 soldiers was off for Texas. Fortunately for the colonists, he took along Stephen F. Austin who had come by way of Matamoros on his return from the legislature at Saltillo. It is safe to conjecture that Austin spent many hours amplifying and emphasizing to Mexia what he had already written to the Mexican authorities concerning affairs in Texas. His argument was stated thus: "There is no insurrection of the Colonists against the Constitution and Government, neither do they entertain ideas endangering even remotely the integrity of the territory." They had not resisted the Mexican government but had fought Bradburn, a petty tyrant who took his orders from Bustamante, the very man Mexia was trying to overthrow. They were loyal Santanistas and had declared themselves so in the beginning. Mexia gave the colonists their cue in a letter of July 16 to John Austin, written after a conference with and, no doubt, in the presence of Stephen F. Austin. Mexia stated:

But if, as I have been assured by respectable citizens, the past occurrences were on account of the colonists having adhered to the plan of Vera Cruz . . . you can in that case assure the inhabitants that I will unite with them to accomplish their wishes, and that the forces under my command will protect their adhesion to said plan.

The colonists, who knew of the coming of the expedition, prepared for Mexia a most lavish reception. He was saluted at the mouth of the Brazos by a salvo of cannon, entertained in the home of John Austin, and assured by reception committees of the loyalty of the Texans. At Brazoria the general was given a dinner and ball; the crowd was "large, cheerful, and convivial," and drank many toasts to Santa Anna. Under such conditions there was nothing for Mexia to do but to return to Mexico. He could not make war on the people who were on his side of the contest and who were treating him like a king.

THE CONVENTIONS OF 1832 AND 1833

Since the insurrection of 1832 was eminently successful, the colonists were not willing to leave matters where they stood. They wanted some concessions from the Mexican government and some assurance that the abuses would not be repeated. Accordingly, on August 22, just a month after Mexia had sailed away, the *ayuntamiento* of San Felipe issued a call to the districts to send delegates to a convention to meet at San Felipe on October 1, 1832. Sixteen districts responded (not counting Goliad, whose delegation arrived too late for the proceedings) and chose 58 delegates. Stephen F. Austin was elected president. Committees were appointed to draft resolutions on various topics. Several resolutions were addressed to the federal government, others to the

Antonio López de Santa Anna. The reactionary dictatorship of this opportunistic general and politician provoked the Texas Revolution. His harsh treatment of the men of the Alamo and Goliad made his name hated in Texas. Defeated and captured by Sam Houston at San Jacinto, he nevertheless became president of Mexico twice again before his death in 1876. (Southwest Collection, Texas Tech University)

state government, and still others applied to local affairs. The convention was emphatic in its protestations of loyalty to the Mexican confederation and constitution. It asked that the state supply titles to settlers east of Austin's colony and that additional *ayuntamientos* be created there; that congress exempt the colonists from tariff duties on necessities for three years; that customs officers be appointed by the alcaldes of the respective jurisdictions; and that the state set aside land for school purposes. It also provided for a committee of the convention which should, together with the *ayuntamiento* of Nacogdoches, investigate the affairs of the Cherokee and other Indians in East Texas. It approved a uniform plan for organizing the militia and suggested plans for defense against the Indians.

The convention placed the greatest emphasis on two requests made of the government at Mexico City: first, the repeal of that part of the act of April 6, 1830, prohibiting Anglo-American immigration; and, second, separation from Coahuila and admission of Texas to the Mexican confederation as a state. There was a lengthy and urgent memorial on each. The convention adjourned on October 6.

76

For reasons not entirely clear, its petitions were never presented to the state and federal governments. The governor instructed the political chief to remind the Texans that the convention was a violation of the constitution and the laws. Santa Anna frowned on it, for he saw in it a tendency of the foreigners in Texas to declare themselves independent of the Republic.

The Texans were not in the least intimidated by this official disapproval. In the convention they had set up a central committee and subcommittees for the different districts. These organizations were known as committees of "safety, vigilence, etc." to keep up "a regular and stated correspondence with each other, on all subjects relating to the peace and safety of the frontier. . . ." In January of 1833 the central committee issued a call for a second convention to meet at San Felipe on April 1st. This second convention chose as chairman William H. Wharton, a radical, which indicates that the moderate, or Austin, faction was now a minority. Only about one-third of the delegates who sat in the second convention had attended the first. The grievances set forth were much the same as those at the preceding meeting, the emphasis again being placed on the repeal of the anti-immigration law and the passage of a law for the separation of Texas from Coahuila.

If the first convention shocked the Mexicans' sense of loyalty and propriety in public affairs, this gathering must have seemed even more improper. It went ahead and framed and approved a state constitution, typically Anglo-American in every important feature, and asked the federal government for approval.[1]

When burdensome public service had to be rendered in colonial Texas, the task generally fell to Stephen F. Austin. On April 22, 1833, Austin set out for the long, expensive trip to Mexico City to present to the supreme government the petitions of the convention.

When he arrived in Mexico City on July 18, President Santa Anna was away from the capital. Austin thus conferred with Vice-President Gómez Farías who, as acting president, received him cordially. The ministry submitted to the House of Deputies the petition asking for a state government. Then a cholera scourge suspended all business at the capital, and Austin, impatient at the delay, on October 1, told Farías bluntly, that unless the government remedied "the evils which threaten that country [Texas] with ruin," the people of Texas would organize a state government without its approval. Farías took this statement as a threat; the two men quarreled, and Austin, while still in a huff, wrote the *ayuntamiento* at San Antonio, urging that body to take the initiative in a plan to organize a state government.

A little later the proprietor was reconciled to Farías, and on Novem-

---

[1] Sam Houston, who had come to Texas that year, was chairman of the committee on the constitution, and David G. Burnet wrote the memorial asking Congress to recognize the instrument.

ber 5 he had a conference with Santa Anna (now exercising the executive power) and his cabinet. He found Santa Anna sympathetic and friendly. The president would not approve separation from Coahuila, but he did assent to almost every other request. He agreed to the repeal of the prohibition on immigration; he would refer to the treasury office a request for better mail service and a modification of the tariff; and he promised to urge the state government to give Texas trial by jury.

Before he left the city on December 10, Austin actually witnessed the repeal of the law against immigration, which was to take effect six months later. On his way back to Texas he stopped on January 3, 1834, to see the commandant at Saltillo on a matter of business. There he was placed under arrest and then taken back to Mexico City. The cause was his letter of the preceding October to the *ayuntamiento* at San Antonio, written, as Austin said, "in a moment of irritation and impatience," suggesting that it take the initiative in the organization of a state government without waiting for approval of the central government. The letter found its way to the governor and finally back to Gómez Farías just after Austin had left Mexico City.

For some time Austin was kept *incommunicado* in the Prison of the Inquisition. He could get no trial, for no Mexican court would accept jurisdiction of his case. Two attorneys, Peter W. Grayson and Spencer H. Jack, were sent to his aid by the people of Texas, bearing many petitions for his release; but all they accomplished was to get him out of prison on bail on Christmas Day, 1834. He was finally released through an amnesty law and left Mexico City in July 1835.

SANTA ANNA AND THE NATIONAL SCENE (1833–1835)

Until the second year of his presidency, Santa Anna had a good record as a liberal. Born in Jalapa in 1795, he became a cadet at the age of fifteen and thereafter was a professional soldier. In the various contests over the supreme authority in Mexico he supported consistently the constitution and popular government. When Bustamante came into power, Santa Anna retired and remained out of the public eye for nearly two years. In January 1832 he prompted the garrison at Vera Cruz to start a revolt, soon became its leader, and finally forced Bustamante to capitulate. He was easily elected president for the term beginning April 1, 1833. He was not inaugurated on that date, however, but let Vice-President Valentin Gómez Farías, an ultra-liberal but woefully lacking in political wisdom, assume the powers of the office. Farías was permitted to exercise the executive power on several occasions. From April 1, 1833, to January 28, 1835, the presidency was exchanged by these two men seven times.

Meanwhile, the reforms to which both men were pledged were being carried out by Farías and a liberal congress. Church appointments were placed in the hands of the state; the clergy was forbidden to discuss political matters; forced collections of tithes were suspended; and plans were inaugurated to reduce the size and the influence of the army. It has been stated previously how Texas profited from this liberal movement.

Obviously, the powerful clerical and army personnel, sustained as they were by the wealthier classes, did not permit these reforms to proceed without challenge. Quietly and surreptitiously they organized and found a leader, strange to say, in Santa Anna himself. The wily politician had permitted Farías to launch a trial balloon of liberalism, while he, in the eyes of the public, was a mere spectator. Seeing that the opposition was very powerful, he realized that as its leader he could make himself dictator. In April 1834 he returned to the capital and took over the supreme power from Farías. This time his coat of executive power was very different from the one he had worn in the past. He repudiated liberalism completely, forced Farías into exile, dissolved congress, dismissed all except one of Farías' cabinet, disbanded legislatures and *ayuntamientos*, and declared void the laws against the privileges of the clergy; and in various other ways he imitated Napoleon Bonaparte, whom he greatly admired. A subservient congress supplemented and legalized what Santa Anna did, and in October 1835 it replaced federalism with a centralist system of government. Among its most offensive acts was a law reducing the number of militia to one soldier for every 500 inhabitants. At word of this, the people of Zacatecas, spirited and known for their love of free institutions, rose in rebellion, but Santa Anna defeated 5,000 state troops led by their governor and permitted his soldiers to plunder the state capital.

AFFAIRS IN TEXAS AND
COAHUILA (1833–1835)

During 1833 and 1834 the state government was generous with Texas. The legislature repealed the law which had prohibited any but native-born Mexicans from engaging in retail merchandising. It divided Texas into three political departments, the capitals to be at Bexar, San Felipe, and Nacogdoches respectively. Texas was allowed three deputies out of the twelve that composed the state congress. The English language was recognized for official purposes, and religious toleration was granted. The court system, which had been the most constant object of complaint, was completely revised. A superior court was created for Texas and trial by jury was established. As stated in a preceding chapter, the new court proved defective, but like the other concessions, it had come of an honest desire to satisfy the colonists.

Except for the disturbances of 1832, when they declared for Santa Anna as a kind of afterthought, the Texans had managed to avoid entanglements in Mexican civil wars. Beginning with 1834, however, these wars came closer home. The two principal sources of strife and agitation were the quarrel between Saltillo and Monclova over the location of the state capital, and the squandering of the public lands of Texas through sales to speculators.

The quarrel over the state capital began in March 1833, when the legislature removed the seat of government from Saltillo in the southeastern corner of Coahuila to Monclova in the north. Later Saltillo set up a rival government, but Santa Anna gave his nod to Monclova and the government remained there. In April 1835 the legislature criticized Santa Anna severely, and the dictator sent his brother-in-law, Martín Perfecto de Cós to break up the state government. On the approach of the national forces Governor Agustín Viesca sought to transfer the government to Bexar, but was arrested on his way by Cós's troops. Other officers and a swarm of land speculators fled to Bexar. By August both the Saltillo and the Monclova factions accepted as governor Rafael Eca y Músquiz, who then moved the capital back to Saltillo.

Most Texans were disgusted with their state government because of its unwise and dishonest land sales. Speculation in Texas lands had been common ever since the passage of the state colonization law of 1825, which permitted a native Mexican to purchase as much as 11 *sitios* for a nominal sum. This speculation was eclipsed, however, by reckless legislation in 1834 and 1835. Representatives John Durst, from Nacogdoches, and J. M. Carbajal, from San Antonio, were implicated in and probably profited from this business. An act of April 19, 1834, authorized the governor to dispose of as much as 400 *sitios* of land for the purpose of maintaining the militia in defense against the Indians. Another law, that of March 14, 1835, empowered the governor to dispose of 400 *sitios* more. The final act in this extravagant series was passed on April 7, 1835, authorizing the governor "to take of himself whatever measure he may think proper for securing the public tranquility. . . ." Apparently the governor thought the situation called for the frittering away additional large blocks of land.

The operations of the partnership firm of Williams, Peebles, and Johnson are typical. In consideration for 400 *sitios* of land they agreed to place and maintain in the field 1,000 men for the defense of the state. Without supplying a single soldier, they issued to about 40 persons certificates calling for the entire 400 *sitios*. The constitutional convention of 1836 nullified a part of these grants but validated others apparently no more meritorious.

As a result of the imbroglio at the capital, the rank and file of Texans failed to see clearly that the basic issue was Santa Anna's intent to discard the constitution and establish himself as a dictator. The land speculators brought alarming reports to the effect that Santa Anna was planning to invade Texas, but most people believed that their talk was merely a cloud to screen their own bad conduct.

One citizen wrote thus:

Williams, Johnson, Carbajal, Bowie and others cry, "Wolf, wolf, condemnation, destruction, war, to arms, to arms!" Williams says, "I have bought a few leagues of land from the Government; but if they don't bring the Governor to Bexar, I shall not be able to get my titles." What a pity....

As late as midsummer of 1835, most Texans would have endorsed the statement of George W. Smyth, land commissioner at Nacogdoches, who wrote in May of that year that he was confident that there would be no war and added: "Come what may I am convinced that Texas must prosper. We pay no taxes, work no public roads, get our land at cost, and perform no public duties of any kind."

Yet there was a small but active war party, and on the other extreme a peace party, likewise small, active, and persistent. The great majority of Texans stood between these two extreme groups, indifferent at first but finding their complacent attitude more and more untenable. Developments during the summer of 1835 favored the war party.

SANTA ANNA FORCES THE ISSUE

The first violent action that led directly to revolution was associated with Anahuac, the seat of the disturbances of 1832. Indeed, the story of Texas during the early summer of 1835 reads strangely like that of 1832. In January 1835, Santa Anna sent a small detachment of soldiers to Anahuac to enforce the collection of customs at that place and at Galveston. The collector at Velasco on the Brazos collected tonnage duties only, while the officers at Galveston and Anahuac, backed by the garrison, insisted on the payment of all duties. Andrew Briscoe, a merchant of Anahuac, and others became disgruntled and declared that no more duties should be collected at that port until collections were enforced equally throughout Texas. As a result of a misunderstanding, a Texan was wounded at Anahuac, and Briscoe and another citizen, De Witt C. Harris, were imprisoned. Meanwhile Cós had heard of the threatening attitude of the people at Anahuac and had determined to reinforce the garrison. He wrote Captain Antonio Tenorio, its commander, to be resolute and of good cheer, that reinforcements were coming. It happened that the courier bearing Cós's letters and other communications of similar vein stopped at San Felipe on June 21. There was much excitement in the community. The people knew of the breaking up of the state government and of the arrest of Governor Viesca and the arrest of the citizens at Anahuac. Already excited over these events, the

William Barret Travis (an artist's conception). A lawyer from Alabama who came to Texas in 1832, Travis was an ardent advocate of the revolt against Mexico. As a colonel in the revolutionary army, he was in command of the small force that died trying to hold the Alamo against Santa Anna in March 1836. James Bowie and David Crockett were among those who died with him. (Texas State Library)

San Felipe war party seized and opened the courier's dispatches. Although the reaction against this extreme measure was sharp, the clique that favored drastic action met, elected J. B. Miller, political chief of the department of the Brazos, to take the chair, and passed resolutions authorizing W. B. Travis to collect a force and drive away the garrison at Anahuac. With some 25 or 30 other hotspurs armed with rifles and a small cannon mounted on a pair of sawmill truck wheels, Travis appeared before the post and demanded its surrender. Tenorio made no resistance and on the morning of June 30 surrendered some 44 men. The prisoners were paroled and treated kindly by the colonists.

This act of Travis and his band was looked upon with pronounced disfavor by the great majority of the people, and it was formally condemned by meetings in no less than seven communities. At a meeting on June 28, the people of Columbia emphatically denounced it as an act calculated to involve the citizens of Texas in a conflict with the central government. They pledged their loyalty to Mexico, and through a committee they asked the political chief to send to Cós assurances of the people's loyalty. More general gatherings at San Felipe on July 14 and 15 adopted resolutions of similar tenor; and J. B. Miller, as if to atone for his alignment with the radicals a few weeks earlier, wrote an apologetic letter to Cós. Then a conference of committees from Columbia, Mina, and San Felipe, met at San Felipe from July 17 to 21, and sent D. C. Barrett and Edward Gritten with conciliatory letters to Cós at Matamoros. The peace party was asserting itself. The agitators were on the defensive.

Cós was not in a compromising humor. He called for the arrest of Lorenzo de Zavala, a distinguished political refugee and enemy of Santa Anna, who had lately arrived in Texas. Then, at the suggestion of Dr. J. H. C. Miller, a busybody who belonged to the extreme peace party, Colonel Ugartechea, Cós's subordinate at Bexar, made out a slate of offenders: F. W. Johnson, who had been prominent in land speculation; Robert M. Williamson, the Patrick Henry of the Texas Revolution, commonly called "Three Legged Willie"; W. B. Travis; and Samuel Williams. Cós insisted that the colonial officials arrest these men and turn them over to the military for trial. He refused to treat with the peace commissioners (who had gone as far as San Antonio on their way to confer with him) until this was done. To the Anglo-Americans, who believed that a person should be tried only by a jury composed of his peers, to turn their fellow citizens over to the mercies of a Mexican military tribunal was unthinkable. Cós, who managed to secure and read copies of the various inflammatory speeches and utterances of the Texans, particularly a Fourth of July address by R. M. Williamson, became adamant. On August 17 he wrote Henry Rueg, political chief at Nacogdoches:

The plans of the revolutionists of Texas are well known to this commandency; and it is quite useless and vain to cover them with a hypocritical adherence to the federal Constitution. The constitution by which all Mexicans may be governed is the constitution which the colonists of Texas must obey, no matter on what principles it may be formed.

Thus did the season for conciliation pass.

In the American Revolution it was the committees of correspondence which began in Massachusetts in 1772 under the tutelage of Samuel Adams that kept the people in touch with developments and finally made possible organized resistance. Similar organizations existed during the Texan Revolution, and without them the colonists could not have been aroused to the point of resistance or have been organized with any degree of effectiveness.

Mina (Bastrop) on the frontier led the communities by appointing on May 8, 1835, its committee of safety and correspondence for the general diffusion of information. Organizations at Gonzales and Viesca were formed a few days later. Before the end of the summer apparently every precinct had such an organization. Holding over from the convention of 1833 was the central committee which served as a guide and clearing body for the local committees.

These committees brought together representatives of the munici-palities for a consultation. Apprehensive about the recent developments, on July 4 the committee of safety at Mina issued an address to the *ayuntamientos* of the department of the Brazos urging that a consulta-tion of the representatives of the different communities be called. A week later the *ayuntamiento* at Columbia urged the call of a consultation with the "utmost expedition." A meeting at San Felipe on July 14 like-wise favored a consultation. It was the people of Columbia who actually called the general meeting. At a gathering of the citizens on August 15, with William H. Wharton, the staunch champion of action, presid-ing, the committee of safety and correspondence was instructed to issue a call for a consultation of all Texans. Three days later the committee framed an address in which it asked that each jurisdiction elect and send five delegates to a consultation to be held at Washington on Oc-tober 15. The tenor of its message is revealed in the sentence: "The only instructions which we would recommend to be given to our repre-sentatives is to secure peace if it is to be obtained on constitutional terms, & to prepare for war—if war is inevitable."

Some three weeks later Stephen F. Austin, free at last and home again, gave the consultation his approval. He accepted the chairman-ship of the central committee of safety of San Felipe and by common consent became the leader of the revolution. The news came that Cós was on his way to Bexar with reinforcements. This destroyed the last hope of peace, and on September 19 the central committee rein-forced the call for a consultation and added: "War is our only re-source. There is no other remedy. We must defend our rights ourselves and our country by force of arms."

Selected Bibliography

The general accounts cited in Chapter 4 are useful. The best accounts for this particular period are D.M. Vigness, *The Revolutionary Decades*, and Frank W. Johnson. *A History of Texas and Texans* (E.C. Barker and E.W. Winkler, eds., 5 vols., Chicago and New York, 1914). Of the more intensive studies, the best are: E.C. Barker, *The Life of Stephen F. Austin*; E.C. Barker, *Mexico and Texas, 1821–1835*; E.C. Barker, "The Organiza-tion of the Texas Revolution," *Publications of the Southern History As-sociation*, V, 1–26; E.C. Barker, "Public Opinion in Texas Preceding the Revolution," *Annual Report of the American Historical Association for 1911*, I, 217–228; O. Morton, "Life of General Don Manuel de Mier y Terán, As It Affected Texas-Mexican Relations," *Southwestern Historical Quarterly*, XLVI, 22–47, 239–254; XLVII, 29–47, 120–142, 256–267; XLVIII, 51–66, 193–218; Merton L. Dillon, "Benjamin Lundy in Texas," *Southwestern Historical Quarterly*, LXIII, 46–62; Robert E. Davis (ed.),

Diary of William Barret Travis, August 30, 1833–June 26, 1834 (Waco, 1966).

The best collections of source materials are: E.C. Barker, *The Austin Papers*; C.A. Gulich, Katherine Elliott, and Harriet Smither (eds.), *The Papers of Mirabeau Bonaparte Lamar* (6 vols., Austin, 1921–1927); E.C. Barker, contributor of a series of important documents in the *Publications of the Southern History Association*, V, 451–476; VI, 33–40; VII, 25–31, 85–95, 200–206, 238–246; VIII, 1–22, 104–118, 343–362; IX, 87–98, 160–173, 225–233; and E. Wallace and D.M. Vigness (eds.), *Documents of Texas History*. For proceedings of the Texas convention see H.P.N. Gammel (comp.), *Laws of Texas* (10 vols., Austin, 1898), I.

Accounts of the disturbances of the early 1830's are E.C. Barker, "Difficulties of a Mexican Revenue Officer in Texas," *Quarterly of the Texas State Historical Association*, IV, 190–202; Edna Rowe, "The Disturbances at Anahuac in 1832," *ibid.*, VI, 265–299; Dr. N.D. Labadie, "Narrative of the Anahuac, or Opening Campaign of the Texas Revolution," *Texas Almanac, 1859*, 30–36; Duncan W. Robinson, *Judge Robert McAlpin Williamson: Texas' Three-Legged Willie* (Austin, 1948); Forrest E. Ward, "Pre-Revolutionary Activity in Brazoria County," *The Southwestern Historical Quarterly*, LXIV, 212–231; Boyce House, "An Incident at Velasco, 1832," *ibid.*, 92–95.

Concerning the "OPQ" letters see "Some Texas Correspondence," *Mississippi Valley Historical Review*, XI, 99–127. Almonte's report on Texas has been translated and edited by C.E. Castañeda in the *Southwestern Historical Quarterly*, XXVIII, 177–222. For affairs at the state capital, see E.C. Barker, "Land Speculation as a Cause of the Texas Revolution," *Quarterly of the Texas State Historical Association*, X, 76–95.

Concerning Santa Anna and national affairs see Frank C. Hanighen, *Santa Anna: The Napoleon of the West* (New York, 1934); Wilfred H. Callcott, *Santa Anna* (Norman, 1936); H.H. Bancroft, *The History of Mexico* (6 vols., San Francisco, 1883–1888).

The best study for this particular period by a Mexican historian is Vito Alessio Robles, *Coahuila y Texas desde la consumación de la independencia hasta el tratado de paz de Guadalupe Hidalgo* (2 vols., Mexico, D.F., 1945–1946).

6

THE TEXAN REVOLUTION, 1835–1836

It has been said that Americans never fought better than they fought in Texas, and with a measure of truth it might be added that never did they manage their affairs worse. By way of excuse for their mistakes it must be pointed out that they were all comparative new-comers; they knew little about one another; except for Austin, they had no leader at the beginning of the contest; and most of their people were without political experience.

The Texan Revolution may be divided into four periods: first, from October 2, 1835, when fighting began in Gonzales, to January 17, 1836, when the revolutionary government collapsed because of discord; second, from January 17 to March 2, when a convention with plenary power proclaimed the Republic of Texas; third, from March 2 to April 21, when the victory at the Battle of San Jacinto made independence a reality; and, fourth, from April 21 to October 22, when Sam Houston was inaugurated the first constitutional president of the republic. A fifth section of this chapter will deal with efforts and problems common to all periods.

FIGHTING FOR THE CONSTITUTION OF 1824

In September 1835 Ugartechea sent five Mexican cavalrymen to Gonzales to get a 6-pounder cannon which had been turned over to the empresario, Green DeWitt, for defense against the Indians. Convinced that the move was to make resistance to Santa Anna's military power more difficult, the alcalde, Andrew Ponton, hid the cannon, put the Mexicans off with the excuse that he had no authority to give it up, and sent runners to other settlements with dispatches calling for aid. Already some Texan volunteers were under arms planning to go against General Cós who had landed at Copano with 400 troops, an advance guard for larger forces that were to follow. These Texans turned aside to Gonzales when they heard that trouble was expected there. Ugartechea reinforced his demand by sending Lieutenant Francisco Castañeda with about 100 troops to take the gun. The colonists, now with a force under Colonel J. H. Moore larger than that which threatened them, crossed the Guadalupe, attacked the troops, and sent them scurrying away toward San Antonio. Thus began the Texan Revolution on October 2, 1835.

At once the cry "on to San Antonio" was raised. Stephen F. Austin was called to take command of the "Army of the People," and on October 12 he took up his march for that place. A force under Captain George Collinsworth captured Goliad with large stores of food and ammunitions. By October 24 the colonists had driven the Mexicans back to San Antonio and had begun a siege of the place. A month later, Austin was relieved of the command by Edward Burleson in order that he might go with a commission to seek aid in the United States. On December 5 a special force of about 300 volunteers led by Ben Milam began an assault on the town, and five days later Cós capitulated. He and his men were permitted to return to Mexico after agreeing that they would not again oppose the reestablishment of the Constitution of 1824. Milam fell at the head of his men on the third day of the attack.

The Texan victory at San Antonio was a brilliant achievement. With less than 500 citizen soldiers they had taken a town held by an army of more than twice their number with every advantage of a defensive position. Their success caused them to place too low an estimate on Mexican fighting ability and to conclude that the war was over.

While these developments were taking place in the field the political scene had shifted rapidly. Texas had two provisional governments and the third was already experiencing some of the difficulties that later caused its dissolution. The first government, ironically enough, is known as the Permanent Council, although its formal existence was for only three weeks. It was organized on October 11 and consisted of the committee of safety of San Felipe and representatives from other communities. Richard R. Royall, of Matagorda, was its president and Charles B. Stewart, its secretary. During its brief existence the Permanent Council served well. It sent supplies and volunteers to the army in the field; it commissioned privateers; it set up a postal system; it

ordered the land offices closed and surveying discontinued; it authorized an agent, Thomas F. McKinney, to go to the United States and
borrow $100,000; and it appealed to the citizens of the United States
for men, money, and supplies. It kept the people of Texas informed
about the revolution and spurred them to greater exertion.

The Consultation, which had been postponed because of the fighting at Gonzales, was organized on November 3, with delegates from the
twelve municipalities of the departments of the Brazos and Nacogdoches, each municipality being entitled to seven members.[1] It denom-
inated itself "The Consultation of the Chosen Delegates of all Texas, in
General Convention Assembled." Here the colonists had to face a fundamental question: What were they fighting for—independence or their
rights as loyal Mexican citizens under the constitution of 1824? A committee could not agree and asked the house for instructions. Then followed three days of debate, described by Gail Borden, Jr., a participant,
as "lengthy and animated yet coolness and moderation pervaded throughout. . . ."

The president, Branch T. Archer, had sounded the keynote in his
opening address, however, when he said that the Texans were not bat-
tling alone but were "laying the cornerstone of liberty *in the great
Mexican Republic.*" Evidently the majority agreed with him, looking
with a single eye to securing aid from the Federalists of Mexico, and
determined that nothing be done to antagonize that party. The body
on November 7 voted 33 to 14 in favor of a "provisional government
upon the principles of the constitution of 1824" and then 33 to 15
against a declaration of independence. The declaration adopted was,
however, a compromise between the majority and the advocates of
an immediate separation. It spoke of Santa Anna's tyranny; of the "natural rights" of the people of Texas; declared that the Texans were
fighting to maintain the federal constitution of 1824; and stated that
they offered their assistance to all Mexicans who would join them in
resisting military despotism. The fifth article is especially suggestive of
more extreme action. The colonists, it stated, "hold it to be their right
. . . to establish an independent government," but they would "continue faithful to the Mexican government so long as that nation is governed by the constitution and laws that were formed for the government of the political association." Another act of the body which constituted a definite step toward separation was the election of B. T.
Archer, William H. Wharton, and Stephen F. Austin commissioners to
the United States to obtain aid. The delegates must have known that

---

[1]The place of meeting had been changed from Washington to San Felipe. The
municipalities of the Department of Bexar, except the municipality of Bexar, later
elected delegates, some of whom participated in the general council that grew out of
the Consultation. Ninety-eight men were named as delegates but only 58 took part
in the Consultation.

their kinsmen east of the Sabine would not send men and money to Texas merely to have a part in a domestic Mexican squabble. In fact, the cause of the friends of the constitution was already lost. That instrument had been superseded on October 3 by a decree of congress which established a centralist form of government for the nation, including the replacement of states with departments controlled by the president.

The Consultation gave its official endorsement to most of the work of the Permanent Council; adopted a plan for the creation of an army and elected Sam Houston commander in chief; and drew up a plan for a provisional government. The plan provided for a governor, a lieutenant governor, and a general council to be composed of one member from each municipality. All officials were to be chosen from the members of the Consultation, the governor and lieutenant governor by the whole body, and members of the council by the delegations from the several municipalities. The most unfortunate part of the instrument was that it failed to delineate clearly the powers of the council and of the governor. The Consultation voted to sustain the army then before Bexar, but declared that the volunteers were not obliged to submit to its control. Thus it confessed its weakness and transmitted to its successor, the Provisional Government, its impotence in this all-important matter.

By the action of the Consultation Texas was deprived of the effective services of her two essential men. Austin, who should have been placed at the head of the Provisional Government, was sent away "in honorable exile" to the United States; and Houston was made a commander in chief without any army. Henry Smith, who had served as political chief of the department of the Brazos, was elected governor and James W. Robinson of Nacogdoches was chosen lieutenant governor. The Consultation adjourned on November 14, to reassemble on March 1, 1836, unless called sooner by the governor and council.

For a month or more the new government wrought creditably and well. It created and filled numbers of offices and completed the framework of the political structure; provided for the organization of a post office and for a little navy; and gave much support and a small measure of direction to the army in the field.

Internal discord soon made it helpless, however, and it became an object of derision. The crisis came over a matter of policy. Like the Consultation, the council favored cooperation with the friends of the constitution in Mexico and believed that the seizure of the Mexican town of Matamoros at the mouth of the Rio Grande would encourage them to resist Santa Anna. It approved a campaign against Matamoros to be led by Frank W. Johnson. Both the governor and General Houston opposed it. After the council had repeatedly passed measures over his veto, Governor Smith determined to cow it into submission or to dismiss it. For a test of his strength he chose the occasion of the receipt of a letter from J. C. Neill, commanding the troops at Bexar, complaining that Johnson and his fellow officer, James Grant, had on leaving with their troops for Matamoros stripped the garrison of supplies and clothing. On January 10, 1836, his message vilifying certain members of the body in most intemperate language was read to the council. Either the council should apologize for its evil ways, said the governor, and agree henceforth to cooperate with him or adjourn until the first of March. The council replied in language quite as severe as the governor's, declared the office of governor vacant, and inaugurated Lieutenant Governor Robinson as acting governor. Smith refused to deliver up the archives and continued to receive much mail addressed to the executive. The council could not secure a quorum after January 17, and thereafter until the convention assembled on March 1 the only semblance of government was an advisory committee which worked with Robinson; but its results were negligible.

A WINTER OF DEFEAT AND DEATH

Developments in the field during the early part of 1836 were fully as discouraging as those at the seat of government. On January 3 after the council had approved the expedition against Matamoros, Johnson informed the body that he had given up the idea. Then the council appointed James W. Fannin, Jr., to lead the force; whereupon Johnson reconsidered and stated that he planned to continue with the expedition. In fact, it was already on the march. The council again approved Johnson's commission but did not withdraw the authorization granted Fannin. Now two men, Johnson and Fannin, had the authority of the council to lead an expedition against Matamoros. Meanwhile, matters had been complicated even more; Governor Smith had ordered General Houston to proceed to Goliad, to take charge of the troops thereabouts, and to advance upon Matamoros.

The force of Johnson and Grant, nearly 500 men composed largely of volunteers from the United States, marched to the vicinity of Refugio, where it established its headquarters. Houston joined it there, learned that the men would not accept him as commander in chief, became even more positively convinced that the expedition was futile, and proceeded to wash his hands of the whole affair by retiring from the army on furlough until March 1. He then went to eastern Texas to treat with the Indians. Before he left the army, however, he succeeded in persuading most of the men to abandon the Matamoros project. The remainder, thereafter nothing but a scouting party of about 150 men that operated in the vicinity of San Patricio and southward, was destroyed almost to a man on February 27 and March 2 by the Mexican cavalry as it advanced northward under José Urrea.

The Alamo. The Texas revolutionaries took the town of San Antonio in December 1835, and three months later about 180 men led by Travis, Bowie, and Crockett died trying to hold the Alamo against Santa Anna's several thousand troops. Their heroic resistance made "Remember the Alamo" the rallying cry of the revolutionary army. (University of Texas Library)

Meanwhile Fannin, who had brought together a force of about 450 volunteers from the United States, never got beyond Refugio and Goliad. He tried to go to the relief of the Alamo which was then being besieged by Santa Anna, but failed because of transportation difficulties. On March 13 and 14 he received an order from General Houston, now authorized by the convention to command all troops in Texas without let or hindrance, to fall back to Victoria. This step he proposed to take, but he was delayed by having to wait for the return of about 180 men of his force who had been sent to aid in the evacuation of settlers in the vicinity of Refugio. The troops which he had sent out were killed or captured by Urrea during the next few days. Fannin, with the main force, began his retreat on March 19. Near the Coleto that afternoon he was surrounded by the Mexicans on an open prairie within half a mile of timber which would have afforded protection. The Americans hurled back the Mexican assaults, but on the following day, faced by superior numbers, they surrendered. The survivors always contended that they surrendered as prisoners of war to be treated according to the policy of civilized nations. The original document in the Mexican archives shows, however, that they surrendered at discretion and placed themselves at the mercy of the supreme government. A week later on March 27, Palm Sunday, the prisoners to the number of about 350 (including some captured elsewhere) were shot. Santa Anna was responsible for the dastardly deed. The massacre aroused sufficient sympathy and pride of citizens of the United States to insure badly needed financial and moral support for the struggling young republic.

In March of 1836, death hovered over every camp in Texas. Even before Fannin's surrender, a debacle equally as tragic as that which destroyed his forces had befallen the little garrison at San Antonio. After the departure of Johnson and Grant, Neill was left with about 100 poorly equipped men. On January 17 Houston ordered James Bowie (then with him at Goliad) to take a small force to San Antonio, destroy the fortifications, and then to retreat. Once there with about 25 men, however, Bowie decided to remain with the defenders. Then, a few days later Governor Smith relieved Lieutenant Colonel William Barrett Travis of his duties as recruiting officer at San Felipe and ordered him to go to the relief of San Antonio. Travis was able to raise only 30 men to take with him. A few other troops arrived there; among them James Butler Bonham, an Alabama lawyer, South Carolina bred; and David Crockett, ex-congressman from Tennessee with a few of his "Tennessee boys." By mid-February there were at San Antonio about 150 effective fighting men.

Internal discord as well as peril from without threatened the post. When Colonel Neill left to visit his family, some of the volunteers chose Bowie as their leader, and Travis took command of the remainder. The result was strife and confusion, for the two men found it difficult to cooperate. The orders to abandon San Antonio were ignored or avoided with lame excuses. As Amelia Williams, historian of the Alamo, has stated, "the place, moreover, seemed to cast some sort of spell over the Texan leaders." "We consider death preferable to disgrace which would be the result of giving up a Post which has been so dearly won," wrote Travis.

On August 1, 1835, Santa Anna issued a formal proclamation announcing the invasion of Texas. At Saltillo, in December 1835 and January 1836 he made preparation for his campaign. While the main force was being organized he sent General Ramirez y Sesma to the Rio Grande, and ordered General José Urrea to Matamoros and to advance thence northward and eastward to protect the right flank of the main army. Urrea's destructive work against Johnson and Fannin has already been mentioned. The dictator concentrated a larger part of his force at Laredo about the middle of February. He was leading against Texas an army of 6,000 men.

After a bitter, exhausting march, the advance forces of Santa Anna's army reached San Antonio on February 23. The Texans took refuge behind the walls of the Alamo and the siege began. Travis (Bowie, co-commandant, became bedridden with typhoid and pneumonia on February 24) sent out many calls for aid, phrased in language forceful and dramatic. He appealed to Andrew Ponton at Gonzales, to Fannin at Goliad, to the convention at Washington on the Brazos, to the people of Texas, and to all the Americans in the world. Several faithful runners risked their lives to keep up communication. The friend of Travis' youth, James Butler Bonham, twice went out and twice came back. His return on March 3, after it was evident that the Alamo was a death-trap, seems to qualify him to head the list of Texan heroes. Yet a roll call of the immortals would have to include, also, the names of the 32 men from Gonzales who managed to enter the post on March 1, the only effective response ever made to Travis' appeals. At dawn on the morning of March 6, Santa Anna took the place by storm, its defenders fighting until death. They had not died in vain; their sacrifice delayed Santa Anna and gave their countrymen a few more precious days to prepare to meet the advancing horde.

FIGHTING FOR INDEPENDENCE

On March 1, 1836, the contesting governors and council, despised and impotent because of quarrels and bickerings, were supplanted by a convention. Realizing that a reconvening of the Consultation would not be adequate to meet the emergency, the council had passed on December 13, 1835, over Governor Smith's veto an act calling for the election of delegates to a convention "with ample, unlimited, or plenary powers as to the form of government to be adopted."

The conditions that confronted the assembly as it gathered that cold March morning in the village of Washington on the Brazos called for courage and statesmanship of the highest order. Urrea's lancers were slashing their way toward Goliad; Santa Anna's legions were wearing out the heroic garrison at the Alamo, and Travis was pleading for aid. There were no troops at Washington and none between Washington and San Antonio, 150 miles away. The life of every delegate was in danger; indeed, all Texas was in peril and the outlook was well-nigh hopeless. Yet several features contributed to the effectiveness of the convention. Among the 59 men who signed the declaration of independence were a few with broad experience and several of superior ability. Robert Potter and Samuel Carson had served in the Congress of the United States from North Carolina, and Richard Ellis and Martin Parmer had helped to make state constitutions before they came to Texas. Other men of less experience, but of equal or greater ability, were Thomas J. Rusk, James Collinsworth, and George C. Childress. Collin McKinney, then seventy years old, but destined to outlive many of his colleagues, and

James Gaines, who had known Texas since the days of Magee and Gutiérrez, did not make outstanding records, but they supplied such wisdom as
comes only with age. One of the most distinguished members was the
Mexican statesman, Lorenzo de Zavala, whose influence apparently was
great. Sam Houston, who was sent as a delegate from Refugio, probably was the most influential member; but he left the convention
to take command of the army on the afternoon of March 6, before
much work had been accomplished.

Another favorable factor was the unanimity of sentiment. The delegates knew that the hour of Texas had struck and that hesitation, doubt,
disputing, and strife would spell her doom. They must adopt a declaration of independence written in unequivocal terms; frame a constitution for the republic they hoped to create; set up a strong provisional government to serve until the constitutional government could
be inaugurated; and take such steps as were necessary to hurl back
the invaders and save their homes from immediate destruction. Even
the immediacy of danger proved an asset, for it spurred the members
to work day and night with all possible haste. An anecdote related in
later years illustrates this fact. Zavala, who had a weakness for speech-
making, began what promised to be a lengthy discourse with the statement, "Mr. President, an eminent Roman statesman once said . . ."
whereupon he was interrupted by Rusk with the comment that it be-
hooved the convention to give less thought to dead Romans and more
to live Mexicans.

Richard Ellis was elected president and H. S. Kimble, secretary of
the body. The first act of importance was the adoption on March 2 of a
declaration of independence, presented by a committee headed by
George C. Childress. Childress is credited with writing the instrument
which follows the main features of the document written by Thomas
Jefferson sixty years earlier.

The constitution, adopted at midnight following March 16, is a com-
posite structure made up of excerpts from the constitutions of the
United States and of several states. Features most nearly unique are:
the term for the president was to be three years (the first constitutional president to serve two years only) and he was not to succeed
himself; the president was not to lead armies in the field except with
the consent of congress; ministers of the gospel were not to hold office; each head of a family in Texas was to be granted a headright
of a league and a *labor* of land;[2] and the institution of slavery was
legalized but the African slave trade was made piracy.

The convention constituted itself the government of Texas and took
steps to meet the emergency. Its most important work in that connection

---

[2]The convention also provided for land bounties to soldiers in amounts of 320
to 1,280 acres, varying with the lengths of service, but this was not incorporated in
the constitution.

was the appointment of Sam Houston "Commander in Chief of all the land forces of the Texian Army, both regulars, volunteers, and militia, while in actual service." Houston left the convention for the field on March 6. A motion by the impetuous Potter that the body adjourn and go to the relief of the Alamo was rejected. The last act of the convention, performed as the candles burned short on the night of March 16–17, was the selection of an *ad interim* government to direct the infant republic until the constitution could be adopted and a regular government inaugurated. David G. Burnet was elected president over Samuel P. Carson by a vote of 29 to 23; Lorenzo de Zavala, vice-president; Samuel P. Carson, secretary of state; Bailey Hardeman, secretary of the treasury; Thomas J. Rusk, secretary of war; Robert Potter, secretary of the navy; and David Thomas, attorney general. They were sworn in at 4:00 A.M. and a few hours later the convention adjourned.

Houston proceeded to Gonzales, where he found on his arrival five days later "three hundred and seventy-four effective men, without two days' provisions, many without arms, and others without any ammunition." He had hoped to go to the relief of the Alamo but learned of the tragic fate of the heroic garrison a few minutes after he reached the town. On learning through Mrs. Suzanne Dickenson, wife of an officer who had been killed in the Alamo, that General Sesma was advancing eastward with a division of Santa Anna's army, Houston determined to retreat. On the afternoon of March 17, he reported his arrival at Burnam's Crossing on the Colorado, near present-day La Grange, with a force of 600 men; and nine days later he took up his march toward the Brazos. About March 28 he arrived at San Felipe, and on April 1 he was at Groce's, some twenty miles up the Brazos where he remained a fortnight.

News of Houston's retreat, carried eastward into the settlements by fleeing civilians and soldiers who left with or without leave to look after their families, created widespread fear. The frontier began to fold back upon itself. Loading their wagons, oxcarts, or sleds, or taking such simple belongings as could be carried on horseback or even on foot, the people set out in a desperate rush to keep ahead of the Mexican army. With fathers and sons in the army, many women and little children had to manage as best they could. It was a season of heavy rain; streams were swollen; ferries became jammed; epidemics prevailed; and the misery and suffering were indescribable. Stern Captain Mosely Baker wept at the sad sight he witnessed as the people trudged by his camp opposite San Felipe. In her reminiscences, Dilue Rose Harris states that there were 5,000 people at Lynch's Ferry at the mouth of the San Jacinto when her family arrived there on April 10.

The government fled with the people. As the Mexican forces advanced, Texan headquarters were removed from Washington to Harrisburg (now within the city of Houston) and from Harrisburg to Galveston

Island. Houston complained at the government for retreating, and Burnet in turn berated Houston. "The enemy are laughing you to scorn," he wrote, "you must fight them. You must retreat no farther. The country expects you to fight. The salvation of the country depends on you doing so." In commenting on his own conduct Houston wrote Rusk on March 29, "I consulted none—I held no councils-of-war. If I err, the blame is mine."

Meanwhile Burnet sent Secretary of State Carson to Fort Jessup, Louisiana, to appeal to General Edmund P. Gaines, who commanded a strong force of United States troops, for aid; but at that time Gaines's troops did not cross the Sabine.

Santa Anna himself with Sesma and a part of the Mexican army arrived at San Felipe, which had been burned by Houston's men, on April 7. Finding the crossings in that vicinity guarded by Moseley Baker's company of colonists, the Mexican president marched down the Brazos with a picked force of troops and gained possession of the ferry at Fort Bend. Here he learned that the Texan government was at Harrisburg just 30 miles away, and hastened toward that place. He arrived at Harrisburg a few hours too late to capture the officials; then hurried eastward and missed them again at Morgan's Point, overlooking Galveston Bay. Then turning northward, he moved up the prairie almost to Lynch's Ferry. On April 20, he pitched camp with open country on his left flank, the San Jacinto River on his right, and Buffalo Bayou and Houston's army before him.

With the aid of the steam boat *Yellowstone*, Houston crossed the Brazos on April 12 and 13. Learning of Santa Anna's advance, he took the road to Harrisburg. On the 18th, while he was in camp near the ruins of the town (Santa Anna had burned it), the faithful scout, Deaf Smith, brought in as captive a Mexican courier with dispatches revealing Santa Anna's plans and movements. Houston thereupon crossed to the south of Buffalo Bayou, left hidden in the woods his sick men and a small guard, and proceeded with more than 900 effective troops to the vicinity of Lynch's Ferry, where Buffalo Bayou joins the San Jacinto. Here he pitched camp with the Bayou at his rear and open prairie on the front and right flank.

Houston's correspondence indicates that in the San Jacinto campaign he had no definite plan. He was well aware that by retreating eastward he gained the advantage of being nearer his major source of supplies and at the same time of drawing the enemy farther away from his base. Also, he was following a Fabian policy, as old as organized warfare, which was to keep out of the enemy's way until the enemy made a mistake. On April 20, Santa Anna made the mistake of placing an inferior force in such a position that organized retreat was impossible. On the next morning, however, Cós with between 500 and 600 troops joined Santa Anna, bringing the total Mexican strength to between

San Jacinto. Near the confluence of Buffalo Bayou and the San Jacinto River on April 21, 1836, Sam Houston surprised a superior force of Mexican troops commanded by Santa Anna, defeated them, captured the commander, and thereby won the decisive battle of the Texas revolution. The monument was built in the 1930's to celebrate the centennial of Texas' struggle for independence. (Reproduced with the permission of the San Jacinto Museum of History Association, San Jacinto Monument, Texas)

1300 and 1400 men, Thus, Houston with a few more than 900 men now faced a significantly larger force.

A minor engagement had taken place on the afternoon of April 20, but neither side was disposed to press the fight. On the afternoon of April 21, the Texans prepared for attack. They formed a line of infantry that extended for 1000 yards and placed a cannon on each wing, their flag in the center, and 60 horsemen under Mirabeau B. Lamar on the extreme right to prevent the Mexicans from breaking away to the prairie. Even a four-piece band was improvised, which at the moment of attack played a few bars from a popular love song, "Will You Come to My Bower I Have Shaded for You?" A rise in the terrain hid the Texans from view until they were within 200 yards of the flimsy Mexican barricades. The shape of the terrain, the Mexican habit of taking a siesta, and the utter contempt in which Santa Anna held the Anglo-American troops, afford the only explanation of one of the most astounding facts in all military history: an army was taken by surprise by a much smaller force advancing for a mile across a prairie in the middle of an April afternoon. Santa Anna had made his second mistake within 24 hours.

The carnage at San Jacinto was indescribable. In his official report Houston stated that the battle lasted but 18 minutes; that 630 of the enemy were killed, 208 were wounded, and 730 were taken prisoner.[3] Only a handful of the Mexicans escaped. Nine Texans were killed or mortally wounded and 34 were wounded. Santa Anna himself was taken prisoner the next day.

READJUSTMENTS AFTER
SAN JACINTO

The defeat of Santa Anna's forces saved the Texan cause for the time, but it did not assure independence. Mexico was still belligerent; there were in Texas about 2,000 Mexican troops that might have to be reckoned with; and Houston was helpless and soon to take a steamer to New Orleans for the treatment of an ankle shattered by a ball as he led the charge. The Texan army was, furthermore, almost as badly disorganized by victory as was the Mexican army on the Brazos by the reports of defeat and death brought on the night of April 21 by a few dragoons who had managed to escape from the San Jacinto battlefield. The testing time was not yet over. The immediate problems before the government were: first, to restore order and establish among the people a sense of security and competence; second, to strengthen,

---

[3]The exact size of the Mexican army at San Jacinto has never been determined. In his report Houston accounts for nearly 1,400 men, but it is difficult to reconcile this number with the Mexican accounts. See Johnson, *Texas and Texans*, I, 448. In their *Heroes of San Jacinto* (1932), Kemp and Dixon have verified the names of 918 participants on the Texan side.

supply, and keep control of the army; and third, to secure from Mexico the recognition of Texan independence, or at least to rid the country of Mexican troops.

Order and confidence returned gradually as the people learned of the completeness of the victory and observed that the government again was functioning. Many persons who had taken part in the "runaway scrape" went back to their homes at once. Government headquarters were removed from Galveston to Velasco where better quarters could be secured. *The Telegraph and Texas Register,* whose plant at Harrisburg had been destroyed during the invasion, resumed publication at Columbia in August. On July 23, President Burnet issued a proclamation calling for a general election to be held on the first Monday in September, for the purpose of establishing a constitutional government.

The gravest problem that confronted the *ad interim* government after San Jacinto was that of controlling the army. The subject is, however, inseparably linked with that of disposing of the prisoner Santa Anna and arriving at some understanding with the Mexicans. Shortly after he had been brought to Houston's headquarters on April 22, the terrified Mexican President entered into an armistice in consequence of which he wrote General Vicente Filisola, second in command, to retire with his troops to Bexar and to order Urrea to fall back to Victoria "pending some negotiations . . . by which the war is to cease forever." This order was not necessary; even as Santa Anna wrote, the Mexican forces were in retreat and the messenger did not overtake Filisola until April 28. Then, at Velasco on May 14, Burnet negotiated two treaties with Santa Anna, one public and one secret. By the terms of the public treaty an end was declared to hostilities; the Mexican army was to retire at once beyond the Rio Grande, and all Texan prisoners were to be released by the Mexicans, the Texans agreeing to release a corresponding number of Mexican prisoners. The chief purpose of the secret treaty was to get from Santa Anna the pledge to use his influence on the Mexican government to secure the execution of the treaty already made and, also, to establish a permanent treaty whereby Mexico should acknowledge the independence of Texas, the boundary of Texas not to extend beyond the Rio Grande. The Texan government in turn pledged itself to release Santa Anna at once, giving him escort to Vera Cruz.

There was widespread clamor that the dictator be put to death, but Burnet courageously determined to carry out the treaty and return him to Mexico. On June 4, after General Santa Anna, his secretary Caro, and Colonel Almonte were aboard the armed schooner of war *Invincible,* a group of disgruntled and ambitious army officers, led by General Thomas J. Green, who had just arrived from the United States with a force of volunteers, compelled Burnet, despite Santa Anna's protest, to remove the Mexicans from the vessel and place them again in confinement.

Developments during the next few weeks did not improve Santa Anna's position. Word came that the Mexican Senate had annulled his treaty and had declared that the government would continue the war; three Texan emissaries, sent to Matamoros under a flag of truce and bearing passports from Filisola, to see if all prisoners had been released, were arrested and added to the Mexican prison rolls; and on June 17, Rusk wrote from the army that Urrea was advancing on Goliad. It was left to President Houston finally to dispose of the prisoner.

Burnet's difficulties with insubordinate troops were not confined to volunteers at the seat of government. After the Battle of San Jacinto, Thomas J. Rusk reluctantly took command of the Texan army and followed the retreating Mexicans as far as Victoria. Word that Santa Anna was to be released provoked an army mass meeting and an insolent and threatening letter to Burnet. Thinking that army morale might be improved by a change of commanders, Burnet sent Mirabeau B. Lamar about July 1 to replace Rusk; but neither the men nor officers would accept him. When a plan of the army officers to arrest and bring him before the army for trial failed, Burnet sought to absorb the energies of the army by encouraging an expedition against Matamoros. This was not carried out. He then sent word to agents in New Orleans to send no more short-term volunteers, and passed the problem of the army on to his successor, Houston.

AID FROM THE UNITED STATES

Expenditures of the Texan revolutionary government were strikingly small. Figures in the audits read more like those of a retail store than of the government of a sovereign state. Virtually every device for raising money known in that day was resorted to. Donations, including one of $7,000 from a committee in New Orleans and two of $5,000 each from persons in the United States, aggregated about $25,000. Many loyal persons pledged land, slaves, and other property to be sold for the benefit of the cause, but little money was raised in that way. Receipts from the sale of land and other property were negligible. Treasury notes, issued to the amount of $150,000, were almost worthless from the date of their issue. The most substantial receipts, about $100,000, came from loans negotiated in the United States by Commissioners Austin, Archer, and Wharton. The revolution was financed largely by those who advanced supplies to the infant government on faith and by the troops who willingly served for little other compensation than the promise of land bounties. By August 31, 1836, the government debt was $1,250,000.

War supplies came mainly from New Orleans. The firm of William Bryan and Company, Texan agents in that city, often used their own funds and impaired their private credit in the interests of the struggle. Also, the Texan merchant, Thomas F. McKinney, who declined the office of commissary general, wrought faithfully in his private capacity toward supplying the troops, and to that end he spent large sums of his own money. The records show heavy shipments of flour, rifles, powder, lead, clothing, and other necessary supplies for the army, without which it could not have continued the struggle.

From east of the Sabine came men as well as supplies. As early as October 26, the Permanent Council addressed the citizens of the United States with an impassioned appeal to come to the aid of "suffering Texas." From New Orleans to Cincinnati friends of the colonists held meetings, raised funds, and sent out forces of volunteers of "armed emigrants." The chief recruiting stations were Louisville, Cincinnati, and New Orleans. Some of the best-known volunteer organizations were the two companies of "New Orleans Greys," in one of which were represented five foreign countries and twelve different states; the Georgia Battalion, composed of men from Georgia and Alabama and strengthened by recruits who joined them on the way to Texas; the "Mobile Grays," originally some thirty men under Captain David N. Burke; the Alabama "Red Rovers," almost seventy men under Captain Jack Shackelford, who arrived at Matagorda early in 1836 armed with muskets from the arsenal of the State of Alabama; the "Mustangs," from Kentucky and Tennessee; and some fifty Tennesseans, among them David Crockett, who arrived at Nacogdoches on January 12, 1836.

For most of these valiant young Americans fate held a tragic ending. A majority of the men who died in the Alamo were lately from the United States, as was true of the forces of Johnson and Grant; and Fannin's men were almost without exception newcomers. After all, the Texan colonists did the most effective fighting. It was they who drove the Mexicans out of Texas in 1835, and they constituted an overwhelming majority of Houston's army at San Jacinto.

The most successful work in recruiting troops abroad for Texas was that of Thomas J. Chambers. Authorized by the council to raise for Texas an "Army of the Reserve," Chambers in February 1836 proceeded to Natchez, Mississippi, and thence to points in Tennessee, Kentucky, and Ohio. Report of the victory at San Jacinto made it comparatively easy, both to secure volunteers and to raise the means to equip them. By December 1836 he had sent 1,915 well-equipped volunteers and, also, quantities of ammunition and other supplies. These forces arrived too late, however, to participate in the battles of the revolution.

In the conveying of men and equipment, as well as in the prevention of the free movement of troops and supplies by the enemy, the Texans were greatly aided by their tiny navy. In fact, the first fighting in the revolution was at sea when the Texan steamboat *Laura*, aided by the armed schooner *San Felipe*, of United States registry, bearing a cargo of munitions to Brazoria, attacked and overcame the Mexican schooner of war *Correo de Mejico* under Captain Thomas M. Thompson. Thompson had antagonized the Anglo-Americans by his arbitrary seizure of ships and cargoes in the vicinity of Velasco. Mexican ships of war and transports continued to operate along the coast and the Texans realized that they must meet them. In November 1835 the Provisional Government authorized privateering and the creation of a navy of four schooners. Meanwhile citizens in the coastal communities had brought and equipped the schooner *William Robbins.* After being granted a letter of marque, Captain W. A. Hurd sailed to Paso Caballo and took the Mexican man-of-war *Bravo*, together with a prize the *Bravo* had just taken. Sentiment in the United States was so pronounced against privateering, however, that the Texans had to discontinue the practice. Texan commissioners then proceeded as authorized to purchase four ships for a navy. A United States revenue cutter was bought in New Orleans, rechristened the *Independence*, and sent to sea under Captain Charles E. Hawkins. The *Brutus* was bought and placed under the command of Captain W. A. Hurd. The Texan government also managed to purchase the privateer *William Robbins*, rechristened the *Liberty*, and the *Invincible*.

In cruising along the Texas coast and convoying shipments from New Orleans, these vessels rendered excellent service. The *Liberty* took as a prize the fine Mexican schooner *Pelicano*, whose cargo consisted largely of munitions for the Mexican army (packed in barrels of flour and apples and consigned to New Orleans in the hope of escaping the Texas blockade). The *Invincible* took a valuable prize off Matamoros and prevented the sending of reinforcements to Santa Anna's army; the *Liberty* took a prize also, sailing under a false manifest.

As the Mexican army advanced, the Texan fleet withdrew to Galveston Bay. In spite of the efforts of the little navy, the Mexicans succeeded in getting quantitites of supplies through to Goliad by way of ship, supplies which were of great aid to the Mexican army. Major Isaac Burton and his detachment of mounted rangers managed to seize three of these Mexican supply ships on June 3, winning the appellation "the horse marines."

Selected Bibliography

A great deal has been written about the Texan Revolution. Of the older general histories, all cited at the beginning of the references for Chapter 4, good accounts may be had in J.H. Brown, H.H. Bancroft, W. Kennedy, H. Yoakum, D.G. Wooten (reprint of Yoakum's text), C.R. Wortham, and H.S. Thrall. Yoakum gives much source material; Thrall has many biographical sketches; Wortham devotes a volume to the Revolution. Of the newer general histories, two are superior: W.C. Binkley, *The Texas Revolution* (Baton Rouge, 1952), and D.M. Vigness, *The Revolutionary Decades;* two others are Vito Alessio Robles, *Coahuila y Texas en la Epoca Colonial* (Mexico, D. F., 1938), and A.J. Houston, *Texas Independence* (Houston, 1938).

Several biographies are extremely valuable in connection with the Revolution. The best is E.C. Barker, *The Life of Stephen F. Austin.* Others are L. Friend, *Sam Houston, the Great Designer* (Austin, 1954); Marquis James, *The Raven: A Biography of Sam Houston* (New York, 1929); E. Wallace, *Charles DeMorse, Pioneer Editor and Statesman* (Lubbock, 1943); Herbert P. Gambrell, *Mirabeau Bonaparte Lamar* (Dallas, 1934); H.P. Gambrell, *Anson Jones: The Last President of Texas* (New York, 1948); O.B. Faulk, *General Tom Green, Fightin' Texan* (Waco, 1963); M.L. Dillon, *Benjamin Lundy and the Struggle for Negro Freedom* (Urbana, Ill., 1966); J.A. Atkins, *David Crockett, the Man and the Legend* (Chapel Hill, 1956).

There is much source material in the *Austin Papers;* the *Lamar Papers;* Amelia W. Williams and E.C. Barker (eds.), *The Writings of Sam Houston* (8 vols., Austin, 1938–1943); W.C. Binkley (ed.), *Official Correspondence of the Texan Revolution, 1835–1836* (2 vols., New York and London, 1936). Useful also is C.E. Castañeda (ed. and trans.), *The Mexican Side of the Texan Revolution* (Dallas, 1928); E. Wallace and D.M. Vigness (eds.), *Documents of Texas History;* John H. Jenkins (ed.), *Recollections of Early Texas: The Memoirs of John Holland Jenkins* (Austin, 1958).

Shorter studies dealing primarily with the early phase of the Revolution include "General Austin's Order Book for the Campaign of 1835," *Quarterly of the Texas State Historical Association* XI, 1–55; Fred H. Turner, "The Mejia Expedition," *ibid.,* VII, 1–28; E.C. Barker, "Proceedings of the Permanent Council," *ibid.,* IX, 287–288; E.C. Barker (ed.), "Journal of the Permanent Council," *ibid.,* VII, 249–278; E.C. Barker, "The Texan Declaration of Causes for Taking Up Arms Against Mexico," *ibid.,* XV, 173–185; E.C. Barker, "The Tampico Expedition," *ibid.,* VI, 169–186; Ralph Steen, "Analysis of the Work of the General Council of Texas, 1835–1836," *Southwestern Historical Quarterly,* XL, 309–333; XLI, 225–240; E.C. Barker, "Don Carlos Barrett," *ibid.,* XX, 139–145; R.S. Lee, "The Publication of Austin's Louisville Address," *ibid.,* LXX 424–442; Katherine Hart and Elizabeth Kemp (eds.), "E.M. Pease's Account of the Texas Revolution," *ibid.,* LXVIII, 79–89.

On the war in the field see: E.C. Barker, "The Texan Revolutionary Army," *Quarterly of the Texas State Historical Association,* IX, 227–261; E.C. Barker, "The San Jacinto Campaign," *ibid.,* IV, 237–345; General John E. Roller, "Captain John Sowers Brooks," *ibid.,* IX, 157–209, contains letters from a soldier with Fannin; Ruby C. Smith, "James W. Fannin, Jr., in the Texas Revolution," *Southwestern Historical Quarterly,* XXIII, 79–90, 171–203, 271–284; Harbert Davenport, "Captain Jesus Cuellar, Texas Cavalry, Otherwise Comanche," *ibid.*, XX, 56–62; Amelia Williams, "A Critical Study of the Siege of the Alamo . . . ," *ibid.*, XXXVI, 251–287; XXXVII, 1–44, 79–115, 157–184, 237–312; M.L. Bonham, Jr., "James Butler Bonham: A Consistent Rebel," *ibid.*, XXXV, 124–136; H. Davenport, "The Men of Goliad," *ibid.*, XLIII, I–41, (an interpretation of the entire Texan Revolution); H.M. Henderson, "A Critical Analysis of the San Jacinto Campaign," *ibid.*, LIX, 344–362; Jewel D. Scarborough, "The Georgia Battalion in the Texas Revolution: A Critical Study," *ibid.*, LXIII, 511–532; Thomas L. Miller, "Fannin's Men: Some Additions to Earlier Rosters," *ibid.*, LXI, 522–532; James Presley, "Santa Anna in Texas: A Mexican Viewpoint," *ibid.*, LXII, 489–512; Walter Lord, *A Time to Stand* (New York, 1961); Lon Tinkle, *Thirteen Days to Glory* (New York, 1958); Sam H. Dixon and Louis W. Kemp, *The Heroes of San Jacinto* (Houston, 1932).

For an account of the convention of 1836 see R.N. Richardson, "Framing the Constitution of the Republic of Texas," *The Southwestern Historical Quarterly*, XXXI, 191–220; J.K. Greer, "The Committee of the Texas Declaration of Independence," *ibid.*, XXX, 239–251; XXI, 33–49, 130–149; Henderson Shuffler, "The Signing of Texas' Declaration of Independence: Myth and Reality," *ibid.*, LXV, 310–332; L.W. Kemp, *The Signers of the Texas Declaration of Independence* (Houston, 1944).

On developments after the Battle of San Jacinto see W.C. Binkley, "Activities of the Texan Revolutionary Army after San Jacinto," *Journal of Southern History*, VI, 331–346.

Concerning the attitude of President Jackson toward the Texan Revolution two points of view are presented in E.C. Barker, "President Jackson and the Texas Revolution," *American Historical Review*, XII, 797–803; and R.C. Stenberg, "The Texas Schemes of Jackson and Houston, 1829–1836; *Southwestern Social Science Quarterly*, XV, 229–250.

J.C. Winston has published in *Southwestern Historical Quarterly* a series of articles on aid from the United States. See XVI, 27–62. 277–283; XII, 36–60; XVIII, 368–385; and XVII, 262–282. See also, C. Elliott, "Alabama and the Texas Revolution," *ibid.*, L, 316–328.

On the Texan navy see Alex Dienst, "The Navy of the Republic of Texas," *Quarterly of the Texas State Historical Association*, XII, 165–203, 249–275; XIII, 1–43, 85–127; Jim Dan Hill, *The Texas Navy* (Chicago, 1937); George G. Haugh (ed.), "History of the Texas Navy," *Southwestern Historical Quarterly*, LXIII, 572–579.

7

THE REPUBLIC OF TEXAS, 1836–1846

The history of the Republic of Texas may be divided logically into two major sections: domestic affairs and foreign relations. Because of the many problems with which the new-born Republic had to cope and the contrasting policies of Presidents Houston and Lamar, each of these sections in turn is subdivided into a number of topics. Domestic affairs is treated under the following subjects: the election of 1836; Houston's first administration; Lamar's administration; Houston's second administration; the land policy of the Republic; contracts of immigrant agents; and immigration and the extension of settlement. The section of foreign relations divides itself naturally into four topics: early efforts to obtain recognition by and annexation to the United States; relations with European nations; relations with Mexico; and the annexation of Texas to the United States.

THE ELECTION OF 1836

Even after the Texan victory at San Jacinto the *ad interim* government had to cope with many critical problems. Restless military officers defied its orders and threatened to replace it with military dictatorship.

Money was scarce; families were destitute; crops had been planted too late, if at all, to yield well; and the government lacked adequate power to deal with problems either at home or abroad. Consequently, in desperation President Burnet and his cabinet, without waiting until December as the convention had proposed, on July 23 issued a proclamation, setting the first Monday of the following September as the date for the election. Three major issues were to be decided: first, ratification of the constitution; second, the election of constitutional officers who would take office provided the voters approved the constitution; and third, whether the new government should seek annexation to the United States.

The ratification of the constitution and a favorable vote on annexation were unquestionably certain; thus the major interest in the election centered in the selection of a president. Since there were no political parties in Texas at the time, the candidates had to depend largely on their general popularity. Henry Smith, the first to announce openly for the presidency, sought to vindicate his policies as head of the Provisional Government. Austin entered the race at the solicitation of William H. Wharton, B. T. Archer, and others. Despite his distinguished and unselfish service to Texas, Austin had become exceedingly unpopular. His early opposition to independence, his support of the government in saving Santa Anna from a firing squad, and the charge that he had not served Texas well while in the United States adversely affected his popularity. It was soon evident, however, that Sam Houston was the people's choice. Just 11 days before the election he formally accepted the nomination by numerous groups throughout the nation. In the election Houston received 5,110 votes, almost 80 percent of the total, Smith 743, and Austin only 587. Mirabeau B. Lamar was elected vice-president. The constitution was accepted overwhelmingly; only 233 voters were in favor of giving Congress power to amend it; and only 93 voted against the mandate requiring the new president to negotiate for annexation to the United States.

HOUSTON'S FIRST
ADMINISTRATION (1836–1838)

Houston stated that he chose his cabinet "with a total disregard to personal preference" and "for the furtherance of the interests of the Country." Austin, long the leader of conservative Texans, who had opposed, until after the revolution was well under way, separation from Mexico was made secretary of state and Henry Smith of the radical or Wharton faction was appointed secretary of the treasury. Austin died about two months after taking office, and Robert A. Irion served at the head of the cabinet during most of the term. Soon William H. Wharton was sent to represent the Republic at Washington. The office of chief justice was established and James Collinsworth was appointed to that post. The chief justice, acting with the four district judges provided for in the law, composed the supreme court. Congress created 23 counties, corresponding in most cases to the old municipalities. A system of courts for counties also was provided, each county to have a chief justice and two associate justices, who were to be selected by a majority of the justices of peace in the county.

At its first session the First Congress passed over Houston's veto an act providing for opening the land offices, which had been closed by the Permanent Council and the Consultation. Before his law went into effect, however, in December 1837 Congress passed over President Houston's veto a comprehensive land office act supplanting all preceding legislation on the subject. This act provided that the offices be opened for the use of old settlers and soldiers on the first Thursday in February 1838; and for all others six months thereafter. Meanwhile, Congress also approved a generous schedule of land grants to soldiers, based on the length of their service, and to immigrants. A more detailed treatment of the land policy of the Republic will be given later in this chapter.

National defense and frontier protection were subjects of considerable legislation during Houston's first administration. Threats of Mexican invasion and fear of hostile Indians caused Congress, in December 1836, to authorize a military establishment of 3,587 troops, a battalion of 280 mounted riflemen, and a chain of forts and trading houses on the frontier. In addition, the president was authorized to receive forty thousand volunteers to meet the Mexican threat.

Houston, however, was more interested in getting rid of the army he had already than in raising new troops. It will be recalled that the army had refused to accept Lamar as commander. Its morale was not improved when Rusk, who was appointed secretary of war, was succeeded by Felix Huston, a military adventurer. President Houston sent Albert Sidney Johnston to succeed Huston, but Huston challenged Johnston, wounded him severely in a duel, and stayed in command. While Huston was away at the seat of government lobbying for a law authorizing a campaign against Mexico, the president took advantage of the situation to furlough all troops except 600, who apparently were also soon disbanded, leaving only the militia and, at times, some Ranger companies as a frontier guard. Thus canny Sam Houston removed the threat of a military dictatorship.

By keeping troops out of the Indian country and using such limited means as were available, Houston managed to avoid serious Indian wars. The most threatening situation was that of relations with the Cherokees. Some of these people had moved into Texas as early as 1819. The Spanish government gave them a vague grant to lands in the vicinity of Nacogdoches; and in February of 1836 when the Texans needed

Sam Houston. Elected Governor of Tennessee in 1827, Houston seemed to have a secure political future when two years later he resigned and moved to what is now Oklahoma to rejoin the Cherokee Indians by whom he had been adopted in his youth. Houston came to Texas in 1833 and became a member of the conventions that declared Texas independent of Mexico and set up a provisional government. Criticized for retreating before the Mexicans, Houston regained popular favor when he defeated Santa Anna at San Jacinto in April 1836, and was elected the first president of the Republic. (E. C. Barker History Center, University of Texas) Shown also, the home the Houstons built in Huntsville, Texas in 1847. (C. C. Springfield, Huntsville)

their friendship, the commissioners Sam Houston, John Forbes, and John Cameron, by authority of the Consultation, negotiated with them a treaty providing for permanent titles to their lands. When the senate, contrary to Houston's admonition, refused to ratify the treaty, the Cherokees and their associated tribes threatened to make trouble. To add to the confusion and uncertainty, Vicente Córdova, a Mexican citizen of Nacogdoches and an agent of the Mexican government, led a band of nearly 600 Mexicans and Kickapoo Indians in a rebellion in the Angelina River vicinity in the summer of 1838. In November General Rusk with a force of volunteers marched against the insurgents. Córdova fled, but the following winter he succeeded in inciting some of the tribes to renew hostilities. The Cherokees did not participate in this affair, but the president was both uneasy about their attitude and solicitous of their rights. His efforts to protect them did not avail, however, and as a result of Lamar's harsh Indian policy, they were expelled in 1839.

Public expenses in Houston's first administration amounted to nearly $2,000,000. There was a wide breach between expenditures and income. A tariff, ranging from a duty of one percent on breadstuffs to 50 percent on silks, was the most productive tax. Tonnage dues and port fees, a direct property tax, poll taxes, business taxes, and land fees each added a little. Inasmuch as this slender income was in the form of audited drafts, the treasury received but little money. These claims, incidentally, had depreciated to 15 cents on the dollar, when an act of June 12, 1837, provided that they might be exchanged at par for ten percent bonds. The poverty of the government at times was embarrassing. For a period, Secretary of the Treasury Henry Smith could not attend to his duties because he had no stationery and no funds with which to buy any. Houston could secure supplies for the army only by pledging his personal credit.

Under such conditions the government resorted to the expedient of issuing paper money. Acts of 1837 required the president to issue promissory notes of the government to the amount of $650,000, payable 12 months after the date of issue and bearing ten percent interest. The notes circulated readily, were not reissued, and suffered little or no depreciation. However, a succeeding issue, "the engraved interest notes" already had depreciated to a valuation as low as 65 cents on the dollar several months before November 3, 1838, when the estimated amount in circulation was $812,454.

The constitutional provision that the first president serve two years only and that no president succeed himself made Houston ineligible for reelection. Long before the election it became evident that Vice-President Lamar would be president. He was the choice of the senate and was endorsed by various persons and groups. The opposition, that is the Houston party, was never able to find a candidate. Rusk was so-

Mirabeau Buonaparte Lamar came to Texas from Georgia to join the revolutionaries in 1835 and took part in the battle of San Jacinto. During his term as the second president of the Republic (1834–41) he secured foreign recognition of Texas independence. He had hoped to make the Republic self-sufficient, but his filibustering expeditions to New Mexico left Texas in financial difficulties. (E. C. Barker History Center, University of Texas)

licited, but he refused to run. Houston's followers then threw their support to Peter W. Grayson, but in early July he died by his own hand. The Houston party then chose James W. Collinsworth, chief justice of Texas, who was too young to meet the constitutional age requirement. Soon after his nomination he was drowned in Galveston Bay, apparently a suicide victim. The vote for Lamar then was almost unanimous.

LAMAR'S ADMINISTRATION (1838–1841)

In his inaugural address and in a 10,000-word message to Congress in December 1838, Lamar indicated that the conservative policies of the two preceding years would be abandoned for a more ambitious public program. Only a few of his proposals, however, were actually adopted.

An act of January 20, 1839, provided that each county should be given three square leagues of land for primary schools, and that 50 square leagues should be set aside for two colleges or universities. A year later a law gave an additional square league to each county, one-half of the proceeds of which were to be used for the benefit of a county academy and the remainder to be distributed among the common school districts. Congress also made land grants to several private institutions. Lands were cheap, and many years were to pass before Texas had even the semblance of a system of public education; but these foundation laws link Lamar, who urged their enactment, eternally with the schools of Texas.

The question concerning the seat of government was carried over from Houston's regime. Burnet had selected Columbia as a temporary capital, and there the first administration under the constitution had its beginning. In December 1836 Congress voted to move the seat of government to the new town of Houston in May 1837, with the stipulation that a permanent location would be designated by 1840. Because of sectional rivalry, the site had not been selected when Lamar became president. Lamar persuaded Congress to locate the capital farther west and farther in the interior and to authorize a commission to designate the exact site. In 1839 the commission agreed on a site at a settlement called Waterloo. The members believed that at that place roads linking the Red River with Matamoros and Santa Fé with the Gulf of Mexico would intersect. Edwin Waller was made the government agent to lay out the capital, which was christened Austin, and in October 1839, the president and his cabinet proceeded to the new town. Four months later it claimed a population of 856.

Frontier defense was left almost wholly to the Rangers and the militia. From January 1 to October 30, 1839, 1,984 militiamen served at one time or another. It must be said that they did the job quite thoroughly. The act of December 1838 provided for a system of frontier posts extending from the Red River to the Nueces River. Colonel William G. Cooke began operations under the terms of the law in the fall of 1840, but only one post, that on the Red River, had been established when the appropriation was exhausted.

Lamar, upon assuming the presidency, immediately inaugurated a drastic change in the Indian policy of the government. He told Congress that the Indians were tenants at will and had no possessory rights in the land; and thus the white people could take the land whenever they desired. Albert Sidney Johnston, the secretary of war, G. W. Bonnell, commissioner of Indian affairs, a majority of Congress, and many others agreed with him and urged an aggressive frontier policy. Consequently, Lamar's administration was marked by the bloodiest Indian wars Texas had known. Yet the fact must be kept in mind that Lamar inherited these wars; hostilities had already begun when he became president. The Cherokees and associated tribes in eastern Texas had been put off with promises for too long, and they were in an ugly humor. Farther west, the Wacos, Tawakonis, and the fierce Comanches, seeing the surveyors enter their hunting grounds deeper each season, were already on the warpath.

Early in 1839 small commands of volunteers took the field, assuming that every Indian they saw was an enemy to be slain. Manuel Flores, who had been active the year before in the Córdova rebellion, and who with a party of about 25 marauders had committed several murders between Seguin and San Antonio, was killed in an engagement with a Texan force near Austin. Certain papers found on his body convinced Lamar and his cabinet that the Cherokees were in treasonable correspondence with the Mexicans, and Lamar determined to expel the Indians from the Republic. The Texan army entered the Cherokee country in midsummer, and after a bloody engagement drove the Indians into Arkansas. The Shawnees, less numerous than the Cherokees, were removed without bloodshed, and the Coshatta and Alabama Indians were removed to other lands in Texas.

More prolonged and bloody was the war with the Comanches, whose tactics of surprise attacks and flight before the white people could strike back made them the most formidable enemy of the frontiersmen. On February 14, 1839, J. H. Moore with three small companies of volunteers attacked a Comanche village at Spring Creek in the valley of the San Saba, and was repulsed. Captain John Bird lost his life, and his company of 35 men was threatened with annihilation near the present Belton by an aggregation of Indians, among whom Comanches predominated. In March 1840 a Comanche chief and a number of warriors were slain at San Antonio, while in a council with representatives of the government. When they heard of this affair, other Comanches killed their white prisoners; in the summer following, they engaged in a destructive raid that was carried as far as Victoria and Linnville on the coast. As they retired to the plains, the Indians were attacked and defeated by volunteers under command of Felix Huston and Edward Burleson at Plum Creek near Lockhart. In the following autumn, Colonel J. H. Moore carried the war into the Indian country. On October 23 he attacked and destroyed a Comanche village far up the Colorado River, probably near the site of Colorado City, killing an estimated 130 Indians. The Comanches thereupon withdrew far from the Texas frontier. By the close of 1840 Indian wars had practically ceased.

Lamar's Indian campaigns cost $2,500,000 as well as the lives of several score of white people and of a greater number of Indians. The justice of his campaigns may be questioned but their effectiveness is beyond dispute. Lamar and his troops opened to settlers the rich Indian lands of East Texas; rid the state of most of its immigrant Indians; and made the country comparatively safe for the advance of surveyors and immigrants.

The financial affairs of the Republic, bad enough at the start, grew constantly worse during the Lamar administration. Tariff duties, which were already quite moderate, were lowered almost to a free-trade basis. Direct taxes and license taxes were levied, but were difficult to collect and brought small returns, especially since they were paid in depreciated currency. Total receipts for the three-year period were $1,083,661, and expenditures were $4,855,213.

Since the autumn of 1836, the government had been trying to borrow $5,000,000, but all that it managed to secure was a loan of $457,380 from the Bank of the United States in Pennsylvania, negotiated by James Hamilton who had been appointed by Lamar to seek loans for the Republic. Lamar himself favored a gigantic Texas bank to be owned and operated by the government, but he never could get Congress to create it. It could not have been placed in operation without the proceeds of the proposed $5,000,000 loan.

The administration resorted to the favorite expedient of moneyless governments—the issue of government paper money. When Lamar assumed office, there was outstanding more than $800,000 of treasury notes, already depreciated by from 15 to 50 percent. Then by the acts of 1839, 1840, and 1841, Congress authorized government noninterest-bearing notes, known as "red backs," which were issued to the amount of $3,552,800. The last act placed no limit on the quantity of such notes other than the amount of appropriations that Congress might vote. By November 1841, they were quoted at from 12 to 15 cents on the dollar.

HOUSTON'S SECOND
ADMINISTRATION (1841–1844)

So radically different from the policies of Houston were those of Lamar that the voters soon came to be divided into two distinct camps: the administration group and the opposition, led by Houston. It was natural, therefore, that Houston, who had since the end of his presidential term served in the House of Representatives, should become a candidate to succeed Lamar. The forces opposing Houston supported David G. Burnet, formerly president *ad interim*, vice-president, and for a period while Lamar was away, acting president.

A few issues to which the press and campaign speakers referred occasionally were the Franco-Texienne bill, which Houston had favored but which his followers now regarded as dead; economy and retrenchment; certain laws to check land speculators and quiet the titles of *bona fide* settlers; protection of the frontier; and the removal of the seat of government. Issues were incidental, however, for the contest took the form of gossip, scandal, and vituperation against the two candidates. The saga of San Jacinto was too widespread and the unpopularity of the Lamar administration too great for the race to be really close. Houston received 7,915 votes to Burnet's 3,616. Edward Burleson, running as an independent, and not altogether acceptable to the Houston forces, was elected vice-president.

The election of Houston and a conservative Congress marked a sharp transition from the ambitious and costly program of the Lamar administration. The Sixth Congress carried economy to the point of parsimony. Offices thought to be unnecessary were abolished; the number of clerks was reduced; and salaries were lowered below a living wage. The Fifth Congress had failed to make any appropriation for the regular army, and military expeditions after 1841 were confined to the maintenance of a few companies of Rangers. The navy continued to call for outlays, and its ships were badly in need of repairs; Congress met this situation in January 1843 by a secret act ordering them to be sold. However, the people of Galveston were enthusiastic about the little fleet of four vessels which had helped to protect Texas from Mexico. They were in sympathy with its commander, Edwin W. Moore, who had been insubordinate, had been declared a pirate, and then dishonorably discharged by Houston. By force they prevented the auction of the four vessels. In June 1846, in conformity with the joint resolution of annexation, the ships of the Texas Navy were transferred to the United States Navy.

Total expenditures for Houston's administration of three years was only a little more than $500,000. All currency laws were repealed by an act authorizing the issue in quantities not to exceed $200,000 in "exchequer bills," which were made the only currency receivable for taxes. Even under these favorable conditions the notes depreciated in value.

President Houston returned to the pacific Indian policy of his first administration. In September 1843 a treaty was signed at Bird's Fort with the Waco, Tawakoni, and other sedentary tribes; and in October 1844 at Torrey's Trading House, near present-day Waco, the southern Comanches agreed to bury the hatchet. Both treaties were ratified by the senate; that with the Comanches was the last treaty of the Republic of Texas.

In keeping with these treaties, the Texan government granted Torrey's Trading House, which looms large in the saga of the Texas frontier, and another trading post on the west fork of the Trinity that was not long maintained, a monopoly of the trade with the Indians on the northwestern frontier. Houston's pacific policy proved effective. The period from his inauguration to annexation to the United States was comparatively free of Indian wars.

More serious than Indian wars was a feud in East Texas that had smouldered for years and flared up in 1839 in a contest between the "Regulators" and "Moderators." It grew out of lawlessness inherited from the Neutral Ground agreement. Affairs in Shelby and neighboring counties, including murders, reached a state of anarchy. Many well-meaning men had become involved in the contest on one side or the other. In 1844 President Houston called out the militia, and partly by force and partly by persuasion succeeded in disbanding the organizations.

In 1844 President Houston saw his administration vindicated by the election of a Houston party man to succeed him in the presidency. Although Dr. Anson Jones publicly criticized some of the president's policies and wrote in his *Memoranda* that Houston did not prefer him as his successor, he was regarded as the administration candidate and his success was a measure of Houston's popularity. The comparatively high tariff, the removal of the government from Austin (which Jones condemned), Houston's Indian policy, and his failure to secure the release of the Texans imprisoned at Perote came in for much censure. Vice-President Edward Burleson was the candidate of the opposition; and, although he denied any such connection, his opponents dubbed him the Lamar party candidate. Jones carried the east, that is, the country east of the Trinity, and Burleson carried the west. The vote was 7,037 for Jones to 5,668 for Burleson.

LAND POLICY OF THE REPUBLIC

The public land policy of the government, because of its absorbing interest to the people throughout the entire period of the Republic and its far-reaching consequences, merits special treatment. The old Texans had hardly returned from the army or from the "runaway scrape" before their kinsmen from east of the Sabine began to join them. On May 16, 1837, *The Telegraph and Texas Register* stated:

Crowds of enterprising emigrants are arriving on every vessel, and so numerous have our citizens already become, that we confidently believe Houston alone could, in case of a second invasion, furnish an army of able-bodied men, nearly equal to that now encamped on the banks of the La Baca.

It was reported that during the following summer and fall, 6,000 immigrants crossed the Sabine at one ferry. Accounts indicate that in 1840 more immigrants arrived than had in any previous year, and that the volume was sustained in 1841 and the early part of 1842. The Mexican invasion of 1842 checked the flow sharply, but by 1844 the fear of invasion had ceased and a veritable stream of homeseekers was arriving almost daily. On October 30 the editor of the *Northern Standard* (Clarksville) stated: "Even now as we write, four wagons are passing the office, from Green County, Illinois, with 'Polk, Dallas, Oregon, and Texas' painted on the covers." Trains of immigrants gathered at the ferry crossings and had to wait for hours while the children amused themselves counting the conveyances. The white population, which was estimated in 1836 by Henry M. Morfit, Jackson's special representative in Texas, at 34,470, including Mexicans, had reached 102,961 by 1847; the slave population, estimated at 5,000 in 1836, had reached 38,753. Adding the 295 free Negroes, the total population of Texas was 142,009.

The explanation for this phenomenal migration is to be found in the liberal land policy of the Republic and the early state government and in the Anglo-American lust for free or cheap virgin land. The government was generous with its public lands. The constitution specified that heads of families (Negroes and Indians excepted) living in the Republic on March 2, 1836, might receive free a square league and a *labor* of land (4,605 acres), and that single men above 17 years of age might receive one-third of a square league. The recipients of constitutional grants were not required to reside on their lands. The Congress of the Republic then granted to immigrants who came after March 2, 1836, and before October 1, 1837, 1,280 acres for heads of families and 640 acres for single men. Later legislation allowed amounts of 640 acres and 320 acres respectively to heads of families and single men who came between October 1, 1837, and before January 1, 1842. It was required of citizens who arrived after March 2, 1836, that they reside in Texas for three years before their title was completed. Additional legislation gave actual settlers who did not own land preemptive rights, that is, the settler could purchase (for the most part at 50 cents an acre) land on which he was living to an amount not greater than 320 acres. Details of the law were changed from time to time; but, except for four years from 1854 to 1858, land could be acquired in Texas by right of preemption from 1845 to 1889.

In their determination to make Texas a nation of homeowners, the legislators went even further. They enacted a limited homestead law in 1838 (which preceded by a quarter of a century the homestead law of the United States). Its scope was enlarged in 1845 and a more general law was enacted in 1854. The usual size of homestead grants has been 160 or 200 acres. The homestead exemption act of 1838 and the homestead exemption provision in the Constitution of 1845 made the home secure from seizure for debt.

The Republic also granted land to its veterans. Volunteers who arrived before August 1, 1836, were allowed the same amount of land as the original colonists, that is, a square league and a *labor* for married men and one-third of that amount for single men. Additional lands were granted to permanently disabled veterans, to those who participated in the Battle of San Jacinto, and to the heirs of the men who fell in the Alamo and in the Matamoros and Goliad campaigns. Soldiers who served the Republic after the Revolution were granted lands varying in quantity from 320 acres, for serving three months, to 1,280 acres for serving twelve months.

The law of December 1837 provided for a board of land commissioners in each county, before whom claimants should appear to obtain certificates designating the amount of land to which they were legally entitled. Certificate holders would then engage a surveyor who was authorized to "locate" and survey the land out of the unappropriated public domain for a fee usually amounting to one-third of the land. The surveyor's field notes were then approved by the county or district surveyor, and certified to the commissioner of the general land office who, if convinced that the requirements of the law had been met, issued a patent. Land certificates for military service were granted through the secretary of war. The system, drawn partly from the Old South and partly from the Spanish and Mexican practice, had the merit of costing the public little as the people who got the land paid the cost. There were, of course, some forgeries and other kinds of fraudulent claims, but the most unfortunate result was that the aim of the lawmakers to place the land in the possession of actual settlers was only partly attained. No residence requirements were attached to certificates issued to old settlers and to soldiers for military service. Speculators and men who made a business of locating lands went into the Indian country, far ahead of the settlements, and surveyed and secured title to lands, so that bona fide settlers who came later found the best country already alienated. An examination of a land map of any county in Central Texas will reveal that the choicest land, that along the streams, passed into private ownership from ten to thirty years before the county was actually settled.

CONTRACTS WITH IMMIGRANT AGENTS

Contracts with immigrant agents was another phase of the land system of the Republic. In its eagerness to secure citizens and to increase its slender income the government granted contracts to immigrant agents much like the *empresario* agreements under the Mexican regime. These contracts were authorized by an act of Congress in February 1841 and by a general colonization law on February 5, 1842. Most important were those made with W. S. Peters and Associates, afterwards known as the Texas Emigration and Land Company; Charles F. Mercer; Henri Castro; and with Fisher and Miller, afterwards transferred to the German Emigration Company. Although the contracts with these companies differed in certain details, they were alike in all essentials. A given area was designated as "the colony," and within the boundaries thus indicated all unappropriated public domain was closed to entry by others until the proprietor had completed his contract, or it had been declared forfeited. The contractor was allowed ten premium sections for each 100 families. He also might secure additional compensation from his colonists for surveying the land, erecting cabins, moving the colonists to Texas, and supplying certain necessities. The Republic, and afterward the state, retained alternate sections, and it was from the sale of these that it expected to secure a money income.

However, the day of the *empresario's* usefulness had passed. It was no longer expedient to close from public entry thousands of square miles of public domain while an *empresario* or proprietary company appropriated the best lands. It was natural that persons holding land certificates would oppose these colonization contracts in every way possible. Accordingly, congress, early in 1844, passed over Houston's veto a bill repealing all laws authorizing colonization contracts and requiring the president to declare forfeited all that had not been complied with strictly.

As finally amended, the contract with W. S. Peters and Associates set aside for the colony more than 16,000 square miles, bounded on the east by a line extending from or near present-day Dallas northward to the Red River. The company met with difficulties posed by dissatisfied colonists, by holders of certificates eager to locate on vacant lands within its boundaries, and by an unfriendly government. By order of the Constitutional Convention of 1845, the attorney general instituted proceedings to cancel the contract, and the subsequent legislation and litigation was too vast to describe here. A legislative committee found that by July 1848 the company had introduced 2,205 families.

Charles F. Mercer's contract, signed just before the act of Congress of January 30, 1844, discontinued *empresario* contracts, called for the location of families in a large area lying mainly south and east of Peters' colony and in that colony, subject to Peters' prior rights. Mercer and Associates met with difficulties similar to those that confronted Peters and the Texas Emigration Company. On October 25, 1848, R. E. B. Baylor, judge of the third judicial district, declared the contract void because of failure of Mercer to meet all of its requirements. Thereafter came legislation and litigation until finally in 1882 the Supreme Court of the United States denied the Mercer associates any compensation whatsoever.

A most energetic *empresario* was Henri Castro, a Frenchman. Castro advertised his colony extensively in Europe and by March 1, 1843, about 300 colonists, mostly from the Rhine provinces of France, had set out for Texas under his direction. The area assigned to him was the Indian-infested country between the Nueces and the Rio Grande, a region made more dangerous by threats of another Mexican invasion. One tract was about 50 miles southwest of San Antonio, and another in Starr County on the lower Rio Grande. Castro laid out the town of Castroville, the first permanent settlement between San Antonio and the Rio Grande, in September 1844, and by 1847 he had introduced 2,134 colonists.

Of great importance in bringing about a large migration of Germans to Texas was the contract with Henry F. Fisher and Burchard Miller. In February 1842 and in January 1844 Fisher and Miller in return for a grant of about 3,000,000 acres lying between the Llano and Colorado rivers contracted to introduce 6,000 colonists. Before introducing any settlers, however, they sold their grant to the *Adelsverein* (Society for the Protection of German Immigrants in Texas), organized in 1842 by a group of German noblemen for the purpose of promoting German immigration to Texas. A German settlement had been made in Texas as early as 1838 when Friedrich Ernst founded Industry in Austin County, but German immigration on a large scale is associated with the *Adelsverein*. Its agent, or commissioner general, Carl, Prince of Solms-Braunfels, who visited Texas in 1844, purchased for the Society the Fisher and Miller lands and, in addition, an extensive area north of San Antonio and a tract on Matagorda Bay. Early in 1845 the Society's first settlers established New Braunfels, named for the Prince. During the next year the Society founded Fredericksburg, about 80 miles north of New Braunfels but outside the Fisher and Miller grant. In fact, before settlement could be made on this tract it was necessary to pacify the Penateka Comanches who had occupied the area for half a century. John O. Muesebach (Baron Ottfried Hans Freiherr von Muesebach), Solms-Braunfels' successor, made a treaty with this Comanche division in March 1847 in which for presents worth $3,000 the Indians agreed to share their country with the Germans. Fredericksburg grew rapidly, and by 1850 its population was 754. Several other German settlements were made in that general vicinity, but the Society never succeeded in inducing a great number of settlers to go into the Fisher and Miller grant. It was too far from the coast and the attitude of the Indians was too uncertain. Sisterdale, Boerne, Comfort, and other settlements were established. By 1860 Germans constituted a majority of the population in three counties of the Austin and San Antonio section and a substantial part of the population in six other counties in the general vicinity.

IMMIGRATION AND
EXTENSION OF SETTLEMENT

The settled area of Texas in 1836 lay approximately south and east of a line running from San Antonio along the old road to Nacogdoches and extending north to the Red River. Each year after 1836 witnessed the extension of settlements into the unappropriated area. At first the most rapid advance was from the northeast, where the settlements about Pecan Point and Jonesborough in present-day Red River County served as a base. It will be recalled that here were located the oldest Anglo-American settlements in Texas, planted at a time when it was thought that the area was a part of the Louisiana Purchase. This section was comparatively unaffected by the threat of Mexican invasion; it afforded wood, rich soil, and good grass; and in 1835 after Captain Henry Shreve had finished removing the raft that obstructed navigation on the Red River, it had an outlet for its commodities. On the Texas side of the river were a dozen landings, which were visited periodically by puffing little steamboats during the high water season from December to July. Although the boats frequently were held up for weeks because of the shallow river, navigation at its worst was more practicable than overland transportation.

In the van of the advancing column of farmers were Indian traders, among them Samuel Fulton and Robert Cravens, who built a trading house at the mouth of Sander's Creek in Lamar County in 1833. Better known were Holland Coffee and Silas Colville who had traded for years in the Indian territory and had established a trading house at Preston Bend in the northern part of Grayson County in 1837. The town of Preston, laid out in 1840, was for a few years an important gateway to Texas and through it came many immigrants.

From Bowie, Red River, and Lamar counties, settlers pushed southward into both the timbered country of Hopkins, Wood, and Van Zandt counties and the prairies of Hunt, Collin, and Kaufman. Dr. Daniel Rowlett and party of Tennessee came by steamboat to Jonesborough in 1835, continued their journey the following spring, and settled in the present Fannin County. From the Red River settlements pioneers entered Hunt County in 1839, and five years later Ben Anderson's store constituted the beginning of Greenville. The supplies for the new town were hauled from Jefferson. In 1842 settlers moved into Collin County, then a part of Fannin, and a little later the Hopkinses made settlements in the county that bears their name. The first settlers of Kaufman County, Dr. William P. King and a company of 40 Mississippians, came by ox train and made a settlement near the town of Kaufman in 1841.

Meanwhile, the advance from the northeast had reached the upper Trinity. John Neely Bryan, a Tennessean, who came through Arkansas and by way of the Red River settlements, pitched his lonely cabin in 1841 near the three forks of the Trinity. Other colonists soon came and the settlement of the three forks was started. Nearby, at Farmer's Branch, Peters' colony headquarters were established; and for a while it outgrew the three forks. Bryan's settlement finally gained the ascendancy, however, and we know the place by the name of Dallas.

While settlers were advancing from the northeast, a similar extension was in process from the southeast along the lower Trinity, Brazos, and Colorado valleys. Parker's Fort, near the Navasota River in Limestone County, had been the center of a settlement established in 1834. The "runaway scrape," followed by the massacre of a number of citizens at Parker's Fort[1] by Indians in 1836 caused the section to be all but depopulated. The dauntless pioneers soon returned, however, and in December of the following year, the region between the Trinity and the Brazos, north of the San Antonio and Nacogdoches Road, was organized as Robertson County. In 1839 a blockhouse was built on Boggy Creek in the present Leon County, and within a year settlers began to move in. The pacification of the Indian tribes by President Houston in 1843 hastened the settlement of the counties along the Trinity, and by the close of 1846 Limestone, Navarro, and other counties in that vicinity had been organized. Navigation of the Trinity River was of some aid to these settlers, but most of their corn and cotton had to be hauled overland to Galveston.

The hostility of the Indians retarded the settlement of the valley of the Brazos above the San Antonio and Nacogdoches Road. A blockhouse near present-day Belton afforded some protection; but it was not until after the Indian treaty of September 29, 1843, that white people were able to live even in partial security in Bell County. The settlement of McLennan County was preceded by the establishment in 1842 of the Torrey Brothers and Associates' trading house on Tehuacana Creek, about eight miles southeast of the present-day city of Waco. In 1845, Neal McLennan, a Scotchman, settled on the South Bosque, a little above the site of the old Waco Indian village. Other settlers came, and in 1849 George B. Erath surveyed the Waco village, and the city of Waco had its beginning. Three years later, George Barnard, who had been associated with the Torreys, established an Indian trading post farther up the Brazos River in present Hood County. The advance of settlers into that area was not far behind.

Because of Indian hostility, settlements along the Colorado River advanced slowly for some time. Hornsby's Bend above Bastrop long was the most advanced point. It was in this vicinity in 1833 that Indians scalped and left for dead Josiah Wilbarger, a man of rugged physique and iron will, who lived for 12 years thereafter. A few farmers had, however, reached the vicinity of Austin when the town was laid out in 1839.

The hostility of the Mexicans as well as the Indian depredations retarded the advance of settlements in southern Texas. For some time after the Mexican invasion of 1836 the counties of San Patricio, Victoria, Goliad, and Refugio were depopulated to such an extent that no district court was held in them. However, in 1839 Henry L. Kinney and

---

[1]Young Cynthia Ann Parker, together with others, was captured on this occasion. She grew to womanhood among the Comanches, became the wife of a chief, and the mother of Quanah, the last great chief of the Comanches. In 1860 she was recaptured and returned to her white relatives, but her affections remained with the Comanches.

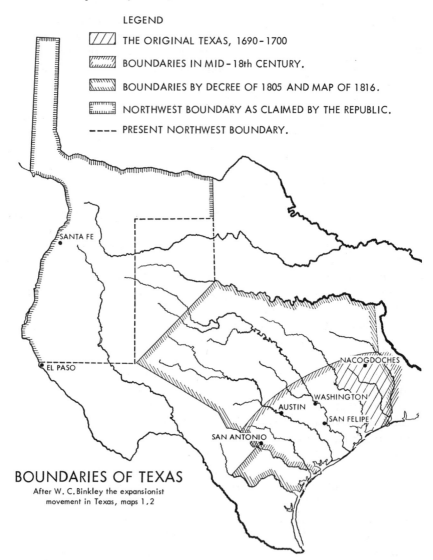

LEGEND

THE ORIGINAL TEXAS, 1690-1700

BOUNDARIES IN MID-18th CENTURY.

BOUNDARIES BY DECREE OF 1805 AND MAP OF 1816.

NORTHWEST BOUNDARY AS CLAIMED BY THE REPUBLIC.

---- PRESENT NORTHWEST BOUNDARY.

SANTA FE

EL PASO

NACOGDOCHES

WASHINGTON

AUSTIN

SAN FELIPE

SAN ANTONIO

BOUNDARIES OF TEXAS
After W. C. Binkley the expansionist
movement in Texas, maps 1, 2

William Aubrey established a trading post in the vicinity of Corpus
Christi at the mouth of the Nueces River. Other traders joined them,
and the place became a trading center. The coming of Taylor's army
in 1845 stimulated its growth, and the impetus continued after the
close of the war with Mexico. The area between the Nueces and the
Rio Grande was not organized into counties until after the Mexican
War, and for sometime thereafter its population was overwhelmingly
Latin-American.

In summary, the frontier line of settlement in 1846, when a state
government replaced that of the Republic, extended from Corpus
Christi to San Antonio on the Southwest, and thence northward through

New Braunfels, Fredericksburg (settled in 1846), Austin, Belton, Waco, Dallas, and Collin County to Preston on the Red River near the present city of Denison. The main reason for such a phenomenal extension of settlement, in the face of danger from Indian attacks and Mexican invasion, was the liberal land policy of the Republic.

RELATIONS WITH THE
UNITED STATES, 1836–1839

The foreign relations of the Republic cannot be understood without giving consideration to the diplomacy of the Texan Revolution. The opinion of most Texans on the subject may be summarized thus: Texas should leave nothing undone to secure the maximum aid from the United States; it should seek recognition by the United States and, if possible, bring about the intervention of that government in its behalf; and it should at the very earliest date possible be acquired by the United States, either by purchase from Mexico or by annexation after independence had been attained.

The commissioners, Austin, Archer, and Wharton, traveling slowly but working zealously in the Texan cause as they proceeded from city to city, arrived at Washington late in March 1836. They were soon replaced by other representatives, but little was accomplished. James Collinsworth and Peter W. Grayson, the last commissioners sent by Burnet, did learn in an informal interview with President Jackson that he had sent Henry M. Morfit, a secret agent, to Texas to secure information.

The vote in the election of September 1836, all but unanimous in favor of annexation, constituted a mandate to Houston to promote that end. Santa Anna, seeking some means to secure his freedom, suggested that he be allowed to go to Washington and to interview President Jackson in the interest of a transfer of Texas to the United States. Houston, who was seeking some excuse to get his prisoner out of Texas, accepted the suggestion; and, in spite of protests of Congress, Santa Anna started with an escort for Washington on November 26. Jackson realized that the ex-dictator's proposal to sell Texas to the United States was now impractical. At Jackson's order Santa Anna was carried to Vera Cruz aboard the United States frigate *Pioneer*.

Houston sent William H. Wharton, with comprehensive instructions from Secretary of State Stephen F. Austin, directing Wharton to secure the recognition of Texas and bring about its annexation to the United States. Memucan Hunt was sent to assist Wharton. To the great disappointment of the Texans, President Jackson, with the report of Morfit before him, in a message to Congress advocated delay in recognizing Texas independence. His reasons for delay were based on doubt as to the ability of Texas to maintain its independence; fear of offending Mexico; and belief that recognition would be regarded as a preliminary step toward annexation. In a private interview Wharton learned, however, that President Jackson would approve recognition if Congress would recommend it. By diligent work and with the aid of various friends, Wharton and Hunt secured the passage of a bill providing expenses for sending a diplomatic agent to Texas whenever the president should deem it expedient. The last official act of President Jackson was to appoint Alcée LaBranche *charge d'affaires* to the Republic of Texas.

Recognition now attained, Texas pressed for annexation. On August 4, 1837, Hunt formally made the offer. John Forsyth, the United States Secretary of State, answered three weeks later, saying that treaty obligations with Mexico prevented the United States from entertaining the subject. Having failed to get annexation by treaty, the issue was introduced in the United States Congress early in 1838 along with a stream of memorials and petitions. The opposition to annexation of Texas was very active. John Quincy Adams, in the House of Representatives, spoke for his counterresolution in opposition to annexation during the morning hours of each session from June 16 to July 7, when Congress adjourned without acting on the measure. Pursuant to Houston's orders Anson Jones, then representing Texas in Washington, announced the "formal and absolute withdrawal" of the offer. The Congress of Texas on January 23, 1839, ratified the withdrawal, and annexation was not again an issue until about three years later.

RECOGNITION BY EUROPEAN POWERS

In the summer of 1837, President Houston, convinced that the United States would not consider annexation, obtained authority from Congress to open diplomatic negotiations with the European powers. He then sent Secretary of State J. Pinckney Henderson as minister plenipotentiary to Great Britain and France to secure recognition and negotiate commercial treaties. Lord Palmerston, British Minister of Foreign Affairs, was disappointingly indifferent. England was opposed to slavery; British capitalists had millions invested in Mexican bonds; and England was not interested in aiding a state that probably would soon join the American Union. Early in 1838 Henderson did, however, secure a convention with Great Britain that provided for trade between that country and Texas. He then took up negotiations with the French Ministry. The withdrawal that autumn of the offer of Texan annexation to the United States and the avowed purpose of Lamar to maintain an independent nation strengthened Texan diplomacy appreciably. President Lamar commissioned James Hamilton, a former governor of South

Carolina with successful experience in diplomacy and business, to negotiate a foreign loan. Hamilton joined Henderson in France, and in September 1839 recognition by France and a commercial treaty with her were secured. Henderson thereupon returned to Texas, but Hamilton remained in Europe as the representative of the Lamar administration, and in September 1840 he signed a treaty with the Netherlands.

Meanwhile, Palmerston had become convinced that Texan recognition would serve Britain's best interest. In November of 1840 he and Hamilton signed a treaty of commerce and navigation, a second treaty obligating England to mediate with Mexico for Texan independence, and still a third giving England great liberty in suppressing the foreign slave trade. Hamilton was never able, however, to secure a loan in Europe.

Thus before the close of Lamar's administration, France, the Netherlands, Great Britain, and Belgium had recognized the independence of Texas, and favorable commercial treaties had been secured from France, Great Britain, and the Netherlands.

RELATIONS WITH MEXICO

As stated previously, President Burnet and Santa Anna on May 14, 1836, signed the Treaty of Velasco which specified that Mexican troops were to be withdrawn south of the Rio Grande, and that the boundary between the two countries would be established by a later treaty, but the territory of Texas should not extend beyond the Rio Grande. The Mexican Congress, however, on May 20 rejected the Treaty of Velasco and announced that it intended to subdue the rebellious Texans. President Houston, convinced that Mexico was too involved in internal difficulties to carry out the threat, furloughed most of the army.

When Lamar became president in December 1838, Mexico's threatening attitude seemed likely to lead to war. Aware of this possibility, Lamar in his first message to Congress stated: "If peace can only be obtained by the sword, let the sword do its work." He would, however, meet with alacrity any move for peace. Indeed, he sought to secure some understanding with Mexico on satisfactory terms. To this end he sent three different agents to Mexico and solicited and secured the diplomatic aid of the United States and Great Britain, all to no avail.

Conditions seemed propitious. France, in order to enforce the collection of her subjects' claims against Mexico resorted to arms (the Pastry War) and kept Mexican ports blockaded for the greater part of 1838 and until March 1839. Anastacio Bustamante, again in power, was a weak executive, and the Federalists in several northern states were defying his government.

Lamar sent Secretary of State Barnard E. Bee to Mexico in May 1839 with authority to offer the Mexican government as much as $5,000,000 if it would recognize Texan independence and the Rio Grande as a boundary. Richard Pakenham, British Minister to Mexico, supported the Texan cause, but to no avail. Bee never got beyond Vera Cruz and did not accomplish anything of consequence. In November 1839 James Treat arrived in Mexico City as the confidential agent of the Texan government. He remained there ten months while the Mexicans gave him just enough encouragement to keep him from leaving. The most important factor in changing the attitude of the Mexicans was the Texas navy, contracted for by the Houston administration and delivered in the spring of 1840. Under its commander, Edwin Ward Moore, it was cruising the Gulf by June and threatening Mexican shipping and Mexican ports. It was well, thought the Mexicans, to continue to encourage Treat as long as his presence would keep the Texas fleet from their ports.

When at last Treat left without accomplishing anything, Lamar recommended war to compel Mexico to recognize Texas. Congress, however, took no action. Then came news of the second treaty of November 1840, whereby Great Britain agreed to mediate between Mexico and Texas, and if successful, Texas would assume $5,000,000 of the Mexican foreign debt to protect the British subjects who held Mexican bonds.

Following the ratification of this treaty, Lamar early in 1841 sent his last emissary, Secretary of State James Webb, to Mexico. Despite pressure exerted by Pakenham the Mexicans refused to receive him, and in June he returned to urge his government to begin hostilities immediately. Lamar then entered into an alliance with the Mexican State of Yucatán, then in revolt against the central government, whereby the government of Yucatán agreed to help maintain the Texan navy. But the alliance proved of little consequence because shortly after it was made Yucatán renewed its allegiance to Mexico.

Mexico's smouldering malice was fanned into active hostility by the expansionist efforts of the Texans. Like many of his contemporaries, Lamar dreamed of a Republic of Texas extending westward to the Pacific. He gave first attention, however, to the territory actually claimed under the terms of the law passed by the First Congress, which fixed the boundary on the south and west at the Rio Grande. He sought to promote trade with the settlements along the Rio Grande, but such an arrangement was not practicable at that time. Several colonizing schemes were given more or less serious consideration. The most important was the Franco-Texienne Company bill, which would have authorized the introduction of 8,000 French families to be located in such a way as to create a shield between the hostile Indians and the outermost Texan settlers. It would have created a semiautonomous state on the border, threatening the unity of Texas. The bill passed the house of representatives, having the support of Sam Houston, then a member of that body, but it was defeated in the senate, probably because of Lamar's opposition.

On the east side of the upper Rio Grande was the major part of the settlements that had long composed the Spanish province and later the Mexican territory of New Mexico. These communities came within the jurisdiction of Texas as defined so generously by Congress, and Lamar proposed to occupy them. His resolution was strengthened by reports from that country that the hold of the Mexican government was weak and that the people desired a union with Texas. After Congress had refused to authorize the expedition, President Lamar, on his own responsibility, proceeded to raise and equip it. At his invitation merchants with a supply of goods made up a caravan to go along, and Lamar bid the party adieu at its camp near Austin on June 21, 1841. Colonel Hugh McLeod commanded the military escort of 270 men and William G. Cooke, ex-senator José Antonio Navarro, and Dr. Richard F. Brenham went along as commissioners of the Texan government. William G. Dryden, a citizen of Santa Fé who had been in touch with Lamar, was to act with the commissioners after the expedition reached New Mexico. They were instructed to take possession of Santa Fé and to set up a government under the authority of Texas. If Mexican troops should oppose them, they were to use force, but only in case they were convinced that the mass of the people opposed the troops and favored the Texans. In fairness to Lamar, it is well to remember that the best information he could secure indicated that the force would be welcome.

The story of the expedition was written by George Wilkins Kendall, editor of the New Orleans *Picayune*, who went with the party for an outing. The vacation he had anticipated turned out to be a desperate experience with heat, hunger, thirst, wild Indians, and cruel Mexicans; his narrative is a classic in travel and adventure. Misfortune dogged the trail of the party as it traveled 1,300 miles, first northward to present-day Wichita Falls, and then northwestward by way of Quitaque to arrive in New Mexico exhausted and at the mercy of the Mexicans. The survivors were made prisoners and marched in most brutal fashion to Mexico City and thence to Perote and other prisons, where they were confined until April 1842.

In the Texan Santa Fé Expedition Lamar had sown the wind and it was for Houston, his successor, to reap the whirlwind. Partly because he did not wish Mexico's claim on Texas to expire by limitation and partly in retaliation at the ambitious move of the Texans, Santa Anna sent an army into Texas in March 1842. The invaders took San Antonio, Goliad, and Refugio, but retired after a day or two, having done little damage. The most unfortunate result was the panic which the affair caused in West Texas, resembling the "runaway scrape" of 1836. President Houston declared a public emergency and ordered the archives of the government removed to Houston. The citizens of Austin refused to permit their removal, thus creating the comical and yet grim "archive war."

The Republic had no regular army, but the militia by the hundreds rushed to San Antonio, and Houston sent W. H. Daingerfield as agent to the United States to secure men, money, and supplies for the invasion of Mexico. He called Congress to assemble at Houston on June 27, delaying the call, as he stated in confidential communications, because he could not "trust their wisdom" in the crisis. When Congress met, it voted for a declaration of war and appropriated ten million acres of land to meet the expense. Houston, determined to avoid a war if possible, wisely pronounced this amount totally inadequate and vetoed the bill.

There was another invasion in September 1842 when General Adrian Woll held San Antonio nine days before retiring on September 20 with a number of prisoners, including a district judge and other officials. Again the militia was called out and began to form up at San Antonio. About the middle of November, 750 men under the leadership of General Alexander Somervell started for Laredo. They took that town on December 8, after which a part of the force disbanded and returned home. The remainder then marched down the Rio Grande until December 19, when Somervell ordered them to retire to Gonzales.

About 300 of the men refused to obey Somervell's orders, organized under Colonel W. S. Fisher, and marched to Mier on the south side of the Rio Grande. There, after a desperate battle with General Pedro Ampudia, they surrendered on December 26. Then followed their march as prisoners into Mexico, their break for liberty, their recapture, and the drawing of the black beans to determine which of their number should compose the one tenth who were to be shot. The survivors were finally imprisoned in the dank Castle Perote with the men of the Texas Santa Fé Expedition and the prisoners from San Antonio who had been taken away by Woll. After many months of confinement they were released by Santa Anna, partly because of the efforts in their behalf of Waddy Thompson, United States Minister to Mexico.

Another Texan expedition against the Mexicans at this time ended only a little less tragically than that against Mier. In the spring of 1843 Colonel Jacob Snively organized a force of 180 men in North Texas and by authority of the president led it to the Santa Fé Trail in an attempt to seize rich Mexican caravans going from Missouri to Santa Fé across North Texas. The leader and a part of his men were captured and disarmed by an escort of United States troops that accompanied the train. Since the seizure was on Texan soil, the government on its demand was reimbursed for the arms taken.

While resisting the popular clamor for war against Mexico, Houston was exerting every effort to secure peace and the recognition of independence. After Woll's invasion in 1842, he urged the governments of Great Britain, France, and the United States to "require of Mexico either the recognition of the Independence of Texas, or to make war upon her according to the rules established and universally recognized by civilized nations." A month later Waddy Thompson, United States chargé in Mexico, urged recognition and offered the good services of the United States in the interest of peace. Nothing came directly through these efforts; but early in 1843 Santa Anna released James W. Robinson, formerly lieutenant governor of Texas, from Castle Perote and sent him to Texas to open negotiations with that government. Robinson conveyed to Houston Santa Anna's offer of peace if Texas would recognize Mexican sovereignty. Houston had no intention of accepting the offer, but it gave him an opportunity to bargain and to play for time while he corresponded with the Mexicans through British diplomatic agents. He proclaimed a truce on June 14, 1843, and both nations later appointed commissioners who signed an armistice on the following February 15. A revival of the movement to annex Texas to the United States, however, brought an end to this armistice four months later.

ANNEXATION ACHIEVED

Perhaps the most important result of the ill-fated Santa Fé and Mier expeditions was that they greatly augmented the interest of the people of the United States in Texas. The result was to revive the subject of Texan annexation which had been dormant since 1838. Houston had sounded the United States government on the subject in March 1842, when his appointee, James Reily, succeeded Barnard Bee as *chargé d'affaires* at Washington. The United States did not respond at the time, but fear of growing British influence caused President John Tyler on October 15, 1843, to open negotiations for annexation by treaty. After John C. Calhoun, who became Tyler's secretary of state in March 1844, gave assurances that the United States would provide protection pending annexation, Houston assented to negotiate a treaty. The treaty was signed on April 12, 1844, by Isaac Van Zandt and J. Pinckney Henderson, who represented Texas, and Calhoun, who represented the United States. On June 8, the Senate of the United States rejected it. Certain slaveholding factions joined free soilers in opposing it. Furthermore, the uncertainty as to the attitude of the public and the disinclination of the senators to make such an important decision on the eve of a national election contributed to its defeat.

Then the subject of annexation went before the American people in the political campaign of that year. Van Buren, the leading Democratic candidate, lost the nomination to James K. Polk, a "dark horse," because he refused to endorse annexation. In the election James K. Polk defeated Henry Clay, the Whig nominee, who opposed immediate annexation.

President Tyler interpreted Polk's election as a mandate from the people for immediate annexation. In December he placed the subject before Congress, and on February 28, 1845, that body passed a joint resolution providing for annexation. Its terms were (1) Texas should become a state in the American Union, if its people approved the step before January 1, 1846, with all questions with other governments concerning its boundary to be adjusted by the United States; (2) the state, when admitted, should cede to the United States its public property, except its public lands which were to be retained and applied so far as necessary to the payment of its debts; (3) as many as four additional states might by the consent of Texas be formed out of its territory, slavery to be prohibited in any state created north of parallel 36°30′. A supplementary provision authorized the President, should he prefer, to withhold the joint resolution proposal and negotiate in its stead another treaty of annexation.

Tyler signed the joint resolution on March 1, and through his agent, Andrew Jackson Donelson, promptly submitted the offer to the Texan government. James K. Polk, who was inaugurated President on the day after instructions had been sent to Donelson, also pressed the offer on Texas and urged that there be no delay. Indeed, it was now the American government's turn to be anxious about the subject, while Jones and his colleagues could be tantalizingly independent.

England and France opposed annexation and sought to maintain an independent Texas. Captain Charles Elliot and Count de Saligny, representing England and France respectively, induced President Jones on March 29 not to commit the government for ninety days, during which Elliot should go to Mexico and secure a treaty guaranteeing Texan independence on the condition that the Republic agree never to unite with the United States. Meanwhile, Jones called Congress to meet on June 16. Public sentiment for annexation was so overwhelming, however, that the president realized he could not delay action. The terms of the joint resolution required that Texas accept the offer through a convention elected for that purpose.

Without waiting for Congress to assemble, Jones issued on May 5 a call for a convention to meet in Austin on July 4. When Congress convened, he submitted to it both the proposal of annexation to the United States and the preliminary treaty with Mexico which Elliot had secured on May 19 and rushed to Washington on the Brazos, the capital at that time. Congress rejected the Mexican treaty, unanimously recommended the acceptance of the offer by the United States, approved the president's proclamation calling for the election of delegates to a convention, and adjourned. The convention then met on July 4, adopted with one dissenting vote an ordinance accepting the terms of annexation, and spent some two months in drawing up a state constitution. On October 13, the voters approved annexation and ratified the constitution by a vote of 4,254 to 257 and 4,174 to 312, respectively.

The constitution was accepted by Congress, and President Polk on December 29, 1845, signed the act that made Texas one of the United States of America.

At a special election on December 15 new state officials were named, and on February 19, 1846, at a ceremony in front of the Texas capitol, President Jones relinquished executive authority to Governor J. P. Henderson. In concluding his address Jones uttered the memorable words: "The final act in this great drama is now performed; the Republic of Texas is no more."

Selected Bibliography

Of the older general histories which have been previously cited, good accounts of the Republic of Texas are included in H.H. Bancroft, J.H. Brown, W. Kennedy, H. Yoakum, H.S. Thrall, L.J. Wortham, and F.W. Johnson. The best recent account is S.V. Connor, *Adventure in Glory* (Austin, 1965). Emphasizing certain phases are William R. Hogan, *The Texas Republic: A Social and Economic History* (Norman, 1946); Stanley Siegel, *Political History of the Texas Republic, 1836–1845* (Austin, 1956); Joseph Schmitz, *Texan Statecraft, 1836–1845* (San Antonio, 1941); E.T. Miller, *A Financial History of Texas* (Austin, 1916); and Edward M. Neusinger, "The Monetary History of the Republic of Texas," *Southwestern Historical Quarterly*, LVII, 82–90; Anson Jones, *Memoranda and Official Correspondence Relating to the Republic of Texas, Its History and Annexation, Including a Brief Autobiography of the Author* (Chicago, 1966); W.P. Webb, *The Great Plains* (New York, 1931).

The best biographies of the period are those of Sam Houston, previously cited; A.K. Christian, "Mirabeau B. Lamar," *Southwestern Historical Quarterly*, XXIII, 153–170, 231–270; XXIV, 39–80, 87–139, 195–234, 317–324; H.P. Gambrell, *Mirabeau Bonaparte Lamar*; H.P. Gambrell, *Anson Jones*; John N. Cravens, *James Harper Star: Financier of the Republic of Texas* (Austin, 1950); Joe B. Frantz, *Gail Borden, Dairyman to a Nation* (Norman, 1951); and E. Wallace, *Charles De-Morse: Pioneer Editor and Statesman*. Useful also are John J. Linn, *Reminiscences of Fifty Years in Texas* (New York, 1883); and *A Biographical Directory of Texas Congresses and Conventions* (Austin, 1941).

On domestic affairs the following are useful: W.P. Johnston,

The Life of General Albert Sidney Johnston (New York, 1878); Charles P. Roland, *Albert Sidney Johnston: Soldier of Three Republics* (Austin, 1964); Mary A. Maverick, *Memoirs* (San Antonio, 1921); W.P. Webb, *The Texas Rangers* (Boston, 1935); A.F. Muir (ed.), *Texas in 1837: An Anonymous Contemporary Narrative* (Austin, 1958); J. Schmitz, *Texas Culture in the Days of the Republic, 1836–1846* (San Antonio, 1960); Tom Henderson Wells, *Commodore Moore and the Texas Navy* (Austin, 1960); Edmund Travis, "When Austin Became the Capital," and other short articles on related subjects in the *Texas Weekly*, May 30 and June 20, 1936; E.W. Winkler, "The Seat of Government of Texas," *Quarterly of the Texas State Historical Association*, X, 140–171, 185–245; E.W. Winkler, "The Cherokee Indians in Texas," *ibid.*, VII, 94–165; D.H. Winfrey, "The Texan Archives War of 1842," *Southwestern Historical Quarterly*, LXIV, 171–184; G.F. Haugh (ed.), "History of the Texas Navy," *ibid.*, LXIII, 572–579; Anna Muckleroy, "The Indian Policy of the Republic of Texas," *ibid.*, XXV, 229–260; XXVI, 1–29, 128–148, 184–206; Jesse Guy Smith, *Heroes of the Saddlebags* (San Antonio, 1951); W. Eugene Hollon and Ruth L. Butler (eds.), *William Bollaert's Texas* (Norman, 1956); D.H. Winfrey (ed.), *Texas Indian Papers, 1825–1843* (Austin, 1959); D.H. Winfrey (ed.), *Texas Indian Papers, 1844–1845* (Austin, 1960).

Sources and specialized studies relating to the land policy, immigration, *empresario* contracts, and extension of settlement are numerous. On these subjects, county and regional histories are essential, and indispensable for their effective use is H.B. Carroll, "Bibliography of Texas Counties," *Southwestern Historical Quarterly*, XLV, 74–98, 260–275, 343–361. Two good works of a regional nature are Lucy A. Erath (ed.), "Memories of Major Bernard Erath," *ibid.*, XXVI, 207–233, 255–280; XXVII, 27–51, 140–163; and James K. Greer, *Grand Prairie* (Dallas, 1935). The best studies on the land policy are Reuben McKitrick, *The Public Land System of Texas, 1823–1910* (Madison, Wisconsin, 1918); A.S. Lang, *Financial History of the Public Lands in Texas* (Waco, 1932); and Thomas L. Miller, "Texas Land Grants to Veterans," *The Southwestern Historical Quarterly*, XLIV, 342–437.

The best source of information on immigration to Texas is the United States census returns for 1850 and the Texas census of 1847, bound with *Laws Passed by the Second Legislature* (Houston, 1848). There is much information in E.E. Braman, *Braman's Information about Texas* (Philadelphia, 1857); and Jacob DeCordova, *Texas, Her Resources and Public Men* (Philadelphia, 1858). Barnes F. Lathrop's *Migration into East Texas, 1835–1860* (Austin, 1949), is an impressive study. B.M. Jones, "Health Seekers in Early Anglo-American Texas," *Southwestern Historical Quarterly*, LXIX, 287–299, shows that many of the immigrants came to Texas because of their health.

Studies dealing with colonizers, their settlers, and their lands include R.L. Biesele, *The History of the German Settlements in Texas, 1831–1861* (Austin, 1930); S.V. Connor, *The Peters Colony of Texas, A History and Biographical Sketches of the Early Settlers* (Austin, 1959); Irene M. King, *John O. Meusebach, German Colonizer in Texas* (Austin, 1967); Terry G. Jordan, *German Seed in Texas Soil: Immigrant Farmers in the Nineteenth Century* (Austin and London, 1966); S.V. Connor, "A Statistical Review of the Settlement of the Peters Colony, 1841–1848," *Southwestern Historical Quarterly*, LVII, 38–64; Nancy Eagleton, "The Mercer Colony in Texas, 1844–1883," *ibid.*, XXXIX, 275–291; XL, 35–57, 114–144; and Julia N. Waugh, *Castroville and Henry Castro* (San Antonio, 1934). On Lamar's efforts to extend the jurisdiction of Texas over Sante Fé, see W.C. Binkley, *The Expansionist Movement in Texas* (Berkeley, 1925); W.C. Binkley, "New Mexico and the Texan Santa Fé Expedition," *The Southwestern Historical Quarterly*, XXVII, 85–107; George W. Kendall, *Narrative of the Texan Santa Fé Expedition* (London, 1845); H. Bailey Carroll, *The Texan Sante Fé Trail* (Canyon, 1951); N. Loomis, *The Texan-Santa Fé Pioneers* (Norman, 1958).

On foreign relations of the Republic of Texas, the most important source material is G.P. Garrison (ed.), *Texan Diplomatic Correspondence* (3 vols.), in *The Annual Report of the American Historical Association for 1907 and 1908* (2 vols., Washington, 1908 and 1911); the best overall survey is J. Schmitz, *Texan Statecraft*. Valuable studies dealing with special phases of the subject include: E.D. Adams, *British Interests and Activities in Texas* (Baltimore, 1910); J.M. Nance, *After San Jacinto; The Texas-Mexican Frontier, 1836–1841 (Austin, 1963)*, a comprehensive study; J.M. Nance, *Attack and Counterattack: the Texas-Mexican Frontier* (Austin, 1964), another impressive study; J.H. Smith, *The Annexation of Texas* (New York, 1912), definitive; Milton Lindheim, *The Republic of the Rio Grande; Texas in Mexico, 1839 1840* (Waco, 1964); Thomas J. Green, *Journal of the Texan Expedition against Mier* (New York, 1845); Ethel Z. Rather, "Recognition of the Republic of Texas by the United States," *Quarterly of the Texas State Historical Association*, XIII, 155–256; Annie Middleton, "Donelson's Mission to Texas in Behalf of Annexation," *Southwestern Historical Quarterly*, XXIV, 247–291; E.C. Barker, "The Annexation of Texas," *ibid.*, L, 49–74; Nancy N. Barker, "The Republic of Texas: A French View," *ibid.*, LXXI, 181–193; L.B. Friend (ed.), "Sidelights and Supplements on the Perote Prisoners," *ibid.*, XLVIII, 366–374, 489–496; LXIX, 88–95, 224–230, 377–385, 516–524; Ralph A. Wooster, "Texas Military Operations against Mexico, 1842–1843," *ibid.*, LVII, 465–484; and D.M. Vigness, "Relations of the Republic of Texas and the Republic of the Rio Grande," *ibid.*, LVII, 312–321.

8

EARLY STATEHOOD, 1846–1861

During the decade and a half between the annexation of Texas and its union with the Confederacy, Texas experienced the most rapid growth in its history. Its population increased more than fourfold and its assessed property more than eightfold. That its cultural progress did not keep pace with its material developments was the result of frontier conditions rather than the lack of fine innate qualities in its people.

Many episodes and developments, both impressive and significant, made the period between annexation and the Civil War rich in history. There is, however, no single theme around which these events can be related with continuity. Thus, this chapter has a topical orientation. The establishment of a new constitutional government obviously was a development of lasting influence. Even more significant was the defeat of Mexico and her recognition of the right of Texas to join the American Union and to the Rio Grande as the boundary. The boundary controversy between the United States and Texas over a part of New Mexico developed into a national crisis. Closely associated with the dispute was the settlement of the debt incurred by the Republic of Texas. Political affairs also call for special treatment, for it was during the period that political parties became active, that Union and state rights factions took the place of old party alignments, and that, like an approaching storm, the controversy over slavery and secession grew increasingly ominous. Meanwhile, the army had made extensive explorations across the unknown western part of the state, and immigrant homeseekers, who came year after year in ever increasing numbers, joined with other thousands of land-hungry "old" Texans to push their settlements into the Western Cross Timbers. Finally, the explorations and the intrusion of the whites into the homeland of the Comanche Indians created an Indian problem that taxed the combined efforts of both the federal and state governments until they were interrupted by secession and the Civil War.

THE ESTABLISHMENT OF
STATE GOVERNMENT

The Texas Constitution of 1845 was well designed and well written. Since it was used as a working model by the framers of the Constitution in 1876, it is in a measure still the fundamental law of the state. Its framers probably constituted the ablest assembly that has ever served the state. Thomas Jefferson Rusk, its president, had made substantial contributions to the Constitution of 1836. J. Pinckney Henderson had served in Houston's cabinet and as minister to England and France, and Isaac Van Zandt had been a member of the Texas Congress and later was sent as minister to the United States. R. E. B. Baylor, a jurist of superior ability, had also served in the Congress of the United States from Alabama. N. H. Darnell had been speaker of the Texas house of representatives; Abner S. Lipscomb had studied law in the office of John C. Calhoun and had been chief justice in Alabama; and Hiram G. Runnels had been governor of Mississippi. José Antonio Navarro, a member of the Convention of 1836, was the only native Texan. Tennessee contributed eighteen members, Virginia eight, Georgia seven, Kentucky six, and North Carolina five.

The framers drew extensively from the Louisiana constitution, which had just been completed, and to some extent from the fundamental laws of other states. Their own Texas Constitution of 1836 seems, however, to have been used as a working model. The governor was to be chosen by the voters for a term of two years, but was not eligible to serve more than four out of six years. Subject to the approval of the senate, the governor should appoint the secretary of state, attorney general, the three justices of the supreme court, and district judges. The comptroller and treasurer were to be chosen by the legislature. Thus, of state officers, only the governor, lieutenant governor, and members of the legislature were elected by the voters. In 1850, however, the state took a long step toward the unwieldy ballot of our own day by providing for the popular election of the attorney general, comptroller, and treasurer.

Under the Republic, the lawmakers had met annually, but the new constitution called for biennial sessions. Representatives should serve two years and should be apportioned among the several districts according to the number of free inhabitants. Senators were to be apportioned on the basis of the number of qualified electors and should serve four years. From the old constitution was carried over the prohibition against ministers of the gospel holding a seat in the legislature. The instrument disqualified from holding public office any person who might thereafter participate in a duel either as principal or as second.

Hostility toward corporations, so prevalent in that day, took the form of requiring a two-thirds vote of both houses to create any kind of a private corporation and forbidding the incorporation of any bank. It was required that all property be taxed in proportion to its value, except such as the legislature might exempt by a two-thirds vote, and that the aggregate amount of debt which the legislature might incur should not exceed $100,000. Married women were made secure in their right to their separate property. Exemption from foreclosure of homesteads not in excess of two hundred acres was allowed.

The election of officers for the new state was held on December 15, 1845. On that day J. Pinckney Henderson was chosen governor over Dr. James B. Miller by an overwhelming vote, and for lieutenant governor Albert C. Horton beat N. H. Darnell by a slender majority. On receiving information that President Polk had signed the act admitting Texas, President Jones called the legislature to assemble in Austin on February 16, 1846, for the purpose of organizing a state government. Three days later in a formal ceremony Jones officially transferred the government to the newly elected state officials.

Governor Henderson promptly named John Hemphill chief justice of the state supreme court, and the first legislature elected Thomas J. Rusk and Sam Houston to the United States Senate. To Houston fell the short term; he was twice reelected. Rusk also was reelected and served until his death in 1857.

Changes and adjustments incident to the transition from republic to state consumed much of the efforts of officers in Texas during Henderson's administration. The postal system was taken over by the United States; and arms, building, and other public property were transferred to the general government.

THE WAR WITH MEXICO

The War with Mexico, which grew out of the annexation of Texas, concerned the people of Texas vitally. As soon as it was evident that Texas would accept the offer of annexation, General Zachary Taylor was ordered with a strong force of United States troops to establish his headquarters at Corpus Christi. Corpus Christi was at the mouth of the Nueces River, the stream that had been set by the Spaniards as the boundary between Texas and Nuevo Santander and which the Mexicans contended was still the boundary. The Republic of Texas, however, by legislative act had designated the Rio Grande as her southern and western boundary, and President Polk supported her claim. When the information reached Polk that the Mexican government had refused to negotiate with his emissary, John Slidell, who had been authorized to obligate the United States to assume the claims of its citizens against Mexico up to $5,000,000 in exchange for recognition of the Rio Grande as the boundary, he decided to call on Congress to declare war and ordered Taylor to move to the Rio Grande. Taylor's movements to the Rio Grande aroused the Mexicans, who sent troops north of that stream. There was a skirmish on April 24, and on May 8 and 9 contingents of American troops clashed with the Mexicans at Palo Alto and Resaca de la Palma, in the general vicinity of Brownsville. Congress, on the basis that Mexico had "shed American blood on American soil," declared war on May 13. Taylor immediately opened an offensive to drive the Mexican forces toward Monterrey. He asked Governor Henderson for two regiments of infantry and two of cavalry, and the legislature gave the governor a leave of absence to take command of the Texan troops who might be mustered into the service of the United States.

In the campaign a number of Texans won distinction. One organization, that of John C. (Jack) Hays, made up largely of old rangers and commanded by such men as Ben McCulloch and Samuel H. Walker, attained renown. Approximately 5,000 Texans were in military service during the war. In the treaty of Guadalupe Hidalgo on February 2, 1848, which ended the war, Mexico recognized the independence of Texas and accepted the Rio Grande as the boundary. She also ceded to the United States for a payment of $15,000,000 the provinces of New Mexico and upper California. The Texas claim to that part of New Mexico east of the Rio Grande soon created a national crisis.

THE TEXAS–NEW MEXICO BOUNDARY CONTROVERSY

It will be recalled that by an act of December 19, 1836, the Texas Congress claimed as the southern and western boundary of the Republic the Rio Grande from mouth to source and thence a line running northward to the 42nd parallel. The claim was exceedingly ambitious. It took in a vast stretch of territory not included in the Texas of Spanish and Mexican days; it cut into the Mexican states of Tamaulipas and Coahuila, according to their boundaries as they had been drawn by the old Spanish decrees of 1805 and 1811; it included territory claimed by the State of Chihuahua; and it proposed to attach to Texas the capital and most of the principal settlements of New Mexico. It was founded in part on the treaty of Velasco made with the prisoner Santa Anna on May 14, 1836, which mentioned the Rio Grande in an indefinite manner. The only other basis for the claim was that of the right of a victorious people to take as much territory of the defeated nation as possible.

The Texans had made no settlements of consequence beyond the Nueces River; efforts to establish commercial relations with settlements along the lower Rio Grande had failed; and the expedition sent to assert jurisdiction over the Santa Fé country had met with disastrous failure.

It will be recalled that the joint resolution of annexation provided that the United States would adjust all questions of boundary that might arise with other governments. A certain amount of recognition was given the Texan claim in the provision that if the state should ever be divided, slavery should not exist in the part of the territory north of parallel 36°30′. President Polk, furthermore, gave assurances that the United States would not allow the Texan rights to the territory to be sacrificed. Also, on December 31, 1845, the United States established a customs district including Corpus Christi and the territory to the west of the Nueces, which was tantamount to recognizing the claims of the state to the region between the Nueces and the Rio Grande.

The War with Mexico soon brought a series of developments that complicated the question of the territorial rights of Texas. In August 1846 Stephen W. Kearny, in command of the Army of the West, occupied New Mexico and established a civil government there with the approval of his superiors and without regard to the claims of Texas. On June 4, 1847, Governor Henderson reminded Secretary of State James Buchanan of the Texan claims. Buchanan replied by stating that the question would have to be settled by Congress, but he assured the governor that the temporary civil government would not affect the claim which, he believed, Texas justly asserted to all territory east of the Rio Grande. Their fears thus quieted, the Texans awaited the outcome of the war.

The treaty of Guadalupe Hidalgo, ratified by the Senate of the United States on March 10, 1848, made the lower Rio Grande the international boundary and put an end to the claims of the Mexican states to territory north and east of that river. Since all of New Mexico was ceded to the United States, the treaty did not in any way settle the claims of Texas to a part of New Mexico. The Texans expected that with the ratification of the treaty all territory east of the Rio Grande would be turned over to them. Meanwhile, the question of the extension of slavery was injected into the subject. The Wilmot Proviso, introduced in Congress, would have prohibited slavery in any territory acquired by the United States as a result of the War with Mexico. Although the proviso was not adopted, it united the men of the South in a determination to open to slavery any territory that might be organized out of the Mexican Cession. The free-soil men soon became aligned against the extreme claims of Texas. If the boundaries the state claimed were permitted to stand, slave soil thus would extend at least as far westward as the Rio Grande. Divided between these two factions, Congress found itself unable to pass any laws whatever concerning New Mexico.

Texas, however, acted promptly and decisively. Its legislature, by an act of March 15, 1848, created Santa Fé County with boundaries including practically all of that part of New Mexico which it claimed; and five days later it voted to ask the United States to sustain through its army the state officers who were to be sent there. Judge Spruce M. Baird was dispatched to organize the new county and to serve as its judge. Far from sustaining the Texan judge, the military and certain civilian leaders conspired to oppose him and used the press to excite the people against him. Just before his arrival, in November 1848, a convention was held at Santa Fé, and petitions were adopted asking that New Mexico be created a territory. On his arrival Baird was informed by Colonel John M. Washington, commanding officer at Santa Fé, that he would sustain the government established in New Mexico by General Kearny "at every peril" until ordered to desist either by the executive or the legislative power of the United States. Baird left the territory for Missouri in July 1849.

Whatever chance the Texans had for securing the support of the federal forces in New Mexico vanished with the end of Polk's administration on March 4, 1849. President Taylor favored granting statehood both to California and New Mexico.

Meanwhile the press and the officials of Texas were growing restive over the situation. In November Governor George T. Wood suggested to the legislature that Texas assert its claim "with the whole power and resources of the state," but neither the governor nor the legislature took any decisive action. Then Peter Hansborough Bell, who had defeated Wood in 1849 by advocating a more aggressive policy regarding the disputed territory, urged that the legislature send to New Mexico a force sufficient to maintain the authority of Texas. In response, the legislature, on December 31, designated new boundaries for Santa Fé County, and created three additional counties to the south of it between the Pecos and the Rio Grande. Then by authority of an act passed four days later, another commissioner, Robert S. Neighbors, was sent to organize the counties. Neighbors went armed with an address by the governor to the citizens of the four counties urging them to lend him such "assistance and protection" as might be necessary. He organized El Paso County without meeting with resistance; but on arriving in New Mexico he found the majority of the people antagonistic and the military not disposed to aid him. The people, moreover, soon were absorbed in efforts to organize a state government for New Mexico, and President Taylor opposed the Texan efforts. Neighbors thereupon returned to Texas, and his report to the governor, made public early in June 1850, caused great excitement. At mass meetings in Austin and other places there were protests, threats of secession, and proposals that the state assert its claim by military force. Governor Bell angrily demanded of President Taylor an explanation of the course the federal government was pursuing in New Mexico and called a special session of the legislature to meet on August 12.

Before the legislature assembled the situation had become even more critical. The people of New Mexico had adopted a constitution for their proposed state with boundaries so extended as to include most of the disputed territory and also some territory unquestionably Texan. President Taylor had died, and his successor, Millard Fillmore, reinforced the army in New Mexico and stated flatly that he would send troops against the Texas militiamen if they attempted to occupy the country. Fillmore did, however, favor a settlement of the controversy and threw the support of his office behind the compromise measures then before Congress. After assembling in August, the legislature heard the governor's message declaring that Texas must assert its rights "*at all hazards and to the last extremity,*" and debated measures to organize the militia and send it into New Mexico.

The crisis finally was brought to an end by the action of Congress. As Congress grappled with the problem, one plan after another was considered and modified or discarded. Gradually sentiment for purchasing a part of the territory at a reasonable price and confirming the claims of Texas to the remainder gained ground. At last the bill written by James A. Pearce of Maryland, which had the support of the entire Texas delegation and of moderate men North and South, was accepted by the Senate and passed by the House on September 6. It fixed the northern and western boundary of Texas as it now stands, providing that it should begin at the intersection of the 100th meridian and the parallel of 36°30′, run west along that parallel to the 103rd meridian, follow that to the 32nd parallel, extend along that parallel to the Rio Grande, and follow that stream to its mouth. Texas was to renounce all claims to territory beyond the boundaries described, for which it would be paid $10,000,000. As amended before final passage, the bill provided for the organization of the Territory of New Mexico. It was one of a series of laws known as the Compromise of 1850.

At first there was considerable sentiment in Texas against accepting the proposition; but a majority of the voters seemed to take the

Peter H. Bell, a native of Virginia, fought at San Jacinto, was a Texas ranger, and fought under General Zachary Taylor in the War with Mexico. He was governor of Texas from 1849 to 1853, and in the controversy that developed over the claims of Texas to the Rio Grande as its western boundary he represented the state's interests with force and energy. (E. C. Barker History Center, University of Texas)

point of view of the La Grange *Monument* that, although the measure was not all the state desired, it was "doubtful whether ten years' trading would give Texas a better bargain than she can now make." At a special election the voters accepted the proposition by a majority of two to one, the legislature in special session approved it, and Governor Bell signed the act of acceptance on November 25, 1850.

SETTLEMENT OF THE
DEBT OF THE REPUBLIC

It will be recalled that according to the joint resolution of annexation, the public lands of Texas were to be used, so far as was necessary, for the settlement of the public debt of Texas. The debt was complex in nature and created considerable ill will against the general government because of the terms of the boundary act. It consisted of two major types of obligations, nonrevenue debt and revenue debt. The nonrevenue debt was made up of the claims of participants in the Texan Revolution or suppliers of the Texas army, nearly all representing at most a few hundred dollars each. The revenue debt consisted of principal and interest owed to holders of Republic of Texas securities. Under the terms of the boundary act, as interpreted by United States officers, the revenue debts were preferred obligations, for which import duties of the old Texan government had been pledged as security. To make sure that these were paid, the federal government retained $5,000,000 in bonds. The state soon paid the ordinary or nonrevenue debt out of the $5,000,000 delivered to it and had about $3,750,000 in bonds left.

The revenue debt, however, was slowly paid. The state proposed to scale the debt, to which many creditors objected; some creditors neglected to file their claims, and the United States officials would not pay any claims until all were in. Final settlement was made by an act of February 28, 1855. Congress estimated that the bonds held for Texas together with accrued interest amounted to $6,500,000. It added to this amount $1,250,000 to reimburse Texas for damages resulting from depredations committed by Indians of the United States in Texas since 1836; thus, there was a total of $7,750,000 in cash to be distributed *pro rata* among the creditors who had not yet been paid. The legislature accepted the offer in February 1856. The $7,750,000 prorated among the holders of the $10,078,703 revenue debt gave each creditor about 77 cents on the dollar. The state contended that such scaling was equitable since the Republic had not received par value for the obligations at the time they were issued.

Of the $3,750,000 in bonds that remained after the nonrevenue debt had been paid, $2,000,000 was set aside as an endowment for the public schools, the greater part of which amount was, in turn, loaned to railroads to aid construction. For six years, beginning with 1852, the state remitted to the counties nine-tenths of its taxes. The constitution required that the remaining tenth be applied to the use of the schools. The counties, in turn, used the remitted tax money for the construction of public buildings and various other purposes. Thus, Texas was able to endow its public schools, promote internal improvements, construct public buildings, and maintain all the while a very low tax rate.

STATE POLITICS DURING THE ERA

While Governor Henderson was commanding Texas troops during the Mexican War, Lieutenant Governor Horton served as governor. Henderson returned in November 1846 and resumed his duties as chief executive. He declined to run for reelection and was succeeded on December 21, 1847, by George T. Wood, a Trinity River planter who had gained popularity as commander of a regiment of volunteers in the campaign against Monterrey. Wood's vote was substantially greater than that of his leading opponent, Dr. J. B. Miller. The chief objects of public attention during the Wood administration were frontier defense, the public debt, and the claims of Texas to the disputed territory east of the Rio Grande. While Wood was governor, Texans for the first time participated in an election for president of the United States. They supported Lewis Cass, the Democratic candidate. Wood was a candidate again in 1849, but was defeated by Peter Hansborough Bell. Wood charged his defeat to the indifferent support given his candidacy by Senator Houston. The anti-Houston forces, among them J. P. Henderson and William B. Ochiltree, opposed him actively. The fact that his opponent advocated a more aggressive policy in asserting Texas' claims to a part of New Mexico may account also for Wood's defeat.

Bell was a veteran of San Jacinto and of the War with Mexico. The first term of his administration was marked by the crisis over the Texas-New Mexico boundary, the exploration of routes across Texas, the establishment of a line of military posts along the frontier, and a popular mandate to keep the capital at Austin. In his campaign for reelection in 1851, the growing jealousy of the South over state rights was reflected. None of his opponents—John A. Greer, M. T. Johnson, T. J. Chambers, or B. H. Epperson (who ran as a Whig)— was in sympathy with the abolitionists, but Bell was known as the most pro-Southern of them all. Subjects of general interest in Bell's second administration were the scaling and paying of the public debt; the land claims of certain emigrant agents and their colonists, growing out of contracts made during the period of the Republic; and frontier defense. Bell's firm stand against the United States, his aggressive frontier policy, and most of his other measures in general met with public approval. A few weeks before the expiration of his second term, Bell resigned to fill the vacancy in Congress caused by the death of David S. Kaufman.

In 1853 several candidates sought to be governor. W. B. Ochiltree, a Whig, expected to win because of a large personal following. To secure the defeat of Ochiltree, M. T. Johnson and another candidate, J. W. Henderson, withdrew and urged their followers to support Elisha M. Pease. Thus Pease, an "old" Texan, especially popular in the southern and western part of the state, was elected.

Pease's platform called for founding a public school system, encouraging internal improvements, and removing the Indians from Texas. The most important act of his administration was the school law of 1854. By its terms the state set aside $2,000,000 of the indemnity bonds which it had acquired from the United States in the settlement of 1850 as a permanent endowment for public schools. Income from the fund was distributed each year on a per capita basis to supplement the receipts from the one-tenth of the annual revenues which the constitution had reserved for the schools. The legislature set aside $100,000 of the United States bonds for endowment of a university, but the proceeds later were absorbed in the state revenue fund. A number of charters were granted to railroad companies, and two Indian reservations were authorized by the legislature.

The Pease Mansion was built by Elisha Marshall Pease, a New England Yankee who came to Texas in 1835 and settled in Bastrop (then called Mina). An outspoken advocate of independence, Pease was a member of the Committee of Safety in Mina and took part in the convention of 1836. Under his administration as governor (1853–57) railroads were encouraged, taxes reduced, the state debt paid off, the state university planned, and a new capitol erected. A Unionist, Pease was appointed provisional governor again in 1867, but resigned because of disagreements over Reconstruction. (Texas Highway Department)

The Pease era is also important in politics because of the rise of political parties in the state and the beginning of party nominations by conventions. No party delineation existed during the Republic and but little during the first years of statehood. Voters generally aligned themselves with the Houston or the anti-Houston leaders. As early as May 1846 an effort was made to organize the Democratic Party, but without results. Both the Whigs and the Democrats held conventions from time to time, but the attendance was slender. The Democratic Convention of 1855 drew delegates from only 12 counties. Shortly after it adjourned, however, a new rival organization, mysterious and baffling in its tactics, came into existence.

Resentment at the powerful political influence wielded by foreigners, especially Irish, had inspired on the Atlantic seaboard a strong nativist movement. Organized initially in a series of secret societies, the followers soon merged into the American or Know-Nothing Party. The new party opposed foreigners holding office and was decidedly anti-Catholic and pro-Union. It obtained many of its followers from the disintegrating Whig Party. First appearing in Texas in 1854, it elected that year a complete slate of city officers at San Antonio. In the following spring its candidate was elected mayor of Galveston, and several newspapers were carrying articles in its support. Under the guise of a river improvement convention, the Know-Nothings met in a convention at Washington on the Brazos, June 11 to 13, agreed on a slate of candidates headed by Lieutenant Governor D. C. Dickson, formed a state organization with R. E. B. Baylor as "grand president," and made plans to extend the order to every community through "subordinate councils" and "committees of vigilance." It got a major boost when Houston publicly expressed sympathy with the aims of the organization.

In less than a week after the Washington convention, the editor of the *State Gazette,* the principal Democratic organ, called a "bombshell" meeting of Democrats at Austin. This gathering denounced all secret political factions, and pledged its support to Pease for governor and H. R. Runnels for lieutenant governor. This meeting gave wide publicity to the Know-Nothing secret convention and drew the line of cleavage between that group and the Democrats. Other Democratic contestants for governor were persuaded to withdraw to avoid splitting the party vote. During a hard-fought campaign Dickson severely attacked the governor for his espousal of the "state plan" for building railroads, his alleged hostility toward the proposed Pacific railroad, and his failure to protect the frontier. Pease beat Dickson by a substantial majority, but the Know-Nothings managed to elect about twenty representatives and five senators to the state legislature. It was stated that the Know-Nothing order supported Lemuel D. Evans, who was elected to Congress, but Evans denied any connection with the party.

In 1856 the Know-Nothing Party held a state convention, open to the public, but its distintegration was by that time clearly evident, and it passed soon out of existence. Its most important effect was to force the Democrats to perfect their party organization and to adopt the practice of nominating candidates by conventions. When the Democrats convened to nominate candidates and select presidential electors, 91 out of 99 counties were represented. With candidates for governor, lieutenant governor, and commissioner of the general land office to be nominated attendance was even better the next year. That convention named Hardin R. Runnels, a wealthy planter of Bowie County, candidate for governor, and Francis R. Lubbock, who had been an active party worker, for lieutenant governor.

Of greater importance even than party alignments was the distinct cleavage that appeared between the Houston and anti-Houston factions. More and more the Houston group referred to themselves as Jackson Democrats or Unionists, while the opposition was often called Calhoun Democrats. Since 1836 Sam Houston twice had been president of the Republic and thrice United States senator. His record had been the subject of both praise and blame, but his supremacy had never been successfully challenged. He antagonized the extreme proslavery leaders in 1848 by voting for the creation of the free-soil territory of Oregon and by refusing to sign John C. Calhoun's protest against what he termed the aggression of the free states. The speeches and debates of Houston and of Rusk (whose record was only slightly less offensive than Houston's to the pro-Southern extremists) created much excitement in Texas in 1849. Then Houston's vote against the Kansas-Nebraska bill (the bill that opened to slavery territory that had been closed to it by the Missouri Compromise) was regarded as treason to the South. His affiliation with the Know-Nothing movement in 1855 likewise made him vulnerable. Apparently believing that he would not again be elected to the United States Senate, he determined to test his strength in a gubernatorial contest before the voters. Accordingly, in May 1857 he announced for governor as an independent, running on his record as a Jackson Democrat or Unionist. Louis T. Wigfall, a proslavery extremist and staunch champion of state rights, debated Houston wherever possible, and when Houston avoided debate, Wigfall and J. P. Henderson followed the old veteran from place to place, answering his arguments. Runnels and the regular Democratic ticket won an overwhelming victory. It was the only defeat in a major contest before the voters that Houston ever suffered. The legislature elected Chief Justice John Hemphill to take his seat in the United States Senate. In 1857 Senator Rusk met death by his own hand, and the same legislature chose J. P. Henderson to fill the vacancy. Soon thereafter Henderson died and Matthias Ward was appointed to succeed him. Wigfall was chosen to succeed Ward in 1858.

During the Runnels administration, 1857 to 1859, frontier defense and the national controversy associated with slavery were all-absorbing subjects, and other issues were eclipsed by the excitement and hatred which they created. The frontier defense problem is treated hereafter in this chapter, but the national controversy and the election of 1859, because of their inseparable connection with secession, are deferred for later consideration.

EXPLORATIONS

At the close of the Mexican War most of Texas west and north of Dallas, Austin, Fredericksburg, San Antonio, and Laredo was an unknown In-

Colonel John S. (Rip) Ford, a South Carolinian by birth, came to Texas in 1836. In the course of a long career he practiced medicine in San Augustine, edited the Texas Democrat and later the State Times in Austin, and served in both the Congress of the Republic of Texas and the state senate. He attained renown as a Ranger, defeating the Indians in two notable engagements, and as an officer in the Confederate Army, commanding the troops that won the Battle of Palmito Ranch, the last land engagement of the War. His nickname Rip came from his practice of introducing death notices during the war with Mexico with "Rest in peace," which in the stress of battle became "R.I.P." (E.C. Barker History Center, University of Texas)

dian country. During the next twelve years, as a result of the efforts of the Texans and the army to find and survey wagon and rail roads across the region and to locate and supply new military posts on the southern border of the nation, the region was extensively explored.

In March 1849 Robert S. Neighbors, a noted Indian agent, with orders from General William J. Worth, and John S. ("Rip") Ford, a famous ranger officer, set out with a party to find a practical wagon road between San Antonio and El Paso. They went by way of the Middle Concho, Horsehead Crossing on the Pecos River, and the Davis Mountains, and returned by way of Guadalupe Pass, the Pecos and Middle Concho rivers, and Fredericksburg. At about the same time Captain W. H. C. Whiting made an army reconnaissance to El Paso. He returned by way of the Davis Mountains, Devils River, and the head of Las Moras River at present Brackettville. The leaders of both expeditions reported favorably on their return routes. Army officers then surveyed and tested the practicability of the two routes. Lieutenant Colonel Joseph E. Johnston moved a train of 250 wagons in one hundred days from San Antonio to El Paso by Whiting's return route. Both routes were marked: the "upper," leading northward to Brady's Creek, thence westward to the Pecos at Horsehead Crossing, up that stream to the mouth of Delaware Creek, near the present Texas-New Mexico line, and westward through Guadalupe Pass to El Paso; the "lower," used more extensively, westward from San Antonio, following the route of Highway 90 to Fort Clark, now Brackettville, thence northwest, crossing the Pecos west of Ozona, and following the general direction of Highway 290 to El Paso. Many emigrants, California bound, used these routes.

Meanwhile, the military was exploring and marking wagon roads across the state farther north. Captain Randolph B. Marcy in April 1849 escorted a party of immigrants to Santa Fé by following the Canadian River across the Texas Panhandle. On his return, Marcy passed through Guadalupe Pass, crossed the Pecos a little below the present Texas and Pacific Railroad crossing, followed the route of the railroad to the vicinity of Colorado City, thence bore slightly northward by the present towns of Stamford and Henrietta, and crossed Red River at Preston, north of Sherman. This route, afterwards known as the Marcy Trail, was long used by emigrants and other pioneers.

In 1853 Congress made an appropriation for surveying practicable routes for railroads to the Pacific. The southernmost of these surveys ran through North Texas and was surveyed in part by Captain John Pope. The route followed substantially the Marcy Trail. Many years were to pass before the railroad was built, but to the exploration and surveys must be credited in part the Southern Overland Mail Service that was extended through that section in 1858.

Camels, introduced into Texas by the United States Army in 1856 and 1857, proved successful in some reconnaissance expeditions in the arid western part of the state. Their use, however, never passed beyond the experimental stage.

IMMIGRATION AND EXTENSION OF SETTLEMENT

It has been stated previously that the frontier line of settlement in 1846 extended from Corpus Christi to San Antonio on the southwest and thence northward approximately through New Braunfels, Fredericksburg, Austin, Waco, Dallas, and Collin County to Preston on the Red River, and that the total population in Texas in 1847, including Negroes but not Indians, was estimated at 142,009. If the liberal land policy and the expectation of annexation had stimulated immigration, annexation and the continuation of the liberal land policy brought a veritable stream of homeseekers. The lure of cheap land in Texas was second only to that of gold in California. During 1845 the newspapers in Missouri, Arkansas, and Louisiana bore strong evidence of migration to Texas. There was a lull in 1846 and 1847 due to the Mexican War, but the news of American success started the wave anew. One day in

December 1848, 300 immigrants crossed the ferry at Washington on the Brazos, and during November 1849 more than 5,000 on their way to Texas crossed the Arkansas River at Little Rock. A year later, the editor of the *Northern Standard* at Clarksville, the northeastern gateway to Texas, wrote: "For the last two weeks scarcely a day has passed that a dozen or more movers' wagons have not passed through our town." The census of 1850 showed 154,034 whites, 58,161 slaves, 397 free Negroes, for a total of 212,592 or an increase of almost 50 percent since 1847.

Year after year the number grew increasingly larger. In December 1858 the editor of the Clarksville *Standard* declared that no less than fifty wagons of immigrants were passing through Clarksville each day. By 1860 the population of the state had jumped to 604,215, almost three times that of 1850. Of this number, 182,921 were Negroes.

Of the 1860 population, almost three-fourths had been born outside of Texas. A majority of the immigrants had come from the states of the Old South, Louisiana, Arkansas, and Missouri. Tennessee had contributed 42,265, more than any other state; Alabama was the next with 34,193. A few had been born in northern states. The foreign born, numbering 43,422, represented almost every country of Western Europe. The Germans and Mexicans constituted by far the largest foreign-born elements, being represented by 20,553 and 12,443, respectively.

Immigrants from Europe, other than the Germans who in 1860 constituted a majority of the population in three counties in the San Antonio-Austin area and a substantial part in six other counties, included French, Czechs, and Norwegians. La Réunion, a French colony, was established in 1855 near Dallas by followers of Victor Considerant, a disciple of the socialist, F. C. M. Fourier. The colonists soon lost their enthusiasm for the frontier and cooperative enterprise, however, and drifted away to other communities. A few Czechs had come to Texas during the period of the Republic; after the revolutions of 1848 in Central Europe, many others to escape Austrian tyranny followed them. Among them were a number of liberal intellectuals who exercised considerable influence on the early development of Texas. A small Norwegian settlement was planted in Henderson County in 1845, but settlers from Scandinavia did not come in numbers until nearly a half-century later.

Obviously, the liberal land policy and the tremendous population increase resulted in a significant extension of settlements during the 15 years of early statehood. The counties of Nueces, Webb, Starr, and Cameron were created in 1848. Their populations seem to have been overwhelmingly Mexican. Election returns for Nueces County showed a total of 44 voters, 37 of whom had Spanish names. Along the Rio Grande, far removed from the main Texas settlements, were a number of communities, including Laredo and Eagle Pass, whose populations likewise were largely Mexican. In 1850 this area and the counties of Cameron, Starr, and Webb had about 13,000 people. Higher up on the Rio Grande were several settlements, including Presidio and El Paso, with about 4,000 persons.

Thousands of new arrivals, joined by other thousands of "old" Texans, advanced the frontier westward deep into the Western Cross Timbers despite Indian hostility and the less favorable physical environment. By 1849 the newly established towns of Sherman, Farmersville, Dallas, Waxahachie, Ennis, Waco, and Fredericksburg marked the western limits of white settlement. During that year the federal government completed the establishment of a line of military posts, generally a few miles in advance of the settlements, to deter the Indians from raiding the whites. Villages sprang up at once near Fort Worth and Fort Croghan (Burnet), but because the infantry sent to the posts were unable to offer protection, the rush to the frontier came to a temporary halt in 1850 with the establishment of Gainesville, Belton, and Uvalde County.

Under pressure to open up new lands for settlers, the federal government in 1851 and 1852 moved its military posts westward more than a hundred miles. As soon as the posts were established, there was a rush to settle the intervening lands. Within two years settlements had been made at Bandera, San Saba, Meridian, Gatesville, Cleburne, and Stephenville; and at the end of another four years Comanche, Hamilton, Weatherford, Jacksboro, and Palo Pinto had been founded.

In 1860 the western extremity of settlement extended irregularly from Henrietta on the north through Belknap, Palo Pinto, Brownwood, Llano, and Kerrville, to Uvalde. The advance halted here not only because of the outbreak of the Civil War and lack of timber and water, but also because of the inability to cope with the hostile Plains Indians.

THE INDIAN FRONTIER

The people of Texas believed that once annexation had been completed the United States would put an end to Indian depredations; but they were soon disillusioned. Troubles with Indians continued for more than thirty years, and were even worse at times than they had been during the Republic. The three sources of frontier defense were the United States Army, state troops, and the frontier citizens.

The United States made a treaty with the Penateka Comanches, the band nearest the whites, in 1846; but because of the outbreak of the Mexican War, Texas was left to defend its own frontiers. Soon after the outbreak of the war, five companies of mounted Texas Rangers were stationed along the frontier from the West Fork of the Trinity to

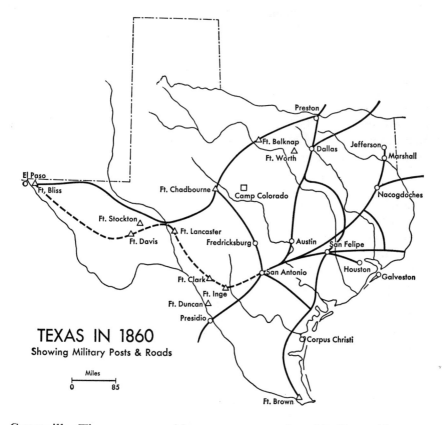

TEXAS IN 1860
Showing Military Posts & Roads

Miles
0   85

Castroville. They were not able to prevent a series of Indian raids, most severe in South Texas, and during 1847 four additional companies were placed in service between San Antonio and the Rio Grande. Other than these nine companies of state troops, the frontier had no protection until after the war.

When the United States began withdrawing its troops from Mexico, it sent seven companies of regulars to replace the state troops. It has been stated previously that in 1849 the War Department put into effect a permanent line of defense. It established between the Rio Grande and the Red River eight military posts to deter the Indians from going into the settlements. From south to north these forts were Duncan at Eagle Pass; Inge, near Uvalde; Lincoln, 55 miles west of San Antonio; Martin Scott, at Fredericksburg; Croghan, near Burnet; Gates, on the Leon River; Graham, on the Brazos River; and Worth, 54 miles due north of Fort Graham, at the present city of Fort Worth. So rapid was the advance of settlements, however, that within less than two years the line of frontiersmen's cabins had passed beyond this cordon. Consequently, beginning in 1851 they were replaced by seven new forts generally along an irregular line about 100 miles to the west. From north to south they were Belknap, on the Brazos at the present town of Newcastle; Phantom Hill, 14 miles north of present Abilene; Chadbourne, on Oak Creek in present Coke County; McKavett, on the San Saba River about 24 miles above present Menard; Terrett, on the North Llano; Mason, at the present town by that name; and Clark, at present Brackettville. Still a third chain of posts, located along or near the Rio Grande, was built for a double purpose, namely, keeping out marauding parties from Mexico and preventing Indians from the United States from harassing the settlements of northern Mexico. Several other posts also were built in strategic points.

A close correlation existed between the number of troops and the extent of marauding operations by the Indians. During 1853, for instance, there were 3,265 soldiers in Texas, the greatest number at any time before the Civil War, and the frontier was comparatively tranquil. During the following year, after many troops had been withdrawn and the country between the Colorado and the Red rivers was defended only by four small companies of infantry and two of dragoons, conditions became so bad that General Persifor F. Smith called on Governor Pease for state troops. At Fort Chadbourne there were only 20 men and they were commanded by the post surgeon.

Meanwhile, the Indian agents were working faithfully, in spite of great handicaps, to keep the red men peaceful. The ablest of these agents was Robert S. Neighbors, who had served the Republic of Texas as an Indian agent and afterwards continued in the service of the federal government, except from 1849 to 1853, until his death in 1859.

In an effort to provide better for the Indians and to restrain them, two reservations were established in Texas in 1855. The state contributed the land, twelve square leagues (69,120 acres). Surviving members of the Caddo, Anadarko, Ioni, Waco, Tonkawa, Tawakoni, and other small tribes, in all about 1,000, were located on a reservation of eight square leagues at the junction of the Brazos and Clear Fork rivers. A reservation of four square leagues for the Penateka Comanches was established on the Clear Fork in present Throckmorton County; but only about 500 Penatekas, not much more than half of that Comanche band, could be persuaded to move onto the reservation. Some of the remainder united with the northern Comanche bands and became even more troublesome.

Conditions near the Indian country improved greatly in 1856. The change seems to have been caused in part by the reservations, but probably it should be credited more to the presence of the greatest aggregation of fighting men that ever represented the United States Army in the Old West—the Second Cavalry, whose roll of officers included Albert Sidney Johnston, Robert E. Lee, George H. Thomas, George Stoneman, and John B. Hood. Johnston and a part of his regiment were ordered to Utah in 1857, and the depredations again became severe. During the following year both the state and federal forces carried the war to the Indians. In April, with a force of 215 rangers and friendly Brazos Reservation Indians under their agent Shapley P. Ross, John S. Ford crossed the Red River into present Oklahoma and on May 12 decisively defeated a large band of Comanches in the Canadian River valley near the Texas-Oklahoma line.[1] In September of the same year, Major Earl Van Dorn led a cavalry force from Texas against the Comanches in the Indian Territory and on October 1 defeated a band of that tribe and Wichitas near the present Rush Springs, Oklahoma. In this campaign also, about 125 friendly Indians from the Brazos Reservation, under the command of Lawrence Sullivan Ross, son of the Indian agent and later governor of Texas, gave substantial aid. Later that year Van Dorn carried his war even farther north and defeated another band of Comanches in southern Kansas.

Meanwhile, in spite of the loyal aid the Indians of the Brazos Reservation had given the troops, the people of the frontier, joined by many persons in the interior, charged that the reservation Indians were taking part in raids on the settlements and demanded that they be removed from Texas. Swarms of angry settlers repeatedly threatened the lives of the reservation people, and only the presence of federal troops prevented a massacre. In the late summer of 1859 the Indians of both reservations were moved to the valley of the Washita River in Indian Territory.

Soon after the removal of the reservation Indians, trouble developed on the lower Rio Grande frontier. In the fall of 1859 Juan N. Cortina, a notorious Mexican bandit, and a large band of followers crossed the Rio Grande and harried Brownsville and the entire lower Rio Grande valley. Two companies of state troops, under the command of John S. Ford, went to the aid of a contingent of federal troops, and after a lively campaign forced the bandit raider to limit his activities to the south side of the Rio Grande.

The removal of the reservation Indians did not bring peace to the frontier. The northern Comanches and the Kiowas, aroused by the attacks from Texas, retaliated that autumn with devastating raids on the exposed settlements. Dissatisfaction over this situation constituted a major factor that led to the defeat of Runnels and the election of Houston as governor that year. Although aggressive warfare against the Indians had been contrary to Houston's nature, he had promised to quiet the Indians and this time neither the whites nor the Indians were in a mood to resort to treaties. Thus, he had to act. By a series of orders he authorized and sent to the frontier by the end of March 1860 seven ranger companies, consisting of more than 500 men. Also, the chief justice in each frontier county was authorized to raise a company

---

[1]As incorrectly located at that time, the 100th meridian, which north of Red River separates the Panhandle of Texas from Oklahoma, was approximately 60 miles east of the true location; thus, Ford may have believed that he was in Texas, but apparently he gave the question of boundary no consideration.

of not more than 25 minutemen, and for a time that spring 23 such companies were available for service. The state force must have numbered more than 1,000 on active duty. At the same time there were 2,651 federal troops in Texas, and 842 others were on the way to the state. Such a sizable force of mounted troops temporarily frightened the Indian raiders away from the frontier, and in May the minutemen were disbanded, but four companies of rangers, were ordered to scout for hostile Indians without regard to state boundaries. Although the rangers remained in Indian territory for nearly a year, they had little noteworthy success except for the defeat of an encampment of Indians in what is now the Panhandle of Oklahoma. One expedition penetrated the Indian country as far as Kansas but failed to accomplish anything of consequence. Meanwhile, the federal troops were likewise active, and by the end of 1860 it appeared that Texas might have peace on its western frontier. However, Texas was on the eve of secession and the final settlement of its Indian problem was to require another 15 years of tough campaigning after the close of the Civil War.

Selected Bibliography

The best general accounts of the period of early statehood are S.V. Connor, *Adventure in Glory*; E. Wallace, *Texas in Turmoil* (Austin, 1965); O.M. Roberts, *A Political, Legislative, and Judicial History of Texas, 1845–1895*, in D.G. Wooten (ed.), *A Comprehensive History of Texas, 1685–1897* (2 vols., Dallas, 1898); and previously cited older works by H.H. Bancroft, J.H. Brown, H.S. Thrall, F.W. Johnson, and L.J. Wortham; for source material, see the *Houston Papers* and the *Handbook of Texas*.

Biographies that are essential for an understanding of the period include those of Sam Houston, previously cited: H.P. Gambrell, *Anson Jones*; Claude Elliott, *Leathercoat: The Life of James W. Throckmorton* (San Antonio, 1938); W.J. Hughes, *Rebellious Ranger: Rip Ford and the Old Southwest* (Norman, 1964); E. Wallace, *Charles DeMorse: Pioneer Editor and Statesman;* J.K. Greer, *Colonel Jack Hays* (New York, 1952); Ben H. Procter, *Not Without Honor: The Life of John H. Reagan* (Austin, 1962); A.L. King, "Louis T. Wigfall: The Stormy Petrel" (unpublished dissertation, Texas Technological College, Lubbock, 1967).

On the Constitution of 1845, see a study by F.L. Paxson in *Southwestern Historical Quarterly*, XVIII, 386–398, and another by A. Middleton, *ibid.*, XXV, 26–62; also see *Debates of the Convention of 1845* (Houston, 1846).

For the War with Mexico and on the frontiers, see W.P. Webb, *The Texas Rangers*; Otis A. Singletary, *The Mexican War (*Chicago,

1960); Justin H. Smith, *The War with Mexico* (2 vols., New York, 1919); J.K. Greer, *Colonel Jack Hays*; Ernest C. Shearer "The Carvajal Disturbances," *Southwestern Historical Quarterly*, LV, 201–230; and H.W. Barton, "Five Texas Frontier Companies during the Mexican War," *ibid.*, LXVI, 17–30.

The controversy over the Texas-New Mexico boundary and the settlement of the debt of the Republic of Texas are dealt with in W.C. Binkley, *The Expansionist Movement in Texas*; E.T. Miller, *A Financial History of Texas*; Holman Hamilton, *Prologue to Conflict: The Crisis and Compromise of 1850* (Lexington, Ky., 1964); Holman Hamilton, "Texas Bonds and Northern Profits: A Study in Compromise, Investment, and Lobby Influence," *Mississippi Valley Historical Review*, XLIII, 579–594; Kenneth F. Neighbours, "The Taylor-Neighbors Struggle over the Upper Rio Grande Region of Texas in 1850," *Southwestern Historical Quarterly*, LXI, 431–463; and C.A. Bridges, "Texas and the Crisis of 1850" (unpublished manuscript, University of Texas Library, Austin).

On the politics of the era, besides the biographies and the general works mentioned above, there is F.B. Sexton, "J. Pinckney Henderson," *Quarterly of the Texas State Historical Association*, I, 187–203; Louis F. Blount, "A Brief Study of Thomas J. Rusk," *Southwestern Historical Quarterly*, XXXIV, 181–202, 271–292; Ralph A. Wooster, "Membership in Early Texas Legislatures, 1850–1860," *ibid.*, LXIX, 163–173; R.A. Wooster, "An Analysis of the Texas Know-Nothings," *ibid.*, LXX, 414–423: S.H. Sherman, "Governor George Thomas Wood," *ibid.*, XX, 260–268; Roy Sylvan Dunn, "The Knights of the KGC in Texas, 1860–1861," *ibid.*, LXX, 543–573; G.L. Crockett, *Two Centuries in East Texas*; E.W. Winkler (ed.), *Platforms of Political Parties in Texas* (Austin, 1916), indispensable to a study of Texas politics; Francis R. Lubbock (C. W. Raines, ed.), *Six Decades in Texas* (Austin, 1900); and Norman G. Kittrell, *Governors Who have Been, and Other Public Men of Texas* (Houston, 1921); James T. DeShields, *They Sat in High Places: The Presidents and Governors of Texas* (San Antonio, 1940); with special reference to education, see J.J. Lane, *History of Education in Texas* (Washington, 1903); Frederick Eby, *The Development of Education in Texas* (New York, 1925); and J.C. Jeffries, "Sketches of Old Baylor," *Southwestern Historical Quarterly*, LVI, 498–506.

For accounts of exploration, see Grant Foreman, *Marcy and the Gold Seekers* (Norman, 1936); "Marcy's Report on His Return from Santa Fé," *West Texas Historical Association Year Book*, I, 30–54; M.L. Crimmins, "Captain John Pope's Route to the Pacific," *Military Engineer* (March–April, 1931); W.J. Hughes, *Rebellious Ranger: Rip Ford and the Old Southwest;* W. Turrentine Jackson, *Wagon Roads West* (Berkeley, 1952); A.B. Bender, "Opening Routes across West Texas,

1848–1856," *Southwestern Historical Quarterly*, XXXVII, 116–135; W.H. Goetzman, "The United States-Mexican Boundary Survey, 1848–1853," *ibid.*, LXII, 164–190; T.L. Connelly, "The American Camel Experiment: A Reappraisal," *ibid.*, LXIX, 442–462; E.B. Lammons, "Operation Camel: An Experiment in Animal Transportation in Texas, 1857–1860," *ibid.*, XLI, 20–49; W.H. Goetzman, *Army Exploration in the American West* (New Haven, 1959).

For immigration and the extension of settlements, most sources and studies cited under these subjects in the preceding chapter are also valuable for the period of early statehood. In addition, see W.C. Holden, *Alkali Trails* (Dallas, 1930); W.J. Hammond and Margaret F. Hammond, La Réunion, *A French Settlement in Texas* (Dallas, 1958); Ermance V. Rejebain, "La Réunion; The French Colony in Dallas County," *Southwestern Historical Quarterly*, XLIII, 472–478; H.R. Marsh, "The Czechs in Texas," *ibid.*, L, 236–240; R.N. Richardson, *The Frontier of Northwest Texas, 1846–1876: Advance and Defense by the Pioneer Settlers of the Cross Timbers and Prairies* (Glendale, 1963); James Day, *Jacob de Cordova: Land Merchant of Texas* (Waco, 1962); B.P. Gallaway, "The Physical Barrier to Settlement in the Western Cross Timbers Frontier," *West Texas Historical Association Year Book*, XLII, 51–58; Mrs. William L. Cazneau (Cora Montgomery), *Eagle Pass or Life on the Border* (Austin, 1966).

Of the large body of material dealing with the frontier and the Indians, the following are among the most useful: R.N. Richardson, *The Comanche Barrier*; W.P. Webb, *The Texas Rangers*; C.C. Rister, *The Southwestern Frontier* (Cleveland, 1928); D.H. Winfrey, *Texas Indian Papers, 1846–1859* (Austin, 1960); E. Wallace and E.A. Hoebel, *The Comanches*; W.C. Holden, "Frontier Defense, 1846–1860," *West Texas Historical Association Year Book*, VI, 35–64; Kenneth S. Neighbours, "Indian Exodus Out of Texas in 1859," *ibid.*, XXXVI, 80–97; A.B. Bender, "The Texas Frontier," *Southwestern Historical Quarterly*, XXXVIII, 135–148; M.L. Crimmins (ed.), "Colonel J.K.F. Mansfield's Report on the Inspection of the Department of Texas in 1856," *ibid.*, LXII, 122–148, 215–257, 351–387; "W.G. Freeman's Report on the Eighth Military Department," *ibid.*, LII, 227–233; Lena Clara Koch, "The Federal Indian Policy in Texas, 1845–1860," *ibid.*, XXXVIII, 223–234, 259–286; XXIX, 19–35, 98–127; W.J. Hughes, " 'Rip' Ford's Indian Fight on the Canadian," *Panhandle-Plains Historical Review*, XXX, 1–26; J.K. Greer (ed.), *A Texas Ranger and Frontiersman: The Days of Buck Barry in Texas, 1845–1906* (Dallas, 1932); T.R.. Havins, *Beyond the Cimarron: Major Earl Van Dorn in Comanche Land* (Brownwood, 1968).

9

PIONEER INSTITUTIONS

By 1861 when the scourge of war ended all progress, the pattern of Texan civilization had been formed; the state's cultural institutions had been established. In many respects they were like those of the Old South, whence a majority of the population had come; but there were many variations and a few distinct differences. Texas, in fact, belonged both to the Old South and the New West. Basic to the state's economy were the slaves and cotton of the South; but whereas in the old states the frontier was a thing of the past, in Texas it still affected all the people either directly or indirectly. Typical of the frontier, Texas was a man's country; men outnumbered women by a ratio of approximately 11 to 9. In contrast to the Old South, the foreign-born population of the state was comparatively high, with German and Mexican elements constituting the largest groups of 43,000 emigrants from foreign lands.

Apparent in the pluralism of the society were several dominant patterns. There were more than a hundred occupations, but Texans were tied closely to the land. Although most were small subsistence farmers, owning few or no slaves, plantation owners and townsmen contributed more to the ideals and cultural institutions of the time. Throughout the state farmer, planter, and townsman alike sought to improve the primitive frontier transportation system. Otherwise, Texans worried about epidemics and disease and amused themselves in rather conventional fashion, but they also acquired a reputation for lawlessness. Meanwhile, they made more positive and longer-lasting achievements in such areas as education, news publication, and religion.

OCCUPATIONS

Manufacturing and crafts provided a living for many antebellum Texans. The Census of 1860 reported 3,449 persons employed in 983 manufacturing establishments. More than 400 men worked in grist and saw mills; and by 1860 the presence of an equal number of wheelwrights suggests the manufacture of wagons, carriages, and other vehicles. In 1860 a plant in Houston manufactured hats; relying primarily on Negro labor, a factory in Harrison County produced textiles. In the crafts the 1,361 carpenters of 1850 doubled in number by 1860, and there were many brick and stonemasons, blacksmiths, and saddle and harness makers.

The professions were represented surprisingly well. In 1850 Marshall, serving a wide area but with a relatively small population of 1,189, had 28 lawyers and 11 doctors. Certainly, of lawyers there was no shortage; the 428 located in Texas in 1850 doubled by 1860. Physicians, though often poorly trained, were likewise plentiful, their number increasing to 1,471 by 1860. But at the same time Texas had only 65 dentists, most of whom traveled from town to town to serve their practice. There were 758 clergymen but as one might expect in a frontier society, only eight architects.

Occupations included both the ordinary and the unusual. Merchants increased rapidly during the fifties, numbering 2,223 by 1860, while 3,541 persons found employment as domestic servants. Four Texans described themselves as "catchers of wild horses," a conventional occupation of the times. Less to be expected were four toymen, six daguerreotypists, three actors, 45 artists, five clockmakers, and six dancing masters.

By far the most common occupation was farming. In 1850 approximately 25,000 of the 43,000 persons who listed occupations called themselves farmers, and no doubt many others were similarly engaged. Farmers and farm laborers accounted for more than half of the 105,491 occupations of 1860. Appropriately, improved land in farms increased from 639,111 acres in 1850 to 2,650,781 acres ten years later; and during the same period the value of farms increased more than fivefold, reaching a total of about $88,000,000.

For the marketplace, the most important crop was cotton. Except for occasional years when pests ravaged the crops, the output in-

Early settlers of Comanche County in west central Texas: a representative group of sturdy ranchers, farmers, and an occasional lawyer, doctor, or preacher who probably migrated from counties in eastern Texas or directly from Tennessee, Alabama, Arkansas, or Louisiana during the period between 1854 (the year of the first settlement) and 1880. (E.C. Barker History Center, University of Texas)

creased each year. It reached 58,072 bales in 1849–1850 and 431,463 a decade later. During the period of the Republic, cotton farming had been confined to the river valleys of the Coastal Plain and to eastern Texas from the upper Neches River northward, where there was limited production. By 1860 these regions still produced the greater part of the crop; but cotton farming was being extended into Central Texas, even though the notion still prevailed that it was a bottomland crop not suited to the black prairies.

Although cotton was the money crop, in early Texas corn was indispensable. To a very large extent it sustained both the people and their animals. With comparatively little cultivation it would grow and yield bountifully in the virgin soils from the Gulf to the Red River. Reports claimed an average yield in early years of 40 to 80 bushels to the acre and that as much as 110 bushels had been grown without the application of manure.

Other food crops included sweet potatoes, wheat, and sugarcane. Next to corn in importance was sweet potatoes, grown not only by the small subsistence farmer but also on the large plantations. Less abundant was wheat, not grown at all in southern Texas and a secondary crop elsewhere. During the period of low prices for cotton that followed the Panic of 1837, the planters near the coast turned to the raising of sugarcane. The industry grew until 1852, when 11,023 hogsheads of more than 1,000 pounds were produced. Because of occasional droughts and freezes it declined thereafter.

During this period there was some organized effort to improve farming. Agriculture societies were formed as early as 1843, but apparently their efforts were not long sustained. The first exposition known actually to have been held was the Corpus Christi fair of 1852. Offering prizes to the value of $3,000, it was sponsored by H. L. Kinney who persuaded Dr. Ashbel Smith, acquainted with similar events in England and greatly interested in agriculture, to act as general superintendent. At Dallas in 1858 the first recorded State Fair of Texas was held. Formally chartered in 1886, it has become one of the leading annual exhibitions of the nation. Thomas Affleck, long active in the improvement of agriculture in the South, in 1858 established Glenblythe near Brenham as a model for Texas plantations. Although lack of adequate markets made the livestock industry of much less importance than the production of field crops, efforts to improve livestock breeds began at an early date. Colonel James Morgan, it is said, brought the first Durham bull to Texas during the Mexican regime. English-bred hogs, sheep, horses, and cattle were imported in 1840; two years later Berkshire pigs were offered for sale. In a land of horses, many were highly bred, some of racing stock; one stallion in the fifties was valued at $6,000. But cattle accounted for most of the value of Texas livestock, placed at $42,825,447 in 1860.

SLAVERY AND THE PLANTATION SYSTEM

In antebellum Texas slavery and cotton cultivation expanded together. Reflecting the widespread belief that white men could not work in the fields during the hot summer, the largest cotton-producing counties contained the largest slave population. Estimated at 5,000 in 1836, the slave population increased at an accelerated pace after Texas became independent. The census of 1860 showed 182,566 slaves and 430,891 white persons. Since 1850 the slave population had increased 214 percent and the white population only 180 percent.

Slaves represented a substantial proportion of Texas capital. In 1850 the average value of a slave assessed for taxes was $362, while in 1860 this amount reached $672, and the aggregate value of all slaves assessed was $108,688,920. The value of slave property thus was about 20 percent greater than the value of the farms of Texas. On the market field hands brought from $1,200 to $2,000 and "plow boys" from $1,000 to $1,500. Good hands could be hired out at from $200 to $300 for the year. Some enthusiasts contended that a good field hand who produced eight bales of cotton could pay for himself in a year.

Rapidly expanding agriculture created a demand for slaves that was never satisfied. Apparently most of the Negroes were brought in by immigrants, and by far the greater number of sales were private transactions involving neighbors only. Yet dealers in Galveston and Houston kept on hand slaves of all ages and held regular auctions; in most communities there were sale or auction days. During the late 1850's there was considerable demand for the reopening of the African slave trade, a move supported by a number of prominent Texans and even by some church groups. The illicit African slave trade, meanwhile, brought in hundreds, perhaps thousands, through Galveston and other coastal points. Free Negroes, who could reside in Texas only with special permission granted by an act of the legislature, were sometimes enslaved, either through kidnapping or legal subterfuge.

Although slaves in western areas nearer the Mexican border may have been subjected to harsh restrictions, they apparently fared somewhat better in Texas than in the older states. Escape was comparatively easy, a condition that made dissatisfied slaves poor property. The high value of the slave not only evoked good care for a valuable piece of property but also gave him a higher standing in both slave and free society. Slave quarters on the plantation generally consisted of a one-room or a two-room cabin for each family, located along a street or about an empty square and near the overseer's house. The food of the slaves was much like that of the poorer whites; bacon and corn bread made up the base of the diet. Some, however, raised gardens and kept poultry. On the best plantations food was served from a common kitchen, especially during the planting and harvesting season. Clothing generally consisted of two suits each year, seldom made of homespun, for the planter considered ready-made articles more economical. Medical attention in most cases was perhaps as good as that available to sick white people. Often slaves were not forced to work on Saturday afternoon and Sunday; and sometimes they were permitted to earn spending money of their own.

In Texas as elsewhere, however, those in bondage longed for freedom. Slaves frequently ran away. Apparently most returned voluntarily and were not punished severely. But a few were arrested and returned while others made their way to Mexico or to Indian Territory. During the decade preceding the Civil War, there was growing uneasiness about slavery, and vigilance committees became common.

Those who profited most from slavery, the planters, made up a small minority of the population. In 1860 there were 21,878 slaveowners in Texas, only 5.7 percent of all slaveowners in the nation. Only 2,163 of these owned 20 or more slaves, and only 54 owned 100 or more. More than half of all the slaveholders owned five or less. Only about 10 percent of the slaveholders and less than 5 percent of all farmers operated on a scale large enough to necessitate hiring an overseer, thereby coming within the planter class.

The influence of the planters was, however, far out of proportion to their number. Nearly all were leaders in their communities, and many exercised state-wide influence. More than any other group they stamped upon early Texas society its distinguishing characteristics.

A study of those planters with more than 100 slaves revealed wide variations in wealth but several relatively consistent characteristics. Property holdings of 47 great planters ranged from $60,000 to more than $600,000; cotton production from less than 250 bales to more than 800; and livestock holdings from $1,400 to more than $53,000. Although all but three were cotton planters, their agricultural practices were surprisingly diversified. Practically all owned cattle and hogs, about half of the group raised sheep, every planter grew corn, more than three-fourths grew sweet potatoes, and a somewhat smaller proportion planted other food crops. The Texas plantation was far from self-sufficient, but it was likewise far from complete dependency on outside sources for many staple products.

The wealthier planters lived better than any other people of their day. They had food in great abundance and variety, and elaborate meals were frequently assembled from garden, woods, and stream, with hot breads, cakes, jellies, preserves, and rare delicacies from New Orleans. As they acquired more property, the planters replaced their log cabins with larger and better constructed buildings of cedar, walnut, or pine, and occasionally of brick. Many of these houses were built during the decade preceding the Civil War. Later generations have sought to imitate their sturdiness, simple lines, and ample proportions. Tastes varied from time to time, but a desire for luxuries remained constant. In 1831, cottonades and candle molds were in especial demand; sideboards, tables, and jewelry were bought in quantity during the forties and fifties; and in 1848 one merchant apparently had difficulty in filling an order for a "Bathing Tub and Pea Fowl Brush."

LIFE ON THE FARMS

For most rural Texans the plantation system was something only to be observed and perhaps envied. Their existence depended upon their own labor; their houses were simple; and their luxuries were few.

The houses built by country people were only slightly better than those of colonial times. Here and there was to be found a frame dwelling well designed and carefully built, but the prevailing type at the middle of the century was still the log cabin. The double log cabin, or dog-run house, was the most popular. It consisted of two rooms under a continuous, gabled roof, separated by an open space or dog run. Commonly a porch extended across the entire front. In addition to serving as a sleeping place for the dogs (and for overflow guests) and providing a space for family and friends to sit during warm weather, the dog run and the porch served as catchalls for saddles, bridles, harnesses, chests, boxes, guns, and a dozen other things. The logs were hand hewn and dovetailed at the corners. As the family grew, a lean-to might be added to the back of one or both rooms. Also a kitchen and perhaps a smokehouse might be built, but they were separate from the main house. Spaces between the logs were chinked with boards and daubed with clay or mortar. The roofs were of clapboards held securely in place by weight poles. Chimneys commonly were made of sticks, covered with mud. Floors, if any, were puncheon. While traveling in eastern Texas in 1855, Frederick Law Olmsted stopped for the night at a comparatively comfortable house; but he could "look out, as usual, at the stars between the logs." Traveler Rutherford B. Hayes, the future president of the United States, described a house he saw in Texas whose walls you "could throw a cat through at random." Olmsted frequently made note of houses having glass windows, but he mentions them in such a way as to indicate that they were the exception rather than the rule. The Germans built better houses than the Anglo-Americans, frequently using stone in their construction. There was much building during the sixth decade of the century and houses of lumber became more common. Often such houses were flimsy, box-like affairs, not as good as the sturdy log cabins they displaced.

For a country that might have produced fruits, vegetables, cereals, and honey in bountiful quantities, and where cattle were abundant, the diet of most early Texans was strangely monotonous. Even by 1860 many farm families lived like the earliest Texans, almost wholly on salt pork, corn bread, and syrup. The most common vegetable was the sweet potato. Many people tasted fresh meat only occasionally and a large percentage of them did not have milk and butter. Except in the northern counties, wheat bread was almost unknown in the poorer homes. Water was secured from a nearby spring or stream or occasionally from a well or cistern.

The farm was substantially, though not totally, self-sufficient. Candles or lard-burning lamps supplied light. Ash hoppers and pork fat supplied materials for soap; corn was ground in steel hand mills; and cotton was carded, spun, and woven into cloth. Within less than five years one Texan recorded in his diary that he made a wheel, a coffin, a reel, a churn, a cradle, a bucket, a pump auger, an ox yoke, and a pair of shoes, in addition to working at the loom, hewing puncheons, and graining deerskins. Isaac Van Zandt, a man of distinction, made in emergencies a saddle, a pair of shoes, candles, and a baby's cradle. Toward the end of the period, however, imported manufactured cloth and ready-made clothing were rapidly supplanting homemade materials.

THE TOWNS

A person coming into Texas, direct from the Northern States might, perhaps, be surprised upon seeing many places called towns in Texas. He would, probably, as has been frequently the case, inquire, "where is the town?"

Thus did Melinda Rankin, a missionary from New England, comment on Texas municipalities in 1850. In truth, the state had no towns to spare. Galveston, with 4,177 inhabitants, was the largest. San Antonio, Houston, New Braunfels, and Marshall followed in the order named. No other town had a population of as many as a thousand. Austin, long buffeted by hostile Indians and the threat of Mexican invasion, was the home of only 639 persons. Through trade with Mexico and growth as an army center, San Antonio had forged ahead by 1860 and could show an aggregate of 8,236 persons. Galveston came second, Houston third, and Austin fourth. Sixteen other towns, making 20 all told, are shown in the eighth census to have had a population of 1,000 or more each.

In 1860 foreigners constituted more than a third of the free population in five of the six largest towns. Occupations varied, but the Irish most often were laborers; the Germans, French, and English were usually merchants or craftsmen; and the Mexicans were generally laborers or cartmen. Most came directly from their native country to make substantial economic progress in their new land. Although many opposed slavery, wealthier foreigners often owned slaves.

The best buildings in a town generally were the hotels. Dr. Ferdinand Roemer found the hotel at Houston "a rather pretentious two-story building," but the interior was so neglected as to remind him that he had reached the "borders of civilization." Service was poor and one was expected to occupy a room with several strangers. The pride of San Antonio was the Menger Hotel on Alamo Plaza, which was opened in 1859. The building of fine cut stone, two and one-half stories high, together with its carpets, decorations, and beautiful furniture cost $16,000. Only wealthy people and professional travelers patronized hotels; the rank and file put up at the wagonyards.

Civic improvement came but slowly. Observers found Houston streets filled with "bottomless" mud and San Antonio streets almost impassable in bad weather. In 1857, however, Galveston paved its most traveled street with shells, and San Antonio spent $1,200 on street improvement and also built some bridges. About the same time San Antonio organized a "Fire Association," and in 1860 installed gas lights.

By 1860 one could purchase in the larger Texas towns almost any article to be had in the stores and warehouses in the East. Advertise-

ments indicate that merchants kept in stock all kinds of farm machinery, carriages, wagons, building supplies, furniture, kitchen supplies, many kinds of cloth and clothing, jewelry, gold and silver plate,
a large assortment of processed foods, ice, quantities of drugs and cos-
metics, and liquors; indeed, an almost endless list of items. There were
jobbers and wholesalers in Texas, but many merchants made their purchases in New Orleans or in other cities.

The scarcity of money and lack of banking facilities constituted a
handicap for business during the period of the Republic and early
statehood, just as it had in colonial times. This condition was aggravated by the provision in the Constitution of 1845 prohibiting the chartering of banks. Various firms carried on certain banking functions.
Among them were the firms of McKinney and Williams, established
at Quintana, at the mouth of the Brazos, just before the Texan
Revolution, and beginning business in Galveston about 1837; R. &
D. G. Mills of Galveston, which had strong financial backing in New
Orleans and New York; and Ball, Hutchings & Company, predecessors
of the modern firm of Hutchings, Sealy & Company. By 1859 several commission firms had located in Austin and Galveston, handling
bills, checks, and exchange on banks of the Old South. There was one
incorporated bank in Texas before the Civil War, the Bank of Commerce and Agriculture, opened at Galveston by McKinney and Williams in 1847, under an old charter of the State of Coahuila and Texas
issued in 1835.

During the early years of the Republic quantities of depreciated
bank notes from the United States circulated in Texas. We have seen that
the paper money issued by the Texan government was even less dependable than was the spurious paper money from the United States.
Promissory notes even were used as money. The commonest hard money
consisted of hammered Spanish dollars (old Spanish dollars with the
royal effigy defaced) and Mexican dollars. The firm of R. and D. G.
Mills took notes of a Mississippi wildcat bank and endorsed them,
placed them in circulation, and maintained at par from $40,000 to
$300,000 of them. Later the quality of bank notes brought in from the
East improved.

TRANSPORTATION

"No one walks in Texas if the distance is more than a mile," said
Dr. Ferdinand Roemer, who visited the country in 1846. Nevertheless,
Texans found inadequate transportation facilities in the vast land to be
one of their more difficult problems, one that for a long time retarded
development in the state. Travelers and merchants depended on coastal
and river traffic, roads, stage lines, and freight contractors. Railroad
construction began in the fifties.

Invaluable for foreign and interstate traffic were the coastal outlets. The most serviceable ports were Galveston and Matagorda. Houston did considerable business through Buffalo Bayou, and Indianola, founded by Prince Carl of Solms-Braunfels in 1844, near the present Port Lavaca, came to be the principal port of West Texas. It was destroyed by a storm in 1875, rebuilt, and destroyed again in 1886.

Some areas relied on the rivers. The Brazos was navigable as far as Brazoria, and occasionally boats went even higher up the river. Red River was navigable to Shreveport and under favorable conditions to Pecan Point and Jonesborough. Through Big Cypress Bayou, Caddo Lake, the Red River, and the Mississippi, Jefferson had water connection with New Orleans. In seasons of abundant rain small boats ascended the Sabine to Sabinetown near San Augustine; the lower Trinity would carry boats of shallow draft; and some cotton was shipped down the San Jacinto. Buffalo Bayou afforded good navigation to Houston. Because of a raft that closed its channel near the Gulf, the Colorado was useless for navigation.

The great majority of Texans depended on such roads as existed. The chief roads, or routes of travel that were called roads, were the old military road, from Red River through Dallas, Waco, and Austin; the old San Antonio-Nacogdoches Road, passing through Bastrop and Crockett; the road from Indianola to San Antonio; and a road from Dallas and vicinity southward to Houston. The roads, which were bad even under favorable conditions, became impassable quagmires in wet weather. Olmsted, who entered Texas from the east, pronounced the road in Leon County "little better than a cowtrack." He described the road from Victoria to Lavaca as "a mere collection of straggling wagon ruts, extending for more than a quarter of a mile in width, from outside to outside, it being desirable in this part of the country, rather to avoid the road than follow it." Yet, all roads were not so nearly impassable. Rutherford B. Hayes in the winter of 1848–1849 recorded in his diary, "Rode 14 miles on good dry roads on the banks of the Brazos [near Columbia]."

Freight contractors and stage lines provided public transportation. Using strong, heavy wagons of bois d'arc, "shaped like boats," with iron axles, wheels five and a half feet high, and tires six inches wide, freighters hauled loads averaging 7,000 pounds. These huge wagons, pulled by teams of 10 to 20 mules or horses or from 20 to 30 oxen, sometimes moved in long trains, occasionally mixed with the smaller carts generally used by Mexican freighters. Freight rates varied with the weather and season, averaging about one cent per mile for each 100 pounds but more in bad weather.

Of the many vehicles used for public conveyances, the stage coach was the most popular. The quality of the coaches, at least on certain lines, was greatly improved during the fifties. Described as large, airy,

Before railroads, both passengers and mail crossed Texas by stagecoach. The San Antonio–San Diego line, established in 1857, was the first to link Texas with the Pacific coast. It operated four-horse coaches and a "fleet" of pack mules. Relay stations with passenger accommodations were set up, but probably none equalled the Winedale Inn near Round Top, pictured above. (Texas Highway Department)

and strong in contrast with the "ordinary hacks," used in the eastern states, they carried as many as nine passengers in the inside and a few on the outside. On the San Antonio-San Diego and the Southern Overland Mail Lines, the famous Concord coaches were used. Travel was nevertheless uncomfortable, sometimes dangerous, and usually expensive. Mud, high water, cold weather, Indian attacks, and robberies combined at times to make travel hazardous. The usual charge for a passenger was ten cents a mile, but some contractors doubled the charges in wet weather.

Stagecoaches radiated from each terminal town. Sawyer and Risher's four-horse coaches left Hempstead at ten o'clock in the morning and arrived at Austin at twelve o'clock at night on the day following. Austin had similar connections with Eagle Lake and Powderhorn (near Indianola) on the Gulf. Stage service was maintained between San Antonio and Eagle Lake, San Antonio and Powderhorn, and San Antonio and

Eagle Pass. Washington and Waco both had stage connections with Hempstead. Nacogdoches was linked with Waco through Rusk and Palestine; a line ran from Palestine to Dallas, and another from Dallas to Fort Belknap. Northeast Texas was served by a line from Clarksville to Waco.

Interstate stage traffic was fast and dependable. In August 1857 a semimonthly mail and passenger service was opened between San Antonio and San Diego, California. The scheduled thirty-day trip cost $200; during the first year there was not a single failure to complete the journey. Better service still was that inaugurated in 1858 by the Southern Overland or Butterfield Mail line, which skirted the settlements of North Texas on its route from St. Louis and Memphis on the east to San Francisco on the west. Stages ran each way twice weekly and completed the journey of about 2,700 miles in 25 days or less.

Federal mail subsidies were largely responsible for the long stage lines. Mail contracts supplied the large expenditures necessary for stage stands, coaches, road repairs, and labor. Mail service otherwise was substantially improved by 1861, though it did not even approximate present-day standards. Wet mail and late mail were common causes of complaint, and post offices were scarce. Not until 1850, for instance, did San Antonio have one.

During the fifties the railroads began both to compete with and to feed the stage and freight lines. Late in 1852 construction on the first railroad line in Texas was begun in Harrisburg, nine miles below Houston. It was the Buffalo Bayou, Brazos, and Colorado, commonly called the Harrisburg Railroad and now a part of the great Southern Pacific system. By 1855 it had been extended 32 miles, from Harrisburg on Buffalo Bayou to Richmond on the Brazos; and five years later it was built into Alleyton near the Colorado. The Houston tap to this line was built by the citizens of that town who taxed themselves for the purpose. Shortly after work was begun on the Harrisburg line, workmen began laying track on a railroad that was intended to link Houston with the Red River, the Houston and Texas Central. By 1860 it had reached Millican, in the Brazos Valley below Bryan, and a branch had been extended to Brenham. Meanwhile Houston and Galveston had been linked by a railroad. The Houston tap and Brazoria Railroad was built to Columbia on the Brazos in 1859, and the following year the Texas and New Orleans was constructed from Houston to Orange on the Sabine.

Railroad building in Louisiana also was of service to Texans. When the New Orleans and Opelousas Railroad reached Berwick's Bay (at present-day Morgan City) during the middle fifties, Cornelius Vanderbilt established regular steamship service between that point and Galveston and Indianola. By this combined rail and water route passengers and mail from New Orleans to Galveston could be transported in twenty-two and a half hours. The principal railroads radiated from

Houston, but there were other lines of less importance elsewhere; from Port Lavaca and Indianola to Victoria and from Shreveport to Marshall.

With all its inconveniences railroad travel was far superior to travel by other conveyances. Reflecting the contrast of the old and the new, the Harrisburg Railroad advertised in 1860 "*The River Bottom and Wet Praries* are NOW BRIDGED, and what was (and is now on some routes) a journey of *days* is now performed in the same number of hours." Charges were five cents per mile for passengers and about a cent per mile for each 100 pounds of freight.

HEALTH

Early-day Texans claimed that their state was the most healthful in America; yet it seems to have been a good place for doctors.

From time to time epidemics took a heavy toll. In the spring of 1833 cholera took 80 lives at Brazoria and nearly depopulated Velasco. The dreaded scourge returned in 1834, ravaging Nacogdoches and taking 91 lives in Goliad. Later cholera epidemics of 1849, 1850, and 1852 particularly endangered the Negro population. In 1846 an epidemic, which may have been typhus, killed scores of people in New Braunfels and Fredericksburg, and also many German immigrants at Indianola on their way to the settlements. Yellow fever appeared from time to time, and next to cholera was the most dreaded disease. The people suffered from many ailments, chills and fever, inflammation of the eyes, summer complaints, rheumatism, biliousness, measles, whooping cough, and small pox.

Although intelligent persons did associate cholera with filth, claims for nostrums and cures were even more extravagant than in our own day, and stores were filled with patent medicines ranging from cancer cures to cough remedies. One merchant said he believed the people used quinine like they used corn meal; they bought it and took it whether they were sick or not. Warning of an impending cholera epidemic, the San Antonio board of health in 1834 prescribed a cleanup campaign, but also recommended a copper amulet to be hung around the neck. Another prescription (almost 100 percent effective, it was claimed!) consisted of water from the boiled peyote cactus, a little lime, and a few drops of laudanum. Later "cures" were little, if any, more scientific than those of earlier years; brandy, cayenne pepper, and mustard were favorite remedies. Perhaps others relied on Vandevee's Schiedam Schnapps, a Holland gin that according to its advertisement not only cured "debility, natural decay, colic, and decline," but also counteracted the "evil effects of overindulgence and excess."

There was, however, some progress in medical science. Although it did not hold a second meeting for 16 years, the State Medical

Association was organized in 1853, with Dr. Ashbel Smith and Dr. J. W. Throckmorton among its more prominent members. In 1854 the distinguished surgeon, Dr. Ferdinand Charles von Herff, of San Antonio, performed a major operation using chloroform.

AMUSEMENTS

The people of Texas brought to their new homes the traditional amusements of the Anglo-American frontier. Athletic contests in which trained teams participated were almost unknown, but there were house raisings, log rollings, shooting matches, bear hunts, wolf hunts, quilting bees, and a dozen other activities where work, sport, and play were mixed. Dancing was popular in country and in town, but the most active church people objected to it. Traveler Rutherford B. Hayes described a dance which began at two o'clock in the afternoon and lasted until four-thirty the next morning. Men and women came on horseback through mud and rain 10 or 15 miles. Hayes found "fewer wallflowers and more life than is usually found in our gatherings."

Balls and formal dinners frequently were given in honor of some distinguished visitor or on some other special occasion. Apparently everybody joined in the patriotic celebrations on July 4, March 2, and April 21. Barbecues, patriotic songs, processions, and fervid oratory were the favorite forms of entertainment. Organizations, such as the Sunday School Union or the Sons of Temperance, sponsored and directed the programs on these occasions. Christmas and New Year's were times for dances, torchlight processions, and other amusements. Thanksgiving was celebrated at various dates according to the proclamation of the President of the United States. The most popular sport, both among rustics and townsmen, was horse racing. Every community had its race track. The track at Velasco was famous in Texas, and well known in New Orleans.

Interest in cultural entertainment was creditable. Most towns had amateur theatrical organizations. As early as 1838 San Augustine had its "Thespian Corps." The distinguished lawyer W. B. Ochiltree was a member and John Salmon Ford, famous as an editor, soldier, and statesman, wrote a play for it. Houston and Galveston each had an active lyceum during the fifties. San Antonio, with its large German population, was a center for artists. The German Casino Association owned a fine building there which was used for theatrical performances, concerts, lectures, exhibits, and dramatic readings. In almost every community, literary societies sponsored debates on ponderous subjects; there were many lectures, both pay and free, and vocal and band concerts. Professional troupes gave performances in all the larger towns. A complete program consisted of a song, a dance, a farce, and a drama. Some of the farces were: "Limerick Boy," "The Irish Tiger," and "The Widow's Victim." Among the dramas were "Cross of Gold," "The Maiden's Vow," and "William Tell."

CRIME, VICE, AND REFORM

Early Texas society, like that of our own day, presented to observers many facets. It was clean and wholesome, base and immoral, or at some level between these two extremes, depending on the point of view of the person describing it.

At an early date Texas acquired a reputation for crime and law-lessness, a reputation not altogether undeserved. The high stand-ards required of citizens by the *empresarios* was not maintained in later years, and many renegades drifted in. The *Houston Telegraph* of January 19, 1842, lists several homicides, and the editor states that they are so frequent as to "foster opprobrium upon the national char-acter." Dueling continued, although the provision against it in the Con-stitution of 1845 reduced the practice. More frequent was the informal duel, where enemies simply "shot it out" at first meeting.

As late as the Republic, the criminal code was harsh and several offenses might be punished by death. One rather notorious woman was sentenced to death for forgery, but President Lamar pardoned her. Whipping and branding were not infrequent. There was no peniten-tiary until 1849. Jails were small and crowded, and jail breaks were common. Law enforcement was lax, a condition which explains why vigilance committees occasionally used direct methods. In 1852 such an organization hanged 12 or 15 persons in the vicinity of San An-tonio, and it was claimed that its work was highly effective in reduc-ing crime.

More common were lesser vices. Gambling was quite prevalent. Gamblers were held in low esteem, but public disapproval apparently was not strong enough to stop their operations. In 1842 the Harris County grand jury found 77 indictments for "playing at cards." The number found by grand juries after 1848 was decidedly less, but the decline probably was due more to greater laxity on the part of the officers than to any change in the habits of the people. Betting on horse races was very common, and occasionally men of some means lost all their property in a single day at the tracks. Drinking was widespread and drunkenness common. In some communities, at least, it was customary for candi-dates to set before voters an open barrel of whiskey. "Profaneness, gam-ing, and intemperance are prevailing vices against which we have to contend," wrote Martin Ruter, the Methodist missionary, of Texas in 1838.

Beyond a doubt, the temperance movement, which entered from

the East shortly after annexation and enlisted the services of prominent churchmen, brought some change. In 1848 M. Yell, Methodist presiding elder, wrote that in a meeting at Caldwell, 67 out of 75 or 80 persons "took the pledge" and in another meeting about 200 signed it. The Sons of Temperance, a national organization opposing the use of alcohol, was organized in Texas in 1848 and in a little more than a year claimed 3,000 members. During the following year it was stated that a majority of the members of the legislature belonged to it. Sam Houston, whose excessive drinking had often been a matter of public comment, had mended his ways, and now worked in behalf of the organization. In 1851 a traveler found local organizations of the Sons in nearly every town and in many rural communities.

Meanwhile there was some legislation on the subject of alcoholic drink. The Republic had found it a troublesome subject and enacted laws requiring license of dealers and a bond guaranteeing that they would keep orderly reputable houses and prevent gambling and quarreling on their premises. A law of 1854 went much further. It permitted the electors of a county by majority vote to forbid the licensing of the sale of liquor in quantities less than a quart, a provision aimed at the saloon. The champions of temperance were not satisfied with such a measure, and in a large convention at Huntsville advocated a "thorough Maine Liquor Law." Of the 41 counties where the subject was submitted to the voters, restrictions of sale was adopted in 35. The law was declared unconstitutional, however, and never went into effect.

EDUCATION

By 1850 there was a strong sentiment for a public school system. People generally were taking a greater interest in education; the agitation of the slavery question was producing an acute sectionalism; and proud Texans were loath to send their children to schools in the North. Even if the parent had to pay tuition, the state, they thought, should contribute funds to make the schools better. In a preceding chapter it was stated that in 1854 the legislature set aside $2,000,000 of the United States indemnity bonds for schools. The law provided for dividing the counties into school districts, but two years later this method of organization was done away with. Thereafter, any group of people might set up a school, employ a teacher, and draw from the state fund each child's money. The share of each child was pitifully small; only 62 cents in 1854 and a dollar and a half the following year. Under the terms of the law it was not even necessary that the people of a community organize and start a public school in order to receive state funds. A parent might select a private school, pay his children's tuition, and at the end of the year receive from the county treasurer the amount of state funds to which he was entitled. In fact, this was done in most cases, with the result that only a few public schools were established.

The most important institutions of learning in Texas before the Civil War were not a part of the public school system. Some were private, wholly under the control of one or two men; others were community enterprises; and a number were under the control of lodges or religious denominations. The Constitution of 1836 did not prohibit private or denominational schools from receiving public aid, and several of these early schools were given land grants by the Republic. There was no classification and no uniformity of standards. Although, with two or three exceptions, their work was confined to elementary and secondary levels, they were called indiscriminately institutes, academies, colleges and universities.

The churches regarded Christian education as an important church function, and they began to establish schools at a very early date. Martin Ruter, the Methodist missionary, had not been in Texas six months when he wrote: "My labor in Texas will be devoted to forming societies and circuits, establishing schools, and making arrangements for a college or university." Schools not under church control generally maintained religious environments. Most of the teachers were preachers. For instance, of the fourteen Presbyterian ministers who came to Texas as missionaries during the Republic, nine engaged in teaching; and as late as 1866, of a list of teachers who attended the Texas teachers' state convention, 18 were ministers and 17 laymen.

The first Protestant denominational school was Rutersville College (named for Martin Ruter), which was established by the Methodists near La Grange. Its preparatory and female departments were opened in January 1840, and its collegiate department for young men in 1841. It was chartered by the Republic and endowed with four leagues of land. For a few years the community was the leading school center of Texas, but about 1850 the school began to decline rapidly. The University of San Augustine, opened in 1842 with a grammar school, a female department, and a college, was widely known for a few years. Associated with it, in 1845 and for some time thereafter, as president of the board of trustees and lecturer in law was Oran M. Roberts, a young lawyer and farmer, lately a graduate of the University of Alabama. Perhaps the most prosperous and best-known school in its day was McKenzie College, founded near Clarksville in 1841. Like others of that day, the school simply grew up around a great teacher, in this case J. W. P. McKenzie. For a period it had as many as three hundred boarding students.

Baylor University, a Baptist school, chartered at Independence by the Republic in 1845, attained a position of leadership at an early

Founded by Colonel R. T. P. Allen, the Bastrop Military Institute was incorporated in 1858 by a board of trustees elected by the Methodist Episcopal Church. The school offered preparatory and collegiate courses of study to such students as Joseph D. Sayers and Sam Houston, Jr. After being closed during the Civil War, Bastrop became the Texas Military Institute in 1868. (Texas Highway Department)

date. It granted 16 degrees in 1858 and 22 in 1859, more for each year than all other schools in Texas combined. Waco University was founded in 1861. The two schools were consolidated as Baylor University, and located at Waco in 1886. The female department of Baylor University became Baylor Female College in 1866 and was moved to Belton in 1886.

From annexation to the beginning of the Civil War, the legislature granted charters to 117 schools and incorporated, in addition, nine educational associations. There were 40 academies, 30 colleges, 27 institutes, seven universities, five schools, three high schools, two seminaries, one collegiate institute, one orphan asylum, and one medical college. Of these only three have survived with anything like a continuous history: Austin College, founded in 1849 at Huntsville through the influence of Dr. Daniel Baker, and moved to Sherman in 1879; Ursuline Academy of San Antonio; and Ursuline Academy of Galveston.

Through their emphasis on discipline, as well as the knowledge they dispensed, these old schools were great civilizing agencies. "Course of study full, instruction thorough, and discipline strict," ran a typical advertisement of the fifties. "A strict discipline rigidly enforced," stated another. The curricula emphasized ancient and modern languages and philosophy. San Augustine University, however, required laboratory work in science and maintained a chemical laboratory and mineralogical cabinet. Even the simplest subjects were described in awe-inspiring terms. Surely parents would be impressed and children terrified on reading that in the city schools of Houston in 1841 were being taught "English, French, Spanish, and Latin, grammatically and etymologically, on the most approved and expeditious principles." Apparently some of the teachers taught everything they had studied; and some, like the Reverend Marcus A. Montrose, graduate of Edinburgh, had had liberal training. At San Augustine University he taught mathematics, Latin, Greek, history, navigation, astronomy, rhetoric, logic, political economy, natural philosophy, chemistry, botany, and geology. In fact, for a period he alone made up the faculty of the university, although he must have been assisted by some of the more advanced students.

Evidently a large majority of early-day Texas youths received their training either in their homes or in "old field schools," unknown beyond the confines of a single community. In spite of the handicaps that confronted teacher and pupil, such training must have been efficient. In 1850 a little less than six percent of the white men of Texas and eight percent of the white women were illiterate. By 1860 illiteracy had decreased to less than four percent among the men and slightly more than five percent among the women.

NEWS PUBLICATION

Although no formal efforts were made to promote adult education, numerous agencies attempted to raise the intellectual level of the people. By 1840 no less than 13 newspapers were being published in Texas, one or two of which were semiweeklies. The *Texas Almanac* of 1857 gives a list of 61 newspapers, five of which were religious, and one, *Port Folio,* of Galveston, literary. The federal census of 1860 reports three daily, three triweekly, and 65 weekly newspapers, and three monthly publications in Texas. The circulation of the weekly papers was 90,615, a number sufficiently large to have reached practically every white person in the state. The most venerable publication was the *Telegraph*, revived at Columbia after the Texan Revolution and moved to Houston in 1837. A neighbor of the *Telegraph*, the *Daily News* of Galveston started in 1842 as a "puny four-page sheet . . . born in a one-room, unpainted shack on the Strand," but lived to become the oldest business institution of Texas. Both the *Dallas News* and the *Galveston News* of our own day trace their lineage to this paper. Under the guidance of Willard Richardson it came to be the greatest champion of the business and commercial interests of Texas, advocating such measures as the repeal of the inhibition against incorporated banks, and a state railroad system. The *State Gazette* of Austin, established in 1849, was edited from 1853 to 1861 by John Marshall, a Calhoun Democrat, associated for a part of the time with William S. Oldham. Marshall and Oldham were brilliant, aggressive men and their paper was noted for its opposition to Sam Houston. Marshall's successor, David Richardson, inaugurated during the Civil War a pony express to carry dispatches from the terminus of the Texas Central Railroad at Hempstead to Austin. Beginning in 1842 Charles DeMorse, soldier, statesman, and editor, published at Clarksville the *Northern Standard*. Its files, unbroken until 1861 and renewed in 1865, constitute the richest source of information extant on early civilization in northeast Texas. Robert W. Laughery's *Texas Republican* at Marshall was well edited and influential. Worthy also were the *Weekly Herald* at Dallas, and the *Chronicle* at Nacogdoches.

The newspapers of early Texas do not meet the standards of our own day. Apparently little or no use was made of such news-gathering agencies as the Associated Press, which was organized in 1848; also, not until the late fifties was there sufficient telegraph mileage to distribute the news well. News from the outside generally came through New Orleans. Many social activities were ignored. It was not deemed good taste to print the names of ladies in newspapers except under very unusual conditions. Yet, more clearly and fully than any other source, these papers describe for us the way of life of that era. They were, furthermore, replete with political news and sharp editorial comment on public affairs, and the people who read them were well informed on important current issues.

Apparently the number of books and magazines increased rapidly during the fifties. The bookstore of Francis D. Allen of Galveston, for instance advertised books: "Standard, Classical, Scientific, Mechanical, School, Historical, Law, Medical, Theological, Agricultural, Poetical, Biographical, Voyages, Novels, etc." One item especially mentioned was Henderson Yoakum's *History of Texas*, which had come from the press a few years before. Richardson and Company sold 10,000 copies of the *Texas Almanac* for 1857, increased the output of the 1858 issue, and published 30,000 copies of 1859, featuring such items as a biographical sketch of General Rusk, and an account of the Texan Revolution. In the census returns for 1850, twelve libraries were listed; the returns for 1860 showed 132. Magazines that were read extensively were *Harper's, Blackwood's, Edinburgh Review, Westminster Review, London Quarterly,* and *Godey's Lady's Book.*

RELIGION

Of all the forces affecting early Texas society none had a greater influence than the churches. As previously stated, itinerant Protestant preachers began their work during the colonial period. It was not until after Texas had her independence, however, that a well-organized missionary program was launched. Methodists and Baptists were in the van; Presbyterians were not so numerous, but their influence was great, and other denominations were active.

When news of the defeat of Santa Anna reached the General Conference of the Methodist Episcopal Church in session at Cincinnati, Ohio, in May, 1836, church leaders were quick to realize that it meant the opening of a mission field rich with opportunities. Martin Ruter, already distinguished by years of service in the church, volunteered as a missionary to Texas then and there. Eighteen months later he crossed the Sabine at Gaines' Ferry and entered Texas. Two other Methodist missionaries, Robert Alexander and Littleton Fowler, had preceded him by a few days; the three worked feverishly, building churches, forming circuits, and organizing classes. Pursuant to an act of the General Conference in 1840, the Texas Conference was organized with 1,878 members and 25 local preachers. In 1844, the same year that the church was divided into a northern and a southern organization over the question of slavery, the East Texas Conference was organized to include the country east of the Trinity, while the remaining territory was continued as the Texas Conference. The Rio Grande mission conference, including the extreme western part of the state, was authorized in 1858. With 30,661 members and 244 traveling preachers, the Methodist church in 1860 was by far the strongest in Texas.

Since Baptists recognized the authority of the local congregation as superior to that of any other body in church matters, it was easy for them to establish churches under frontier conditions. There were preachers and deacons among the immigrants and they frequently organized churches without the aid of a visiting missionary. The sect encountered difficulties, however, because of the presence of two factions, missionary and antimissionary. The first antimissionary church in

Texas was Pilgrim Church, brought intact in 1834 by immigrants from Illinois under Daniel Parker. The first missionary Baptist church was organized at Washington early in 1837; and at once it sent an appeal to organized Baptists in the United States to send missionaries. "Dear brethren, we ask you again," said the fervent Texans, "come over into Macedonia and help us!" People in the East read the appeal, and James Huckins of New Hampshire was sent in 1840. Already the home Mission Society of New York had sent W. M. Tryon; and Z. N. Morrell had begun preaching in the Republic in 1835. Churches and associations were organized rapidly and a state convention was formed in 1848. By 1860 there were approximately 500 Baptist churches in Texas. The denomination had 280 church buildings, as compared with 410 for the Methodists. Baptists, however, led all denominations in the number of church publications.

Presbyterian mission work was begun in 1837 under the especial patronage of the Synod of Mississippi. Hugh Wilson of North Carolina and W. C. Blair of Kentucky were among the early missionaries, and in 1840 came Daniel Baker, whose name looms large in the annals of Texas. Already Presbyterian churches had been established near Independence, and at Houston, Austin, and Galveston. A Presbytery was organized in 1840 and in 1851 the Synod of Texas came into being. In 1857 the Presbyterians had 2,261 members in Texas and by 1860 they had 72 church buildings.

The Episcopal Church sent R. M. Chapman of New York as missionary to Texas in 1838. For a time he made Houston his home but he preached in Galveston one Sunday each month. By 1860 there were 19 Episcopal church houses in Texas. The Christian Church grew rapidly during the decade before the Civil War. In 1850 it owned only five buildings; ten years later it had 39. The Catholics maintained churches in Nacogdoches, San Augustine, and probably in other Texas communities continuously from colonial times. A Catholic church was established in Houston shortly after the Texas Revolution, and by 1860 there were 33 Catholic church buildings in the state.

The churchmen brought with them to Texas practices that had been developed in the United States and tried for a century—protracted meetings, basket meetings, and camp meetings. Sermons were usually long and fervent. The ladies gave suppers, "refreshment parties," "fairs," and bazaars to raise money for the church. There were union meetings, but sectarianism was strong and apparently increased after the period of the Republic. The Protestant leaders advocated a strict observance of Sunday, but evidently did not succeed in bringing it about. Melinda Rankin complained that the day was ignored by many people, and at Crockett, Olmsted found all stores open on Sunday and was told that it was the merchants' best day.

Sunday schools, which apparently were maintained by the more active churches of all Protestant denominations, constituted powerful agencies for Biblical and moral training as well as for enlarging the intellectual horizons of the people. Information concerning effectiveness and methods is meager, but it is evident that their work was by no means confined to the study of the Bible. It would appear that union Sunday schools were more numerous than those maintained by the separate denominations; the American Sunday School Union (nonsectarian) began work in Texas in 1846. The best Sunday schools had libraries; the union school at Brownsville had 1,000 volumes and another at Austin had 1,300. It was stated that wherever a Sunday school was established it generally was followed by Bible classes, temperance societies, and educational interests, and that it served as a "focus where all good influences have converged."

In the society of early days the churches were the greatest civilizing agencies. They brought the people together, clean and in their best apparel. At church the men exchanged greetings and talked on subjects ranging from the weather and crops to the political issues of the day. Here chatted farmers' wives and daughters, tired of drudgery and starved for companionship. The churches, moreover, set the moral standards for many of the people. They attacked immorality of every type; their leaders praised or condemned almost all conduct and every institution. It cannot be said that they always had their way on moral issues, but the most reckless individual dared not ignore them.

The effectiveness of the early churches must be credited in large measure to the quality of their leaders, worthy and courageous men with a selfless devotion to duty. Some were educated, representing the highest culture of their day: Martin Ruter, who committed his church to the cause of education in Texas; Daniel Baker, founder of Austin College; and James Huckins, who wrote his sermons in beautiful, forceful style. The majority had little schooling; they were men of the people who brought spiritual comfort to the most destitute places. One of these, Noah Byars, the gun smith at Washington on the Brazos, who became a preacher, organized in all sixty churches.

Closely associated with the churches and next to them the most influential social agencies were the lodges. Freemasonry had barely been planted before the Texas Revolution uprooted it. With typical Anglo-American resilience the Masons reestablished their order within less than a year. Representatives of Holland Lodge of Houston, Milam Lodge of Nacogdoches, the McFarland Lodge of San Augustine, all of which had been organized by authority of the Grand Lodge of Louisiana, convened at Houston in December 1837 and organized the Grand Lodge of Texas. The order was supported by many distinguished Texans, including Anson Jones and Sam Houston. By 1860, 252 lodges had been organized, one for practically every community, and the order numbered nearly 10,000. Children of poor masons were provided assistance for attending school, and the lodge maintained or sponsored a score or more of schools. The Independent Order of Odd Fellows was introduced into Texas from Louisiana in 1838, chiefly through the efforts of Jacob De Cordova, publisher and land agent. It grew slowly at first, but there was rapid expansion in the fifties and by 1860 there were 74 active lodges and more than 3,000 members. A noteworthy service for that age was the protection it offered members in the form of sick benefits and benefits for the orphans of deceased members.

Selected Bibliography

Much has been written about Texan pioneers. Good general references are J.D. DeCordova, *Texas; Her Resources and Public Men*; the *Texas Almanac* (Galveston) for 1857 through 1862; C.C. Rister, *Southern Plainsmen* (Norman, 1938); W. Gard, *Rawhide Texas* (Norman, 1965); L.B. Friend, "The Texas of 1860," *Southwestern Historical Quarterly*, LXII, 1–17; Earl Fornell, *The Galveston Era* (Austin, 1961); and R.N. Richardson, *The Frontier of Northwest Texas, 1846–1876*.

For contemporary accounts see Marilyn McAdams Sibley, *Travelers in Texas, 1761–1860* (Austin, 1967), and "Bishop Morris in Texas, 1841–1842," *East Texas Historical Journal*, III, 149–168; A.F. Muir (ed.), *Texas in 1837: An Anonymous Contemporary Narrative*; Mary Austin Holley, *The Texas Diary, 1835–1838* (J.P. Bryan, ed., Austin, 1967); R.S. Lee, *Mary Austin Holley: A Biography* (Austin, 1962); Frederick L. Olmsted, *A Journey Through Texas* (1857; James Howard, ed., Austin, 1962); F.R. Lubbock, *Six Decades in Texas*; Charles Michael Gruener, "Rutherford B. Hayes' Horseback Ride Through Texas," *Southwestern Historical Quarterly*, LXVIII, 352–360; and Melinda Rankin, *Texas in 1850* (Boston, 1950).

Some studies of life and institutions are W.R. Hogan, *The Texas Republic*, and his "Pamelia Mann, Texas Frontierswoman," *Southwest Review*, XX, 360–370; J.B. Frantz, *Gail Borden*; W.P. Webb, "Christmas and New Year in Texas," *Southwestern Historical Quarterly*, XLIV, 357–379; J.W. Schmitz, *Texas Culture in the Days of the Republic, 1836–1846* (San Antonio, 1960); Dorothy Kendall Bracken and Maurine Whorton Redway, *Early Texas Homes* (Dallas, 1956); Kenneth W. Wheeler, *To Wear A City's Crown: The Beginnings of Urban Growth in Texas, 1836–1865* (Cambridge, 1968); Roy B. Broussard, *San Antonio during the Texas Republic: A City in Transition* (El Paso, 1968); Caroline Remy, "Hispanic-Mexican San Antonio, 1836–1861," *Southwestern Historical Quarterly*, LXXI, 564–570; A.F. Muir, "Intellectual Climate of Houston during the Period of the Republic," *ibid.*, LXII, 312–321; William Seale, *Texas Riverman* (Austin, 1966); and D.H. Winfrey, *Julian S. Devereux and Monte Verdi Plantation* (Waco, 1962). Scholarly analysis of population characteristics may be found in three articles by R.A. Wooster: "Notes on Texas' Largest Slaveholders, 1860," *Southwestern Historical Quarterly*, LXV, 72–79; "Foreigners in the Principal Towns of Ante-Bellum Texas," *ibid.*, LXVI, 208–220; and "Wealthy Texans, 1860," *ibid.*, LXXI, 163–180.

For economic developments see Robert L. Jones, "The First Iron Furnace in Texas," *Southwestern Historical Quarterly*, LXIII, 279–289; and Charles H. Dillon, "The Arrival of the Telegraph in Texas," *ibid.*, LXIV, 200–211. A.L. Carlson tells the history of Texas banking in the *Texas Monthly*, IV, 481–499, 615–641; V, 74–102. See also Mary Rena Green, *Sam Maverick, Texan, 1803–1870* (San Antonio, 1952). Transportation in early Texas has received considerable study. See Ralph Moody, *Stagecoach West* (New York, 1967) for a general treatment; also, J.W. Williams, "The Butterfield Overland Mail Road Across Texas," *Southwestern Historical Quarterly*, LXI, 1–19; and Emmie Giddings Mahon and Chester V. Kielman, "George H. Giddings and the San Antonio-San Diego Mail Line," *Southwestern Historical Quarterly*, XLI, 220–239. For railroads good studies are C.S. Potts, *Railroad Transportation in Texas* (University of Texas *Bulletin*, No. 119; Austin, 1909); and S.G. Reed, *A History of Texas Railroads* (Houston, 1941). See also P. Briscoe, "The First Texas Railroad," *Quarterly of the Texas State Historical Association*, VII, 279–285; A.F. Muir, "Railroads Come to Houston, 1857–1861," *Southwestern Historical Quarterly*, LXIV, 42–63, and his "The Destiny of Buffalo Bayou," *ibid.*, LXVII, 19–22; and Eugene O. Porter, "Railroad Enterprise in the Republic of Texas," *ibid.*, LIX, 363–371.

On slavery and plantations, see Abigail Curlee, "The History of a Texas Slave Plantation, 1831–1863," *Southwestern Historical Quarterly*, XXVI, 79–127; Karl E. Ashburn, "Slavery and Cotton Production in Texas," *Southwestern Social Science Quarterly*, XIV, 257–271; and E. Fornell, "Agitation in Texas for Reopening the Slave Trade," *ibid.*, LX, 245–259. M.L. Dillon ably presents the activities of an early abolitionist in Texas in *Benjamin Lundy and the Struggle for Negro Freedom.* Later effects of the slavery issue are discussed in Wesley Norton, "The Methodist Episcopal Church and the Civil Disturbances in North Texas in 1859 and 1860," *Southwestern Historical Quarterly*, LXVIII, 317–341.

Pioneer medicine is dealt with in George Plunkett Red, *The Medicine Man in Texas* (Houston, 1930); J.V. Haggard, "Epidemic Cholera in Texas, 1833–1834," *Southwestern Historical Quarterly*, XL, 216–230; P.I. Nixon, *A Century of Medicine in San Antonio* (San Antonio, 1936), *The Medical Story of Early Texas* (San Antonio, 1953), and *A History of the Texas Medical Association, 1853–1953* (Austin, 1954). See also Ashbel Smith, *Yellow Fever in Galveston* (Austin, 1951), and B.M. Jones, *Health Seekers in the Southwest, 1817–1900.*

The best history of education in Texas remains F. Eby, *The De-*

velopment of Education in Texas, but see also C.E. Evans, *The Story of Texas Schools* (Austin, 1955); Mrs. Jonnie L. Wallis (ed.), *Sixty Years on the Brazos* (Los Angeles, 1930), an account of a schoolboy in old Washington; Rev. William M. Baker, *The Life and Labours of the Reverend Daniel Baker* (Philadelphia, 1859); F.B. Baillio, *A History of the Texas Press Association* (Dallas, 1916); Murl L. Webb, "Religious and Educational Efforts Among Texas Indians in the 1850's," *Southwestern Historical Quarterly*, LXIX, 22–37; H.B. Carroll, *Masonic Influence on Education in the Republic of Texas* (Waco, 1960); James David Carter, *Masonry in Texas: Background, History, and Influence to 1846* (Waco, 1958); and John C. English, "Wesleyan College of San Augustine," *East Texas Historical Journal*, III, 141–148. A glimpse of early schools may be had in Emily Jones Shelton, "Lizzie E. Johnson: A Cattle Queen of Texas," *Southwestern Historical Quarterly*, L, 349–366. See also Jefferson Davis Bragg, "Baylor University, 1851–1861," *ibid.*, XLIX, 37–65, and "Waco University," *ibid.*, LI, 213–224.

On religion and the churches see C.E. Castañeda, as listed in Chapter 2; and *The Historical Magazine of the Protestant Episcopal Church*, September, 1941; Macum Phelan, *A History of Early Methodism in Texas, 1817–1866* (Nashville, 1924); W.S. Red, *A History of the Presbyterian Church in Texas* (Austin, 1936); J.M. Carroll, *A History of Texas Baptists* (Dallas, 1923); L.R. Elliott (ed.), *Centennial Story of Texas Baptists* (Dallas, 1936); Mary Angela Fitzmorris, *Four Decades of Catholicism in Texas, 1820–1860* (Washington, 1926); G.L. Crocket, *Two Centuries in East Texas*; Stephen Daniel Eckstein, *History of the Churches of Christ in Texas, 1824–1950* (Austin, 1963).

Useful manuscripts in the University of Texas Library are: Louise C. Cezeaux, on social life in early Texas; Abigail Curlee, on slavery; D.T. Carlton, on the early cotton industry; Mary H. Ellis, on social conditions about 1850; Dorthy K. Gibson, about early San Antonio; Dorothea Bright, concerning early Houston; William F. Ledlow, on Protestant education in Texas; and Carl F. Wilson, on Baptist educational efforts.

10

SECESSION AND WAR, 1860–1865

Ninety percent of the white immigrants to Texas had come from the Old South, bringing with them pronounced opinions on their institutions and rights. Thus, as the rancorous controversy over slavery divided the nation into two well-defined camps, it was natural that the state should join the proslavery group.

Other issues demanded attention, however, and it was not until 1857 that the electorate became aligned in conservative and radical or Unionist and state rights groups. In that year the state rights faction gained control of the Democratic Party. The Whig Party was no more; gone also was the Know-Nothing organization which had been basically Unionist in spite of its zeal for state rights. Henceforth the friends of the Union had no organization. Houston's defeat by Runnels in 1857 may be attributed in part to that fact. During the next two years the regular Democrats became more aggressive and gravitated toward the position of the extreme proslavery group east of the Mississippi. The legislature authorized the governor to send delegates to a Southern convention if it should be deemed expedient. John Marshall, chairman of the state Democratic committee, kept up a barrage of editorials in the *State Gazette* advocating the reopening of the African slave trade. The party convention of 1859 refused to endorse a proposal so extreme, but it did favor the acquisition of Cuba "as a measure which self-protection imperatively demands," it applauded the decision of the Supreme Court in the Dred Scott case, holding that Congress could not legislate slavery out of the territories, and it nominated Runnels for reelection.

Against this organization, Houston, running as an independent on a platform endorsing the Constitution and promising allegiance to the Union, threw into the contest all the strength of his personal popularity and skill as a campaigner. Ex-governor Pease supported him, as also did J. W. Throckmorton, B. H. Epperson, and other old-time Whigs. Touring the state in a buggy, wearing an old linen duster, on hot days sometimes appearing without a shirt, the old warrior made a mighty appeal to the people. In this his last political battle, he defeated Runnels by nearly 9,000 votes, 35,257 to 27,500. By a much narrower margin, Edward Clark, running with Houston as an independent, managed to defeat Lubbock for lieutenant governor. No doubt various factors affected the results of the election. Houston's personal popularity weighed heavily, as did also the dissatisfaction of the people on the frontier who charged Runnels with neglecting to protect them. The conclusion seems inescapable, nevertheless, that the state rights leaders had moved too rapidly for the majority of the voters.

Events thereafter strengthened the hands of the extreme pro-Southern faction. John Brown's raid on Harper's Ferry in October 1859 antagonized and alarmed the people and may account in part for the choice by the legislature of Louis T. Wigfall to represent Texas in the Senate. In the Democratic state convention of April 1860 the state rights leaders, having gained complete control, abandoned restraint. Texas as a sovereign state had the right, they stated, "to withdraw from the confederacy, and resume her place among the powers of the earth as a sovereign and independent nation." The platform deplored "the unnatural efforts of a sectional party at the North to carry on an 'irrepressible conflict' against the institution of slavery" and implied that the election of a Republican president would bring about a dissolution of the Union. This body sent to the national Democratic convention in April at Charleston such staunch champions of the slaveholders' cause as H. R. Runnels, F. R. Lubbock, Guy M. Bryan, R. B. Hubbard, and Tom Ochiltree. At that convention, when Stephen A. Douglas, leader of the Northern Democrats, insisted on a platform endorsing his theory of popular sovereignty in the territories, the delegates from Texas and seven other Southern states withdrew. At an adjourned session at Baltimore, the Democrats from the South nominated John C. Breckinridge, of Kentucky, as their candidate for president and Joseph Lane for vice president; the Northern Democrats chose Stephen A. Douglas and Herschel V. Johnson. At its convention the Republican Party adopted a resolution to the effect that slavery could not legally exist in a territory and selected Abraham Lincoln and Hannibal Hamlin as its nominees.

None of these tickets suited the conservative Southerners, in whose ranks, be it said, were most of the large slaveholders. At Baltimore they organized the Constitutional Union Party, dedicated to the principle that secession would be ruinous to the South and that her only hope lay in fighting for her rights in the Union. On the first ballot Sam Houston received 57 votes as against 68½ for John Bell of Tennessee. Bell was nominated on the second ballot and Edward Everett was chosen as his running mate. Houston permitted his name to go before the country as "the People's candidate," but on August 18 he withdrew formally.

During the eventful year of 1860 public excitement in Texas reached the stage of hysteria. Severe fires, of incendiary origin it was alleged, occurred at Dallas, Denton, Waxahachie, Kaufman, and various other points in North Texas. The fires were charged to abolitionists and linked with stories of slave uprising, poisonings, and assassinations—generally greatly exaggerated if not wholly unfounded. Vigilance committees sprang into action. At Dallas three Negroes were hanged in the presence of a large crowd; three white men, presumably abolitionists, were hanged in Fort Worth because they had been "tampering" with slaves. A growing spirit of intolerance by 1860 pervaded the entire state.

A secret order known as the Knights of the Golden Circle was introduced into Texas in 1860 and soon had established a number of local lodges or "castles." The plans of the organization seem to have been to make slavery more secure in the South, particularly by incorporating into the Union additional slave states from Mexican territory. Two poorly organized filibuster movements against Mexico in 1860 never got beyond the borders of Texas. The Knights did, however, supply organized forces that took an active part in the secession movement.

While in the grip of this psychosis, the people were obliged to make a fateful decision at the polls. The Lincoln-Hamlin ticket did not receive any votes in Texas, and Douglas and Johnson got only 410 votes. Bell's vote was 15,463 and that of Breckinridge, 47,548. The pro-Southern faction had won an overwhelming victory in the state and had suffered a humiliating defeat in the nation.

SECESSION

Lincoln's election drew the issue sharply. The Unionists had no organization but among them were able men: Sam Houston, David G. Burnet, E. M. Pease, J. W. Throckmorton, John and George Hancock,

E. J. Davis, and A. J. Hamilton. The burden of their argument was that the election of Lincoln, although unfortunate, did not warrant secession and that the South could better protect its interests in the Union than out of it. Houston wrote: "Mr. Lincoln has been constitutionally elected, and, much as I deprecate his success, no alternative is left me but to yield to the Constitution."

But each day the conservatives lost ground and the radicals grew stronger. The party soon to be in power had been born in opposition to the extension of slavery, and its leader, now the president-elect, had said publicly that slavery must ultimately be abolished. Southern leaders had given warning that Lincoln's election would mean the dissolution of the Union; to yield at this late date would, they thought, constitute a surrender of their rights. Some of their utterances showed a lack of restraint, but they were effective in the crisis. The editor of the Navarro *Express* wrote: "The North has gone overwhelmingly for Negro *Equality* and Southern Vassalage! Southern men, will you submit to the degradation?"

Various petitions, editorials, and letters were directed at Governor Houston urging him to convene the legislature or call a convention. These steps he refused to take, being determined to make no move that would give aid and comfort to the secessionists. The radicals took matters into their own hands and proceeded with haste and determination. At Austin on December 3, a group of leaders including George M. Flournoy, O. M. Roberts, of the supreme court, Guy M. Bryan, W. S. Oldham, and John Marshall drew up an address to the people of Texas calling on the voters of each representative district to select, at an election to be held on January 8, two delegates to a state convention. Similar resolutions were adopted in several other meetings throughout the state. The elections were held and the convention met as called on January 28, 1861. Meanwhile, Houston had convened the legislature on January 21 in extraordinary session. The legislature ignored Houston's claim that the recent election was illegal, and authorized the convention to act for the people, subject only to the condition that the question of secession be submitted to the voters.

The convention lost no time in dealing with nonessentials. Under O. M. Roberts as president, it approved on the second day by a vote of 152 to 6 a resolution stating: "It is the deliberate sense of this Convention that the State of Texas should separately secede from the Federal Union." A committee on Federal relations then drew up an ordinance of secession which declared that the ordinance of 1845 by which Texas had accepted annexation "is hereby repealed and annulled." The proposed ordinance was to be submitted to the voters on February 23, and unless rejected by a majority of the votes cast, was to take effect on March 2, exactly 25 years after independence had been declared. The vote on the ordinance was taken at noon on February

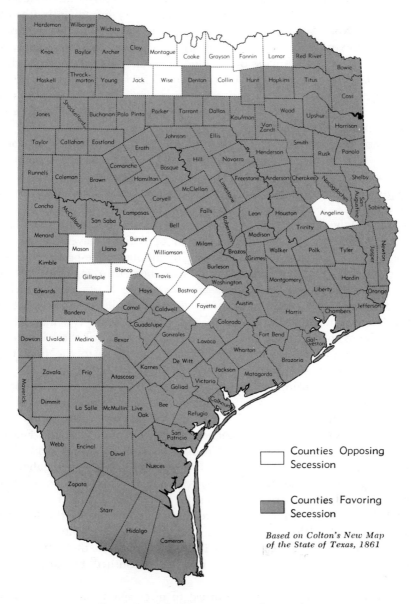

Counties Voting against Secession

From Ernest Wallace, *Texas in Turmoil* (Austin, 1965), p. 70. Reprinted with the permission and assistance of Steck-Vaughn Company, publisher.

1, in the presence of packed galleries. The scene had its dramatic incident. As the roll of delegates was called, only very infrequently was the response "No." Among those who voted thus was J. W. Throckmorton who while voting violated the no-discussion rule. A hiss and applause followed, to which he made the memorable retort: "Mr. President, when the rabble hiss well may patriots tremble." The final vote was 166 to 8.

On the following day the convention drew up a "declaration of causes." It alleged that (1) the general government had administered the common territory of the Union in such a way as to exclude the Southern people from it; (2) because of the disloyalty of the people of the North and the "imbecility" of their government, incendiarism and outlawry were rampant in Kansas; (3) the United States had failed to protect Texas against Indian and Mexican bandits and had refused to reimburse it for expenditures made in defending itself; (4) the people of the North had become hostile to the Southern states and "their beneficent and patriarchal system of African slavery, preaching the debasing doctrine of the equality of all men, irrespective of race or color"; (5) the slaveholding states were now in a minority, unable to protect themselves against the fanatics of the North who preach a "higher law" than the Constitution; (6) and finally the extremists of the North had elected as president and vice-president "two men whose chief claims to such high positions are their approval of these long continued wrongs, and their pledges to continue them to the final consummation of these schemes for the ruin of the slave-holding states."

In South Carolina and the old Gulf states the separating movement had attained even greater momentum than it had in Texas. At Charleston on December 20, 1860, a special state convention had formally dissolved the union between South Carolina and the Federal government. Soon Mississippi, Florida, Alabama, Georgia, and Louisiana followed; representatives of these commonwealths were about to form a government at Montgomery, Alabama. Technically Texas could not act until the voters had spoken at the polls. Before it adjourned on February 5 the convention, nevertheless, took time by the forelock, and sent seven delegates "in order that the views and interests of the people of Texas may be consulted with reference to the Constitution and provisional government that may be established by said convention."

The Texas convention adjourned to meet again on March 2, after the election. It projected itself during the interim by leaving in session a powerful select group called the Committee on Public Safety. The legislature adjourned also, to convene again on March 18.

In the brief period between adjournment and the election many of the delegates took part in the campaign on the ordinance of secession. Judge Roberts issued an appeal to the voters to support secession, and twenty thousand copies of the "Declaration of Causes" were distributed. In the cause of secession, state rights journals of long standing, such as the *Telegraph* (Houston), the *Galveston News, State Gazette* (Austin), and *Texas Republican* (Marshall) were soon joined by more conservative papers such as the *Dallas Herald*. The thin line of Unionists made a noble fight. Twenty-four opponents of secession, from the convention and the legislature, issued an address to the people of Texas urging that they oppose secession, at least until further efforts had been made in the direction of compromise. Supporting such speakers against secession as Houston, Throckmorton, and John Hancock were the *Southern Intelligencer* (Austin), the *Bastrop Advertiser*, the La Grange *True Issue*, and the *Weekly Alamo Express*.

The secessionists amassed a vote of 46,129; their opponents, 14,697. Ten counties in the vicinity of Austin showed antisecession majorities, a fact to be attributed to the large German population, to several Unionist newspapers, and to the efforts of such leaders as Sam Houston, A. J. Hamilton, and John Hancock. Throckmorton and a few associates managed to carry eight counties in northern Texas, where lived a large immigrant population from northern and border states. With only a few exceptions, the heavy slaveholding counties yielded huge majorities for secession.

By their vote on February 23, the electors approved secession; they had taken no action on joining the Confederate States of America. In the minds of most people, however, the two steps seem to have been inseparably linked. The convention reassembled on March 2. Three days later it "approved, ratified, and accepted" the provisional government of the Confederate States of America by a vote of 109 to 2 and directed the Texas delegates at Montgomery to apply for admission to that government. The application was not necessary; already the Confederate Congress had passed an act to admit Texas.

The stride of the secessionists was too rapid for Governor Houston. Thus far he had followed them reluctantly; but when the convention called on him along with other state officers to take the oath of allegiance to the Confederacy, he insisted that it had no authority and defied it. Thereupon, the convention on March 16, 1861, declared the office of governor vacant and made Lieutenant Governor Edward Clark governor. President Lincoln offered to aid Houston if he would oppose the convention with force, but the Governor, unwilling thus to bring on civil war, rejected the proposal. The convention ratified the constitution of the Confederacy on March 23 and three days later adjourned *sine die*.

While the convention was directing the course of secession it did not neglect the state's interest in respect to military affairs. Distributed along the frontier at 21 widely separated posts were about 2,700 Federal troops under the command of Major General D. E. Twiggs, with headquarters at San Antonio. Twiggs, a Georgian in sympathy with the

South, in anticipation of the crisis asked his superiors for instructions, but no orders were given him. Then he offered his resignation, which was accepted; but before he had turned his command over to Colonel C. A. Waite, his successor, he was confronted with a critical situation. The Committee on Public Safety, acting under authority of the Secession Convention, boldly demanded that he surrender to its representatives all public arms and munitions of war under his command. When Ben McCulloch, military commander representing the convention, led an armed force into San Antonio, Twiggs and the commissioners came to terms. It was agreed that the Federal troops, 160 in number, should evacuate San Antonio and surrender to representatives of the Committee all Federal property, that the troops should retain their side arms, camp and garrison equipage, and the facilities of transportation, all to be delivered upon their arrival at the coast. On February 18 Twiggs agreed to the evacuation of all other forts in Texas under similar terms. Henry E. McCulloch received for the Texans the surrender of the northern posts, and John S. Ford took over the posts in the southern part of the state. Thus did the convention by a series of bold strokes and without the firing of a shot put out of action more than ten percent of the regular army of the United States and acquire military supplies and other property valued at $3,000,000. In Texas secession was off to a good start.

After the firing on Fort Sumter, April 12, 1861, and President Lincoln's call for volunteers to suppress the insurrection, both the Texan and Confederate authorities took the position that they were no longer bound by the terms of evacuation made in February. The Federal troops who were still in Texas at the time were held as prisoners of war until paroled or exchanged.

AT THE BATTLE FRONTS

Texas was a border state in the Confederacy, exposed to attack from the north, west, and south. In May 1861, the immediate threat of invasion from the north was removed when W. C. Young, a former sheriff and a resident of Cooke County, led a volunteer regiment of Texas cavalry across the Red River and took Forts Arbuckle, Cobb, and Washita without the firing of a shot.

The problem of protection from the Indian raids that had troubled Texas for a century and a half was never adequately solved by the state and Confederate governments. A Texas regiment under John S. Ford was taken over by the Confederate government and assigned the task of guarding the Rio Grande frontier from Fort Brown, near the Gulf Coast, to Fort Bliss, near the site of El Paso. During 1861, however, companies of minutemen bore the brunt of Indian warfare. Early in

1862 they were replaced by the Frontier Regiment, a state organization under James M. Norris. Norris established a chain of sixteen posts along the frontier from the Red River to the Rio Grande and a regular patrol along the line. The Frontier Regiment was reorganized in 1863, with J. E. McCord as commander. Since the patrols had not been successful, McCord replaced them with scouting expeditions in hope of surprising the Indians. In December 1863, the frontier defense system was again changed. The Frontier Regiment was transferred to Confederate service; a part of it, under the command of Colonel James Bourland, was assigned to defend the frontier along the Red River, and the remainder was sent to the Houston area. To offset the loss, the men in frontier counties liable for military duty were enrolled and required to give a part of their time to protecting the frontier. Bourland's troops gave some aid to the frontier forces, but most of the burden fell on the state troops.

A raid into Young County in October 1864 by Comanche and Kiowa Indians was very destructive. People in the frontier communities moved into stockades for protection—"forting up" they called it. Ironically, the bloodiest battle with the red men during the Civil War resulted from an attack on an inoffensive party of about 1,400 Kickapoo Indians who were skirting the Texas settlements in their migration from the Indian Territory to Mexico. In January 1865 at the Indians' camp on Dove Creek, a tributary of the South Concho, 370 state troops were repulsed with heavy losses. During the last two years of the war deserters added to the threat of hostile Indians by creating confusion on the frontier.

The most aggressive campaign in which Texans participated was that into New Mexico. John R. Baylor, commander of a detachment of Texas troops, after having occupied the Federal posts between Brownsville and El Paso, marched into New Mexico and on August 1, 1861, issued a proclamation establishing the Territory of Arizona which was to comprise that part of New Mexico lying south of the 34th parallel. Later, with Baylor as governor, a constitutional government was established, and for a short while Confederate troops occupied the country as far west as Tucson. Simultaneously, General H. H. Sibley, with three regiments of Texans, sought to drive the Federals out of New Mexico. He defeated a force of over 3,800 at Valverde on February 2, 1862, and took Albuquerque and Santa Fé. On March 28, however, at Glorietta Pass the Federals checked his advance and destroyed his supply train. As a result of this and other disasters, he was obliged to retire from the territory. When with the shattered remnant of his troops he returned to San Antonio in the summer of 1862, the territorial government retreated with him. Thus ended the dream to extend the Confederacy to encompass a port on the Gulf of California and the gold and silver mines of the West.

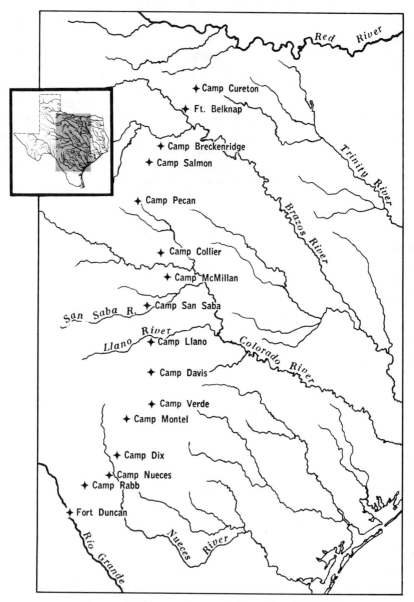

Texas Military Posts during the Civil War

From Ernest Wallace, *Texas in Turmoil* (Austin, 1965), p. 236. Reprinted with the permission of Steck-Vaughn Company, publisher.

Defense of the Texas coast constitutes one of the most brilliant chapters in the story of the Confederacy. In July 1861 the Federal blockade was extended to include Texas. Before a formidable enemy force, state and Confederate troops evacuated Galveston in October 1862. Then John B. Magruder, fresh from the Peninsula Campaign before Richmond and now in command of the Department of Texas, determined to recover the town. With two riverboats armored with cotton bales, and 300 veterans of Sibley's New Mexico campaign serving as marines, he moved against it by sea. A land force was concentrated at Virginia Point, opposite Galveston. On January 1, 1863, the combined forces took Galveston with a loss of 26 killed and 117 wounded. The Federals suffered the loss of two warships and 414 men killed or captured. Four Federal gunboats made their escape.

Fighting also took place about Sabine Pass, the outlet for both the Sabine and the Neches rivers. In September 1862 a Federal blockade patrol forced the Confederates to abandon it. After retaking Galveston, the Confederates on January 21 reoccupied the place and fortified it as well as their limited means would permit. Admiral David G. Farragut and General N. P. Banks then made plans for a major campaign against Texas that would begin with the retaking of Sabine Pass. Four gunboats and 17 transports bearing about 1,500 troops for the initial landing attacked it on September 8, 1863. To meet this formidable force, Lieutenant Dick Dowling had two small gunboats and a garrison of 46 men! Yet he disabled and captured two enemy craft, took about 350 prisoners, and turned back the entire expedition. His victory was a severe blow to the morale of the North and augmented doubts about the efficiency of the Federal Navy. The *New York Herald* credited it, together with the Federal defeat at Chickamauga, with lowering the credit of the United States to the extent of raising the price of gold 5 percent.

Banks' next thrust was more successful. With a combined naval and land force of about 7,000 men he moved against the lower Rio Grande, where the Confederate garrisons were pitiably weak. Beginning with the taking of the island of Brazos de Santiago off the mouth of the Rio Grande on November 1, 1863, seizures were extended to include Brownsville, Corpus Christi, Aransas Pass, Indianola, and other points, until Galveston and Sabine Pass were the only ports left to the Confederates.

In the spring of 1864 Banks made his last campaign against Texas. From Alexandria, Louisiana, 25,000 well-equipped veterans, sustained by a powerful flotilla of gunboats, moved up the Red River. Banks planned to unite this army with 15,000 men under General Frederick Steele, who was moving southward from Little Rock. It was expected that the combined forces would crush all opposition and extend their operations over all northern Louisiana, southern Arkansas, and eastern Texas. The Confederate shops at Marshall and Henderson and the rich East Texas farm country constituted choice prizes. With a large part of his best troops drawn away to sustain the flagging Confederate cause in the East, General E. Kirby Smith, in command of the Trans-Mississippi Department, worked desperately to form an army to cope with Banks. Magruder in Texas sent him every man he could spare; and as the regiments hastened eastward old men and beardless boys were enlisted to offset losses by death, disease, and desertion. With 8,000 cavalrymen, Sterling Price stopped Steele at Camden, Arkansas. Richard Taylor, in immediate command of the army that faced Banks, had a force made up largely of troops from Texas, Louisiana, Arkansas, and Missouri, including Walker's division of Texas infantry and Tom Green's brigade of cavalry. On April 8, with 11,000 effective troops, he attacked and all but routed Bank's army at Mansfield, Louisiana, 50 miles below Shreveport, taking 2,500 prisoners. The Confederates were repulsed on the following day at Pleasant Hill, but Banks hastily retreated to the east side of the Mississippi.

In the summer of 1864, the Confederate forces under John S. Ford recaptured Fort Brown and forced the Federals in South Texas to withdraw from the mainland. The last battle of the Civil War was fought when the Federals in the spring of 1865 attempted to recapture Fort Brown. At Palmito Ranch near Brownsville on May 13 Ford with a force of 300 met and defeated two Negro regiments and a company of unmounted Texas (Union) cavalry. From the 111 prisoners he took in that engagement Ford learned that General Robert E. Lee had surrendered more than a month before.

Even after Joseph E. Johnston had surrendered the last major Confederate army on April 18, 1865, Governor Murrah, General Kirby Smith, and other leaders insisted that the war be continued in the West. That was the decision on May 13 of the conference of the representatives of Trans-Mississippi states held at Marshall after Grant had insisted on the same terms of surrender that were granted to General Lee. Thereafter Smith, Magruder, and Murrah made various unsuccessful efforts to secure more favorable terms. Meanwhile the armies of the West melted away, and General Smith, left without an army, formally surrendered the Trans-Mississippi Department at Galveston on June 2.

SUPPLYING MEN

In Texas there was a pronounced tradition that young men should join the colors in an emergency, and as early as September 30, 1861, ten regiments of Texas troops had already been organized. It was thought at first that Texans would not be needed east of the Mississippi. Early in 1862, however, Governor Lubbock received a call for 15 regiments of infantry, and these, he stated in his memoirs, were made up of volunteers "in a few months." He thought Texas had about 20,000 men in military service before conscription went into effect.

The first Confederate conscription act was passed on April 16, 1862, applying to men from 18 to 35 years of age. In September of that year the age limit was raised to 45, and a later act extended the limits from 17 to 50. On December 25, 1861, the state provided for the enrollment and organization of the militia; an act of March 7, 1863, provided that the militia might be transferred into Confederate service for a period of no more than a year. A state act of May 28, 1864, provided for the transfer of state troops to Confederate service, except officers of the state government and privates not subject to the Confederate conscription laws.

There were liberal exemptions, especially for officeholders and persons supposedly indispensable in the professions, agriculture, and industry. Certain Texans were exempted also for frontier defense. The law, furthermore, permitted the hiring of substitutes. Beyond a doubt the lax exemption policy and the provision permitting a man to hire a substitute had a bad effect on the morale of the troops and the people behind the lines.

Texas contributed significantly in manpower to the Confederate military effort. She furnished one general (Albert Sidney Johnston), three major generals (S. B. Maxey, John A. Wharton, and Tom Green), 32 brigadier generals, and 97 colonels. It is impossible to determine the number of men who saw military service either as state or Confederate troops during the war. Even Governor Lubbock, who should be a dependable authority for the period when he was chief executive, gives figures that are difficult to reconcile. In February, 1863, he stated that Texas had in actual service 68,500 men, including 6,500 state troops. His figures evidently included a number of duplications, particularly among those who volunteered for state duty and afterwards entered Confederate service. According to the census of 1860, white males in Texas between the ages of 18 and 45 numbered 92,145. Some 58,533 men were recruited in the cavalry alone. Probably two-thirds of those who served remained west of the Mississippi.

Texans fought on every battlefront and a host of witnesses vouch for their valor. For mobility, and heroic daring, the organization named after B. F. (Frank) Terry was unsurpassed; Ross's Texas Brigade fought well on both sides of the Mississippi; Hood's Texas Brigade broke the Federal lines at the Second Battle of Manassas and at Gaines' Mill, Virginia, and became the first division of Longstreet's famous corps. The war exacted of the state a cruel toll. Among the uncounted host who did not return were Ben McCulloch, who fell at Pea Ridge; Albert Sidney Johnston, killed at Shiloh; and two-thirds of Terry's Texas Rangers, whose graves might be found in half a dozen states.

THE STATE AND THE CONFEDERACY

Party activity ceased during the war. Unionists, pacifists, and defeatists were obliged to keep their counsel, for secessionists were completely in the ascendency. No party nominations were made in 1861. In the race for governor, Francis Richard Lubbock, who had served as lieutenant governor during Runnels' administration, defeated Edward Clark, the incumbent, by only 124 votes. John M. Crockett, mayor of Dallas, was elected lieutenant governor. At the same election, congressmen were chosen to represent the state at Richmond. Louis T. Wigfall and W. S. Oldham were elected to the Confederate Senate. John H. Reagan accepted an appointment as postmaster-general in President Jefferson Davis' cabinet.

State efforts during Lubbock's administration were centered on winning the war. The governor supported the Confederacy with all his power, and most legislation pertained to defense. A military board consisting of the governor, comptroller, and treasurer was authorized to dispose of the bonds of the United States then held by Texas or to use other means in purchasing military supplies. Other acts suspended all laws for the collection of debts, validated bonds issued for military purposes, authorized special county taxes for war purposes, appropriated money for equipping troops, and authorized the receipt of Confederate notes and treasury warrants for taxes.

Confederate reverses, Lincoln's Emancipation Proclamation, and "signs of a latent dissatisfaction at the existing state of things if not a positive disloyalty to the Confederacy" caused Lubbock to call an extra session of the legislature for February 2, 1863. That body doubled taxes, and appropriated $600,000 for the use of needy families of soldiers and $200,000 as a hospital fund for sick and wounded Texans in the Confederate armies.

In 1863 Lubbock entered the Confederate service and did not stand for reelection. The race soon became a contest between T. J. Chambers (candidate for the fourth time) and Pendleton Murrah, a Harrison County lawyer. Murrah, more emphatic than Chambers in his promise to support the Confederate cause in every way possible, defeated Chambers by a vote of 17,511 to 12,455, the total vote being only a little more than half that cast in the preceding election. F. S. Stockdale, who had helped draft the ordinance of secession, was elected lieutenant governor. The election results revealed no special dissatisfaction with the course of events at Richmond.

Every war governor proclaimed his loyalty to the Confederacy and his determination to work with it harmoniously. The Texas Supreme Court upheld the constitutionality of the Confederate conscription law. It declared constitutional the act abolishing substitution in the

Oran M. Roberts (above left): *judge, secessionist leader, governor, and professor of law at the University of Texas where he was awarded the title "the Old Alcalde." Thomas J. Rusk* (above right): *secretary of war during the Texas revolution, and one of the first two United States Senators from Texas. Ashbel Smith* (right): *Yale graduate, physician, secretary of state of the Republic of Texas, Confederate colonel, and a leader in the cause of education.* (University of Texas Library)

army, even though it violated the obligation of contract. General P. O. Hébert, with the approbation of Governor Lubbock, proclaimed martial law for the entire state in order better to enforce the conscription law. His decree was, however, soon annulled by the Secretary of War.

The most serious clash of authority grew out of the Texas law of 1863, which provided for organizing into companies for defense all men of military age in frontier counties and for exempting them from conscription under the Confederate laws. Obviously the proposed exemption was in conflict with the Confederate constitution, but Murrah insisted on its enforcement. Then, when General Kirby Smith, desperately in need of troops to repel Banks in Louisiana in the spring of 1864, called on Murrah through Magruder to send more men, the governor quibbled over certain relatively unimportant matters until it was too late for the state troops to be of service.

In defense of Murrah it should be said that as the war progressed the Trans-Mississippi states were thrown more and more on their own resources, and it was natural that he should hesitate to transfer men from state control to the Confederate authorities.

As the war proceeded complaints of neglect of the West by the Confederate government became more emphatic. The governor of Arkansas stated in June 1862 that if the western states were not to be protected the sooner they knew it the better. At the request of President Davis, Governor Lubbock and Governor Claiborne F. Jackson of the Confederate government of Missouri met at Marshall, Texas, in July 1862 and framed a request to the Richmond government for a commanding general for the Trans-Mississippi West, for money, and for arms and ammunition. The government at Richmond gave them a commanding general and a fiscal agency for the department. E. Kirby Smith, commander of the Trans-Mississippi Department, called another conference of western state representatives at Marshall for August 15, 1863. The conference, presided over by Governor Lubbock, favored more friendly relations with the French in Mexico; agreed on a plan of exchanging cotton for supplies in Mexico; suggested that Confederate notes be reissued for meeting military expenses; and recommended that in his department General Smith "assume at once and exercise the powers and prerogatives of the President of the Confederate States."

In connection with the purchase of cotton and the plan of exchange approved by the Marshall conference, another sharp conflict arose between state and Confederate authorities. Pursuant to an act of Congress, the Confederate government in 1863 began to impress cotton to be hauled to the Rio Grande and exchanged for necessary supplies. The Marshall conference approved a plan, which Smith had already put in operation, whereby the Confederacy was to acquire and dispose of cotton through a bureau with headquarters at Shreveport. Under this arrangement the planter or other holder would be asked to

James S. Hogg (left) *earned a reputation as champion of the people's rights when he served as Attorney General and Governor of Texas during the last quarter of the nineteenth century, the period when big business was being brought under public control. John H. Reagan* (right) *served Texas, The United States, and the Confederate States of America with distinction. He resigned as United States Senator to accept the chairmanship of the first railroad commission of Texas in 1896.* (University of Texas Library)

sell half of his cotton, after which the other half would be exempt from impressment. Owners were to be paid for their cotton in certificates redeemable in cotton bonds or by such other methods as the Confederate Congress might provide. To compete with Smith's bureau the Texas Military Board under Governor Murrah's "state plan," would contract for all of a planter's cotton, transport it to the Rio Grande, and there give half of it back to the owner, paying for the other half in state bonds. Obviously, the Confederate Cotton Bureau could not compete with the state under such a system, and the importation through Mexico and Texas of arms and other materials equally vital would have to cease. Through an act of February 6, 1864, the Confederate Congress seized control of the situation by prohibiting the exportation of cotton, tobacco, and certain other commodities except under regulations made by the President. At a conference in July 1864 Governor Murrah and General Kirby Smith arrived at an understanding, and thereafter Murrah cooperated to the fullest extent.

The financial condition of the state during the war is difficult to describe accurately. Most of the transactions were made in depreciated Confederate currency and equally depreciated state treasury warrants. Net expenditures—that is, warrants actually paid by the treasurer from August 31, 1861, to June 8, 1865—aggregated $4,863,790.55, more than three-fourths of which were attributable to the war. Total net receipts for the same period were $8,161,298. About 40 percent of the receipts had been derived from a wide variety of taxes, 8 per cent from the sale of bonds, 38 per cent profits on the penitentiary, and 14 per cent from miscellaneous sources. In the treasury on August 1, 1865, was $3,368,510 (most of which was in the form of worthless money), and there was a debt of about $8,000,000. In its desperation the state government had used special trust monies, such as the school fund and the university fund to the amount of almost $1,500,000. A commentary both on the confusion of the times and the poverty of the state is the fact that when certain persons looted the state treasury on the night of June 11, 1865, all that they found of value and negotiable was $5,000 in specie.

Far greater than the burden of state taxes was the burden of Confederate taxes, which during the four years from 1861 through 1864 amounted in Texas to $37,486,854.

THE PEOPLE AT HOME
DURING THE WAR

The rank and file of Union sympathizers in Texas at the time of secession may be classified in three groups: (1) those who accepted the decision of the state electorate as binding upon them and sustained heartily the efforts of the Confederacy; (2) those who tried to remain neutral; and (3) a few who left the state or tried to do so. J. W. Throckmorton, who became a general in the Confederate armies, is, perhaps, the most widely known representative of the first class. Of those who tried to remain neutral the largest group consisted of Germans in settlements near the coast and in the counties west of Austin. Many of these people, it is true, volunteered and became superb soldiers for the Confederate cause, but among them were large groups who never became reconciled to secession. North Texas, with its heavy immigrant population from the free states and border slave states, also had many persons who opposed the war. For protection against Indians and for avoiding conscription, the Germans organized the Union Loyal League in 1861, but later were forced to disband it. A few determined to leave the state, and in August 1862 about 65 Germans on their way to Mexico were attacked by Confederate forces and 34 of them were killed. In Colorado, Austin, and Fayette counties, Germans and some Anglo-Americans organized to resist the draft, but General Magruder declared martial law, arrested the leaders, and quelled open resistance.

It was in the northern part of the state that the war psychosis became most severe. In 1862 a secret organization popularly referred to as the Peace Party was discovered. Its aims were to avoid the draft, to provide a spy system for the Northern army, and to prepare the way for an invasion of North Texas by Federal troops. Spies visited its meetings and soon the excited people were repeating in whispers reports that its leaders were planning arson, murder, and a general reign of terror. The Confederate military forces joined civilians in a grim campaign to destroy the movement in its infancy. About 150 men were arrested and tried at Gainesville by "people's courts," which were neither military nor constitutional. Some confessed; 40 were hanged, most of them on no other charge, it seems, than membership in the organization. The Wise County people's courts were more deliberate; only five men were hanged there. In Grayson County 40 men were arrested, but J. W. Throckmorton interceded with a plea for justice, a court of investigation reviewed their cases, and all but one were released.

Many outspoken critics of the war were arrested, in most cases by the military under laws that had suspended the writ of *habeas corpus*. Of such cases the best known is that of Dr. Richard R. Peebles, of near Hempstead, and four other prominent citizens who were arrested in October 1863, on charges of plotting treason against the Confederate government. Peebles and two associates were exiled to Mexico.

Numbers of Unionists managed to leave Texas early in the war and many others made their way to Matamoros where they were rescued by Federal ships. Others hid themselves in isolated places, where soon they were joined by deserters from the state and Confederate forces.

By February 1863 the problem of desertion had become so serious that General Magruder was urging Governor Lubbock to aid him in suppressing it. Eight months later, Henry E. McCulloch, in command of the northern submilitary district, estimated that there were 1,000 deserters in his territory and declared that he did not have sufficient troops to arrest them. He offered them special inducements to join the army and succeeded thus in enlisting 300; but he found that these "bush soldiers" had a weakness for returning to the brush! Soon deserters were so numerous in Wise, Denton, and neighboring counties that they intimidated loyal citizens. Sterner measures apparently brought about improvement in 1864, but during the last few weeks of the war conditions grew distinctly worse.

The story of the disloyal and dissatisfied minority must not be permitted to obscure the fact that the overwhelming majority of Texans at home and at the front supported until the end the waning Confederate cause with a selfless devotion that may well prove an inspiration to all posterity.

The war forced radical readjustments in farming. The demand for cotton declined and that for food crops increased. Newspapers urged the planting of more corn. There was some agitation for laws to compel changes in acreage to meet the emergency, but no such legislation was enacted. From time to time there was a shortage of farm labor, and the families of poor soldiers frequently found it difficult to work their farms. Crops were good during the years of the war, and except in a few isolated cases, no one suffered for food. Salt, an absolute necessity for livestock and the preservation of meat, became so scarce that a soldier's salary for a month would not buy a sack; the Grand Saline in Van Zandt County, the Brooks salines, and a few other sources supplied most of the state. The frontier people visited Ledbetter's Salt Works, near the site of Albany, the salt flats along the upper Brazos, and the salt lakes in the vicinity of El Paso.

Of medicines and hospital supplies there was never enough. In 1864 a serious effort was made by the military authorities to encourage the growing of poppies for opium, and the press frequently called the attention of the public to shrubs and plants of medicinal value. Through ladies' aid associations loyal women did their best to supply bandages and other equipment for the wounded; much clothing also was contributed. Relief committees received donations and distributed funds and goods for the benefit of the wives and children of soldiers. In 1863 it was said that the citizens of Houston were contributing nearly $3,000 a week to this purpose. People soon learned to make various substitutions in food and clothing. The ashes of corncobs served as soda; parched sweet potatoes, rye, and okra were substitutes for coffee; women learned to make hats and fans out of shucks and straw; and the spinning wheel again came into use. The people took great pride in their self-sufficiency. Governor Lubbock was inaugurated in a homespun suit; and the "homespun dress that Southern ladies wear" became a theme of song and story.

The shortage of manufactured goods was a great handicap. An arsenal, which turned out a few cannon, and a cap and cartridge factory were established in Austin. Many corporations for the manufacture of goods were chartered, but most of them never reached production. The largest cloth factory was at the penitentiary in Huntsville. Iron foundries were opened near Jefferson and Rusk, and the tanning industry increased rapidly. Likewise the output of wagons, ambulances, harness, and saddles increased sharply. By 1863 many newspapers were forced to suspend publication for want of paper.

As the Federal blockade became more effective, the flow of imports and exports to and from the South was reduced to an intermittent trickle. Cotton, the chief export commodity, was hauled to the Rio Grande over different routes and in such quantities that one observer declared that "the chaparral would be almost white in places from the lint detached from passing bales." In spite of the costs and hazards of the trade, men would undertake it, for cotton in 1862 at the Rio Grande brought from 20 to 72 cents per pound, and in 1864 the price in New York ranged from 72 cents to $1.90 per pound. On their return the cotton wagons brought sugar, coffee, cloth, nails, and sometimes medicines and military supplies.

Imported consumer goods were in great demand but there never was enough to go around. After the arrival of a shipment, stores were more badly crowded than the present-day bargain counters on the morning of a special sale. Mrs. Maverick, of San Antonio, relates that she "went and stood wedged up and swaying about till near 12," when, at last, she managed to get "one bolt of domestic cloth, one pr. shoes and 1 doz. candles for $180.00." Although that particular merchant's stock had cost $60,000 in specie, she thought it would be exhausted within a week. As the value of the currency declined and prices soared there was much complaint about "unfair and unjust speculators."

Men of nonmilitary age and women made brave efforts to keep up the morale of their communities, in spite of the reports of Confederate reverses and the tragic news from sons and husbands that they received from time to time. There are accounts of Christmas celebrations as in ordinary times, of parties and receptions for returned soldiers, and of "war meetings" with stirring speeches and "dinner on the grounds." It was the zeal and courage of the people behind the lines, quite as much as the efforts of the men in the field, that sustained for four years the Confederate cause against overwhelming odds.

Selected Bibliography

The best general accounts of Texas during the Civil War are in D.G. Wooten, F.W. Johnson, J.H. Brown, H.H. Bancroft, and E. Wallace, *Texas in Turmoil*, all previously cited. An excellent but very brief survey of Texas in the Civil War is Allan C. Ashcraft, *Texas in the Civil War: A Resume History* (Austin, 1962).

The chief sources for secession are E.W. Winkler (ed.), *Journal of the Secession Convention of Texas, 1861* (Austin, 1912); and *War of the Rebellion, Official Records, Union and Confederate Armies* (130 vols., Washington, 1880–1900). Accounts of some merit by participants, in addition to O.M. Roberts' in D.G. Wooten's work, are F.R. Lubbock, *Six Decades in Texas*; and E.L. Dohoney, *An Average American* (Paris, Texas, 1907). The best studies on secession are: C.W. Ramsdell, *Reconstruction in Texas* (New York, 1910); C.W. Ramsdell, "The Frontier and Secession," reprinted from *Studies in Southern History and Politics* (Columbia University Press, 1914); C.W. Ramsdell, *Behind the Lines in the Southern Confederacy* (Baton Rouge, 1944);

Laura W. Roper, "Frederick Law Olmstead and the Western Texas Free Soil Movement," *American Historical Review*, LIV, 58–65; C. Elliott, *Leathercoat: The Life of James W. Throckmorton;* Anna Irene Sandbo, "Beginnings of the Secession Movement in Texas," *Southwestern Historical Quarterly*, XVIII, 41–73; A.I. Sandbo, "The First Session of the Secession Convention of Texas," *ibid.*, 162–194; R.A. Wooster, "Analysis of the Membership of the Texas Secession Convention," *ibid.*, LXII, 322–335; C. A. Bridges, "The Knights of the Golden Circle," *ibid.*, XLIV, 287–302; Dunn, "The KGC in Texas, 1860–1861," *ibid.*, LXX, 543–573; C. Elliott, "Union Sentiment in Texas, 1851–1865," *ibid.*, L, 449–477; Frank H. Smyrl, "Unionism in Texas, 1856–1861," *ibid.*, LXVIII, 172–195; Floyd F. Ewing, "Origins of Union Sentiment on the West Texas Frontier," *West Texas Historical Association Year Book*, XXXII, 21–29; Floyd F. Ewing, "Unionist Sentiment on the Northwest Texas Frontier," *ibid.*, XXXIII, 58–70.

Accounts of Texas troops in the war include Robert Lee Kerby, *The Confederate Invasion of New Mexico and Arizona, 1861–1862* (Los Angeles, 1958); C.P. Roland, *Albert Sidney Johnston: Soldier of Three Republics;* O.B. Faulk, *General Tom Green: Fightin' Texan;* W.J. Hughes, *Rebellious Ranger: Rip Ford and the Old Southwest;* Ludwell Johnson, *The Red River Campaign: Politics and Cotton in the Civil War* (Baltimore, 1958); E. Wallace, *Charles DeMorse: Pioneer Editor and Statesman;* C. Elliott, *Leathercoat: The Life of James W. Throckmorton;* Stephen B. Oates, *Confederate Cavalry West of the Mississippi River* (Austin, 1961); James L. Nichols, *The Confederate Quartermaster in the Trans-Mississippi* (Austin, 1964); J.B. Hood, *Advance and Retreat* (New Orleans, 1880); Victor M. Rose, *Ross' Texas Brigade* (Louisville, 1881); V.M. Rose, *The Life and Services of General Ben McCulloch* (Philadelphia, 1888; Austin, 1958); Walter P. Lane, *The Adventures and Recollections of General Walter P. Lane* (Marshall, 1887); August Santleben, *A Texas Pioneer* (New York, 1910), in the Union service; Xavier Blanchard DeBray, *A Sketch of the History of DeBray's (26th) Regiment of Texas Cavalry* (Waco, 1961); Harold B. Simpson (ed.), *Touched with Valor: Civil War Papers and Casualty Reports of Hood's Texas Brigade* (Hillsboro, Texas, 1964); Marcus J. Wright, *Texas in the War, 1861–1865* (Harold B. Simpson, ed., Hillsboro, Texas, 1965); W.H. Watford, "Confederate Western Ambitions," *Southwestern Historical Quarterly*, XLIV, 161–187; S.B. Oates, "Recruiting Confederate Cavalry in Texas," *ibid.*, LXIV, 463–477; Alwyn Barr, "Texas Coastal Defense, 1861–1865," *ibid.*, LXV, 1–31; A. Barr, "The Battle of Calcasieu Pass," *ibid.*, LXVI, 59–67; Allen W. Jones, "Military Events in Texas during the Civil War, 1861–1865," *ibid.*, LXIV, 64–70; C. C. Jeffries, "The Character of Terry's Texas Rangers," *ibid.*, LXIV, 454–462; F.H. Smyrl, "Texans in the Union Army, 1861–1865," *ibid.*, LXV, 234–250; Charles C. Cumberland, "The Confederate Loss and Recapture of Galveston, 1862–1863," *ibid.*, LI, 109–130; E.C. Barker and Frank Vandiver, "Letters from the Confederate Medical Service in Texas, 1863–1865," *ibid.*, LV, 378–401, 459–474; Theophilus Noel, *Autobiography and Reminiscences* (Chicago, 1904); W.C. Holden, "Frontier Defense in Texas during the Civil War," *The West Texas Historical Association Year Book*, IV, 16–31; Harry M. Henderson, *Texas in the Confederacy* (San Antonio, 1955); John P. Dyer, *The Gallant Hood* (New York, 1950); R.N. Richardson, *The Frontier of Northwest Texas*; Richard Taylor, *Destruction and Reconstruction* (Richard B. Harwell, ed., New York, 1955).

Phases of home life and public affairs during the Civil War are dealt with in Mrs. E.M. Loughery, *War and Reconstruction in Texas* (Austin, 1914); Thomas North, *Five Years in Texas* (Cincinnati, 1871); Grover C. Ramsey (comp.), *Confederate Postmasters in Texas, 1861–1865* (Waco, 1963); Alma D. King, "The Political Career of William Simpson Oldham," *Southwestern Historical Quarterly*, XXXIII, 112–133; C.W. Ramsdell, "The Texas State Military Board, 1862–1865," *ibid.*, XXVII, 253–275; Robert W. Shook, "The Battle of the Nueces, August 10, 1862," *ibid.*, LXVI, 31–42; Carland Elaine Crook, "Benjamin Théron and French Designs in Texas During the Civil War," *ibid.*, XLVIII, 432–454; Thomas L. Miller, "Texas Land Grants to Confederate Veterans and Widows," *ibid.*, LXIX, 59–65; Sam Acheson and Julie Ann Hudson O'Connell (eds.), "George Washington Diamond's Account of the Great Hanging at Gainesville, 1862," *ibid.*, LXVI, 331–414; Thomas Barrett, *The Great Hanging at Gainesville* (Austin, 1961).

Scores of county histories deal with certain phases of the war. Brief biographies of the governors of Texas may be found in J.T. DeShields, *They Sat in High Places; The Presidents and Governors of Texas*. Many excellent unprinted studies are available in the university libraries in Texas.

11

RECONSTRUCTION, 1865–1874

On June 19, 1865, General Gordon Granger with the first contingent of occupation troops arrived at Galveston and in the name of President Johnson proclaimed the authority of the United States over Texas. He declared that the slaves were free;[1] that all acts of the Texas government since secession were illegal; and that officers and men of the late Confederate army should be paroled.

A few troops were sent into the interior and a greater number were concentrated on the Rio Grande as a threat to the French in Mexico. The troops were supposed to restore the authority of the United States in Texas and preserve order. For some weeks they did neither. No organized resistance arose, but the confusion incident to the breakup of the Confederate armies continued unabated. Generals Kirby Smith and Magruder and Governor Murrah, along with many other prominent ex-Confederates, had fled to Mexico and no state government whatsoever existed.

A month after the landing of Granger, A. J. Hamilton, ex-congressman and staunch Unionist, arrived to serve as provisional governor. Thus was inaugurated the era of reconstruction, and thereafter for

---

[1]President Lincoln's preliminary emancipation proclamation had been announced on September 22, 1862. Texas Negroes, however, observe June 19 as the date of their emancipation.

almost five years the policies of the state government were dictated from Washington and were not in harmony with the views of the majority of Texas' citizens. The entire reconstruction period, enduring for a little less than nine years, may be divided as follows: (1) presidential reconstruction, including the provisional government, from June 19, 1865, to August 20, 1866, when President Johnson declared the insurrection at an end in Texas; (2) constitutional government subject to annoyance by the military from August 20, 1866, to March 1867; (3) congressional reconstruction, from March 1867 when the reconstruction program of Congress was begun, to April 16, 1870, the date that "all civil authority" was remitted to the officers of Texas; and (4) radical rule and its overthrow, from April 16, 1870, to January 17, 1874, the date that Richard Coke, Democrat, succeeded E. J. Davis, Republican, as governor of Texas.

PRESIDENTIAL RECONSTRUCTION

Northern leaders were divided over how reconstruction should be accomplished. President Lincoln held that secession was illegal and that reconstruction was thus the responsibility of the executive branch of the government. Congress, on the other hand, maintained that the Confederate states by secession had forfeited their statehood and, since it alone had the power to admit new states, that therefore it had the power to reconstruct. In conformity with his ten percent plan, permitting the establishment of new loyal governments, Lincoln accorded presidential restoration to Tennessee, Louisiana, and Arkansas. He also granted legitimate status to the refugee loyalist government of Virginia, and by a pocket veto killed the Wade-Davis bill in which Congress had countered with its plan. Nothing further was done to reorganize Southern state governments until after the end of the war.

On May 29, 1865, President Andrew Johnson prescribed in two proclamations a process of reconstruction for the remaining Confederate states which was essentially the same as Lincoln's. The Amnesty Proclamation excluded 14 classes, including high ranking military and civil officers and persons whose taxable property was worth over $20,000; the second proclamation provided for the restoration of civil government in North Carolina. During the next few weeks the President issued proclamations identical to the latter for each of the remaining six former Confederate states. The Texas proclamation, in which Hamilton was named provisional governor, was issued on June 17.

Governor Hamilton set out to establish the state government anew in its entirety. He appointed James H. Bell, a former member of the supreme court, secretary of state, and William Alexander attorney general, both Union men. As rapidly as practicable, Union men, with a few exceptions, were appointed to the district, county, and precinct offices throughout the state. In keeping with President Johnson's plan of reconstruction the governor called an election of delegates to a constitutional convention to convene on February 7, 1866. Under the President's plan four conditions had to be met before he would accept the work of the convention: the abolition of slavery; the establishment of the civil status of the new freedman; the repudiation of the ordinance of secession; and the repudiation of debts, both state and Confederate, incurred in behalf of the war.

When the convention assembled, two old factions, Unionists and secessionists, faced each other under new conditions. John Hancock, I. A. Paschal, and E. Degener were sitting opposite such confirmed rebels as H. R. Runnels and O. M. Roberts. Between them was a group, larger than either, inclined to be conservative and to avoid any permanent alignment with the opposing factions. J. W. Throckmorton, a moderate who had been both a Unionist and ex-Confederate brigadier, was chosen president.

The convention spent much time in trying to decide what disposition to make of the ordinance of secession. Obviously, it was no longer in effect, but was it null and void from the date it was enacted, or did it become null and void as a result of the war? The question was never answered. By a vote of 55 to 21 the convention finally simply acknowledged the supremacy of the Constitution of the United States and declared void the ordinance of secession without reference to time.

The most important subject with which the convention dealt was the status of the Negro. The questions of abolition and civil rights were combined in a single ordinance. The convention agreed that slavery no longer existed and that it could not be reestablished in Texas, but it formally refused to approve the Thirteenth Amendment to the Constitution of the United States on the basis that it already had been ratified and declared in force. It was agreed, also, that Negroes must be made secure in person and property. Their right to testify in court was the subject of sharp debate. As finally written, the constitution gave the Negro the same right before a court as a white person, except that his right to testify was abridged in cases where Negroes were not involved. On the whole, it was more generous toward the former slaves than was the fundamental law of any other state of the late Confederacy.

The convention was expected to repudiate the war debt; otherwise, it would be tantamount to recognition that secession and the war were legitimate. It went further and canceled all the state debt incurred during the war. This measure brought much criticism from the conservative press, for the state had incurred obligations in no way connected with carrying on the war. In defense of nullification it was pointed out that the debt had been acquired in violation of the Constitution of 1845, and that nearly all warrants were in the hands of speculators. Men of both parties voted for repudiation.

Before it adjourned, the convention approved all laws and all acts of officers of the Confederate state government not in violation of the Constitution of 1845 and without any direct relation to the war. The work of the convention was done through the passage of a series of ordinances. At first it delegated unto itself legislative and constituent power supreme and final; but on March 27, after it had declared secession null and void, had canceled the war debt, and fixed the status of freedmen, it voted to submit to the electors amendments to the Constitution of 1845. Among the changes proposed was a plan to lengthen to four years the terms of most officers, to give constitutional status to county courts, and to provide for a possible division of the state.

In an election on June 25 to choose constitutional officers, the Unionists or radicals supported E. M. Pease for governor, and the conservatives stood behind J. W. Throckmorton. The contest was heated, but the candidates did not differ so widely as their followers. Throckmorton upheld the reconstruction policy of President Johnson and opposed Negro suffrage in any form. Pease adopted a mild tone. He agreed that the Negroes were not qualified to exercise the privileges of citizenship, but favored, as a matter of expediency, granting the right to vote to those who could read and write. His followers, however, blatantly charged the conservatives with disloyalty and with planning to drive the Union men from the state. Envisioning defeat in Texas, they allied themselves with the radicals in Congress and sought to delay the restoration of the state to the Union. Throckmorton received 49,277 votes to Pease's 12,168. By a comparatively close vote the amendments to the constitution were ratified.

CONSTITUTIONAL GOVERNMENT
UNDER DIFFICULTIES

The newly elected Eleventh Legislature, conspicuously conservative, convened on August 6, 1866; three days later Governor Throckmorton and Lieutenant Governor G. W. Jones were inaugurated, and on August 20, President Johnson proclaimed the insurrection in Texas at an end.

The legislature had the task of naming two United States senators. By a decisive vote, it chose over the leading Unionist candidates the elderly David G. Burnet, a Unionist in 1861 who had come out of retirement to denounce vehemently the radicals, and O. M. Roberts, who had been the president of the Secession Convention. Neither Burnet nor Roberts could take the "iron-clad" test oath required of all United

States officials by an act of July 2, 1862. Neither the senators-elect nor the three representatives-elect who later joined them in Washington were seated. Then, following the suggestion of Governor Throckmorton, the legislators did not act on the Thirteenth Amendment to the Constitution of the United States and refused by an overwhelming vote to ratify the Fourteenth. Ignoring the warning of John H. Reagan[2] that the radical Republicans were gaining control of the government and would demand racial equality in the South, they proceeded to pass laws on the subject of apprenticeship, vagrancy, and labor contracts, all of which were calculated to keep at least a part of the freedmen in a state of peonage. Neither the apprentice nor vagrancy acts met with strong opposition, but the labor law was especially offensive to champions of Negro rights. Its tenor may be judged by the provisions that laborers should not leave home without permission, or have visitors during working hours, and that they must be obedient and respectful. Men who had been brought up in a society based on slavery could see nothing wrong or inappropriate in such laws. For the slaves there had been slave codes; now that the slaves were freedmen, there should be codes for freedmen. The Texas legislature exercised much restraint and avoided the extremes of the "black codes" of some other states.

More and more the radical Republicans distrusted the ex-Confederates. Numerous reports told of the mistreatment of the former slaves and the insults to Union men. The spirit of rebellion in the South had not been broken, said the men of the North. The radicals would provide guidance for the Negro in their own way; they would reconstruct the South under a plan that would destroy the political power of the old slavocracy and place all government in the hands of loyal men.

In the South the agencies of the radicals were the army, which policed the country and set up courts that interfered with the civil government, and the Freedmen's Bureau. The Freedmen's Bureau, created pursuant to an act of Congress of March 3, 1865, was clothed with authority to take control of all affairs relating to freedmen, refugees, and abandoned lands in the conquered states. In December of that year the Bureau was set up in Texas under General E. M. Gregory, assistant commissioner. Toward the end of the summer there was much complaint that the Negroes were breaking their contracts. Gregory set to work with enthusiasm. He admonished the Negroes to work; he required that labor contracts be registered with the Bureau; and he did his best to dispel the notion that each Negro would be given "forty acres and a

[2]John H. Reagan, Postmaster-General of the Confederacy, spent several months after the war in a Northern prison. There he came to realize that if the South were to avoid a most severe reconstruction program it must safeguard the rights of the freedmen. His open letter of August 1865 suggesting limited Negro suffrage was received in Texas with derision. A later letter, written from his home near Palestine, only added to the irritation produced by the first.

mule" out of the lands of former masters. The Bureau did some relief work among freedmen and it provided night schools for several thousand of them. Its most important work was, however, to supervise contracts and protect the Negro from unscrupulous employers. Another activity, which was most offensive to whites, was its interference with the courts in cases in which Negroes were involved. In fact, Bureau officials gave the state government scant consideration.

Governor Throckmorton contended that President Johnson's proclamation of August 20, 1866, declaring the insurrection in Texas at an end, reestablished the supremacy of the civil over the military authority. The constitution was on the governor's side, but with the President's prestige diminishing each day and the strength of the radical Republicans increasing, constitutional rights were of little avail. While the provisional government had been in existence the army officers did very much as they pleased, and their practices were not changed with the inauguration of a civil regime.

The governor set to work to make the best of a bad situation. He sought to restore law and order; to secure the removal of the garrisons from the centers of population, where they were interfering with civil government, to the frontier, where they were needed; and to bring an end to the courts of the Freedmen's Bureau and the interference of the military in civil affairs.

To a limited extent, Throckmorton succeeded in getting a better distribution of the troops for the protection of outlying communities. Less effective were his efforts in trying to stop the interference of the military and the Freedmen's Bureau in civil affairs. There were in Texas three kinds of courts: the military courts, which claimed jurisdiction in all cases involving soldiers and federal employees; the Freedmen's Bureau, which claimed jurisdiction in all cases relating to Negroes; and the constitutional courts, which claimed jurisdiction in all criminal and in most civil cases. Although the Bureau was helpful in forging the new relationship between the Negro worker and his white employer, its partisan actions in interfering with the normal procedures of law, often with the support of the military, were sometimes flagrant in their disregard for justice. A Bureau agent arrested and fined D. L. McGary, editor of the Brenham *Banner*, for unnecessary abuse and ridicule of the Bureau, its wards, and its agents. McGary refused to pay the fine and went to jail. Throckmorton appealed to J. B. Kiddoo, head of the Bureau in Texas, and secured McGary's release. The editor finally had the last word: "The Bureau's jurisdiction is confined to refugees, freedmen, and abandoned lands. . . . We are not a refugee—we are not a freedman: perhaps we may be abandoned lands." The agent who arrested McGary later was indicted and jailed for lawless acts in Guadalupe County but was released by federal troops.

In spite of the furor and rancor it caused, the Freedmen's Bureau operated a system of Negro schools that must have had a salutary effect. In January 1866 it had 16 schools attended by 1,041 students, and in June the numbers had increased to 100 schools and 4,447 students. When the Bureau ceased operation in 1870 the Negro enrollment in schools had grown to 6,499 pupils, but its accomplishments were rather disappointing.

Almost without exception trouble developed wherever Negro troops were stationed. For a while Negro troops at Victoria controlled the county jail and made it impossible to hold in prison there a Negro or a Union man. They burned Brenham, and neither the soldiers nor their officers were ever brought to justice. Only occasionally was a soldier turned over to civil authorities for trial for violating the laws of the state. Persons who posed as Union men might expect to receive almost any favor at the hands of the troops. Meanwhile, lawless persons who hated both the Negroes and the Union men added to the problems of the military, the Bureau, and the governor.

CONGRESSIONAL RECONSTRUCTION

The radical Republicans in Congress watched the progress of Johnson's reconstruction program with rising resentment and hostility. It was moving too rapidly to suit them; it was turning the state governments of the late Confederacy back into the hands of the former slaveholders; it threatened to place the Negro and the ex-Union man at the mercy of ex-rebels; and it would add to the Democratic Party a phalanx of 11 states, at least a part of which would return with a greater representation in Congress than when they seceded. Through pride and failure to comprehend fully their own peril the men of the South had strengthened the cause of the radicals. They had honored with high office prominent leaders of the Confederacy. Several states had passed black codes calculated to reduce the Negro to serfdom. They had failed to prevent occasional race riots and many acts of lawlessness, which a few prejudiced observers from the North and other self-seeking politicians of the South exaggerated beyond all measure; and, with the exception of Tennessee, they had refused to ratify the Fourteenth Amendment.

In the election of 1866 the radical Republicans gained control of Congress and thus could carry out their own reconstruction program. Ignoring all that had been done by the President and the states, they proposed to place the government of the late Confederate states in the hands of Negroes and a small minority of white men who professed loyalty to the radical cause. They would reverse the political order by suppressing the people who had always run the government and by placing in control men who were, in the main, ignorant, inefficient, and irresponsible. In short, they would stand the social pyramid on its apex. The First Reconstruction Act, passed over the President's veto on March 2, 1867, contained the heart of their program. It declared inadequate and illegal the existing governments in the Southern states; it divided the South into five military districts; it granted the commanding generals authority superior to state laws and civil officials; it called for a constitutional convention, the delegates to be elected by voters of both races, exclusive of those disqualified as former rebels; it required that the convention frame and the qualified voters ratify a new constitution granting Negro suffrage and otherwise acceptable to Congress; and it required that the legislature elected under the new constitution should ratify the Fourteenth Amendment.

The commanding generals might continue with the civil officers as they were or replace them by their own appointees. General Philip H. Sheridan, then stationed at New Orleans as commander of the Military Division of the Southwest, was given charge of the Fifth district made up of Louisiana and Texas, and under him General Charles Griffin was made commander of the subdistrict of Texas.

Throckmorton pledged Sheridan and Griffin his cooperation, but from the very beginning they were determined to get rid of him as soon as it became expedient. Griffin first became offended with the governor when he refused to comply with his most extraordinary request that he pardon the 227 Negro convicts in the penitentiary. A Bureau official had visited the prison and accepted without reservation the statement of the Negroes that their offenses were trivial. The radical press fought Throckmorton vindictively, and designing Unionists, sought in every way possible to undermine his influence. On July 19, Congress passed an act which removed the last doubt as to the power of the commanding generals to remove all civil officers; and on July 30 Sheridan declared Throckmorton "an impediment to reconstruction," removed him, and appointed in his stead ex-governor E. M. Pease.

Meanwhile, Griffin had brought the civil government completely under his control. A rule that jurors take the "iron-clad" test oath[3] barred most men otherwise qualified to serve and threw the courts into the greatest confusion. It was in connection with the registration of voters, however, that Sheridan and Griffin were most tyrannical. The reconstruction act of March 2 had disfranchised only those persons who were excluded by the Fourteenth Amendment from holding office. A second reconstruction act of March 23 imposed this same restriction more emphatically by requiring the voter to take an oath to the effect that he had never held a state or federal office or taken an oath to support the Constitution of the United States and thereafter engaged

---

[3]"That I have never voluntarily borne arms against the United States; . . . have voluntarily given no aid, countenance, counsel, or encouragement to persons engaged in hostility thereto; . . . have not yielded a voluntary support to any government . . . hostile or inimical thereto."

in insurrection or rebellion against the Union. Sheridan, with the connivance of General Grant, applied this regulation most rigidly, even after the attorney general of the United States ruled that the law excluded only those who had taken an oath to support the Constitution of the United States and afterwards supported the Confederacy. For instance, persons who, without having been required to take the oath, had served in such capacities as mayors of cities, school trustees, or even sextons of cemeteries, and who had later taken part in the rebellion were disfranchised.[4]

Texas was fortunate in the selection of provisional governors. We have seen that A. J. Hamilton, the first military governor, was a Texas citizen seasoned by years of public service. E. M. Pease had been even better prepared. Long a resident of the state, he had served four years as its chief executive. He was, says Ramsdell, "the most moderate of all those who had the confidence of the military authorities; and . . . his advice carried weight as Throckmorton's could not."

After Throckmorton's removal came the dismissal of other state and many local officers. Indeed, it was difficult to find enough "loyal" men to fill the vacancies, but as rapidly as possible the state was purged of the influence of the Democrats. On September 15 Griffin died of yellow fever, but his successor, J. J. Reynolds, quickly swept the state clean of all "rebel" officials. In November, General W. S. Hancock succeeded Sheridan as commander of the fifth military district. Hancock, more generous toward the Southern people than Sheridan, notified civil officials to return to their normal functions and permitted the registration of about 5,000 additional voters.

When the registration of voters for the election of delegates to a constitutional convention had been completed, the rolls showed about 59,633 white voters and 49,479 Negro. It was estimated that the number of men disfranchised was from 7,500 to 10,000. The Republicans, organized in the Loyal Union League and in the Grand Army of the Republic, sought by various plans and designs to gain complete control of the Negroes. Opposed to them was the Ku Klux Klan, which in Texas was not affiliated with the organization by that name in the Old South, but local organizations by various names sought to destroy the political influence of the ex-slaves by threats and intimidation. The accepted method of the Ku Klux Klan was to operate by having ghostlike horsemen parade through Negro settlements at midnight; to make dire and mysterious threats against ill-disposed Negroes, but actually to do no violence. Like all such organizations, the Klan at times got beyond the control of responsible leaders and there was violence.

The election was held from February 10 to 13, 1868. The law re-

---

[4]By the third reconstruction act of July 19, 1867, Congress wrote into the law substantially the Grant-Sheridan interpretation and gave to local registration boards broad discretionary powers to register or reject an applicant.

quired that a majority of the registered voters had to participate in the election in order to make it effective. The Democrats proposed to stay away from the polls, hoping thereby to defeat the reconstruction program. As some stated, they preferred "Yankee rule to Negro rule." Unfortunately for the plan, some of the Democratic leaders lost confidence in it, and at a meeting early in January advised their followers to vote against a convention and for delegates who would oppose Negro suffrage. The vote was 44,689 for the convention and 11,400 against it, the total being a little more than half of the total registration. Thus the conservatives lost the election and failed to invalidate it.

The convention assembled at Austin on June 1, 1868. Of its 90 members only six had served in the convention of 1866. Carpetbaggers (adventurers lately arrived from the North) were relatively unimportant; only six or eight delegates could be so classed. Twelve conservatives, led by L. D. Evans, an exiled Unionist during the war, and nine Negroes attended the convention. The Republicans were composed of two distinct factions differing widely on important issues. A. J. Hamilton, the leader of the moderate Republicans, had the unwavering support of Supreme Court Judges Colbert Caldwell and Livingston Lindsay and of Judge M. L. Armstrong, a Democrat. Of the radical Republicans the leaders were Morgan C. Hamilton (brother of A. J. Hamilton); Edmund J. Davis, president of the convention, who had commanded a regiment of Union cavalry during the war; James P. Newcomb, who had been an antisecessionist editor; Edward Degener, the leader of the Germans in Texas; J. W. Flanagan and his son Webster Flanagan; and G. T. Ruby, an educated Negro from New England, who was president of the Union Leagues in Texas. One of the chief subjects of controversy was the old question of the status of the secession ordinance. The extreme Republicans favored an *ab initio* resolution, that is, a declaration that the ordinance was null and void from the date of its passage. The proposal, as finally adopted, validated all acts of the Confederate state government not in violation of the constitution and laws of the United States and Texas, or in aid of the rebellion.

The body spent much time chartering railroads, debating proposals to divide Texas into two or three states, and hearing complaints of lawlessness. It ran out of funds and adjourned from August 31 to the first Monday in December. Money with which to complete its deliberations was raised by a special tax. During the recess, Grant's overwhelming victory in his campaign for the presidency added to the already demoralized state of the Democrats and strengthened the Republicans.

When the convention reconvened in December, the delegates spent most of their time wrangling over division of the state. In January 1869 the convention, after refusing to accept a "Constitution for the

State of West Texas" prepared by Davis and six other radical delegates, voted to send a committee to inform Congress that division was necessary. Just ten days before it adjourned, the body arrived at the task for which it had convened and finished the constitution. Factional strife prevailed until the end, when 45 of the 90 delegates signed the completed instrument on February 8, 1869.

The constitution, as finally adopted, disfranchised only persons disqualified by the Constitution of the United States, and it permitted unrestricted Negro suffrage by providing that a person's political status should not be affected by "race, color, or former condition." It provided for much centralization of authority. The governor should hold office for four years and should appoint the secretary of state, the attorney general, and the judges of the courts. County courts were abolished. The convention did more for public education than any like body that had preceded it by providing that all proceeds from the sale of public lands should be added to the permanent school fund and that the available fund should be used for the education of all children from six to eighteen years of age, irrespective of race and color. The schools were granted in addition proceeds of a poll tax and one-fourth of the revenue from annual state taxes.

If the spirit of the times be taken into account, the Constitution of 1869 was not a bad instrument. It was so conservative in tone that the radicals opposed it and tried to discredit it with the Grant administration. Unsuccessful in this, they executed an about-face, endorsed the instrument, and nominated E. J. Davis for governor and J. W. Flanagan for lieutenant governor. To oppose the constitution meant defeat, and to join the moderate Republicans would destroy their party. In opposition to these political buccaneers the moderate Republicans and the Democrats supported A. J. Hamilton as their candidate for governor. The conservatives made a valiant fight, but the odds against them were staggering. Through the Loyal Union League the Negroes were aligned solidly with the radicals. General J. J. Reynolds, military commander in Texas, stacked the registration boards with Davis men, and many Democrats refused to take part in the election because they believed that Congress would not recognize the new government if Hamilton were elected or because they simply would not vote for any Republican.

The election was held on Tuesday, November 30 and the three days following. There was little violence, but there were many irregularities. General Reynolds never made public the returns, but the vote that he certified was 39,901 for Davis and 39,092 for Hamilton. Hamilton always believed that he was counted out. The constitution was adopted by a huge majority—72,466 as against 4,928. The radical Republicans elected three congressmen; the fourth Texas congressman, J. C. Conner, a Democrat, was an army officer and carpetbagger.

When Reynolds' alliance with the radicals became known in September 1869, Governor Pease resigned in protest. Reynolds then proceeded to rule the state without a governor until January 8, 1870, when he appointed the successful candidates for state office to the respective offices for which they had been elected to serve as provisional officers until their constitutional terms should begin. He convened the legislature on February 8. That body promptly ratified the Fourteenth and Fifteenth Amendments and elected Morgan Hamilton and J. W. Flanagan to the United States Senate. On March 30, 1870, President Grant signed the act of Congress admitting Texas senators and representatives; the executive officers of Texas dropped the qualifying title "provisional"; and on April 16, 1870, General Reynolds formally brought military rule to an end by remitting authority to the civil officers.

Texas had been restored to the Union; but it was not until four years later, when a government was established that had the confidence of the majority of the people, that reconstruction actually ended.

RADICAL RULE AND OVERTHROW

Pursuant to the call of Governor Davis, the Twelfth Legislature convened on April 26, 1870, and proceeded to write into law the radical Republican program. The first session ended on August 15, but the body assembled again on January 10, 1871, and continued until May 31. One of the first acts of the legislature was to postpone until November 1872 the regular election, which for congressmen should have been held in the fall of 1870 and for state officers in 1871. The excuse for the measure was that it made the dates for state and congressional elections coincide; the effect was to increase by one year the term of the radical officers elected in 1869. The most despotic act of the radicals was committed by the 15 members of their faction in the senate. When the opposition of the eleven Democrats and three conservative Republicans made it difficult to put through their legislative program, they arrested and excluded temporarily a part of the minority and even expelled one member. The house evidenced lack of restraint almost as lamentable when on May 10, 1871, it removed its speaker, Ira H. Evans, because he opposed certain measures of the extremists.

The legislature proceeded rapidly. It provided for the organization of the militia and gave the governor power to declare any county under martial law. Under the control of the governor it placed also a state police force of 258 men. The so-called enabling act authorized the governor to fill offices made vacant by the act readmitting Texas into the Union, including state, district, county, and city. One citizen estimated that Davis appointed, either directly or indirectly, 8,538 temporary or permanent employees or officers. Much patronage was provided; provision was made for a public printer, an official state journal, and county or regional newspapers that were to be designated to print public notices.

The legislators with almost reckless disregard for taxes and indebtedness promoted railroad construction. They authorized cities to vote bonds as an aid. In a law later declared unconstitutional they promised to the International Railroad Company, which was to build across the state, eight percent state bonds to the amount of $10,000 for each mile constructed. Over Davis' veto a similar provisional grant was made to the Southern Pacific and Southern Transcontinental Railway companies. Since the Constitution of 1869 prohibited the legislature from granting lands to railroads, the extensive public domain could not be used as a subsidy for construction. This restriction, however, was removed in 1873 by a constitutional amendment. Subsequently, a legislature controlled by Democrats granted 20 sections of land per mile and tax exemption for 25 years to the International Railroad Company in lieu of the bond subsidies and settled claims of the Southern Pacific and Southern Transcontinental Railway companies in similar fashion. The substitution of land for bond subsidies and other vetoes by Governor Davis saved the state from being burdened by a huge, long-term debt.

Of all abuses associated with the E. J. Davis administration, those remembered with greatest resentment pertained to the activities of the state police and the imposition of martial law. The police force evidently had within its ranks numbers of criminals or other persons too weak or venal to exercise authority with restraint. In a few cases policemen arrested men on little or no provocation and killed them as prisoners in cold blood. At other times they started riots and created a reign of terror. The use of Negro policemen to preserve order at elections and even at political meetings of the conservatives did more to create racial hatred in Texas than did any other practice. Less widespread, but more severe when it did apply, was Governor Davis' declaration of martial law. The killing of a citizen by a Negro policeman brought rioting in Limestone and Freestone counties. The governor placed troops over the region and declared it under martial law in the fall of 1871. The cost of occupation was met by a tax of three cents on each $100 of property valuation in the occupied area. Evidence indicates that the whole procedure was an unnecessary injustice.

The state police rendered certain services in the interest of law and order. Even the conservative press occasionally praised the men for chasing outlaws and dealing with other desperate criminals. For the 14 months that ended September 17, 1871, the police reported 3,475 arrests; during the same period eight of their men had been killed in line of duty. Nevertheless, the majority of substantial citizens were opposed to the state police, and their attitude in turn emboldened the criminals.

Not all the laws of the radicals were discreditable. Indeed, these men designed a constructive program of social and economic legislation for Texas which under more favorable conditions might have been successful. They sought to provide a public road system and levied taxes for that purpose. They enacted a homestead law. They were generous in appropriations to provide state troops to supplement the inadequate frontier defense provided by the federal forces. Theirs was the first administration to envision a genuinely public, free school system. In making attendance compulsory and levying taxes adequate for the maintenance of the schools they were half a century ahead of their time. The system was most unpopular, however, because it was costly and highly centralized.

Before it had been completed, the political structure of the radicals showed signs of disintegration. The Republicans had gained control of the state by a slender margin, and their victory was due to the demoralized state of the Democratic opposition. Their power rested mainly on Negro suffrage, a support that was soon cut away by the persuasion and intimidation of the opposition. Their use of the militia and state police was bitterly resented, and their legislative program was unpopular.

Democrats and conservative Republicans united in attacking the radicals. In September 1871 the representatives of 94 counties met in Austin as a taxpayers' convention to protest the extravagance of the administration. Such men as A. J. Hamilton, Morgan Hamilton, and E. M. Pease united with ex-Confederates to show that the Davis administration was flagrantly violating the constitution and laws and was bankrupting the state. At a special election in October 1871 (made necessary because the legislature in violation of the constitution had postponed the general election until November 1872) the Democrats elected all four of their candidates for Congress; this in spite of Davis' supervision of the polls by peace officers and militiamen and the efforts of the canvassers to reject enough votes to win a seat for one Republican. In 1872 Horace Greeley, the Democratic nominee for president, outran President Grant in Texas by almost 20,000 votes; the Democrats again won all seats in Congress and gained control of the legislature. It was at this election, incidentally, that the voters chose Austin as the permanent capital.

When it assembled in Austin on January 14, 1873, the Thirteenth Legislature proceeded to repeal the basic laws of the radical program. It began by enacting a new printing law which withdrew official patronage and thereby helped to destroy a whole school of subservient radical newspapers. Over the governor's veto it repealed the hated police act; it rewrote the militia law in such a way as to remove the power of the governor to declare martial law; and reduced substantially the appointive powers of the governor. It simplified requirements for the registration of voters and provided for precinct voting and one-day elections. The offensive school system of the radicals was reshaped by a law abolishing the board of education and school supervisors and reducing the power of the state superintendent. Before it adjourned, the legislature provided for a general election of state officers for the first Tuesday in December 1873.

The election brought the final test of the strength of the radicals. Davis and R. H. Taylor headed the Republican ticket, running against Richard Coke and R. B. Hubbard, the Democratic nominees. The campaign was hard fought with both sides resorting to fraud and intimidation. The Loyal Union League threatened Negroes who voted the Democratic ticket; the Democrats ordered Negroes to stay away from the polls; and white men under age voted. Coke's vote was reported as 85,549 against 42,663 for Davis. The other state contests and most county contests were won by the Democrats.

The radicals made their last stand before the courts. They sought to invalidate the election on the ground that it was unconstitutional since, pursuant to the terms of the law passed by the Thirteenth Legislature, the polls were open for one day only while the constitution called for four-day elections. The state Supreme Court, in what became known as the semicolon court case, upheld their contention.[5] Its decision, however, was ignored by the general public, and Coke and Hubbard were inaugurated late at night of January 15, 1874. Davis appealed to Grant, but the President advised that it would "be prudent as well as right" to accept the verdict of the voters. Davis refused to recognize the new administration and certain members of the Thirteenth Legislature sought to organize that body as the constitutional law-making agency. For several days it seemed that bloodshed was inevitable. Davis was supported by some of his state police and Negro militia.

Citizens, armed and grim, under such leaders as Henry E. McCulloch and John S. ("Old Rip") Ford, sustained Coke. A local militia company, the Travis Rifles, also took the side of the new governor. At last, after Davis had received another message from the Attorney General of the United States, stating positively that President Grant would not sustain him against Coke, he retired under protest.

The financial record of the radicals was bad. Money appropriated under the printing act, the police law, the school law, frontier de-

---

[5]The justices, all Davis appointees, based their decision on the grammatical force of a semicolon in an article of the constitution: "All elections for state, district, and county officers shall be held at the county seats of the several counties until otherwise provided by law; and the polls shall be opened for four days...." The court ruled that the semicolon in the article had the force of a period, and, therefore, the legislative statute establishing one-day elections was unconstitutional. Thus the election was null and void.

fense, and the payment of expenses for long legislative sessions amounted to millions. Through state taxes there was raised in 1871 and the three years following nearly $4,000,000. Besides the state *ad valorem* taxes and other levies, there were burdensome local taxes. In 1871 these combined rates amounted in some instances to as much as $2.17 on the $100 of valuation, an increase of 1450 percent over 1866. Meanwhile, it had become necessary to resort to borrowing and the public debt was increased by more than $2,000,000.

EFFECTS OF RECONSTRUCTION

The nine years of confusion, uncertainty, and strife that followed the collapse of the Confederacy proved woefully destructive to the private fortunes of many Texans. The war itself had bankrupted numbers of persons; and the minority of planters and small farmers who had managed to hold on to their estates through the war found themselves land poor, with their livestock depleted, their property in slaves destroyed, and without an adequate supply of labor. Of all their problems, that of securing labor was greatest. Even after liberal allowance is made for the prejudices of the white men of that day against free Negro labor, it is impossible to escape the conclusion that the freedmen were very inefficient. To many of the former slaves freedom meant freedom from work. Thousands of acres lay idle. Land values fell to 20 percent of 1860 prices. Cotton, practically the only money crop, declined in value from 31 cents per pound in 1866, to 17 cents in 1870, and to 13 cents in 1875. The total production of cotton declined from 431,000 bales in 1859 to an average of 343,000 bales for the years from 1866 to 1870, both inclusive.

Improvement came gradually. The Freedmen's Bureau was removed from Texas in 1868, which helped matters somewhat. Work for wages gave way to leasing or renting, where Negro labor was involved, and by 1870 the sharecropping system was becoming common. Under this practice landowners supplied the laborers with all houses and farming equipment and took as their share from one-half to two-thirds of the crop. Improvement in the agricultural situation is reflected in the production of cotton, which by 1873 was exceeding 500,000 bales per year. Following the discovery that cotton would thrive on the rich uplands of North Texas, the increase in acreage was rapid. Immigration stimulated the production of all farm commodities. During this period southern and western Texas became comparatively prosperous by the pouches of gold brought back by drovers who took each year hundreds of thousands of cattle to northern markets. The industrial development of the country is reflected in the railroad mileage, which increased from 395 in 1865 to 1,650 in 1874.

Economic losses through the war and reconstruction were soon overcome, but the damage to political and social institutions was more enduring. The people could not forget that radical Republicans in Congress had imposed on the South a harsh program designed, it seemed, more for political purposes than for the general welfare. Thus, the Republican Party in the state was all but destroyed by the reaction against the Davis administration, and a one-party political system consequently has prevailed for a century.

Most unfortunate of all were the effects of reconstruction on the Negro who became the victim of the strange experiment of standing the social pyramid on its apex. It must be said to his credit that he bore the responsibilities of his new freedom as well as might have been expected, but that fact did not protect him from the hatred of many white men who resented the child-like vanity and the insolence he sometimes displayed. The conservative white people associated universal Negro suffrage with the hated radical government, and by indirect but effective means they proceeded to abolish it.

Racial relations were seriously aggravated by reconstruction; and the evil effects of it have not been overcome altogether even to this day. Before the Civil War, to mistreat a Negro stamped a white man as belonging to the uncouth backwoods class whom the Negroes described as "po' white trash"; during the reconstruction era the Negro-hater often became a hero.

Selected Bibliography

The best extensive studies of reconstruction are C.W. Ramsdell, *Reconstruction in Texas*, and E. Wallace, *Texas in Turmoil*. Good sketches of reconstruction may be read in S.S. McKay, *Seven Decades of the Texas Constitution in 1876* (Lubbock, 1942); L.J. Wortham, *A History of Texas*; F.W. Johnson, *Texas and Texans*; and O.M. Roberts, *A Political, Legislative, and Judicial History of Texas, 1845–1895*. Excellent biographical studies of participants in the Civil War and reconstruction include B.H. Procter, *Not Without Honor: The Life of John H. Reagan*; C. Elliott, *Leathercoat: The Life of James W. Throckmorton*; W.J. Hughes, *Rebellious Ranger: Rip Ford and the Old Southwest*; E. Wallace, *Charles DeMorse: Pioneer Editor and Statesman*; John L. Waller, *Colossal Hamilton of Texas: A Biography of Andrew Jackson Hamilton* (El Paso, 1968).

Other useful book-length studies are W.C. Nunn, *Texas under the Carpetbaggers* (Austin, 1962); W.C. Nunn, *Escape from Reconstruction* (Fort Worth, 1956); Marion H. Farrow, *The Texas Democrats* (San Antonio, 1944); and D. Richardson, *Texas as Seen in 1870* (Shreveport, 1870).

Of the writings of participants, see O.M. Roberts, "The Experiences of an Unrecognized Senator," *Quarterly of the Texas State Historical Association*, XII, 87–147; John H. Reagan, *Memoirs, with Special Reference to Secession and the Civil War* (W.F. McCaleb, ed., New York, 1906); and A.W. Terrell, *From Texas to Mexico in 1865* (Dallas, 1933).

Valuable specialized studies published as articles include W.A. Russ, Jr., "Radical Disfranchisement Texas," *Southwestern Historical Quarterly*, XXXVIII, 40–52; C. Elliott, "The Freedman's Bureau in Texas," *ibid.*, LVI, 1–24; George Shelley, "The Semicolon Court of Texas," *ibid.*, XLVIII, 449–468; Billy Bob Lightfoot, "The Negro Exodus from Comanche County, Texas," *ibid.*, LVI, 405–416; O.A. Singletary, "The Texas Militia during Reconstruction," *ibid.*, LX, 23–35; J.R. Norvell, "The Reconstruction Courts of Texas," *ibid.*, LXII, 141–163; and J.E. Ericson, "Delegates to the Texas Constitutional Convention of 1875: A Reappraisal," *ibid.*, LXVII, 22–27.

The most essential documents may be found in W.L. Fleming (ed.), *Documentary History of Reconstruction* (2 vols., Cleveland, 1906–1907); H.P.N. Gammel, *The Laws of Texas*; and E. Wallace and D.M. Vigness (eds.), *Documents of Texas History*.

There are many miscellaneous items pertinent to the period. The *Texas Almanac* for the years of the reconstruction period contains a voluminous amount of statistical, factual, and even descriptive information. W.P. Webb has a chapter on the state police in *The Texas Rangers*; Sam Acheson, *35,000 Days in Texas* (New York, 1938), a history of the *Dallas News*, brings out the flavor of the reconstruction era; John C. McGraw, "The Texas Constitution of 1866" (unpublished dissertation, Texas Technological College, Lubbock, 1959) is an excellent reference; and E. Wallace, *Ranald Slidell Mackenzie on the Texas Frontier* (Lubbock, 1965), covers the frontier Indian problem from 1871 to 1879. For an account of E.J. Davis' appeal to the courts, see J.H. Davenport, *The History of the Supreme Court of the State of Texas* (Austin, 1917). Short biographical sketches of the governors of the reconstruction era are in J.T. DeShields, *They Sat in High Places*.

12

THE TRIUMPH OF DEMOCRATIC CONSERVATISM, 1875–1890

With the election of the Democratic legislature in 1872 and of Governor Coke in 1873, political power came into the secure grasp of those seeking to redeem the state from radical rule. Only the judiciary remained a Republican stronghold, and it proved to be a temporary one. Legislative maneuvering soon removed several district judges, who were replaced with Democrats. Moreover, a constitutional amendment adopted at the recent election had terminated the service of the three incumbents of the supreme court and had raised the number of judges from three to five. Within a month after his inauguration, Coke named five Democrats to fill the vacancies, including Oran M. Roberts as chief justice.

The triumph of the redeemers initiated more than a decade of conservative government. Reflecting the attitudes shared by most white Texans, these conservative Democrats sought where possible to wipe out the last vestiges of radical rule, the most obvious being the Republican-written Constitution of 1869. Suffering under the miseries of the Panic of 1873 and identifying expansive governmental expenditures with radical extravagance, they promoted public economy and retrenchment, sometimes to the point of parsimony, but simultaneously they encouraged the exploitation of the public lands and the construction of railroads. Initially preoccupied with legacies of reconstruction such as crime and public indebtedness, they soon found another perplexing challenge. Agrarian unrest, provoked by the emergence of a commercial economy characterized by falling prices, tight credit, and strangling freight rates, would be a persistent problem.

Although the conservative Democrats failed to cope successfully with the problems of agrarian discontent and their policies otherwise were sometimes shortsighted, the period was not without substantial progress. Gone were the radical Republican days when a majority of the people were hostile toward public officials. Certainly, old enmities were being forgotten. When U.S. Grant and Phil Sheridan visited Texas in 1880, they were received cordially, and Sheridan apologized for having once said that if he owned Texas and hell he would "rent out Texas and live in hell." Crime was reduced; personal and property rights were made comparatively secure; new institutions were established; foundations were laid for a public school system; and finally the low prices and the business stagnation that followed the Panic of 1873 gave way in the early eighties to a period of temporary prosperity.

THE CONSTITUTIONAL CONVENTION OF 1875

Upon winning control of the legislature in 1872 Democrats agreed with something approaching unanimity that there must be a new constitution. Critics found the Republican origins of the Constitution of 1869 sufficient cause to discard it, but they offered more substantial reasons. Dissatisfied with the judicial system, they wanted elected judges, shorter terms, and fewer courts. Advocating a return to the old law, they sought repeal of the road tax and the maintenance of roads by personal service under overseers in the various communities. They hoped to abolish voter registration regulations and to require that all executive officers be elected to two-year terms. Taking the Constitution of 1845 as a working model, they advocated a biennial legislature with severely limited powers, especially concerning taxation and indebtedness, and a governor with substantially reduced authority.

Partially inspired by a desire to limit expenses, an abortive effort to remodel the fundamental law in 1874 through a legislative joint-commission delayed the calling of a constitutional convention. The senate accepted the work of the commission, headed by Senator J. L. Camp and Representative J. B. Sayers; but the house, arguing that the method was too autocratic, failed to adopt it. Acting on the advice of Governor Coke, the legislature then submitted the question of a constitutional convention to the people. On the first Monday in August 1875 the voters approved the convention and elected three delegates from each of the 30 senatorial districts.

Perhaps the evaluation placed by the San Antonio *Herald* on the convention delegates who assembled in Austin on September 6, 1875, was as sound as any generalization could be. "We know," observed the newspaper, "that the convention has relatively but a few able men in its composition, but those we deem very able, with sound clear judgment." Certainly the roll of delegates bears impressive testimony that the old Texans were again in the ascendancy. Seventy-five were Democrats, and only 15, including six Negroes, were Republicans. Forty-one were farmers, and 29 lawyers. Eight had participated in the secession convention of 1861; 19 had served in the Texas legislature, two in the Congress of the United States, one in the Confederate Congress, and one in the cabinet of Jefferson Davis. More than a score had held high rank in the Confederate Army, and three had been officers in the United States Army. One had served in the constitutional convention of 1845 and another in the convention of 1866, but significantly, none had sat in the convention of 1869.

Among the more distinguished were John S. Ford, noted editor and Texas Ranger; John H. Reagan, Postmaster General of the Confederacy and congressman-elect to the United States House of Representatives; Lawrence Sullivan Ross, famed Indian fighter destined to become governor of the state and president of Texas A&M College; Charles DeMorse, gifted editor and ex-Confederate colonel; and Thomas Nugent, who became a leader in the farmers' revolt of the 1890's. Presiding over the convention was E. B. Pickett of Liberty County, ordinarily president *pro tem* of the senate.

Particularly influential in the convention proceedings was a bloc of 40 or more delegates who were members of the Patrons of Husbandry. This powerful and militant farmers organization, better known as the Grange, had been introduced into Texas in 1873 by the establishment of a subordinate Grange at Salado in Bell County. Spurred by the Panic of 1873 membership climbed rapidly until by 1876 the order claimed 45,000 members. Although the Grange as such did not take part in politics, Grangers frequently acted collectively for or against certain issues or candidates. In the convention, constitutional provisions reducing taxes and expenditures, crippling the embryonic public school system, prohibiting the state from chartering banks and restricting corporate and railroad practices would reflect the ideals of the Grangers.

From the beginning the convention manifested a determination to promote measures of economy and retrenchment. Obviously rural delegates who were having difficulty making a living in the depressed times would show little sympathy for generous salaries for public officials, whose tasks seemed easier than their own, or for heavy taxes, when any seemed burdensome and oppressive. Thus, hinting of frugal principles to be incorporated into the fundamental law, the delegates voted themselves only five dollars per day when members of the legislature had been receiving eight, refused to have the proceedings of the convention printed because of the expense, and even refused to employ a stenographer when they could not secure one for less than ten dollars a day. Surely, few would quarrel with Delegate W. P. McLean's remark that "if future State Governments prove burdensome and onerous, it ought not to be the fault of the Convention."

THE CONSTITUTION OF 1876

In keeping with a trend in the making of state constitutions in evidence since the early nineteenth century, the Constitution of 1876 is longer than the fundamental laws which preceded it, and it contains many provisions which the framers of earlier instruments left to the discretion of legislatures. It changed the framework of government in several important respects. The legislature was to be composed of two houses, the senate to consist of 31 members and the house of representatives never to exceed 150. The term of senators was reduced from six to four years. In calling for biennial sessions instead of sessions each year, as under the Constitution of 1869, the framers returned to the practice in vogue before the day of the radicals. The lawmakers should receive a mileage allowance and five dollars a day for the first 60 days of each regular session and two dollars a day thereafter. Like the Constitution of 1845, the new instrument limited severely the powers of the legislature. It was forbidden to incur indebtedness to an amount greater than $200,000, and the maximum tax rate, except for the payment of debt, was set at 50 cents on the $100 of valuation. An important limitation was the requirement that all property be taxed in proportion to its value. The legislature was forbidden to give or to lend the credit of the state to any person or corporation, or to make appropriations for private or individual purposes. The maximum duration of all offices it might create was two years. A reaction against conditions of the war and reconstruction periods was reflected in the statement that the writ of *habeas corpus* "is a writ of right" which shall never be suspended.

The article describing the executive department provided for seven officers: a governor, lieutenant governor, secretary of state, comptroller, treasurer, commissioner of the land office, and attorney general. All, save the secretary of state, were to be elected by the voters. The maximum salary, that of the governor, was set at $4,000 a year, $1,000 less than he was then receiving. In vain did John H. Reagan, Charles DeMorse, and others plead for higher salaries, contending that such parsimony would in the long run prove costly. Terms of the executive officers were fixed at two years, with no prohibition against reelection.

The governor's powers and duties were set forth in considerable detail. He might convene the legislature in extraordinary session, call out the militia and declare martial law to suppress insurrection, and fill various vacancies by appointment, subject to approval of the senate by a two-thirds vote. He was given power to veto laws and veto items in appropriation bills, but his veto might be overridden by a two-thirds vote of both houses. It was declared that the governor as the chief executive of the state should cause the laws to be "faithfully executed," but the powers granted to him were not equal to such great responsibility. He was given no control over local officers and other elective state executive officers.

The judicial article reflected a reaction against the courts of the reconstruction era. When the convention met, there were 1,600 undecided cases before the supreme court, and many regarded a number of the judges appointed by Governor Davis to be notoriously incompetent. Accordingly, the new constitution provided that all judges be elected by popular vote, with terms of four and six years for district judges and judges of the higher courts respectively. The number of district courts was reduced to 26. Establishing a dual system of appellate courts the convention provided for a supreme court, with power to review civil cases only and for a court of appeals with appellate jurisdiction over all criminal cases and certain classes of civil cases.

By an amendment adopted in 1891 a court of civil appeals was established to remove some of the burden from the supreme court, and the old court of appeals was made the court of criminal appeals, a jurisdiction it still retains. Other courts of civil appeals have been added since that time; in 1969 there were fourteen.

Following the leadership of Pennsylvania and other northern states, the convention declared railroads to be common carriers, forbade consolidation of competing lines, and authorized laws to prevent unjust discrimination and to establish maximum freight and passenger rates. The delegates, not realizing that the regulation of railroads was as much an administrative as a legislative problem, made no provision for a commission with regulatory powers. This oversight was corrected by a constitutional amendment in 1890. In order to promote the construction of new mileage, the legislature might grant public land to railroads to an amount not in excess of 16 sections for each mile of road constructed; it was forbidden, however, to grant state funds or bonds to railroads. The convention also provided for homestead grants of 160 acres to heads of families and half that amount to single men over 18 years of age.

Suffrage provoked a heated debate in the convention. The most serious contest was over the proposal, supported largely by East Texas delegates, to make payment of a poll tax a prerequisite for voting, the chief purpose obviously being indirect disfranchisement of Negroes. A substantial majority, including all but one of the Republicans, defeated the move, such a requirement not becoming law until the adoption of an amendment in 1902. Otherwise, nobody objected to permitting aliens to vote, if they had resided in the state one year and had declared their intention of becoming citizens, but a petition sent in by an Eldorado woman praying that women be given the ballot provoked bitter denunciation of woman suffrage.

Economy and retrenchment were apparent in the discussion over the state supported immigration bureau. Authorized in the Constitution of 1869 and eager to secure immigrants, the bureau had spent money freely. Considering the retention of the immigration bureau, the convention divided along sectional and political lines, western delegates and Republicans fighting for continuation, while others, led by the frugal Grange, successfully demanded its demise. Thus, a useful public institution was destroyed at the very time it was most needed to bring settlers to the millions of acres of public domain.

More controversial and more affected by demands for economy were provisions regarding public education. Texas had never had a satisfactory public school system, measured even by the standards that prevailed in the nineteenth century. Even now, in the convention some contended that education was a private duty, that no man should be taxed to educate another's child. Supporters of public education overruled that argument, but provisions for education were not as generous as those under the Constitution of 1869. Indeed, possibly the radical Republicans of 1869 had been too ambitious, but surely the conservative Democrats of 1876 were too cautious. The convention authorized the legislature to contribute to the support of the public schools a poll tax of one dollar and not more than one-fourth of the *ad valorem* and occupation taxes. Rejecting the centralization prevailing under the radicals, it abolished the office of state superintendent, eliminated compulsory attendance, established segregated schools, and made no provision for local school taxes. Apparently the delegates saw no inconsistency between these provisions and their declaration that the legislature should "establish and make suitable provisions for the support and maintenance of an efficient system of public free schools." But an aroused *Galveston News* acidly observed that the convention, after "decreeing universal suffrage, had now also decreed universal ignorance."

The convention was more generous with school endowments, a fact that accounts in part for the slender support provided for maintenance. It set aside as a perpetual fund all monies, lands, and other property previously granted to the schools, all alternate sections of land reserved by the state out of grants made to railroads, and one half of the public domain, and all monies to be derived from the sale of these lands. All told the land granted amounted to about 42,500,000 acres and the permanent school fund invested in securities at that time was

$3,256,970. Largely as a result of the sale of land and oil royalties and leases, this endowment had grown to $755,365,793 by 1968.

To the University of Texas, yet unborn, the convention gave with one hand and took away with the other. By a law of 1858 the school would have been entitled ultimately to about 3,200,000 acres, a part of which had already been located and surveyed within the rich domain of north central Texas. The delegates repealed this provision and gave the university a million acres of land to be selected from the public domain unappropriated at that time, an exchange very disadvantageous both as to the quantity and the quality of the land. Only additional grants by the legislature and the fortuitous discovery of oil on some of the lands kept the university from suffering severely. Mainly from income from oil lands, the university permanent fund on August 31, 1968 had reached $516,099,544.

ADOPTION OF THE FUNDAMENTAL LAW

Ratification of the Constitution of 1876 was accomplished without effective opposition but without impressive enthusiasm. Only one delegate expressed hearty approval, declaring that the constitution was "the noblest instrument ever submitted to the verdict of a free people." The six Republicans remaining in the convention joined five Democrats in a vote against adoption, and many other delegates were opposed to portions of the document. Nevertheless, by a vote of 53 to 11 the convention adopted the constitution on November 24, 1875. Previously, arrangements had been made to submit it to the voters for their approval. Beginning in 1878 biennial elections were to be held on Tuesday after the first Monday in November. But the convention had postponed the general election that was to be held in the autumn of 1875 to the third Tuesday in February, 1876, at which time the voters were not only to choose their officials but also to express their opinion of the new constitution.

Anticipating some criticism, the convention issued a statement praising its handiwork and explaining that economies would save the state $1,500,000 annually. Significantly, the delegates felt obliged to defend at length the measures on public education, the part of the constitution that had been attacked by the press more severely than any other. The statement pointed to the extravagance of the former school system and the poverty of the state, emphasizing the generous permanent school fund.

Some opposition to ratification did develop. By a vote of 674 to 176 the state Democratic convention evaded endorsement, and the Republican convention denounced the document in a unanimous vote. Opponents claimed that the constitution crippled education; that its provision eliminating the immigration bureau would retard development; and that in failing to make the payment of a poll tax a prerequisite to voting, the instrument would surrender to Negro rule a large number of counties in the black belt. However, Governor Coke and much of the state press, together with the powerful Grange, backed ratification. In a mood for change, the voters probably would have ratified a much poorer instrument. The vote for adoption in a remarkably quiet election was 136,606 to 56,652.

All in all the constitution complied with public opinion quite faithfully. Biennial sessions of the legislature, low salaries, no registration requirement for voters, precinct voting, abolition of the road tax and a return to the road-working system, a homestead exemption clause, guarantees of a low tax rate, a more economical school system with schools under local control, a less expensive court system, popular election of officers—all these were popular measures with Texans in 1876.

The constitution, a logical product of its era and a fairly adequate pattern for government for the period in which it was made, was nonetheless an enduring fundamental law with many unfortunate features. Limitations on the powers of the legislature have made necessary many amendments to the original instrument, most of them giving the legislators additional power. It seems unfortunate also that the constitution did not give the governor more power. Actually, he is not the chief executive of the state but is rather a peer among equals. It is true that he is regarded as the political leader of the commonwealth and his influence may be very great; but he does not have the power to modify appreciably the policies and practices of other elective officers, and many appointive officers are wholly beyond his control.

Changes to meet the needs of an evolving society have come through amendments submitted to the voters by the assent of two-thirds of the members of each branch of the legislature at a regular session and approved by a majority vote of the electors. Thus, it is state policy to fix in the constitution by amendment ceilings on taxes, on salaries, and on various expenditures, to define minutely the powers, rights, and prerogatives of various state agencies, to assume that state legislatures are not to be trusted, all of which makes necessary more and more legislating by the people themselves. Although during the first half century of the instrument few amendments were added, adoptions have come to an ever increasing pace in recent times. Of 99 submitted up to September 1928 only 43 were adopted. Up to 1969, however, 298 have been submitted, and of this number 191 have been approved by the voters, an average of about two per year since 1876.

Efforts to effect a complete revision have accomplished little. No provision was made in the document for calling another constitutional convention, but legal authorities have generally agreed that this can be done only by the approval of the voters after the question has been submitted to them by a vote of two-thirds of the members of both houses. At different times there has been considerable agitation for a new constitution, but when the question was submitted to the voters in 1919 only nine percent of them were sufficiently interested to express an opinion. Created at the urging of Governor John Connally and under the authority of the house but without the cooperation of the senate, a commission presented to the legislature in January 1969 proposals for comprehensive constitutional changes.

POLITICS AND PERSONALITIES, 1875–1890

For nearly a decade and a half following the adoption of the Constitution of 1876 politics were characterized by the same tone of conservatism that prevailed in the convention. Democrats, who won state and local elections with monotonous regularity, differed on various particulars, but most generally agreed that economic retrenchment was more necessary than aggressive reform. Appropriately, in a state whose population was predominantly rural, political conflicts focused on the problems of the farmer; elected officials concentrated on such matters as law enforcement, debt retirement, and disposal of the public lands.

Although composition of the state legislatures varied and the number of Negro representatives declined thereafter, the legislature elected in 1878 may be viewed as fairly typical of the age. Business and professional men, mostly attorneys, accounted for 64 members, while 44 were farmers or involved in activities related to farming. More than 90 percent were native born southerners, 11 were born in Texas, and at least half had served in the Confederate Army. Negroes among the delegation numbered five. Nine of the legislators were members of the Grange, and ten formerly had endorsed Whig policies. An overwhelming majority were Democrats, but there were nine Republicans and seven independents.

Throughout the period the Republican party, torn by factional quarrels even when in power, continued to deteriorate as an effective political organization. The party elected scattered local officials, a few state legislators, and occasionally even a congressman, but by and large it found little success at the ballot box. Temporarily Republican leaders joined with agrarian reform groups in a marriage of convenience to oust the Democrats, but usually they concentrated on establishing their power within the party in order to assure their control over federal patronage in Texas. Factional conflicts of this type were intensified by differences over the role of the Negro in the party. Without the Negro the party faced little but frustration and defeat, but white Republicans found Negro leadership and control unpalatable, if not totally unacceptable. Nevertheless, after the death of E. J. Davis in the mid-1880's the most powerful figure in the party was Norris Wright Cuney, Negro customs collector of Galveston and one of the more perspicacious politicians of his time.

Cuney's influence reflected the continued activities of Negroes in politics. After regaining power white Democrats evaded disfranchisement of the Negro, feeling that the black vote could be controlled or outnumbered. But in 14 counties located along the Gulf Coast and in East Texas Negroes constituted a majority of the population, and in 13 others they amounted to nearly one-half. Thus several counties for a time were controlled by a Negro electorate. Beginning with Harrison County in 1878, and followed subsequently by others, notably Fort Bend County in 1888, white Democrats used organization, intimidation, and other means, sometimes extra-legal, to eliminate these local pockets of Negro power. But extensive curtailment of Negro suffrage through sophisticated laws awaited a later day. Meanwhile, Negroes participated in politics, often without effectual strength but sometimes holding office. Primarily they operated in the Republican Party, but they also formed a significant portion of the strength of another, the Greenback Party.

The Greenback party, a threat more serious to Democratic suzerainty than the Republican challenge, was a voice of agrarian discontent calling for various reforms. It was particularly powerful in a West settled recently by poor farmers who had remained poor. Unlike the Grange, which operated usually within the Democratic party, the Greenbackers formed their own. Organized originally in the midwest as early as 1874 to protest the resumption of the payment of gold for greenbacks (paper money without specie backing), the Greenback Party spread rapidly after passage of the Federal Resumption Act of 1875. Greenbackers, who wanted "more money and cheaper money," argued that a gold monetary standard was deflationary and an undue hardship on debtors, a status common to many farmers. Advertising an intention to protect the poor man against bankers and bondholders, the party demanded that the general government issue more greenbacks as legal tender and redeem all treasury notes and outstanding bonds with such money. In Texas Greenbackers advocated an income tax, a better school system, a reduction of salaries of state officers, the abolition of useless offices, a repeal of the "smoke-house tax" on farm commodities, the regulation of railroads, and various other reforms. Several of these proposals were adopted during the progressive era of the early twentieth century.

Introduced into Texas in 1877, the party made its first campaign the following year, electing two senators and ten representatives to the legislature and indirectly assisting the election of a number of Republicans. Its strength declined somewhat in the election of 1880, but the Greenbackers regained new hope in 1882 with the arrangement of an alliance with the Republicans. This so-called Independent movement was in ideology as absurd as the marriage of the owl and the pussy cat, for the two factions had nothing in common save opposition to Democrats. Nevertheless, the move gave the Democrats their biggest fright of the decade though Democratic candidates, with only rare exceptions, swept the election on all levels. Efforts to perpetuate the Independent coalition through the election of 1884 were only partially successful, and thereafter the coalition and the Greenback Party faded from Texas politics.

Indeed, between 1875 and 1890 major state offices were controlled by a parade of conservative Democrats. Sam Bell Maxey, an "ultra-simon-pure-secession-anti-reconstruction Democrat," was elected to the United States Senate in 1874, there to remain until 1887. Granger favorite Governor Coke was reelected in 1876, only to resign in December of that year to accept the other seat in the United States Senate where he remained until 1895. When Lieutenant Governor Richard H. Hubbard, a Georgia-born ex-Confederate officer who succeeded Coke as Governor, sought reelection on his own in 1878, he found a crowded field. Critics proffered charges impugning Hubbard's integrity and wisdom, while James W. Throckmorton, who had served as governor in the early days of reconstruction, and W. W. Lang, master of the state Grange, also vied for the nomination. A deadlocked convention brought the selection of Oran M. Roberts, elderly ex-Confederate colonel, then chief justice of the supreme court and known affectionately as the Old Alcalde. Frugal and legalistic but strong-willed and aggressive, Roberts easily defeated W. H. Hamman, his Greenback opponent, an accomplishment he repeated in 1880, winning over both Hamman and E. J. Davis, the Republican nominee.

When in 1882 Roberts refused suggestions that he accept a third term, the Democratic nomination went instead to Judge John Ireland of Seguin. A native of Kentucky, ex-member of the Know-Nothing Party, and ex-Confederate colonel, Ireland was an intense and intelligent man of integrity often called "Ox-Cart John" in tribute to his opposition to railroad land grants. His opponent, George W. ("Wash") Jones of Bastrop, was a delightful addition to the political wars. Jones had been a Unionist but had served as a Confederate colonel. A Democratic Lieutenant Governor in 1866–1867, he had been elected to Congress as a Democrat in 1878, had won reelection as a Greenbacker in 1880, had welcomed Republican support on all occasions, and was now running as an Independent. If party regularity was not one of Jones's virtues, he was nonetheless widely respected for his honesty and engaging oratorical talent. He was awkward but kind, earnest but humorous, shrewd but forthright. The somewhat colorless Ireland, who wisely declined to speak against him on the same platform after an early debate, won the gubernatorial election, but the contest was the closest of the decade, Ireland receiving 150,891 votes to Jones's 102,501. In a repeat race in 1884, however, Jones's votes declined and Ireland's increased substantially.

The practice of electing conservative governors was perpetuated through the end of the decade. With his campaign directed by railroad attorney George Clark, a shrewd and successful conservative political manager, Lawrence Sullivan Ross won the nomination from a field of five candidates and an easy election in 1886. Agrarian discontent had increased significantly by 1888; but Ross, not a reactionary but certainly no reformer, again won by a margin of almost three to one, this time over Marion Martin, the candidate of an incipient farmers protest movement.

A number of factors explain the ease with which conservative Democratic elements maintained their political domination. Challenge from outside the party was limited by the lingering memories of reconstruction radical Republican government. Republican factionalism and Democratic adoption of some agrarian reform programs advocated by third party movements likewise reenforced the Democracy. No doubt fraud and ballot box irregularities sometimes accounted for Democratic victory. Until 1891 the constitution did not call for voter registration. But even after that date a voting list in one county contained the names of several national leaders and Jefferson Davis! Radical insurgence within the party was controlled to a degree by nominating practices. Candidates generally were chosen by conventions, primaries not coming into widespread use until near the end of the century, and politicians already in power often found conventions easily manipulated. Finally, essentially conservative policies such as promotion of railroads, frugal expenditures, and low taxes were policies attractive to most Texans, even those who wanted more extensive reforms such as railroad regulation and augmented state services.

PUBLIC POVERTY

Poverty-stricken public finances constantly plagued the government of Texas during the decade following the adoption of the Constitution of 1876. When Coke was inaugurated governor in January 1874, the state debt, including some items of doubtful validity, was $3,167,335. The receipts for that year were not sufficient to meet half of the state's expenditures, and state warrants were quoted at from 65 to 80 cents on the dollar. Industry and commerce, not yet recovered from the Civil War and reconstruction, were prostrated by the Panic of 1873. Taxes were already too burdensome. No new sources of revenue were available, and it seemed that the only way to balance the budget was to reduce the outlay.

With the cooperation of the legislatures, Governors Coke and Hubbard wrought manfully to reduce expenditures, but their economies were offset by increased demands on the treasury—funds for buildings for the new agricultural and mechanical college, pensions for veterans of the Texan Revolution, frontier defense, and interest charges. The treasury did not operate on a cash basis until the spring of 1879, by which time the state's indebtedness had increased to approximately $5,500,000.

Taking office in 1879, Governor Roberts insisted that the legislature balance the state's budget at any sacrifice and made several suggestions toward that end. He would refund state bonds and lower the interest rate; reduce the outlay for veterans pensions; make the penitentiaries self-supporting; and most extreme of all, lower the appropriation to the public schools from one-fourth to one-fifth of the general revenue. To increase income he would provide for a better system of tax assessment and collection; and in order to hasten the payment of the public debt, he favored sale of the unappropriated public lands to any person in any quantity desired. On his own part, he discontinued the payment of rewards for the arrest of criminals, and followed a liberal policy of reprieves and pardons to relieve the crowded prison system.

The legislature responded readily to a part of Governor Roberts' suggestions. It adopted a law offering for sale in any quantity the public domain at 50 cents an acre, one-half the receipts to go to the permanent school fund and the remainder to be applied to the public debt. It passed laws to improve the collection of taxes, to provide fees for government services, and to broaden and increase occupation taxes. Toward reducing expenditures, it lowered substantially the appropriation for the maintenance of the state frontier force. The legislators exceeded the governor's wishes by discontinuing pensions altogether and substituting instead the grant of a section of land to each indigent veteran, an amount later raised to two sections.

But to enforce completely his program of economy, Governor Roberts found it necessary to use the veto. When lawmakers failed to lower the appropriations to the public schools from one-fourth to one-fifth of the general revenue as he had recommended, the governor vetoed the school item. Sharp criticism was hurled at him, but he stood firmly by his policy of retrenchment. At a special session in June 1879 the legislature reenacted the measure fixing the school appropriation at one-sixth of the general revenue. In 1881, during Roberts' second term, it raised the school appropriation to one-fourth of the general revenue, but lowered the rate from 50 to 40 cents on each $100 of valuation and diverted a part of the public school revenue to the Sam Houston Normal School.

At the end of his administration the Old Alcalde could report with pride that the public debt had been reduced by more than a million dollars, that the annual interest burden had been cut by a third, and that there was a liberal operating surplus in the treasury. Probably he found the greatest satisfaction of all in the fact that the *ad valorem* tax rate had been reduced from 50 to 30 cents on each $100 of valuation. The achievement was one made at considerable cost, however, for public lands were disappearing into the hands of speculators, and state services, particularly education, were operating at a minimal level.

John Ireland, who took the oath of office in January 1883, differed with his predecessor in several important matters. He opposed the rapid sale of public lands and favored reserving them to meet the needs of homeseekers in future years. He opposed the state's purchasing its own bonds at high prices in order to hasten the extinction of the debt; he urged a more persistent enforcement of the criminal laws; and he promised to follow a less liberal pardoning policy. In the matter of economy, however, he was disposed to continue the Roberts program. The voters themselves in 1883 broke the spell of public parsimony by approving an amendment to the constitution authorizing special state and local school taxes, but the legislature continued to provide funds only with great reluctance, denying for example in 1883 and in 1885 appropriations out of general revenue for the maintenance of the University of Texas.

Surely the state finances improved substantially during the 1880's, an accomplishment due in part to the sale of public lands, economies in government, and more effective tax laws. But in fact the state's financial record merely indicated the extraordinary increase in wealth and general prosperity. In many significant areas Texas wealth increased from two to threefold between 1875 and 1890, growth appropriately reflected on the tax rolls.

LAW ENFORCEMENT

In respect to government the greatest accomplishment during this period was the victory for law and order. Except in the extreme western part of the state, depredations by marauding Indians did not constitute a serious problem after 1875; but sufficient unto the new day were the evils thereof. Mexico was in a state of war and confusion, and Juan N. Cortina, the Mexican bandit who commanded scores of brigands and had long troubled the border, was now stealing Texas cattle to supply the Cuban market. The criminal and lawless elements which had become so powerful in the interior of Texas during the reconstruction era did not yield readily to the authority of the new government. With the rapid extension of the cattle industry into western Texas during the late seventies, the frontier was no longer a line extending from north to south through the center of the state, but a vast area hundreds of miles in length and breadth where the cowboys carried arms for self-protection but did not always use them in the interest of law and order.

Often the spirit of rowdyism and the yearning to establish a reputation as a "tough" caused young men who were not criminals at heart to become so in fact. Thus certain frontier characters would occasionally "take a town" just to see its inhabitants "hunt cover." More desperate and generally more dangerous was the professional criminal. During the seventies and eighties the far-flung ranch headquarters and isolated cow camps afforded concealment and a measure of protection for numbers of renegades and desperados. In 1876 the Adjutant General compiled a list of 3,000 fugitives from justice and noted that other names were arriving by every mail. In his message to the legislature in 1879 Governor Roberts stated that there was "an amount and character of crime and civil wrong entirely unprecedented in this country."

One of the commonest and most widely practiced crimes was horse theft. The editor of the *Frontier Echo* (Jacksboro) estimated that there had been 100,000 horses stolen in the state during the three years preceding March 8, 1878, that 750 men were regularly engaged in the business, and that not more than one in ten was ever caught and brought to justice. The Northwest Texas Stock Association (which later became the Texas and Southwestern Cattle Raisers' Association), organized at Graham in 1877, devoted considerable effort to suppressing cattle theft, but for several years the results were discouraging because men of wealth and influence were doing a considerable part of the stealing. The Panhandle Stock Association, organized at Mobeetie in 1881, attacked the problem more successfully, but often this organization found it difficult to secure convictions.

Stage robbery became almost an epidemic between 1876 and 1883. On one occasion near Fort Worth in 1876, highwaymen held up a stage, lined up the passengers along the side of the road, and proceeded to take their money and other valuables. Suddenly a freighter's outfit and a private carriage came up. The new arrivals were made to join the others, and the loot taken aggregated $7,000. The robbers then shot their own horses and made away on animals belonging to their victims.

Feuds presented defenders of law and order with one of their most perplexing problems. For instance, in the spring of 1874 feudists in DeWitt County were defying local officers and making it impossible to convict their friends in court. Their method of avoiding conviction was a simple one; they merely murdered unfavorable witnesses. A bitter feud took place in Mason County in 1875 between the Germans and the Anglo-Americans. Meanwhile, the Horrell and Higgins feud of nearby Lampasas County, which had begun in 1873, grew in intensity. During the chronic quarrel each side scored killings, and the clans were so powerful that local peace officers and even the local courts were helpless to deal with them.

To cope with lawlessness of various types, vigilantes, more or less formally organized, were found in almost every community. Such a group at Denison seems to have been quite active; the Hill County vigilantes warned thieves in open letters; and during one week at Fort Griffin in 1878 vigilantes were credited with shooting one man in his jail cell, with hanging another, and with being responsible for the disappearance of a third.

But of all agencies suppressing crime in Texas the Texas Rangers were the most effective. From the Gulf to the Panhandle they terrified evildoers and brought a sense of security to the men who obeyed the law. The dauntless Captain L. H. McNelly and his Rangers made it possible at least to hold court in the DeWitt County feuds. Major John B. Jones restored order in the Mason County dispute, though he could not remove the cause of the trouble. In Lampasas County he arrested the leaders of that feud and persuaded them to enter into a peace covenant that temporarily preserved law and order. When Kimble County became notorious as "the worst section of the country there is for men to work in and a better hiding place for rascals than any other part of Texas," the Rangers entered the county and soon arrested 41 men. In 1879 Captain George W. Arrington, a Ranger, was sent with a force to the Panhandle where, working with another great hater of cattle thieves, Charles Goodnight, he played a leading part in bringing first order and then law to the High Plains.

Improvement in law enforcement was not left altogether to the peace officers. Court procedure was made more effective. A law of 1876 made it more difficult for the defense in criminal cases to stack the jury with men who were incompetent, venal, or biased. The number of district attorneys was substantially increased in 1879. When cases continued to stack up in the appellate courts, thereby encouraging crime, filling jails with criminals whose cases were pending, and promoting lynch law, the legislature in 1879 provided for appointive commissioners of appeals to assist the supreme court and court of appeals by deciding certain civil cases to clear the way for criminal matters. This plan was continued until 1892, when the system of courts of civil appeals still in effect today was devised.

Another law helped to stop the theft of land through the forging of evidence of title, a nefarious business that had grown to large proportions. Later, more than 30 such criminals were sent to the penitentiary and many others were driven from the state.

THE PUBLIC LANDS

If establishment of law and order was the state government's greatest accomplishment during this period, formulation of a wise and far-sighted public land policy may very well have been one of its least satisfactory achievements. In 1876 the state still retained a public domain of 61,258,461 acres. Distribution of these lands brought conflict and confusion and provoked charges of fraud and speculation. In 1881 state officials discovered that railroad land grant commitments exceeded land available for that purpose by 8,000,000 acres. Meanwhile, state policies on sale of school and otherwise unappropriated lands produced a political if not necessarily an economic crisis.

Governor Roberts, the Old Alcalde, bore primary responsibility for the crisis. Honest, well-meaning, and unselfish, but a fiscal conservative in the ultimate sense of the word, Roberts would not tolerate deficit spending and was determined to eradicate or to reduce substantially the public debt of $5,500,000. To help defray the cost of public education and to pay the state debts, he persuaded the legislature to pass the so-called Fifty-Cent Law whereby unappropriated lands could be purchased by anyone for 50 cents an acre in any quantity. The terms allowed the prospective buyer to control the lands for 150 days without paying any part of the purchase price. Receipts from the sale of these unappropriated lands were to be divided equally between the public schools and payment on the state debt. In a separate law school lands suitable for farming were to be sold for one dollar an acre in blocks of one-quarter to one section and grazing lands sold up to a maximum of three sections per purchaser. Subsequently, an 1881 amendment raised the price of farming lands to two dollars an acre and the maximum amount of grazing lands purchaseable to seven sections.

Critics of these land laws declared them to be an open invitation to speculation and fraud, that the heritage of the people was being wasted for an absurdly small return, and that corporations and syndicates would soon own most of the western area of the state. Typical of the critics was the venerable Charles DeMorse who, in indignation over the sacrifice of the public domain, resumed publication of his Clarksville *Standard*.

In sympathy with the clamor, the Ireland administration in 1883 put through legislation that established a Land Board to investigate frauds, terminated the sale of large blocks of land, provided for sale by auction but for minimum prices of two and three dollars per acre according to type, and offered liberal credit terms to bona fide settlers.

Actually, the damage done by the notorious Fifty-Cent Law was largely indirect. Less than two million acres of land were sold under its provisions, probably because Land Commissioner W. C. Walsh, who objected strenuously to it, blocked many sales by means that were, if not strictly illegal, certainly unanticipated by the legislature. More important, the law depressed land prices to almost giveaway levels. Much of the acreage that fell into the hands of speculators was not purchased directly from the state but from railroads and Confederate veterans and widows at prices of as little as 15 cents an acre. Furthermore, the law produced little revenue, less than a million dollars.

Modification of the Roberts administration's land policies did not eliminate Ireland's problems with the public domain. Fence cutting, discussed elsewhere, and leasing of public lands caused trouble throughout the decade. An 1883 regulation of the land board provided that school lands and those reserved for eleemosynary institutions might be leased on competitive bidding with a minimum price of four cents an acre. When it became apparent that ranchers conspired to pay only the minimum, the land board raised the price to eight cents and many ranchers paid nothing. Ireland proposed a compromise of five cents, but vetoed a law to that effect because it failed to limit quantities and restricted public transit. The affair deteriorated into a political wrangle with differences between the land board, the governor, and the ranchers. Suits to force ranchers to pay the leases and to abandon illegal enclosures of land not owned or leased proved of little value when the state was compelled to try its cases before West Texas cowboy juries controlled by the ranchers.

The state land board was abolished in 1887, and the entire responsibility of administering the public lands was placed on the commissioner of the general land office, subject to the approval of the governor in some matters. Among other changes, the new law provided that school lands were to be classified by state agents rather than by local surveyors, and made some modifications in minimum prices. In an effort to prevent speculation, each purchaser of agricultural land was required to swear that he desired to "purchase the land for a home." It was also specified that he must reside on the land at least six months each year for a period of three years before the state would pass title to him. These provisions were retained in all subsequent legislation, and, according to the statement of Commissioner of the General Land Office John J. Terrell, made in 1908, have been the occasion of "untold perjury." Notwithstanding the rigid precautions of the law, in western counties the number of sales exceeded greatly the number of settlers. The greater part of the land went into the ownership of the ranchmen. Misrepresentation and perjury are reprehensible, yet the history of the American frontier reveals that such practices generally arise when a government, dominated by men of older regions, attempts to impose on a new country a pattern that does not suit its needs. Agriculture was either in its infancy or unknown in West Texas at this time. The country apparently was not suited to anything but cattle raising, an industry that had developed under an economy of large-scale production which called for extensive landholdings. Hence, in the ranching country there was not sufficient sentiment to enforce the state land laws. Before the repeal of this act in 1895, however, 6,400,000 acres had been sold subject to its provisions, the large part of which was later forfeited in order to secure better terms.

In short, if in a frontier society acquisition of a population is of highest priority, and if in depressed circumstances reasonable revenue from the disposal of the public domain is a logical objective, Texas public land policy between 1876 and 1890 failed to measure up on either count. The failure is particularly strange, considering the preoccupation of the administration with fiscal prudence and the dominance of farmers in the population.

PUBLIC IMPROVEMENTS
AND EDUCATION

During the decade following 1876 slow but evident improvement was made in the physical plants of the state's institutions. The first hospital for the insane had been built at Austin in 1856 and a sister institution was completed at Terrell in 1885. A state orphans home was provided at Corsicana in 1887. During the same year the interest of the Negro was recognized in the founding of the school for deaf and blind colored youths at Austin. The crowning achievement of the building program is the capitol in Austin, authorized in 1879 and completed in 1888. For this imposing structure made of Texas granite the state exchanged 3,050,000 acres of land located in the Panhandle that became the famous XIT ranch.

The enforcement of the law soon crowded the penitentiary and focused attention on the state's prison problem. A new penitentiary was completed at Rusk about 1883, with the idea of smelting iron ores in that vicinity, but the results were disappointing. Governor Roberts apparently hoped to lessen the prison burden by a liberal policy of pardons, but his plan provoked much opposition; his successor, John Ireland, was less generous toward the convicts. In 1871 Texas tried the prison lease system, under which the state leased the penitentiary to private individuals. The lessees were to employ the convicts in any way they wished, subject only to the mandates of the state inspectors, who were supposed to see that the prisoners were not abused and that the prison property was not damaged. This was perhaps the worst system practiced in modern times. The death rate of convicts doubled and the number of escapes per year more than tripled. In the year 1876 alone, 382 convicts made their escape, a condition that aggravated seriously the problem of crime in the state. Pursuant to the recommendation of a legislative investigating committee, the lease was terminated in 1876, but the lease system was not abolished until 1883.

The plan of 1883 is described as the contract-lease system. It was better than the old lease plan but far from satisfactory. Under the new arrangement the state retained control of the prison and prisoners, but leased to private operators the shops within the penitentiary walls, and also hired out gangs of convicts to railroad construction foremen, planters, and others. The Huntsville industries were not successful. It was charged that their product was inferior and they were boycotted. Likewise the iron industry at the Rusk prison proved to be a white elephant in the hands of the state. Meanwhile intelligent people were coming to realize that as long as the labor of convicts was used to promote the interests of private capitalists abuses would exist. It seemed, therefore, that the only course left to the state was to buy and operate its own farms. Harlem Farm, a tract of 2,500 acres, was purchased for $25,000 in 1885. It was located in Fort Bend County, 100 miles from Huntsville and a much greater distance from Rusk. Thus the Texas prison system began farming as a last resort and without plan or design, but prison farming as well as prison manufacturing was to present difficulties.

The most enduring foundations of this period pertain to public education. Both state higher education and the present-day public school system began at this time. The first institution of higher learning was the Agricultural and Mechanical College, established near Bryan in 1876. It is a land-grant college, now named Texas A&M University, and owes its origin to the Morrill Bill passed by Congress in 1862, by which Texas received 180,000 acres of land to establish a college for the study of agricultural and mechanical arts. Texas accepted the offer in 1866, but the school was not opened until 1876, just after the constitutional convention had declared it would be a branch of the University of Texas. A school for Negro youths under the management of the board of regents of the Agricultural and Mechanical College was established in 1876. At that time no Negro students sought training in agriculture, and in 1879 the school was reestablished as Prairie View Normal School. It was not until 1899 that agricultural and industrial departments were added for both boys and girls. Sam Houston Normal Institute at Huntsville had its beginning in 1879 when the state matched a donation of $6,000 from the Peabody Board and the citizens of Huntsville made available the campus formerly used by Austin College there.

It has been stated in a preceding chapter that the Republic of Texas set aside 50 leagues of land for the endowment of two universities. A bill establishing the University of Texas was passed in 1858, but the Civil War stopped all development and the project was postponed for another 20 years. The Constitution of 1876 granted a million acres of land to the University and its branches but contained no provisions to compel the actual organization of the school. The State Teachers Association, organized in 1878 when Governor Roberts called a meeting of the state's teachers under the presidency of Dr. William Carey Crane, was instrumental in developing sentiment for establishing the University. At a meeting of the association at Mexia in 1880, a committee was appointed to present to Governor Roberts a plan for organizing the school. On this committee were the ablest educators of that day: Oscar H. Cooper, W. C. Crane, S. G. Sneed, R. W. Pitman, Smith Ragsdale, J. G. James, and O. N. Hollingsworth. The governor sent the report of the committee to the legislature with his endorsement; the legislature carried out the plan substantially in the law approved March 30, 1881, providing for the establishment of the school. In an election the voters selected Austin as the site for the main university and Galveston for the medical branch. The main university was opened in 1883 and its medical branch in 1887.

Of wider public interest, if not of greater importance than the beginning of teacher education and higher education, was the revolution of the public school system during the early eighties. In keeping with the constitutional pattern, the legislature in 1876 adopted the community school system. This strange institution is without a parallel in the history of education in America. The "community" had no boundaries and no means of acquiring and controlling property. After a school had been established there was no assurance that it would be continued, for it had to be reorganized each year.

Governor Roberts' veto of the school appropriation bill in 1879 aroused public sentiment that soon became overwhelming in its demand that the schools be given some income independent of an uncertain share in the general revenue. Among the leaders who promoted an interest in public education were O. N. Hollingsworth, secretary of the state board of education, who initiated the *Texas Journal of Education*; Barnas Sears of the Peabody Board, who had made possible model schools in 18 communities distributed throughout the state; Dr. Ashbel Smith, a friend of education since the days of Mirabeau B. Lamar; R. C. Burleson, president of Waco University and state agent for the Peabody Board; and William Carey Crane, president of Baylor University. The reforms were actually attained during the Ireland administration by a constitutional amendment adopted in 1883 and a law enacted the following year. The amendment repeated the provision in the original constitution granting to the public schools a poll tax of one dollar and adding to this one-fourth of the state occupational taxes. It provided also that the legislature should levy a special school tax, not to exceed 20 cents on the $100 of valuation, but sufficient with the income from other sources to maintain a school term of at least six months. It permitted also two-thirds of the qualified property taxpaying voters of a district to vote a local tax, not to exceed 20 cents, for the maintenance of schools and the erection of buildings. The limitation upon the amount of district tax did not apply, however, to incorporated cities or towns.

The following year witnessed the complete rewriting of the school law. The law of 1884 provided for an elective state superintendent of instruction with limited supervisory power over all public schools, and placed the schools under the immediate supervision of county judges. It provided that counties, except 53 that were exempted, should be divided into school districts that should have the privilege of voting a local tax according to the provision of the constitution. It extended the scholastic age to include the years from eight to 16, both inclusive; it required that teachers hold certificates; and it prescribed a system of registers and reports.

Progress under the new system was slow. Immigration and a high birth rate caused the scholastic population to increase more rapidly than the available school fund. Especially discouraging was the indisposition of the people to vote local school taxes. "The chief effect of the law of 1884," says Frederick Eby, "was to lift the responsibility for educational progress from the state as a whole and to place it upon the local communities." Thus the common country schools remained poor and inefficient, with improvement confined largely to the towns and cities. The legislation of Ireland's day was a noble start, but there lay ahead of the public schools a long and rough ascent which they have not surmounted even to this day.

For Negroes, segregated in their schools by the Constitution of 1876, provisions for education were even more inadequate. Negro education in Texas for a time compared favorably with that of other southern states, and illiteracy declined from more than 75 percent in 1880 to less than 40 percent in 1900. By 1900, however, Texas ranked fifth among southern states in enrollment of Negro students and daily attendance and third in the number of Negro teachers. There were a number of able Negro leaders, such as R. L. Smith, a graduate of Atlanta University and aide to Booker T. Washington, who diligently sought educational gains, and some white leaders recognized the merit of the cause. But often the white community was either disinterested or openly unsympathetic. Generally, Negro schools labored under the burden of inadequate financial resources and poorly trained personnel. Until the nineties laws required that funds be divided equitably between white and Negro schools, but violations of the rule were not unknown. Complaints that many Negro teachers were deficient in training were often heard. Yet significant improvement of Negro faculties could scarcely have been expected. As late as 1900 secondary training for Negroes in Texas was not inadequate; it was practically nonexistent. A Negro in Texas seeking an education during these years likely could learn the rudiments of reading and writing; he probably would find little opportunity beyond those humble beginnings.

Selected Bibliography

Seth Shepard McKay has written several authoritative works on the Constitution of 1876. He wrote *Making the Constitution of 1876* (Philadelphia, 1924); he brought together and edited newspaper accounts of the convention as *Debates of the Texas Constitutional Convention of 1875* (Austin, 1930); and he wrote *Seven Decades of the Texas Constitution* (Lubbock, 1943). See also his "Some Attitudes of West Texas Delegates in the Constitutional Convention of 1875," *West Texas Historical Association Year Book*, V, 100–106. For other studies see E. Wallace, *Texas in Turmoil*; S.D. Myers, Jr., "Mysticism, Realism, and the Texas Constitution of 1876," *Southwestern Political and Social Science Quarterly*, IX, 166–184; Ralph Smith, "The Grange Movement in Texas, 1873–1900," *Southwestern Historical Quarterly*, XLII, 297–315; and J.E. Ericson, "Delegates to the Texas Constitutional Convention, of 1875: A Reappraisal," *ibid.*, LXVII, 20–27. The Constitution with amendments is published and indexed biennially in the *Texas Almanac*.

For the course of politics the manuscript of C.A. Barr, "Texas Politics, 1876–1906," in the Library of the University of Texas is most useful. See also E.W. Winkler, *Platforms of Political Parties in Texas*; F.R. Lubbock, *Six Decades in Texas*; S. Acheson, *35,000 Days in Texas*; E. Wallace, *Charles DeMorse*; Paul Casdorph, *A History of the Republican Party in Texas, 1865–1965* (Austin, 1965) and his "Norris Wright Cuney and Texas Republican Politics, 1883–1896," *Southwestern Historical Quarterly*, LXVII, 455–464; and B.H. Procter, *Not Without Honor, the Life of John H. Reagan*. A well-written general account of the era is B.M. Jones, *The Search for Maturity* (Austin, 1965).

On state finances the best sources are E.T. Miller, *Financial History of Texas*; A.S. Lang, *Financial History of the Public Lands in Texas*; R. McKitrick, *The Public Land System of Texas, 1823–1910*; and "Memories of a Land Commissioner, W.C. Walsh," *The Southwestern Historical Quarterly*, XLIV, 481–497. Considering economic matters primarily is J.S. Spratt, *The Road to Spindletop* (Dallas, 1955).

There is a historical sketch of the Texas penitentiaries by Carl Rosenquist in the *Handbook of Texas*, II, 411–413. See also C.S. Potts, "The Convict Labor System in Texas," *Annals of the American Academy of Political and Social Science*, XXI; W.C. Holden, "Law and Lawlessness on the Texas Frontier, 1875–1890," *Southwestern Historical Quarterly*, XLIV, 188–203; W. Gard, *Frontier Justice* (Norman, 1949); C.L. Sonnichsen, *I'll Die Before I'll Run* (New York, 1961); and Jack Martin, *Border Boss: Captain John R. Hughes* (San Antonio, 1942).

On the history of education see F. Eby, *The Development of Education in Texas,* and C.E. Evans, *The Story of Texas Schools.* In this connection see also H.Y. Benedict, *A Source Book Relating to the University of Texas* (Austin, 1917); George Sessions Perry, *The Story of Texas A & M* (New York, 1951); W.J. Battle, "A Concise History of the University of Texas, 1883–1950," *Southwestern Historical Quarterly,* LIV, 391–411; George P. Garrison, "The First Twenty-five Years of the University of Texas," *ibid.,* LX, 106–117; and E. Bruce Thompson, "William Carey Crane and Texas Education," *ibid.,* LVIII, 405–421. Valuable for information on Negro education and other aspects of Negro life during thirty years is Lawrence Rice, "The Negro in Texas, 1874–1900" (unpublished manuscript, Texas Technological College; Lubbock, 1967).

13

THE ADVANCE
OF THE FRONTIER

In 1860 the frontier, except for some settlements along the Rio Grande near Presidio and El Paso, extended along a line from Henrietta southward through Belknap, Palo Pinto, Brownwood, Kerrville, and Uvalde, to Brackettville. During the Civil War there was no farther advance. A decade later this line was still the cattleman's farthest westward extension, but many of the earlier settlers, as a result of the ravages of marauding Indians, had retreated eastward. A line drawn from 30 to 150 miles east of it would delineate the area having less than one inhabitant per square mile. Such a line, running, from the common boundary of Cooke and Montague counties irregularly to Bandera and thence to the Gulf a few miles south of Corpus Christi, may be designated as the farmers' frontier. About 40,000 people lived to the west of it in 1870; a decade later the number had increased to 165,000. Within 20 more years the number was nearly 500,000, and by the middle of the twentieth century the area west of the line was the home of about one third of the population of the state. Although many of these people settled within this vast area as a result of the colonizing efforts of railroad and land companies, the overwhelming majority did so on their own initiative, each trusting in his own strength and in a kindly Providence as he made his way into the new country.

Stages in the westward movement included the subjugation and removal of the Indians, the expansion of the range cattle industry, the conversion of the open ranges into big pastures, the advance of the subsistence farmers, the development of commercial farming, and the growth of industry. The two latter, being dependent upon transportation, had to await the building of railroads and highways to get their products to distant markets. Meanwhile, the stubborn contest between the white and the red men for possession of the land and the short interlude before the arrival of the railroads, when cattlemen challenged by only a few bold and hardy subsistence farmers held supremacy over the newly-won empire of grass, constitute a colorful and significant segment in the history of Texas and the American West.

THE DEFEAT AND REMOVAL OF THE INDIANS

After the collapse of the Confederacy, the state organization for frontier defense gradually ceased operation, and for several months thereafter the western settlers were left without protection. The Indians, soon aware of the situation, scourged the frontier as never before in history, driving the line of settlements eastward in some places 100 miles. The country west of a line drawn from Gainesville to Fredericksburg was abandoned by all but a few of the most courageous settlers, who moved into stockades. The worst raids were made on moonlit nights, and the soft summer moon became a harbinger of death. Charred rock chimneys stood guard like weird sentries, symbolizing the blasted hopes of pioneers and often marking their nearby graves. A Waco newspaper in April 1866 claimed that not more than one-fifth of the ranches in its vicinity were still occupied, and later that year a large group of citizens in a mass meeting at Denton resolved to abandon their homes unless help had arrived before November. Incomplete reports from county judges covering the period from May 1865 to July 1867 showed that 163 persons had been killed by Indians, 43 carried away into captivity, and 24 wounded. These figures did not include Wise and Young counties whose combined population declined from 3,752 in 1860 to 1,585 in 1870.

Upon the inauguration of the constitutional government in August 1866 the legislature promptly authorized the raising of a thousand Rangers, but General Sheridan would not allow it. However, Governor Throckmorton's persistent efforts to persuade Sheridan and the Washington government to place at least a part of the four thousand troops it had in Texas on the frontier met with a measure of success. In September a cavalry detachment was sent to Fredericksburg, and by the end of the year Federal troops had reoccupied Fort Mason, Fort Dun-

Established in 1867, Ft. Griffin was an important link in the chain of military posts along the frontier. Troops from this fort were called on to escort government mail, surveying parties, and cattle drives, and to punish Indians for their forays into white settlements. The town that grew up around the fort attained fame as headquarters for buffalo hunters, cowboys, and frontier adventurers, but declined rapidly after the fort was abandoned in 1881. (Texas Highway Department)

can, Fort Inge, Fort Clark, and Camp Verde to provide protection against marauding Apaches and bands from Mexico to the western settlements between the Colorado River and the Rio Grande. Within another year several of these posts had been abandoned for more favorable sites, and the remainder of those maintained before the war had been reoccupied, all on a permanent basis. The line ran from Fort Richardson (at Jacksboro) through Griffin (near Albany), Concho (at San Angelo), McKavett (near Menard on the upper San Saba River), and Clark (near Brackettville) to Duncan (at Eagle Pass). An extreme western line was marked by Fort Stockton (near the present town of Fort Stockton), Fort Davis (near the present town of Fort Davis), and Fort Bliss (near El Paso).

The protection afforded by the military was inadequate. The troops were poorly disciplined and too few in number; many officers were lazy and inept, and often were unduly restrained by their superiors; and the policy was strictly defensive—to keep the Indians out of the settlements by scouting maneuvers instead of by attacking their villages. Furthermore, the distance between the posts was too great for the soldiers to prevent the Indians from crossing the line.

In defense of the Army, however, it must be said that its delay in establishing permanent posts and in adopting an aggressive policy was partially due to Indian agents who convinced Washington officials that peace could be had by treaty-making and the appointment of Quakers as Indian agents. If the Indians could be induced to keep the peace, forts and war would be unnecessary. Consequently, Congress authorized a commission to secure a lasting peace among all the Plains Indians. At Medicine Lodge Creek, Kansas, the commissioners in October 1867 met with the Cheyennes, Arapahoes, Kiowas, Kiowa-Apaches, and Comanches in what seems to have been the most colorful council ever held between Indians and whites in the American West. Satanta, the principal leader of Kiowa raiding parties into Texas, insisted that western Texas belonged to the Kiowas and Comanches and that he did not want to give up any part of it; and Ten Bears, a Comanche chief who realized that the Indians must accept the terms offered by the commissioners or be destroyed, blamed the Texans who had taken his country and pleaded that his people might be allowed to continue their nomadic way of life. They argued in vain. According to the treaty of Medicine Lodge Creek, the Indians present agreed to accept reservations in the Indian Territory and to cease their depredations. The defiant warriors, nevertheless, continued to raid. Some of the Kiowas and about half of the Comanches refused to move onto the reservation. In fact, the fierce Kwahadi Comanche band was not represented at the Medicine Lodge Creek council and did not recognize the treaty. Later that year a government agent who visited them at present-day Quitaque reported that the band had about 15,000 horses, 300 or 400 mules, and innumerable stolen cattle, and that 18 parties were at the time raiding the Texas frontier.

Nevertheless, President Grant, upon assuming office in 1869, was won over by the peace advocates and appointed as Indian agents Quakers who maintained that in dealing with the Indians kindness and reason would be more effective than force. Quaker Lawrie Tatum, a strong devotee of the peace policy who became the new agent at the Kiowa-Comanche Reservation, soon found, however, that his wards would not listen to reason unless compelled by armed force. Unrestrained by troops, the reservation became a sanctuary for restless braves who slipped away to plunder in Texas. Beginning in the fall of 1870, they repeatedly ravaged the Texas frontier, killing 14 persons during the following spring.

Best known of their audacious raids is the Salt Creek massacre of May 1871 when a band of Kiowas attacked a wagon train between Jacksboro and Fort Griffin, killed or wounded most of the 12 teamsters, and stole the mules. For the Indians the time of the attack proved unfortunate. General of the Army William Tecumseh Sherman, escorted by Randolph B. Marcy, Inspector General of the Army, had passed the site only a few hours before the brutal attack and was at Jacksboro. The two generals were inspecting the frontier to see for themselves if conditions were as bad as had been reported. Marcy thought they were. He noted in his journal that the Indian raiders, unless punished, would soon have the country between Belknap and Jacksboro totally depopulated. By the time the wounded teamster who had managed to escape and make his way to Jacksboro had finished with his description of the tragedy, Sherman likewise was convinced that the Indian menace on the Texas frontier had not been exaggerated. The Indian raiders were followed to the reservation where at least one of their leaders (Satanta) was boasting of his exploits. Sherman ordered the arrest of the raiding chiefs. Satanta and Big Tree were brought back to Jacksboro, tried in accordance with the laws of Texas, convicted of murder, and sentenced to be hanged. Governor Davis, however, commuted the sentence to imprisonment, and the chiefs were paroled in August 1873.

As a result of the Salt Creek massacre, the War Department unleashed its troops against the Indians off the reservation where the peace advocates had no authority. To lead the offensive, General Sherman fortunately had transferred to the Texas frontier Colonel Ranald Slidell Mackenzie, regarded by U.S. Grant as the most promising young officer in the Army at the end of the Civil War, and his tough Fourth Cavalry regiment. In the autumn of 1871 Mackenzie led an expedition northwest, from old Camp Cooper on the Clear Fork of the Brazos to Blanco Canyon, where he harassed the Kwahadi Comanches under Quanah Parker but was unable to prevent them from escaping unharmed across the High Plains in a heavy snowstorm. In April of the following year at Howard Wells in Crockett County, Indians, apparently Comanches, killed 16 members of a wagon train party and afterwards held off two companies of troops who tried to punish them. In July Mackenzie renewed his campaign. After following two routes across the dangerous and unexplored plains in an effort to catch some cattle thieves, on September 29 he decisively defeated a camp of Comanches who had participated in the attack at Howard Wells. As a result of their defeat and the imprisonment of their captured people, the Comanches and Kiowas remained peaceful for more than a year.

With the Comanches and Kiowas seemingly anxious for peace, General Sherman and Lieutenant General Philip H. Sheridan, Commander of the Division of the Missouri, sent Mackenzie and his Fourth Cavalry to the Rio Grande border to put a stop to raiding in the area between San Antonio and the Rio Grande by Kickapoo and Apache Indians living in Mexico. By 1873 these Indians, it was estimated, had murdered a number of citizens and inflicted damages amounting almost to 50 million dollars. The troops quickly destroyed three of their villages, captured some of the Indians, and established an effective border patrol. By the end of the year, Indian raids along the Rio Grande had ceased, and Mackenzie resumed his job of driving the Indians from northwestern Texas.

Suddenly realizing in the spring of 1874 that reservations and advancing buffalo hunters meant the end of their old way of life, the Indians of the southern plains renewed their attacks on the Texas frontier. The new war erupted in June when several hundred Comanches and Cheyenne warriors and perhaps a few Kiowas attacked a buffalo hunter's stockade, known as Adobe Walls, in present-day Hutchinson County. Superb marksmen among the 28 buffalo hunters in the stockade, armed with their "big fifty" buffalo guns, were more than a match for the red men. Although repulsed with heavy losses in their initial attack, the Indians were determined to keep white men off their favorite hunting grounds. They again began hitting the isolated settlers along the Texas frontier with vindictive fury. When General Sherman learned of the situation, he persuaded President Grant on July 26, 1874, to turn the Indians, even those on the reservation, over to the military thus putting an end to the Quaker peace policy.

When in August the deadline for the Indians to enroll at the agencies had passed, the Army moved against the remainder. The majority of the proud and stubborn natives took refuge in the wild canyons and breaks along the eastern edge of the *Llano Estacado*. There they were pursued relentlessly by well mounted, well armed, and thoroughly seasoned troops, led for the most part by officers who had learned in the school of experience the way of Indian warfare and guided by Indian scouts who could follow a trail like bloodhounds. Altogether, 46 companies, about 3,000 men, marching in five commands from as many directions converged on the headstreams of the Red River in the eastern Panhandle of Texas where they found the Indian encampments.

Colonel Nelson A. Miles with 750 men moved southwestward from Camp Supply, Indian Territory, toward Palo Duro Canyon. Opposite the junction of Tule and Palo Duro canyons on August 30, he defeated about 500 Indians, burned their village, and chased the fleeing hostiles to the head of Tule Canyon before turning back to scout again the region nearer his supply camp. Major William Price with four companies of cavalry moved from Fort Union, New Mexico, down the Canadian River to join Miles. Near Sweetwater Creek in the eastern Panhandle he won, though terribly scared, a skirmish with a group of Indians in flight from the reservations. From September to November Lieutenant Colonel John W. Davidson with nine companies of troops searched the country between his Fort Sill base and the main fork of the Red River almost to the Caprock without engaging the Indians in battle, but he returned to the reservation over 300 Comanches who surrendered to him. Simultaneously, Lieutenant Colonel George P. Buell, while scouting up the Red River, destroyed two large Indian villages and a considerable quantity of supplies.

The most effective and dramatic blow to the last bid of the tribes of the southern plains to retain their nomadic way of life, however, was delivered by Mackenzie. After establishing his base at his old supply camp on the upper Brazos River near the present town of Crosbyton, Mackenzie with about 500 men, including a detachment of Indian scouts, headed northward along the edge of the Caprock for the head-streams of the Red River. After beating off an attack by Comanches at Tule Canyon and an all-night march, on September 28 in a daring, almost reckless, display of courage Mackenzie led his men down a narrow path to the bottom of Palo Duro Canyon. Here he defeated five villages of Comanches, Kiowas, and Cheyennes, burned their lodges and huge quantities of supplies needed for survival during the ensuing winter, and captured 1,424 horses and mules. Flushed from hideouts which their medicine men had assured them could not be found by blue-coated troopers, many of the Indians sought safety at the water-holes on the *Llano Estacado*. Mackenzie, however, did not intend that they should find safety anywhere except on the reservation. Early in November he surprised and defeated a band of Comanches near the present town of Tahoka. Most of the Indians, however, had gone already or were on their way to the reservation, and the Red River War was over. By June 1875 the remainder had straggled to Fort Sill and surrendered, the last being a large band of Kwahadies led by Quanah Parker. Very few Indians had been killed or taken captive; but left without lodges and supplies or horses to acquire replacements, they could no longer continue their nomadic existence. Thereafter, only a few ever stole away from the reservation to raid in Texas, and the damage they did was negligible.

On the southwestern frontier, from the vicinity of Laredo to the outskirts of El Paso, another five years was to elapse before the Indian problem was settled. In the eastern portion of that section, the Apaches and Kickapoos from Mexico renewed their destructive forays after Mackenzie and his Fourth Cavalry had been removed. To stop the marauding by Indians based in Mexico, Sherman sent Mackenzie to Fort Clark early in 1878. Mackenzie quickly established at strategic sites a number of subposts, reactivated his system of effective border patrol, and in June led an expedition across the Rio Grande in search of the renegade Indians. The reappearance of this aggressive leader on the border influenced Mexican President Porfirio Díaz, who wanted to attract United States capital to Mexico, to assist in the efforts to break up the raiding. Before the end of the year, affairs along the Rio Grande border were "most satisfactory."

Further west, the frontier enjoyed comparative peace in 1875, due in part to a successful scouting expedition led by Lieutenant Colonel William R. Shafter, but the next year Victorio at the head of a band of Apaches from New Mexico began raiding in Texas. In 1879 Victorio left the reservation and from his hideouts at isolated watering places on both sides of the Rio Grande made life and property insecure for all who had dared to settle within or attempted to travel across the Trans-Pecos country despite the protective efforts of the federal troops and the Texas Frontier Battalion. Benjamin H. Grierson, in command of United States troops, and George W. Baylor, with a contingent of Texas Rangers, cooperating with the commander of a Mexican military force, pursued relentlessly the hostile Apaches on both sides of the international border. In October 1880 Victorio, the last of the troublesome leaders of the Apaches, was cornered and killed by Mexican troops, thereby concluding the final elimination of the Indian barrier to the settlement of western Texas.

As during the pre-Civil War years, the defense efforts of the federal government were supplemented by the state. In 1871 the legislature authorized the minute-company plan which permitted citizens in 24 frontier counties to organize and equip themselves and receive limited pay. The plan, however, was not successful, and in 1874 the state created two organizations of Rangers destined to attain renown. The first, the Special Force of Rangers under the command of L. H. McNelly, who always spoke softly but firmly, was sent in the spring of 1875 to the lower Rio Grande where several hundred brigands under Juan Cortina were committing murders and stealing cattle daily. The Ranger captain soon reported that his men had slain near Brownsville an entire party of 12 cattle thieves. On one occasion he crossed the Rio Grande with 30 men, moved against Las Cuevas Ranch, where several hundred bandits and soldiers were established, and recovered some of the stolen cattle. His aggressive and fearless action brought a measure of security to several South Texas counties.

The other famous fighting organization was the Frontier Battalion, commanded by Major John B. Jones, a stern, unassuming but highly efficient officer whose strongest drink was black coffee and favorite beverage was buttermilk. Although created, like the Special Force of Rangers, to deal principally with lawless white men, the Frontier Battalion took the field in time to have an important part in bringing to an end Comanche and Kiowa raids in Texas. Jones placed his six companies in camps along the frontier in positions calculated to offer maximum protection. From these camps scouts and patrols were kept constantly on the move to intercept any Indian raiding party that might be trying to make its way into the settlements. At Lost Valley, near the Jack-Young County line, on June 12, 1875, 27 Rangers under the command of Jones himself fought 100 well-armed Indians for an entire day. In this instance the Rangers were obliged to send a runner to Fort Richardson (Jacksboro) for aid, but normally they were able to deal successfully with any Indian force they encountered. During the first six months of its existence the Frontier Battalion had 15 engagements with Indians, killed 15 Indians, wounded ten, captured one, followed 28 trails, and recovered livestock valued at $5,000. When the Red River War was over, the Frontier Battalion concentrated its efforts very effectively against lawless white men.

A bizarre but significant episode closely associated with the problem of Indian removal and the advance of the Texas frontier was the extermination of the buffalo, or bison. This large, shaggy animal, which roamed the grassy plains in millions, constituted the Plains Indians' source of existence. In addition to food, clothing, and shelter, the buffalo robes provided an important trade commodity. Although 199,870 buffalo robes reached New Orleans in 1828, the peak year, the number of buffalo killed before the end of the Civil War made no apparent reduction in the size of the immense herds nor gave the Indians cause for alarm. Beginning in 1870, however, when experiments showed that buffalo hides could be made into good leather, the demand for hides increased sharply. Buyers gathered at convenient points near the buffalo range and offered good prices for all hides. Hunters, who were superb marksmen, penetrated the plains, beginning near the railroad lines in Kansas, and wrought havoc with the Indians' "cattle."

Having slaughtered most of the buffalo in Kansas, they moved in 1873 from Dodge City to the Panhandle of Texas where they found a massive herd. The attack on their supply post at Adobe Walls in June 1874 only checked their operation for that season. By the end of the year several hunters had taken a long, circuitous route around the Indian country and had entered the range from the east by way of Fort Griffin. Before the end of 1875 J. Wright Mooar and his brother John, Joe S. McCombs, and others were hunting in the vicinity of the present towns of Sweetwater, Colorado City, and Haskell. During the 1875–1876 season an estimated 1,500 hunters were engaged in their deadly work. The magnitude of their operation is revealed in the volume of business at the supply base. In one day in 1877, the hunters bought at F. E. Conrad's general mercantile store in Fort Griffin, guns and ammunition to the amount of $2,500. Another supply base, Rath City, or Reynolds City, in Stonewall County, had a hide business alone that year valued at $100,000. Other bases and camps that became towns included Buffalo Gap, Hide Town (Snyder), and Mobeetie. During two months at the peak of their kill—December 1877 and January 1878—the hunters took at least 100,000 hides from the Texas range. During the following season, however, only a few small herds could be found, and by 1880 the buffaloes were gone.

Frontiersmen long engaged in lively arguments over the comparative effectiveness of the three factors that helped to rid the plains of Indians: the United States Army, the Texas Rangers, and the buffalo hunters. Each made some contribution. The Army broke up large-scale resistance to authority; the rangers made raiding too hazardous for even the most reckless warrior; and the buffalo hunters destroyed the Indians' larder and opened the way for the herds of the cattlemen.

THE CATTLE KINGDOM

Before the farmers could establish themselves on the lands vacated after the Civil War by the retreating Indians, except in the Cross Timbers where there was a small supply of timber and water, new inventions and discoveries had to be made. While they impatiently waited the adaptations for a relatively short interval of less than three decades, the cattle kingdom arose, flourished, and declined on the free or cheap but nutritious grass that covered the plains. Texas is logically associated with cattle. Texans took over from the Spaniards the open-range cattle industry, modified it somewhat, and transmitted it from Brownsville to Montana. Besides furnishing a large part of the nation's beef supply, Texas cattle stocked the middle and northern plains. The techniques, the lingo, and other aspects of the culture of the cattle kingdom contributed significantly to the history of the West.

When the first soldiers and priests came, they brought along cattle. The Spanish cattle were the progenitors of the wild cattle that in later years were to be found in various parts of the state, and also of the famous longhorns, a type that evolved in southern Texas and came to be known throughout the West. Apparently, cattle brought in from the Old South in the early nineteenth century affected materially the strain of animals on the range. But whether they were the lanky longhorns of South Texas or the better built round-barreled "Texas cattle," they were hardy and able to protect themselves; they made fairly good beef when fat and furnished their own transportation to market. Except for roundups at branding time they were given no attention and needed none.

The open-range cattle industry had its beginning in South Texas between San Antonio and Brownsville and between Matagorda Bay and Laredo. In climate this region is unsurpassed as a range for cattle that are given practically no care. Some large herds were there during the Spanish era; in 1774 at Goliad, Mission La Bahía Espíritu Santo claimed 15,000 and Mission Rosario 10,000 head.

After the retreat of the Mexican Army following Santa Anna's defeat at San Jacinto, many Mexicans withdrew from the country between the Nueces and the Rio Grande, and Anglo-Americans gradually entered the region. In a preceding chapter mention was made of H. L. Kinney, an adventuresome Irish-American from Illinois, who established a trading post at the site of Corpus Christi in 1839 and soon engaged in ranching. Kinney hired a retinue of followers both to work and to fight, and for many years he was a veritable lord of the marches. The war with Mexico brought a number of prominent Anglo-Americans to this area, among them Captain Mifflin Kenedy and Captain Richard King who enlarged his initial Santa Gertrudis tract of 75,000 acres into the famous King Ranch of more than a million acres. Many gold seekers on their way to California passed through Corpus Christi and created a limited market for the cattle. In spite of marauding Indian bands and even more destructive Mexican bandits, the cattle increased rapidly, and a few cattlemen prospered. In 1860 there were an estimated 3,786,433 cattle in Texas, six times as many cattle as people.

After the war with Mexico, the range-cattle industry spread into the vast prairie region marked today by such cities as Dallas, Ft. Worth, and Denton. John Chisum, later the best-known cattleman in New Mexico, owned a herd in Denton County during this period. By 1861 the cattlemen had extended their domain westward, appropriating the best ranges in the western Cross Timbers, from San Saba County to Clay County. The Civil War halted their westward march, but in 1867, with the reestablishment of a line of military posts, the rangemen began appropriating the rolling plains. By 1876 they had reached or passed the 100th meridian, from Kimble County in the Edwards Plateau to Childress County in the eastern Panhandle.

Meanwhile, the industry had swung around the high plains and was well established along the slopes of the Rocky Mountains and the valleys farther west. The career of Charles Goodnight illustrates this movement. Goodnight went to Palo Pinto County in the Cross Timbers of West Texas in 1857. A few years of trail driving, scouting, and ranger service made of him one of America's finished plainsmen. With Oliver Loving in 1866 he drove a herd by the Concho-Pecos River route to New Mexico, opening the Goodnight (or Goodnight-Loving) Trail. He soon drove herds by this route into Colorado, and in 1869 established his home near Pueblo. After business reverses had brought losses and the range had become crowded, Goodnight turned again to

Texas. He moved his herd southwestward to the Texas Panhandle. The fierce Comanches, who had formed a barrier against white intrusion into that country, had been driven by the soldiers to a reservation, and Goodnight felt confident that he could successfully deal with any small bands that might slip back to their old haunts. He entered the Palo Duro Canyon in 1876, and in partnership with John Adair, an Irish capitalist, established the JA Ranch.

Goodnight had selected a range with a fairly adequate supply of water. The scarcity of water was a great handicap for the cattlemen. Indeed, the plentiful grass was useless without the control of water. Surface water was impounded in tanks where there were creeks and draws, but for several years after the Indians had been removed, ranchers doubted that the millions of acres of fine grass on the High Plains could ever be grazed because of the lack of water. Fortunately, underneath most of the area lay an ample supply. Before it could be used, however, it was necessary to locate this supply and devise methods for making it available.

As early as 1855 Captain John Pope of the United States Army, while surveying for a railroad route, drilled for water on the high plains. A well near where the Texas-New Mexico boundary crossed the Pecos River showed plentiful water, but at a depth too great to be practical. A few railroads utilized underground water, and in 1881 the Quaker settlers dug a well in Blanco Canyon and found an abundance of shallow water. Within the next two years several good wells were drilled in the San Angelo country and one in Schleicher County. In 1884 a cattleman had six wells drilled on his land in Lubbock County and proved that wells with windmills were practical for watering cattle. Within five years all the High Plains was cattle country.

Texas cattle were much easier to raise than to sell. During the Spanish era they were worth very little and could scarcely be disposed of at any price. Occasionally a herd was driven to Louisiana, notwithstanding the fact that trade with that province was forbidden, and at times dried beef was carried by pack train to cities in Coahuila. After the Texan Revolution, Anglo-Americans entered the business in the lower Nueces country, occasionally drove a herd to the East, and shipped cattle in considerable numbers to New Orleans. Nevertheless, cattle were of so little value that many thousands were slain for their hides and tallow. To conserve these commodities, packing plants were established along the coast of Texas, a dozen or more shipping their products through Rockport alone in the early seventies. A few pens, vats, ropes, pulleys, salt, and containers for the meat products constituted the equipment. Although some of the choicest meat was salted and pickled, millions of pounds, after being cooked to render out the tallow, was fed to hogs or dumped into the sea. Naturally, daring and resourceful men sought to get the cheap Texas steer to the tempting northern market. Before the Civil War a few drovers had proved that trail driving to the railheads in Missouri was practical. Left at the end of the war with very little money and an overabundance of cheap cattle, Texans in great numbers renewed their efforts to reach the affluent markets of the North by means of the long drives. In 1866 an estimated 260,000 cattle were started on the trail for Sedalia and other railroad stations in Missouri, from which they could be shipped to eastern markets.

But the Texans met with unforeseen perils. In southern Missouri and eastern Kansas bands of farmers turned them back or broke up their herds, contending that the Texas cattle destroyed their crops and transmitted to their animals the dreaded Texas fever. By following a circuitous route west of the farmers' frontier, some of the herdsmen managed to reach St. Joseph and from there shipped their cattle to Chicago. By midsummer of the next year, however, the Kansas Pacific Railroad had extended its line beyond the farmers' frontier, and at Abilene, Kansas, herds could reach the railroad without interference.

Each year for more than two decades thereafter, thousands of Texas cattle were driven to railroad stations in Kansas to be shipped to eastern markets. During the first few years of the drives fortunes varied; then the year 1874 and the decade following constituted a prosperous era for the cattlemen. A combination of factors created a strong market. Only a part of the cattle driven out of Texas went directly to the slaughter pens. Men soon discovered that the rich grasses of the northern plains would sustain and fatten cattle, and at the cow towns of Kansas, purchasers of stock cattle competed with those who bought for beef. Also, the process of refrigeration, which made it possible to ship dressed beef across the ocean, came into practice in 1875. By 1882 good steers brought five and one-half cents a pound on the Chicago market, at that time the highest price ever paid in the United States. The boom lasted until 1885 when a severe winter, followed by a drought, forced many owners to sell their animals on a market that already was weak, thereby causing the industry to collapse. Thereafter, trail driving declined rapidly. Vexing quarantine regulations and barbed wire fences made it more difficult and more costly each year.

Estimates of the number of cattle driven over the trails vary. The 1880 census estimates the drives to Sedalia, Missouri, for 1866 at 260,000; the drives to Abilene, Kansas, 1867–71 at 1,460,000; to Wichita and Ellsworth, Kansas, 1872–75, at 1,072,000; to Dodge City and Ellsworth, Kansas, 1876–79, at 1,046,732; to Dodge City, Caldwell, and Hunneville, Kansas, 1880, at 382,000. More conservatively, Joseph Nimmo in *Range and Ranch Cattle Traffic, 1866–1884*, estimates the total of cattle driven over all the trails from 1866 to 1884 at 5,201,132.

The perils of the trail loom large in the literature of the cattle kingdom. The monotonous fare on the trail; the lonely night guards; the storms with their wind, hail, and lightning; the stampedes when the roar of the ten thousand charging hoofs and the clatter of half as many sharp-pointed horns reminded the rider that his life depended on his surefooted horse; cold wind that chilled men to the marrow and blistering sun that scorched the earth; the swirling water of swollen streams; and the hazards of marauding Indians were experiences that caused many a trail driver to swear that he would quit for good at Abilene, Ellsworth, or Dodge City. Yet when it next came time for the drive, he was usually ready to go again.

Trail driving was economical. Eight, ten, or a dozen men with few supplies and only a small amount of equipment could deliver a herd of 2,000 or more animals from Texas to the railheads in Kansas at a cost per head of 50 to 60 cents, a small fraction of the charge for shipping by rail. Thus, during the later years many herds were driven past Texas railroad stations and on to Kansas to get them as near as possible to eastern markets before shipping by rail.

There were several major cattle trails to the North, each with a number of branches in Texas used by drovers in reaching the main route. The first was the Sedalia Trail which started near Matagorda Bay and passed through or near Austin, Fort Worth, Denison, and Fort Smith. As a result of unfortunate experiences in Arkansas, the drovers, after crossing the Red River, followed a more westerly course by the Shawnee village to Baxter Springs and thence around the farmers in eastern Kansas to St. Joseph or to Abilene.

The best known of the group was the Chisholm Trail, named for Jesse Chisholm, a Cherokee Indian trader, which began in South Texas, ran by Austin and Lampasas, passed between Fort Worth and Weatherford, crossed the Red River near present Nocona, and thence ran along or near the 98th meridian across Indian Territory to Caldwell, Kansas. Here extensions led to Abilene, Wichita, Newton, and other points. As the farmers moved westward, they forced the cattlemen to seek new routes and new shipping termini. For instance, Abilene, Kansas, was the chief shipping point from 1867 through 1871; Wichita to the south and Ellsworth to the west displaced it in 1872; and after 1876 Dodge City received most of the herds on their way to the eastern markets.

The Dodge City or Great Western Trail, formed at Mason by the junction of three important branches that came from the southeast by Lampasas, from the south by San Antonio, and from Bandera to the southwest, led northward through Coleman and Fort Griffin, crossed the Red River near Doan's Store north of Vernon, and then continued in an almost straight line to Dodge City, Kansas. An extension of the trail was used for driving many cattle from Dodge City to stock the vast northern ranges of western Nebraska, Wyoming, and even Mon-

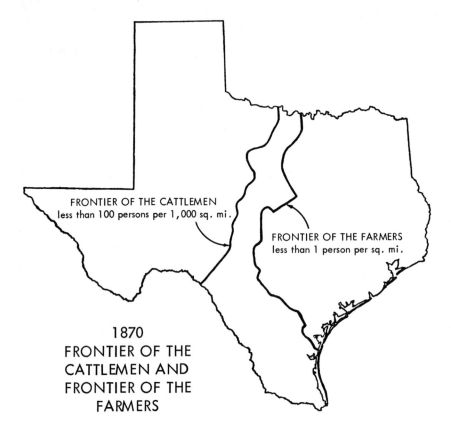

FRONTIER OF THE CATTLEMEN
less than 100 persons per 1,000 sq. mi.

FRONTIER OF THE FARMERS
less than 1 person per sq. mi.

1870
FRONTIER OF THE
CATTLEMEN AND
FRONTIER OF THE
FARMERS

tana. Reference has already been made to another major trail farther
west that Goodnight and Loving opened in 1866. The Goodnight-Lov-
ing (or Pecos) Trail went westward up the Middle Concho, along the
Great Comanche War Trail across the waterless stretch to the Pecos
River at Horsehead Crossing, and thence up the Pecos into New Mexico.
Within a few years, it had been extended by way of Raton Pass and
Denver into Wyoming and Montana.

THE BIG PASTURE COUNTRY

The open-range cattle industry spread with marvelous rapidity; its
decline was even more rapid than its spread.[1] The crowded ranges, the
westward advance of farmers and railroads, the introduction of barbed
wire, and the utilization of drilled wells and windmills for obtaining
water economically transformed the open range into a country of big

[1]These statements apply to raising cattle on the unfenced range and not to enclosed ranching and stock farming. The latter business has continued to our own day.
There were more beef cattle in Texas in 1960 than there were in 1880 or 1890.

pastures. In brief, it ceased to exist about 1890 when the ranges had been enclosed by fences. Thus, the forces that promoted fencing call for some consideration.

The very success of the open-range cattle industry led to its destruction. Reports of huge profits attracted Eastern and European capitalists as well as many small investors. Numbers of syndicates, such as the Texas Land and Cattle Company, the Matador Land and Cattle Company, Hansford Cattle Company, the Capitol Syndicate Company, and the Espuela Land and Cattle Company, invested millions in the business. These concerns had the money to buy their lands and to fence them. Furthermore, the ranges soon became crowded. Protracted droughts interspersed by severe blizzards from 1885 through 1887 and quarantine laws by northern states against Texas cattle either decimated many herds or forced owners to sell thousands of gaunt animals, thereby bringing about a disastrous collapse in the cattle market. Fencing seemed to be the logical solution for the problems. Even before barbed wire, which offered a cheap and effective fencing material, had come into use, cattlemen in South Texas were enclosing their better grasslands with smooth wire or with boards.

Fencing was hastened greatly by at least three factors: the extension of railroads into West Texas; the invention and sale of barbed wire; and the discovery of an adequate groundwater supply and the use of windmills to make it available.

The Texas railroad system is described more at length elsewhere in this volume. It must suffice to state here that every large division of West Texas secured a railroad during the decade of the eighties. The Corpus Christi, San Diego, and Rio Grande line was completed as far as Laredo in 1881; at about the same time the International and Great Northern connected San Antonio with Laredo. On January 1, 1882, the Texas and Pacific joined the Southern Pacific at Sierra Blanca, making possible transcontinental rail traffic across Texas by way of Dallas, Fort Worth, and El Paso. Less than two years later, the Southern Pacific linked El Paso and San Antonio. The Santa Fe was built westward to San Angelo in 1888, and in the same year the Fort Worth and Denver tied the upper Red River valley and the Panhandle with two connecting railroad terminals. The network of railroads made practicable the importation of fencing material, though some ranches were still more than 100 miles from the nearest line, and within another decade the best range lands had been fenced with barbed wire. J. F. Glidden, a farmer of De Kalb, Illinois, invented barbed wire in 1873.[2] Henry B. Sanborn, a salesman for the Glidden wire and later the founder of Amarillo, at first found it difficult to sell his product in Texas, but by

---

[2]Other persons were working on the same idea and it is difficult to apportion credit fairly for the product among the different inventors and promoters.

Ranching. Cattle were introduced into Texas by the Spanish explorers and counted for the principal wealth of the missions. Herds increased during the Civil War when they were neither tended nor thinned. Barbed wire, first available to Texans in quantity in 1879, revolutionized land values and made it possible to open homesteads in frontier plains areas. Texas still leads the nation in the production of cattle, sheep, and goats. Also shown here, cowboys on the 3-million acre XIT Ranch that was given as payment for construction of the state capitol, and a bunch of Herefords, an improved beef breed. (University of Texas Library)

1880 there were a few barbed wire fences in a number of counties, including Clay and Montague in North Texas and Coleman and Runnels farther westward. Three years later practically all the cattle country of South and Central Texas had been enclosed, and fencing was well under way in the Panhandle and North Texas.

Opposition to fencing swelled with its spread. The first lands to be fenced naturally were those having a supply of surface water. It was soon evident either that the fencing movement had to be stopped or else those who did not fence would be ruined. The commissioners court of San Saba County asked the legislature to prohibit by law the building of barbed wire fences; and in 1888 the stockmen's association of Nolan and Fisher counties approved a resolution that the land west of the 100th meridian was "fit only for grazing" and that fences should not be allowed. Some men, however, expressed their resentment more violently by cutting the fences. Public sentiment generally supported the fence cutters. In many cases large proprietors had fenced in land that did not belong to them and had closed public roads. Fences displaced many cowboys who had neither the inclination nor training for another kind of work. Rustlers opposed fences because they made theft more difficult. Furthermore, "nesters" and small farmers who pushed ahead into the cattle country might find themselves entirely surrounded by a fence without an outlet or in turn have their own fences cut by those who resented their bold intrusion into the domain of grass. More significantly, the public resented fencing because the movement was led by large cattle companies mostly owned by eastern and foreign capitalists. This sentiment was well expressed by a contemporary newspaper editor who, after branding fence cutting as an evil, charged it to the fallacious and dangerous policy of the state in selling off its domain in such large tracts, "creating principalities, pashalics, and baronates among a few capitalists and arousing a spirit of agrarianism among the poorer classes."

During 1883 fence cutting occurred in more than half the 171 organized counties of the state. It was most serious along the agricultural frontier, marked by Clay County on the north, Coleman and Brown counties in the center, and Frio and Medina counties farther south. In some areas sentiment was so evenly divided that the local officers and the Texas Rangers were helpless.

To deal with the problem, Governor John Ireland called a special session of the legislature. Early in 1884 it made fence cutting a felony, but required that gates be placed every three miles along a fence. It also made unlawful the enclosing of land not owned or leased. Although in some localities four years later not a fence was left uncut, the legislative enactments, the energetic efforts of a few sheriffs and the Texas Rangers, and a growing public sentiment for law and order combined to put an end by the close of the decade to the destructive orgy. The damages to fences has been estimated as high as $20,000,000, a tremendous financial loss, but even more consequential was the unfavorable publicity which discouraged investments and immigration.

The crowded ranges, the westward advance of farmers and railroads, the introduction of barbed wire, and the utilization of drilled wells and windmills transformed the open ranges into big pastures. In the conversion, some of the cattle companies were faced with the problem of consolidating their holdings. A few had managed to secure compact tracts of lands, but many of the large concerns had fenced in land they did not own. They bought a large part of their land from the railroad companies, paying from 25 cents to one dollar an acre for it. Interspersed with the sections of railroad were alternate sections of school land, which the ranchmen might lease but could not purchase, except in small quantities, for the law limited the amount of school land that one person could buy from the state. The ranchmen bought as much school land as possible; but still there generally was land open to settlers in every large pasture. Immigrants in time sought out and purchased or squatted on these lands. The ranchmen ultimately bought out the "nesters," and a number of big, consolidated ranches emerged.

Most famous among them was the King Ranch which has been mentioned elsewhere. Nearby, Mifflin Kenedy, a former partner of Richard King, established a ranch that encompassed most of Kenedy County. In northwest Texas the JA Ranch under Goodnight's able direction by 1887 had 40,000 cattle and 700,000 acres of land under its control. Thomas Sherman Bugbee, who began grazing cattle in the Texas Panhandle in 1876, eventually expanded his Shoe Bar Ranch to 450,000 acres. Within another decade several other very large ranches were operating in the area. The Matador, a Scottish syndicate, at its peak owned 861,000 acres in Texas; the Spur, a British company adjoining the south side of the Matador, obtained a total of 439,972 acres; and the XIT, a Chicago based syndicate and the largest of the Texas ranches, located the 3,050,000 acres transferred to it for building the state capitol along the border of New Mexico from Hockley County on the south to the Oklahoma line on the north. J. W. Williams, an authority on the subject, listed 19 ranches in 1954 with a range of more than 150,000 acres each. The list included the previously mentioned King and Kenedy ranches, the W. T. Waggoner Estate, the West Cattle Company, and the Burnett ranches, all with ranges in excess of 400,000 acres.

On the enclosed pastures, select breeding of animals, impossible under the open-range system, soon came into practice. Durham, Angus, and Hereford cattle replaced the Spanish longhorns, but the Herefords soon dominated. In time the ranchmen began experimenting with crops to supplant their pastures of grass. At first they planted sorghum, then grain sorghum, and eventually wheat on larger and larger farms.

Closely associated with the advancing frontier and the cattle industry was the raising of sheep and goats. Sheep, like cattle, were brought to

Texas during the early Spanish era and were first raised on a large scale in Texas in the country south of San Antonio. In fact the sheep industry was confined principally to that region until about 1880. Almost without exception, the sheepmen appeared after the cattlemen had established themselves. This fact, as well as the disposition of sheep to eat the grass so short that a cow could not subsist on it, made sheep raising unpopular in the cattle country, and sometimes there were clashes and bloodshed between the sheepmen and cattlemen.

The rapid growth of the sheep industry is reflected by the fact that in 1870 there were 1,223,000 sheep in Texas, whereas in 1880 there were 6,024,000, a larger number than at any time thereafter until 1930. The number, after declining to less than two million in the early twentieth century, increased to nearly eleven million during World War II, and in 1960 was over six million, making Texas the nation's leading producer of sheep.

Angora goats that produce quality mohair were brought to America and to Texas from Turkey in 1849. Goat raising became concentrated chiefly on the Edwards Plateau. In 1960 Texas goats numbered over three and one-third million and constituted three-fourths of the goat numbers of the nation.

THE ADVANCE OF THE FARMERS

In 1870 the extreme western line of the farmers' frontier extended from the common border of Montague and Cook counties irregularly to the vicinity of Bandera and thence to the coast a few miles below Corpus Christi, comparatively close to the cattlemen's frontier. But, as we have seen, within another decade the cattlemen's frontier had left the farmers' frontier hundreds of miles behind. The cattlemen appropriated the choice watering places and best grass lands, but generally there were not enough persons to form communities and establish local governments. The lawmakers created counties (54 by one act in 1876), and geographers marked them on maps in checkerboard fashion; but the herdsmen generally had to wait for the coming of at least a few farmers before they could secure the 150 signatures required to organize a county. For land records and judicial purposes most of these western counties were attached to older counties to the east until a few farmers arrived to augment the adult male population.

Although they advanced more slowly, the farmers came in far greater numbers than did the cattlemen, and their movement gained momentum after the marauding Plains Indians had been confined to the reservations. An estimated 400,000 immigrants entered Texas in 1876, many of whom went directly to the frontier. At the end of the next year the western line of farms ran from Henrietta in Clay County southward through Archer, Young, Stephens, Comanche, Mills, San Saba, and Mason counties. By 1880 it extended from Vernon through Haskell, Jones, Taylor, Runnels, Coleman, and Mason counties. Within the three-year interval farmers by the thousands had settled within the long, triangular region formed by the Red River and these two lines. The increase in population was phenomenal. Jack County, which had only 694 inhabitants in 1870, had 6,626 in 1880. Taylor County was without white population altogether until about 1874, but by 1880 it was the home of 1,736 persons. Apparently, most of the frontier settlers during the 1870's came from older communities in Texas, but other states, particularly of the Old South, were well represented.

During the late seventies and early eighties several colonies of farmers moved to western Texas, some locating far in advance of the other settlements. The best known included a group of 400 Germans from the vicinity of Indianapolis, who settled in 1878 in Baylor County; Lewis Henry Carhart's Christian Colony, which located in 1879 in the vicinity of the town of Clarendon; a colony of Quakers from Ohio and Indiana, who, under the leadership of Paris Cox, in 1879 established a settlement on the High Plains in Lubbock and Crosby counties; and a colony of German Catholics from Anderson County, who were induced by the Texas and Pacific Railroad to locate in 1881 at the present-day town of Stanton. Unacquainted with the country, the crops and the methods of tillage called for, and beset by droughts and plagues of grasshoppers, most of these pioneer farmers did not succeed, but their heroic efforts paved the way for others who came later and profited by their experience.

With the coming of railroads in the eighties, the farmers' frontier abruptly ceased its comparatively orderly and solid advancement. No matter where the rails ran, settlers soon followed. The Texas and Pacific Railroad in 1880 overtook the line of settlements in Taylor County. Within a year Abilene, Sweetwater, Colorado City, and Big Spring were flourishing towns, and the better lands in their vicinity were soon occupied by farmers. A terrible drought in the mid-eighties halted the farmers' advance only for its duration; when it broke in 1887, the tillers of the soil arrived in greater numbers than ever. The mainstream of this new wave of settlers followed the Fort Worth and Denver Railroad along the upper Red River valley and across the Texas Panhandle. Almost by the time the line reached Texline on the border of New Mexico in 1888, Quanah, Childress, Memphis, Clarendon, and Amarillo had become service centers for farmers.

By 1890 the farmers had located in numbers throughout the region east of the 100th meridian and near the railroads. A decade then passed before there occurred any significant westward advance. Settlement of the productive region around Lubbock, about midway between the Texas and Pacific and the Fort Worth and Denver railroads, in the Concho valley around San Angelo, and along the Pecos River was delayed until the turn of the century. The advance of agriculture into South and Southwest Texas is likewise a twentieth century movement and will be given more consideration in connection with the economic development of the state.

Selected Bibliography

A general survey of frontier defense and the Indian problem may be found in C.C. Rister, *The Southwestern Frontier*; R.N. Richardson and C.C. Rister, *The Greater Southwest* (Glendale, 1934); and E. Wallace, *Texas in Turmoil, 1849–1876*. Major studies devoted primarily to the subject include R.N. Richardson, *The Comanche Barrier*; E. Wallace, *Ranald S. Mackenzie on the Texas Frontier*; W.S. Nye, *Carbine and Lance, The Story of Old Fort Sill* (Norman, 1937); C.C. Rister, *Fort Griffin on the Texas Frontier* (Norman, 1956); J.E. Haley, *Fort Concho and the Texas Frontier* (San Angelo, 1952); W.H. Leckie, *Military Conquest of the Southern Plains* (Norman, 1963); R.G. Carter, *On The Border with Mackenzie* (New York, 1961); and Dan Thrapp, *The Conquest of Apacheria* (Norman, 1967). Valuable studies of Indian tribes include E. Wallace and E.A. Hoebel, *The Comanches*; M.P. Mayhall, *The Kiowas* (Norman, 1962); and A.M. Gibson, *The Kickapoos: Lords of the Middle Border* (Norman, 1963). The Indians' side of the story is presented by Thomas C. Battey, *The Life and Adventures of a Quaker among the Indians* (Boston, 1875); and W.S. Nye, *Bad Medicine and Good: Tales of the Kiowa* (Norman, 1962). Considerable source material dealing with the subject is published in J.M. Day and D.H. Winfrey, *Texas Indian Papers, 1860–1916* (Austin, 1961); E. Wallace, *Ranald S. Mackenzie's Official Correspondence Relating to Texas, 1871–1873* (Lubbock, 1967); E. Wallace, *Ranald S. Mackenzie's Official Correspondence Relating to Texas, 1873–1879* (Lubbock, 1968); Joe E. Taylor (ed.), "The Indian Campaign on the Staked Plains, 1874–1875; Military Correspondence from War Department, Adjutant General's Office, File 2815–1874," *Panhandle-Plains Historical Review*, XXIV, 1–216; XXV, 1–360. A few of the many articles dealing with specialized phases of the subject are Adrian N. Anderson, "The Last Phase of Colonel Ranald S. Mackenzie's 1874 Campaign against the Comanches," *West Texas Historical Association Year Book*, XL, 71–82; Frank Temple, "Colonel B.H. Grierson's Victorio Campaign, *The West Texas Historical Association Year Book*, XXXV, 99–111; E. Wallace and A.N. Anderson, "R.S. Mackenzie and the Kickapoos: The Raid into Mexico in 1873," *Arizona and the West*, VII, 105–126; G. Derek West, "The Battle of Adobe Walls (1874)," *Panhandle-Plains Historical Review*, XXXVI, 1–36; Donald Whisenhunt, *Fort Richardson, Outpost on the Texas Frontier* (El Paso, 1968); Ernest R. Archambeau, "The Battle of Lyman's Wagon Train," *Panhandle-Plains Historical Review*, XXXVI, 89–102.

For the story of the shortest-lived frontier industry, see M. Sandoz, *The Buffalo Hunters* (New York, 1954); W. Gard, *The Great Buffalo Hunt* (New York, 1959); and Charles L. Kenner, "A History of New Mexican-Plains Indian Relations" (unpublished dissertation, Texas Technological College; Lubbock, 1966).

Historical literature of the range cattle industry is voluminous. General studies are Ernest S. Osgood, *The Day of the Cattleman* (Minneapolis, 1954); E.E. Dale, *The Range Cattle Industry* (Norman, 1930); E.E. Dale, *Cow Country* (Norman, 1942); and James Cox, *The Cattle Industry of Texas and Adjacent Country* (St. Louis, 1895). Bearing especially on Texas is W.C. Holden, *Alkali Trails*; Coleman McCampbell, *The Saga of a Frontier Seaport* (Dallas, 1934); Billy M. Jones, *The Search for Maturity* (Austin, 1965); Robert M. Utley, "The Range Cattle Industry in the Big Bend of Texas," *The Southwestern Historical Quarterly*, LXIX, 419–441.

There are several historians of the cattle trails: W. Gard, *The Chisholm Trail* (Norman, 1954); J. Marvin Hunter and George W. Saunders (eds.), *The Trail Drivers of Texas* (Dallas, 1925); Harry Drago, *Great American Cattle Trails* (New York, 1965); Andy Adams, *The Log of a Cowboy* (Boston, 1931); Emerson Hough, *The Story of the Cowboy* (New York, 1923); Jimmy M. Skaggs, "The Route of the Great Western (Dodge City) Cattle Trail," *West Texas Historical Association Year Book*, XLI, 131–143.

Ranches and cattlemen have been popular subjects for writers. Among the best are Lewis Atherton, *The Cattle Kings* (Bloomington, 1962); Tom Lea, *The King Ranch* (2 vols., Boston, 1957); William M. Pearce, *The Matador Land and Cattle Company* (Norman, 1964); J.E. Haley, *The XIT Ranch of Texas* (Chicago, 1929; Norman, 1953); Cordia Sloan Duke and J.B. Frantz, *6,000 Miles of Fence: Life on the XIT Ranch of Texas* (Austin, 1961); William Timmons, *Twilight on the Range: Recollections of a Latterday Cowboy* (Austin, 1962); Lewis Nordyke, *Cattle Empire* (New York, 1949); W.C. Holden, *The Spur Ranch* (Boston, 1934); J.E. Haley, *Charles Goodnight, Cowman and Plainsman* (Boston and New York, 1936), an excellent biography; J.E. Haley, *George W. Littlefield, Texan* (Norman, 1943); W.C. Holden, *Rollie Burns: or an Account of the Ranching Industry on the South Plains* (Dallas, 1932); J.W. Williams, *The Big Ranch Country* (Wichita Falls, 1954); Laura V. Hammer, *Short Grass and Longhorns* (Norman, 1943); L.F. Sheffy, *The Life and Times of Timothy Dwight Hobart, 1855–1953* (Canyon, 1950); L.F. Sheffy, *The Francklyn Land and Cattle Company: A Panhandle Enterprise, 1882–1957* (Austin, 1963); A. Ray Stephens, *The Taft Ranch* (Austin, 1964); Charles Kenner, "John Hittson: Cattle King of West Texas," *West Texas Historical Association Year Book*, XXXVII, 70–81; H.T. Burton, "A History of the J.A. Ranch," *Southwestern Historical Quarterly*, XXXI, 89–115, 221–260, 325–364; XXXII, 26–66; J.M. Skaggs, "John Thomas Lytle: Cattle Baron," *ibid.*, LXXI, 46–60; David B. Gracy, II, "George Washington Littlefield, Portrait of a Cattleman," *ibid.*, LXVIII, 237–258.

Several other phases of the cattle industry have attracted authors. Some excellent studies in this miscellany are W.P. Webb, *The Great Plains*; Frank S. Hastings, *A Ranchman's Recollections* (Chicago, 1921); R.D. Holt, "The Introduction of Barbed Wire into Texas and the Fence Cutting War," *The West Texas Historical Association Year Book*, VI, 65–79; Henry D. McCallum, "Barbed Wire in Texas," *Southwestern Historical Quarterly*, LXI, 207–219; W.C. Holden, "The Problem of Maintaining the Solid Range on the Spur Ranch," *ibid.*, XXXIV, 1–19; T.R. Havins, "The Passing of the Longhorns," *ibid.*, LVI, 51–58; T.R. Havins, "Texas Fever," *ibid.*, LVII, 147–162; J. Fred Rippy, "British Investments in Texas Lands and Livestock," *ibid.*, LVIII, 331–341; W. Gard, "The Impact of the Cattle Trails," *ibid.*, LXXI, 1–6; Lowell H. Harrison, "British Interest in the Panhandle-Plains Area, 1878–1885," *Panhandle-Plains Historical Review*, XXXVIII, 1–44; Gene M. Gressley, *Bankers and Cattlemen* (New York, 1966); J.B. Frantz and Julian Ernest Choate, *The American Cowboy: The Myth and the Reality* (Norman, 1955).

Two authoritative works on the sheep industry are Edward Norris Wentworth, *America's Sheep Trails* (Ames, Iowa, 1948); and Winifred Kupper, *The Golden Hoof: The Story of the Sheep of the Southwest* (New York, 1945); also, see Harold M. Gober, "The Sheep Industry in Sterling County," *West Texas Historical Association Year Book*, XXVII, 32–57. For the correspondence of George W. Kendall, Texas' leading sheep rancher, see H.J. Brown, *Letters from a Texas Sheep Ranch* (Urbana, Illinois, 1959).

Preeminent among the accounts of the settlement of West Texas is W.C. Holden, *Alkali Trails*; R.N. Richardson, *The Frontier of Northwest Texas, 1846 to 1876*; B.M. Jones, *The Search for Maturity*; Robert Lee Hunt, *A History of Farmer Movements in the Southwest, 1873–1925* (College Station, Texas, 1935); dealing with various phases of the subject are Mrs. S. C. Miller, *Sixty Years in the Nueces Valley, 1870–1930* (San Antonio, 1930); Stuart McGregor, "Migrations of Population in Texas" (reprinted from the *Dallas News*), *Bunker's Monthly*, September, 1929, 271–279; R.C. Crane, "Early Days in Fisher County," *West Texas Historical Association Year Book*, VI, 124–169; Walter B. Stephens, *Through Texas* (reprint of a series of letters published in *The St. Louis Globe Democrat*, 1892); Mary L. Cox, *History of Hale County, Texas* (Plainview, 1937); Willie N. Lewis, *Between Sun and Sod* (Clarendon, Texas, 1938); Nellie W. Spikes and Temple Ann Ellis, *A History of Crosby County* (San Antonio, 1952).

14

THE COMMERCIAL REVOLUTION, 1870–1930

In the span of a man's lifetime, 1870–1930, the economic transformation of Texas assumed the proportions of a revolution. Most of Texas in 1870 was either unpopulated or inhabited by subsistence farmers who could do little more than produce for their own needs. Transportation facilities were primitive with only about 500 miles of serviceable railroads. Industrial production was for the most part limited to small shops catering to the demands of self-sustaining communities.

But change, eagerly sought in the name of progress, was accomplished with dramatic speed. By 1904 Texas contained more miles of railroad track than any other state. Spurred by land hunger and encouraged by the potential markets represented in the expanding rail lines, settlers rushed forward into western and southern areas. Although subsistence agriculture did not disappear entirely, farmers turned more and more to a commercial market economy, usually concentrating on the production of a single cash crop—cotton. Meanwhile, the pace of industrialization quickened. The value of Texas industrial production by 1901 amounted to more than half of the value of agricultural goods. Commercial agriculture continued to provide a living for a majority of Texans for the next several decades, but after the discovery of lush oil production at Spindletop, industry became more and more a dominant element in the economy. By the twenties the value of industrial production exceeded that of agriculture. With industrialization came its usual concomitants—the rise of the city and the beginnings of organized labor.

BUILDING THE RAILROADS

To the Texans of the late nineteenth century, the railroads appeared to be the key to progress and prosperity. Living in a land of almost limitless expanse and almost nonexistent natural transportation media, farmer and townsman alike recognized the necessity of a cheap, fast, and dependable means of marketing, one available apparently only through railroads. Without the market afforded by the rails there would have been little point in mining coal at Thurber nor in raising cotton at Sweetwater. Wagon freight rates averaged one dollar per 100 pounds per 100 miles. With cotton bringing about 35 dollars a bale in 1876, wagon freight from north Central Texas to Galveston would have absorbed more than half of the value of the crop. Rail freight rates, though often discriminatory, were never after 1879 more than 50 cents per 100 pounds per 100 miles and declined more or less consistently from that figure.

Thus, Texans understandably courted the builders of the roads. Citizens of Brenham, for example, were agreeable to a railroad's demand for a right-of-way through the county and $150,000 in cash. For a time Fort Worth granted bonuses to all railroads building into the city. For the communities already built and those still only existing in dreams, the railroad meant population and profit. When the railroad bypassed a community, the town was in almost all instances doomed to a certain and often a swift death. Citizens were drawn to the market place found in the rail terminals.

In addition to the enticements offered by local communities on their own authority, cities and counties, authorized by an 1871 state law, used public resources amounting to more than two million dollars to subsidize much of the cost of railroad building. In 1856 a law was enacted authorizing the lending of school funds to railroads to the amount of $6,000 per mile; under this law nearly two million dollars was loaned to the railroads. During reconstruction, from 1869 through 1871, the legislature voted bonds to railroads, but most of these obligations were later paid in land. In fact, by far the greatest bounty to railroads came from the public lands. From 1854 until 1882, except for the period from 1869 to 1873 when it was prohibited by the constitution, Texas maintained a policy of liberal land grants. In most cases the amount of land given was 16 sections for each mile of road constructed. About 41 railroad companies received state land, first and last, before the repeal of the land-grant act in 1882. The greatest single beneficiary was the Texas and Pacific which was given 5,167,360 acres. Approximately 32,150,000 acres of the state's public domain were disposed of in this way, an area as large as Alabama.

The wisdom of such generous land grants was at the time, as it has been since, a moot question. Its critics have contended that the aid was more generous than necessary, that it caused the building of some lines that were not needed, and that in many instances the lands granted to railroads were retained by holding companies, thereby retarding the development of the country. It must be said, however, that most of the railroads never received any real benefits from their lands. The railroad corporations were undercapitalized; the lands could not be converted into cash; the companies were forced into receiverships; and the land was sold at a few cents an acre. The railroads promoted rapid settlement and development of the country, the goal of every Anglo-American commonwealth.

Construction of the bulk of the state's major railroads was accomplished in the span of two decades. Only 11 short railroad lines, aggregating a little less than 500 miles, had been constructed in Texas before the Civil War. Most of these lines radiated from Houston, and not until 1872 were railroad connections made with other states. The debacle of Civil War brought an end to railroad building, and only one line, the Houston and Texas Central, made any progress before the state was readmitted to the Union in 1870. The years from 1870 to 1873, inclusive, witnessed substantial railroad building; but the Panic of 1873 and the consequent decline in available credit is reflected in the small increase of mileage in 1874 and 1875. Partial recovery from the panic and the repeal of the inhibition against granting lands to railroads in 1873 brought about a substantial increase in mileage each year from 1876 to 1882. In the latter year new construction amounted to more than 2,000 miles. The act of the legislature in 1882, discontinuing forever the granting of land bounties, probably accounts for the fact that only 66 miles were constructed in 1883. The next year saw a great increase in building, however, and by the close of 1890 the state had 8,710 miles of railroads.

The first railroad to penetrate northern Texas was the Houston and Texas Central. From its terminus at Millican, it reached Corsicana by 1871. The arrival of its first train in Dallas on July 16, 1872, afforded the people of that city the occasion for a great celebration, including a barbecue of buffalo meat. By the first of January following, it had reached Denison. Later it became a part of the great Southern Pacific system.

While the Houston and Texas Central was being built northward, the Missouri, Kansas, and Texas (the Katy), a Kansas corporation, was extending its line southward through the Indian Territory to the Texas border. Late in 1872 it bridged the Red River and soon thereafter was halted in a cornfield where now stands Denison. These two roads, the Houston and Texas Central and the Katy, linked the Texas seaboard with Kansas City, St. Louis, and other markets in the North and East.

The International and Great Northern Railway, which grew out of the consolidation of two lines in 1873, soon afforded service across Texas from northeast to southwest. Longview in East Texas was united with Hearne on the Houston and Texas Central by December, 1872. The line was extended to Austin in 1876, and thence to San Antonio, and to Laredo, where it connected with the Mexican National Railroad in the early eighties. The International and Great Northern became a part of the Gould system, all lines of which were connected directly or indirectly with the St. Louis, Iron Mountain, and Southern Railway at Texarkana.

In a strange way yellow fever enters the story of the Gulf, Colorado, and Santa Fe Railroad. Galveston had no railroad outlet that did not pass through Houston. Tiring of the strict quarantine against the fever which Houston enforced almost every season to the great injury of trade, leading citizens of Galveston determined to build their own railroad directly into the interior. The road was incorporated in May 1873, and by 1878 it had been built to Richmond. By the close of 1881 one branch had reached Fort Worth; five years later, when control passed to the Atchison, Topeka, and Santa Fe, one branch had been extended eastward to Dallas and another westward to Brownwood. In 1887 the Fort Worth branch was extended to connect with the main Atchison system at Purcell, Oklahoma.

Three great railways were constructed across West Texas during the eighties. The Galveston, Harrisburg, and San Antonio Railroad acquired additional lines and charter rights authorizing the establishment of a line to San Antonio and to El Paso. The enterprise had the support of C. P. Huntington, T. W. Peirce, and others interested in the construction of a southern transcontinental railroad, and it was pushed with vigor. The line was built into San Antonio in 1877, and in 1880 it was extended westward toward El Paso, to meet three years later the Southern Pacific which was being built eastward from that place. In the meantime Houston had been linked by rail with New Orleans. These railroads, together with the Houston and Texas Central and some other smaller lines, became a part of the Southern Pacific system.

The Texas and Pacific Railway company was formed in March 1872 by the consolidation of three companies that owned a certain amount of trackage and had valuable franchise rights, including a charter from Congress. In 1873 the main line was opened from Longview to Dallas giving Dallas a direct route to the East. Westward extension was halted near Dallas by the Panic of 1873. Aided by the people of Fort Worth, the railroad reached that city in 1876, after which there was more delay.

In 1880 Jay Gould and Russell Sage took charge of the Texas and Pacific and it was built westward rapidly. General Grenville M. Dodge, who built the Union Pacific, was in charge of construction. Meanwhile Huntington's Southern Pacific Railroad had been chartered to build eastward until it effected a junction with the Texas and Pacific. From San Francisco this line reached the Arizona border in May 1877 and continued its construction eastward. Each road built with all possible haste in order to obtain a maximum amount of government subsidy. By 1880 the Southern Pacific had reached El Paso; and, as already stated, the Galveston, Harrisburg, and San Antonio Railroad soon closed the gap between San Antonio and El Paso. This extension completed the southern transcontinental service between San Francisco and New Orleans. At Sierra Blanca, 92 miles east of El Paso, the westbound Texas and Pacific had met the eastbound Southern Pacific by January 1, 1882. Here the famous Huntington-Gould agreement providing that the two lines should share jointly the track from Sierra Blanca to El Paso was made. Other parts of this agreement, kept secret for many years, were comprehensive. They called for the distribution of traffic and the pooling of receipts between certain lines of the two great systems, and promised that neither side would build lines to compete with the other. It is thought that the agreement retarded railroad building in Texas for many years. In 1881 the Texas and Pacific had acquired a line from Shreveport to New Orleans, providing direct connection between El Paso and New Orleans over the Gould system.

What the Southern Pacific did for the southern part of the state and the Texas and Pacific for the northern part, the Fort Worth and Denver City did for the Panhandle. Construction of this line provided railroad facilities for Wichita Falls in 1882. After considerable delay, the road reached Amarillo, and was extended on to Texline in 1888. For a while this road was a part of the Union Pacific system, but in 1893 it was sold to the Colorado and Southern, a part of the Burlington system.

SETTLEMENT OF WESTERN
AND SOUTHERN TEXAS

Conquest of the Indians, liberal land laws, and building of the railroads combined to provide a momentum to the pace of westward migration that did not subside until western and southern Texas was populated. As previously noted, by the close of the seventies the Indian barrier to settlement was removed, and by the nineties most areas in the state had been tapped by the railroads. Land laws thereafter were directed toward the interest of people in the western part of the state. The farmers' frontier was seldom very far behind that of the cattleman. A law of 1897 reduced the minimum price of agricultural lands to $1.50 per acre, provided extended terms of one-fortieth down and 40 years on the balance at three percent interest, and gave previous buyers an opportunity to forfeit their original purchases and to buy the same land under the new and more advantageous terms. A law of 1901, which allowed one person to purchase four sections of agricultural or grazing land by filing at local county seats, produced some land rushes and conflicts between cattlemen and farmers. However, a more orderly system was created in 1905 by a law requiring publication of prospective sales of school lands, minimum values, and competitive sealed bids, a procedure that brought prices as high as 22 dollars an acre.

Actually, these land rushes marked the end of the old controversy between the cattlemen and the farmers. As long as there was free grass or land in quantity to lease, the cattlemen opposed the advance of the farmers. They told the agrarians that the right side of the soil was already up and that to turn it was both poor business and a crime against nature. But once they had acquired legal possession of their lands, the ranchmen had no reason to oppose the coming of the farmers or of anybody else who would develop the country and increase the value of all land.

The railroads, which inaugurated costly programs aimed at peopling the country, probably accomplished more in that direction than all other agencies combined. They had agents in eastern centers who distributed tons of printed materials; some railroads ran exhibition trains; some erected immigrant depots, where people might stay while selecting their lands; some established demonstration farms; and all of them favored immigrants with their transportation rates. Once settlements were established the people became enthusiastic about the country, and newspapers sometimes proclaimed its wonders in language unrestrained.

When, at about the turn of the century, the people of the North Central Plains began to recover from the immigration fever, it spread to the High Plains where it raged intermittently for decades. The best school and railroad lands passed into the ownership of farmers and the supply was exhausted early in the century. In 1908 the Commissioner of the General Land office reported that trainloads of prospectors, speculators, and investors were invading Andrews, Dawson, Ector, Gaines, Midland, and Yoakum counties, eager to buy land at from 12 to 22 dollars an acre. During the two years preceding August 1, 1908, they had purchased 6,383,263.77 acres of school lands. The commissioner reported in 1912 that the asylum lands (which had been dealt with in a fashion similar to the school lands) had been sold, and in 1920 he announced that "the sale of all surveyed school lands was practically completed . . . this year." But already ranchmen had begun cutting up their pastures and selling off land in small tracts. Real estate companies occasionally made of this development a land boom, much like those in regions to the east a decade or two earlier. Homeseekers were brought in by trainloads; public conveyances were not adequate to accommodate them and private vehicles had to be pressed into service. Land values sometimes increased from 50 to 100 percent within a few months.

While farmers were establishing themselves on the high Plains, others were moving with equal effectiveness against the domain of the cattleman in southern Texas. They practiced both dry farming and irrigation, but irrigation drew in the greater number, especially in the lower Rio Grande valley.

The growth of this region started with the building of the St. Louis, Brownsville, and Mexico Railroad in 1904. Thereafter the production of fruits and vegetables by irrigation increased rapidly, though irregularly. By 1910 a few commercial citrus fruit orchards had been set, and in 1914 it was discovered that by budding grapefruit and oranges on the native orange stock one could produce a tree adapted to the Rio Grande soil and climate. An amendment to the state constitution in 1917 and subsequent liberal acts of the legislature encouraged the organization of irrigation and drainage districts; thousands of farmers from North Texas migrated to the Rio Grande valley during the decade following World War I.

During the decade following 1918 a major land boom developed in this region. The general prosperity, in which the farmers shared at least in part, and the restoration of order along the Mexican border combined to create an ideal condition for real estate agents. Old irrigation projects were enlarged and new ones were established, so that each season huge blocks of pastureland were marked like gridirons by life-giving ditches. Unlike the promoters of earlier years, the Rio Grande valley sought only the well-to-do or the rich immigrants. Indeed, in no other area of Texas was the disparity between wealthy landowner and abysmally poor laborer, usually of Mexican descent, as apparent as in the valley. Poor men could not purchase these high-priced lands. From North Texas cities agents ran excursion trains of Pullman cars and diners only, frequently making the passengers their guests, without charge for transportation or meals. At times, land sales on a single excursion of this kind aggregated more than a million dollars. Between 1920 and 1930 the population of the lower Rio Grande valley (Cameron, Hidalgo, and Willacy counties) more than doubled.

To a considerable degree, population of the west depended upon the development of new agricultural techniques. Irrigation, the key to survival in the Rio Grande valley, could not be practiced extensively elsewhere in western Texas until the 1930's. Meanwhile, drought was a persistent and ominous threat. Drought in 1886 and 1887 brought some of the poorer settlers near to starvation. Public and private funds afforded some relief, but most survived on their own resources or with the help of more fortunate neighbors. Other devastating droughts returned in 1917 and 1918 and again in 1933 and 1934. Nearly as destructive were the years of subnormal rainfall that turned promising yields into disappointing near-failures. The farmer of the west never conquered the threat of parching drought until the advent of irrigation, but through dry-farming techniques and careful selection of crops and varieties, he reduced its effect. By the 1880's grain sorghums such as milo maize and Kaffir corn were being grown as substitutes for corn on the Spur Ranch in the rugged lands east of the Caprock. Wheat, a relatively drought-resistant plant, soon became the principal crop of northwest Texas.

Though it advanced at a somewhat slower pace, cotton, likewise drought-resistant, by 1900 was being grown in western areas, especially along the Texas and Pacific Railroad. Concentration of cotton production in West Texas, however, would not come until the middle of the twentieth century.

COMMERCIALIZATION OF AGRICULTURE

The revolutionary change in the nature of agriculture that occurred during these decades was in many respects as significant as the expansion of the farmers' frontier. By the seventies there was an apparent trend away from self-sufficiency toward commercialization wherein the farmer concentrated on production of commodities for market and in turn purchased many of his necessities.

Although Texans produced a variety of crops for the marketplace, cotton dominated the emergence of the commercial agricultural economy. In the late nineteenth century and early decades of the twentieth, the average Texan was more familiar with the cotton sack and hoe than with the lariat rope and branding iron; he was a farmer, not a rancher. In 1880 farmers on slightly less than two and one-half million acres produced a cotton crop valued at about 57 million dollars. In 1928 almost 17 million acres brought a return of $446,687,000. By 1910 approximately half of the cultivated acreage in the state was devoted to cotton; ultimately the commodity would be grown in 238 of the 254 counties. In comparison, cattle production did not begin to keep pace. Cattle numbers almost doubled between 1880 and 1900, reaching ten million head, but declined thereafter to slightly more than five million in 1930.

Cotton production expanded in the face of innumerable problems and persistent opposition. The vagaries of nature—worms, boll weevils, Johnson grass, root rot, dry weather, wet weather—were enough to try the patience and to test the will of the most determined farmer. Moreover, critics repeatedly questioned the wisdom of expanding production and often the intelligence of the producer. Farm organizations, editors, agricultural colleagues, and self-appointed advisors who volunteered their counsel persistently condemned specialization in general and cotton farming in particular. Cotton farming, they contended, was responsible for oppressive mortgages, exhausted fertility, rising tenancy, and declining income. Diversification, as they used the term, in essence a return to the self-sustaining farm, would ease the burden of the farmer. The cotton farmer paid no heed.

Although some critics argued that ignorance accounted for the cotton farmer's stubborn refusal to restrict his acreage, the reasons were actually more complex and convincing. Prices declined, but cotton almost always returned more income per acre than other crops suited to his labor, land, and machinery resources. Cotton was the most dependable of the southern crops; contrary to popular opinion, it did not exhaust the soil as quickly as many other crops. And the machinery for marketing cotton was more advanced than for other commodities.

Few farmers, whether they raised cotton or other products, found the market place with its enticing opportunities an avenue to substantial wealth. Returns fluctuated unpredictably from one year to the next; variables such as prices, costs, mortgages, and weather frequently combined to leave the farmer looking anxiously to "next year" rather than rejoicing in the present. But between 1880 and 1920 agricultural wealth for the state as a whole increased steadily from decade to decade, even spectacularly, and remained fairly stable during the twenties. From less than $1,000 in 1880, the value of the average farm increased to more than $7,000 in 1930. Total value rose from less than two hundred million dollars in 1880 to more than three and one-half billion in 1930. Since the size of the average farm increased only about 20 percent, the expanded value represented primarily new acres brought into production and an increase in value per acre from about five dollars in 1880 to almost $30 per acre in 1930.

THE GROWTH OF INDUSTRY

Although Texas possessed vast natural resources, industry in 1870 was still confined primarily to small shops that seldom supplied a market beyond the immediate community. Industrial workers made up less than one percent of the population. During the next several decades, however, the pace of industrialization quickened, depending mostly on manufacturing related to agriculture and exploitation of basic natural resources. After the turn of the century a number of organizations were formed to promote the growth of manufacturing.

Processing of agricultural products was one of the major businesses in the late nineteenth century. Into the eighties flour milling was the leading industry, ranking ahead of that of lumbering. Meanwhile, manufacture of products from cottonseed steadily increased in importance, ranking second in the state's industrial economy in 1900. Meat packing, which began at Victoria in 1868, was soon extended to other communities and numbers of small plants added to the output. It is said that the first application of ice to the packing industry was at Denison, where a plant was established in about 1875. A small packing plant was built at Fort Worth in 1884; six years later the Fort Worth stockyards were opened; and thereafter the packing business in that city expanded rapidly. The first modern plants in Texas were two establishments located at Fort Worth in about 1901. In later years smaller plants began to operate at Dallas, San Antonio, El Paso, Amarillo, and other cities. Textile manufacturing began before the Civil War when the famous frontier businessman, John F. Torrey, set up a cotton mill at New Braunfels. A plant manufacturing cotton goods was operated in the penitentiary for a number of years during and after the Civil War. At later dates plants were established at Dallas, Sherman, and Post, but they remained comparatively unimportant.

One of the early Texas industries was lumbering. With more than 20 million acres of timberland to supply them, pioneers soon started their sawmills turning. Peter Ellis Bean had a sawmill near Nacogdoches in 1829, and there were several in Texas at the time of Colonel Almonte's visit in 1834. With the coming of the railroads after the Civil War, the lumbering business attained huge proportions. By 1900 Orange and Beaumont had come to be important sawmill centers; in 1900 the mills of Orange alone were cutting 700,000 feet of lumber a day. Production of the Texas mills passed the billion board feet total in 1899 and reached a maximum of more than 2,250,000,000 in 1907. Thereafter, because of the depletion of the forests, the total declined, but Texas continued to rank from sixth to eighth among the states in the production of lumber.

After 1880 mining operations contributed significantly to the industrial economy. Coal deposits existed in many regions of the state, but commercial mining was concentrated in Palo Pinto and Erath counties where Thurber was the center of activity. In 1900 the value of coal mined amounted to more than the combined value of all other mineral products. Commercial coal production continued until the 1920's. Other mineral products of substantial value mined by 1900 included salt in the Grand Saline area, iron ore at Rusk and Jefferson, and limestone and granite at various sites. Sulphur was first produced in paying quantities in Texas in 1912 at Freeport in Brazoria County.

But it was oil, the state's greatest mineral resource, that dominated the development of an industrialized Texas. The presence of petroleum in paying quantities was discovered by accident in Nacogdoches County as early as 1867, and at Corsicana about 30 years later. There were a few other early discoveries, but they are of little consequence, except for the fact that they may have stimulated the search for oil. In fact, the petroleum industry in Texas is a twentieth century business. It began at Beaumont, when on a January day in 1901 a well drilled by Captain Anthony F. Lucas, oil prospector from Louisiana, roared in with a stream of oil that spouted 200 feet into the air. This gusher was the first in Spindletop, a field that produced 12,421,000 barrels in 1902 alone. Other Gulf Coast fields raised Texas oil production to 28,136,189 barrels in 1905. The output declined for a number of years thereafter, notwithstanding the discovery of the Petrolia field in 1904 and the Waggoner or Electra field in 1911.

The discovery of oil at Ranger in 1917, through the enterprise and

Forests of iron and steel. Beginning in the 1920's, Texas led the nation in oil production; and it still has a large share of the nation's oil and gas reserves. Oil·field machinery like that pictured above is a familiar sight in many parts of the state. (Texas Highway Department)

persistence of W. K. Gordon of the Texas Pacific Coal and Oil Company, raised Texas oil production to new high levels. The opening of the Ranger field was a matter of world-wide importance, for it added substantially to the oil supply of the United States and her allies during the crisis of World War. Then came the Burkburnett, Breckenridge, Desdemona, and other discoveries that brought the output almost to 100,000,000 barrels in 1920. The early twenties saw a series of fields along the Balcones Fault, among them were the Luling, Mexia, and Powell producing areas.

Meanwhile, wildcatters (individuals or corporations who seek to discover new fields) were exploring the western part of the state. They were rewarded by the Big Lake discovery in Reagan County in 1923, and the McCamey, Crane-Upton, Winkler, and Yates pools in the Pecos River country. When the great wells of the Yates pools in Pecos County, and the Westbrook-Hendricks field, in Winkler County, began to spout in 1926, they alarmed the entire oil fraternity. One well on a test flowed 6,316.6 barrels an hour, or at the rate of 127,598 barrels a day. It was said that the potential production of these fields was from three to five million barrels daily, more oil than the entire United States was then producing! About the same time oil production was opened on the High Plains in the Panhandle north and east of Amarillo. The market could not absorb such floods of oil; men realized that some kind of restriction on production was the only means by which the industry could avoid total collapse. Leadership in such conservation measures logically belonged to Texas, for in 1928 the state led the nation with an output of 257,320,000 barrels of oil valued at almost that many millions of dollars.

Closely associated with oil production was that of natural gas. The commercial use of natural gas in Texas dates from the early years of the twentieth century. Corsicana and Marshall were the first towns to secure natural gas distribution systems. In 1910 a pipe line was completed 130 miles from the Petrolia field to supply Fort Worth and Dallas. Various other towns and cities secured this service during the next 15 years, though the gas companies encountered many difficulties, chief of which was that of securing a dependable supply of gas. During the twenties significant technical improvements were made, and in 1927 the great Panhandle gas field was discovered.

Also allied with oil production was the refining and manufacture of various petroleum products. It seems that the first oil refinery in the state was constructed at Corsicana in 1890. Flush production at Spindletop likewise led to the building of refineries. Most major companies soon operated refining units, and from the earliest history of the industry, there have been numbers of small independent refineries. Forty-three refineries in 1919 produced petroleum products valued at $241,757,313. In the next decade the number of refineries more than doubled and their capacity in barrels per day tripled.

In Texas, as elsewhere, industries tended to consolidate into a few large companies that controlled a major part of the market. Reflecting the trend toward commercialization, the number of flour mills declined about 50 percent in the last three decades of the nineteenth century, but capital investment increased fourfold and the value of the annual production about sixfold. Like the grasslands of West Texas, the timberlands of East Texas came to be owned by comparatively few people. After 1879 timberlands were classified separately from grazing and agricultural lands, and (where they had been set aside for the schools) gradually could be bought in small quantities at five dollars an acre. Soon they were purchased by nonresidents. Capitalists of vision, among them, H. J. Lutcher, G. B. Moore, and John H. Kirby, made heavy investments which later brought them large fortunes. The Kirby Lumber

Company, chartered in 1901 and the first multimillion-dollar industrial corporation in the state, from its formation dominated the lumber business. In some respects the early Texas oil booms in the twentieth century challenged the near-monopoly held elsewhere by the Standard Oil combination. But out of Spindletop and subsequent discoveries came similar gigantic oil companies such as Gulf, Texaco, Humble, and Mobil.

THE EMERGENCE OF ORGANIZED LABOR

With the development of a commercial economy clearly underway, some workers in Texas began to look to unity as a means of protecting and advancing their interests. Sometimes organizations such as the Screwmen's Benevolent Association of Galveston, formed originally as a worker's insurance group, evolved into labor unions seeking shorter hours, higher wages and control of the job. Otherwise, typographers and railroad workers apparently were among the most active leaders in the early formation of unions in the state. By the 1870's organization of railroad brotherhoods in the state was underway, and there were scattered militant groups to be found in a few other industries. Until the mid-seventies general public sentiment toward labor unions was either neutral or even perhaps sympathetic. However, primarily because strikes on the railroads during the seventies brought inconvenience to the farmer and merchant, public opinion had become definitely antilabor by the end of the decade.

In the 1880's the Knights of Labor, a national organization, represented both an industrial and a political force of consequence. Claiming 300 locals and 30,000 members in the state, the Knights opened their membership to farmers and allowed Negroes to join. Probably the Knights organized the highest percentage of nonfarm laborers ever brought into unions in Texas, perhaps amounting for a short time to 50 percent of the nonfarm workers. By 1886 three-fourths of all organized labor in the nation, about 700,000 workers, belonged to the Knights.

Although officially opposing the use of the strike, the Knights resorted to the weapon on several occasions in Texas. Alarming many persons who regarded them as "revolutionary" anyway, the Knights called a strike of the dock workers of the Mallory line in Galveston. About the same time a strike on the railroads controlled by the tycoon, Jay Gould, was called, but the differences were soon adjusted by an agreement favorable to the strikers. However, the Gould organization was apparently determined to crush the Knights. Precipitating the Great Southwest Strike of 1886, the Texas and Pacific, a Gould road, fired a foreman in the shops at Marshall, in violation of a definite agreement, the workers, alleged. The Knights in response called a strike with about 9,000 men going out, a large number of them in Texas. After a clash at Fort Worth over the movement of a freight train where blood was shed and property destroyed, Governor Ireland ordered state militiamen and Rangers to the area, and the disturbance soon subsided. Meanwhile the Texas and Pacific Railway had passed into the hands of a federal receiver and the strike was ruled in contempt of court. Failure of the Great Southwest Strike, charges of responsibility for the Hay Market Square riots in Chicago, and poor business operations thereafter brought a rapid decline in the organization.

A strong militant labor organization in Texas from about 1890 to about 1915 was the United Mine Workers. In the mines of Erath and Palo Pinto counties working conditions were exceedingly bad and the pay was low. The situation was all the more difficult to improve because a large percentage of the laborers were newly arrived immigrants. In the 1880's the Knights of Labor sought to aid the workers, without success, but in 1890 the Knights formed locals under the United Mine Workers and brought about improvements. For two decades and more—until competition of oil forced the closing of the mines—the United Mine Workers constituted the dominant force in the Texas coal mine region. At its peak, soon after 1900, 4,000 miners belonged to the union. Oil workers in the Gulf Coast oil fields were organized by the American Federation of Labor in 1905.

In fact, with the formation of the Texas State Federation of Labor in about 1900, organized labor in Texas for a time had a leader and a spokesman. Although only a fraction of Texas organized labor was affiliated with it, the Texas State Federation of Labor had 783 organizations representing 50,000 members in 1920. Thereafter it declined. Some have laid its decline to the open shop campaign pursued by business establishments and chambers of commerce of that period, and to the unfriendly open port law of 1920, enforced vigorously by state officials; others have laid its decline to bad management, including ill-advised strikes. By 1927 membership in the state federation had declined to 25,000. Efforts to cooperate with farm organizations failed. Laborers generally were faring better than farmers.

URBANIZATION

Paralleling the emergence of a commercial economy in Texas was the rise of cities. In 1870 only 6.7 percent of the people lived in incorporated urban areas of 2,500 population or more. By 1900 urban incorporated centers contained 17.1 percent of the population; and by 1930 the figure had climbed to 41 percent.

The appearance of urban centers is perhaps even more impressive when the growth of individual cities is considered. In 1870 only two towns, Galveston with a population of 13,818 and San Antonio with one of 12,256, contained more than 10,000 people. Houston counted slightly more than 9,000; Dallas had an estimated 3,000; and Fort Worth was a village of about 500. By 1900 eleven towns claimed more than 10,000 people. San Antonio was the largest city with 53,321, followed by Houston, Dallas, Galveston, and Fort Worth. In 1930 Houston, Dallas, and San Antonio each contained between two and three hundred thousand people, a total of more than 10 percent of the state's population. In addition, there were 33 cities with population figures in excess of 10,000.

Although other factors were involved, transportation facilities and oil accounted for much of the growth of these population islands. Houston, Dallas, and Forth Worth exploited their strategic locations in the railroad network to become leading market centers. In one decade after the Houston ship channel was opened in 1919, the city's population more than doubled. Similarly, cities that lost their advantage in the transportation system either grew slowly, remained stagnant, or declined. Jefferson, once connected to the sea by way of Caddo Lake and the Red River, was a busy port town of more than 4,000 in 1870. When clearing of debris reduced the level of the lake to a point where commercial navigation could not be sustained and railroads opened up competitive markets elsewhere, Jefferson's population declined by more than one-fourth.

Oil likewise brought spectacular growth. Port Arthur expanded from less than 1,000 in 1900 to 50,000 in 1930. In West Texas oil discoveries during the twenties actually built towns such as Pampa, Borger, McCamey, and Wink, and substantially added to the population of Amarillo, Abilene, San Angelo, and others.

Texas cities in their growth often acquired a distinct character and identity. San Antonio, perpetuating its early pattern of expansion, retained its military installations and historic sites and sustained a steady growth rate but a somewhat leisurely atmosphere. Dallas became a financial and mercantile center, widely known for its cultural achievements and aspirations. Fort Worth, generally regarded as a city of the west, developed extensive livestock market and packing facilities as well as the sobriquet of "Cowtown." Houston, perhaps because of its more varied economy and sprawling explosive growth, could not be placed with assurance under a single label. In all of these cities, and in a host of smaller ones, could be found substantial evidences of the ubiquitous oil industry.

Before the turn of the century the services and conveniences associated with urban life were available in the Texas cities. By 1900 all cities had telephone exchanges, and practically all were linked together with telegraph systems. The electric light and power industry was not quite as advanced. Galveston had a power plant in the early 1880's and other cities soon had electric service; but the power these plants generated was insignificant in comparison with the output of our own day. The production of power was a local industry until about 1913, when the Texas Power and Light Company constructed a transmission line from Waco to Fort Worth and Dallas. Soon various small concerns were consolidated, and outlying communities were supplied by high-voltage transmission lines radiating from huge plants. Electric power was no longer a monopoly of the cities; every town and hamlet could be served by the "high lines." Development was very rapid after the first World War; it was hastened by the availability of oil and gas for fuel and the discovery that lignite could be used for fuel to produce electric power. During the twenties the West Texas Utilities Company extended its service to 100 towns and cities. Meanwhile, the oil industry had made natural gas available to most urban communities.

CONSEQUENCES OF COMMERCIALIZATION

The development of a marketplace economy significantly complicated the financial, political, and social structure of rural and urban Texas. The transition added emphasis to some issues in political affairs, while other traditional problems faded away. Moreover, new pressure groups and factions emerged, reflecting not only the changing character of agriculture but also the emerging industrial and urban community.

More than ever before the people were subject to the variables of economic forces that reached far beyond the boundaries of the state. The Panic of 1893 brought several years of depression in both rural and urban areas, with prolonged suffering unparalleled in previous economic recessions. After ten years of comparative prosperity in the first decade of the twentieth century, cotton prices, generally the barometer of economic health during these years, broke in 1911. An industrial depression in 1913–1914, followed by the outbreak of World War I brought prices of cotton ruinously low. Despite efforts of the state to support cotton prices with the creation of a public warehouse system, prosperity did not return until forces outside the state brought a rising price level in 1916.

With the approach of the twentieth century, some problems of an older day, such as protection from Indians, disappeared only to be replaced by more complex questions. Tariffs, rail rates, corporate monopoly, depression, mortgages, declining prices, rising costs, city government, and working conditions for labor would be major problems of the new age. Resolution of these problems led to the formation of pressure groups, sometimes with conflicting objectives or viewpoints. Particularly active during the nineteenth century and even later were the farmers' organizations. Organized labor for a time wielded substantial influence during the early years of the twentieth century. Business interests, acting individually and collectively, vigorously pursued their own particular objectives. Thus politics between 1870 and 1930 was to a marked degree the story of the interaction of these often conflicting forces.

Selected Bibliographies

For a general study of economic affairs in Texas between 1875 and 1900, J. Spratt, *The Road to Spindletop*, is unsurpassed in scope, detail, and insight. Other general works of value are Ralph Steen, *Twentieth Century Texas: An Economic and Social History* (Austin, 1942); B.M. Jones, *The Search for Maturity*; and S.S. McKay and O.B. Faulk, *Texas After Spindletop* (Austin, 1965). Rich in economic information is the *Texas Almanac*.

The two standard studies on railroads are S.G. Reed, *A History of Texas Railroads*, and C.S. Potts, *Railroad Transportation in Texas*. See also Ira G. Clark, *Then Came the Railroads* (Norman, 1958); Vera L. Dugas, "A Duel with Railroads: Houston vs. Galveston, 1866–1881," *East Texas Historical Journal*, II, 118–127; Donald Everett, "San Antonio Welcomes the 'Sunset'—1877," *Southwestern Historical Quarterly*, LXV, 47–60; and Ralph Traxler, Jr., "The Texas and Pacific Railroad Land Grants," *ibid.*, 357–370.

The abundance of literature on the settlement of western and southern Texas permits listing only a sampling here. Classic studies are W.P. Webb, *The Great Plains*; W.C. Holden, *Alkali Trails*; R.N. Richardson and C.C. Rister, *The Greater Southwest*; and C.C. Rister, *Southern Plainsmen*. See also W.C. Holden, "Experimental Agriculture on the Spur Ranch, 1885–1904," *The Southwestern Social Science Quarterly*, XII 16–23; and Riley E. Baker, "Water Development as an Important Factor in the Utilization of the High Plains," *ibid.*, XXXIV, 31–34. For southern Texas see J. Lee Stambaugh, *The Lower Rio Grande Valley of Texas* (San Antonio, 1954). On the public land system see A.S. Lang, *Financial History of the Public Lands in Texas*; R. McKitrick, *The Public Land System of Texas, 1823–1910*; and R.D. Holt, "School Land Rushes in West Texas," *West Texas Historical Association Year Book*, X, 42–57. An account of the transition from ranch to farm is found in D.B. Gracy, II, *Littlefield Lands: Colonization on the Texas Plains, 1912–1920* (Austin, 1968). The effects of drought are portrayed in Richard King, *Wagons East: The Drought of 1886* (Austin, 1965).

The evolution of a commercial economy in agriculture and industry is emphasized in J. Spratt, *The Road to Spindletop*, cited above, and supported in detail by Samuel Lee Evans, "Texas Agriculture, 1880–1930," (unpublished manuscript, 1960, University of Texas Library). However,

B.P. Gallaway, "Population Trends in the Western Cross Timbers of Texas, 1890–1960: Economic Change and Social Balance," *Southwestern Historical Quarterly*, LXVII, 376–396; and Neal Baker, Jr., "Red River County, Texas, in the 1920's: A Landlocked Frontier," *ibid.*, LXX, 443–460, suggest that subsistence agriculture remained at least a hope, if not a reality, for some Texans. For additional information on industry see V.L. Dugas, "Texas Industry, 1860–1880," *ibid.*, LIX, 151–183; Edwin L. Caldwell, "Highlights of the Development of Manufacturing in Texas, 1900–1960," *ibid.*, LXVIII, 405–431; Dwight F. Henderson, "The Texas Coal Mining Industry," *ibid.*, LXVIII, 207–219; Robert S. Maxwell, "The Pines of Texas: A Study in Lumbering and Public Policy, 1880–1930," *East Texas Historical Journal*, II, 77–86; and William R. Johnson, *A Short History of the Sugar Industry in Texas* (Houston, 1961).

Considering the importance of the industry, the large number of studies on oil is to be expected. C.C. Rister's *Oil! Titan of the Southwest* (Norman, 1949) is the standard general work, and a colorful account of the first important discovery in Texas is William A. Owens, "Gusher at Spindletop," *American Heritage*, IX, 34ff. Those seeking additional sources should consult Walter Rundell, Jr., "Texas Petroleum History: A Selective Annotated Bibliography," *Southwestern Historical Quarterly*, LXVII, 267–278, which lists and describes more than sixty studies published through 1962.

Unfortunately, published materials on organized labor in Texas are scarce. Pioneering studies have been made by Ruth A. Allen who has published *Chapters in the History of Organized Labor in Texas* (Austin, 1941); *The Great Southwest Strike* (Austin, 1942); and *East Texas Lumbering Workers, An Economic and Social Picture, 1870–1950* (Austin, 1961). Dealing primarily with an earlier period but useful for later years is James V. Reese, "The Early History of Labor Organization in Texas, 1838–1876," *Southwestern Historical Quarterly*, LXXII, 1–20.

Likewise, scholarly studies in urban history are still scarce. *Houston: A History and Guide* (Houston, 1942), compiled by the Federal Writers' Program of the Works Projects Administration in the State of Texas, is useful, but see also for a more specialized aspect of the city, Marilyn Sibley, *The Port of Houston* (Austin, 1968). For twentieth century developments, see James Howard, *Big D is for Dallas* (Dallas, 1957). A superior study both in scope and insight is Lawrence Graves (ed.), *History of Lubbock* (Lubbock, 1962).

15

IN THE AGE OF
REFORM: 1890–1910

By 1890 the demands for reform in political and economic affairs could no longer be ignored or rejected. Texans in the next two decades adopted laws regulating business, expanding education, reforming the electoral system, and making other changes designed to meet the needs of the emerging modern society. In the nineties the primary impetus for reform was agrarian unrest. Seeking the elimination of economic inequities and the expansion of political democracy, the more militant agrarian radicals organized a third party, the People's or Populist party, while other reformers sought similar goals within the Democratic party.

With the decline of agrarian protest, sentiment for reform subsided temporarily, only to be revived after 1900 with the spirit of the progressive movement. Progressivism of the new century was not merely a renewal of agrarian protest. The strength of the movement was broader, with more emphasis on the role of businessmen, teachers, and professional people, and new organizations such as the State Federation of Labor and the Texas Local Option Association. The goals were more complex. Business regulation continued to be a primary objective, but progressives also stressed humanitarian reforms, reorganization of municipal government, expansion of education, and other changes affecting not only the rural but also the urban population. In short, progressivism reflected the growing importance of industrialization and urbanization in the social and economic structure. Nevertheless, twentieth century Texas progressivism preserved a strong rural influence. Many of the goals and some of the leadership of former years were the same; moreover, a new agrarian organization, the Farmers' Union, was one of the more effective reform pressure groups.

Reform, however, was not the only element determining the course of politics during these years. The divisions in Texas over the issue, deep-seated and at times bitter, lasted until 1910, in some respects much longer, and on occasion, as in the election of 1892, the dichotomy of reform versus conservatism was apparent. But often the political alignments and battles were more complex. Except for the Populist challenge, most political conflicts took place within the Democratic party. In the one-party structure personal and factional rivalry sometimes disregarded ideology for the sake of political expediency, forming alignments not particularly related to the matter of progressive change.

THE PRELUDE TO REFORM

During the first two decades following the Civil War the prevailing attitude in Texas toward big business was friendly. We have seen that the Constitution of 1876, though framed by a convention controlled by farmers, contained no provisions hostile to organized wealth. It is true that the Grange and the Greenback party repeatedly criticized the Democratic administration, contending that they were too generous toward corporations and failed to control them, but the dominant party continued with its program of encouragement to capital and a minimum of regulatory measures. The demand for regulation increased, however, and during the later eighties the number of malcontents grew rapidly.

As in former years, the center of dissatisfaction was among the farmers; this group, let it be remembered, constituted a majority of the people. Since the Civil War the ills of the farmer had been many and real. The price of cotton, the great money crop of Texas, declined from 31 cents a pound in 1865 to less than five cents in 1898. In 1887 Texas farmers received approximately $88,000,000 for a crop of 1,600,000 bales, whereas in 1890 they received only $68,000,000 for a crop of 2,000,000 bales. It seemed that the more the farmers made the less they had. The supply of money in circulation, limited anyway, seemed unreasonably diminished when the Coinage Act of 1873 eliminated subsequent coinage of silver into money. Meanwhile, taxes and interest charges on mortgages never diminished and the cost of many other articles the farmer had to buy increased from year to year. It was easy for him to believe that the corporation that held a mortgage on his farm charged him exorbitant interest; that the railroads were exacting too large a share for hauling his crops; and that the middlemen were appropriating too much for services, some of which he deemed unnecessary.

Amid the disintegration of the first farmers' movement, the Grange and the Greenback party, arose a second, the Farmers' Alliance. The Farmers' Alliance was founded in Texas in about 1875 and was reorganized in 1879. In 1887 it became a national organization and soon its strength was estimated at from one to three million members. At a state meeting at Cleburne in 1886, the Alliance set forth a political program in a series of "demands." After a preamble which referred to "the shameful abuses that the industrial classes are now suffering at the hands of arrogant capitalists and powerful corporations," the program "demanded" among other measures that the public school lands be sold only in small grants to actual settlers; that railroad property be assessed at its full value; and that an effective interstate commerce law be enacted. Two years later the Alliance called for an antitrust law as well as more effective regulation of railroad rates.

Meanwhile the Alliance, and to a lesser extent the Knights of Labor, were affecting the pronouncements of the Democratic party. The party's platform as it was framed in 1886 called for the sale of land "in tracts of reasonable size" to bona fide settlers only; favored laws correcting various abuses practiced by the railroads; and, most extreme of all, contained a plank that stockholders of a corporation be made liable to the amount of 100 percent assessment on their stock to pay the debts of the corporation. In 1888 the Democratic convention adopted a stronger plank on railway regulation and called for an antitrust law. Then two years later the Democratic candidate for governor, running on a platform calling for the abolishment of the national banking system, free coinage of silver, and a state railway commission, received the endorsement of the Alliance. All these proposals were of the essence of the Alliance. At last, the agrarian reformers had triumphed; they felt that they had captured the Democratic party.

Meanwhile, certain Texans wrought manfully for reforms in the national government. In Congress, Robert Q. Mills, chairman of the Committee on Ways and Means, proposed a tariff reform measure that passed the House of Representatives in 1888 and became the Democratic manifesto in the national campaign of that year. More successful as a national reformer was the veteran John H. Reagan, who, as member of the Senate in 1887, was co-author of the Interstate Commerce Act, which marked the beginning of Federal regulation of railroads.

Prohibition was another active reform movement of the period. Introduced into Texas in about 1870 were the United Friends of Temperance and its juvenile society, the Bands of Hope, whose members pledged total abstinence from drink and sought to cultivate public sentiment against the liquor traffic. In 1882 the Woman's Christian Temperance Union, which grew rapidly in the state, entered the campaign for prohibition with great fervor. Meanwhile, the Grange had declared against the sale of intoxicating liquor, and the Greenback party had denounced the Democrats for failing to submit the question to the voters. After dodging the issue as long as possible, the legislature submitted to the voters in 1887 an amendment that would replace the local option law of 1876 with state-wide prohibition. With both the prohibitionists and their opponents organized, the campaign was heated and bitter, but the amendment was defeated in the election of August 1887 by a vote of 220,627 to 129,270. For the next 24 years the forces of moral reform could not muster strength enough to force another prohibition election, but they steadfastly refused to allow the issue to die. Meanwhile, reform was accomplished in a variety of other areas.

REFORM TRIUMPHANT: JAMES STEPHEN HOGG

For more than a decade James Stephen Hogg was instrumental in determining the tone of the Texas government. First elected to state office in 1886 as attorney general in the administration of Lawrence Sullivan Ross, Hogg stood in striking contrast to the conservative governor. Thirty-five years old, son of a Texas statesman and Confederate brigadier, and left an orphan at twelve, Hogg had grown to manhood in his native East Texas during the troublous reconstruction era. He had not passed the intermediate grades when he left Peyton Irving's school in Tyler in 1866. Unaided, he made his way at such jobs as he could secure; years as a typesetter and printer furnished the background for a sympathetic understanding of the problems of the common people. After serving as prosecuting attorney and spending a few years in private law practice, Hogg was elected attorney general. He realized that the dominant question in Texas was the regulation of corporations. On that issue he soon appropriated the center of the political stage, and was elected governor in 1890 on a platform distinguished by severe planks against the abuses of big business.

Men who knew him were never indifferent to Jim Hogg. The corporation lawyers soon learned that he was a dangerous antagonist, and as a stump campaigner he had few equals. He knew the mind of the common man and how to appeal to it with fluent speech and expressive vernacular. Newspapers of the opposition charged that his frequent "by gatlings" (his nearest approach to profanity) and the earthy epithets he hurled at his enemies "were offensive to the ladies who honored him with their presence," but the ladies and all others continued to go to hear him. First and last he was a commoner. In the scant shade of a picnic arbor he could hold crowds for hours while he berated the railroads and denounced the discrimination against farmers. When the heat became severe he would doff his coat, fling off his suspenders, and gulp from time to time water from a pitcher or a bucket. His public record was punctuated with incidents that made good news and kept him ever in the public eye. When the Southern Pacific Railroad in 1894 deliberately stranded seven hundred marchers of Coxey's Army at a West Texas desert station, a Hogg ultimatum defying the awesome corporate power forced the road to convey the men across the state.

After he became attorney general in 1887, Hogg first directed his efforts against certain insurance companies that were operating in unlawful fashion. Some of them were premium companies doing business without sufficient capital and reserves; others were mutual assessment companies. Attorney General Hogg drove about 40 of these from the state and compelled certain others to pay taxes and to obey the laws.

Hogg also contributed to the passage of antitrust measures. There had long been a widespread conviction that monopolies or "trusts" conspired to fix prices and to eliminate competition. Farmers' organizations complained of the "cotton-bagging trust"; there were charges that the packers constituted a "beef combine"; and there was much resentment against land corporations. Agitation on the subject in Congress, moreover, inspired legislation on the state level. Hogg assisted in framing the Texas law. Enacted on March 30, 1889, it was the second antitrust law in the nation, being preceded four weeks by a similar law in Kansas. With labor and farm organizations exempted, the law carried heavy penalties against combinations of any kind for the purpose of restricting trade, fixing prices, or limiting production. The law was extended in 1895 to apply to insurance companies, and subsequent changes in 1899, 1903, and 1907 added to the severity and effectiveness of antitrust regulation.

Hogg's greatest efforts were directed toward the regulation of railroads. The article on railroads in the Constitution of 1876 seems to have been borrowed largely from the Pennsylvania Constitution of 1873. It declared railroads to be public highways and common carriers; authorized the legislature to pass laws to "correct abuses, and prevent unjust discrimination and extortion" in rates and fares; required the railroads to maintain offices where their books were to be open to inspection; forbade the consolidation of competing lines; and authorized the legislature to set by law reasonable maximum rates. The power over the railroads reserved to the state was altogether adequate, except that it did not provide for their regulation by a commission. Under its rate-making authority the legislature in 1879 set the maximum freight rate, and in 1882 passenger fares were reduced from five to three cents per mile. These regulations were not adequate, however, and apparently little effort had been made to enforce some of them prior to Hogg's administration as attorney general. He found various abuses and proceeded against the railroads with such vigor that he was charged with trying to drive capital from the state. He compelled one railroad that had ceased to operate to revive and continue its service. He forced the dissolution of the Texas Traffic Association, a pool through which nine railroads with headquarters outside of the state were controlling all Texas lines save one, setting rates and prescribing the service that should be given. He also dissolved the International Traffic Association and the International Weighers' Association, combinations similar to the Texas Traffic Association. Through various suits and official actions he lessened the control which certain out-of-state corporations had over the Texas railroads, and compelled the Texas railroads to reestablish their general offices in the state.

The best efforts of Attorney General Hogg were not sufficient, however, to secure effective railroad regulation. Realizing this fact, Hogg worked aggressively while he was attorney general to secure the enactment of a railroad commission law and while he was governor to sustain the power of the commission after it had been established. Since the constitutionality of such a measure was in doubt, the legislature in 1889 gave up the idea of establishing a commission by law and submitted to the voters a constitutional amendment that would settle all questions as to the legality of such an agency.

At once the commission amendment became a leading political issue. An organization of businessmen, known as the State Freight Rate Convention, endorsed it, and the Farmers' Alliance favored it. In his campaign for governor in 1890 Hogg championed it with the zeal of a crusader. He showed by a series of comparisons and contrasts how unreasonable certain of the Texas rates were; how lumber, for instance, could be shipped from the East Texas forests to Nebraska cheaper than to Dallas. The opponents of the commission rallied behind Gustave Cooke, of Houston; but the Democratic convention nominated Hogg by an overwhelming vote. The convention also endorsed the railroad commission, and the voters adopted the amendment in the November election.

Acting under the leadership of Hogg, the legislature in April 1891 set up a commission with power to make classifications and to fix rates and fares. As originally established the commission was to consist of three members appointed by the governor, but by constitutional amendment which became effective in 1894 the commission was made elective. John H. Reagan resigned his seat in the United States senate to accept the chairmanship.

The commission enjoyed a measure of success. It secured the reduction of freight rates and claimed credit for the increase of milling and manufacturing in the state and of saving a million dollars on the shipment of cotton in two seasons. The railroads, however, contending that the rates were confiscatory, brought suits in 1892 to restrain the commission from enforcing its orders; and for nearly two years it was impotent. The long fight in the courts ended in victory for the state, and in July 1894 the body again took up the work of rate regulation.

While litigation over rate regulation was underway, the commission acquired additional authority. Realizing that the question of rates was inseparably linked with that of railroad capitalization, Governor Hogg pointed out that the railroads were increasing their obligations on an average of $30,000,000 annually without making any improvements of consequence. Since they would endeavor to maintain rates high enough to pay interest and dividends on this increased capitalization, the increase was in effect a charge against the shippers of the state. To correct this evil, the legislature, at Hogg's behest, in 1893 passed a law authorizing the railroad commission to ascertain the value of all property and franchises belonging to each railroad and to regulate and control the issue of securities. The law proved especially effective in enabling the commission to hold down the capitalization of new railroads.

Meanwhile a bitter political controversy had raged over the railroad commission issue. In the gubernatorial campaign in 1892, the railroads and most leading newspapers supported George Clark, of Waco, a railroad attorney. Clark had opposed the commission amendment in 1890 as "wrong in principle, undemocratic and unrepublican"; its only function, he said, was to harass the railroads. Now he accepted the commission as an established fact but insisted that it should be conservative, completely democratic, and elective, and that the law should be liberalized to permit the railroads to appeal to the courts. Hogg defended the commission and attacked his opponent with all of the tactics of the versatile stump speaker that he was. At the famous "Street Car Barn Convention" in Houston in August 1892 the Democrats divided, one group nominating Hogg, the other Clark; and in the autumn of the year the warring factions continued their campaign before the voters. Although one wing of the Republican party supported Clark, Hogg was reelected by a substantial majority.

Other reforms of the Hogg administration, or "Hogg laws" as they were often termed, affected a variety of issues. In response to Governor Hogg's urgent plea, the legislature in 1891 passed a law prohibiting foreigners from owning lands in Texas. The supreme court declared it unconstitutional on a technicality, and in the following year the legislature enacted another alien land law. Another law, which became effective in 1893, prohibited the organization of corporations for the special purpose of dealing in lands, and required that such corporations already in existence should dispose of their lands within 15 years. All other corporations were required to sell within 15 years all land not necessary to enable them to carry on their business. The law was easily contravened and failed to accomplish its purpose. Otherwise, Hogg promoted prison reform, the establishment of a Board of Pardon Advisors, extension of the school term from four to six months, additional revenue for the University of Texas, and a law forcing railroads to segregate facilities for Negroes and whites.

Leaving office in 1895, Hogg spent the final decade of his life amassing a fortune, though he did not abandon his interest in public affairs. His zeal as a reformer perhaps diminished somewhat; indeed, his wealth came in large measure from the interests he had sought as a reformer to control. Nevertheless, the position of James Stephen Hogg as the symbol of Texas reform remained deservedly unshaken.

THE CHALLENGE OF POPULISM

Reforms either promised or accomplished by Governor Hogg and the Democrats quieted for a time criticism from the Farmers' Alliance, but the Democrats did not go far enough to suit the more militant of the agrarian radicals. Government ownership of railroads and similar proposals found little sympathy among Democratic leaders. Governor Hogg refused even to name a leader of the Farmers' Alliance to the newly created railroad commission. Moreover, Hogg and his followers in the Democratic party refused to endorse the favorite program of the Texas Alliance, a subtreasury plan whereby the general government should make loans to farmers directly at a nominal rate of interest with farm produce as collateral. In fact, the Democratic leaders in 1891 read out of the party those Alliance men who supported the subtreasury plan.

Thus, disenchanted with Hogg and snubbed by the Democrats, before the elections of 1892 the Farmers' Alliance evolved in effect and purpose into a new third party, the People's or Populist Party, organized not only in Texas but elsewhere over the land by similar dissident groups. The People's party grew rapidly. When the Democratic convention chose Grover Cleveland, the conservative, sound-money champion as its standard-bearer in 1892, many of the Democratic faithful were alienated along national lines. The hard times of the early nineties, reinforced by the economic catastrophe of the Panic of 1893, fed the discontent, enlisting thousands of small farmers in the Populist cause. With this formidable strength, the Populists contested each election in Texas for several years, their rivalry with the Democrats at times comparable in bitterness to that of reconstruction days.

The list of reforms supported by the Populists was lengthy and comprehensive. Some were adopted from earlier reform movements, others from the Democrats, and some were Populist innovations. Demands of the People's party emphasized government regulation of business, public ownership of railroads, free coinage of silver, abolition of the national banking system, and establishment of the subtreasury system. The Populists supported laws to improve the status of the laborer and to implement a graduated income tax. To further democracy, they advocated direct election of United States senators and other federal officers, limiting all officeholders to two terms, and the use of referendum and recall. But Texas Populists, perhaps for political expediency, did not take up the cause of woman's suffrage and state-wide prohibition.

Populism, however, was more than a platform of an organization; it was also an attitude, a crusade, the determined effort of those who felt oppressed to use the machinery of government to ameliorate their miseries. In a very real sense an example of class-consciousness in politics, the Populists at times oversimplified their problems and their solutions, but the problems were real and the solutions were not without merit. A rural movement, almost half of the leaders in Texas were farmers. Strongest among the poorer farmers of East and West Central Texas and among some laboring groups, Populism had little attraction for most business and professional men. Its greatest appeal was to the alienated, to those who felt that they could no longer depend on traditional institutions to protect their interests, to advance their cause.

Basing their program on doctrines of economic and political equality, the Populists struck telling blows at various abuses of the prevailing order. Seventy-five weekly newspapers, among them *The Southern Mercury*, printed at Dallas, carried the gospel of populism to every part of the state. A corps of stump speakers, led by a few men of superior ability, for example, Thomas L. Nugent, Jerome Kearby, T. P. Gore (who later represented Oklahoma in the United States Senate), and James H. ("Cyclone") Davis, served as ardent evangelists of the new gospel. Many of their leaders were Protestant preachers, who not only appropriated the camp meeting, the hymns, and the religious fervor of the pioneer churches, but took from the Bible many of their utterances and arguments.

As the campaigns became more and more acrimonious, Populists and Democrats resorted to various political tricks. The People's party made a strong bid for the vote of Negroes, many of whom were naturally attracted anyway by doctrines suited to their interests. Leaders of both parties, however, sometimes purchased the services of white and black men who were influential in controlling the Negro vote (" 'fluence men," they were called), and distributed among the Negro voters many petty bribes. If the Democrats were a little less active and successful in their appeal to the Negro voter, they were as guilty as the Populists of using corrupt practices to control the Mexican vote in South Texas.

Although the Populists did not gain control of the state government, they had some success at the ballot box. The party's maximum strength in the legislature came immediately after the election of 1894, when it had 22 of the 128 members in the lower house and two senators. In the gubernatorial campaign of 1894 Populist Thomas Nugent received nearly one-third of the vote. Two years later Jerome Kearby, aided by the Republicans, threatened Democratic supremacy more seriously than had any candidate since reconstruction. Kearby polled 238,692 votes to 298,528 for Governor Charles A. Culberson, the Democratic incumbent. More successful in local campaigns, the Populists elected large numbers of county and precinct officers.

After 1896 the Populist party faded quickly from Texas and national politics. With William Jennings Bryan as their standard-bearer, the Democrats on the national level had sealed the doom of the third party by appropriating its chief plank, free coinage of silver, and a number of other proposals which the Grange, the Greenback party, the Farmers' Alliance, and the People's party had advocated over the years. Moreover, the wave of prosperity that appeared in Texas near the turn of the century did much to silence the voices of discontent.

While successfully meeting the challenge of Populism, the Democratic administration had cautiously perpetuated the reform programs of Governor Hogg. Between 1895 and 1899 Governor Charles Culberson, former attorney general and son of a well-known United States congressman, signed laws regulating primary elections, strengthening anti-trust regulations, adding to the authority of the railroad commission, improving the judicial system, setting aside school lands for a Negro university, and modifying the collection of delinquent taxes. He occasionally thwarted efforts toward corporate consolidation in the state. In a dramatic move he called a special session of the legislature to outlaw prizefighting in Texas. But primarily for fiscal reasons, Culberson vetoed a number of measures, many of them furthering the cause of reform. Neither an enthusiast nor an opponent of reform, his administration was thus a logical transition from the preceding reform-minded regime of Governor Hogg to the relatively conservative era that followed.

REFORM QUIESCENT:
SAYERS AND LANHAM

Although the reform impulse was not entirely absent, the years between 1898 and 1906 reflected a noticeable lack of strife and a tone of conservatism. With the Populists fading and the Republicans quarreling, Democratic rule was virtually unchallenged. In the Democratic party much of the tumult usually associated with gubernatorial politics was eliminated by the shrewd and efficient manipulations of Colonel Edward M. House, a well-to-do planter and railroad builder who made politics his avocation and surpassed the professionals in it. A veteran of the electoral wars who had helped reelect Hogg in 1892 and had directed Culberson's campaigns in 1894 and 1896, House skillfully guided the campaigns of governors Joseph Sayers (1899–1903) and Samuel Willis Tucker Lanham (1903–1907). House, unknown to most Texans, was not a leader of a political machine in the usual sense, but relying on careful, thorough organization and the assistance of a few intimate and powerful friends, he exerted a degree of influence without parallel in Texas politics.

Indications of declining enthusiasm for reform were abundant. Leading newspapers, never strong supporters of progressivism anyway, spoke out confidently about the dangers of stringent regulation of business. Corporate consolidations and manipulations generally were viewed with more sympathy, sometimes with approval. The number of reforms enacted into law was limited; perhaps more significant, lack of enforcement rendered many ineffectual.

In part the leadership of governors Sayers and Lanham was responsible for the resurgence of conservatism. Both were genteel, high-minded men; both were ex-Confederates, the last to serve as chief executive of the state; and both had rendered their previous public service mainly in Congress. Both brought to the office mature judgment and high idealism but little imagination; by temperament and training, neither was a zealous crusader for change.

But other forces contributed to the decline of progressive fervor. The conservative mood was a natural reaction to the agitation and drive of the Hogg era; and the Spanish-American War diverted the attention of many Texans. Moreover, an attitude more favorable toward business prevailed. Oil discoveries including the fabulous Spindletop excited the hopes of Texans and enticed a welcome flow of capital to the state. Other industries such as the lumbering companies of East Texas, nearing their peak level of production, bolstered the state's economy. Indicating the growing importance of the commercial community, the proportion of members of the legislature who were farmers declined from about one-half in the early nineties to about one-third after 1900. Political leaders such as Colonel House, though surely not subservient to corporate interests, nevertheless did not harbor the suspicious convictions about business common among the agrarian rebels of the nineties. Texas remained a rural land, but the industrial age was fast approaching.

Despite the conservative temper of the times, some worthwhile reforms were accomplished. The legislature adopted several laws protecting labor. An 1899 statute exempted organized labor from antitrust regulations; in 1901 the legislature outlawed the use of blacklists to control union organization and the use of company script that could be spent only at company stores. In 1903 laws limiting the hours of railroad employees and requiring certain safety measures on street railways were passed. That same year the first Texas law regulating child labor was adopted. Unfortunately, enforcement of labor laws was often weak and erratic.

A state banking system, prohibited for many years by the Constitution of 1876, was established during the Lanham administration. In 1904 the voters ratified a constitutional amendment permitting the state to charter banks, and the legislature of the following year established a commission of insurance and banking. Directed by Thomas M. Love, a native of Missouri and progressive politician of Dallas, the commission supervised the chartering of more than 500 banks during the next five years.

Tax reform, sought unsuccessfully during the Sayers administration, was partially accomplished in the second Lanham term. The general property tax had provided the greater part of the state's revenue and valuations had not kept pace with the increasing demands. Railroad properties, for example, were evidently undervalued; the greater portion of intangible properties escaped taxation. In response to Governor Lanham's request, the legislature in 1905 raised taxes on intangible assets of railroads and certain other industries. Laws providing for franchise taxes and levies on gross receipts of express companies, sleeping-car companies, pipelines, utilities, and similar concerns were also adopted.

Guided by a peculiar mixture of progressive and reactionary goals, the legislature reorganized the state's election system. Prior to 1903 party candidates in some counties were nominated by primaries and in other by conventions. In either case, abuses were widespread. Unscrupulous party officials sometimes failed to give adequate notice of impending conventions; occasionally the meetings were at places and under conditions that made it impossible or impractical for the rank and file of voters to attend. Relying on proxies and other devices, corporation attorneys and other special interests wielded an undue influence. Dates of party primaries were sometimes manipulated to the advantage of particular candidates; ballot box frauds were common.

Many abuses were practiced at primary and at general elections. Although the constitution authorized the legislature to provide for punishing fraud and preserving the integrity of the ballot, little had been done to eliminate such practices as the purchase of votes, extravagant campaign expenditures, and dishonest election returns. In 1895 the legislature passed a law which regulated primary elections in those counties where they were held, but it was inadequate. The law was changed in 1897 and again two years later, but it did not attack the abuses prevalent in that day. Registration of voters was assured, however, by the constitutional amendment adopted in 1902 which made a poll-tax receipt or exemption certificate mandatory for voting.

During the Lanham years the legislature took hold of the problem in earnest. Two laws, named after Judge Alexander W. Terrell, their author, affected both primaries and general elections. The first became effective in 1903; and the second, repealing the first and passed in 1905, constitutes the foundation of Texas election laws to this day. The first law did not make the primary election mandatory but permitted a political party to determine for itself whether it would nominate its candidates by a primary or a convention. The most important features of the second and more comprehensive law may be stated thus: it set forth in great detail who should be permitted to vote both in primary and general elections; it required candidates to file within ten days after a primary or general election itemized statements of expenditures; it made mandatory a primary for parties which polled at the last general election 100,000 or more votes (the Democratic party); it set forth minute regulations for the governance of parties and required that primaries be held the fourth Saturday in July; it provided that county and precinct nominees be determined by the results of the primary, but that the county committee might call a second primary, the voters to make their choice from the two leading candidates; and it required that nominees for state and district offices still be chosen by conventions.

Subsequent legislation modified these rules. In 1907 a law required that in all cases the candidate receiving the highest number of votes be declared the nominee. Thus the primary election had come to be the nominating agency; party conventions were mere canvassing bodies. A 1913 law provided for a second primary in which the voters should select from the two candidates receiving the most votes when no candidate for the United States Senate received a majority in the first contest. In 1918 this provision was extended to all state and district contests and made optional in county races.

Although the electoral reforms made at the turn of the century eliminated many abuses, the changes in some respects were made at the expense of democracy. The poll tax discouraged poor people of all kinds from voting, but Negroes generally fared worse than others. Inspired by a long-standing fear of Negro suffrage that was reinforced by the events of the Populist years and the rising tide of racial antagonism prevalent near the end of the century, white politicians deliberately sought to eliminate the Negro from politics. By the early 1900's most Democratic primaries, which were usually tantamount to election, were open only to white voters. For the next several decades Negroes would be denied an effective voice in the politics of the state. Not until the Supreme Court of the United States ruled white primaries unconstitutional in 1944 and the poll tax unconstitutional in 1966 was the Negro assured of his place at the polls. Progressive electoral reform, indeed, progressive reforms in general did little to improve the life of the Negro.

Public welfare services and education, which perhaps needed improvement even more than the electoral system, received some attention during the Sayers and Lanham years. The Pasteur Institute for the prevention of rabies was organized in 1903, and the Abilene State Hospital for epileptics began receiving patients in 1904.

Limited improvements were made in education. The legislature in 1901 authorized the state board of education to invest the permanent school fund in the building bonds of independent school districts. Availing themselves of this opportunity, many communities changed their organization from common to independent school districts and erected substantial school plants. Also, most independent school districts voted a local tax for school purposes. By November 1904 about 90 percent of the 381 or more districts then in existence had provided for local taxes.

Unfortunately, country schools, most of which were organized as common school districts, lagged far behind urban programs. Primarily because of conditions in the rural schools, Texas in 1901–1902 ranked from 28th to 42nd among the states of the nation, according to the various tests that were used at the time to determine the adequacy of the school system. In 1900 towns and cities spent $8.35 for the education of each child; the country schools spent only $4.97. The average term of 162 days in town and city schools was almost twice the average of 98 days found in rural areas. A strange and unreasonable restriction in the constitution limited the taxing authority of country districts to 20 cents on the $100 of valuation while allowing independent school districts to vote as much as 50 cents. Emphasizing the tragedy of inadequate rural schools was the fact that they served more than three-fourths of the school-age population.

During this period the state continued its war against the trusts. More stringent antitrust acts were passed in 1899 and 1903, and state attorneys successfully prosecuted a number of violators. Indeed, the Texas antitrust policy was more severe than that of the federal government. Of the 119 prosecutions brought under the Texas statutes up to 1915, 84 were settled by compromise with penalties exacted in 74 of these totaling $3,324,766. In comparison, federal antitrust laws in effect about the same period of time brought 187 prosecutions with fines or penalties in 33 cases amounting to only $548,881.

The most famous Texas antitrust case involved the Waters-Pierce Oil Company, a Missouri corporation with Standard Oil affiliations. In 1897 the attorney general brought suit for violations of the Texas antitrust act. A verdict revoking the firm's permit to do business in the state was upheld by the United States Supreme Court in 1900. Then, claiming that it had reorganized and had severed all ties with the Standard Oil combine, the company secured a new Texas license, though not without the objections of some Texans like Jim Hogg, who questioned the sincerity of the Waters-Pierce officials. Subsequently, a suit brought by the state of Missouri in 1905 revealed that a majority of the stock of the company, though registered in the name of an individual, actually belonged to the Standard Oil Company. Acting quickly, the state of Texas sought and obtained a judgment for ouster and penalties of $1,623,900. When the decision was affirmed by the court of last resort, the corporation paid a fine aggregating $1,808,483.30, the largest ever collected by the state, and the properties of the firm were sold at auction.

Meanwhile, the case had provoked an even greater controversy—Baileyism. While a candidate for the United States Senate in 1900, Congressman Joseph Weldon Bailey, ignoring the possible conflict of interest, urged Governor Sayers and the state attorney general to allow Waters-Pierce to return to the state. Though he did not receive a fee for this service, he was employed by Henry Clay Pierce in other matters. Furthermore, he had borrowed $5,000 from Pierce, who, unknown to Bailey, had placed the note on company records.

Almost immediately some questioned the propriety of Bailey's intervention, but not until new investigations in 1905 and 1906 publicly disclosed the relationship between the senator and the oilman did the state divide into angry camps of pro- and anti-Bailey men. Though Bailey was unopposed for reelection in the Democratic primary of 1906, critics argued that the legislature should ignore the primary and refuse to return him to the senate. Bailey in response contended that the whole affair was a conspiracy to deprive the nation of his great services.

By a vote of 108 to 39 the legislature reelected the senator, but meanwhile, a legislative investigating committee was studying the ethics of the colorful figure. The Texas senate, taking the affair out of the hands of its committee, quickly exonerated him, but the house committee divided in its report. Not satisfied with this victory, Senator Bailey announced that he would make the selection of the Texas delegation to the Democratic national convention in 1908 a test of his strength; none but Bailey men should go to the convention. Both the Bailey and the anti-Bailey forces organized and waged a contest with heat and rancor that has rarely been equalled in the annals of Texas politics. By an overwhelming vote Bailey and his slate of delegates won. Nevertheless, differences still rankled, and no doubt the controversy would have flared up again in 1912 if Bailey had not voluntarily retired to private life.

THE REVIVAL OF REFORM:
THOMAS M. CAMPBELL

A definite swing away from conservatism was apparent in the gubernatorial contest of 1906. For the first time in more than a decade, Colonel House refused an active role in the contest, and none of the candidates had a decided advantage. Each of the four major contenders favored a war on the trusts, an antilobby law, tax reform, and generous support for the state's institutions. Emerging the victor from a rather evenly divided race was a lawyer from Palestine, Thomas M. Campbell. Generally regarded as the most progressive of the candidates, Campbell had the endorsement of ex-Governor Hogg, who had voiced repeatedly his dissatisfaction with the attitude of the Sayers and Lanham administrations toward big business, and the last minute support of Senator Bailey. Armed with the support of farmers, labor, and various others, Campbell energetically promoted tax reform, insurance regulation, improvements in education, additional laws protecting labor, and a number of other changes. Though sentiment for reform declined in his second term and he was unable to perpetuate the control of progressives beyond his own administration, he nonetheless in large measure justified the confidence of Hogg.

Tax reform, begun under Lanham, continued in the Campbell years. Most important was a 1907 "full rendition law" requiring that property be rendered for taxation at its "reasonable cash market value." This law also created an automatic tax board consisting, as amended in 1909, of the governor, comptroller, and treasurer, and gave to the board the power to set the tax rate for general revenue and school purposes within the constitutional limits. The full rendition law very nearly doubled the value of property on the tax rolls, but it also provoked anguished protests, not only from corporate interests but also from land-owning farmers.

Other aspects of Campbell's fiscal program were likewise somewhat controversial. The governor's plea for an income tax had little success; he did obtain a light inheritance tax, but it produced more complaints than revenue. In the interest of economy he vetoed appropriations in 1909 to the amount of $1,700,000; some items were for badly needed improvements. At the end of his administration, the automatic tax board lowered the tax rate to an unrealistic level, leaving a deficit of nearly a million dollars for the next governor. Moreover, it should be noted that the laws of the Lanham and Campbell period did not shift the tax burden extensively. The general property tax continued to produce the greater part of the state's operating revenue, and real estate continued to bear approximately two-thirds of the tax burden placed on property. Not until the coming of the automobile and the development of the oil industry did Texas succeed in placing the larger share of the burden on natural resources and on the production and exchange of goods.

Regulation of insurance companies was a signal accomplishment. Comprehensive codes for life, health, accident, home, and fire insurance were adopted. Furthermore, the Robertson Insurance Law enacted in 1907 required life insurance companies to invest in Texas securities at least 75 percent of their reserves set aside for insurance policies on the lives of Texas citizens. When they failed to defeat the bill, 21 insurance companies withdrew from the state, contending that its requirements were harsh and unreasonable. As a matter of fact, other states had similar requirements; furthermore, of the $40,000,000 reserves held by the companies, less than $1,000,000 had been invested in Texas. Some of the companies returned after the commissioner of insurance and banking modified certain regulations. Others continued with great persistence to work for the repeal or the modification of the law, but it was not repealed until 1963.

In a related area the state in 1909 established an insurance program protecting funds deposited in state banks. A few bank failures during the Panic of 1907 had centered public attention on the need of greater protection for small depositors. For a number of years the plan worked quite successfully, but numerous failures in the early 1920's threw a heavy strain on the system, and it was abolished in 1927.

Progressives made additional improvements in the public school system. Organized in 1907, the Conference for Education in Texas discussed school problems, held mass meetings, scattered information throughout the state and sought in various other ways to awaken the people to the needs of the schools. Its work was reinforced and extended by the state department of education, the Congress of Mothers, parent-teacher associations, and other agencies. In 1908 the friends of school improvement made certain distinct gains; noteworthy was the constitutional amendment that permitted common school districts to use funds derived from taxation for the equipment of buildings. Far more important, they abolished the constitutional requirement calling for a two-thirds vote, and provided that a simple majority of taxpaying voters might impose a tax on a school district. The greatest victory won that year was the change in the constitution raising the limit of taxation from 20 to 50 cents on the $100 of valuation in common school districts. During the first year after these amendments were put into operation, local taxation in the rural districts increased 35 percent. Local taxation, in fact, between 1905 and 1910 increased 153 percent.

Reforms in municipal government, a prominent feature of progressive change elsewhere, were most noticeable during the Campbell administration. The commission system of government, first used in Galveston in 1901, was encouraged by the governor who approved 13 city charters containing the plan. Though demands for similar practices on the state level accomplished nothing, practically every city charter issued under Campbell provided for more direct democracy through the use of the initiative, referendum, and recall.

A number of other progressive measures were adopted. Campbell, who had consistently advocated greater regulation of corporations, in 1907 signed a law strengthening antitrust restrictions. Several laws improving conditions for labor were passed; the legislature created the state medical board and the state board of health. Campbell also approved laws giving towns of 2,000 population or more power to regulate utilities; restricting free passes by railroads; promoting pure food; prohibiting nepotism in state administration; against lobbying; and several acts for the improvement of roads.

Prison reform was the last major change of the Campbell administration. Spurred by a series of articles on prisons carried in certain state newspapers in 1908 and 1909 and the charges of Oscar B. Colquitt during his successful campaign for governor in 1910, Campbell called a special session of the legislature after the election. An investigating committee of state senators and representatives had found conditions in the state penal system intolerable. Convicts had been shot or whipped to death for trivial offenses; women prisoners had been abused; tasks set were unreasonable; food was poor; clothing inadequate; and sanitation abominable. The financial affairs of the system were in such confusion that it was impossible to audit the books.

Acting on the recommendation of the committee, the legislature abolished the contract-lease system, whereby the services of convicts were sold to different private employers. Management of the system was placed under the direction of three commissioners appointed by the governor; to supervise financial affairs a prison auditor was to be selected by the attorney general, the state treasurer, and the comptroller. Stripes were to be abolished except for the worst class of prisoners, sanitation and medical service improved, and each convict paid ten cents a day for his labor.

With the close of the Campbell administration shortly after the enactment of these prison reforms, the progressive movement in Texas was in many respects nearing an end. Prohibition, absorbing much of the energy of Texans after 1908, would dominate the election of 1910 and political affairs for sometime thereafter. But the progressives had already in countless ways turned the services of government to the benefit of the many rather than the few. In Texas, as elsewhere, they had not succeeded in every instance in their quest of reform. Despite the laws calling for corporate regulation, giant corporations would grow larger and more powerful. Nevertheless, the more obvious abuses had been eliminated; the most pressing needs had been met.

Selected Bibliography

General studies dealing with these years are S. Acheson, *35,000 Days in Texas*; B.M. Jones, *Search for Maturity*; and S.S. McKay and O.B. Faulk, *Texas after Spindletop*.

Very useful are the biographies of figures active in the era. For James S. Hogg see Robert C. Cotner (ed.), *Addresses and State Papers of James Stephen Hogg* (Austin, 1951) and *James Stephen Hogg, A Biography* (Austin, 1959); and H.P. Gambrell, "James Stephen Hogg; Statesman or Demagogue?" *Southwest Review,* XIII, 338–366. See also B.H. Procter, *Not Without Honor: The Life of John H. Reagan;* Mrs. C. Nugent, *Life Work of Thomas L. Nugent* (Stephenville, 1896); Wayne Alvord, "T.L. Nugent, Texas Populist," *Southwestern Historical Quarterly,* LVII, 65–81; S. Acheson, *Joe Bailey: The Last Democrat* (New York, 1932) and R.N. Richardson, *Colonel Edward M. House: The Texas Years, 1858–1912* (Abilene, 1964).

Concerning reforms, on railroad regulation there are M.M. Crane, "Recollections of the Establishment of the Texas Railroad Commission," *Southwestern Historical Quarterly,* L, 478–486; Robert L. Peterson, "Jay Gould and the Railroad Commission of Texas," *ibid.,* LVIII, 422–432; and J.R. Norvell, "The Railroad Commission of Texas: Its Origin and History," *ibid.,* LXVIII, 465–480. The standard work on trust legislation is Tom Finty, Jr., *Anti-trust Legislation in Texas* (Dallas and Galveston, 1916). See also O.D. Weeks, "The Texas Direct Primary System," *Southwestern Social Science Quarterly,* XIII, 95–120; E.T. Miller, *A Financial History of Texas;* and *The Report of the Prisons Investigating Committee* [first special session of the Thirty-third Legislature] (Austin, 1910). Difficult to classify but a reminder that Texans were concerned about things other than politics and economics is Charles Carver, *Brann the Iconoclast* (Austin, 1957).

On politics and political parties see Roscoe C. Martin, *The People's Party in Texas* (Austin, 1933); Ralph Smith, "The Farmers Alliance in Texas," *Southwestern Historical Quarterly,* XLVIII, 346–369; E.W. Winkler, *Platforms of Political Parties in Texas;* and S.S. McKay, *Texas Politics, 1906–1944* (Lubbock, 1952). For reform efforts in a national context see John D. Hicks, *The Populist Revolt: A History of the Farmers' Alliance and the People's Party* (Minneapolis, 1931), and Richard Hofstadter, *The Age of Reform From Bryan to F.D.R.* (New York, 1955).

Particularly valuable are a number of manuscripts in various libraries. Bob Holcomb's study of Joe Bailey is in the Library of Texas Technological College, and in the Library of the University of Wisconsin is James Tinsley's work on the Progressive movement in Texas. In the University of Texas Library are Alwyn Barr, on Texas politics from 1876 through 1906; Charles Chamberlain, on A.W. Terrell; George P. Huckaby, on Oscar B. Colquitt; R.L. Peterson, on the Railroad Commission; R.L. Wagner, on Charles Culberson; and H.L. Crow, on the Texas penal system.

16

CRUSADES AND COMPLACENCY, 1910–1930

Crusades and complacency characterized Texas politics in the score of years between the progressive era and the great depression. Many Texans joined the crusade for prohibition with enthusiasm; practically all supported the great crusade of the first World War; and not a few endorsed the reactionary crusading of the Ku Klux Klan. It was, moreover, an age of dramatic social, technological, and economic change. Yet, it was in some respects an era of complacency. Particularly in the twenties, politics was largely the story of governors who sought reforms, reforms which were in the main moderate and reasonable and generally needed, but which indifferent legislators and a still more indifferent electorate would not accept. Prohibition, a world war, the impeachment of a governor, and the rise of a hooded tyranny contributed diversity. But basic problems associated with the rapid pace of industrialization and urbanization and a corresponding decline in the role of agriculture provided an element of continuity.

OSCAR BRANCH COLQUITT

Having the support of most opponents of prohibition in the Democratic gubernatorial primary of 1910, railroad commissioner Oscar Branch

Colquitt captured 40 percent of the vote, the nomination, and subsequently the general election. A former Hogg man, the governor was nevertheless generally regarded as the most conservative man in the race. Most assuredly, he was not a crusader. Promising a relaxation of political agitation, he received the support of some corporate interests. Once in office, his record in part fulfilled conservative expectations. He attempted to block some labor legislation; he vetoed a city charter providing for initiative and referendum and denounced direct democracy as "socialistic, un-American"; and curbed appropriations for higher education and frowned on the introduction of free textbooks in the public schools.

Yet the Colquitt years were not without progressive achievements. Additional penal reforms were adopted; two hospitals for tuberculosis patients were authorized and one established; and a training school for delinquent girls was founded. Crude but well-aimed was a law permitting counties to provide poor houses and poor farms for indigents. There were laws regulating child labor, promoting factory safety, and limiting the hours of women workers. Most important was the workmen's compensation act requiring that persons employed in most industries be insured against accidents and setting forth rules for compensation in case of injury.

An old vexing problem returned during the Colquitt administration. Provoked by a series of Mexican revolutions beginning in 1910, violence erupted along the Rio Grande and rumors of a Mexican insurrection in the United States were heard. Ill will and confusion persisted on the border until long after the first World War. An investigating committee of the United States Senate reported that between November 1910 and October 1919 500 Americans lost their lives in the Mexican troubles; of these, 62 civilians and 64 soldiers were killed along the American side of the river. Governor Colquitt twice sent state troops to the Rio Grande; they were soon supplanted by federal soldiers. A thousand Texas Rangers stationed along the border afforded a measure of protection, but violence did not cease until several months after the close of the war. Following a sweeping legislative investigation in which it was charged that the Rangers had maltreated peaceful Latin American citizens of the United States, a law of March 31, 1919, reduced the force to four regular companies of 17 men each.

Less dramatic than rumored insurrection but certainly serious were the state's financial problems during the Colquitt years. When the outgoing administration set tax rates too low, Governor Colquitt inherited a deficit of nearly a million dollars. A rising cost of living necessitated an increase in salaries. New departments and new institutions and repairs on buildings at the older institutions required heavier outlays. Various calamities, especially a fire at the Agricultural and Mechanical College, augmented the normal expenses. The penitentiary seemed the most hopeless of all state institutions, requiring the state legislature in 1913 to authorize $2,000,000 in bonds to pay debts, make repairs, and add improvements. Reelected in 1912 without much difficulty, Colquitt during his second administration vetoed appropriations to the amount of $3,500,000, but even then it was necessary to raise the state tax rate. State expenditures, in fact, more than doubled between 1903 and 1914.

PROHIBITION: THE TRIUMPH OF
A MORAL CRUSADE

Although discouraged temporarily by their severe defeat in 1887, prohibitionists soon renewed their fight, directing their efforts mainly toward local option. The Texas Local Option Association was organized in Dallas in 1903, and in 1907 the Anti-Saloon League entered Texas. To meet their challenge, the powerful Texas Brewers' Association raised between 1902 and 1911 by assessment of its members more than two million dollars. In 1907 the Retail Liquor Dealers' Association was organized, its members pledging themselves to obey all laws as the only way to stop the march of prohibition. Nevertheless, through the extension of local option, the prohibitionists gained ground steadily. During the nineties they drove the saloons out of most of North and West Texas and in the following decade they began to make inroads into South and Southeast Texas. The constitutional amendment of 1902 requiring a poll tax for voting was regarded as a victory for the prohibitionists. Encouraged by their triumph, prohibitionists turned their aims toward a statewide ban, only to encounter among some of its former opponents a strange and new enthusiasm for local option.

By 1908 prohibition had become the all-absorbing political issue. In fact, from the primary campaign of 1908 when the question of statewide prohibition was again submitted to the voter until the first World War, there were in effect two Democratic parties in Texas, one prohibitionist, the other antiprohibitionist. True, there was no formal division; there was only one set of party committees; and there was only one Democratic primary. But the factions were so pronounced that every prominent leader was forced to join one side or the other, and the great rank and file of voters took their places in the respective camps to fight one another with greater vehemence than ever Democrat had fought Republican since the time of E. J. Davis.

The forces were evenly matched. In the primary election of 1908 the prohibitionists won by a slender margin, but the brewery interests were able to defeat the submission of a constitutional amendment by the legislature. When the entire question was fought out again in the primary election of 1910, the prohibitionists again committed the party to submission. In the selection of candidates, however, they were not so successful. Better organized than their opponents, the antiprohibitionists centered their votes on Colquitt, who was elected by a large plurality over three opponents, two of them ardent prohibitionists who split the votes. Thus, in its primary the Democratic party called for a prohibition amendment and at the same time made sure of the election of an antiprohibitionist governor.

When the legislature submitted the prohibition amendment to the voters and designated July 22, 1911, as the day for the election, the two factions aligned themselves for another desperate contest. With great fervor Cone Johnson, William Poindexter, Thomas M. Campbell, Thomas H. Ball, and J. D. Sandefer, among the lay leaders, and preachers such as J. B. Gambrell, George W. Truett, and George C. Rankin campaigned for the cause. Among its leading opponents were Jake Wolters, Nelson B. Phillips, Charles K. Bell, and Governor Colquitt. By a close vote, 231,096 for to 237,393 against, statewide prohibition again failed.

Although they kept up the fight, the prohibitionists in Texas made little headway for sometime. However, suits filed by Attorney General B. F. Looney in 1915 revealed that the brewers had violated the state's antitrust laws and had used funds in elections in corrupt fashion. Then came the impeachment of the governor in 1917 and evidence indicating that the brewers had shown him favors. Moreover, prohibition became a patriotic issue, a measure with which to win the World War. A law which became effective on April 15, 1918, forbade the sale of liquor within ten miles of any place where troops were quartered. Shortly thereafter a state-wide law closed all saloons. Then, beginning July 1, 1919, a federal law prohibiting the sale of intoxicating liquor anywhere in the nation went into effect; and on January 16, 1920, the Eighteenth Amendment to the federal constitution made prohibition a national policy. Meanwhile, the legislature of Texas had ratified the 18th Amendment, and on May 24, 1919, the voters of Texas had adopted a prohibition amendment to the state constitution by a vote of 188,982 to 130,907. Traces of the rift caused by the issue would linger nearly as long as the experiment. But other dramatic national and state issues had already diverted the interest of voter and politician alike.

THE BIRTH OF FERGUSONISM

In 1914 there appeared in Texas politics a man destined to stir the emotions of the people for a generation. Rising from miserable poverty and a meager formal education, James E. Ferguson by 1914 was a successful Temple banker, lawyer, and businessman; but he was a virtual unknown in state politics. Yet, Ferguson who would be often called "Farmer Jim" was twice elected governor, serving from January 1915 to September 1917. Through his wife, Governor Miriam A. ("Ma") Ferguson, he guided many policies of the state from January 1925 to January 1927 and again from January 1933 to January 1935. In addition to his successful campaigns, he was a candidate for governor in 1918, for president of the United States in 1920, and for the United States Senate in 1922; besides the years when she was elected, Mrs. Ferguson ran for governor in 1926, 1930, and 1940. Meaning different things to different people, "Fergusonism" became a familiar term to the Texas voter. Critics angrily denounced the Fergusons as unprincipled demagogues; but to their loyal supporters they were undaunted crusaders seeking justice for the oppressed.

Believing that the majority of Texans were tired of the prohibition controversy, Ferguson announced as a candidate for governor in the primary of 1914 with the declaration that he would hold aloof from both prohibition political factions and make this campaign on other and more important issues. Although he posed as a businessman's candidate, the principal plank in Ferguson's platform appealed to tenant farmers. For many decades tenantry in Texas had been increasing. In 1880, 37 percent of all farms were operated by tenants; in 1900 the percentage had increased to 49; and in 1910 it was 62.6 percent. While their number had increased, the lot of tenants was growing harder and their outlook more discouraging. The time-honored custom of the landlord's taking a rental of one-fourth of the cotton and one-third of most other crops was not being followed uniformly in Texas. In the richer farmland regions the practice of charging higher rentals, or the customary one-third and one-fourth plus a money bonus was increasing. Ferguson proposed to fix by law farm rentals at one-third and one-fourth and to make a higher rate illegal. He opened his campaign at Blum, Hill County, a tenant community; of the 155 speeches which he delivered before the primary election, only ten were made in towns and cities. In the primary he defeated Thomas H. Ball, of Houston, who was supported by the prohibition wing of the party. In November he was elected governor with little opposition.

Ferguson's first administration was characterized by harmony and an imposing list of constructive laws. Of the 160 general laws enacted during the regular session of the 34th legislature in 1915, the governor vetoed only five. Ferguson was easily reelected in 1916, and the first five months of his second administration witnessed a continuation of a constructive legislative program. The governor's rental plank was readily enacted into law in 1915. But apparently never rigidly enforced, it was declared unconstitutional in 1921. Interesting and indicative of a new era was a law setting automobile speed limits at 15 miles an hour in towns and 18 miles an hour in the country. More significant, and in view of subsequent developments, more incongruous, were a number of laws substantially improving educational services.

Governor Ferguson's popularity declined during his second administration, but he still had a large following both in the legislature and among the rank and file of voters. In March 1917 the house of representatives investigated charges of irregular conduct on the part of the governor and discovered some questionable transactions; the committee, nevertheless, recommended that the charges be dropped. The regular session of the legislature completed its work and adjourned; but developments soon indicated that the governor would not be allowed to finish his second term.

Although charges of corruption and incompetence were leveled at Ferguson, both friend and foe have usually agreed that he would not have been impeached if he had not antagonized the exstudents of the University of Texas. The governor's quarrel with the university began as early as 1915 when he attempted to dictate to Acting President W. J. Battle the interpretation of the appropriation law for the school. In the following year he apparently became piqued because he was not consulted by the regents in their selection of a president for the university. Later, he demanded that the regents dismiss President Robert E. Vinson and several other faculty members, threatening the veto of the entire university appropriation otherwise. The regents, supported by the powerful exstudents association, refused to yield. The governor was not bluffing; in June 1917 just after the legislature had adjourned he vetoed the appropriation. Although the attorney general declared the veto void on a technicality, the fight between Ferguson and the university was then eclipsed by a movement to impeach the governor.

Responding to rising sentiment for impeachment proceedings, on July 23 the Speaker of the House issued a call for a special legislative session. He had no constitutional authority for such an act, but Governor Ferguson made the session legal by issuing a call after it became evident that the legislature was going to meet anyway. When the legislature convened, the house impeached the governor on 21 articles. On September 24 the senate convicted Ferguson on ten charges. The most serious counts held that Governor Ferguson had appropriated to his own use certain state funds; that he was guilty of irregularities in connection with deposits of public funds in the Temple State Bank, of which he was a stockholder; and that during his campaign in 1916 he had secured currency to the amount of $156,500 from sources unknown. It was discovered later that most of this money had been borrowed from the brewing interests and apparently had never been repaid. The court of impeachment removed Governor Ferguson from office and prohibited him from holding office again in Texas, a restriction that would bring strange developments in later years.

Despite the ban on his holding office, Ferguson returned to the political wars the following year, contesting Will P. Hobby, the lieutenant governor who had taken his position after his impeachment, for the

Democratic gubernatorial nomination. Ferguson campaigned with enthusiasm, venting his ire on the University of Texas in particular. One professor of the school, he declared, had devoted two years to an attempt to grow wool on the back of an armadillo. Faculty members were "educated fools," "butterfly chasers," and "two-bit thieves"; crooks and grafters controlled the school's administration. Governor Hobby was a "political accident." The "political accident" won the nomination with a comfortable margin of almost 70 percent of the vote. But the state had not heard the last of Farmer Jim Ferguson.

TEXAS IN THE FIRST WORLD WAR

The impeachment of a governor in Texas took place in the midst of a titanic military contest in Europe that was shaking the foundations of civilization. When the submarines of Germany took the lives of United States citizens, Texans, along with other Americans, became aroused. When Congress declared war on Germany on April 6, 1917, sentiment in Texas in support of the measure was overwhelming.

Politics determined that Texans would play a prominent role in the world conflict that dominated the second term of President Woodrow Wilson. It was the Texas delegation in the Democratic national convention at Baltimore in 1912, the "immortal forty," that voted for Wilson first and last and possibly insured his nomination. Later Wilson appointed Thomas Watt Gregory, of Austin, Attorney General and David F. Houston, formerly a Texan, Secretary of Agriculture. Albert Sidney Burleson, of Austin, served as Postmaster General and during the war directed the government's operation of the nation's telephone and telegraph systems. Colonel E. M. House was for some time probably the President's most trusted and important private counselor and personal representative. Thomas Love of Dallas served as Assistant Secretary of the Treasury; and many other Texans held positions of great honor and trust.

Within the state the military demands of war were quite apparent. Thousands of soldiers were training in four large camps (McArthur at Waco, Logan at Houston, Travis at San Antonio, and Bowie at Fort Worth), and in officers' training schools at Leon Springs and Kelly Field. A number of aviation schools scattered over the state provided many citizens with their first view of an airplane. Almost one million Texans registered for military service. Through the selective service law and voluntary enlistment, 197,389 served in the army, navy, and marine corps, with only a few opposing or evading the draft. Women made their contribution, providing 449 nurses for the service. Of those Texans in the armed services, more than 5,000 lost their lives.

At home the state council of defense sought to make the resources of Texas available for the war effort. Created in May 1917, and consisting of 39 representative citizens under the chairmanship of O. E. Dunlap of Waxahachie, the council was a branch of the National Council of Defense. Its work was distributed among the major committees; cooperating with it were 240 county councils and approximately 15,000 community councils. The services of these committees were placed at the disposal of the directors of various drives for Liberty Loans and support of the Red Cross; these committees assisted in promoting wholesome recreation for the soldiers, and in doing various other things to add to the comfort of the troops and improve their morale. The publicity committee of the council directed war information; kept available a staff of "four-minute men" for various campaigns; distributed pamphlets; urged the conservation of food; and remained on the alert for disloyal acts and utterances. After the war, the council aided returning soldiers in securing employment.

Independent of the council of defense but cooperating with it was the Federal Food Administration in Texas. Its first campaign in the fall of 1917, which aimed at getting housewives to sign cards agreeing to conserve flour, sugar, fats, and meats, was not so successful as had been expected. Then the emphasis was shifted from the homes to the merchants, and each dealer was requested to conform to the "fifty-fifty" rule which required the sale of one pound of wheat substitute for every pound of wheat flour. This procedure was more successful although in some cases it was necessary to impose penalties on merchants. From April 15 to June 15, 1918, a "wheat fast" was imposed on Texas, during which period no flour was shipped into the state and such stocks as could be spared were shipped to the Allies. Thus, some Texans found themselves eating cornbread even for breakfast.

The war effected a number of more significant changes. Inflation brought a soaring cost of living not always matched by comparable increases in incomes, though farm prices generally advanced. A permanent change was the rapid increase in public expenditures, expenditures which failed to decline when the war ended. In 1913 the government of Texas spent approximately $13,000,000 for all purposes; by 1919 this amount had increased to $27,000,000.

The war is also credited with bringing about woman suffrage. The legislature provided partial suffrage by an act permitting women to vote in the primaries of 1918. In the following year, however, the voters rejected a woman suffrage amendment to the state constitution. The Texas legislature, nevertheless, ratified the nineteenth amendment to the Constitution of the United States providing for woman suffrage. The amendment became operative in August 1920.

Predictable but regrettable was a spirit of fear, intolerance, and enforced conformity. Following the example set by the general government, the state legislature at a special session in 1918 enacted a drastic law to promote loyalty. To utter criticisms against the United States government, its flag, its officers, or the uniform of soldiers or to question the wisdom of the entrance or continuance of the United States in the war was an offense punishable by fine and imprisonment. The election law was changed to deny the ballot to foreign-born persons not naturalized. It was required that all classes in the public schools, the study of foreign languages excepted, be conducted in English; that all schools devote at least ten minutes each day to the teaching of patriotism; and that the United States flag be displayed from a flagpole in every school yard. The law of 1923 requiring that the Constitution of the United States and of Texas be taught in all public schools and that all teachers be citizens of the United States was, beyond a doubt, a belated product of the war mood.

Indeed, the excesses of superpatriotism ranged from the absurd to the tragic. In keeping with the spirit of the times was the recommendation of a legislative investigating committee that all books and periodicals of recent date in the state library extolling the greatness of Germany be immediately destroyed or securely boxed and put out of the way. Governor Hobby in 1919 vetoed the appropriation for the German department of the University of Texas, observing that elimination of such courses would promote purer Americanism. In some communities the obsession for conformity led to terror. "Influential and esteemed" citizens of a central Texas town, for example, flogged six of their neighbors who declined to join the American Red Cross. A newspaper editor in a nearby community endorsed the action, remarking that "whipping may convert some, while others are beyond conversion and should be shot." Texans found that crusading may beget intolerance.

THE POLITICS OF COMPLACENCY

"You are assembled here in a new era. You have problems to deal with that concern a new age." Thus did Governor William P. Hobby, in a message to the legislature in 1919, evaluate the importance of that time and occasion. Two years later, in the midst of a short financial depression, Governor Pat M. Neff expressed a similar feeling in language even more startling: "We are pioneering today," he said to the legislature, "amid the rocks and reefs and whirlpools of the most disturbed and uncertain financial ocean the world has ever known. These are testing times. The affairs of men are shifting. Things are abnormal. The world is at a turning point in civilization. . . ."

Indeed, the sense of change was very pronounced in the postwar years. Most Texans seemed to feel that with the defeat of Germany and the triumph of democracy, time had turned a page and begun a new chapter. The old order had passed; a new era had come bringing sharp changes in the affairs of men and nations. In a sense this was true; it was the dawn of a great boom. As men went from the army and navy back to civilian life, they were easily absorbed by industry. The depression of 1920 was short-lived, and Texas shared the general prosperity that soon returned. New plants were erected for the manufacture and processing of goods, land values doubled, millions were invested in public utilities, and thousands of new oil wells belched forth their black gold. The great state highway system was constructed, destined to be used by an ever-increasing number of foreign and Texan-owned cars. New colleges were built, and thousands of youths crowded the old ones; the public school system grew larger and more creditable each year. Prices of farm commodities lagged behind those enjoyed by industry, but bountiful crops tended to offset the price handicap. Texas was prosperous during the "mad decade," and people paid no heed to timid prophets here and there who told them that ahead were lean years that would devour the fat ones.

Thus for business and industry the decade following the close of the first World War did constitute a new era; but in politics and political institutions there was little to distinguish it from the years that preceded it. A few new government agencies were added and some of the old ones were enlarged, but there was little suggestive of the "new era" which Governor Hobby thought he saw ahead. In many respects the governors recognized the political demands of the emerging industrial and urban society. But a reluctant legislature and a complacent electorate refused to respond.

Complacency in politics was apparent even before the end of the war. In February 1918 a legislative investigating committee made a report suggesting various changes in the state government. All interests and efforts were absorbed in the war and nothing came of the report at that time. One of its recommendations was, however, adopted in 1919 with the creation of the state board of control, consisting of three members appointed by the governor for a term of six years. The board was made the budget agency for the state and given control of some of its insitutions. Many students of government regretted that its powers were not more extensive.

After the war Governor Hobby advocated several important reform measures. Some educational improvements were made, but little else was done. Hobby suggested a civil service commission, complete revision of the judiciary article in the constitution, and amendment of the constitution to authorize the state to lend its credit to heads of families to enable them to purchase homes. Indeed, he proposed that the constitution be rewritten. None of these measures was adopted. The question of a constitutional convention was submitted to the voters in 1919 and defeated. The governor's plan to aid persons in acquiring homes was endorsed by the voters in the Democratic primary, but it never became law. The voters also rejected constitutional amendments providing for woman suffrage, eliminating the fee system as a means of compensating certain officers, providing for the separation of the Agricultural and Mechanical College from the University of Texas, bonding the state for the construction of roads, enlarging the taxing power of counties and cities for public improvements, and increasing confederate pensions. Caught by the spell of the new era, the legislature might propose changes, but the people disposed of them in their own way by rejecting ten of the 13 constitutional amendments submitted.

Proclaiming a new democracy, Pat M. Neff entered the race for governor in 1919 subject to the action of the Democratic primary of the following year. The dignified and devout Waco lawyer knew Texas politics at first hand, for he had served as speaker of the house of representatives in 1903 and 1904. His chief opponent in the Democratic primary was Joe Bailey, who returned to politics after eight years of retirement to base his campaign largely on opposition to the Wilson national administration, woman suffrage, and most of the trends in government that had appeared during the last decade. Neff championed the great causes Bailey opposed, and he also favored a graduated land tax and other proposals that scandalized the staunch champions of the old Democratic party. Bailey led in the first primary, but in the runoff Neff won by a majority of 79,376. In spite of opposition from organized labor, Neff was renominated and reelected in 1922.

The new democracy was triumphant but the people were not ready for any drastic changes. Through various messages to the legislature Governor Neff advocated a number of reform measures. Among them were the reorganization of the state's administrative system in order to eliminate extravagance and duplication of effort, various enactments to halt the crime wave, a constitutional convention, and fundamental changes in the state tax system. The governor got practically nowhere. Although some offices were eliminated or consolidated, the legislature refused to modify greatly the organization of the state administrative system. There was no constitutional convention and no important change in the tax system. Neff's concern with what he termed the worst "crime wave" in the history of Texas received similar treatment. He thought the chief cause of this condition was the suspended sentence law which had been enacted in 1911 and amended in 1913. He asked for its repeal—without results. Likewise he wanted the legislature to empower the attorney general to institute proceedings for the removal of any local peace officer who did not enforce the law. The only action on the subject was a feeble measure permitting a district judge to remove a county officer for certain causes, but not for intoxication if it resulted from drinking liquor prescribed by a licensed physician! Neff, however, did his part to keep prisoners in the penitentiary. He disbanded the board of pardons, made his own investigations within prison walls from time to time to determine who merited clemency, and granted very few pardons. In this respect his administration was in striking contrast with those of Hobby and the Fergusons.[1]

Otherwise some permanent improvements were made. Governor Neff, an ardent champion of good roads, must be given a share of credit for the expansion and improvement of the highway system. Likewise, he used his influence effectively to promote the conservation of natural resources. The state park system had its beginning in 1923 with the creation of a nonsalaried park board. A harsh comment on the lack of foresight of those who had gone before is the fact that the State of Texas, which once had owned millions of acres of land, was obliged to solicit donations of a few hundred acres here and there in order that its people might have access to recreational facilities.

THE KU KLUX KLAN AND THE RETURN OF FERGUSONISM

In 1921 there appeared in Texas an organization that was the subject of bitter controversy for several years. The Ku Klux Klan had its beginning near Atlanta, Georgia, in about 1915, taking the name of the famous organization of reconstruction days and making white supremacy one of its slogans. It was, however, more akin to the various nativist movements that have arisen among the American people from time to time, notably Know-Nothingism of the 1850's, than it was to the original Ku Klux Klan of reconstruction days. In fact, the Klan in Texas was as much as anything else an effort to impose social and moral conformity on a society in rapid transition from the farm to the city. The Klan made little headway until after the first World War, when various conditions combined to promote its spread. The nation had been made aware of the presence of millions of foreign-born persons, commonly called "hyphenated Americans," whose loyalty had been impeached, in many cases unjustly, be it said, and after the war there arose sharp resentment toward everybody and everything foreign. Protestant in sympathy, the Klan was distinctly anti-Catholic and anti-Jewish. It declared war on crime and corrupt officials, a phase of its program that appealed to thousands of men who had little sympathy for its racial and religious intolerance. It gained its maximum growth in Texas during 1921 and 1922, at a time when Governor Neff (not in sympathy with the Klan) was writing and

[1]From January 1915 to September 1917 Governor James E. Ferguson granted 1,774 pardons and 479 conditional pardons; from August 1917 to January 1921 Governor W. P. Hobby granted 1,319 pardons and 199 conditional pardons; from January 1925 to September 1926 Governor Miriam A. Ferguson granted 384 pardons and 777 conditional pardons. The period covered in Mrs. Ferguson's first administration (January 1925 to September 1926) does not include the time during which the governor exercised the pardoning power most liberally.

speaking against the "greatest crime wave" in Texas history and giving credence to the estimate that "not ten percent of those who violated the law was arrested, and not half of those who are arrested are convicted." The Klan went further, assuming for itself the responsibility of protecting "virtuous womanhood," "premarital chastity" and "marital fidelity," "respect for parental authority," and "abstinence from alcoholic beverages."

Covertly the Klan entered politics and soon its power was felt in almost every community. In 1922 it gained control of many local offices, and participated in the campaign for the United States Senate. That year several candidates sought to succeed United States Senator Charles A. Culberson, who had served continuously since 1899, but was prevented by poor health from making an active campaign. The strongest contenders were Earle B. Mayfield, member of the Texas railroad commission; and James E. Ferguson, who had left the Democrats in 1920 to run for president of the United States on his own American party ticket, but returned to the Democratic party two years later. Mayfield admitted that he had belonged to the Klan, and it was generally understood that he was supported by it, whereas Ferguson attacked the organization severely. Mayfield received the nomination, and disgruntled Democrats, uniting with the Republicans behind George E. B. Peddy, a Houston attorney, failed to defeat him in the general election.

In the election of 1924 the Klan played a part even more important. It supported Judge Felix D. Robertson of Dallas; and Ferguson, disqualified from holding the governorship by the terms of his impeachment in 1917, entered the race through his wife, Mrs. Miriam A. Ferguson. Robertson and Mrs. Ferguson survived the first primary, and the race became the keenest the state had seen in many years. The Klan was powerful but it had already lost ground. In their zeal to impose moral conformity, the Klansmen had frequently taken the law into their own hands. From almost every community came reports of hooded men, working by night, serving as their own sheriff, judge, and jury, and flogging persons, driving them from their communities, or otherwise terrifying them. The Klan denied connection with most of these outrages, but it must be said that its masked parades and secret conclaves had inspired many of them. In the primary Mrs. Ferguson defeated Robertson by nearly 100,000 votes. Another minority of the Democratic party was now dissatisfied and this group united with the Republicans in an effort to defeat Mrs. Ferguson in the general election. The bolters supported George C. Butte, dean of the University of Texas law school. Mrs. Ferguson defeated him by more than 100,000 votes to become the first woman governor of Texas.

During this second era of Fergusonism (1925–1927) reform took a holiday. James E. Ferguson, who determined the policies his wife followed, was disposed to pursue a conservative course. No drastic proposals appeared in the governor's messages and no outstanding laws were enacted. Ferguson's liberal pardoning policy—two thousand acts of executive clemency, counting furloughs and extensions, during twenty months —evoked much gossip and unfavorable comment. An investigating committee found that most of the governor's pardons were issued on the recommendation of her husband, some of them before the beneficiaries reached the prison. The chief attack by the enemies of the administration was, however, aimed at the highway commission, a body composed altogether of appointees of Mrs. Ferguson and dominated by the former governor who sat with it whenever important matters were up for consideration. It was alleged that favoritism, rather than the best interests of the state, was the determining factor in the letting of contracts for the construction of roads. Several contracts were cancelled as the result of suits brought by Attorney General Dan Moody, who became the chief antagonist of the Fergusons.

A crusader for reform, in 1926 Dan Moody entered the campaign for governor against Mrs. Ferguson. The Fergusons were confident, but the Attorney General was able to defeat her by a substantial majority to become the next governor of the state.

MOODY'S REFORM PROGRAM

In Dan Moody the friends of reform had an able spokesman. Although he was the youngest governor who ever served Texas (elected at the age of 33), he had been seasoned by experience as a local prosecutor and by two years in the exacting office of attorney general. As district attorney in Williamson County, Moody had attained a state-wide reputation for his vigorous prosecution of certain members of the Ku Klux Klan who had committed acts of violence, a distinction that brought him the office of attorney general.

He proposed a broad reform program that represented in the main the best ideals of the progressive forces of his day. He advocated a number of measures calling for important changes in the constitution and laws of the state. He supported a change in the constitution to permit the legislature to enact laws separating the subjects of taxation. He proposed that the judiciary article of the constitution be rewritten so as to raise the number of justices of the supreme court from three to nine. He would reorganize the state government and give the governor power to appoint the important executive officers who were now elected under the Constitution of 1876. He pointed out that these officers "are entirely independent of the Governor, and administer their respective offices under no executive supervision, without any co-ordination, and in the past there has been actual friction among themselves or with other departments."

With these appeals Moody was no more successful than had been his predecessors who advocated the same or similar reforms. The governor's most earnest and persistent plea was for a civil service law that would secure the tenure of experts and employees in minor administrative positions against changing administrations. In one message to the legislature he devoted more than three closely printed pages to arguments against the spoils system. No law on the subject was ever placed on his desk.

The perennial problem of prisons and prison management demanded attention during this period. Prison properties consisted principally of the main plant at Huntsville and about 77,000 acres of land located in several widely separated farms, a great deal of which was subject to overflow. It was necessary that about seven-eighths of the prison population, which had grown to more than 3,000, be kept on these farms. During Neff's administration the legislature had favored centralizing the system, and had authorized a commission consisting of the governor, attorney general, and commissioner of the general land office to secure a site within 75 miles of Austin where the entire system could be consolidated and made primarily industrial. Nothing came of this plan, however, since Governor Neff thought the system should be centralized on lands already owned in Brazoria and Fort Bend counties.

During Moody's administration the prison population increased to 4,500, and the system continued to lose money. Pursuant to the recommendation of Governor Moody, who favored a centralized system with less farming and more industrial projects, the legislature created a centralization commission to make a study of the Texas system and those of other states and to formulate a plan that would settle the vexing problem.

Unfortunately the commission, which failed to agree on any plan, submitted majority and minority reports to the legislature called in special session in early 1930. The result was a compromise measure which fell far short of the complete reorganization and concentration which the governor and other champions of reform had advocated. The plant at Huntsville was to be improved by providing better facilities for sanitation and medical care of prisoners and installing equipment for additional industries. The farms were to be improved by "units," taking one or two farms at a time and providing sufficient quarters, hospitals, and other facilities to modernize that particular part of the system. Meanwhile the voters by constitutional amendment authorized the legislature to set up any method for control of the prisons that in its judgment seemed wise. In keeping with this amendment the legislature in 1927 created a new governing body of nine members with power to select and employ a manager, who should be in charge of the entire system and be responsible to the board. After Lee Simmons, a Sherman businessman, was appointed manager in 1930, the prison system thereafter showed marked improvement.

Limited administrative and judicial reforms were adopted in other areas. The Fortieth Legislature (1927) made some progress toward reform of the court system in an act continuing the commission of appeals to aid the supreme court. The act specified also that the supreme court should make semiannual equalizations of the dockets of the 11 courts of appeal. A constructive measure enacted by the 41st Legislature (Moody's second term) provided for a state auditor and efficiency expert, to be appointed by the governor and clothed with his authority to audit all departments of the state government.

In the election of 1928, for the first time in history the interest in the contest for the presidential electoral vote in Texas was keener than the interest in state and local races. Governor Moody received a majority vote in the first primary over Louis J. Wardlaw who was supported by the Fergusons. But early in the year the presidential candidacy of Governor Alfred E. Smith of New York, a Catholic and an outspoken opponent of prohibition, threatened the unity of Texas Democracy. The Republicans also were, as usual, divided; one group, led by R. B. Creager, supported Herbert Hoover, and was opposed by a faction under the leadership of Congressman Harry M. Wurzbach. The "Harmony Democrats" chose Governor Moody as their leader and at the state convention prevailed against the "Constitutional Democrats," led by Thomas Love, who sought to instruct the state delegation against Smith. After Smith was nominated at the national convention in Houston, the anti-Smith forces organized with Alvin S. Moody, of Houston, as chairman. The regular Democrats organized with James R. Young of Kaufman County as their leader. Most of the party leaders stayed with the regular organization; but they were not able to match the strength of the bolters who united with the major Republican faction in a campaign for Hoover that resembled the prohibition crusades of other years. Hoover's plurality was 26,000; he was the first Republican to receive an electoral vote in Texas. It has been said that the chief issue in the campaign of 1928 were "the three P's"—prosperity, prohibition, and prejudice. In this election Tom Connally defeated Earle B. Mayfield for the United States Senate.

Moody's first term was, perhaps, the most prosperous period the state had ever known. But during the last year of his administration the state began to feel the pinch of the depression and panic that had begun in 1929 with the collapse of the stock market and spread to all parts of the nation. The brunt of the depression, however, was borne by the Sterling and Ferguson administrations (1931–1935).

EDUCATION

Even against the obstacle of political complacency, the educational system of Texas made substantial progress during these years. To be sure,

The lack of a public school system was one of the grievances listed in the Texas Declaration of Independence, and the Constitution of the Republic of Texas stipulated that Congress provide such a system. Despite the support of President Mirabeau B. Lamar and Governors E. M. Pease and James S. Hogg, among others, the Texas public education system was relatively poor, and the one-room school house was still very common in 1914 (the date of the photograph shown at right). Not until the automobile was in general use was it possible for widely separated families to send their children to larger and better equipped schools that offered more specialized education. (E. C. Barker History Center, University of Texas)

by most criteria that could be used to evaluate public schools, Texas continued to lag behind the national norms. But through constitutional reforms, added local responsibility, expanded resources, and consolidation public education came nearer than before to meeting the needs of a modern society. Creation of new institutions of higher learning and dramatic growth of older ones were additional evidence of a maturing educational structure.

In 1915 the legislature, at last recognizing the handicap under which the rural schools were operating, took a long step toward equalizing educational opportunities between town and country. That year a law written by J. M. Wagstaff and others was enacted appropriating $1,000,000 for the special benefit of rural schools, to be used during the ensuing biennium. A constructive feature of the law was the requirement that before a rural school district could qualify for special aid it should levy a local school tax of 50 cents on the $100 of valuation. The measure had the effect of stimulating greatly the levying of local school taxes in rural districts where they were most needed. Legislatures continued the practice until 1949, when the Gilmer-Aiken school program went into effect. Ferguson's administration also gave the state its first compulsory school law, which went into effect in the fall of 1916. In 1918 a constitutional amendment authorizing free textbooks was adopted; at the same time the constitutional maximum for the state ad valorem school tax was raised from 20 to 35 cents on the $100 of valuation. In 1920 the voters removed the greatest barrier to an adequate school system set by the Constitution of 1876 when they abolished entirely the limit on the tax rate that communities might levy for school purposes.

The state continued to be somewhat more generous in its support of the schools. When the schools found themselves in financial straits in the depression of 1920, the legislature came to their relief with a special appropriation of $4,000,000. This special aid, together with the increase in revenue from other sources, raised the state's per capita scholastic apportionment from $7.50 to $14.50. Legislatures thereafter continued to supplement the school fund by special appropriations.

These expenditures, more generous than those of earlier years, did not lift the Texas school system from its low rank when compared with other states. A survey of the schools, authorized in 1923 and conducted under the general supervision of George A. Works of Cornell University, brought forth a number of recommendations, most of which the legislators and voters did not see fit to adopt. One notable change, to be credited at least in part to the survey, was a constitutional amendment authorizing the legislature to abolish the ex-officio board of education consisting of the governor, comptroller, and secretary of state. A law of 1929 provided for a board of nine members to be appointed by the governor and to exercise certain powers not vested in the former ex-officio board. The superintendent of public instruction was still elected by the voters of the state, and he shared with the board of education a great deal of the power and responsibility associated with the public schools.

By the twenties a trend toward consolidation was apparent. The building of a state highway system and the improvements of lateral roads during this period made it possible for communities to take advantage of a law of 1915 which permitted the consolidation of schools whenever a majority of the voters of two or more districts favored it. In 1925 the legislature empowered county trustees to make consolidations under certain conditions. These powers granted to voters and trustees, together with the provisions authorizing the transportation at public expense of students who lived at a distance, constituted the beginning of the end of the "little red schoolhouse." By 1930, 1,530 consolidations had been made.

Unfortunately, with the pattern of segregation as rigid as ever, Negro schools, already far behind those for white students, failed to share appreciably in the educational gains. Between 1905 and 1930 the salaries of white teachers in rural areas increased $8.98 per scholastic; salaries of Negro teachers per student increased sixteen cents. In 1930 Negro teachers in rural and city schools received in salary approximately one-third as much per scholastic as their white colleagues. Provisions for secondary education for Negroes were limited indeed. Negroes constituted approximately one-third of the scholastic population of East Texas. Yet more than 97 percent of the high schools of East Texas were for whites only.

During these years the junior college movement, associated with

Texas since its infancy, expanded rapidly. In 1897 the Baptist State Convention established a correlated system of higher educational institutions, with Baylor University and Mary Hardin-Baylor College as senior schools and Howard Payne College, Rusk College, and Decatur Baptist College as two year institutions. A little later the Methodists developed a similar organization in connection with Southwestern University. Other denominations entered the field, establishing a number of church-controlled junior colleges by 1920. About the same time the state created junior colleges at Stephenville and Arlington. With the founding of El Paso Junior College in 1920, Texas cities entered the junior college educational field. By 1940 there were in Texas 39 recognized junior colleges (public, state, church, and private) with an enrollment of more than 10,000 students.

Full term colleges and universities also grew in number and size. During the early decades of the twentieth century, the state established a college for women at Denton and acquired, founded, or authorized normal schools at Canyon, Commerce, Kingsville, and Alpine. In 1923 the state normal schools were made teacher's colleges. The same legislature authorized the establishment of Texas Technological College at Lubbock, thus meeting the demand for a university pressed by the citizens of that section for many years.

The twenties saw the most rapid growth the state colleges had known. Each year brought additional thousands of students to tax the facilities of institutions already overcrowded. A constitutional amendment approved in 1930 permitted regents of the University of Texas to borrow from the school's permanent fund for the purpose of erecting buildings. Meanwhile, the university temporarily solved its problem by erecting flimsy wooden structures dubbed "shacks" by the students. In a sense, the shacks symbolized the position of education in Texas at this point: progress had been made, the need for improvement had been recognized, but there remained much to do.

Selected Bibliography

General studies on this period are R. Steen in F.C. Adams (ed.), *Texas Democracy* (4 vols., Austin, 1937); S.S. McKay, *Texas Politics, 1906–1944;* S. Acheson, *35,000 Days in Texas* and *Joe Bailey: The Last Democrat;* R. Steen, *Twentieth Century Texas; An Economic and Social History;* and S.S. McKay and O.B. Faulk, *Texas after Spindletop*.

References on border troubles are W.P. Webb, *The Texas Rangers;* and C.C. Cumberland, "Border Raids in the Lower Rio Grande Valley, 1915," *Southwestern Historical Quarterly*, LVII, 285–311.

For special studies on the Fergusons see R. Steen, "The Ferguson War on the University of Texas," *Southwestern Social Science Quarterly*,

XXXV, 356–362; Ouida Ferguson Nalle, *The Fergusons of Texas* (San Antonio, 1946); H.G. James, "The Removal of Governor Ferguson of Texas by Impeachment," *National Municipal Review*, VI, 725–726; W.F. McCaleb, "The Impeachment of a Governor," *American Political Science Review*, XII, 111–115; and Octavia F. Rogan, "Texas Legislation, 1925," *Southwestern Political and Social Science Quarterly*, VI, 167–168.

Activities of two other governors are described in James Clark, *The Tactful Texan: Governor W.P. Hobby* (New York, 1958); and in Emma M. Shirley, *The Administration of Pat M. Neff, Governor of Texas, 1921–1925* (Waco, 1938). Also see S.A. MacCorkle, "The Pardoning Power in Texas," *Southwestern Social Science Quarterly*, XV, 218–228; and O.D. Weeks, "The Election of 1928," *ibid.*, IX, 337–348.

Texas' part in the first World War is treated, inadequately, in Army and Navy History Company, *History of Texas World War Heroes* (Dallas, 1919). For the operation of the draft law see Second Report of the Provost Marshall General to the Secretary of War (Washington, D.C., Government Printing Office, 1919). Two useful studies in manuscript in the University of Texas Library are Henry George Hendricks on the Federal Food Administration in Texas, and Oran E. Turner on the Texas Council of Defense.

For additional reading on other crusades, see H.A. Ivey, *Rum on the Run in Texas* (Dallas, 1910), biased but of value; Elizabeth A. Taylor, "The Woman Suffrage Movement in Texas," *Journal of Southern History*, XVIII, 194–215; and Charles C. Alexander, *Crusade for Conformity: The Ku Klux Klan in Texas, 1920–1930* (Houston, 1962).

Texas' place on the national scene is touched upon in Arthur Link, "The Wilson Movement in Texas, 1910–1912," *Southwestern Historical Quarterly*, XLVIII, 169–185; Dewey Grantham, "Texas Congressional Leaders and the New Freedom, 1913–1917," *ibid.*, LIII, 35–48; R.N. Richardson, *Colonel Edward M. House: The Texas Years, 1858–1912;* W.P. Webb and Terrell Webb, (eds.), *Washington Wife: Journal of Ellen Maury Slayden from 1897–1919* (New York, 1962); Lee N. Allen, "The Democratic Presidential Primary Election of 1924 in Texas," *Southwestern Historical Quarterly*, LXI, 474–493; Tom Connally and Alfred Steinberg, *My Name is Tom Connally* (New York, 1954); and Bascom M. Timmons, *Garner of Texas; A Personal History* (New York, 1948).

17

DEPRESSION, RELIEF AND SECURITY, 1930–1941

In the early autumn of 1929, after a long period of soaring prices, the New York stock market turned downward. On October 23 a sharp drop precipitated much selling, and on the next day panic seized the exchanges of the nation. Although Texans suffered their share of losses in the stock market crash, their immediate injuries were not as great as those that followed later. The price of cotton dropped from 18 cents a pound in 1928 to less than six cents in 1931. Many farm laborers and tenants, dispirited and broken, gathered in towns and cities, hoping either to share in direct relief or to draw slender wages on public works projects. Merchants, manufacturers, and shopowners laid off hands, adding to the rolls of the unemployed.

In many cases relatives and friends helped for awhile and local charity organizations did the best they could; but all such efforts proved to be inadequate. Thousands of individuals and not a few families took to the highways, "hitchhiking" from place to place. Many were without funds, and persons living near arteries of travel were often compelled either to give them food or turn them away hungry. Swarms of unfortunate people sought protection in abandoned buildings, caves, dugouts, and shanties made of discarded boxes.

It was believed generally that the period of financial stagnation would be of short duration, as those following the panics of 1907 and 1920 had been. President Hoover was unduly optimistic and thought that local relief agencies could supply adequate aid. Chambers of commerce of some cities sent out goodwill parties to neighboring towns and villages, assuring the people that the depression would soon end. But a financial crisis in Central Europe in 1931 rebounded to our shores and aggravated our problems, and the depression deepened.

Conditions gradually grew worse and with the closing of all banks in March 1933, the depression reached every farm and hamlet in the nation. President Roosevelt's positive action in dealing with the bank crisis and his assurance that the general government would apply its vast resources toward relief and recovery restored a measure of confidence, but it did not bring the nation out of the financial doldrums. "Prosperity is just around the corner" came to be a trite, sorry joke. Progress toward recovery was uneven until midsummer 1935; thenceforth improvement was rapid until the autumn of 1937, when a recession that continued through much of the following year wiped out a considerable part of the gain. Not until the gigantic defense program of 1940-1941 stimulated demands for labor and goods did the economic society attain "recovery," and even then many thousands of workers, continued to be unemployed.

Meanwhile, acting both directly and through the states, the United States government had inaugurated the most ambitious social and economic legislative program in history. The treatment of the farm program and other conservation measures is deferred to the next chapter. The present chapter will include a survey of public affairs in Texas during the period of deepest depression, from 1930 through 1934; an examination of the all-absorbing questions of relief and security from 1935 to 1941; and the consideration of other public issues that have appeared in recent years.

THE VAGARIES OF POLITICS (1930-1935)

The history of the gubernatorial campaign of 1930 sustains the exaggerated statement that the Democratic party in Texas chooses its candidate for governor by lottery. Twelve persons filed for that office, and it seemed that of a half-dozen or more any two might qualify for the second primary. Thus the voters might be compelled to choose the lesser of two evils. Governor Moody supported Ross Sterling of Houston, who was completing his fourth year as chairman of the highway commission. James E. Ferguson, as usual, was in the race through the candidacy of his wife. In the first primary, Mrs. Ferguson led the ticket and Sterling ran next to her. After a bitter contest preceding the second primary, Sterling was nominated by a majority of about 100,000. His chief claim to the office was the promise of "a business administration to meet the demands of a growing State, by a successful business man." In the general election he defeated without difficulty William E. Talbot, the Republican nominee. Edgar E. Witt was elected lieutenant governor and Morris Sheppard was returned to the United States Senate.

During Sterling's administration (January 1931 to January 1933) emergency followed emergency, and one crisis had not passed before another appeared in the offing. Taxes were in arrears; state income fell off sharply; expenditures were nearly as high as ever; and Sterling was obliged to use the veto severely. A deluge of oil from the East Texas field created a crisis for that industry in the summer of 1931, and the legislature in its first called session tackled that problem. In the following year a called session (the fourth called by Sterling) attacked again the same problem. The remedial laws on this subject and the governor's use of troops to enforce them are discussed in a later chapter.

In his election campaign Sterling had advocated a state road bond issue of $350,000,000. The legislature refused to submit to the voters the constitutional amendment authorizing the bond issue; but in a called session in September 1932 it did appropriate one-fourth of the proceeds of the state tax on the retailing of gasoline to be used in paying local obligations that had been incurred in the improving of state highways. Thus, the state relieved the counties in a part of their indebtedness.

Governor Sterling worked faithfully in the interest of Texas and brought to bear on public affairs the rich experience of a varied business career; but the times bred discontent, and in 1932 the voters were ready for a change. Sensing the dissatisfaction, James E. Ferguson again entered the contest. In supporting his wife's campaign he said to the voters: "Two years ago you got the best governor money could buy, this year you have an opportunity to get the best governor patriotism can give you." He added that when his wife was governor he would "be on hand picking up chips and bringing in water for mama." He charged that Sterling had wasted state highway funds; he attacked him for invoking martial law; and he proposed certain drastic changes in state taxes. Former Governor Moody and other prominent Texans worked diligently for Sterling, but in the second primary Mrs. Ferguson beat him by a few hundred votes out of a total of nearly a million.

The Forty-third Legislature, which convened in January 1933, found that the depression was aggravating old problems and creating new ones. State income had been reduced several million dollars annually by the constitutional amendment, now in effect, exempting from state taxation homesteads to the value of $3,000. The governor recommended a sales tax of three percent; but the legislature, like its successors until 1961, refused to adopt such a measure. By slashing salaries and effecting a few other economies, general appropriations were reduced about 21 percent.

But, notwithstanding economies, the administration found it difficult to make ends meet and municipalities and school districts every-where were impoverished. The urgent need for more revenue accounted in part for a measure, enacted as a rider on an appropriation bill in 1933, making betting on horse racing legal. The act, denounced in the pulpits of the state and by many editors and businessmen, was repealed in 1937 by a special session of the legislature called by Governor Allred for that purpose. In their opposition to the return of the legal sale of liquor the forces of reform were not so successful. Texas joined in ratifying the Twenty-first Amendment to the Constitution of the United States which ended national prohibition, December 5, 1933. Then the Forty-fourth Legislature submitted an amendment repealing state prohibition, and the voters ratified it in August, 1935.

It is difficult to evaluate objectively Mrs. Ferguson's second adminis-tration. Relations between the legislature and the executive were not harmonious, and the lawmakers distrusted the governor and her hus-band. The return of the Fergusons' policy of liberal pardons and paroles for state prisoners was attacked from various quarters. It must be said, however, that the administration was economical and apparently met with much greater public approval than did Mrs. Ferguson's first ad-ministration as governor.

Governor Ferguson did not seek reelection in 1934. For the first time since 1914, Texas voters were not confronted directly by "Ferguson-ism." In the second primary Tom F. Hunter, an oil man of Wichita Falls, was defeated by his former fellow townsman, James V. Allred, who was completing his second term as attorney general. Although Allred was relatively liberal and is sometimes referred to as "Texas' last liberal gov-ernor," his platform was more conservative than those of his opponents, several of whom leaned toward changes in the state's tax system that would have transferred the burden from homeowners and small busi-ness establishments to natural resources and big business. All candidates favored, or at least refused to oppose, old age pensions. Hunter, who had proposed what he termed a "blended tax" on the wealthy, charged that the "interests" (power trust, oil companies, and chain stores) caused his defeat. In the same primary Joseph W. Bailey, Jr., made a spirited but unsuccessful effort to wrest from Tom Connally his seat in the United States Senate. President Roosevelt gave the incumbent his nod of approval by referring to him as "my old friend, Tom Connally."

By the beginning of Governor Allred's term, January 1935, the New Deal relief program was well under way and President Roosevelt's plans for national social security had been announced. The governor urged "planned recovery" for Texas and to that end a Texas planning board was established for a period of four years. The board proper was com-posed of nine business and professional men and state officials, and asso-ciated with it through ten committees were a number of representative citizens. It set out to prepare a comprehensive program for the conservation and utilization of the resources of the state. Not less than a dozen boards and commissions were created by the legislature to aid in carrying out projects associated with the program of relief and security in its various forms.

RELIEF

As the depression deepened, it soon became evident that private relief organizations and such antiquated public agencies as poor farms could not care for the increasing number of persons who had no means of support. Governor Sterling in 1931 suggested public works as a means of providing indirect relief, but of greater immediate value was his committee for the relief of unemployment, which functioned through the commission of labor and placed many thousands of cotton pickers that year.

Meanwhile, the federal government had attacked the problem in a program calling for billions of dollars for direct relief and work relief, much of which was to be spent through state and local agencies. There were two means of approach; the first by making grants to the states for general relief; and the second by carrying on a works program that would serve the double purpose of relieving unemployment and "priming the pumps" of business and industry. The first aid was extended late in 1932 under a law authorizing the lending of Federal Reconstruction Finance Corporation funds to state and local bodies for relief activities. Through various state and local agencies, both public and private, these funds were used to provide work on different projects, supposedly of public value. By April 20, 1933, Texas had received through the Reconstruction Finance Corporation approximately $7,000,000 for direct relief and work relief of the unemployed. At that time it was estimated that 267,000 persons, or bread earners representing a million of the population were unemployed. An unemployment census taken in 1933 showed that 105,045 families, representing 7.1 percent of the total population, were on relief at that time. Although it was serious, the condition in Texas compared favorably with that of the nation as a whole, where 10.3 percent of the people were on relief. The RFC insisted that the state should share with the general government the burden of relief. The legislature accordingly submitted to the voters a constitutional amendment to authorize the issuance of bonds not to exceed $20,000,000 for the relief of unemployment. The bonds were issued and sold from time to time. The last of these "bread bonds" were issued during the Allred administration. The Legislature also established a Texas relief commission as a coordinating and administrative organization through which the various agencies worked. County relief boards also were provided to make plans for roads and other public improvements through which needy persons might be given employment.

The Federal Emergency Relief Administration, created by the act of May 12, 1933, provided the states with funds for both direct relief and work relief. Through this agency and through the RFC, which continued to provide funds, Texas received for the aid of its destitute in 1933 and 1934 approximately $50,000,000. Unfortunately, the number of persons calling for relief did not diminish in proportion to the improvement in the general economic situation. On September 20, 1934, there were in Texas 246,849 relief cases, representing about a million people.

While these agencies were meeting the pressing needs of the people who had neither property nor jobs, a broader program of government spending was launched which was designed both to furnish employment and to revive business and industry. From 1933 through 1938 the Civilian Conservation Corps paid to 110,000 boys and war veterans salaries aggregating approximately $25,000,000. The National Youth Administration was established in 1935 to administer a program of assistance to young people. Under the National Industrial Recovery Act, a Federal Emergency Administration of Public Works (PWA) organized and coordinated a gigantic system of public building. The RFC loaned funds both to private business establishments and to construction firms for the purpose of financing public and public-guaranteed projects. In May 1935, work relief was coordinated in a Works Progress Administration, which made possible construction and rehabilitation of all kinds of public property and provided hundreds of white-collar activities.

For the calendar years 1933 through 1936 the United States supplied through various agencies $10,667,379,186 for relief and works programs. Of this sum $351,023,546, or about 3.03 percent was spent in Texas. During the same period state and local funds used for relief and work programs in Texas amounted to $80,268,595. Expenditures continued with some variations but without any substantial decrease. The various works programs left some results of enduring value in Texas. For instance, PWA alone listed in its "physical accomplishments" up to 1939, 510 public buildings, 998.7 miles of new highway pavement, and improvements in 135 parks and playgrounds.

General relief functions were transferred from the Texas Relief Commission to the Welfare Department in September 1939, and during the following four years the administration of general relief cost $1,300,000. For the sound of mind and able-bodied, war industry ended the need for aid from the state.

SOCIAL SECURITY

In June 1934 President Roosevelt declared that the security of its men, women, and children was the first objective of the nation. A month later he appointed a committee on economic security and out of its study, as well as the hearings of Congress, came the National Social Security Act, signed August 14, 1935. The law was revised and amended in important features in 1939 and at subsequent dates.

The most important provisions of the act were to provide support for persons past 65 years of age (later made optional at 62) by public assistance, or old age pensions, to be provided by state and federal contributions, and by benefit payments, or old age survivors insurance, based on earnings, weighted in favor of the oldest and poorest people, to be financed by contributions made by both employers and employees; to give aid for a limited period to unemployed bona fide workers, in those fields of employment not excluded, from a fund created by a payroll tax on employers; and to make grants to states, more or less by matching state and federal funds, for a number of purposes, including aid to the blind, aid to families with dependent children, and aid to permanently and totally disabled persons.

In the main the act called for state and federal cooperation and made it necessary that a state provide adequate agencies and funds in order to participate in its various services. One important service, namely old age survivors insurance (not to be confused with old age pensions), was made entirely a federal matter, and was in no way made dependent on state cooperation. Under the plan provided, worker and employer contribute monthly to build up for the worker an endowment fund to assist him and to aid his dependents during his declining years. The plan was weighted heavily in favor of people who were approaching retirement age. In 1966 this plan was extended to include medical care. The scope of old age benefits has been extended by subsequent legislation until nearly all workers (including the self-employed) contribute to the fund and will be entitled to share in its benefits after retirement.

The welfare service of the state is administered by the Department of Public Welfare. Some public problems come and go, but the problem of the aged, the blind, the totally disabled, and of needy children are abiding ones. In the matter of aid to the unfortunate Texas is frugal if not parsimonious. Cost of administration is low and in most of the categories the state stands near the bottom in the average payment to the recipient. Still the program in the state costs more than $200,000,000 a year, about one-fourth of which is paid by the state. On January 1, 1967, 229,329 aged Texans received old age assistance at a cost to the state of $14,168,963 per month. At this time 782,781 Texans were recipients of old age survivors' insurance.

A TURBULENT POLITICAL ERA (1935–1941)

The most difficult problem the Allred administration had to face was that of old age assistance. The constitutional amendment, authorizing public assistance to persons above 65 years of age, did not specify the amount of the pensions (except for the maximum state contribution of 15 dollars) or set any definite standards for determining who should receive them. The pension program was to be "under such limitations and restrictions and regulations as may be deemed by the legislature expedient. . . ." Furthermore, the amendment made no provision for raising additional funds necessary to meet the payments. During Allred's first term (1935–1937) three special legislative sessions were devoted to the subject; it consumed much of the regular session of 1937 and it was the principal reason for a called session in September of that year. Before the end of September following the beginning of payments in July 1936, applications approved had reached 80,718 and the old age assistance commission estimated that the number would eventually reach almost 150,000. The governor asked the legislature to vote additional taxes for the pension fund. It increased the revenue, and deliberalized the law sufficiently, it was estimated, to cut the rolls to 80,000. To deliberalize was easier said than done, however, and on June 1, 1937, aged Texans receiving pensions numbered 125,772. At that time the legislature conducted an investigation of the old age assistance commission, and it was evident that the subject of pensions was in politics.

Pensions and taxation, subjects necessarily linked together be it said, drew sharp attention in the gubernatorial campaign of 1936 when Allred sought reelection. Texans had heard a great deal of Huey Long's "share the wealth" program in Louisiana; they were well acquainted with Dr. Francis E. Townsend's plan to pay a pension of $200 a month to most persons past 60 years of age; and Father Charles E. Coughlin's National Union for Social Justice was then active. The candidates accordingly leaned toward a more generous pension policy. Governor Allred, who advocated pensions for the aged needy only and but few new taxes, was more conservative than his opponents, and the fact that he was nominated in the first primary by receiving more votes than the four opponents combined indicates that the Texas voters were still in a conservative mood.

The governor was obliged, nevertheless, to appeal to the Forty-fifth Legislature, which convened in January 1937, for additional revenue. During the depression the legislature had reduced the state's general fund by allocating to the public schools more than the constitutional minimum of one-fourth of the occupation taxes. The colleges and almost all other state institutions needed more money. The number of mental patients in the state's hospitals was increasing by five hundred a year; and a less liberal pardon policy raised the prison population during Allred's first term from 5,800 to 7,000. Expenditures for the centennial celebration, interest and principal payments on relief bonds, increased aid to rural schools, the partial restoration of predepression salaries, and the payment of old age pensions called for more revenue. The voters had, moreover, authorized workmen's compensation for state employees, had planned a teacher retirement fund, and, apparently, would soon authorize the state to care for needy blind and for dependent children.

Allred proposed to raise most of the additional revenue by an increase in all the taxes on oil, gas, and sulphur. The legislature refused to increase taxes; in keeping with the spirit of the times, it showed a weakness for imposing new burdens on the general revenue fund without providing additional income. In appropriating it was as bold as a lion; in taxing, timid as a lamb.

The return of legalized liquor brought problems equally as difficult as those of the prohibition period. When the voters in August 1935 repealed the state prohibition amendment they rejected a plan for state liquor dispensaries. Shortly thereafter the legislature provided for taxing and licensing dealers, prohibited the sale of heavy liquors by the drink, provided for local option elections, and placed the administration of the traffic under a liquor control board. Soon there were complaints of violations by dealers, especially of the provision of sale by drink; and subsequently each legislature has had to deal with the question in one or more of its phases. The status of liquor in counties and cities which were dry at the time that state prohibition was enacted in 1919 was not affected by the repeal of the amendment, and local option again became an issue in many communities. Revenue from the sale of liquor, about $6,000,000 a year, was of substantial aid in paying social security obligations.

Pursuant to a mandate of the voters in a constitutional amendment of 1932, Texas celebrated in 1936 the 100th anniversary of her independence. The state appropriated $3,000,000 for the use of the centennial commission and the United States government matched it with an equal amount. The WPA also made contributions. The public funds were divided between the main exposition at Dallas and various other historical and commemorative projects in different communities. A considerable part of the money was spent in erecting numerous monuments to historical personages and placing markers at historic sites.

In the Texas gubernatorial race of 1938, politics and showmanship combined to produce one of the most spectacular campaigns in history. Among the thirteen candidates were such veteran campaigners as Attorney General William McCraw, Railroad Commissioner Ernest O. Thompson, and Tom F. Hunter. About a month before the election it became evident that W. Lee O'Daniel of Fort Worth was reaching more people than all other candidates combined. He applied to the race for governor the same tactics he had used in selling flour by radio: popular music interspersed with comments and an occasional short, informal speech. Whether it was the promise of a businesslike administration, the castigation of professional politicians, the music, the candidate's homely philosophy, or the promise of pensions that drew the votes has not been determined; it is only known that for the first time since the Texas primary law was adopted did a candidate for governor, making his first race, poll more than half of the votes.

Governor O'Daniel's promise to give a pension to every old person made pensions the chief issue of his administration. After the election the campaign promise was pared down to a proposal to give only to needy persons past 65 years of age an amount sufficient to raise their income to 30 dollars a month. Likewise, the governor soon abandoned the hope, often expressed to the voters, that the new taxes would not be necessary, and proposed to the legislature that an enlarged pension program be financed by a tax of 1.6 percent on all transactions. The lawmakers dubbed the proposal a sales tax (anathema in Texas at that time) and attacked it bitterly. The affair widened the breach already existing between the governor and the legislature. The legislature liberalized pensions but failed to provide additional revenue and the problem became even more vexing. In spite of vetoes of items aggregating more than $5,000,000 the deficit in the general fund continued to increase.

Six candidates challenged O'Daniel's bid for reelection in 1940. Although they attacked his record and his plan for raising revenue, his opponents did not directly attack his proposal for more liberal pensions. Texas had developed a "share the wealth" movement of its own, and the candidates did not dare to resist it. O'Daniel was renominated by an overwhelming vote and reelected in November, 1940.

Like the lawmaking bodies that had preceded it for a decade, the Forty-seventh Legislature, which convened in January 1941, found that the problem of taxation was its chief worry. It could not, like its predecessors, take up the question, debate it, and drop it. The general fund, which supplied most of the higher educational, eleemosynary, judicial, and administrative agencies, showed a deficit of $25,000,000. There were predictions that Texas would be deprived of all federal pension money unless it raised more funds to meet the increasing demand of its own liberal pension laws. The teacher retirement payments had not been matched by the state; the electors demanded that it care for its destitute children and the blind. After extended debate there was passed and given executive approval an omnibus tax bill calculated to bring $22,000,000 additional revenue annually. Approximately one half of the amount was to come from increased taxes on the production of oil and gas and the remainder from a variety of sources. This measure doubled the old age pension income but did not quiet the agitation over pensions.

When a seat in the United States Senate was made vacant by the death of Morris Sheppard, in 1941 the governor appointed as his successor, until an election could be held, Andrew Jackson Houston, the eighty-seven year old son of the hero of the Battle of San Jacinto, who was also once a member of the United States Senate. Houston did not live to complete his short appointive term. Meanwhile, several candidates entered the race, one of the last being the governor himself. Although he was elected, his prestige was seriously impaired, for he defeated by only a few hundred votes Congressman Lyndon B. Johnson, an "old friend" of President Roosevelt's. Again, in the Democratic primaries of 1942 he defeated ex-Governors Dan Moody and James V. Allred, after a hard-fought campaign in which it was charged that O'Daniel had failed to support adequately President Roosevelt's defense and war policies.

Lieutenant Governor Coke R. Stevenson, who twice had been elected speaker of the house and twice elected lieutenant governor, was inaugurated governor in August 1941. In September the legislature was convened for the purpose of reallocating state highway funds, the first called session since September 1937. The one-cent tax on the retailing of gasoline was now more than sufficient to pay the interest and sinking fund obligations of the county road bonds which had been assumed by the state. Under an act of this special session, the state continued to meet the payment of interest and sinking funds on such county bonds as had been voted before January 1, 1939. The surplus that remained was to be divided equally between the state highway fund and the counties of the state. The counties thus were provided with additional revenue for constructing lateral roads.

During the 1930's the influence of Texans in the national government became greater than ever before. John Nance Garner, who had served continuously in the House of Representatives since first he took the oath of office before Speaker Joe Cannon in 1903, was elected speaker in 1931. In the year following he was nominated and elected vice-president, and was reelected in 1936. In presiding over the Senate his great personal influence and broad acquaintance with legislative tactics were brought to bear on most of the measures that made up the New Deal. A movement was launched to nominate him for President in 1940, but the movement declined as it became increasingly evident that President Roosevelt would again accept the nomination.

Another influential Texan in Washington was Jesse Jones of Houston, chairman of the RFC from 1933 to 1939. In 1939 he was appointed administrator of the powerful Federal Loan Agency and in 1940 was appointed Secretary of Commerce. In 1933 Texans held the chairmanships of six major committees in the House of Representatives. They were: Marvin Jones, Agriculture; Sam Rayburn, Interstate and Foreign Commerce; Hatton W. Sumners, Judiciary; Fritz G. Lanham, Public Buildings and Grounds; J. J. Mansfield, Rivers and Harbors; and James P. Buchanan, Appropriations.

For the first time since Joseph D. Sayers held the post before the turn of the century, a Texan was chairman of the powerful Committee on Appropriations. Rayburn became majority leader and later speaker. Morris Sheppard succeeded his father, John L. Sheppard, in the House of Representatives in 1902, and when death ended his services in 1941 he had fulfilled one of the longest careers in the history of Congress. Since 1913 he had been a Senator. He is best remembered for his persistent championing of the cause of national prohibition; but his most enduring service was in promoting President Roosevelt's New Deal in the Senate. He was, furthermore, chairman of the Committee on Military Affairs and was recognized as the foremost authority in Congress on military needs. Senator Tom Connally, chairman of the Committee on Foreign Relations, was a staunch spokesman for the administration in the enactment of the gigantic defense program and the war measures of the 1940's.

Selected Bibliography

The best accounts of public affairs in Texas during the depression years are those of S.S. McKay in writings previously cited. The *Dallas News* and the *Texas Weekly* (Dallas), a lively sheet edited for some years by Peter Molyneau, are most useful. See also S.A. MacCorkle, "The Pardoning Power in Texas," *Southwestern Social Science Quarterly*, XV, 218–228; Carl M. Rosenquist, "Some Special Problems of Social Security in Texas," *ibid.*, XVII, 274–280.

The annual reports of the Texas Department of Public Welfare give the most complete accounts of the aid given by the state to certain classes of citizens. The *Annual Report* for 1949 is especially useful for the period preceding that date. On federal aid during the depression years, see E.A. Williams, *Federal Aid for Relief* (New York, 1939). On Texas relief, see Booth Mooney, "925,000 Texans Getting Government Aid," *Texas Weekly*, November 11, 1939, pp. 6–7.

A satisfactory review of social security is given in *Social Security Act: its First Twenty-five Years*, reprinted from the Social Security *Bulletin*, August 1960, by the Social Security Administration, United States Department of Health, Education, and Welfare. For the impact of medical insurance on the program, see "Social Security—Past, Present, Future," *Newsweek*, April 12, 1965, pp. 88–90. For unemployment compensation, see Carey C. Thompson, "Unemployment in Texas," *Southwestern Social Science Quarterly*, XXXV, 93–106.

For Texans in Washington see Bascom Timmons, *Jesse H. Jones* (New York, 1956) and *Garner of Texas* (New York, 1948); C.D. Dorough, *Mr. Sam, A Biography of Samuel T. Rayburn* (New York, 1962).

18

INDUSTRIALIZATION CONTINUES: MANUFACTURING, MINING, AND TRANSPORTATION

Through its history far into the twentieth century, Texas was notable both for its vast natural resources and for its comparatively small industrial output. Since the time of Stephen F. Austin its leaders had decried the lack of industries and urged that more labor and capital be directed toward the processing of raw materials and the manufacture of goods. A certain amount of manufacturing, however, was carried on from the beginning. The census of 1850 revealed an industrial output worth $1,000,000. Each decennial census thereafter showed an increase, and a most extraordinary gain was made between 1880 and 1890. The census of 1900 gave the value at $92,894,433.

MANUFACTURING

The twentieth century brought even greater interests in manufacturing, and various organizations worked ardently to stimulate its growth—the Federated Commercial Clubs of Texas, the Texas Commercial Secretaries Association, the Texas Industrial Congress organized in 1910, and later the Texas Manufacturers Association. After the first World War, these organizations were joined by three influential regional chambers of commerce; that for West Texas, which came into existence in 1919, another for East Texas, and still another for South Texas organized soon thereafter. Besides these general agencies, the chamber of commerce of every town and city was on the alert to secure new industries.

Growth was slow but steady. The value added to goods by manufacturers in 1909 was about $95,000,000 and during the following decade it tripled. There was no gain of consequence in the depression decade preceding 1940; but the second World War and the years that followed brought stupendous increases, so that the estimate for 1967 exceeded ten billion dollars.

Lumbering, one of Texas' oldest industries, continued near mid century to be of major importance. During most years after 1939 production equalled or exceeded a billion board feet per year and the growing of timber was offsetting the depletion of forests through lumbering.

In addition to lumber, Texas forests in recent years have produced quantities of timber for crossties, poles, piling, pulpwood, and other uses. By 1965 pulpwood alone aggregated one and two-thirds million cords, a third of which was in the form of chips saved from sawmill operations. More than half the lumber produced was being used in Texas and the 1,800 plants using wood were employing some 40,000 persons.

An important industry associated with forests is the manufacture of paper. At Orange in 1911 Edward H. Mayo achieved the distinction, as far as is known, of being the first person to make sulphate paper out of yellow pine, a discovery that made possible the development of a large industry. In 1937 the Champion Paper and Fibre Company established a large pulp mill near Houston and three years later extended its operations. This plant soon began to supply paper for *Life* magazine. Meanwhile the Southland Paper Mills began to produce newsprint near Lufkin and later built a plant in Harris County. In 1967 at least five mills were producing paper in Texas and two additional ones were under construction. The value added by the manufacture of paper and paper products exceeded $150,000,000.

Industries related to agriculture, often initiated in the nineteenth century, have expanded considerably in recent years. Cattle feeding increased greatly after 1950; the 278 lots operating in 1967 had capacity for a million head. Meanwhile, with the decline in the importance of terminal markets and the establishment of auction markets in dozens of communities, the marketing of livestock underwent a great change. Likewise meat packing was decentralized; there were 37 federally-inspected plants in 1965. The people employed in manufacturing or processing food and related products exceeded 75,000, making it the leading industry in respect to the number of workers used. An important business is that of cottonseed processing, which turns out quantities of oil used in manufactured products and cake for cattle feed. Textile manu-

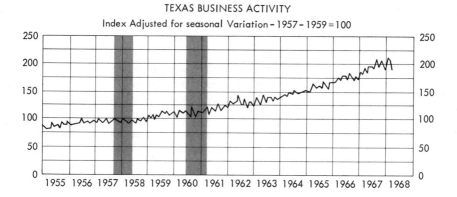

TEXAS BUSINESS ACTIVITY
Index Adjusted for seasonal Variation - 1957 - 1959 = 100

In spite of short periods of reversal, the trend of Texas business activity was consistently upward from 1955 to 1968. A chart for the period of 1940–55 would show substantially the same trend. Since 1940 Texas has known the longest era of unbroken prosperity in its history. (Shaded areas indicate periods of decline of total business activity in the United States. This graph is based on bank debits reported by the Federal Reserve Bank of Dallas and adjusted for seasonal variation and changes in the price level by the Bureau of Business Research.) (Courtesy of *Texas Business Review*)

facturing likewise has grown in recent years, with plants in 18 communities employing some 4,600 people.

The wealth of materials in Texas for certain types of manufacturing is not equalled elsewhere. There are refinery gases, yielding butylenes and other petrochemicals; petroleum, supplying benzol and ethylene; natural gas, from which come many products, among them the carbon black essential in rubber making; sulphur for vulcanizing; and salt, lime, and clays.

Even during the depression years the chemical industry in Texas had thrived. Chemical production went with the oil and gas industry hand and glove. Such operations as acidizing wells, gas and oil refining, the making of lubricating oils and of synthetic rubber called for quantities of chemicals. The production of alkalies in Louisiana and Texas in the 1930's was brought about because of the abundance of raw materials and the development of alkali-consuming industries such as rayon, cellulose, acetate, pulp and paper, aluminum, soap, glass, and oil refining. Alkali plants in turn brought a rising demand for chlorine and metallic sodium. The Southern Alkali Corporation opened an ammonia-soda plant at Corpus Christi in 1934, producing heavy alkalies, soda ash, caustic soda, and later chlorine. World War II stimulated the demands for its products.

The making of elastomers, including synthetic rubber, has become an industry of first magnitude. The Monsanto Chemical Works at Texas City, built for the purpose of producing, among other commodities, styrene, toluene, and other chemicals for synthetic rubber manufacture, was destroyed by the explosion of a chemical laden ship in the harbor April 16, 1947. The explosion, one of the major disasters that Texas has known, killed 512 people. The plant was rebuilt with greater capacity.

The chemical industry in Texas expanded rapidly during the 1960's. An authority has stated that there was hardly a week during 1965 when some chemical company failed to announce a new Texas plant or a multimillion dollar expansion of one already in place. The value of chemical plants along the Gulf Coast in 1967 was estimated at five billion dollars. At that time Texas ranked second in the nation in values added by the manufacture of chemicals.

The smelting of metal at El Paso had been carried on since 1883; and in the decade and a half following 1939, an impressive volume of metal production was developed in Texas. At El Paso the Phelps-Dodge Corporation refined 30 percent of all copper refined in the United States. The Dow Company plant at Freeport, established in 1940 for the manufacture of magnesium and some 60 to 70 other products from sea water, was enlarged from time to time by purchasing government owned factories and building new ones.

The Aluminum Company of America (Alcoa) began production in Texas with a plant at Point Comfort, Lavaca Bay, and later established a huge plant at Rockdale, Milam County, using the abundant lignite deposits there as fuel. Among other products it produced powdered aluminum for rocket fuel. At Gregory, near Corpus Christi, the Reynolds Company established an $80,000,000 aluminum plant. During and after World War II steel production and the making of steel products increased substantially, represented by Lone Star Steel (merged with Philadelphia and Reading), United States Steel, Sheffield, and LeTourneau Steel Company. One outgrowth of local steel production was the development of an industry manufacturing equipment for the oil industry. Centered in the Houston area, it is the world's largest, employing some 45,000 men.

Stimulated by war, the aircraft industry in Texas grew at a speed truly remarkable, and then, after the wars ceased, gave promise of retaining much of its wartime stature. The industry centered in the Dallas and Fort Worth section. North American Aviation Company located a large plant at Grand Prairie which began to turn out the AT-6 (the "Texan") plane in 1941. The plant was completed, employment reached 30,000, and the Mustang P-51 and the B-24 Liberator were produced. In 1942 the Consolidated Vultee Aircraft Corporation (Convair) was opened near Fort Worth. Before the end of World War II it was employing over 30,000 people and had produced over 3,000 Liberator B-24's. The plant continued with reduced force after World War II, expanded production during the Korean War, and in 1955 went into the production of supersonic bombers.

The Texas Engineering and Manufacturing Aircraft Company (Temco) entered Grand Prairie following the withdrawal of North American and soon had additional plants in Garland and Greenville. Chance-Vought, a gigantic airplane manufacturing company, moved to Grand Prairie in 1948 from Stratford, Connecticut, and specialized in the production of military aircraft. In 1951 Bell Aircraft moved its helicopter division from Buffalo, New York, to Hurst and continued to produce helicopters.

Other industries that added substantially to the wealth of Texas in the era following World War II were automobile assembling; clothing manufacture; making containers from paper, wood, glass, plastics, and metal; the production of electronic navigation and guidance systems; radar and communication equipment; arms and munitions parts; and the refining of crude oil and manufacture of various materials made from it.

During the second third of the twentieth century, with values added aggregating five billion dollars, manufacturing affected Texas immeasurably. It was the most important feature in making Houston the largest city in the South; it brought many thousands of people to the Houston, Galveston, Beaumont, Port Arthur Complex. It made the Dallas and Fort Worth vicinity almost solidly metropolitan. Between 1940 and 1960 it was a leading factor in more than doubling the population of San Antonio, El Paso, Corpus Christi, Amarillo, Lubbock, and Wichita Falls.

MINING AND OIL PRODUCTION

With its quantities of petroleum, natural gas, natural gas liquids, cement, sulphur, and a score of other materials, Texas has led all states in recent years in the value of its mineral products. The production of sulphur was begun at Freeport as early as 1912 and has grown to be a hundred million dollar business. Oil, discovered at Nacogdoches in 1867 and big business in Texas after the field discovered at Spindletop in 1901, has become more and more important with each decade.

With Texas leading the petroleum-producing states of the nation after 1928, oil production generally edged upward until 1937. Production was increased greatly in the 1930's through the discovery of the East Texas field, the most sensational oil field in history, by Columbus Marion ("Dad") Joiner, a veteran wildcatter. Subsequent drilling proved that the field was 42 miles long and from four to eight miles wide, and that it included approximately 200 square miles of territory, every acre of which produced oil. Although there were numbers of other discoveries after 1930, they were not so sensational. The finding of the Canyon Reef, in the Pennsylvania formation in Scurry County in 1948, brought on a drilling program that revealed some 70 new fields in West Texas in the three years following. The Neches Field in Anderson and Cherokee counties and a number of fields in Grayson County were outstanding developments of the 1950's.

Texas crude oil production reached the billion barrels per year mark in 1951, and thereafter through 1967 the annual output did not miss that mark greatly. In 1966 the state was producing a little more than a third of the nation's oil. The world output of oil had grown larger, however, so that Texas was producing only about nine percent of it.

No major fields had been discovered in Texas after 1960, and the estimated oil reserves tended to decline. Perhaps the most promising area for future development is the offshore fields along the Texas coast. Texas' claims to these offshore oil fields extends out only about ten and a half miles, however. In 1968, production was being sustained in many inland fields by the practice of secondary recovery in which the operators put water or gas into oil formations to increase the output.

The large exportation of gas from the state began with the construction of a high-pressure pipeline to Denver in 1926. Other lines were built to the larger cities of the Mississippi Valley until the depression of the 1930's sharply reduced the practice. The laying of lines was revived during World War II and after the war the business grew apace. In 1966 Texas produced nearly seven trillion cubic feet of gas, a substantial part of which was piped beyond state lines to at least three-fourths of the states and Mexico. Liquids, valued at more than half a billion dollars, were taken from the gas by scores of plants at different points in the state. In 1963 products refined in Texas began flowing from Gulf Coast plants to eastern seaboard markets through what an authority has pronounced the "world's largest privately financed project—the 1,600-mile Colonial Pipeline, 36 inches in diameter, with a capacity of 600,000 barrels a day."

Oil refining, a major industry by the 1920's, with the advent of cracking has become a chemical process. Although a few small refineries continued to operate, by 1960 the industry in the main had been concentrated along the Houston ship channel and near Port Arthur and Beaumont, fed by a network of pipelines from the different fields of the Southwest. In 1966 about 85 percent of the Texas oil output of a billion barrels annually was being refined in the state.

Of all Texas industries, oil and the business associated with it have been most spectacular. It was the foundation for the industries that created the great industrial complex along the Gulf Coast. More than any other factor it made cities of such towns at Tyler, Wichita Falls, Abilene, San Angelo, Amarillo, Lubbock, Midland, and Odessa. It raised the population of Winkler County from 81 in 1920 to 5,784 ten years later, and it quadrupled the population of Gregg County in the East

Mineral-based plants have led Texas industrial development for many years. The greatest concentration is along the Gulf Coast where more than five billion dollars is invested in petrochemical manufacturing (right). The investment in refining equipment (below) is also large: 90% of the crude oil recovered in Texas is processed in refineries in this area. (Texas Highway Department)

Texas oil field between 1930 and 1940. Its benefits were widespread. Ranchers, farmers, and other royalty owners received annually an aggregate of several hundred million dollars from lease bonuses, rentals, and royalties. In the middle 1960's oil in Texas was creating an income of four billion a year and paying more than a fifth of state taxes.

The relative position of the chief source of income in Texas is set forth in the following data for the years 1955, 1963, and 1965. It will be observed that the farm income showed a substantial increase, the income from minerals increased only slightly, and that from manufacturing grew about 40 percent in a period of six years.

	1957	1965
Cash farm income including government payments	$1,835,958,000	$2,669,118,000
Minerals	4,484,539,000	4,717,036,000
Manufactures (values added)	5,039,313,000	7,086,283,000 (1963)

TELEGRAPH, TELEPHONE, AND ELECTRIC POWER

The oldest of the agencies providing instantaneous communications is the telegraph. It is interesting to note in passing that Samuel F. B. Morse offered to the Republic of Texas in 1838 his invention of the electric telegraph. Texas did not take any steps to accept the offer, however, and Morse withdrew it some 22 years later. Meanwhile in 1854 the state had chartered the Texas and Red River Telegraph Company, which offered service from New Orleans to Marshall and thence to Galveston.

Telephone use in Texas has grown remarkably since World War II. It took the Southwestern Bell Telephone Company, the largest in the state, 69 years to reach its millionth installment. Just seven and one-half years later it installed its two millionth telephone, and by January 1, 1967, it had 3,857,992 instruments in service.

In the twentieth century lines were built to many rural homes and the era of the party line, a great social agency, was begun. Rural telephone service declined in later years, but was revived through cooperatives after World War II, so that by 1960 more than half of Texas farms had telephones. At the beginning of 1967, 136 telephone companies were operating 4,786,956 telephones in Texas, about 80 percent of them being a part of the Bell system.

The growth of the electric light and power industry during the last quarter century has been phenomenal. At the beginning of 1967 the 12 investor-owned electric utility companies had a combined investment of about four billion dollars. Indicative of the rapid growth of the business is that their generating capacity had increased fivefold since 1952. Rural electrification made rapid headway, largely through credit supplied by the Federal Rural Electrification Administration. As of October 1966, 97 percent of Texas farms had electricity, supplied principally by 76 electric distribution cooperatives.

LATER PHASES OF RAILROAD CONSTRUCTION

In a preceding chapter an account of Texas railroads during the era of their founding was given. It was stated that by 1890 railroad lines in the state totaled more than 8,000 miles, and that by the close of the century the total was nearly 10,000 miles. Steady building went on during the first and second decades of the new century, until by 1920 the total mileage, excluding yard, track, and sidings, was 16,000. Railroad building in the twentieth century has consisted mainly of extension of trunk lines and the building of feeder roads. A few projects of major proportions have been carried on, however; for example, the Kansas City, Mexico, and Orient was completed by 1913 from Wichita, Kansas, to Alpine, and the extension of the Gulf, Colorado, and Santa Fé from Coleman to Lubbock was added in 1911. The last revival of railroad building was in 1925, when the Southern Pacific built into the lower Rio Grande valley and the Santa Fé, Rock Island, and Fort Worth and Denver roads did some building in the South Plains. These developments brought competitive railroad service to the two last great Texas regions where it had not prevailed before.

Texas railroad mileage reached a peak of 17,000 miles in 1932 but by 1965, it had shrunk almost two thousand miles and trackage was being abandoned each year. The most drastic change in railroad history was during the 1960's when the railroads ended passenger train service except that between large cities. Bus and air travel had appropriated so much of the passenger business that the railroads found the operation of passenger trains brought losses that they could not continue to bear.

There has been a great deal of consolidation of railroad lines in recent years so that six extensive systems control the greater part of Texas mileage; the Burlington, the Katy, the Southern Pacific, the Missouri-Pacific (with its affiliate, the Texas and Pacific), the Rock Island, and the Santa Fé.

The early twentieth century also witnessed the building of a number of electric interurban railroads, offering rapid passenger transportation between cities. The electric railroads could not, however, compete with motor busses which came into use during the 1920's and ran over smooth, broad highways provided at public expense.

Serving both to feed and to compete with railways are the bus and truck lines of Texas. Public transportation by motor vehicles on highways had reached the big business stage by 1927, when motor busses were placed under the supervision of the state railway commission. This act, said to have been a pioneer measure among the states of the Union, was followed by a law extending control of the commission over truck lines. The lean depression years served to stimulate truck and bus transportation and when the war years brought better economic conditions they shared them. Far more people were riding busses than trains in the 1950's. After reaching a maximum of over 25 million passengers in 1944, the passenger business of the railroads dropped to 4,374,915 persons in 1954. In 1952, the busses in Texas transported 37,834,608 persons. Data for more recent years are not available, but we have seen that the competition of the busses has almost put the railroads out of the passenger train business. Passenger busses, running on schedules, link every town and city in the state. In 1966, with 1,116,548 trucks registered, Texas ranked second in the nation, and trucks evidently carried a substantial part of Texas freight. Dependent entirely on trucks for shipping were 2,608 communities, 39 of them county seats.

THE HIGHWAY SYSTEM

Since earliest times the vastness of Texas has contributed to its transportation difficulties. Even at present the greater part of its territory is so thinly settled that the per capita cost of its roads is very high. Its public roads date from the colonial era, but its highway system is distinctly a product of the twentieth century. Highway improvement is the result of the use of automobiles and has been in keeping with the number of motor vehicles owned by Texans. A few automobiles were used in Texas cities as early as 1900. By 1905 one met them occasionally on country roads, where the malodorous, noisy contraptions frightened teams and caused many a runaway and wreck. An act of 1907 limited their speed to 18 miles per hour and required that a machine stop on meeting a horsedrawn conveyance (if the driver signaled) and wait until the conveyance had passed. This act of 1907 required also that automobiles be registered in the county where the owner resided. Ten years later another law provided for the creation of the state highway department and required that all motor vehicles be registered with it. That year registration totaled almost 200,000. With few exceptions the number has increased annually until for 1966 it was estimated at 6,435,500, about 14 percent being commercial vehicles.

The legislative history of the Texas highway system can be outlined in five important steps: (1) the constitutional amendment of 1904 and the laws of 1907 and 1909 which authorized a county or its subdivisions to vote bonds for road construction; (2) the act of 1917 which created the state highway commission; (3) the act of 1925 which gave the state control of the highway system; (4) the assumption by the state in 1932 of the interest and sinking fund obligations on bonds previously voted for state highway improvement by civil subdivisions; and (5) the adoption of a policy in July of that year which required that the state thereafter build and maintain the state highway system without calling on the counties for the cost.

Except for the fact that it was the act of the federal government rather than of the state, the interstate highway system, started in 1944, might make a sixth step. It is necessary to give some explanation of these several developments.

Until 1907 the public roads were built and maintained by community or county taxation and the personal service of the men between the ages of 18 and 45 who chanced to live along them; there was no provision for issuing road bonds. Laws enacted in 1907 under authority of a constitutional amendment adopted in 1904 authorized a county or a road district to vote bonds for highway construction. Thus, improved roads were purely local projects. Counties and their subdivisions could build them; the state could not, for it had no income for that purpose and it could not issue bonds. After 1907, however, improvement was rapid. Good roads associations were formed, and by 1912 approximately one-fourth of the 130,000 miles of road in the state was graded and more than 5,000 miles surfaced. Split-log drags were in common use, and were often applied without expense to the communities by farmers living along the road. By 1914 the counties all told were spending $5,000,000 a year on roads, in addition to funds derived from bonds.

In 1916 Congress began to aid in road construction, and the Texas motor registration law, passed the next year, provided the state with a small road fund. The initiative in road building still lay with the county or community, however, and not with the agencies in Austin or in Washington.

The idea behind federal road appropriations was to bring about a national system of highways made up of "designated" roads in the several states. The states should build the roads, aided by funds distributed by the United States Bureau of Public Roads. To share in these federal funds a state must have a highway department. Texas, accordingly, created one by the act of 1917.

Stimulated by state and federal aid, the counties increased their bond issue and much mileage was constructed. A great defect of the program, however, was that backward or thinly settled counties failed to build roads, with the results that improved stretches were broken by gaps of unimproved mileage. In 1923 Governor Neff stated that in the whole state there was hardly to be found 100 miles of continuous good roads. For the traveler in Texas, the smooth path of pavement led but to the mudhole. Texas had no highway system worthy of the name.

An act of Congress in 1921 made necessary a radical change in the control of the state highway system. It provided that a state might designate not in excess of seven percent of its road mileage to benefit from federal aid, and that the designated mileage must be under the exclusive control of a state agency in matters of design, construction, and maintenance. There were at that time about 182,816 miles of public roads in Texas, and the seven percent designated for federal aid amounted to 12,797 miles. By acts in 1923 and 1925 the Texas Highway Commission was reorganized and its power strengthened. The commission designated about 18,000 miles of Texas highways to be placed under complete state control. This designated mileage making up the state highway system has been increased from time to time. On January 1, 1967, there were 25,583 miles of primary highways and some 36,000 miles of farm-to-market and ranch-to-market road.

Moody's administration (1927–1931) was characterized by great progress in road construction. Gibb Gilcrist, an efficient state highway engineer, worked under the direction of a commission of able men composed of R. S. Sterling of Houston, Cone Johnson of Tyler, and W. R. Ely of Abilene.

The tax on the sale of gasoline was raised by stages to five cents per gallon, three-fourths of which went to highways and one-fourth, by constitutional requirement, to the schools. For a period the policy that was followed called for building roads by contributions, one-third each by the local, state, and federal governments, or one-half each from local and state sources in cases where the road had not received federal designation.

About 1928 it was realized that under such a program the state could never close the unimproved gaps in cardinal highways. Sentiment gained headway in favor of the state's shouldering all the burden of highway construction, leaving the counties free to use their funds for the improvement of local roads. Beginning with July 1932, the highway commission voted that counties no longer would be required to make contributions toward the construction and maintenance of state highways. Their funds henceforth were to be spent on local roads; the highway system at last had become exclusively a state project. Later this policy was modified to the extent of requiring that the local agency furnish the right of way, or a substantial part of its cost. A federal policy of matching funds for farm-to-market roads resulted in the rapid building that was taking paved highways to the great majority of the state's rural communities. By the mid twentieth century Texas had an excellent highway system and it was a gigantic business. The annual budget of the State Department of Highways in 1966 was $470,946,064, about 40 percent of which was derived from federal funds. Texas shared in the Federal Interstate Highway System, authorized by Congress in 1944, to the extent of some three thousand miles, more than half of which had been completed by 1969.

TEXAS PORTS

A great stimulus to commerce during this century has been the development of a system of deep-water ports. Because the rivers of the state are shallow and bars shut in the estuaries along the 375 miles of coastline, its natural ports were poor. We have seen that even in the early years, when light sailing craft and small steamers prevailed, the ports were not adequate. During the period of the Republic and early statehood, Houston, at the head of navigation on Buffalo Bayou, and Galveston were the leading ports. Southeast Texas shipped much cotton, lumber, beef, and tobacco through Sabine Pass. Before the building of railroads the western settlements were served by Port Lavaca, Indianola, Matagorda, Texana, and Corpus Christi. The thin line of settlements along the lower Rio Grande found an outlet through Brownsville and Brazos Santiago. North Texas was served by Jefferson and to a lesser extent by Clarksville. As a shipping point Jefferson was second only to Galveston. Small steamers loaded with cotton, wheat, hides, and lumber managed to thread their way through Big Cypress across Caddo Lake and down the Red River to New Orleans. On their return, the boats brought goods for distribution in communities as far west as Dallas, Fort Worth, and Weatherford. With the building of the railroads in the early 1870's, these communities secured a more rapid and more direct outlet and, in spite of the heroic fight by Jefferson businessmen to hold their trade, the town declined. The coming of railroads explains in part also the rise on the Gulf Coast of new ports such as Beaumont.

With the increase in the draft of boats and the greater demands for safety, the natural ports of Texas became more and more inadequate. The federal government, joined in later years by local navigation districts, spent large sums of money on Texas harbors. As early as 1883 a project was begun to deepen the channel of Galveston Port. Improvements were made from time to time, including a system of jetties, extending to sea about eight miles. By the early twentieth century a 25 foot channel had been provided and by about 1927 it had been increased to 35 feet. For many years Galveston ranked second only to New York in exports and was the greatest cotton-shipping source in the world. By 1910 the Sabine and Neches system and the ports at Freeport, Port Aransas, and Houston had been improved.

In the annals of man-made ports no story is more impressive than that of Houston, the city to which men brought the sea. A channel eighteen and one-half feet deep was made possible by a Congressional appropriation in 1899, but it could not be used by oceangoing vessels. About 1908 its citizens inaugurated a movement to secure a deepwater channel. A few years later, funds supplied by the Harris County Navigation District matched a federal appropriation, and improvement was begun in earnest. By 1925, $10,600,000 of federal money and local funds to an amount one-third as great had been spent to complete the entire channel, 55 miles from the Houston harbor to the outer bar, 30 feet in depth. Thereafter the increase in the tonnage of the port was phenomenal, but even the improved channel was not deep enough. In 1935 a project was launched to make it from 34 to 36 feet deep.

Houston has led the ports of Texas both in imports and exports and has become the second or third port in the nation. In 1965, 13 major ports accounted for about 95 percent of the total domestic and foreign commerce of Texas, which amounted to 190,888,300 tons. About one-third of this was handled by the Port of Houston, with Beaumont, Port Arthur, Corpus Christi, and Texas City ranking high. Among the more important foreign exports were basic chemicals, oil products, steel products, sulphur, cotton, grain sorghums, rice, and wheat. Some important imports from abroad were petroleum, inedible molasses, coffee, and tropical fruits. Commerce along the Texas Gulf coast has been greatly facilitated by the completion of the Gulf Intercoastal Canal from the Sabine River to the Rio Grande, with connections eastward to Apalachee Bay, Florida.

ARMED FORCES ESTABLISHMENTS

Since the beginning of statehood, except for the era of the Confederacy, Texas has had a substantial share of the United States Army within its borders. At times during the 1850's more than ten percent of all federal troops were stationed in Texas. San Antonio became a military center in 1849 when the first United States Army garrison arrived there and restored the ruined Alamo Mission. Soon the city was headquarters for the Eighth Military District. Fort Sam Houston was established in the 1870's and enlarged from time to time. In recent years it has housed headquarters for the Fourth United States Army. Many famous soldiers have served there, among them Theodore Roosevelt, John J. Pershing, and Dwight D. Eisenhower.

Fort Bliss, another old renowned military center, located in El Paso, is the second largest post maintained by the United States Army. In 1967 one of the segments of its broad program was the training of 5,000 missilemen per month in the use of surface-to-air Nike and Hawk missiles. Forty thousand military and 4,800 civilians maintain it. Nearby is William Beaumont General Hospital maintained by the army, visited by 400,000 outpatients a year.

Fort Hood, in Central Texas, opened as Camp Hood in 1942; it is home for the largest concentration of armor in the free world. Thirty-five thousand soldiers are maintained there. Fort Wolters, which began as Camp Wolters in 1941, is best known as a United States Army Primary

Helicopter Center, where several thousand men are maintained in training. The Red River Army Depot, near Texarkana, established in 1941 is a gigantic base for army supplies. Besides a military contingent of considerable size there are some 6,200 civil service employees.

The Navy, too, has establishments. The state's share of the "mothball fleet" is maintained at the Inactive Ships Maintenance Facility at Orange, and there are naval air training installations at Corpus Christi, Beeville, and Kingsville.

AVIATION

Climate and topography combine in Texas to create almost ideal flying conditions, and the state has witnessed much pioneering activity in the field of aeronautics. It was on March 3, 1910, that people stood with mouths agape as Otto Brodie flew a plane over the Dallas Fair Park. Five years later, Lester Miller, experienced as an exhibition flier, and his partner, W. A. Southworth, began to build airplanes in Dallas, and soon turned out a number of the pusher biplane type. In 1916, under authority of a permit from the Postmaster General, they carried a load of mail from Dallas to Fort Worth.

During the first World War the government centered its pilot training in Texas, and Kelly Field, near San Antonio, became the nation's training camp for pilots. Thereafter a large percentage of the airmen of the armed forces received instruction in this state. In 1930 Randolph Field, "the West Point of the Air," was completed near San Antonio at a cost of $11,000,000 and is one of the greatest aviation centers in the world. Rivaling it in size and importance is the training field for naval aviators at Corpus Christi, completed in 1941 at a cost of $44,000,000.

During World War II the armed forces of the nation made Texas the greatest training region for airmen on earth. Randolph Field, Kelley Field, and Brooks Field, all near San Antonio, were enlarged; Ellington Field, near Houston, was rebuilt; and additional air fields were established at Wichita Falls, San Angelo, Lubbock, Midland, San Marcos, Amarillo, and other cities. National headquarters of the American Air Force Training Command was in Fort Worth, a command which at peak strength in January 1944 had more than a million men and women under its jurisdiction. From January 1, 1942 to May 1, 1944, over 200,000 airmen were trained in Texas, 45,000 of them pilots, over 12,000 bombardiers, and about the same number navigators. There were more than 50 air fields and stations in the state.

After World War II Texas continued to be headquarters for airmen. San Antonio, with its several bases, and Carswell Field at Fort Worth were among the largest in the country. A school of aviation medicine was established at Randolph Field.

In 1967 there were not less than 14 air force bases in Texas, including such diverse establishments as Carswell (Fort Worth) and Dyess (Abilene), heavy bomber and tanker bases; Brooks (San Antonio), medical research and education; Goodfellow (San Angelo), security service; Lackland (San Antonio), military training and Women's Air Force training; and Reese (Lubbock), undergraduate pilot training.

In the 1960's a new dimension was added to the Texas share in defense and scientific attainment. The National Aeronautics and Space Administration established a Manned Spacecraft Center on Galveston Bay, in the vicinity of Houston. From this center much of the coordination of the nation-wide field work in the development, testing, and operation of advance spacecraft was to proceed.

Military installations and the presence of large numbers of service men have affected Texas profoundly. Construction projects running into hundreds of millions of dollars have stimulated greatly the economy of communities directly affected and of the entire state in a substantial way.

Troops with their families and friends contributed greatly to the growth of San Antonio, El Paso, Abilene, Amarillo, Big Spring, Lubbock, Wichita Falls, and a score of other cities. The payroll of the military is a sure and dependable stay for business. For the fiscal year ending June 30, 1966, the Department of Defense spent $58,391,000,000, or 42 percent of the national budget. Of this amount more than $1,283,000,000 was allotted for military and civilian payrolls in Texas. Texas was second among the states in the matter of wages and military disbursements from the federal government to the military and defense agencies and personnel. The armed forces, furthermore, added to the social and cultural life of the communities with which they were associated.

The impetus gained from the program of the armed forces in Texas may explain in part the large amount of commercial flying. As early as 1925, all the larger cities had well-equipped flying fields, and every town of consequence had its landing field. First and last, many concerns have had a part in commercial air transportation, but competition has forced consolidation, and most of them either have been merged into a few large corporations or have long since gone out of business.

Passenger carrying was begun in 1928 by the Texas Air Transport, Dallas to San Antonio and Fort Worth to Galveston. Braniff Airways entered Texas in the fall of 1930, and in 1934 began carrying mail from Chicago to Dallas and later to other major cities. Meanwhile, in 1930 American Airways, later American Airlines, had come into existence through several mergers, linking Los Angeles with Atlanta through Dallas. By 1939 Delta Airlines provided service eastward to the old South; Eastern Airlines had connected Houston and Brownsville by plane with the Atlantic states; Chicago and Southern had linked Houston with Memphis; Continental Airlines was flying from Denver to El Paso; Transcontinental and Western Air, Incorporated was crossing the Texas Panhandle; and Pan American Airlines was providing service southward through Mexico to South America.

New airlines reached the state and the old ones in service were consolidated from time to time. Service was extended, until by 1965 12 United States based airlines were operating in the state through 34 airfields. With 5,635,179 passengers, Texas ranked fourth in the nation in emplaned passengers.

Selected Bibliography

The best general reference for this chapter is the *Texas Almanac*. The *Texas Business Review*, published monthly by the Bureau of Business Research, The University of Texas, Austin, is invaluable. Especially useful are Edwin J. Foscue, "The Pulp and Paper Industry of East Texas," April, 1967, 105–109; Stanley A. Arbingast, "Notes on the Industrialization of Texas: Synthetic Rubber," September, 1952, 16–17; Raymond A. Dietrich, "Market Structure Changes in the Livestock-Meat Industry, with Special Reference to Texas," March, 1968, 68–74; Stanley A. Arbingast, "Military Payrolls and the Texas Economy," March, 1967, 76–78.

On the history of oil good references are C.C. Rister, *Oil! Titan of the Southwest* (Norman, 1949), comprehensive and authoritative; W. Gard, *The First Hundred Years of Oil and Gas* (Dallas, 1966); Craig Thompson, *Since Spindletop* (Pittsburgh, 1951); Henrietta M. Larson, *History of Humble Oil and Refining Company* (New York, 1959); Alfred M. Leeston, John A. Chrichton, and John C. Jacobs, *The Dynamic Natural Gas Industry* (Norman, 1963).

Texas Highways, official journal of the Texas High Department, Austin, Texas, and *Texas Parade*, published at Austin monthly with the endorsement of the Texas Good Roads Association, are rich sources of information on Texas roads. In the *Texas Almanac, 1968–1969*, pp. 469–473, may be found a good brief account of Texas ports. The *Texas Almanac, 1968–1969*, pp. 299–301, gives considerable information on aviation and air travel in Texas.

19

WAR, READJUSTMENT, AND TENSION, 1941–1969

On December 7, 1941, the armed forces of Japan attacked Pearl Harbor and drew the United States into the global war that had started in Europe in September 1939 when England and France resisted the German dictator Hitler. For months the nation had been moving toward hostilities; Congress had appropriated funds for a two-ocean navy, had enacted the first peacetime conscription law in American history, and had aided the enemies of Hitler and Mussolini with almost every agency short of declaring war.

The government of Texas and the people loyally supported the national war effort. In keeping with its finest traditions, the state's men and women responded to the call to arms; its oil kept ships, trucks, tanks, and planes moving against the enemy; its industries were strengthened and harnessed for the cause of freedom; everybody was needed in the war effort and the people loyally did their part. Soon the rate of industrial activity was the highest ever known and the total income surpassed all previous records. In spite of the many heartbreaking experiences of war, material prosperity generally prevailed, and after the victory was won the problems of postwar readjustment were made easier by expanding industry, high prices for farm commodities, and a generous federal policy of providing schooling or on-the-job training for veterans. As in most of the rest of the nation, the Texas economy continued to expand; full employment, high wages, and high prices have continued as late as 1969, constituting the longest unbroken period of abundance in American history.

Prosperity did not bring tranquility to the state, however. As in other years farmers protested that they were not sharing fairly in the general abundance, and called for greater freedom in their farming practices, or more controls, as their interest and points of view varied. Labor unions chafed at restraints and penalties they considered unfair, and grew stronger regardless of them. The public school system, growing costlier each year and declining in efficiency, was completely reorganized. There were pleas, fervent and often repeated, for better care of children; the friends of the needy aged were not reconciled to the aid accorded them; and the blind and the crippled had their champions.

Although there was relatively little violence in Texas in the 1960's, several cities and a number of college campuses witnessed marches, gatherings, and various other manifestations of dissatisfaction with "the establishment." The aims of the protesters were often poorly defined, but calls for more freedom, more democracy, and more generous treatment of minorities and unfortunate people seemed to be paramount. In their demands for equality of treatment, minority groups often were sustained by the nation's highest tribunal. The ghost of racial strife and hatred, never altogether downed since the days of reconstruction, grew sorely threatening at times in some communities, but there were few major clashes in Texas.

Charges of brutality were made against law enforcement officers at times; and there were accusations of laxity of law enforcement, bribery, and embezzlement made against officers in high places and in low and some of the charges were sustained. Personal animosities along with public issues provoked rancor and strife and split political parties. Again and again the state's one-party system was sorely tried.

PUBLIC AFFAIRS DURING
THE WAR YEARS

Texans accepted with a modicum of grumbling the austerity that war imposed. Although Governor Stevenson was critical of the rationing program, he sought to promote the war effort. He called for rigid economy in all agencies of government and entered into a no-strike covenant with organized labor that prevented work stoppages in Texas. Attorney General Mann announced that the severe Texas antitrust laws would not be pressed against concerns seriously engaging in production.

In its session of 1943 the legislature cut appropriations to most state agencies and reduced substantially expenditures for senior colleges, which were then low on faculty and men and women students alike.

As the war proceeded various federal agencies brought their efforts to bear on the people. The War Manpower Commission in Texas, with some twelve regional directors, sought to see that all qualified people were employed, and that those deferred from military service worked at essential jobs. The National Office of Price Administration, in charge of rationing and price ceilings, used the staff and pupils of the public schools to bring about sugar rationing. Later rationing was extended to meats, fats (including butter), canned goods, coffee, shoes, and gasoline. One state agency, the powerful Railroad Commission, in charge of the production of from 40 to 50 percent of the nation's gas and oil, occupied a strategic position in the nation's war effort. It was both faithful and effective, and managed to cooperate with Harold L. Ickes, Secretary of the Interior and Petroleum Administrator for War.

In spite of the "freezing" of rents, salaries, and wages and the restraints on prices, the cost of living rose moderately during the war; but since almost every employable person was busy, family incomes increased by a fourth or a third, and the rank and file of people were in relatively good circumstances.

For the Forty-ninth Legislature, which assembled in January 1945, the problem of state finance was delightfully simple. Income had outrun expenditures so far that a $42,000,000 deficit had been eliminated by economies and increased revenues, and had been changed to a surplus. Appropriations surpassed those of any preceding legislature in history; the body made available an additional $13,000,000 for the state school per capita apportionment, gave rural school aid $28,000,000 for the biennium, and submitted a proposed constitutional change to raise to $35,000,000 the ceiling on social security payments.

Before the legislature adjourned on June 5, 1945, it was evident that the war's end was near; thousands of veterans had returned home and tens of thousands would follow them. Texas laws allowed them free voting privileges, the renewal of drivers' licenses without examination, and the privilege of attending state colleges without charge. Already the federal G.I. Bill of Rights was in effect, providing aid for schooling or training, and these privileges were later extended to veterans of the Korean War, the cold war, and the war in Vietnam. Texas voters ratified an amendment to the constitution authorizing bonds for the purchase by the state of land to be sold to veterans. The program has since been extended from time to time. These bonds were the Texan answer to the urge for a blanket state bonus to veterans.

The tang of change was in the air; for the new day the old constitution seemed inadequate in many respects. Bales of proposed constitutional amendments were submitted to each legislature after World War II. In the Forty-ninth Legislature 84 proposals were introduced and eight of these were submitted to the voters (not including one proposing a constitutional convention). The voters approved amendments extending favors to veterans, raising to nine the number of supreme court justices, and raising the ceiling on social welfare payments.

It was during the war years that the cleavage between Texas conservative and liberal Democrats developed fully. As "Jeffersonian Democrats," the opponents of President Roosevelt and the New Deal were in evidence as a minority group in 1936; the candidacy for the presidency of the staunch Texas Democrat, John Nance Garner, held the factions together in 1940; but President Roosevelt's determination to seek a third term prevented the Garner-for-President movement reaching far beyond Texas. Added to their objections to Roosevelt and the New Deal, the conservative Texas Democrats had a grievance against the Supreme Court in 1944; namely, its decision in *Smith v. Allwright* (321 U.S. 649) that the Texas Democratic Party's rule excluding Negroes from its primaries violated the Fifteenth Amendment. When the conservatives, in control of the Texas convention in May, sought to make a party test of opposition to the Supreme Court's decision, the convention split, and the conservatives organized later as "Texas Regulars" made a futile effort against the Roosevelt-Truman ticket.

These factional contests had their repercussions in the state Democratic executive committee and to a limited extent in the legislature. Texas war governor, Coke R. Stevenson, a conservative Democrat, managed to hold aloof from them. He was easily reelected in 1944, and expressed publicly his satisfaction when his successor, Beauford H. Jester, a moderate conservative, was elected in 1946.

TEXAS AND TEXANS IN THE WAR

Long before the day of Pearl Harbor Texas was a huge training field for the armed forces. The first peacetime draft in American history went into effect on October 16, 1940, when 17 million Americans registered. Of the state army organizations transferred to federal service the Thirty-Sixth Division and the Fifty-Sixth Cavalry Brigade were all-Texas units. Texas posts became headquarters of importance. San Antonio, long a soldiers' center, was during a considerable part of the war headquarters of the Third Army, which trained men from Arizona to Florida. It was also headquarters for the Fourth Army, which prepared men for overseas combat service in nine states. The Eighth Service Command, serving as the operating agency for army service forces in Texas and adjoining states, had its headquarters in Dallas. For a period the army had as many as 15 training posts in Texas and prisoner of war camps came to number 21. For defense of the Gulf Coast and Mexican border areas, the Southern Defense Command, with headquarters at Fort Sam Houston, was maintained during most of the war. The great training program in Texas for airmen has been described elsewhere.

Beauford H. Jester (left), was elected governor of Texas in 1946 and again in 1948. He died in office in 1949. Here he is shown with Harry Truman and a fellow Texan, John Nance Garner. In a close national election, 750,000 Texans voted for Truman and 280,000 for his Republican opponent, Thomas E. Dewey. Garner was Vice-President from 1933 to 1941. (E. C. Barker History Center, University of Texas)

It is estimated that one and a quarter million men in all branches of the service were trained in Texas, among them more than 20 combat army divisions. Probably as many as three-quarters of a million Texans, including 12,000 women, served in all branches of the armed forces. Of these about a fourth were in the Navy, Marine Corps, and Coast Guard combined. More than 8,000 Texas women served in the Women's Army Corps (WAC); about 4,200 in the Women Accepted for Voluntary Emergency Service (WAVES); and others in the SPARS and the Marines.

The Selective Service act of September 1940, applicable to men between the ages of 21 and 36, was extended after the United States entered the war to include all men between the ages of 18 and 45. Secretary of the Navy Frank Knox stated in December 1942 that Texas was contributing a larger percentage of men to the fighting forces than any other states, a circumstance perhaps due to the fact that the great majority of Texans are acquainted with the history of their state.

Texan organizations came to be known around the world. The 36th Division, a Texan force, sent to Java an organization whose epic experiences caused it to be known as the Lost Battalion. The division landed at Salerno, being the first American force to enter Europe, and in 400 days of combat advanced through Italy, France, Germany, and into Austria. Texas also had a special claim on the 90th (Texas-Oklahoma) Division, the 112th Cavalry Division, the 103rd Infantry Regiment in the Pacific theater, and the Second Infantry Division and the First Cavalry Division in the European theater.

Wherever they went Texans seemed to have been very much in evidence. The 36th Division carried the Texas flag and often displayed it. Where Texas troops were congregated, natives sometimes spoke of the "Texas Army." Many Texans were recognized for valor as well as enthusiasm. Lieutenant Audie Murphy, of Farmersville, became the "most decorated" soldier of World War II. The Congressional Medal of Honor went to him and some 29 other Texans. Six Texans received the Navy's Medal of Honor, among them Commander Samuel D. Dealey, killed in action, and known as the "most decorated man in the Navy."

Many military officers of renown were Texans or had once called Texas home. Oveta Culp Hobby was director of the Women's Army Corps. The state could claim at least 12 admirals and 155 generals, among them Chester W. Nimitz, Commander in Chief of the Pacific Fleet, and Dwight David Eisenhower, Supreme Allied Commander in Europe. Texans fought on every front and paid their share of war's cruel toll. Their war dead for all branches of the service aggregated 23,022. The seriously wounded and permanently injured numbered many more.

MEN AND ISSUES OF THE POSTWAR YEARS

As the gubernatorial campaign of 1946 began to shape, Homer Price Rainey, former President of the University of Texas, who had been dismissed from that post after a long, bitter controversy with the Board of Regents, seemed to be the strongest of a long slate of candidates. Railroad Commissioner Beauford Jester proved to be a better campaigner, however, and was nominated in the runoff primary. Although Jester had the support of the conservative or anti-Truman element of the party, his middle-of-the-road course prevented an open breach with the liberals.

Like his predecessors in office, Governor Jester opposed emphatically any new taxes. Still, the expanding economy and general prosperity that prevailed placed the executive in the happy position of being able to recommend substantial increases in appropriations without being obliged to suggest new sources of revenue. In 1949 in his "Report to the People" by radio, the chief executive could point to the doubling of appropriations for hospitals and orphanages, the opening of two new tubercular hospitals, a new school for feeble-minded children and senile women, and an institution for delinquent Negro girls. Under the constitutional amendment limiting appropriations to anticipated revenue, which had become effective in 1945, the comptroller refused to certify a number of appropriations made near the end of the session.

Of great importance in the history of higher education was the constitutional amendment, submitted by the legislature and ratified by the voters at the polls appropriating five cents of the Confederate Veteran's pension tax to a fund for constructing buildings for the fourteen state colleges. Eleven laws enacted by the legislature in 1947 having to do with organized labor, most of them opposed by the labor unions, are dealt with elsewhere.

Many Texas conservative Democrats opposed Truman as they had opposed Roosevelt. Indeed, with the President they associated the Fair Employment Practice Committee, the CIO Political Action Committee, and other features and groups which they had opposed consistently. Governor Jester worked for harmony, however, and there was no party division when the national Democratic convention nominated Truman in 1948. The number of those who supported the Republican and Dixiecrat tickets evidently was not large.

Jester was reelected governor without making a campaign. For the seat in the United States Senate to be vacated by W. Lee O'Daniel, who did not seek reelection in 1948, Congressman Lyndon B. Johnson opposed former governor Coke R. Stevenson, in a contest close, acrimonious, and undecided until a federal court ordered Johnson's name placed on the ballot as the Democratic nominee.

In the longest session the state had known, from January 11 to July 6, 1949, the Fifty-first Legislature enacted many laws, some of them probably of enduring value. In an effort to improve the pitiable conditions in the institutions for the mentally ill it created the Board for Texas State Hospitals and Special Schools and gave it supervision over state mental hospitals and state schools for handicapped children. A Youth Development Council was set up to have charge of schools for juvenile offenders. The body enacted an antilynching law, adopted a controversial basic science law, setting forth minimum requirements for all persons in medical and health work, and provided for the licensing of chiropractors.

During this session state appropriations for the biennium, when supplemented by various federal grants, aggregated a billion dollars; so the session was the first to be called a "billion dollar legislature." Like its predecessors the body refused to vote new taxes, and in order to keep expenditures within the limits of income, Governor Jester vetoed second year appropriations for state hospitals and special schools. Two of its measures were far reaching in effect: the modernization of the state prison system and the reorganization of the state public school system through the Gilmer-Aiken school laws. The school system will be dealt with in a later chapter; a brief sketch of prison improvement follows.

Because of limitations brought about by the war and its aftermath, the Texas prison system, never a high-ranking one, had deteriorated rapidly. The growth of the prison population—a gain of one thousand, or 29 percent in 1946 over the preceding year—added greatly to all problems. The board secured O. B. Ellis, an experienced prison administrator, who drew up the Ellis plan for rehabilitating the system. In 1949 the legislature appropriated $4,290,000 for improvements; subsequent legislatures continued to supply funds so that each year two or more units were modernized. Through the prison rodeo and other agencies of self-help, funds were raised to improve the morale of the men. In 1957 the name was changed to State Department of Corrections. Prison population continued to grow, necessitating the enlarging and improving of the plants periodically. In 1966 the average number of prisoners was 12,765, a slight decrease from that of the preceding year. Even though the cost of operation in recent years has been relatively low, the system has ranked high.

SHIVERS AND THE INTERPLAY OF
NATIONAL AND STATE ISSUES

On July 11, 1949, Governor Jester died of a heart attack, and Lieutenant Governor Allan Shivers succeeded to the office. Shivers was just forty-one, but ten years in the state senate and two as lieutenant governor had seasoned him. A called session of the legislature in 1950 was made necessary by failure of the body to complete appropriations for the second year of the biennium.

The governor called for additional taxes as the only way of meeting the demands for increased expenditures. "If we are going to appropriate in the spring," he said, "we must tax in the winter." Shivers pleaded for large appropriations to hospitals to improve old plants and add new. Too many mentally ill people were in jails because of inadequate hospital space. The legislature followed with relatively generous appropriations for the operations of state hospitals and dedicated to a hospital building program for seven years the additional tax of a penny a pack on cigarettes, calculated to yield about $5 million a year. Other additional taxes were levied.

The next legislature, the fifty-second, meeting in 1951, found that still more taxes were needed. Two agencies worked on the budget for that year: the Board of Control, as it had been accustomed to do for some years, and the Legislative Budget Board, or Council, created by the preceding legislature from its own members. All agreed that additional revenue must be found, and again levies in the Omnibus Bill of 1941 were raised, and a gathering tax on natural gas pipelines of approximately one-half cent per 1,000 cubic feet was added. Unfortunately the courts later declared this tax unconstitutional as being in effect a state levy on interstate commerce, and the natural gas interests avoided their equitable share of taxation.

This legislature enacted the first redistricting law in thirty years. Another act, which was the object of much criticism, was the safety inspection and driver responsibility law designed to force unsafe cars off of the road and also to give the public a modicum of assurance that drivers were responsible for the damage they might do to others.

More and more the political stage in Texas came to be appropriated largely by national and international issues and by state-federal relationships. President Truman continued to decline in the esteem of Texas conservative Democrats. Charges of corrupt practice and the infiltration of communism were hurled at his administration. There was also much criticism of his policies in the Korean war. In June 1950, Russian- and Chinese-backed North Koreans invaded South Korea. The United States under the auspices of the United Nations went to the aid of the South Koreans and the "police action" became a bloody war. In order to avoid more serious international complications, the President determined to fight in Korea on a limited scale only. In April 1951 General Douglas MacArthur, commander in Korea, was dismissed as a result of differences over this policy, and many Texans along with millions of other Americans became even more critical of the President.

Resented by Texans more deeply than any other act of the President, however, was his veto of a law of Congress giving Texas title to her tidelands, believed to be rich in oil deposits. Early opinions held almost unanimously that the state owned the land beneath the marginal sea, commonly called the tidelands, until Secretary of the Interior Harold Ickes formally challenged the claim in 1937. In August 1947, the Supreme Court of the United States held that the State of California did not have the right to exploit its tidelands through oil leases and other means because the federal government had "paramount right and power" over this domain. In 1950 the court by a vote of 4 to 3 (two not voting) handed down a similar decision against Texas. It was a heavy blow, for these lands were being leased already for oil and gas development, and nearly $10,000,000 in lease bonuses had been received.

As already stated, President Truman vetoed an act of Congress in 1946 recognizing the rights of the states to lease these lands; and when a similar act was submitted to him in 1952, he vetoed that also. By way of completing the account of these lands it may be stated that on May 22, 1953, President Eisenhower signed a quitclaim bill, restoring the tidelands to state ownership and extending ownership to "historic limits."

For Texas and the west coast of Florida, where the rule of Spanish law still prevailed, "historic limits" meant three Spanish leagues or about ten and a half miles.

For many Texans the subject of the tidelands became a prime factor in the Presidential election of 1952. The Democratic party split that year; the liberal wing bolted; the conservatives led by Shivers kept control of the party organization and refused to support Governor Adlai Stevenson, the Democratic nominee for president, after Stevenson had indicated no sympathy for the claims of the states to the tidelands. That year Texas Republicans had a breach also between the forces supporting Senator Robert A. Taft for president and those supporting General Dwight D. Eisenhower. Later the factions united, joined with the conservative Democrats and carried the state for Eisenhower. Two million Texans voted that November, the greatest turnout to the polls the state had known. Eisenhower carried the state by a majority of over 100,000, winning the second Republican victory in Texas within a quarter of a century. Shivers was easily renominated that year over his chief opponent, the liberal judge Ralph Yarborough. Most of the Texas state offices were not sought by Republicans in 1952; by a system of "cross filing" they placed in their columns on the ballot the names of the Democratic nominees. That year Attorney General Price Daniel defeated Congressman Lindly Beckworth, a pro-Truman or liberal Democrat, for the seat in the United States Senate of Tom Connally, who withdrew from the race.

With the support of the conservative Democrats, Shivers, in a campaign for his third full term as governor, defeated Ralph Yarborough again in 1954, in an acrimonious contest that was settled by the second primary. Yarborough awaited the renewal of the contest in 1956.

LAXITY AND CORRUPT PRACTICES

The Fifty-third Legislature in 1953 held out against a tax increase, but its favorite project, a $600 a year increase in teachers' salaries was negated because the state comptroller would not certify the prospect of funds to meet it. The legislature made some improvement in the state's cumbersome administrative organization. The state board of control was abolished and a new board created whose duties were to be policy-forming and not administrative. By constitutional amendment, which became effective in 1955, a state building commission was set up, with authority to arrange for all state building sites and control the planning and constructing of buildings for state purposes. The Fifty-fourth Legislature in 1955 created a commission on higher education with supervisory powers over the curricula and budgets of state supported colleges and universities. By authority of constitutional amendments the legislature set the terms of county officers at four years and raised the salary of legislative and state administrative officers. The state continued to improve its employees' retirement system and teachers' retirement, and made eligible the transfer of credits between the two.

This legislature could not avoid the levying of additional taxes. For the second time in two years, the corporation franchise tax was raised, this time from $2 to $2.25 per hundred. The remainder of the $100 million additional revenue for the biennium was to be raised by increasing the sales taxes (Texans prefer to call them "occupation taxes") on cigarettes, gasoline, and beer. Of this amount, $41 million was to go for road and highway purposes and $59 million to the general revenue fund.

A series of events brought before the legislature in 1955 the subject of insurance, which it dealt with at length. Following the enactment of the Robertson insurance law of 1907, which caused the withdrawal of a majority of the out-of-state insurance companies then operating in Texas, many insurance companies were chartered in the state and they, along with the outside companies that remained, prospered. By 1954 the state had some 1,875 insurance companies, 1,202 of them Texas based. Of the 793 legal reserve life insurance companies in the nation in July 1953, 215 were in Texas.

Texas insurance laws were lax, and left the way open for fly-by-night promoters and operators. The sale of insurance company stock, not under official supervision, was excepted from the terms of the Texas Securities Act ("Blue Sky Law") which closely regulated the sales of most corporation stock.

Failures of insurance companies, never uncommon, became more frequent after World War II. In 1955, Lieutenant Governor Ben Ramsey reminded the lawmakers that during the last ten years 86 Texas insurance companies had failed, largely because of an inadequate insurance code. The legislature enacted 22 laws on the subject, providing for more effective regulation generally, raising the minimum capital requirements of insurance companies, and reorganizing the board of insurance commissioners. Legislation similar to the Federal Securities Act placed the sale of insurance stock under the board of insurance commissioners.

Failures continued, however—among them United Services Trust and Guaranty Company with approximately 128,000 depositors and stockholders, and the ICT corporation, a concern that controlled some 74 insurance and finance companies in 22 states and Alaska—and in 1957 the lawmakers complied with Governor Daniel's request that he be authorized to appoint an entirely new insurance commission. This legislature enacted 16 laws designed to improve the insurance situation in Texas. Meanwhile Texas insurance companies were subjected to an audit, and more than 100 were denied, temporarily or permanently, permits to continue in business. Investigations of the failures brought before the public an unwholesome relationship between certain Texas lawmakers and some corporations. For instance, nine members of the Texas senate had received legal fees or other income from the United Services Trust and Guaranty Company.

The line of cleavage in the Texas Democratic party between conservatives and liberals continued. Some commentators laid it to such developments as the Supreme Court decision admitting Negroes to Democratic primaries, the political activity of one and a quarter million Latin-Americans, and to the part of organized labor in politics, all of which built up the liberal or left wing of the party and made conservatives more disposed to bolt. Still, such an explanation cannot be reconciled with the fact that in the Presidential contests when conservative Democrats and Republicans united they carried most cities and counties where the Negro, the Latin-American, and the organized labor influences were strongest.

The liberals, or loyalists, controlled the Democratic state presidential convention in 1956. Shivers refused again to support Stevenson, the Democratic nominee, and threw his strength to Eisenhower. Eisenhower and Nixon again carried the state by a majority about twice that of four years before. This year Senator Price Daniel became a candidate for governor, running against Ralph Yarborough and a field of other candidates. Yarborough had the support of organized labor and a majority of the liberal Democrats. In the contest he charged Daniel, along with Shivers, with responsibility for certain irregularities of the veterans land board, of which Daniel and Shivers were ex-officio members when Daniel was attorney general. The $100 million program, by which the state purchased land for resale to veterans that has been mentioned before, was placed under the direction of a veterans land board, composed of the commissioner of the general of the land office, the governor, and the attorney general. Reports of irregularities and frauds in the work of the commission brought investigations by grand juries and senate and house committees. Bascom Giles, commissioner of the general land office, who had just been elected to his ninth term, was sent to the penitentiary for six years on charges of misrepresentation and perjury. By a small margin, Daniel defeated Yarborough for governor in a second primary; then over a slate of opponents Yarborough was elected to the United States Senate to take the seat Daniel had vacated to become governor.

The Fifty-fifth Legislature in 1957 worked under trying conditions. Its legislation on the subjects of water and agriculture are dealt with elsewhere. It was brought out that many legislators were employed more or less regularly by corporations, some of which maintained very active lobbies in Austin. Charges of bribery were hurled freely; one representative who resigned in the face of the charge was convicted in court. The legislature enacted into law for the fiscal years ending August 31, 1958, and August 1, 1959, budgets well beyond a billion dollars.

On November 5, 1957, Texas voters approved constitutional amendments liberalizing retirement, disability, and death benefits for state employees; and increasing the state's share in pensions to the aged.

PARTY AND PERSONAL RIVALRY

The election of Ralph Yarborough to the United States Senate in 1957 encouraged the liberal Democrats. Under the leadership of Mrs. R. D. ("Frankie") Randolph of Houston, Democratic national committeewoman, Jerry Holleman, president of the Texas A.F.L-C.I.O., and others, they organized the "Democrats of Texas" (DOT). Outstanding among a list of demands they made of the party were the abolition of the poll tax, greater liberal representation in party affairs, and loyalty to the national Democratic party. Joined by other liberals in 1958, the DOT gave Yarborough an overwhelming victory over his conservative opponent William A. Blakley (charged with being the candidate of big business) in Yarborough's contest for a regular term in the Senate, and he was elected in November. In contrast, Governor Price Daniel, generally regarded as a moderate conservative, was continued in office by a generous margin, and he dominated the Democratic State Convention.

The great Republican victory in Texas in 1956 was followed by a series of losses. The party elected only one congressman in 1958, Bruce Alger of Dallas. As the decade drew to a close, the outstanding feature in Democratic circles was the bid for the presidency by Lyndon Baines Johnson, the Texan who was now majority leader in the United States Senate and who had the endorsement of Sam Rayburn, the powerful Speaker of the House of Representatives, and of Governor Price Daniel. To promote Johnson's candidacy, the legislature moved the party primaries up to May and changed the convention system so that Senator Johnson's name could appear on the ballot as the incumbent candidate for senator, while on the same day precinct conventions could endorse him for the presidency.

Texas elections in 1960 did not follow any one line of cleavage. Seeking a third term for governor, Daniel, described by an authority as "a political moderate to the right of center," easily defeated his conservative opponent, Jack Cox, who had the support of former governor Allan Shivers, and Daniel was elected in November with little opposition. Liberal Democrats gained a few seats in the legislature. In his dual race for the Senate and for President, Johnson met with mixed results. John Tower, a youthful teacher in Midwestern University at Wichita Falls, his Republican opponent for the Senate, polled nearly a million votes. Notwithstanding Johnson's vote of 1,306,625, the Tower vote was surprisingly great. Johnson's candidacy was endorsed generally by the Democratic precinct and county conventions. With little opposition the state convention chose a delegation pledged to Johnson; the Johnson-Rayburn-Daniel team proved invincible. The DOT (now calling themselves Democrats of Texas Clubs) made an unsuccessful fight, not directly on Johnson's candidacy, but in an effort to require of all state convention delegates an individual written pledge that they would support all Democratic candidates in the election of 1960. Only a general loyalty resolution was, however, passed by the convention.

Although Senator Johnson traveled 31,250 miles in his campaign for the Democratic nomination for President, the chief reliance of his supporting organization was not his campaign speeches but his experience in government, his leadership so well proved in the Senate, the political strength and prestige of his supporter, Speaker Rayburn, and the youth and inexperience of his leading opponent, Senator John F. Kennedy of Massachusetts.

In the Democratic National Convention at Los Angeles in 1960 the united efforts of the Texas delegation were of no avail. Johnson got only 409 delegate votes, mainly from the South; John F. Kennedy was nominated on the first ballot. Kennedy then appealed to Johnson to be his running mate. Johnson assented, a decision that was puzzling to many of his followers because of what appeared to be the wide ideological differences between him and Kennedy. Many Texans were disgruntled also at the strong civil rights plank in the national party platform. Not a few liberals, furthermore, were dissatisfied with Johnson.

Relative harmony prevailed among Texas Republicans in 1960. Mention has been made of the strength Tower demonstrated in his contest for Johnson's Senate seat. The state party organization centered its efforts on carrying Texas for the national Republican ticket, headed by Vice President Richard M. Nixon, with Henry Cabot Lodge, III, his running mate.

Texas was a pivotal state. Leaders of both parties conceded that the contest would be close and that Texas' 24 electoral votes might well determine the election. Both parties had good organizations and their candidates did not ignore Texas.

There was, nevertheless, considerable discord. In September the Democratic State Convention adopted a platform at variance with that of the national party. The Texans supported the Texas right-to-work law (hated by organized labor), the oil depletion allowance (which lessened the federal income tax on oil production), and advocated states rights generally. Still many conservative Democrats declared against the party ticket. In contrast the Texas Republicans were generally harmonious. Allan Shivers campaigned for Nixon and Lodge.

The 1960 presidential election brought out a record vote in Texas

(2,311,845) and in the nation (69,000,000). The Kennedy-Johnson ticket carried the state by a slender margin of 24,019 votes. The vote in the nation was exceedingly close also. The Kennedy-Johnson electoral vote was 303 to 219 for their opponents, but their majority was only 112,881.

Republican victories of 1952 and 1956 in Texas had been mainly at the presidential level. They were defeated in the contest of 1960, but their outlook was not unpromising: Nixon and Lodge had polled the greatest Republican vote in Texas in history. Party workers set out immediately to increase their strength in the state legislature and in Congress. It was a great Republican victory when their candidate defeated the Democrat, William A. Blakley, the former United States Senator, for the Senate seat vacated by Lyndon Johnson. The party made a spirited fight in 1962 in its efforts to build in Texas a two-party system, and the results were not altogether negative. They gained a second congressman and several house seats in the legislature; and in the race for governor their candidate, Jack Cox, made an excellent showing against the victorious John B. Connally, who had resigned as Secretary of the Navy to make the race for governor. Connally had the support of Lyndon B. Johnson, and it was commonly said that he ran at Johnson's behest. In an upsurge in Dallas County in 1962, Republicans won six seats in the Texas House.

Along with a few victories that raised high hopes in Republican ranks, dissension appeared to plague the party in Texas. Many conservative Democrats were joining the party which may help explain its tending toward the extreme right. The conservative political philosophy of Senator Barry Goldwater of Arizona coupled with his opposition to federal interference on the race issue gave him a large following in Texas. His nomination as the Republican candidate for president in 1964 marked the ascendency of conservative Republicanism in the nation, and conservative Texans followed him with enthusiasm; but many Republicans were loath to support him and he had no appeal for moderate Democrats who were getting into the habit of voting for Republican candidates for president.

Likewise, among Texas Democrats discord seemed always to prevail or to be lurking nearby. Before he defeated Jack Cox, the Republican nominee for governor in 1962, John Connally had outdistanced Governor Daniel, who was seeking a fourth term, and in a runoff contest had beaten Don Yarborough, the leading Texas liberal Democrat. Connally sought support from conservatives and liberal-moderates alike, with a measure of success. Still, the relationship between Senator Ralph Yarborough, the outstanding Texas liberal Democrat, and Vice President Johnson was described as "cool," and it was soon evident that Yarborough and Connally were not getting along harmoniously. Besides differences in ideology, each sought to control the Democratic Party in Texas.

A TEXAN BECOMES PRESIDENT

A tragic event in Dallas on November 23, 1963, affected profoundly the course of public affairs in Texas and the history of the world. While the people of the city and of the state were receiving him with enthusiastic hospitality, a hidden assassin shot and killed President Kennedy and seriously wounded Governor Connally, who was riding with him. Within two hours after the death of President Kennedy, Lyndon Baines Johnson, a native Texan, took the oath of office that made him President of the United States.

Through the prestige of the presidency, Johnson, who has been described as being both liberal and conservative, was able to suppress to a degree factionalism in Texas' Democratic ranks for a period. In the Democratic primaries of 1964 the influence of the President, working through and with Governor Connally, prevailed. It has been stated already that Connally was easily nominated and elected governor for another term. Senator Ralph Yarborough won the nomination for another term and defeated his Republican opponent, George Bush. Connally's control of the presidential Democratic state convention was complete, and the 120-member delegation was sent to Atlantic City with instructions to "put forth every effort" to secure Johnson's nomination.

Conservatism prevailed in Texas Republican ranks and there was little opposition in the state convention to Senator Barry Goldwater. The Republicans worked manfully to win Texas again in 1964. Goldwater visited the state six times. Johnson's strength proved invincible, however, and there was relative harmony in Democratic ranks. Even former Governor Allan Shivers supported the Johnson-Humphrey ticket. A record vote of 2,558,000 was cast, with the Republicans having less than a million votes. Professor O. Douglas Weeks, an authority, has entitled his account of the election: "Texas in 1964: A One-Party State Again?"

Apparently Governor Connally's sweeping victory in 1964 strengthened his influence with the legislature and enabled him to continue with his planning for the state and to secure the enactment of an impressive legislative program. He set up a Planning Agency Council with an intergovernmental coordinator and planning consultants to promote better cooperation on the part of state agencies. In response to his suggestion the legislature authorized councils of governments whereby counties, cities, schools, and other political subdivisions of the state might coordinate their efforts and cooperate. He encouraged the establishment of community centers to cooperate with the Department of Mental Health and Mental Retardation. Under his leadership an antituberculosis program was centered in South Texas, especially for children of migrant workers. A State Fine Arts Commission was established. The

Texas Water Commission was reconstituted as the State Water Rights Commission. Compulsory school attendance was raised to include 17-year-olds; and the legislature approved the governor's plan for taking over the James Connally Air Force Base, near Waco, and establishing there a technical institute.

Most of Connally's important proposals called for the submission to the voters of constitutional amendments. Chief of these was an amendment to increase the term of the governor and other state-wide administrative officers from two to four years. His arguments for this amendment are impressive and significant: it would lessen the enormous financial burdens of running for a state office; it would give public officers more time to attend to affairs of state and cope with the increasing costs and complexities of government. He referred to the increasing federal program requiring state planning and administration, the higher education facilities act, and the elementary education act, all adding to the burdens of state officeholders.

The voters did not approve the governor's four-year term proposal, nor did they favor the annual sessions of the legislature, proposed during this era. They did approve an increase in pay for the state lawmakers, remuneration not to exceed $4,800 a year, with mileage and a per diem. They also liberalized the state welfare program, raised the state property tax to give the state colleges more building funds, liberalized the teacher retirement program, and authorized a state student loan fund.

In compliance with the mandates of federal judges the legislature redistricted the state for both houses of the legislature and for Congress. For state representative and congressional districts the work had to be done over in 1967.

PROSPERITY AND PROBLEMS

Although its per capita income was considerably below the national average in the 1950's and 1960's, Texas was relatively prosperous. Still, growth and prosperity seemed to breed problems that fully matched some of those of leaner years. School enrollments were increasing from the kindergarten through the university, and the cost of education ballooned each year. Penal and eleemosynary institutions called for increased appropriations each biennium with appeals that were compelling. Highways needed huge sums and the park system was starved. The growth and complexities of state government were amazing: there were some 70 state agencies in 1965 and the legislature that year added 17. State expenditures increased from $103,672,473 in 1930 to $1,860,633,760 in 1966. The greater part of the state's income was derived from constitutional taxes and other revenues dedicated to certain purposes, such as the motor fuel tax that is divided between the roads and the schools. The pressing problem of the legislature was that of securing funds to carry on the state government and supplement the constitutional funds through general appropriations.

In 1959 there was a prolonged contest in the legislature over a bill to raise additional taxes. A study commission had recommended a complete revision of the state's tax system, but that course was not seriously undertaken. The liberals wanted additional taxes on business, such as levies on gross receipts, franchises, and the production of oil and gas; and they were positively opposed to taxes on consumers. The conservatives were not so afraid of consumer taxes but were wary of taxes on business. Governor Daniel proposed a combined select sales tax and certain business taxes, a solution unsatisfactory to both factions. The impasse continued through the regular legislative session and through two called sessions. As finally enacted in a third special session, the law raised the tax on cigarettes and some other consumer items, increased franchise taxes, levied gross receipts taxes on certain businesses, and provided for a tax on natural gas aimed (unsuccessfully) at the pipeline companies.

With the opening of the legislature in January 1961 the problem of state finances again loomed great. It seemed imperative that teachers have a raise. The voters also had approved medical aid for the aged and that called for substantial outlays. Governor Daniel called for a one-cent payroll tax as the easiest way to get the additional $300,000,000 for the biennium. The lawmakers rejected his proposal, but finally after a prolonged and bitter contest laid on his desk a two-cent general sales tax, exempting groceries and a few other items. The governor did not sign the act but permitted it to become a law. A corporations tax and a tax aimed at gas pipelines was also enacted. At a called session the lawmakers gave the public school teachers a raise averaging $810 a year, which would absorb $149,000,000 of the estimated $350,000,000 that the new taxes would produce.

Notwithstanding the substantial increase in revenue through the sales tax and other levies, Governor John Connally, who took office in January 1963, felt impelled to ask the lawmakers for additional money and a new tax law was calculated to bring in $33,000,000 more. Still, for the first time in recent years a state administration was relieved of the necessity of making new taxes its leading issue. Connally directed his attention mainly to long-range planning for Texas and called on the legislature at this and following sessions (it will be recalled that he won an overwhelming victory in 1964) to enact laws and submit constitutional amendments to promote his program. A Tourist Development Agency was established, which apparently succeeded in increasing the coming of people to visit the state. Parks and wildlife conservation were merged under a commission and more funds provided for park development. More aid was extended to disabled persons. The state was authorized to extend greater aid in the building of reservoirs and the storage of water.

Connally's program featured the improvement of education beyond the high school. A 25-member committee to make a study of education beyond the high school was appointed and its recommendation led to strengthening of the Texas Commission on Higher Education, which acts as a coordinator for the colleges and universities. The governor sought to secure greater appropriations for the colleges and universities, to promote the founding of more junior colleges, and to offer greater facilities for vocational training generally. The University of Houston was made a state university, and Angelo State College at San Angelo and Pan American College at Edinburg were made senior colleges.

Before completing the account of the Connally program it seems in order to take brief notice of the Texas political scene. In 1966 the political outlook was changed substantially when federal courts ruled that the poll tax voting requirement (which Texans had consistently refused to change) was unconstitutional, whereupon the legislature enacted a law eliminating the poll tax. Over the objection of many liberals, the new law required that voters register annually. Apparently the elimination of the poll tax had little effect on the results of the primaries or the general election. Connally was elected overwhelmingly for a third term and other conservative candidates fared well.

The recommendations the governor made to the legislature in 1967 were followed in part only. The body did not assent to his proposal to license the sale of liquor by the drink or to license betting on horse races. One innovation of this administration was somewhat startling and may have had far-reaching results: when the two houses seemed to be making little progress toward agreeing on the biennial appropriation bill, the governor called on them to vote appropriations for one year only. The recommendation was accepted and, as in the era of the Republic of Texas, lawmakers enacted a general appropriation bill for one year only. Of significance in this connection is the fact that the voters had rejected an amendment to the constitution providing for annual legislative sessions.

Connally appealed to the legislature to authorize a constitutional convention. He pointed out that the fundamental law restricts and withholds from the legislature so many powers that it has become necessary to submit to the voters a confusing and almost innumerable list of proposed amendments. He might have added that in 1965 27 were submitted of which 20 had been adopted and that the constitution had been amended some 178 times. Parenthetically, it may be added that seven of the fourteen amendments voted on in November, 1968, were defeated.

The lawmakers did not, however, submit to the voters the question of a constitutional convention. Through the cooperation of the House, a 25-member commission was set up to recommend a new constitution or major revisions in the old one. The Legislature accepted the governor's recommendation that the constitution be amended to allow bonds

The second United States President born in Texas (Dwight D. Eisenhower was the first), Lyndon Baines Johnson made his home state the base for a long and distinguished political career. Elected to Congress in 1937, to the Senate in 1948, to the Vice-Presidency in 1960, he became president when John F. Kennedy was assassinated and was elected for the next term in 1964. The University of Texas awarded him a degree as a distinguished American statesman as well as the state's most illustrious citizen of the day. After deciding not to seek re-election, Johnson returned to Texas in 1969 where he planned to engage in writing and lecturing. (E. C. Barker History Center, University of Texas)

of as much as $75,000,000 to purchase and develop parks, and the amendment was adopted by the voters. The electorate also authorized the issuing of more bonds for land purchases by veterans. Another amendment, adopted by the voters in November 1968, would abolish all state property taxes other than ten cents on the $100 for college buildings. The legislature approved limited participation in medical aid to the needy, called Medicaid.

A called legislative session, made necessary because the body in 1967 had made appropriations for one year only, ended in early July 1968. The budget for the fiscal year beginning in September was about $2,500,000,000. Federal grants to the state—highways, public health, public welfare and education—absorbed about a fourth of the budget. As in all preceding sessions in recent years, the lawmakers had been obliged to levy new taxes, principally by raising the sales tax to three cents. The voters had authorized an amendment to the constitution enabling cities to vote a sales tax of one cent, and most cities had taken advantage of the provision. Thus, on most purchases other than groceries, the rank and file of Texans henceforth would pay four cents taxes on the dollar.

The outlook of Texas politics was changed greatly in 1968 when both Governor Connally and President Johnson announced that they would not seek reelection. Half a score of candidates sought the Democratic nomination for governor and nearly two million voters took part in the primary. Lieutenant Governor Preston Smith, a conservative, and Don Yarborough, an outstanding liberal, entered the run-off. Yarborough advocated a minimum wage of $1.25, a state poverty corps, and increased state aid to the aged, to the disabled, and to dependent children. Some of Smith's billboards read, "Continue Conservative Government."

Results were disappointing to the liberals. The "new voters" they had counted on either did not vote or had fragmented their strength. Smith's vote was 756,909 against Yarborough's 620,726. In November Smith easily defeated the Republican nominee, Paul Eggers.

Led by Governor Connally, the conservative Democratic forces controlled the state presidential convention and sent to the national convention at Chicago a delegation of 104 instructed to support the governor as a favorite-son candidate. At Chicago the Texas liberals contested unsuccessfully the seating of the regular delegation. Vice President Hubert Humphrey won the nomination on the first ballot. The Texan delegation unanimously supported the Vietnam plank in the national platform that opposed a reversal of the administration policy. (It was reported unofficially at about this time that the war had taken the lives of some 1,700 Texans. Texas voters were eager to see it brought to an end but were not in a humor for surrender.)

Texas Republicans united by supporting Richard Nixon and his running mate Spiro T. Agnew, who were nominated in the national convention in Miami. George C. Wallace, former governor of Alabama, headed the new American Party in the contest. The Democrats carried Texas by a close vote and by a margin even more slender Nixon and Agnew carried the nation. Wallace's vote in Texas and in the nation was relatively small.

Selected Bibliography

The writings of S.S. McKay on Texas politics of the twentieth century are very useful: *W. Lee O'Daniel and Texas Politics, 1938–1942* (Lubbock, 1944); *Texas Politics, 1906–1944* (Lubbock, 1952); and *Texas and the Fair Deal, 1945–1952* (San Antonio, 1954). The Texas Institute of Public Affairs, The University of Texas, has published reviews of the work of several legislatures since 1953. It has also published O.D. Weeks, *Texas Presidential Politics in 1956* (Austin, 1957); *Texas in the 1960 Presidential Election* (Austin, 1960); and *Texas in 1964: A One-Party State Again?*

(Austin, 1965). Useful also is *Party and Factional Division in Texas* by James R. Soukup, Clifton McCleskey, and Harry Holloway (Austin, 1964); and *A History of the Republican Party in Texas* by P.D. Casdorph (Austin, 1965).

Fighting by Texans in World War II is related in *The Infantry Journal*, March, 1944, being an account of the Thirty-Sixth Division (Paris, France, 1944); "The Thirty-Sixth Division at Salerno," is related by Major James E. Taylor, *Southwestern Historical Quarterly*, XLVIII, 281–285.

For accounts of the tidelands and the issues involved, see Ernest R. Bartley, *The Tidelands Oil Controversy* (Austin, 1953).

In connection with scandals in insurance see: The Texas Legislative Council, "Insolvency in the Texas Insurance Industry; Insurance, Texas' Frauds and Failures," *Time*, May 31, 1954, p. 64; "Those Texas Scandals," *The Saturday Evening Post*, November 12, 1955, pp. 19ff; D.B. Hardeman, "Shivers of Texas: A Tragedy in Three Acts," *Harpers*, November, 1956, pp. 50–56; Ronnie Dugger, "What Corrupted Texas?" *Harpers*, March, 1957, pp. 58–78.

Concerning Lyndon B. Johnson and Texas Politics, see Rowland Evans and Robert Novak, *Lyndon B. Johnson: The Exercise of Power* (New York, 1966).

20

CONSERVATION

The natural resources of Texas are surpassingly great. They have brought to the state a measure of wealth and general prosperity. Some have, however, been eroded, wasted and dissipated by improper use and the problems of conserving them against deterioration and bringing about their most effective use is ever foremost. Human resources are even more important than those supplied by nature, and the two are inseparable. The struggle by individuals, groups, and organizations to bring about and maintain the proper and profitable use of the land and its output is a part of this story of conservation. Any account of conservation, therefore, may well begin with the land and with the people who use it.

EFFORTS OF THE FARMERS TO HELP THEMSELVES

It will be recalled that the Grange, the first general organization of farmers, entered Texas in 1873 and claimed 50,000 members by 1877. Its ambitious plans for helping its members by establishing stores, mills, and factories failed. Inadequate capital, dangerous extension of credit, and bad management generally brought ruin. The experience of the Farmers' Alliance a decade later, furthermore, was much the same.

For more than a decade after the passing of the Farmers' Alliance,

Texas farmers had no organization. Then in 1902 Isaac Newton (Newt) Gresham, a Rains County farmer, and nine of his neighbors organized the Farmers' Educational and Cooperative Union of America. According to its charter its aims were "to assist them [the farmers] in marketing and obtaining better prices for their products, for fraternal purposes, and to cooperate with them in the protection of their interests." Its rapid growth must have surprised even its founders, for by 1905 the Union claimed 120,000 members in Texas and 80,000 in other states and territories. After 1909 the Texas organization was known as the Farmers' Union of Texas.

Far more ambitious than preceding organizations, the Farmers' Union made efforts to regulate both cotton acreage and cotton prices, but it is impossible to tell what results these efforts had. It lacked both the money and the organization to carry through such an ambitious plan. In 1906 and 1907 the Farmers' Union established stores in different communities and attempted to unite them in a common sales system with headquarters in Houston. The Panic of 1907 caught the Houston agency with thousands of bales of cotton, and the severe loss it suffered on the sale of this commodity put an end to the agency. In later years the organization set up a central clearinghouse for selling and buying, but the Panic of 1914 forced it out of business. Thereafter the Farmers' Union declined rapidly. It was revived after World War II and became the most militant farmers' organization.

These farmers' organizations left certain enduring results. The influence of the Grange and of the Farmers' Alliance in politics has been described in an earlier chapter. The Farmers' Union could not claim credit for any major legislation, but it exercised considerable influence at the state capital. Furthermore, in addition to the direct benefits certain members received from these organizations, all farmers profited indirectly. The cooperatives forced independent competing merchants to pay more for the farmer's produce and to sell him goods at a lower margin of profit.

After the price debacle in 1920, Texas farmers, again seeking an organization that might improve their lot, formed two competing groups —the Farm-Labor Union and the Farm Bureau Federation. The first chapter of the Farm-Labor Union was organized at Bonham in 1920 by a small band of cotton farmers in financial straits. Confining its membership strictly to "dirt farmers," it spread rapidly through Texas and into Oklahoma, Louisiana, Alabama, Mississippi, and Florida. By the close of 1925 its membership had reached 160,000. Bad management and its failure to set up an adequate marketing system, together with the rise in farm prices which improved the condition of its members, brought an end to its activities soon thereafter. Its leaders had proposed a plan for pooling commodities and selling through a national agency, but the plan was never fairly tried.

In contrast with the failure of the Farm-Labor Union has been the success of the Farm Bureau Federation, which was organized on a national basis in 1919. By 1922 no less than 44 state farmers' organizations had united with it. In Texas the Farm Bureau Federation had its beginning in 1920, and grew rapidly. Failure of a cotton pool sponsored by members and leaders in 1926 brought discredit to the Texas Bureau and thereafter it virtually collapsed. A few faithful members kept together a skeletal organization, however, until 1933 when the Farmers' Protective Committee was organized. This committee later became the Texas Agricultural Association, an organization comparatively weak and ineffective. The state was then seriously handicapped for want of an agency qualified to speak for Texas farmers on various vital questions national in scope. This situation was corrected in 1936, when the Agricultural Association was enlarged and affiliated with the American Farm Bureau Federation.

The Texas Farm Bureau grew and reached a membership of more than 100,000 in the 1960's. It has worked for the promotion of agricultural education and research, for the improvement of animal health laws, better farm-to-market roads, and various other proposals in the interest of farmers. It has opposed minimum wage laws for agricultural employees, has favored the eventual elimination of crop controls and price supports, and is generally regarded as the most conservative of the major farm organizations.

GOVERNMENT AID—EDUCATION AND EXPERIMENTATION

If land grants for homesteads be excepted, the first aid extended to the farmers of the United States by state and federal governments was through education. We have seen that the Morrill Land Grant College Act of Congress, passed in 1862, made possible the Agricultural and Mechanical College of Texas, which was opened in 1876. Scarcely less important than the Morrill Act was the Hatch Act of 1887, providing aid for agricultural experiment stations in the states. During the next year Texas established an experiment station and made it a part of the college. Soon substations were founded; every natural region of the state had one or more such establishments, where specialists learned the most practicable farming methods and sought to make their knowledge available to the people. The general government continued to subsidize research in agriculture as carried on at the state experiment stations. The Adams Act of 1906, the Purnell Act of 1925, and the Bankhead-Jones Act of 1935, each brought larger allotments to Texas. Its share of such funds in 1940 reached approximately $150,000. Still more aid was provided the states by the Research and Marketing Act of 1946. Soils and their uses, methods of tillage, the combatting of pests and diseases, and the care and feeding of livestock are a few of the scores of subjects dealt with in the reports of the stations. The work of Dr. Mark Francis, in connection with the control and eradication of Texas tick fever among cattle, has within itself more than warranted all the money spent for research in Texas.

About the turn of this century a few leaders realized that men could be taught more effectively on their own farms than on farms maintained by the state. Such a leader was Seaman A. Knapp, who founded the home demonstration movement in 1903, a movement which soon became national in scope. With the aid of citizens, Knapp, a distinguished scholar connected with the United States Department of Agriculture, established at Terrell a "community demonstration." He secured a small appropriation from the United States Department of Agriculture, and with the aid of the Fort Worth and Denver Railroad, the community demonstration farm plan was extended.

The agricultural demonstration work thus started was both broadened and intensified during the next decade. The men working with Knapp were assigned counties, and the day of the county agent was ushered in. A state law of 1911 authorizing counties to match state and federal funds to support extension work caused the program to be stabilized. The boys' cornclub movement was started in 1908, and soon girls' clubs were organized. Home demonstration work had its beginning about 1912, the year that all extension agencies were centered in the Agricultural and Mechanical College. The short course for farmers offered at the College soon came to be widely attended and to serve very effectively the improvement of farming.

The scope and effectiveness of these agencies increased greatly during the quarter of a century following 1915. Vocational training provided in the high schools has contributed also to the improvement of farming in Texas. The National Vocational Education (Smith-Hughes) Act of 1917 provided money to help pay the salaries of teachers of vocational subjects, and set forth requirements as to methods of teaching far superior to those which had previously been used in most schools. The teaching of agriculture has been extended to practically all high schools where it is needed.

GOVERNMENT AID—PRICE
AND COMMODITY CONTROL

In an earlier chapter it was brought out that, notwithstanding disaster such as floods and price fluctuations, the early years of the twentieth century were relatively prosperous ones for farmers. Growing cities and the consequent enlarging of markets brought to them an affluence greater than they had ever known. Sharp price breaks, such as those in the price of cotton in 1908, 1911, and 1914, were temporary and prices soon recovered. Between 1910 and 1920 farmlands doubled in value, and cultivated acreage increased nine percent, as compared with an increase of five percent for the preceding decade. Expansion in Texas was much greater than it was in the nation as a whole; harvested cropland increased from 18,384,910 acres in 1910 to 25,027,773 in 1920, or a little more than 30 percent. A considerable amount of this newly farmed land was marginal and would not yield a profit except under conditions extremely favorable.

Deflation, which set in in 1920, pressed heavily against the structure of agricultural prices during the following decade. Unlike the manufacturers, the farmers of the nation experienced little of the prosperity that followed recovery in 1922.

Meanwhile, in an effort to bolster agriculture, Congress passed several laws. The Capper-Volstead Cooperative Act of 1922 exempted agricultural associations and cooperatives from prosecution under the Sherman antitrust law; and the Federal Intermediate Credit Act passed the next year made available for farmers new credit resources. President Hoover signed the Agricultural Marketing Act of 1929, which rejected the price-fixing and subsidy features of earlier proposals and centered on the idea of curtailing production through voluntary cooperation under government auspices. Farmers were to be organized in cooperative marketing associations which would stabilize prices by the handling and disposing of marketing surpluses. Under the direction of a Federal Farm Board, a revolving fund of $500,000,000 was set up to lend money to cooperatives whenever it became necessary. Cooperatives were formed rapidly, and in its first year the board made loans to 132 of them.

Of all commodities, wheat and cotton, the two leading crops in Texas, proved costliest. Efforts to keep up the price of wheat failed and in spite of a loss by the Federal Farm Board of $150,000,000 cotton was selling at five cents a pound in 1932, a price ruinously low for the growers.

The Roosevelt administration attacked the farm problem with the most elaborate program in history. In fact, it made relief for agriculture a sort of cornerstone for the entire New Deal structure. The heart of the plan was to provide farmers with purchasing power equal to that of the prewar years; to create a condition whereby they should have parity income based on the period from August 1909 to July 1914—that is, their economic condition should, as nearly as possible, be made as favorable relative to other industries as it was during the five years next preceding the beginning of the first World War. In order to attain this goal, farm production was to be adjusted to meet market requirements, and surpluses were to be held off the market to prevent their destroying the price structure. Closely associated with this part of the program were a plan for conserving the soil by the proper use of lands withdrawn from the production of staple crops; better credit facilities for farmers; and federal aid for the relief and the rehabilitation of the poorest part of the agricultural population. This program was put into effect under the Agricultural Adjustment Act of May 1933. For every acre taken out of production the farmers were to receive compensation from a fund to be raised by taxes levied on the processing of agricultural commodities. The average rental paid on cotton land was eleven dollars per acre. In addition the growers were given a chance to make a profit by taking an option on the cotton the government already held.

Under the 1933 program it was proposed to take out of production not less than 10,000,000 acres, approximately 3,000,000 bales. It was midsummer before the plan was put into effect and it was necessary that the farmers who signed the contracts plow up from one-fourth to one-half of their growing crops. This New Deal plan for attaining prosperity through destruction puzzled many people and brought forth much criticism. More shocking still was a part of the plan adopted later for rehabilitating the livestock industry, under which cattle were shot on the range and their carcasses left to rot. About 10,400,000 acres of cotton were taken out of production, nearly 40 percent of which was in Texas. Texan growers shared in the payments to an amount of $44,580,877.37. As Will Rogers expressed it, they found that being paid not to farm was more profitable than farming.

The farmers cooperated, but nature did not. The crop was 13,000,000 bales, nearly 3,000,000 greater than had been expected. It was evident that a more effective plan of control was necessary. This plan was provided in April 1934 by the Cotton Control Act, commonly called the Bankhead Act. Under this law the voluntary features of the cotton program were abandoned and the farmers were completely regimented.

In January 1936 the Supreme Court declared unconstitutional and null and void the Agricultural Adjustment Act. Congress promptly passed the Soil Conservation and Allotment Act, under which the growers of wheat, corn, cotton, and tobacco might continue to receive grants from the United States government, provided they continued to divert from the growing of staples a part of their lands and practiced such measures as terracing, fertilizing, and planting leguminous crops.

This plan was only partly effective in preventing surpluses. By this time the Supreme Court had become more sympathetic toward the new program, and Congress passed the Agricultural Adjustment Act of 1938, which fixed as a permanent policy the minute control of agriculture by the federal government. Under its terms producers of the more important staples were to receive benefit payments in order to restore parity income measured by the 1909–1914 standard. When necessary to sustain prices, loans might be made on commodities. Parity payments, made available by subsequent legislation, were to be made only to those producers who did not exceed their acreage allotments, and payments were to be limited to the amount required to bring the return to the farmer up to 75 percent of parity price. In other words, the farmers would be assured that a bale of cotton produced in 1939 would purchase at least three-fourths as much goods as a bale of cotton produced during the period from 1909 to 1914. By 1940 cotton acreage had been reduced about 50 percent, but production had been reduced only about 10 percent since 1930.

While aiding farmers with subsidies, the federal government provided for the extension of credit facilities. The Emergency Farm Mortgage Act of 1933 liberalized the loan policy of the land banks, both with respect to the security demanded on loans and the rate of interest (lowered to four percent). Then, in order to enable the land banks to provide this additional credit, the Farm Mortgage Refinancing Act of 1934 was passed, creating the Federal Farm Mortgage Corporation, under the direction of the Farm Credit Administration. Additional federal credit for agriculture to the amount of $2,000,000,000 was thus provided. This credit enabled many farmers to hold onto their homes when otherwise they would have lost them through foreclosure. Credit for farm operations was provided under the Farm Credit Act of 1933, which authorized the organization of production credit associations. Under the plan farmers and stockmen are allowed to organize cooperatives and on members' notes borrow from the federal intermediate credit banks at a rate of about five percent interest. By 1938, 100,000 Texas farmers were taking advantage of these facilities. Credit was extended also to cooperative purchasing and marketing associations.

To aid low income farmers, the Farmers' Home Administration was established in 1937 under the direction of the Department of Agriculture. It lent money for purchasing livestock, fertilizer, and other equipment calculated to make farmers self-sustaining. Also it made loans at very low rates of interest for purchasing farm homes and making improvements. More recently it has extended credit to rural groups for installing water and sewerage systems.

During the second third of the twentieth century trends in agriculture continued with little interruption. The number of Texas farms declined greatly and their size increased proportionately, from about a half million in 1935, averaging 274.86 acres to 205,109 farms in 1964, averaging 690.9 acres. By 1966 the average farm represented an investment of nearly $100,000. There was even a greater change in farm tenantry; tenants numbered 301,660 in 1930, a little more than a third of them sharecroppers. By 1964 there were only 37,080 tenants, and sharecroppers were not reported. The most impressive change of all was in farm population. In 1940 about one Texan in three lived on a farm; in 1966 estimates were that only about 560,000 out of 10,500,000 inhabitants, or about one in eighteen, lived on a farm.

Apparently the shift in population away from the farms, together with the consequent enlargement of units, with increased mechanization, and with better methods and management have strengthened agriculture economically. Crop values have increased greatly and comparison of the outputs of major crops bears evidence of substantial growth. The exodus of people from the farms has, however, raised certain sociological and political questions of grave concern. The traditional American concept is that farmers constitute a stay and ballast of society and that the decline of rural population is a serious social loss. More indisputable is the fact that farmers, who until well into the twentieth century outnumbered those of all other vocations combined, have become a relatively small minority and political power has shifted from the country to the cities.

When prices dropped after World War II and price supports were restored, farmers continued to plant huge crops in order to secure the 90 percent of parity payments. To reduce this practice a flexible price support plan was adopted. Also, beginning in 1956 under the "Soil Bank" Act, farmers leased to the federal government for a period of years almost 20 percent of the crop land of the state, taking it completely out of production. Still farmers of Texas and of the nation produced larger crops than ever and surpluses continued. As late as 1969 farmers (by their own vote) continued to farm with the limitations of allotments, quotas, and price supports.

Texas farm income in 1966, including government payments through the Agricultural Stabilization and Conservation Service and the value of commodities consumed on the farm, was estimated at $2,711,411,000, an increase over that of the preceding year. Their expenses, which were estimated at $1,913,200,000, were increasing much faster than the farmers' income.

Although only about eight percent of Texas' population was engaged in producing agricultural commodities in 1968, a segment of the population far greater was dependent on it more or less for a livelihood. About 12 percent of the people derive all or a substantial part of their income from supplying ranchmen and farmers, and about 20 percent are connected directly with the processing and distributing of agricultural commodities.

THE CONSERVATION OF SOIL AND TIMBER

Under the New Deal farm program the regulation of production and of prices has been linked directly with a less controversial subject, the conservation of soil and water and other resources associated with them. Farmers are paid for terracing, contour ridging, contour listing, the construction of reservoirs, the growing of leguminous and cover crops, and various other soil-building and soil-conserving practices. Efforts to cope with the problem of soil depletion are, however, older than the Agricultural Adjustment Administration.

A survey by the Soil Conservation Service of the United States Department of Agriculture showed that about 132,000,000 acres in Texas (about three-fourths of the entire area) were suffering from erosion. Ruined for further immediate crop production were 11,000,000 acres; severely damaged land aggregated 53,500,000; and 67,500,000 acres were slightly damaged. Rain in Texas comes periodically in downpours, occasionally amounting to several inches within a single hour. At such times sloping land that is cultivated and even rolling pasture land that is heavily grazed is slashed and cut by myraids of rivulets and gullies, until after a few years the topsoil is washed away and the land becomes almost worthless. Geographers have pointed to the great areas in China, once fertile but now made desolate by erosion, and to the ruins of cities in the Near East that were once surrounded by productive lands; but widespread interest in the problem has been slow in developing. Anglo-Americans have had plenty of land. When a field has worn out they have just cleared and plowed a new one. Now very little arable land is left untouched by the plow, the price of land has risen continuously for a quarter century, and the need for taking proper care of land is being more generally realized.

A few people, however, recognized the gravity of the problem at an early date. Howard Duke, a Newton County farmer, constructed a farm terrace in 1882, and other East Texas farmers imitated his practice. The Farmers' Cooperative Demonstration Work, now known as the extension service, began efforts to educate farmers on the subject as early as 1910. In 1927 the Federal Farm Land Bank made terracing a part of its credit extension agreement, and soon the United States Department of Agriculture established erosion-control experiment stations in Texas. The United States Soil Conservation Service, created by the Department of Agriculture in 1935, began to apply to the problem the vast resources placed at its command, and the Agricultural and Mechanical College cooperated with it. In order that Texas might get maximum benefit from the federal agencies, the legislature in 1939 passed a state soil conservation law under which landowners may by their own vote establish soil conservation districts. Local, state, and federal agencies provide technical personnel, labor, and equipment, and under the direction of a board of supervisors the conservation work in the district is carried on systematically. Nearly all of the state has been organized in conservation districts. Until about 1930 terracing crop lands to prevent erosion was the main feature of the service. It has been broadened to include such practices as contour plowing, crop rotation, and the growing of legumes, with the federal government making payments to encourage the improvements. By 1960 25,000,000 acres of range land had been improved.

Although there is very little virgin timber left, the more than 10 million acres of forest land in eastern Texas represents one of the state's

With modern equipment and conservation practices, timber industries (among the oldest in Texas) still contribute substantially to the economy of the state. (Texas Highway Department)

greatest natural resources. Very little was done by way of conserving the timberlands until the Texas Forest Service was created in 1913 and placed under the direction of the Agricultural and Mechanical College. In the following year federal cooperative aid for fire prevention was secured and a skeleton organization was perfected. Demonstration and research facilities were provided in 1924 when the state acquired its first forest. Later, forest nurseries and research laboratories were established.

An important step in the development of forests in Texas was the purchase of forest land by the federal government, pursuant to an invitation extended by the legislature in 1935. In 1955 the four national forests represented a total of 658,112 acres, excellently kept.

With the cooperation of the federal government and land owners, the state maintained a fire prevention service with 83 fire towers. Under the Cooperative Forest Management Act of 1950, aid was extended to farmers and other owners of forest lands to enable them to care for their timber better. Seedlings were sold to them at cost and expert advice was provided on various features. By 1966 tree farms in Texas aggregated nearly 4,000,000 acres and timber was being grown faster than it was being cut.

WATER

Of all the factors affecting the movement of population and the comfort and prosperity of the people none has been more important than water. Abundant springs and running streams made easy the settlement of East Texas; in many parts of Central and West Texas settlement was retarded because of the difficulty of securing water. It will be recalled that the High Plains were not appropriated until well drills and windmills tapped the bountiful veins of underground water.

A most valuable natural resource is the Texas underground water supply. There are sources such as those underlying the Edwards Plateau, from which pour the great springs at San Marcos and New Braunfels; the Trinity sands, underlying much of Central Texas; underground water formations in the Gulf Coastal Plain, which supply municipalities and much of the water for rice growing; and the Ogallala formation underlying much of the High Plains.

The problem of flood control and of the equitable distribution for irrigation, municipal supply, and industry have brought about the enactment of a number of laws pertaining to the surface waters of Texas. In 1909 the state took notice of the water problem by creating the office of State Reclamation Engineer, whose work would deal chiefly with levee construction and the problems of the lower river channels. Four years later the Board of Water Engineers was established and given jurisdiction mainly over water-shortage problems. The conservation amendment to the constitution in 1917, and the legislative acts that followed, encouraged the organization of conservation or reclamation districts.

With respect to control, Texas drainage basins may be divided into three classes: the Canadian and Red River basins, which belong to the Mississippi River system and are shared with other states; the Rio Grande and its tributaries, representing watersheds that lie partly in Texas and partly in other states and Mexico; and those watersheds between, lying wholly or almost wholly in Texas.

The first conservation districts were organized in somewhat haphazard fashion. The program was not coordinated; each community, whether its problem was that of irrigation, drainage, or flood control was disposed to consider its own immediate interests with little regard to those of other localities or to the program as a whole. Gradually it came to be recognized that the entire area within the watershed of a stream constituted a unit for all water use and control; that in such a district water storage, irrigation, industrial use, municipal supply, the building of levees, and the generation of electric power were inseparably linked.

In 1929 the Brazos River Conservation and Reclamation District (since 1953, the Brazos River Authority), the oldest large Texas conservation district, was created with generous powers for the purpose of conserving and exploiting the waters of the entire Brazos River water-shed. No other Texas agency has been endowed with powers so great. It has constructed Possum Kingdom Reservoir, near Mineral Wells, Whitney, near Hillsboro, and Belton, near that city. These are multiple purpose reservoirs; that is, they are designed for flood control, for water storage, and, except Lake Belton, for the generation of electric power. The largest water conservation and utilization agency on the Colorado River is the Lower Colorado River Authority, which has constructed multiple-purpose dams and made the Colorado River a string of lakes for a hundred miles above Austin.

With Dallas and Fort Worth and a vast additional metropolitan area in its scope, the Trinity River watershed has been the site of reservoirs for half a century. By 1955 nine large reservoirs had been built—or were being built—with a total storage capacity of 6,431,200 acre feet. Among them was the huge Lewisville Dam project in Denton County that would hold some 2,250,000 acre feet of water. These reservoirs of the Trinity basin cost all told about $105 million, the contribution of the federal government running a little more than half.

The scores of water authorities and regional and municipal districts cannot be named in these pages. During the early 1960's it was reported in the state there were not less than 200 major reservoirs, each with a capacity of 5,000 acre feet or more. Some outstanding projects were Lewisville Dam on the Trinity River, the McGee Bend Reservoir on the Neches in Jasper County; Lake Houston on the San Jacinto, Toledo Bend on the Sabine, and Lake Corpus Christi on the Nueces.

Compacts between Texas and neighboring states and between the United States and Mexico have made possible such great man-made lakes as Texoma on the Red River, and Falcon and Amistad on the Rio Grande, each impounding four or five million acre feet of water, enough to cover some eight standard-sized Texas counties to a depth of a foot.

As the middle years of the twentieth century passed, Texans developed a thirst for water that could not be quenched. No matter how much water a city, community, or region had, it seemed never to have enough. Industries were in some cases vying with farmers for water, and farmers were looking for more water or hoping to keep what they had. The Wagstaff-Woodward Law of 1932 placed the claims of cities to water ahead of all other interests. Still, industrialists near the coast protested to the governing agencies when cities in northern and western Texas asked for permits to impound and use more water. The Texas Water Commission estimated in 1961 that the state was using 29,000,000 acre feet annually, nearly half of which was nonconsumptive, that is, it was used to generate electric power. Cities were using about a million and a half acre feet, industries a little less and irrigators about 12,000,000 acre feet.

The need for water was aggravated in the 1950's by persistent drought, a condition that necessitated some direct drought relief and generous loans from federal agencies. The drought quickened interest in water conservation. The building of reservoirs was hastened. Voters authorized the issuing of bonds worth hundreds of millions of dollars to enable the state to aid in water storage, and the state strengthened its administration of water affairs. The Board of Water Engineers was succeeded by the Texas Water Commission; a Water Rights Commission was set up to deal with the distribution of water among users; the problems of water pollution were turned over to a special agency; and a Texas Water Development Board was created and assigned the task of formulating a water plan for Texas. Meanwhile the Water Conservation Association and a dozen other statewide or regional organizations were seeking to provide more water.

In theory, at least, the work of the several agencies, state and federal, supported by the different private organizations, was pointing toward a complete and adequate system of soil conservation, flood control, water storage, water use and electric power generation. Working with other agencies, the Soil Conservation Service would promote the maximum absorption of water by the earth where it fell. Small dams on the drainage basin fringes would lessen the impact of floods by impounding temporarily great quantities of water and retaining continuously enough for local needs. Great multiple purpose dams along the major streams would retard the waters and lessen flood damage, store great amounts for municipal use, industry, recreation, irrigation, and power, and fill with water river beds which in droughts either were dry or supplied only a trickle of water. The drought had proved the incalculable benefits of the reservoirs; then, in the spring of 1957 torrential rains proved that the system lessened flood damage, although it did not prevent it.

It was generally agreed by those persons who made even a superficial study of the problem that the water supply available in Texas would not prove adequate for the years to come. After working intensely for months, the Texas Water Development Board came forth early in 1966 with a plan for meeting Texas water needs for the next half century. The board's proposal called for a massive program of additional impounding of water and an elaborate redistribution of the supply, shifting it from basin to basin in order to supply major metropolitan areas and the coastal industrial region, with enough water left for adding a half million irrigated acres in the lower Rio Grande Valley.

Citizens of the northern and western parts of the state protested that the plan left them out. There was no proposal for getting additional water to the Rolling Plains and the High Plains. The great irrigation belt of the Lubbock and Plainview country, producing more from commodities than all the remainder of Texas combined, would be left without water if and when its wells failed to produce water from the Ogallala underground reservoir.

Whereupon the citizens of West Texas formed an organization dedicated to bringing in water in quantities through rivers and canals from the lower Mississippi. A new plan more in keeping with the interests of northern and western Texas was presented in 1968 and the legislature submitted it to the voters.

THE CONSERVATION OF OIL AND GAS

Many decades before the vast mineral resources of Texas had been discovered men had given thought to their conservation. Recognition of the possibility of the presence of minerals is revealed in much of the legislation pertaining to Texas lands. Under the Spanish and Mexican law, title to minerals was not conveyed when land was deeded to the individual, but remained fixed in the state. The Republic of Texas and the State of Texas pursued this policy until 1866. In the constitution framed in that year minerals were released to owners of the soil; this provision was incorporated in the two later constitutions. An act passed in 1907 provided that land classed as mineral land could be sold for agricultural or grazing purposes only on the express condition that the state retain its right to the minerals. This plan permitted the state to enlarge greatly its mineral land classification while, at the same time, it offered the lands for sale for agricultural or grazing purposes. The state did not, however, retain all of this mineral interest. By the Relinquishment Act of 1919, it vested in the owners of the surface fifteen-sixteenths of the oil and gas and made the owners the agent of the state for leasing purposes. Thus the state retained a one-sixteenth royalty interest for the benefit of the public school and the asylum funds. Income from oil and gas is adding substantially to the endowments of both the public schools and the University.

The first Texas law to regulate the production of oil and gas was enacted in 1899, just four years after the first commercial production of petroleum at Corsicana. It required that water be cased off from oil-bearing formations, that abandoned wells be plugged, and that gas not be permitted to escape. More adequate efforts at regulation followed the adoption of the constitutional amendment of 1917 which enlarged greatly the control of the legislature over natural resources. The pipe-line law of 1917 was enacted, providing for the organization of the oil and gas division of the Railroad Commission, with power to supervise common carrier pipe lines and regulate their rates. Two years later the oil and gas conservation law was enacted. Under its terms the Railroad Commission issued regulations calculated to prevent waste in the production of oil and gas, and after some delay the rules were enforced through agents and supervisors. Work was confined chiefly to requiring drilling reports of operators, to preventing injury to oil and gas formations by permitting water seepage, and to preventing the drilling of a well too close to a property line or to another well.

By 1925 oil operators throughout the nation were being handicapped by lack of markets. That year the Borger field was opened. In the year following the Texas Panhandle produced more than 23 million barrels; the old Beaumont (Spindletop) area took on new life and flowed 13 million barrels; the Seminole field in Oklahoma was brought in; and before the year had ended the Yates pool in Pecos County and the Hendricks in Winkler County had been tapped. Thenceforth rich new discoveries followed one after the other so closely that the market did not become adjusted for several years. By the end of 1927 the Texas fields were producing more than 700,000 barrels a day. It was generally agreed that if the wells in Pecos and Winkler counties should be permitted their maximum flow, it would triple the output for the entire state.

It was with such problems of production that the operators turned to the Railroad Commission for aid. By assent of the commission, producers in the Yates field entered into a voluntary agreement in 1927, fixing the total production of the field and prorating it among the several producers. In the Hendricks field a similar agreement was arrived at during the following year. New production continued to exceed the growth in demand, however, and, after a statewide proration hearing in 1930, the commission issued an order limiting the production of the state to 750,000 barrels daily. The order was attacked in the courts on the contention that it was not designed to prevent the waste of oil but to fix the price. It was, however, upheld by the Travis County district court.

Meanwhile there came a flood of oil from the East Texas field, which, it will be recalled, was discovered by "Dad" Joiner in September 1930. The commission was slow in asserting its authority in the new field; and when it did so, many operators either ignored its orders or attacked them by suits in the federal courts. Thus there was inaugurated a train of litigation over oil production that seemed interminable. During three special sessions the legislature gave much time to the problem. Rules made by the Railroad Commission were modified and repealed repeatedly, and the decisions of the courts were not consistent. For a period in 1931, many wells were opened completely; the production mounted to a million barrels daily (a third of the nation's requirements), and the price declined to ten cents a barrel. Then Governor Sterling placed the field under martial law, sent in the National Guard, and controlled production until February 1932, when a three-judge federal court ruled that he was acting without authority.

The cause of conservation was strengthened when the federal government, first by an executive decree and later by an act of Congress, prohibited the shipping of illegally produced oil across state boundaries. The state laws were improved; the courts became more sympathetic with regulation as the judges were forced to learn more about the oil business; and the plan of proration set forth in the order of the railroad commission in April 1933 was finally upheld by the federal courts. At last proration had become a reality. Although it was obliged to contend with many lawsuits, the commission managed to prevent the oil industry from destroying itself by producing oil faster than consumers could use it. Proration was applied throughout the state. Under the state's conservation laws the commission took "nominations," that is, estimates by the Federal Bureau of Mines and statements by the buyers as to the amount of oil that would be needed; then it allocated that demand among all the wells in all the fields of the state in proportion to the ability of each to produce. The purpose of the commission, as stated by Ernest O. Thompson, senior member, was to leave in the earth "the least possible amount of oil never to be recovered by man," and it has been highly successful.

Conservation was extended beyond state boundaries in 1935, when, with the approval of Congress and the President, Texas and five other oil-producing states entered into an interstate compact to conserve oil and gas. The compact stated that it was confined to the prevention of physical waste of oil and gas, to making recommendations that would promote the maximum ultimate recovery from the petroleum reserves, and that it was not "for the purpose of stabilizing or fixing the price thereof." Like the Texas Railroad Commission, the interstate body has, however, been disposed to favor the restriction of production to market figures.

During recent years problems associated with the conservation of natural gas have received much attention. During the early 1930's a number of stripping plants were established in the Texas Panhandle for extracting gasoline from natural gas. The process was exceedingly wasteful, for after the recovery of its small gasoline content, the gas (nature's perfect fuel which could never be replaced) was blown into the air. A law passed in 1935 stopped that practice, and also compelled manufacturers of carbon black from natural gas to use for that purpose only "sour" gas, which is not suited for use as a fuel. Some natural gas is produced in connection with the production of oil. Formerly much gas was wasted by the producers of oil by being flared or popped into the air, for the want of a market. In 1947 the Texas Railroad Commission moved against this practice and reduced it substantially.

Selected Bibliography

On the cooperative phase of the farm movement see Ralph Smith, "The Cooperative Movement in Texas," *Southwestern Historical Quarterly*, XLIV, 33–54. *Farm Bureau Policies* and other publications of the Texas

Farm Bureau (Waco), provide some information about the background of the organization. Useful also is William Tucker, "The Farmers Union . . . ," *Southwestern Social Science Quarterly*, XXVII, 45–63, and a leaflet distributed by the national headquarters of the Farmers Union, Denver, Colorado, entitled "The Farmers Union Past and Present."

The beginning of demonstration work in Texas is related in H.R. Southworth, "The Later Years of Seaman A. Knapp," *West Texas Historical Association Year Book*, X, 88–104. A satisfactory account of the New Deal farm program is given in Henry Bamford Parkes and Vincent V. Carosso, *Recent America, Book II* (New York, 1963). See also *Agricultural Research in Texas Since 1888* (College Station, 1956).

For an account of soil conservation, the *Annual Reports* of the Agricultural Extension Service, Texas A&M University, are most useful.

On water conservation, floods, and droughts much has been written in recent years. Among the best sources are: W.P. Webb, *More Water for Texas* (Austin, 1954); Robert Lee Lowry, *Surface Water Resources in Texas* (Austin, 1958); John R. Stockton, S.A. Arbingast, Richard G. Henshaw, Jr., and Alford G. Dale, *Water for the Future* (Austin, 1959), a publication of the Bureau of Business Research, The University of Texas; Raymond Lee Nance, *Drought of the 1950's, With Special Reference to the Midcontinent* (Washington, 1965). Bulletins and reports of the Texas Water Development Board provide the latest information on the subject.

The long and involved history of the conservation of oil in Texas is dealt with by R.E. Hardwicke, *Legal History of Conservation of Oil in Texas*, and Maurice Cheek, *Legal History of Conservation of Gas in Texas* (Mineral Law Section, American Bar Association, 1938). A briefer study is that of James P. Hart, "Oil, the Courts, and the Railroad Commission," *Southwestern Historical Quarterly*, XLIV, 303–320. Concerning the East Texas oil field, see Ruel McDaniel, *Some Ran Hot* (Dallas, 1939). A study of the tidelands question has been made by Ernest R. Bartley, *The Tidelands Oil Controversy* (Austin, 1953). The work of the Texas Railroad Commission is brought out in *Three Stars for the Colonel* [Ernest O. Thompson] (New York, 1957) by J.A. Clark. On the subject of oil in the Southwest, C.C. Rister's *Oil! Titan of the Southwest* (Norman, 1949) is outstanding.

21

PUBLIC PROBLEMS AND AGENCIES FOR BETTERMENT

A high birth rate and continuous immigration raised the population of Texas from 818,579 in 1870 to 5,824,715 by the census of 1930. During the doldrums of the great depression the increase slowed down but revived again thereafter to reach 7,711,794 in 1950 and 9,679,177 a decade later. One unofficial estimate made by an authority in 1967 was 10,838,502. About 94 percent of population growth in recent years has been the result of an excess of births over deaths.

URBANIZATION ADDS TO PROBLEMS

A pronounced movement of people to cities has been in evidence in recent decades. Between 1960 and 1967, 66 percent of the counties gained in population, cities and industries being mainly the cause of gains. Most of the counties that failed to gain were rural, with no large cities and without industries of importance. Population growth in the 1960's was less rapid than in the preceding decade.

Urban residents, that is persons living in places of 2,500 people or more or in densely populated fringes around cities of 50,000 or more, made up approximately 75 percent of the state's population in 1960, as compared with 70 percent for the nation as a whole. The United States

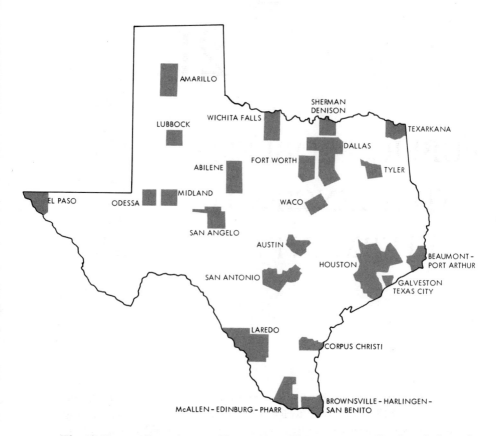

The 23 Metropolitan Areas of Texas, 1966. These areas are distributed through-
out the state, but the bulk of the population is in the eastern third. (Courtesy
of The Texas Research League)

census for that year listed 23 standard metropolitan statistical areas in
Texas, each consisting of one city or more and one county or more. The
population of these areas, as estimated for 1967, ranged from San Angelo (Tom Green County) with 75,710 people to Houston (Harris,
Brazoria, Fort Bend, Liberty, and Montgomery counties) with 1,766,315
inhabitants. Other great metropolitan centers were Dallas (Dallas, Collin, Denton, Ellis, Kaufman, and Rockwall counties) with 1,415,170
people; San Antonia (Bexar and Guadalupe counties) with 869,123 people; and Fort Worth (Tarrant and Johnson counties) numbering 651,613.
About eight out of every ten Texans lives in the 23 metropolitan statistical areas. All but six of the areas had shown a gain since 1960, but the
increase was at a slower rate than in the preceding decade.

The march to the cities has accentuated old problems and added
new ones. Fortunately no region of Texas is subject to excessive smog,

but with the increase of traffic and industry air pollution had to be reckoned with. At least a start was made by the state in the Clean Air Act passed by the legislature in 1967. The cities also have taken some action in this direction. Water contamination, arising both from the wastes of industry and the sewage of cities, imperiled vegetable and animal life as well as the health of people. The state Water Quality Board was given increased power over water pollution.

As cities grow, the quality of housing becomes of greater importance. The very detailed census of housing in 1960 revealed interesting and important facts about the living conditions of the people of the nation. Some 60 percent of the dwellers in the larger cities of Texas owned their homes, a wholesome and encouraging feature. The census indicated also that, although city dwellers lived in better homes than their rural neighbors, from 20 to 30 percent lived in places that failed to meet the standard of being "sound with all plumbing facilities." In one or more parts of every city these substandard houses, crowded with people with inadequate incomes, created slums that were breeders of crimes and various other sorts of social ills. Through Urban Renewal and other aid extended by the federal government to individuals and communities some improvement was made, but the slums remained.

As the cities grew, the need for more revenue invariably outdistanced the added income made possible by the presence of more people. Street building and maintenance, fire and police protection, parks, recreation facilities, and school buildings and school maintenance burdened them greatly, especially so since about the only source of revenue that they had was the general property tax which rested almost wholly on real estate. Hence, when the legislature in 1967 authorized a sales tax of one percent for cities if voted by the electorate, most Texas cities adopted it. In this connection it is pertinent to state that the average personal income of Texans rose from $1,925 in 1960 to $2,511 in 1966, but still was relatively low as compared with that in other states.

The burgeoning of cities also had its effects on the political structure of the state. It left the rural areas over-represented in the legislature and in Congress. The legislature was loathe to redistrict the state; indeed a constitutional provision limited the number of legislators to be elected from any one county. In the 1960's this condition was changed as a result of decisions of federal courts setting forth the "one man, one vote" principle so that the balance of political power in the state shifted to the cities.

THE RACES: INTEGRATION

The largest non-Caucasian group in Texas is the Negro, numbering 1,187,125 in 1960 and representing a little more than 12 percent of the population. For a century Negroes resided mainly on the farms of eastern Texas, where their ancestors had been brought as slaves. During World War II and after there was a pronounced exodus of the black people both out of the state and to cities within the state. These people found employment in towns and cities, so that by 1960 79 percent of Texas Negroes lived in municipalities. Here they were segregated in districts and many of them could maintain only very low living standards.

Pursuant to an act of the legislature, public schools for Negroes were first provided in 1870. The schools long operated under severe handicaps, such as poorly trained teachers, poor schoolhouses, short terms, and unequal distribution of school funds. The Gilmer-Aiken laws of 1949 removed most of the legal handicaps. In addition to the Prairie View Agricultural and Mechanical College for Negroes, the state established in 1947 the Texas State University for Negroes, named Texas Southern University in 1951. In 1957 there were not less than eight independent colleges for Negroes and four public junior colleges.

A decision of the Supreme Court of the United States aimed at racial segregation in the schools changed radically race relations in Texas and other states, especially states of the South. Texas was directly affected in the case of an earlier decision in which the Supreme Court directed the University of Texas to admit a Negro, H. M. Sweatt,[1] to its law school. This decision opened to Negroes the graduate and professional schools of the university. Far more sweeping was the decision of May 1954, pertaining to the public schools. Basing its opinion squarely on the Fourteenth Amendment, which guarantees to all persons the equal protection of the laws, the court held that even if the schools that were maintained by the state for Negroes were in every respect just as good as those for whites, segregation itself deprived the children of the minority group of equal educational opportunities, and added: "To separate them [Negro children] from others of similar age and qualifications solely because of their race generates a feeling of inferiority. . . . We conclude that in the field of public education the doctrine of separate but equal has no place."

The court indicated a willingness to move slowly in applying its doctrine, and left the approach to the lower federal courts. Tension began to mount in Texas in 1956. In the July Democratic primary certain issues were submitted in language favorable to the segregationists, and a large majority of voters favored stronger laws against intermarriage between whites and blacks, laws exempting white students from attending integrated schools, and interposition by the state to avoid the effects of certain decisions by the United States Supreme Court. Here and there threats of violence occurred when schools opened in September, but

---

[1]*Sweatt* v. *Painter*, 339 U.S. 629 (1950). The decision pertaining to the public schools is *Brown* v. *Board of Education of Topeka*, 347 U.S. 483 (1954).

happily the serious disturbances were few. At Mansfield the presence of Negro students in the high school pursuant to a federal court order brought a threat of mob action; Governor Shivers sent in State Rangers with orders that persons whose presence was calculated to lead to riot be sent elsewhere. The Negroes discontinued their attempts to attend the school. A mob of outsiders repeatedly sought to prevent Negroes from entering Lamar College at Beaumont, but did not succeed. Early in 1957 Governor Daniel approved an act of the legislature making mandatory the assent of the voters of any school district before the races could be mixed in the schools. The penalty provided was the withdrawal of all state aid for the district. Before the year ended another law was enacted providing for the closing of any public school at which troops, either federal or state, were stationed.

But legislation against integration and disapproval of it in many communities only delayed it. Its proponents appealed to the federal courts, and federal judges, by authority of the Supreme Court of the United States, uniformly ordered school districts to present plans for desegregation. Governor Price Daniel did not attempt to interpose state authority against the federal agencies. The movement made slow progress, however. Most of the larger school districts submitted plans calling for one-grade-a-year integration. By April 1963 it was reported that 176 of 890 biracial school districts had integrated and an estimate in the autumn of 1966 was that some 100,000 of the state's 400,000 Negro students were in classes at formerly all-white schools. The junior colleges were opened to black students and in 1965 the Southwest Athletic Conference dropped the color line.

There was a substantial increase in the number of Negroes elected to local and state offices. Notable was the election of Miss Barbara Jordan to the state senate from Houston.

Some hotels, restaurants, theaters, and stores resisted integration stubbornly and had to cope with demonstrations, picketing, "sit-ins," and various other forms of disapproval and opposition. The agitators were mainly young people, many of them college students, both white and black. Gradually the barriers were removed, and in most establishments Negroes were accepted.

Labor unions were slow to remove color and race lines. As late as 1962 the statement of George Meany, the national labor leader, "if you pay your dues you should be treated equally," was more the ideal than the practice in Texas. Gains were made, nevertheless. For instance, it was reported that Latin-Americans in San Antonio, who formerly had been excluded, made up 35 percent of craft union membership, and plans were underway to have Negroes accepted as craftsmen. At different points in the state complaints about discrimination continued to be voiced, however.

Although Texas communities did not altogether escape violence resulting from racial clashes, it was gratifying that, with the second largest Negro population of any state in the nation, Texas escaped large-scale rioting such as plagued Los Angeles, Detroit, and Newark. Many alert and dedicated community relations committees aided the cause of law and order.

The Latin-American population of Texas, composed almost entirely of people either Mexican born or of Mexican descent, increased rapidly during the twentieth century. In 1910 it made up a little less than six percent of the total. In 1960 white persons with Spanish surnames numbered 1,418,000, being more than 14 percent of the total and the fastest growing ethnic group in the state. During the early twentieth century these people resided mostly in San Antonio, El Paso, Corpus Christi, and communities of the lower Rio Grande valley. Beginning with World War II, however, they were disposed to move in numbers to Houston, Dallas, Fort Worth, and other cities in the different parts of the state.

In San Antonio and other old cities and communities in South Texas lived certain relatively small groups of proud and aristocratic people of superior culture, mainly of Spanish origin. Some of their ancestors came to Texas long before the Nordics had set foot on its soil. These people, together with a large middle class of Spanish lineage, have made substantial contributions to the civilization of Texas and among them are to be found some of its sturdiest citizens. Much larger than the groups already named were the farm laboring class. Many of these people were migratory. It had been their practice to spend the winter in South Texas and move northward in spring to work in harvests, even going into Colorado, Michigan, and Minnesota for work on the sugar beet farms. In recent years, however, opportunity for employment in agriculture has diminished and many of them have turned to industry. Still, in 1965, Texas had the largest home-based migrant labor force in the United States—127,000 workers.

Alleging discrimination, at times during the 1940's the Mexican Government refused to give Texas a quota for seasonal labor migration, with the result that each season tens of thousands of Mexican workers entered Texas illegally. They were commonly called "wetbacks," on the supposition that they had swum the Rio Grande at unguarded points (a compliment the shallow river rarely merited: swimming was not necessary). Because they were at the mercy of their employers, "wetbacks" were often mistreated. In 1943 Governor Stevenson created the Texas Good Neighbor Commission and the legislature later placed it on an enduring basis. By education, persuasion, publicity, and such authority as it could exercise, the commission brought about a better relationship between the peoples on the two sides of the Rio Grande. Furthermore, conditions were improved by an international convention guaranteeing Mexican laborers (*braceros*) treatment in keeping with the best United States standards. In this connection it should be noted that a treaty in 1966, the Chamizal agreement, involving Texas at the international level, was calculated to improve relations between the United States and Mexico. After long negotiation a tract of several hundred acres, being a part of the City of El Paso, was ceded by the United States to Mexico in exchange for a lesser tract, on the ground that the area was originally Mexican soil that had been cut away by the vagaries of the Rio Grande.

THE SCHOOLS—THE MINIMUM FOUNDATION PROGRAM

In other chapters of this book the slow and uneven progress of public education in Texas has been described. We have seen that although the Constitution of 1876 endowed the schools with many acres, it shackled them by failing to make provision for a direct state *ad valorem* school tax or for local support of schools except in towns and cities. Then friends of the public schools secured in 1883 the constitutional amendment authorizing an *ad valorem* state tax especially for school purposes, not to exceed 20 cents on the $100 of valuation, and also permitting local taxes not to exceed that amount. Thereafter progress through legislation was halted for a generation; but in 1908 an amendment made possible a tax of as much as 50 cents in common school districts; in 1918 the constitutional limit of the state *ad valorem* tax was raised to 35 cents and free textbooks were authorized; and two years later another amendment removed the 50-cent tax limit on common school districts.

As these restrictions were removed the communities responded readily, and local support increased from about $3,000,000 in 1909–1910 to more than $31,000,000 in 1928–1929. Thereafter local support lagged, and increases were borne by the state. Of the $72,977,299 spent on public school operation in the fiscal year ending August 31, 1939, the state supplied more than half. For that year the state per-capita apportionment was $22, which for the 1,563,679 scholastics amounted to $34,400,938.

Likewise the state broadened substantially its support of education when the legislature in 1941 authorized an appropriation of $50 per student to all public junior colleges.

In 1912 the Houston school district took pupils from the elementary grades at the beginning of the sixth year and placed them in an intermediate school for the next three years of their training. The result was a junior high school, the first to be established in Texas and one of the first in the nation. The idea spread slowly in Texas at first, but gained momentum after 1920, and by 1940 more than a hundred junior high schools had been established.

In 1936 there were in the state approximately 309,000 illiterate adults, representing five percent of the population. Both by way of attacking that problem and providing work for teachers, the federal government supplied funds for the employment of 2,000 teachers in special schools for adults, and a great effort was put forth to teach every illiterate person to read and write. The program met with some success but did not solve the problem of illiteracy in Texas.

Until about 1930 only a few school systems in Texas maintained more than eleven grades. The desire of school leaders to conform to the practice in most other states and the difficulty that many high school graduates found in securing employment during the depression years combined to strengthen a movement to add a twelfth year to the public school course. The movement toward the twelfth grade was so pronounced that by 1941 schools representing more than one-half of all the scholastics of Texas either had put the practice into effect or had made plans to adopt it. The war delayed the movement, but during the postwar years the twelve-grade system was adopted generally. Another important change in the Texas public schools during the twentieth century was the broadening of the curriculum. The first two decades brought the introduction of such vocational subjects as manual training, domestic science or home economics, agriculture, and training for business. Since 1920 not only have these subjects received greater emphasis but the schools have made place for music and other fine arts.

School expenditures continued to grow. The state per capita apportionment had been increased from about $3.50 in the late nineteenth century to $55 by 1947; the cost of rural aid from about $4,000,000 for the biennium of 1935–1936 to $28,000,000 for the biennium a decade later. Still Texas public schools remained near the bottom of the scale of state school systems. Many of the schools seemed to be making but little improvement. The state had some of the best and many—too many— of the poorest school systems in the nation.

Rural aid had, furthermore, come to be a subject of controversy. It was limited to country schools, and representatives from the cities insisted that it was unfair. In 1945 the legislature was deadlocked for several days over the question. It seemed that efforts to equalize the schools by the per capita apportionment and the rural aid law had failed. Many leaders believed the time had come for a new comprehensive plan calling for the reorganization of the entire school system.

After various studies had been made, in 1947 the legislature created a commission to continue the study and present a program for action. Leaders were Representative Claude Gilmer and Senator A. M. Aiken, and their names are linked with the legislation that grew out of the study.

Senate bill number 115, submitted to the legislature in 1949, provided for the reorganization of school administration, setting up an elective state board of education to consist of one member chosen from each of the state's 21 congressional districts. The board should appoint the commissioner of education and the board and commissioner should head the Texas Education Agency and have general control of the public school system.

Senate bill number 116 established a minimum foundation school program and prescribed formulas for making it operative; that is, the state would see to it that all persons of school age were given a minimum of nine months schooling, under teachers meeting at least minimum training requirements and in an environment conforming to certain standards.

Senate bill number 117 created a foundation school fund to finance the state's share of the minimum foundation program. Under the law schools were to be financed jointly by state funds and local district funds under an intricate formula which was designed to allocate proportionately larger sums of state aid to the relatively poorer districts.

Some wholesome effects of the new system were soon in evidence. It eliminated many hundreds of inoperative or "dormant" school districts; it helped to improve school attendance; it placed a premium on academic training and thereby stimulated thousands of teachers to get more schooling; it provided a means for enforcing minimum salary schedules; and it removed much of the political pressure in the distribution of funds.

On the other side of the ledger, the minimum foundation program increased greatly the costs of the schools. Before the law went into effect state aid was about $108,200,000 per year; in 1949–1950, the first year of the Gilmer-Aiken program, it was $141,200,000 and it continued to rise thereafter. To meet the state's share, the legislature has at times felt impelled to appropriate to school use one percent a year of the permanent school fund, or endowment.

Following its creation by the legislature in 1949, the Texas Education Agency, composed of an elective 21-member State Board of Education, the State Commissioner of Education, J. W. Edgar, and the State Department of Education worked in various ways to improve the public schools of Texas. They emphasized productive living and citizenship. Furthermore, the factor of national defense loomed great in public education. After the Russians in 1957 placed satellites in orbit around the earth there was a persistent demand for more study and more effective teaching in the schools from the kindergarten through the university. Naturally the greater emphasis was placed on the sciences, but all fields of learning felt the impact of the urge to make schools and schooling a more serious business. One result was that the Texas Education Agency in 1966 was able to report more pupils staying in school longer.

Special programs for the instruction of retarded children reached a substantial number of the less fortunate young people. Programs to assist educationally deprived children were established in many communities in the form of pre-school instruction for non-English-speaking children, and a number of schools provided bilingual teachers. County-wide schools for the deaf were increased, and multidistrict cooperatives in reading instruction, physical education and health services were set up. Holding promise for substantial improvement of education in Texas were the regional Education Service Centers, established in 1967 for supplying teaching materials and the latest teaching techniques and consultation service to teachers and school officials. Teachers' salaries were raised periodically, largely as a result of the efforts of the powerful Texas State Teachers Association. Even so, the state's school system in the 1960's was still rated low in many important features.

HIGHER EDUCATION

In the field of higher education as well as that of the public schools, the war and its aftermath brought changes and readjustments. During the war college enrollments had shrunk a third, a half, or even more. In 1944 Congress enacted the "GI Bill of Rights," offering discharged veterans generous opportunities, such as government unemployment compensation and guaranteed loans for those starting in business, and stipends, together with the payment of tuition, fees, and book costs, for veterans who wished a college education or "job training." These benefits were later extended to veterans of the Korean War. A host of ex-servicemen turned to the colleges, and enrollments were increased two-, three-, and even fourfold. The return of the veterans simply accentuated a growth the colleges had been experiencing, with only occasional interruptions, since they were founded.

It will be recalled that the first institution of higher learning in Texas was the Agricultural and Mechanical College (now A&M University), which opened in 1876, together with the Prairie View Agricultural and Mechanical College, a branch for Negroes. The University has attained prestige in the fields of agriculture, engineering and allied subjects and directs the Texas Agricultural Extension Service and the Agricultural Experiment Station with its numerous substations. The university also offers a wide program in the liberal arts and sciences.

Early in the twentieth century Texas normal schools were made colleges and later four of them, East Texas State, North Texas State, Southwest Texas State, and West Texas State, were entitled universities. Other relatively large state universities are Midwestern, Houston, and Texas Southern. Texas Woman's University offers undergraduate and graduate programs for women only.

The University of Texas has become an institution of great size and prestige. Membership in the American Association of Universities for many years has given it a voice in setting the academic standards of the nation. The main University campus at Austin heads a gigantic system, with branches at Arlington, Dallas, El Paso, Galveston, Port Aransas, and San Antonio. Another rapidly growing multipurpose university is Texas Tech University, which opened in 1925. In addition to agriculture, engineering, law, and other vocational fields, it offers a wide program in the liberal arts and sciences.

Two hundred thousand students taxed the facilities of Texas' 22 state colleges in the late 1960's and problems of adequate financial support grew with each session of the legislature. The college coordinating board recommended that six additional colleges be established within a decade or a little longer. For the year 1967–1968 the budget for all the state colleges aggregated $321,000,000.

In El Paso in 1920 the municipal junior college made its appearance. By 1940 there were 20 public junior colleges in the state and in 1968 there were 39 with 76,000 students. The state commissioner of higher education predicted that by 1985 there would be 305,000 students in 73 junior colleges.

Charged with the responsibility of recommending new junior colleges, of supervising the Texas college system generally by way of preventing excessive duplications of programs that are unduly costly is the college coordinating board of eighteen members, advised by the commissioner of higher education.

Rice University, not linked with the state or a church, is widely recognized for scholarship and academic excellence.

The U. S. Manned Spacecraft Center shown here was established in 1961 on land donated by Rice University. The Center includes research laboratories, astronaut training facilities, management offices, maintenance shops, and the famous "Mission Control Center." In 1967 the Center employed more than 4500 people at a payroll of 50 million dollars, and by 1966 had awarded nearly 5.4 billion dollars in contracts, many of them to Texas firms. (Texas Highway Department)

We have seen that the relative importance of churches in the field of education has declined; yet they have continued to found schools and, in some instances at least, to strengthen those established in earlier years. In 1969 Baylor University was the largest of some sixteen colleges and universities maintained by the Baptists in addition to an academy and a theological seminary. Southern Methodist University, established by the Methodist Episcopal Church in 1915, was the largest of nine Methodist schools. The Presbyterians had Austin College and Trinity University; the Church of Christ, Abilene Christian College and several small schools; the Disciples of Christ maintained Texas Christian University; and Saint Mary's University was the largest Catholic school. The private and denominational schools are still important in Texas higher education. In the academic year 1969–1970 they provided for about 20 percent of the state's college students. In addition to their emphasis on religious training, several do outstanding work in music, drama, and other fine arts.

THE CHURCHES

The growth of Texas churches generally has kept pace with the population and at times has exceeded it. In 1890 church members represented 30.3 percent of the population; by 1916 the percentage had increased to 40; and in 1968 the Texas Council of Churches reported a total of 4,864,162, a figure considerably less than half the total population. Not all churches reported their membership, however, and many that did report counted resident members only. The Baptist bodies led, with nearly a million and three-quarters members; Roman Catholics numbered more than a million and a quarter; and United Methodists aggregated about 800,000. Churches of Christ, Disciples of Christ, Presbyterian, Protestant Episcopal, and Lutherans were represented by large numbers.

Notwithstanding certain distinct differences, the work and methods of the larger Protestant bodies during the last three-quarters of a century have had many characteristics in common. They have maintained Sunday schools and designed their buildings to promote more effective Sunday school work. By 1926 Sunday school enrollment had passed well beyond a million. The churches also maintained auxiliary organizations for young people, among which were the Young People's Fellowship of the Protestant Episcopal Church, the Christian Endeavor of the Presbyterians, and the Baptist Training Union. Certain churches had brotherhoods or other special organizations for men, and most of them, one or more organizations for women. Almost without exception they emphasized the importance of maintaining a zealous and active laity to aid a ministry that was better trained than any ministry that had preceded it, and better paid than any ministry since the disestablishment of churches in the eighteenth century.

Although the state has taken over much of the burden that the churches once bore almost alone, the churches still carry on extensive work in child care and the maintenance of hospitals. In 1968 there were some 30 church-related homes for children and some of the church-related hospitals were among the foremost institutions of healing in the state.

ORGANIZED LABOR

The labor unions, which declined somewhat during the 1920's, were aroused from their lethargy by the advent of the great depression. For their own preservation workers had to be alert. A friendly federal government also helped. Organized labor aided in the repeal of prohibition; it secured favorable amendments to the Texas eight-hour law; it helped in delaying the adoption of a general sales tax and in securing a law against the sale of prison-made goods.

Texas labor leaders generally were disturbed during the 1930's by the widespread organization of company unions (anathema to the major labor groups), and the coming of the rival union, the Congress of Industrial Organizations (CIO). Governor O'Daniel was unfriendly to the major unions, and following his denunciation of "labor racketeers," the legislature in 1941 enacted an antiviolence law, making it a penitentiary offense for a union laborer to commit any act of violence while engaged in a strike.

The Manford Act, of 1943, regulated labor organizers, labor's participation in politics, and required some unions to hold annual elections of officers. In 1947 a veritable shower of laws regulating unions came to Governor Jester, some of which he had advocated. Chief of these: the check-off of the workers' union dues, to be paid directly to the union, was forbidden, except by the assent of the worker; the "right to work" law made it unlawful to require union membership of any employee; picketing was rigidly regulated and mass picketing outlawed; strikes by public employees was forbidden; secondary strikes, picketing, and boycotts were forbidden; the picketing of utilities was prohibited; and labor unions were brought under trust-law regulations. This was the year also that Congress passed the Labor-Management Relations Act (Taft-Hartley Law), which made substantial changes in the body of federal law regarding labor. Even this was not the end. In 1951 a law enacted provided beyond the shadow of a doubt that there be no closed shops in Texas—no sort of a labor agreement could require that workers belong to a union.

Labor leaders declared that these laws had taken away from organized labor all the gains of 47 years; that the gains they made at the bargaining table were lost at the legislative table. Even so, organized labor continued to exercise power in Texas. Its strength was increased greatly in 1957 when the American Federation of Labor and the Congress of Industrial Organizations united. Although there was not always harmony between the two elements, they managed to work together and exert considerable influence on the course of public affairs. Their Committee on Political Education (the political arm of the organization), backed by 175,000 members, and more had to be reckoned with at the polls and in the legislative halls. Their forces evidently supplied a substantial part of the vote that elected Ralph Yarborough to the United States Senate in 1957; and although most of their other candidates for state and national offices have not been so successful, their influence has been felt in every election.

LODGES, CLUBS, AND SOCIETIES

The Masonic orders, well represented in Texas during the pioneer era, had attained by 1967 a membership of 241,706 in 972 lodges located in practically every city and town in the state. The Odd Fellows likewise had grown stronger through the years, and the Knights of Pythias, the Woodmen, and other lodges continued to be active. Through homes and orphanages these orders and their auxiliary organizations for women provided a measure of security for their members and yielded a stabilizing influence generally.

During the past 50 years the lodges have had to compete with luncheon service clubs for the time and efforts of business and professional men. Paul P. Harris, a Chicago lawyer, sought to provide through an organization of city men the same friendliness, comradeship, and understanding that had prevailed in the towns from which many of them had come. The result was Rotary, which in 1912 became an international organization. The first Rotary Club in Texas, and the 39th ever founded, was formed in Dallas in 1911. Growth of the organization was rapid, and it has wielded great influence in the state. During the first World War the Lions, an organization dedicated to community service, was formed, and soon it also became international in scope. It has one or more clubs in practically every town and city in the state. Other organizations with similar purposes are Kiwanis, Optimists International, and Exchange Clubs.

The American Legion, formed in 1919 of veterans of the first World War, has from the beginning exercised considerable influence in Texas. Many posts have constructed buildings, provided facilities for recreation, and carried on various programs of community betterment. The organization has directed its energies especially to the teaching of loyalty and patriotic observance. The Veterans of Foreign Wars, an organization with purposes similar to those of the American Legion, has had rapid growth in Texas.

Among the agencies promoting adult education none has rendered greater service than the Texas Federation of Women's Clubs. "Ladies' reading circles" and "ladies' literary societies" were organized in different communities during reconstruction or earlier and some of these organizations took the form of clubs, a few of which are still in existence. A woman's congress held in Dallas in 1894 probably strengthened the urge to form a state-wide organization. In 1897 the Woman's Club of Waco called a convention of representatives of the different clubs of the state and the result was the Texas Federation of Women's Clubs. By 1917 the organization claimed 30,000 members. It continued to grow and by 1969 it represented some 80,000 clubwomen. Along with their program of study, the clubwomen directed their efforts toward securing public libraries. They were aided in this undertaking by the University of Texas and the Texas State Teachers Association. By 1907 (the end of ten years) they had helped to establish 65 libraries. In addition to its library work, the Federation promoted legislation in the interest of rural education, compulsory school laws, the protection of women and children in industry, and Texas heritage work.

Along with other Americans, Texans are confirmed "joiners." Apparently everybody belongs to at least one organization, and the average for adults of the middle and higher income brackets surely is three or more. Under the heading "Texas Statewide Civil Organizations," The *Texas Almanac* for 1968–1969 names some 500 groups or associations. The list does not include national and sectional organizations that do not maintain headquarters in Texas, nor does it include the thousands of purely local organizations.

There is the Texas State Teachers Association, a powerful group that long has wielded great influence in legislation. Included also are the State Bar and the State Medical Associations, organizations of great strength. There are learned societies, such as the Texas Academy of Science, and the Texas Philosophical Society, which was founded during the Republic and revived in 1936. There were three geological societies and six organizations of engineers; one state-wide historical association and half a dozen regional ones. There were organizations as unrelated as barbers and cattle raisers, Red Men and skeet shooters, veterans, and zionists. They provide outlets for the innumerable interests and emotions of the people and are channels of communication and cooperation. Better perhaps than any other source they reveal the nature of our civilization. They are the institutions of a free people and could not thrive except in an atmosphere of freedom.

Selected Bibliography

For population trends, the United States Census returns constitute the chief source. More usable are data from the census supplied by the *Texas Almanac*.

Useful on urbanization is a publication of the Texas Research League, *Metropolitan Texas: A Workable Approach to its Problems*, (Austin, 1967). A good sketch of the history of Negro education in Texas is in the *Handbook of Texas*, I, 544–545. On the Negro in Texas politics, of some value is Donald R. Matthews and James W. Prothro, *Negroes and the New Southern Politics in State and Nation* (New York, 1949); and Paul Casdorph, *A History of the Republican Party in Texas, 1865–1965*. Much has been written on the subject of integration in Texas but little of it has enduring value. Worth reading are Alan Scott, "Twenty-five Years of Opinion on Integration in Texas," *Southwestern Social Science Quarterly*, September, 1967, pp. 155–163; Greg Olds, "Integration in Texas: Some Gains Made," *The Texas Observer*, October 28, 1966, pp. 1–7.

On Spanish-speaking people, Pauline R. Kibbe's *Latin Americans in Texas* (Albuquerque, 1946) is still useful. A good brief summary is that of Ronnie Dugger, "The Texas Mexicans," in the *Texas Observer*, December 9, 1966, pp. 3–4.

Some sources on education in Texas are C.E. Evans, *The Story of Texas Schools* (Austin, 1955); James T. Taylor, "Gilmer-Aiken Program and State Finances," *East Texas*, January, 1950, p. 9; Texas Research League, *Texas Public Schools Under the Minimum Foundation Program, An Evaluation, 1949–1954*. Recent developments are set forth in the biennial *Report* of the Texas Education Agency.

Good sketches of the colleges and universities extant at the time of publication may be found in the *Texas Handbook*. For later developments, the catalogs and other publications of the institutions are the best sources.

Some references on the history of churches in Texas are Colby D. Hall, *Texas Disciples* (Fort Worth, 1953); J.M. Dawson, *A Century with Texas Baptists* (Nashville, 1947); and Knights of Columbus, *The Church in Texas Since Independence, 1836–1950*.

22

LITERATURE AND
THE ARTS

Critics have pointed out that literature in every section of the United States in its course of development tends to follow the same pattern. The chief controlling influence has been the frontier, which has touched at one time or another every community from Jamestown to Los Angeles. At first the people write of some form of adventure. After a few basic institutions are established, another era begins; the literary output increases; the old subjects continue to be popular but new ones are added and writing is much in evidence. Finally, through research, students make available the rich indigenous materials pertaining both to the past and the present; and gifted persons, aided by such tools, produce a worthy literature.

THE BACKGROUND OF
TEXAS LITERATURE

If Texas literature follows this general outline of development, the year 1860 probably serves as the close of the first era and 1900 as the end of the middle period. Granted this similarity to other regions with regard to the development of literature, Texas writings have certain distinct characteristics. Both with respect to quality and quantity, writings of fact have surpassed those of fiction, because, as J. Frank Dobie has pointed out, the facts of Texas history dwarf in comparison the products of the most imaginative minds, and show their influence in stories of daring and adventure, which are especially pronounced in Texas writings.

Several historical factors are the cause of this type of writing. First, Texas is a land of pronounced natural contrasts. Its forests of oak and pine to the east give way near the center of the state to bald prairie, and the prairie soon becomes a plain. Farther west, mountains present another contrast that has not been without its influence on the institutions of the people. The climate, likewise, varies from section to section; the east has abundant rainfall, droughts occasionally work destruction in the center of the state, while the west never has enough rain.

Second, Texas has been a land of contests. In George P. Garrison's *Texas; A Contest of Civilizations*, this thesis is well sustained. Archeology shows that centuries before white men came to Texas, people of the timber had to fight to defend their wicker huts, patches of corn, and pumpkins from the more savage men of the plains, and that the plainsmen often fought against the people of the mountains. White men's written records describe the century of conflict between the Spaniards and the Indians, and the wars which both fought against the men who came from east of the Sabine River.

Third, the Texas frontier, that pulsating region where civilization touched hands with savagery, has a long and eventful history. With the exception of New Mexico, no other state was subject to the frontier influence for so long a time. The frontier problems of the people of San Antonio, for instance, began when it was settled in 1718. The Indians were still taking scalps near San Antonio more than a century and a half later. Texas, furthermore, has a special claim on two industries that afforded a high degree of adventure—range cattle and oil.

Fourth, paradoxical as it may seem, parts of the state were developed very rapidly. In a preceding chapter, we have seen that, once their movement got under way, the cattlemen appropriated West Texas in less than a decade. Then came the railroads, building ahead of settlement and laying out towns to suit their convenience. After them came farmers who, within a few years or even a few months, changed the way of life in many a county. Finally, the discovery of oil has within a month, a week, or even a day remade communities and the affairs of men. One wonders if these rapid changes have not contributed in Texas saga and writings to the popularity of the tall tale: stories of exaggerated achievement or fantastic occurrences generally growing out of a grain of truth.

The plan of treatment in the following pages is substantially that generally followed by the Texas Institute of Letters in making awards to writers: to take note of writings by Texas authors, or writings on a Texas subject.

WRITINGS BEFORE 1860

The First writers about Texas were the explorers, the earliest of whom was Cabeza de Vaca. It will be recalled that during the 1530's he made his way with three companions through Texas and on as far as the outposts near the western coast of New Spain. He wrote an account of his wanderings and in 1542 published his *La Relación* in Spain. The work has been translated into English and edited by Fanny and Ad. F. A. Bandelier. Its historical value has undoubtedly kept it alive, for it has no special literary merit.

The settlement of Texas by Anglo-Americans brought forth many books of description. Mrs. Mary Austin Holley, cousin of Stephen F. Austin, wrote down in vivid style her impressions of the new land, and included a sketch of its history. Her second work, which is more complete than the first, was published in 1836 as *Texas*. Her text is reproduced in Mattie A. Hatcher's *Letters of An Early American Traveller* (1933), and her life story is told by Rebecca Smith Lee in *Mary Austin Holley*. Mrs. Matilda C. F. Houston, an English woman who visited this country about 1843, wrote *Texas and the Gulf of Mexico*, a most interesting and informative account of the Galveston-Houston region. Representative of German scientists who wrote about Texas was Dr. Ferdinand Roemer, whose *Texas*, published at Bonn in 1849, is the best contemporary account available of the frontier at that time. A few years later came Frederick Law Olmstead, a landscape artist and engineer with broad interests. His *A Journey Through Texas* describes the state as he saw it through critical eyes. George Wilkins Kendall, founder and associate editor of the New Orleans *Picayune*, who accompanied the Texan Santa Fé expedition of 1841, recorded in his history of the journey experiences that represent practically every element of adventure and peril that could have befallen men on the southwestern frontier. Kendall later became a citizen of Texas and engaged in ranching.

Before Texas had emerged from the cradle, men were writing its history. The best work of the early writers was William Kennedy's *Texas* (1841), written by an Englishman who had come to Texas to secure information about the new country. A superior work, published fourteen years later, was Henderson Yoakum's *A History of Texas*.

The frontier scene in Texas early attracted the attention of a number of writers of fiction. Adventure looms large in the works of all these authors. Best remembered of these, perhaps, is Mayne Reid, an Irishman by birth, who came to America in 1840. His *Headless Horseman*, a tale based on a southwest Texas legend, probably is the best of his works.

Of early Texas poetry little has endured. Mirabeau B. Lamar's "Daughter of Mendoza" was popular; James T. Lytle's "Ranger's Song" is still read, as is Reuben M. Potter's "Hymn of the Alamo."

THE LATE NINETEENTH CENTURY

The last third of the nineteenth century witnessed a substantial increase in Texas writings and some improvements in quality. As was true of the preceding era, the best works pertained to adventure. Some reminiscences dealing largely with the times of the Texan Revolution and early statehood have genuine historical value. Z. N. Morrell, a pioneer Baptist preacher who came to Texas in 1836, wrote in his *Flowers and Fruits of the Wilderness* a lively narrative of his long career on the frontier. Likewise in reminiscences of *Fifty Years in Texas*, John J. Linn gave much information about the Texan revolution; and equally interesting is Noah Smithwick's *The Evolution of a State*. John C. Duval's *Early Times in Texas* seems destined to endure. Some years earlier he had written a book quite as meritorious, *The Adventures of Big Foot Wallace*, the biography of a famous ranger who had come to Texas in 1836 to avenge the death of his brother, who had been killed at Goliad a few months before. The element of adventure and the simplicity of style make Duval's work appeal especially to boys; but people of all ages have found his narrative fascinating. Containing less of the element of adventure, but associated with a wider scene are Francis R. Lubbock's *Six Decades in Texas* and John H. Reagan's *Memoirs*. Both men were long prominent in the public affairs of Texas. William Cowper Brann wrote and published in the 1890's, first in Austin and later in Waco, the newspaper, *Iconoclast*, in which he purported to combat hypocrisy, intolerance, and other evils.

During this period books of travel were relatively less important than they were earlier. However, *On a Mexican Mustang Through Texas,* by Alex E. Sweet and J. Armory Knox, two newspapermen, is entitled to mention. Their writings show the influence of Mark Twain. N. A. Taylor's *The Coming Empire* or *Two Thousand Miles in Texas on Horseback* contains less satire, and is more trustworthy and dependable than the book by Sweet and Knox. Taylor's book, written after the author had made a trip on horseback through western Texas, was published under the names of H. F. McDanield and N. A. Taylor.

It has already been observed that the frontier era did not close in Texas until near the end of the nineteenth century. For two decades and more following the Civil War, men who sought adventure did not have to leave the state to find it, adventure of the hardest frontier style. Thus authors continued to write of contemporary experiences, or of the exploits of an early period, or of both. J. W. Wilbarger filled a fat volume entitled *Indian Depredations in Texas* with accounts of border tragedies. This book was a precursor of James T. DeShields' *Border Wars of Texas*, published in the twentieth century. N. A. Jennings, a New York newspaper man who came to Texas and served with the Rangers on the frontier in the eighties, wrote of some of his own experiences in *A Texas Ranger*. In 1886 Charles A. Siringo, a real cowboy who could interest readers, published his *Texas Cowboy* or *Fifteen Years on the Hurricane Deck of a Spanish Pony*. As a paperback thriller its sale ran into many thousands; and it pointed the way for many other writers who have, since that day, dealt with similar themes in books, both of fact and of fiction. In 1927 Siringo's story reappeared along with other of his writings as *Riata and Spurs*.

By no means does all of Texas literature of adventure deal with legitimate enterprise or with men on the side of the law. The "bad man" theme has always been popular. The later frontier period brought forth Henry C. Fuller's, *The Adventure of Bill Longly,* the story of a notorious killer. Sam Bass, a train robber, who has since his death become the Robin Hood of Texas, was the subject of a biography published anonymously in 1878. The gruesome record of John Wesley Hardin was written by himself. W. M. Walton wrote *The Life and Adventures of Ben Thompson,* sometime city marshal of Austin and noted for fights in which he was not always enforcing the law.

Many poems were written during this period, but few of them bear evidence of talent. John P. Sjolander, a Swedish-American, has been called the "greatest pioneer poet of the Southwest." Crude but genuine and apparently destined to endure is William Lawrence (Larry) Chittenden's "Cowboy's Christmas Ball." Sam H. Dixon compiled and edited *Poets and Poetry of Texas*, and Francis L. Allen published a collection known as *Lone Star Ballads*.

The late nineteenth century also is characterized by many works of fiction. Although few of these have any enduring value, there are some notable exceptions. Mrs. Molly E. Moore Davis, the wife of a New Orleans editor, began her writing in Texas and her best work has a Texas setting. *Under the Man-Fig*, probably her best-known novel, deals with the destructive effects of gossip in a small town. William Sidney Porter, known as O. Henry, came to Texas from his native North Carolina in 1882. Two years on a ranch in La Salle County and a decade in Austin, where he held various jobs, supplied much of the experience and setting for the literary work that made him one of the great short-story writers of all time. His collection of stories, *Heart of the West*, published during the first decade of the twentieth century, is based almost wholly on Texas scenes.

TWENTIETH CENTURY WRITINGS OF FACT

As was true of earlier periods, most of the best-known books written by Texas or about Texas in the early twentieth century were nonfiction. History continued as a popular field. The Texas State Historical Association, organized in 1897, maintained *The Quarterly of the Texas State Historical Association,* which in 1912 became *The Southwestern Historical Quarterly.* George P. Garrison, and Herbert E. Bolton contributed much to the success of this publication; and under the editorship of E. C. Barker, which lasted a quarter of a century, it came to be recognized as one of the foremost historical quarterlies in America. Then edited in turn by W. P. Webb, H. B. Carroll, and Joe B. Frantz, it was enlarged and its circulation extended. In 1952 the Association published *The Handbook of Texas,* a monumental reference work of two volumes covering every phase of Texas history. The Texas State Historical Survey Committee, the state agency for the preservation of history established in 1953, has published some history and encouraged research and publication. *Texana,* a quarterly featuring Texas history, published by Robert E. Davis, has attained recognition. A number of Texas regional organizations have maintained substantial publications in history; among these are the East Texas *Historical Journal; Publications* of the Texas Gulf Coast Historical Association; the Panhandle Plains *Historical Review; Southwestern Studies* by the University of Texas at El Paso; and the *West Texas Historical Association Year Book.*

Herbert E. Bolton, most noted of all historians of the Spanish Southwest, published some scholarly studies pertaining to Texas, among them *Texas in the Middle Eighteenth Century* and *Athanase de Mézières and the Louisiana-Texas Frontier.* Charles W. Hackett translated and edited the ponderous and informational *Treatise on the Limits of Louisiana and Texas,* written by the Spanish priest Pichardo; and C. E. Castañeda wrote *Our Catholic Heritage in Texas* (6 volumes), a comprehensive history of the Catholic Church, with the history of Texas supplied as a framework of reference. In his *Texas, A Contest of Civilizations,* a relatively brief interpretative study, George Pierce Garrison brought to bear on the subject years of research and historical training. Eugene C. Barker's printed scholarly articles would fill several volumes; and his contemporary, Charles W. Ramsdell, earned a place among the foremost authorities on the Old South and the War Between the States. Relatively lengthy histories of Texas were written by Louis J. Wortham and Clarence R. Wharton.

As the history of the commonwealth has lengthened and become more complex, historians have been disposed to center on periods and regions. Julia Kathryn Garrett chose the filibusters and the short-lived first Texas Republic in her *Green Flag over Texas.* W. R. Hogan wrote the *Texas Republic, a Social and Economic History;* Stanley Siegel wrote *A Political History of the Texas Republic*; and Joseph W. Schmitz dealt with the foreign relations of the Republic in his *Texas Statecraft.* John S. Spratt, in *The Road to Spindletop,* has dealt with Texas industry from 1875 to 1901, the pre-oil age. Ralph Steen has given emphasis to social and economic topics in his *Twentieth Century Texas.* Begin-

ning with the book *Seven Decades of the Texas Constitution of 1876,*
S. S. McKay wrote four books setting forth in detail much recent Texas political history. A readable comprehensive history of Texas was written
by six historians under the editorship of Seymour V. Connor: Odie B.
Faulk, *A Successful Failure* (1519–1810); David M. Vigness, *The Revolutionary Decades* (1810–1836); Seymour V. Connor, *Adventures in Glory*
(1836–1849); Ernest Wallace, *Texas in Turmoil* (1849–1875); Billy M.
Jones, *The Search for Maturity* (1875–1900); and S. S. McKay and Odie B.
Faulk, *Texas after Spindletop 1901–1965.*

The great size and diversity of Texas have invited regional writ-
ings. The best known of these is W. P. Webb's, *The Great Plains,* setting
forth a new interpretation of the vast region between the 98th meridian
and the Rocky Mountains. Dealing with more restricted regions are Carl
C. Rister's *Southern Plainsmen;* George W. Crockett's *Two Centuries in
East Texas;* W. C. Holden's *Alkali Trails* (West Texas); James K. Greer's
Bois d'arc and Barbed Wire (Central Texas); Rupert N. Richardson's
The Frontier of Northwest Texas; J. Evetts Haley's *Fort Concho;* Carl
C. Rister's *Fort Griffin;* and C. G. Raht's *The Romance of the Davis
Mountains and the Big Bend Country.* Books having to do with relatively
small areas written with sympathy and understanding, are Sallie Rey-
nolds Matthews', *Interwoven* and John Graves', *Goodbye to a River.* In
contrast, Paul Horgan, in *Great River* has dealt with the entire Rio
Grande basin.

The subject of Indians has received considerable attention from
Texas writers. Rupert N. Richardson wrote chiefly of one tribe in
The Comanche Barrier to South Plains Settlement and Ernest Wallace
and E. Adamson Hoebel dealt with both history and ethnology in *The
Comanches, Lords of the South Plains.* Mildred P. Mayhall has published
a historical study of the Kiowas; *The Indians of Texas* by W. W. Newcomb, Jr., is a survey of the entire subject.

Writings on cowboys and the cattle industry have grown beyond
measure. Cattlemen by the hundreds have written their experiences or
had them set down by others. J. Marvin Hunter and George W. Saunders
published two volumes of such material in *Trail Drivers of Texas.*
Among the better known of J. Frank Dobie's books is *The Longhorns,*
an exciting story of the most historic breed of cattle that the world has
known. Closely linked with the industry is another J. Frank Dobie book,
The Mustangs. Wayne Gard has written *The Chisholm Trail. Charles
Goodnight, Cowman and Plainsman,* by J. Evetts Haley is the life story
of a notable and most unique cattleman, a book in keeping with the stature of the subject. Haley has also written *George W. Littlefield, Texan.*
Most readable also is W. C. Holden's *Rollie Burns.* The big ranches, too,
have their histories. W. C. Holden wrote *The Spur Ranch;* J. Evetts Haley,
The XIT Ranch; and Lewis Nordyke is the author of another book on
the same subject. The story of the J. A. Ranch has been told by Harlie

True Burton; and in *The Big Ranch Country,* J. W. Williams has sketched the history of a number of ranches still in existence. Tom Lea, author and artist, wrote an illustrated history of *The King Ranch,* a "spread" of vast dimensions in South Texas.

There has appeared a growing body of creditable writing on Texas business and industry. An excellent medium for articles in this field has been the *Texas Business Review,* a monthly publication of the Bureau of Business Research of the University of Texas, launched in 1926. A scholarly, comprehensive book is Carl C. Rister's *Oil! Titan of the Southwest.* Gerald Forbes dealt with a lesser area in *Flush Production: The Epic of Oil in the Gulf Southwest.* Joe B. Frantz wrote the history of a pioneer business in *Gail Borden, Dairyman to A Nation.* Craig Thompson has written a history of the Gulf Oil Company, and Henry M. Larson and Kenneth Wiggins Porter have told the story of Humble. The standard history of Texas railroads is that by St. Clair Griffin Reed. The history of the Fort Worth and Denver Railroad has been written by Richard Clayton Overton in *Gulf to the Rockies.* History of another railroad vitally linked with Texas is Vincent Victory Masterson's *The Katy Railroad and the Last Frontier.*

Although they have drawn on a wide range of human experience, writers of Texas biography have tended to favor subjects from the heroic age. *The Raven,* a biography of Sam Houston by Marquis James, has been widely read. More authoritative is Llerena Friend's *Sam Houston, The Great Designer.* Eugene C. Barker's *Life of Stephen F. Austin* is still in print after some forty years.

In recent years Texans of later times have been given more attention by writers. The earliest of this list was Sam Hanna Acheson's *Joe Bailey, the Last Democrat.* More recently has appeared Robert C. Cotner's *James Stephen Hogg,* Ben Procter's *Not Without Honor* (John H. Reagan), T. Dwight Dorough's *Mr. Sam* (Sam Rayburn), Ernest Wallace's *Charles De Morse, Pioneer Editor and Statesman,* and Rupert N. Richardson's *Colonel House: The Texas Years.*

Action and adventure have appealed to the writers of *Texana* of all generations. W. P. Webb's *The Texas Rangers* is widely read. More recently have appeared *The Gallant Hood* by John P. Dyer; *Albert Sidney Johnston, Soldier of Three Republics* by Charles P. Roland; *Mighty Stonewall* (Stonewall Jackson) by Frank Vandiver; and *Thirteen Days to Glory,* an account of the siege and fall of the Alamo, by Lon Tinkle. In his *Ranald S. Mackenzie,* Ernest Wallace has told well the story of Texas' last great Indian war.

During the 1960's some autobiographical writings linked with Texas have been at times sympathetic and more frequently critical: William A. Owens' *This Stubborn Soil;* Willie Morris' *North Toward Home;* and David Nevin's *The Texans: What They Are—and Why.*

Interpretive writing on Texas and Texans has increased greatly during the last quarter century. In his *Big Country Texas*, Donald Day has sought to explain the country and its institutions through history, politics, and folklore. Joseph Leach in *The Typical Texan: Biography of an American Myth* has sought to find in history, novels, and biography a true account of Texan character. Frank Goodwyn's *Lone Star Land: Twentieth Century in Perspective* deals with the social changes Texas has known in the light of its culture, geography, and history. The cowboy, a type inseparably linked with Texas, is appraised by Joe B. Frantz and Julian Ernest Choate in *The American Cowboy: The Myth and the Reality*.

Some Texas authors have gained recognition for writings on subjects far beyond the periphery of Texas. Katherine Anne Porter's novels and stories have been read throughout the English speaking world. Frances S. Mossiker twice won the Carr P. Collins award with books on French history: *The Queen's Necklace* and *Napoleon and Josephine*.

The Texas Institute of Letters, organized in 1936 in keeping with the observance of the centennial of Texas independence, came to be an effective agency in encouraging writing and improving its quality. Perhaps J. Frank Dobie gave it its watchword when he wrote: "Great literature transcends its native land, but there is none that I know of that ignores its own soil. All great literature plumbs and soars to the elementals. Texas authors need not be antiquarians; in the rich soil of the novel there has not been even a furrow plowed."

Soon the Institute began offering awards to authors, giving consideration to writings either "by a Texas author or on a Texas subject." It has offered the Carr P. Collins award for the best book on Texas, and several other awards have been given consistently.

Linked with the Texas Institute of Letters for more than two decades and determining its policies in a great measure was the Austin literary "Triumverate," Bedicheck, Dobie, and Webb, that constituted what is perhaps the nearest thing to a school of writers that Texas has known. They have been mentioned already, but their importance in Texas literary history merits repetition, for their writings and their influence raised substantially the standards for Texas authors. Intimate friends and boon companions, they spent many hours together, often around a fire under a canopy of stars. Roy Bedicheck, a naturalist, twice won the Collins award of the Texas Institute of Letters, first, with his *Karankawa Country* and, second, with *Adventures with a Texas Naturalist*. The range of Frank Dobie's writings was remarkably broad: cowboys and the cattle industry, folklore, and themes of nature. Three times he was recognized as the author of the best Texas book of the year. His most enduring writings, perhaps, are those pertaining to animals: the coyote, the longhorns, and the mustangs. Walter Prescott Webb wrote convincingly on such diverse subjects as *The Great Plains, The Texas Rangers*, the contrasts in the economy of the North, South, and West in

Divided We Stand, and *The Great Frontier,* a study of the frontiers of the world.

TWENTIETH CENTURY FICTION AND POETRY

Much Texas fiction pertains to the past, especially to frontier adventure and the heroic age. In her two novels, *On the Long Tide* and *Tell of Time,* Laura Smith Krey has chosen the Texas Revolution and the Reconstruction periods as backgrounds. In her *Star of the Wilderness,* Karle Wilson Baker has followed the career of a Texan woman during early colonial times. Monte Barrett in his *Sun in Their Eyes* dealt with the filibusters. A similar book is Edith Kirkland's *Divine Average.* Andy Adams wrote about cowboys.

During the middle decades of the twentieth century Texas novelist were writing on an increasingly varied list of subjects. In *Wetback* Claud Garner attacked the injustice often done Mexican immigrants who have crossed the Rio Grande unlawfully. William A. Owens' *Walking On Borrowed Land* is a plea for better understanding between the races. David Westheimer, in *Summer on the Water,* deals with the humor and tragedy of a family in a summer colony near Houston. Madison Cooper's *Sironia, Texas* has to do with the intimate affairs of the people of a town. In *The Brave Bulls* Tom Lea deals with the interplay of courage and fear in the mind of a matador hero. In *Hound Dog Man* Fred Gipson took a boy and his dogs through commonplace experiences, with a style suggestive of Mark Twain and Booth Tarkington. Loula Grace Erdman's *The Years of the Locusts,* a story of farm people, won a prize of $10,000 from a national publisher. In keeping with the spirit of the age, Larry McMurty's 1967 novel, *The Last Picture Show,* set in a fictional Panhandle oil field and ranching community, is a critical portrayal of personalities limited by a provincial environment. In a similar vein, Garland Roark wrote of the skulldugery of two East Texas oil promoters in *Drill a Crooked Hole. North to Yesterday,* a tragicomic novel about a cattle drive, written by Robert Flynn, was given the Jesse H. Jones Award by the Texas Institute of Letters in 1968. The New York *Times* termed it one of the twenty best books of the year.

Texas authors have built up a substantial body of children's literature. Some of the best work in this field is Siddie Joe Johnson's *Texas; the Land of the Tejas* and Janette Sebring Lowrey's *Silver Dollar.*

Texas folklore, perhaps as rich and varied as any in the world, did not attract attention of writers until the twentieth century. Fittingly the first volume in this field was John A. Lomax's *Cowboy Songs and Other Frontier Ballads,* published in 1910. Later Lomax took up the search for Negro songs, preserving them, along with others, on 10,000 phonograph records. He was acclaimed the greatest ballad hunter, and his book, *Adventures of a Ballad Hunter* received a Texas Institute of Letters Award in 1947. The Texas Folklore Society has published more than 30 volumes. Perhaps the leading writer of Texas folklore has been J. Frank Dobie, with such books as *Coronado's Children, Tales of Lost Mines and Buried Treasure in The Southwest,* and *Tongues of Monte.*

A survey by the Texas Federation of Women's Clubs in 1968 revealed 31 professional poets in Texas and 448 who classed themselves as amateurs.

Representative of the best poetry is Karle Wilson Baker's verse collected in *Blue Smoke* and other compilations. "Lights," one of her poems of the sea, is as musical as Charles Kingsley's best verse. Another talented Texan, Grace Noll Crowell, author of 24 volumes of poetry, with her *White Fire* won the first annual book publication contest of the Poetry Society of Texas. Her poem, "The Day Will Bring Some Lovely Thing," has supplied mottoes in many lands. The poems of Lexie Dean Robertson, who won the same prize at a later date are well known. With her "Planter's Charm," that carries the odor of hot newly plowed soil and reveals the yearnings of those who toil in it, Fay M. Yauger won the annual prize offered by the Poetry Society of America in 1933.

Heroic action has appealed to Texas poets. In his "Message from Tunisia," David R. Russell recounted the deeds of men who fought that men hereafter might "Greet dawn in freedom, know the peace of spring." In similar vein wrote Arthur M. Sampley in "Night Flight." Vaida Montgomery wrote of the open spaces, the desert, and the stampede. In his *A Cloud of Witnesses* Ramsey Yelvington dealt with the men of the Alamo. More reflective, singing of themselves in their verses, were Frances Alexander and William D. Barney. In a similar vein Vassar Miller three times won the poetry award of the Texas Institute of Letters.

JOURNALISM, RADIO, AND TELEVISION

Texas has had a number of magazines first and last, but the rate of mortality has been high and the mean life span short. *Farm and Ranch* (Dallas), which began publication in 1883, contributed much to the improvement of agriculture and rural life in the state. *The Texas Magazine,* founded in Houston under the editorship of Frank Eberle in 1909, lasted about four years. It contained articles of quasi-popular nature on history; biography, government, politics, the professions, and industry. Of the two outstanding literary magazines in the state the oldest is *The Southwest Review,* founded in Austin in 1915 and later moved to Dallas, where it is sponsored by Southern Methodist University. The quality of its articles is high and it is a worthy exponent of the life and lit-

erature of the state. In 1958 *The Texas Quarterly* was established by
members of the faculty of the University of Texas. It carries a wide
range of narratives, biographies, poems, and art and provides an outlet
for a number of talented writers.

The publication of books is a business of importance in Texas. The
University of Texas Press and the Southern Methodist University press
are among the better known publishers. Carl Hertzog of the University
of Texas Press at El Paso is widely known as a designer of books.

Of the larger newspapers, only the *Galveston News* has survived
since the days of the Republic. Its daughter, the *Dallas News*, is better
known in our own day. The *Dallas News* has maintained a conservative
policy. The Bay City *Matagorda County Tribune* celebrated its one-
hundredth birthday in 1945; and the *Victoria Advocate* is nearly as venerable. Several newspapers in smaller cities have continued from early
statehood until our own times. Among them are: the *Rusk Cherokeean,*
the *Huntsville Item*, the *Henderson Times*, the *Gonzales Inquirer,* and
the *Bastrop Advertizer*.

The troublous post Civil War era witnessed the founding of the
San Antonio Express (1865), one of the most distinguished newspapers in the Southwest, and its neighbor, the *Austin Statesman*. Several of
the leading newspapers of the state were founded in the 1880's. Among
them are: the *El Paso Times,* the *Houston Post*, the *Fort Worth Star-
Telegram*, the *Abilene Reporter-News*, and the *Amarillo News-Globe*.
Few Texas newspapers have been outstanding, but many have been
creditable.

Radio broadcasting was introduced in Texas in 1920, when WRR, a
20-watt station owned by the city of Dallas, was erected. The Texas Quality Network was established in 1934, and included stations WOAI (San
Antonio), WFAA (Dallas), WBAP (Fort Worth), and KRRC (Houston).

The Lone Star Chain of six stations had its beginning in 1938, and
the Texas State Network of 16 stations was established the same year. The
Mutual Broadcasting system also was organized. Texas has come to be
well covered by radio. Not counting amateur, police, or aeronautical
operations, there were 409 radio stations in the state in 1967. The first
television station in Texas, WBAP-TV, Fort Worth, began operating
September 27, 1947; a year later WFAA-TV, Dallas, had its beginning.
By 1967, 66 stations brought television within reach of most Texans.

THE THEATER, ARCHITECTURE,
ART, AND MUSIC

The interest of Texans in the theater, first in evidence during the period
of the Republic, was sustained in later years. An opera house was opened
in Galveston in 1871, one in Dallas two years later, and by the close

of the century every town of consequence had stage facilities. At one time or another there appeared on Texas billboards the name of almost every distinguished actor who played in the United States during the late nineteenth and the early twentieth centuries. Among these were Joseph Jefferson, noted for his portrayal of Rip Van Winkle; Edwin Booth, renowned Shakespearean actor; and Sarah Bernhardt, the greatest actress of her generation. Others were Richard Mansfield, Maude Adams, and Ethel Barrymore.

As motion pictures became popular about 1910 legitimate stage productions declined in Texas as elsewhere. Road tours from New York and Chicago were made into the state occasionally, however, and at least one Texan, Harley Sadler, managed to maintain a traveling troupe that played each season before thousands of people intermittently through the depression and World War II.

In 1909 Stark Young organized the Curtain Club at the University of Texas, and this group and similar organizations in other schools and colleges helped to keep alive the art of acting. After the first World War, the little theater became a community project in most towns and cities. Of such organizations the oldest and best-known in Texas is one in Dallas, founded in 1921. For three successive years, beginning in 1924, it won the Belasco Cup offered in a national tournament in New York. Other flourishing little theater groups are found in Houston, San Antonio, Austin, Fort Worth, and Galveston. During recent years amateur actors in a large number of communities have organized as community players for the purpose of giving productions.

Texas has contributed its share of the stars of the stage and of motion picture, among whom are Maclyn Arbuckle, Tom Mix, Ann Sutherland, Mary Brian, Joan Crawford, Madge Bellamy, Ginger Rogers, Charlotte Walker, Bebe Daniels, Mary Martin, Gene Autry, Fess Parker, Jayne Mansfield, Kathy Grant, Eli Wallach, and Pat Hingle. Other Texans connected with the motion picture industry were Howard Hughes and King Vidor.

Texas has had very little architecture that is distinctive. A few of the old mission chapels that have stood since the Spanish era are beautiful and impressive, but they do not equal some of those of Mexico. A few fine old homes erected by the earliest planters are still standing. Their high central hallways and spacious front porticos with Greek columns bear evidence of the aristocratic tastes of their builders, but their plan and pattern were imported from the Old South.

One critic has stated that the nearest approach to an indigenous architecture in Texas is represented by a few stone houses dating from the colonial era. Comparatively small and unpretentious, these houses are both sturdy and beautiful and are described as having "wide verandahs and porches along the wings that run off to the rear on the west side, forming shady courts and little gardens full of flowers and potted plants." Others contend that most typically Texan is the ranch house, a long, one-story stone structure well supplied with porches.

Of public buildings, the most impressive still is the great state capitol at Austin, made of native granite. In the twentieth century, Texans have witnessed the building of a few churches artistic in design, occasionally an impressive structure on a college campus, and a few hotels and other commercial buildings that are creditable. Although cities tended to decentralize during the middle decades of the twentieth century, skyscrapers continued to delineate their business districts.

Perhaps the first artist worthy of commemoration in Texas was Pedro Huizar, the sculptor-architect who carved the famous window of the sacristy, commonly called the Rose Window at Mission San José at San Antonio, a work that would have been a credit to any artist of any age.

In her *Painting in Texas: The Nineteenth Century*, Pauline A. Pinckney has given sketches of the lives and the works of some 75 artists who left something enduring worthy of mention. José Sánchez, a Mexican army officer who visited Texas in 1828, did vivid sketches of some of its scenes and people. James Strange's portraits of the captives Santa Anna and Almonte are creditable. Among the relatively large number of German intelligentsia who located in Texas in the 1850's were a few artists of superior talents. Among these were Herman Lungkwitz and Richard Petri. Lungkwitz is best remembered perhaps for his landscape scenes, Petri for his Indians. Carl G. von Iwonski did portraits and groups of people.

A contemporary of the German artists was the Frenchman Theodore Gentilz of Castro's colony, painter of Indians. A distinguished artist also was the French woman Eugenie Lavender, who won acclaim at the French court before she came to Texas in 1851. Best known of her work is "Saint Patrick," in the Cathedral at Corpus Christi. Another well-known Texas artist is H. A. McArdle, whose pictures "Battle of San Jacinto" and "Dawn of the Alamo" hang in the state capitol and are viewed by thousands of people each year. A contemporary of McArdle is William H. Huddle, whose "Surrender of Santa Anna" also hangs in the state capitol. Robert Jenkins Onderdonk left some superior portraits and paintings of scenes in the vicinity of both Dallas and San Antonio. His son, Julian, who died in 1922 at the age of 40, was probably Texas' most distinguished painter. His landscape scenes (notably "Dawn in the Hills") have attained a measure of renown. With his *A Picture Gallery* Tom Lea won the Carr P. Collins award for the best nonfiction book given by the Texas Institute of Letters in 1968.

In Texas sculpture one name stands supreme—Elisabet Ney. She came to the state with her husband, Dr. Edmund Montgomery, about 1870. In her native Bavaria she had already attained fame. Best known to Texans are her statues of Stephen F. Austin, Sam Houston, and Albert

Elisabet Ney—beautiful, talented, and willful—learned sculpture in Munich and Berlin where she cast busts of such famous men as Schopenhauer, Garibaldi, and King William I of Prussia. She moved to the United States with her British husband in 1870, and settled in Texas two years later. Unhappy on a remote plantation, she received commissions from the state for busts of Stephen Austin and Sam Houston which enabled her to move to a studio in Austin. One of her best works, a statue of General Albert Sidney Johnston, is now in the state cemetery; but it was her last work, a statue of Lady Macbeth, that won her the fame she frankly enjoyed. (E. C. Barker History Center, University of Texas)

Sidney Johnston. Of higher quality, however, are her imaginative works; for example, the group which she called *Sursum*, now in the Art Institute of Chicago, and her statue of Lady Macbeth, now in the National Museum in Washington. After Miss Ney's death, her studio in Austin was made a museum, and it has become a shrine for Texas artists and lovers of art. Several other Texans by birth or by adoption have attained some recognition in sculpture. Bonnie MacCleary, born in San Antonio, has supplied requisitions for statuary from the Irish Free State, Puerto Rico, and numbers of Texas communities. William M. McVey, of Houston, has shaped monuments to James Bowie, David Crockett, and other Texan heroes whose services to Texas were commemorated in 1936. Pompeo Coppini executed 45 monuments in various cities of the United States, among them the centennial monument in the Alamo Plaza in San Antonio, and the Littlefield Memorial in Austin.

Widespread interest in art in Texas may be measured from the organization in 1911 of the Texas Fine Arts Association, in Austin. During recent years this interest has grown. Most large Texas cities have art museums. Also, the colleges have art departments, and art is an increasingly popular subject in the public schools.

Along with the earliest dramatic productions came music. At the Houston Theater, in 1838, Madame Thielman, a popular singer, rendered "Does Your Mother Know You Are Out?," "Come Dwell with Me," and "Love Was Once a Little Boy." There were musicians of ability in Victor Considerant's French colony, near Dallas. Among them was A. Bureau, who had directed music in a Paris theater. In 1850 the first German singing society was organized, and in 1853 was held the first *saengerfest* in the Southwest.

The state has had a few distinguished composers. The compositions of Franz Van Der Stucken, born in Fredericksburg about 1855, are widely known. Carl Venth, European born and trained, came to Texas in 1909 and continued his work as composer, violinist, and conductor that made him world famous. David W. Guion, born in Ballinger in 1895, was Texas' best-known composer. Recognizing that the Indian, the cowboy, the Negro, and the pioneer furnish rich sources for folk music, he drew heavily on such material. Guion made a great variety of arrangements of Negro spirituals and it has been said that he brought "Turkey in the Straw" into the drawing room. "The Hills of Home," by Oscar J. Fox of San Antonio, was widely sung.

In twentieth-century music Texas made some substantial contributions. Kidd-Key College Conservatory at Sherman gained recognition for excellence and became widely known. Dallas, Houston, and San Antonio had major symphony orchestras, Dallas, Fort Worth, and San Antonio each had a civic opera company. There was unprecedented development of music education at the high school level through the Interscholastic League and through the rapid growth of the fine arts departments in all major institutions of higher learning. A Texas musician, Irl Allison, conceived and promoted a national program of preparatory piano instruction through the National Guild of Piano Teachers. One student who shared in this training was Van Cliburn, who gained world renown as winner of the Tschaikovsky Piano competition in Moscow in 1957.

Selected Bibliography

A wide selection of writings by Texas authors may be found in Martin Shockley, ed., *Southwest Writers Anthology* (Austin, 1967). The following evaluations of Texas writings are of value: Mabel Major, Rebecca W.

Smith, and T.M. Pearce, *Southwest Heritage: A Literary History* (Albuquerque, 1948); Mabel Major and T.M. Pearce, *Signature of the Sun, Southwest Verse, 1900–1950* (Albuquerque, 1950); J. Frank Dobie, *Life and Literature of the Southwest* (Dallas, 1952); "The Southwest, a Cultural Inventory," *Saturday Review of Literature*, May 16, 1942. Most libraries have files of *Book Review Digest*, published monthly (New York) and compiled annually since 1905. William Vann, *The Texas Institute of Letters* (Austin, 1966) is the best source on Texas writings since 1936.

On early newspapers the best source is *Texas Newspapers, 1813–1939*, which is Volume I of the San Jacinto Museum of History Association *Publications* (Houston, 1941).

For the fine arts, see Esse Forrester O'Brien, *Art and Artists of Texas* (Dallas, 1935); Pauline A. Pinckney, *Texas Artists of the Nineteenth Century* (Austin, 1967); Lota M. Spell, *Music in Texas* (Austin, 1938); Marjorie Goodman Sullivan, "Carl Venth–Music Master," *Bunker's Monthly*, IV, 304–318; Charles Jeffries, "Early Texas Architecture," *ibid.*, 905–915. Of some value is Federal Writers' Project, *Texas: A Guide to the Lone Star State* (New York, 1940).

For an evaluation of three noted Texas writers, see Ronnie Dugger (ed.), *Three Men in Texas: Bedicheck, Webb, and Dobie* (Austin, 1967).

APPENDIX

GOVERNORS OF TEXAS[1]

1691–1692	Domingo Terán de los Ríos
1693–1716	Texas unoccupied but included in Coahuila.
1716–1719	Martín de Alarcón appointed governor of Texas on December 7, 1716. (On August 5, 1716, he had been appointed governor of Coahuila.)
1719–1722	The Marqués de San Miguél de Aguayo, governor of Coahuila and Texas
1722–1726	Fernando Pérez de Almazán
1727–1730	Melchor de Media Villa y Ascona
1730–	Juan Antonio Bustillo y Zevallos
1734–	Manuel de Sandoval
1736–1737	Carlos Benites Franquis de Lugo
1737–	Fernández de Jáuregui y Urrutia, governor of Nuevo León, governor extraordinary and *visitador*
1737–1740	Prudencio de Orobio y Bazterra (*governor ad interim*)
1741–1743	Tomás Felipe Wintuisen
1743–1744	Justo Boneo y Morales
1744–1748	Francisco García Larios (*governor ad interim*)
1748–1750	Pedro del Barrio Junco y Espriella
1751–1759	Jacinto de Barrios y Jáuregui. Barrios was appointed governor of Coahuila in 1757, but was retained in Texas until 1759 to complete a task.
1759–1766	Angel de Martos y Navarrete
1767–1770	Hugo Oconór (*governor ad interim*)
1770–1778	The Baron de Ripperdá
1778–1786	Domingo Cabello

[1]The list of governors holding office before the Texan Revolution is based on Herbert E. Bolton, *Guide to Materials for the History of the United States in the Principal Archives of Mexico* (Washington, D.C., 1913) pp. 478, 479. Bolton makes the statement that "there are some imperfections in the results, in spite of care, for the materials for compiling a correct list are still mainly unprinted." In a few instances information made available subsequent to the publication of Bolton's study has removed doubt as to the terms of governors.

1786	Bernardo Bonavía appointed July 8, but apparently did not serve.
1787–1790	Rafael Martínez Pachecho appointed February 27; removal approved October 18, 1790.
1788	The office of governor was ordered suppressed and the province put under a presidial captain.
1790–1799(?)	Manuel Muñoz
1798(?)	Josef Irigoyen, apparently appointed but did not serve.
1800(?)–1805	Juan Bautista de Elguezábal
1805–1810	Antonio Cordero y Bustamante
1810–1813	Manuel de Salcedo
1811 (Jan. 22–March 2)	Juan Bautista Casas (revolutionary governor)
1814–1818	Christóbal Domínguez
1817–	Ignacio Pérez and Manuel Pardo (*governors ad interim*)
1817–1822	Antonio Martínez
1822–1823	José Felix Trespalacios
1823(?)–1824	Luciano García

GOVERNORS OF COAHUILA AND TEXAS

1824–1826	Rafael Gonzáles
1826–1827	Victor Blanco
1827–1831	José María Viesca
1831–1832	José María Letona
1832–1833	Juan Martín de Beramendi
1834–1835	Juan José Elguezábal
1835–	Agustín Viesca
1835–	Ramón Eca y Músquiz

PROVISIONAL GOVERNORS DURING THE TEXAN REVOLUTION[2]

| Nov. 14, 1835–March 1, 1836 | Henry Smith |
| Jan. 11, 1836–March 1, 1836 | James W. Robinson[3] |

[2]This list of Texas chief executives is taken in part from the *Texas Almanac*, 1936, p. 317. Later information courtesy Ray Barrera, Secretary of State.

[3]Robinson was elected by the council after Smith had been deposed and the office of governor declared vacant by the council. Thereafter both men claimed the right to exercise the executive authority.

PRESIDENTS OF THE REPUBLIC OF TEXAS

March 17, 1836–Oct. 22, 1836	David G. Burnet
Oct. 22, 1836–Dec. 10, 1838	Sam Houston
Dec. 10, 1838–Dec. 13, 1841	Mirabeau B. Lamar
Dec. 13, 1841–Dec. 9, 1844	Sam Houston
Dec. 9, 1844–Feb. 19, 1846	Anson Jones

GOVERNORS AFTER ANNEXATION

Feb. 19, 1846–Dec. 21, 1847	J. Pinckney Henderson
May 19, 1846–Nov.–, 1846	A. C. Horton[4]
Dec. 21, 1847–Dec. 21, 1849	George T. Wood
Dec. 21, 1849–Nov. 23, 1853	P. Hansborough Bell
Nov. 23, 1853–Dec. 21, 1853	J. W. Henderson[5]
Dec. 21, 1853–Dec. 21, 1857	Elisha M. Pease
Dec. 21, 1857–Dec. 21, 1859	Hardin R. Runnels
Dec. 21, 1859–March 16, 1861	Sam Houston[6]
March 16, 1861–Nov. 7, 1861	Edward Clark
Nov. 7, 1861–Nov. 5, 1863	Francis R. Lubbock
Nov. 5, 1863–June 17, 1865	Pendleton Murrah[7]
July 21, 1865–Aug. 9, 1866	Andrew J. Hamilton (provisional)
Aug. 9, 1866–Aug. 8, 1867	James W. Throckmorton[8]
Aug. 8, 1867–Sept. 30, 1869	Elisha M. Pease
Jan 8, 1870–Jan. 15, 1874	Edmund J. Davis[9]
Jan. 15,1874–Dec. 1, 1876	Richard Coke[10]
Dec. 1, 1876–Jan. 21, 1879	Richard B. Hubbard
Jan. 21, 1879–Jan. 16, 1883	Oran M. Roberts
Jan. 16, 1883–Jan. 18, 1887	John Ireland
Jan. 18, 1887–Jan. 20, 1891	Lawrence Sullivan Ross
Jan. 20, 1891–Jan. 15, 1895	James S. Hogg
Jan. 15, 1895–Jan. 17, 1899	Charles A. Culberson

[4]Lieutenant Governor Horton served as governor while Governor Henderson was away commanding troops in the war with Mexico.

[5]Lieutenant Governor Henderson became governor when Governor Bell resigned to take his seat in Congress, to which he had been elected.

[6]Houston refused to take the oath of allegiance to the Confederacy and was deposed. He was succeeded by Lieutenant Governor Edward Clark.

[7]Murrah's administration was terminated by the fall of the Confederacy. Murrah retired to Mexico, and for a period, May-June, 1865, Lieutenant Governor Fletcher S. Stockdale was acting governor.

[8]Throckmorton was removed by the military. Pease, provisional governor who succeeded him, resigned September 30, 1869.

[9]Davis was appointed provisional governor after he had been elected governor.

[10]Coke resigned to enter the United States Senate and was succeeded by Lieutenant Governor Hubbard.

Jan. 17, 1899–Jan. 20, 1903	Joseph D. Sayers
Jan. 20, 1903–Jan. 15, 1907	S. W. T. Lanham
Jan. 15, 1907–Jan. 19, 1911	Thomas M. Campbell
Jan. 19, 1911–Jan. 19, 1915	Oscar Branch Colquitt
Jan. 19, 1915–Aug. 25, 1917	James E. Ferguson (impeached)
Aug. 25, 1917–Jan. 18, 1921	William P. Hobby
Jan. 18, 1921–Jan. 20, 1925	Pat M. Neff
Jan. 20, 1925–Jan. 17, 1927	Miriam A. Ferguson
Jan. 17, 1927–Jan. 20, 1931	Dan Moody
Jan. 20, 1931–Jan. 17, 1933	Ross S. Sterling
Jan. 17, 1933–Jan. 15, 1935	Miriam A. Ferguson
Jan. 15, 1935–Jan. 17, 1939	James V. Allred
Jan. 17, 1939–Aug. 4, 1941	W. Lee O'Daniel (resigned to enter U.S. Senate)
Aug. 4, 1941–Jan. 21, 1947	Coke R. Stevenson
Jan. 21, 1947–July 11, 1949	Beauford H. Jester (died)
July 11, 1949–Jan. 15, 1957	Allan Shivers
Jan. 15, 1957–Jan. 15, 1963	Price Daniel
Jan. 15, 1963–Jan. 21, 1969	John Connally
Jan. 21, 1969–	Preston Smith

UNITED STATES SENATORS

Houston Succession

Feb. 21, 1846–March 4, 1859	Sam Houston
March 4, 1859–July 11, 1861	John Hemphill[11]
Feb. 22, 1870–March 3, 1877	Morgan C. Hamilton
March 3, 1877–March 3, 1895	Richard Coke
March 3, 1895–March 3, 1901	Horace Chilton
March 3, 1901–Jan. 8, 1913	Joseph W. Bailey (resigned)
Jan. 8, 1913–Feb. 3, 1913	R. M. Johnson (filled vacancy on appointment)
Feb. 13, 1913–April 9, 1941	Morris Sheppard (died)
April 21, 1941–June 26, 1941	Andrew Jackson Houston (died)
Aug. 4, 1941–Jan. 3, 1949	W. Lee O'Daniel
Jan. 3, 1949–Jan. 20, 1961	Lyndon B. Johnson
Jan. 20, 1961–June 15, 1961	William A. Blakley
June 15, 1961–	John G. Tower

[11]Succession was broken by the secession of Texas. Louis T. Wigfall and W. S. Oldham represented Texas in the Confederate Senate. On August 21, 1866, the Texas legislature elected David G. Burnet and Oran M. Roberts to the United States Senate, but they were not allowed to take their seats.

Rusk Succession

Feb. 21, 1846–July 29,1857	Thomas J. Rusk (died)
Nov. 9, 1857–June 4, 1858	J. Pinckney Henderson (died)
Sept. 29, 1858–Dec. 5, 1859	Matthias Ward (filled vacancy on appointment)
1859–1861	Louis T. Wigfall
Feb. 22, 1870–March 3, 1875	James W. Flanagan
March 3, 1875–March 3, 1887	Samuel B. Maxey
March 3, 1887–June 10, 1891	John H. Reagan (resigned)
Dec. 7, 1891–March 30, 1892	Horace Chilton (filled vacancy on appointment)
March 30, 1892–March 3, 1899	Roger Q. Mills
March 3, 1899–March 4, 1923	Charles A. Culberson
March 4, 1923–March 4, 1929	Earle B. Mayfield
March 4, 1929–Jan. 3, 1953	Tom Connally
Jan. 3, 1953–Jan. 15, 1957	Price Daniel (resigned to become governor)
Jan. 13, 1957–April 19, 1957	William A. Blakley
April 19,1957–	Ralph W. Yarborough

INDEX

Van Zandt, Isaac, 135
Velasco, Battle of, 74
Veterans: legislation for after World War
    II, 360; irregularities of Veteran's
    Land Board, 369; "G.I. Bill of
    Rights," 406
Veterans of Foreign Wars, 411
Vial, Pedro, 32
Vietnam War, 378
Vigilance committees, 171, 185
Vigness, David M., 419

Waco, Texas, 121
Wagstaff, J.M., 325
Wagstaff, R.M., 391
Wagstaff-Woodward Law, 391
Wallace, Ernest, 419
Wallace, George C., 378
Ward, Matthias, 146
Wardlaw, Louis J., 324
War with Mexico, 137
Water: in wells on plains, 259; resources
    of Texas, 390; early legislation on,
    390; Brazos River Authority, 390–391;
    other authorities, 391; major reser-
    voirs, 391–392; interest in quickened
    by drought, 392; agencies for conserv-
    ing, 392; plan for the future, 392–
    393
Water Commission, Texas, 391
Water Conservation Association, 392
Water Quality Board, 399
Water Rights Commission, 374, 392
Waters Pierce Oil Company, 303
Webb, James, 26
Webb, Walter P., 418, 419, 421
Weeks, Oliver D., 373
Western Boundary of the Louisiana Pur-
    chase, 34
Westheimer, David, 422
West Texas Chamber of Commerce, 342
West Texas Historical Association, 418
West Texas State University, 406
Wharton, Clarence R., 418
Wharton, John A., 195
Wharton, William H., 84, 123
Whiting, Captain W.H.C., 147
Wichita Falls, Texas, 355
Wigfall, Louis T., 146, 196

Wilbarger, John W., 416
Wilbarger, Josiah P., 121
William Beaumont General Hospital, 354
Williams, J.W., 420
Williams, Sam, 83
Williamson, Robert M., 83
Wilkinson, General James, 34
Wilson, Woodrow, 315
Winedale Inn, 167
Winkler County, 346
Wolters, Jake, 312
Woman suffrage, 316
Woman's Christian Temperance Union,
    293
Women's clubs in Texas, 411
Wood, Governor George, 139, 142
World War I: Texas in, 315; council of
    defense, 315–316; food administration,
    316; restrictive legislation during, 317;
    Texans' armed forces, 375
World War II: Texans' share in, 357; era
    of prosperity, 359; work of War Man-
    power Commission, 360; Office of Price
    Administration, 360; Texas a great
    training area, 361; Texas units in
    armed forces, 361–362; Texans recog-
    nized for valor, 363; Texans in high
    commands, 363
Worth, General W.J., 147
Wortham, Louis J., 418

XIT Ranch, 264, 266

Yarborough, Don, 372, 378
Yarborough, Ralph, 367, 369, 370, 373,
    410
Yauger, Fay M., 423
Yelvington, Ramsey, 423
Yoakum, Henderson, 415
Young, James R., 324
Young, Stark, 425
Youth Development Council, 364
Yucatan-Texas alliance, 126

Zavala, Lorenzo de: 56, 94, 95